THEORY
and
PRACTICE
of
AMERICAN
DEMOCRACY

THEORY
and
PRACTICE
of
AMERICAN
DEMOCRACY

NATIONAL, STATE, & LOCAL EDITION

FRED KRINSKY & GERALD RIGBY

University of Southern California

Dickenson Publishing Company, Inc., Belmont, California

THEORY AND PRACTICE OF AMERICAN DEMOCRACY
(National, State, and Local Edition)

by Fred Krinsky and Gerald Rigby

L.C. Cat. Card No.: 67–16694

Printed in the United States of America

Preface

   This volume is designed for the many teachers of American government who want to develop a more sophisticated course but are frustrated in finding readily available materials for it. It is doubtful that there can be a truly introductory course in American democracy at the college or university level, as most of our students have not only studied our democratic system more or less systematically and certainly repetitively throughout their school years, but also have *lived* in it, been a part of it, received it uncritically through a kind of educational osmosis. At the same time this inheritance of knowledge, or pseudo-knowledge, about democracy presents special problems for both the student and the instructor. Much of what the student knows is misinformation, misconception, or just plain untrue. There is a real problem of unlearning that which substitutes for genuine understanding of democracy. Therefore the most important goal of a course in democratic government is to assist the student to conceptualize, analyze, and evaluate the ideas and problems that are essential to an understanding of democracy.

   A text on the theory and practice of American democracy must first of all assist the instructor. It must not be so encyclopedic, so fact-oriented, that the instructor has to spend much of his time trying to serve as an index for the student in his effort to answer the question, "how much of this must I know?" Nor would a group of selected readings without a guiding commentary, no matter how individually significant, serve these purposes.

   The present volume is designed to be a central source of in-depth commentaries on the most important aspects of American democracy, with illustrative selections from the best of the literature. It is the authors' belief that the student should be introduced to the best of the contributions of social scientists who have turned their attention to problems of American democracy. He may do this through a reading of both the original materials and the commentaries which organize and elucidate the central ideas of each topic. The readings are reproduced exactly as the original author wrote them, including his footnotes and explanatory comments. The extensive, annotated bibliographical references and the questions suggested for additional consideration will further assist the student.

The volume begins with an exposition of classical or traditional democratic thought, together with several selections designed to argue the virtue of this approach. We then discuss American democracy in both theory and practice in order to evaluate and restate democratic theory. The last part of the volume turns to substantive questions of major policy areas—economic, foreign policy, and civil liberties. The difference between this and the usual text or book of readings lies primarily in the level and significance of the materials and ideas considered. The materials emphasize process and dynamics, not institutions. The student is invited to analyze, evaluate, question, and understand American democracy *as it is,* not to master a mass of detail or commit to memory a series of platitudes about democracy. He is invited to develop for himself a meaningful theory of democracy. Finally, he is stimulated to consider some of the vital substantive policy questions facing our society.

A note on organization: numbers in brackets throughout the text refer to the corresponding reference in the section entitled "Suggested Additional Readings" for each chapter. These references have been carefully selected and annotated to make the search for supplemental reading profitable. Use of these readings will materially increase the value of this volume to both student and instructor. At the end of each chapter are included several important questions for further consideration. These illustrative questions will serve both to summarize and highlight major contributions of the commentary and reading selections and to suggest profitable avenues for further study and discussion.

A special word of appreciation must go to Joseph L. Dana of Dickenson Publishing Company for his tireless efforts in guiding us through the seemingly endless maze of negotiation that production of a book such as this requires, and to our families for their support and understanding.

FRED KRINSKY

GERALD RIGBY

University of Southern California

Contents

Democratic Theory and Democratic Life 1

Americans in the mid-twentieth century have the particular advantage of living in what has been called an open society. Our entire social fabric is permeated with a spirit of initiative, creativity, and dynamism. Self-government is a motive force behind this dynamic system. Before this system was made operative, however, the foundations were laid by a long history of thought and action. At least since the time of ancient Greece, men have speculated on the nature of government—what it is and what it ought to be—and have experimented with a variety of forms. The American citizen of today inherits their wisdom and a storehouse of practical knowledge. [17, 21, 22]

Democracy has always been a controversial concept with no universally accepted definition. It refers generally to the popular control of government, sometimes as direct democracy and sometimes as representative democracy. Today it is thought of not merely as the political machinery of government but as a complete way of life. Specifications of its nature have been legion; for example, democracy has been variously explained as a form of government based upon self-rule of the people; as government based upon freely elected representatives with an executive responsible to the people; as a way of life emphasizing the equality of all individuals and their equal right to life, liberty, and the pursuit of happiness; and even as a particular economic system, ranging from complete laissez-faire to extensive collective control over economic decisions.[1]

The word itself derives from two Greek words, *demos,* meaning the people, and *kratos,* referring to authority or rule. It is also related to the Greek word *deme.* The *demes* were the voting districts in the ancient Athenian democracy. "Democracy," then, means the rule of the people.

Yet this definition does not begin to explain the meaning of democracy.

---

[1] To these traditional categories there has now been added the idea of "totalitarian democracy." The best exposition of this concept can be found in J. L. Talmon, *The Rise of Totalitarian Democracy* (New York: Frederick A. Praeger, 1952).

Before that is possible we must first explore our inheritance of democratic thought from those who have struggled with both the concept and the process down through the ages.

In this chapter will be examined, first, what may be called classic or traditional democratic theory, and second, some of the most challenging ideas of recent and contemporary philosophers of democracy. The aim is not a survey of the history of democratic thought but rather an introduction to the product of that history—an understanding of democratic theory in its traditional form as it bears upon the kinds of philosophical questions presently engaging serious theorists.

In later chapters the product of contemporary empirical and theoretical investigations will be applied to what may be termed a realistic democratic theory. There is no conflict between the best of the traditional and the best of the contemporary statements of democratic theory; indeed, failure to understand and utilize both would be a serious handicap to understanding what democracy is all about.

DEVELOPMENT OF TRADITIONAL DEMOCRATIC THEORY

The classic expression of democracy was the Athenian city-state. This was a direct democracy governed by a popular assembly and a council made up of members from each of the tribes. Candidates were selected in the local districts and then chosen by lot. A board of generals was elected by vote; these magistrates had short terms and were ineligible for re-election. The judicial system was one of popular courts.

These early democratic states, including the Roman Republic, although functioning as democracies, were nevertheless systems based on slavery, which was justified on the basis that it permitted the citizens leisure to devote themselves to questions of public interest. Women, foreigners, and slaves were not allowed to vote. Generally the situation was one of benevolent domination of the poor by the rich.

The Middle Ages did little to further the functioning of democracy, except to carry forward the Christian idea of a "higher law" limitation on the temporal sword, a beginning of the idea of constitutionalism. The growing power and wealth of the Italian cities, as well as the growth of the national state during the Reformation, provided greater social and cultural opportunities with a corresponding increase in the spirit of liberty and creativity. Although the Renaissance and the Reformation strengthened the absolutist power of their period, the new spirit of inquiry increased the emphasis on the individual.

Seventeenth-century England may be regarded as the birthplace of modern democracy. A history of the Magna Carta, common law, and a tradition of local self-government prepared the English for the ideals of liberty. [2, 4, 16] With the Puritan Revolution of 1648 and the Glorious Revolution of 1688 the divine right of kings gave way to the temporal rights of Englishmen. The writings of John Milton and John Locke were filled with thoughts on liberty and freedom as well as the dignity of man's reason. Locke's two basic principles were that the individual is the basis of society and that government is a trust dependent on the free consent of the governed.

Although democracy as we know it today came slowly, English history reflects a gradual development toward limited government. Control of the country was in the hands of a parliament with a house of commons growing in power and an increasing electorate; individuals were protected by a bill of rights; tolerance and abolition of censorship were finally acknowledged; judges and courts were increasingly independent of the Crown; the ideas of nonconformity and individualism were growing.

The New World benefitted from the heritage of England transplanted to a more mobile and individualized society. The American colonists struggled with the mother country for their rights as Englishmen, but, in the absence of the classes and institutions of a feudal society, this conflict created a new surge toward democracy in the colonies. [15] The ideas of reason, natural rights, and freedom expressed by Englishmen had a profound effect on the new nation in establishing its ideological foundation.[2]

AMERICAN DEMOCRATIC DEVELOPMENT

Early American democratic thought was based on a premise that political liberty is the prerequisite to all other freedoms and liberties. And political liberty was related to the idea that men have certain rights which are inviolate and above the secular power of the government. In this view, a government justifies its existence only by protecting each man's inalienable rights and dignity.

These ideas were included in the Declaration of Independence by Thomas Jefferson, who was thoroughly acquainted with the works of Locke and Rousseau. The Constitution of 1789, however, was something of a reaction against the intense democratic feeling of 1776, and emphasized protection of property rights. [9] Significant restraints were imposed on the democratic elements of society; guarantees against excessive popular participation were numerous. For example, while the House of Representatives was to be elected by the people of the states, the Senate was to be elected by the state legislatures. All appointments and treaties had to have the approval of this upper chamber, and no law could be passed without its concurrence. Neither the president nor the vice-president was elected popularly but through an electoral college. Voting requirements were left to state determination, and many states had restrictive property requirements and/or religious tests for voters. Government control by the people, with their tendency to democratic excesses, was counterbalanced by the experience and education of the propertied classes.

With the election of Thomas Jefferson as president in 1800, the slow process of democratization of America began in earnest, and aristocratic elements began to disappear or at least lose their pre-eminence in political affairs.

---

[2] These ideas also affected the French, who watched the events across the ocean. They, too, were soon to be involved in a similar struggle which would rock the foundations of Europe. The French Revolution, symbolized by three words describing the democratic effort —liberty, fraternity, and equality—was to spread the feeling of individual liberty, self-determination, and self-expression. Napoleon's armies helped spread this spirit through Europe, sowing seeds of nationalism and liberty which, though lying dormant for the moment, were to flower in both the old and new worlds.

Property requirements for voting were lowered and gradually abolished. The Civil War and the resulting constitutional amendments abolished slavery and, nominally at least, gave the Negro full political rights. In 1920 the constitutional right to vote was granted to women, although some states had already granted women that privilege. With the development of political parties and the use of national conventions for nominations as well as state conventions for choosing the presidential electors, the election of the chief executive passed indirectly into the hands of the people. In 1913 the Seventeenth Amendment had established the popular election of United States senators.

Much of the democratic spirit in America was the result of the influence of the frontier and the abundance of free land which tended to develop individual enterprise, self-reliance, and a love of liberty. In addition, the great stream of immigrants from all countries which flowed into the United States made America into a "melting pot" where men of different cultures and faiths could live side by side and profit from it. [6]

FORMS OF POLITICAL DEMOCRACY

Political democracy may vary in its methods of popular participation. Direct democracy, which consists of popular deliberation, discussion, and execution of policy, is a form in which every member of the community may participate; the government is directly dependent on the activity of the people. Direct democracy existed in the earliest Greek city-states, the old Swiss cantons, and the New England towns of early America. Today, however, with modern industrialization, and the size and population of modern nations, it has become obsolescent, although certain direct democracy processes, such as the initiative, the referendum, and the recall, by which the voters may enact laws directly, vote on laws passed by the legislative branch, and remove elected officials, are still in use today.

Direct democracy has been considered dangerous and unstable by people of the educated and wealthier classes who fear the ignorance of the uneducated masses. The effect of a demagogue on the people could be alien to the purposes of a democracy as their interests become subordinate to his will.

Many of the American founding fathers were fearful of the excesses of direct democracy and felt that representative democracy would be safer. [19] Power to govern would not be exercised by the people directly but delegated by them to representatives who would be capable of governing wisely and democratically but without the dangers of excessive popular involvement.

Democracy as we have come to know it involves an indirect, representative, constitutional form of government (although the constitution need not be written), characterized by an open competition for political power in which the votes of the mass of the people determine who shall govern. Public opinion is organized rather than immediate and spontaneous as in a direct democracy and is expressed through representatives of political parties who compete for office. The existence of a minority is an integral element in such a system of government, and compromise and opposition go hand in hand. Thus policy is evolved from the conflicts of various interest groups.

In this kind of system, power is characteristically, though not necessarily, divided among the executive, the judicial, and the legislative branches of the government, the latter usually being bicameral. The forms of the executive may vary: often there is either a prime minister and a cabinet which are responsible to the legislature, or, as in the United States, an independently elected president and an appointed cabinet. The form of the judiciary, too, may vary, but the important fact is that the citizen enjoys certain rights which are protected by law and abridgeable only by due process of law. The whole political process is bound within a framework of custom, law, charter, or constitution, imposing regularized restraints on government. Discussion, compromise, and freedom of expression and association are institutionalized to facilitate the competition for power out of which develops a governing party or coalition which will assume the temporary responsibility for government. It is this type of democracy with which the remaining chapters of this volume will deal.

Democracy's uniqueness lies not in its structural differences from other forms of government but in its approach to the concept of freedom.[3] Democrats look upon freedom not simply as a claim made by one person upon other people or upon government but rather as something which emerges from man's inner being. A nation cannot be free in its relationship to its government unless it consists of people who *feel* free. The foundation of freedom is creative doubt. Once a man begins to doubt, and can stand up to his doubts, he will perceive that he does not know everything, that it is impossible that he know everything, and that he is likely, in the course of time, to change his opinions and reactions—and thus add to his own personal enrichment. He will further understand that there may be other opinions which, even though opposed to his point of view, can help to clarify the truth and improve society as well. The emotional matrix of freedom is this: I and the circle of which I am a part know only part of the truth, not all of it. The whole truth can be arrived at only if there are others who discern other aspects of the truth. Public debate and political opposition *elevate* me and the people in my circle. My opponent, if only he admits my right to be, is my antagonist and friend at one and the same time.

Democracy, basically, is a political *method* of deciding what men and measures shall rule, rather than a program of what shall be done. The democratic state is self-limiting, and, therefore, a system of individual rights is basic to it. These rights define the non-political areas in which men are free to express their differences, as long as they do not obstruct liberty; opinions are not curtailed merely because they are strange or offensive to a segment of the population.

Although democracy is primarily a political method, it is also held by some to be an end product, although dissimilar methods are advocated for its achievement. There are those, such as Harold Laski, who feel that socialism is most compatible with democracy; there are others, such as Friedrich Hayek, who consider capitalism most congruous to democracy. These differences of opinions can only be settled by trial and error, not by argument. But it is incontestable that social democracy does make political democracy easier by

[3] For some of the ideas and phrases appearing in the next few pages we would like to give tribute and credit to the men who inspired them—Harold Laski, T. V. Smith, Max Lerner, and J. L. Talmon.

removing tensions and prejudices. Majority rule works smoothly only when the minority is not permanent and embittered or handicapped beyond its tolerance limits but when it knows that it can always freely organize an effective opposition.

Respect for human personality is a motivating force of political democracy and its non-political offshoots. Democratic theorists believe in the dignity of man and thus oppose slavery. Democratic purpose is, in part, the development of the personality of each individual. It is associated with liberty and equality of men before the law; this is an equality of opportunity rather than of wealth or personal capabilities. Democracy presupposes that no one group has a monopoly of wisdom or importance; that there are no legitimate privileges based on wealth, birth, race, or faith; and that individual recognition should be based on accomplishment and merit.

The search for social truth and social well-being is quite unlike the search for truth in the scientific laboratory. In the field of the "exact" sciences, it is possible, even essential, to reach a definite conclusion within the context of the conditions and experiments of a particular time. Not so in politics or social action. Here, the reckoning with doubt is axiomatic to all social planning and progress. The existence of the political antagonist is the foundation of social health—his disappearance or suppression is a sign of stagnation, or an ossification of the creative spirit and the disintegration of society. Political antagonists must exist, for their differences as well as for the things they espouse in common; nor is one antagonist ever completely in the right. Mutual tolerance and sympathetic attention to each other's arguments are vital to the general welfare.

DEMOCRACY IN THE UNITED STATES

The United States today may be called a democracy. Its existing institutions and practices are broadly characteristic of democratic government. It has a system of relatively unrestricted suffrage, and a set of operative checks—institutional and political—on the exercise of power by government. Elected representatives act through delegated power, and government is limited so as to leave room for, even perhaps to maximize, individual freedom. There is a meaningful competitive party system with a basic set of guarantees of civil liberties and immunities from arbitrary governmental restraint.

There may be, however, a considerable gap between the ideal envisioned by traditional democratic theorists and the actual practice in our society. Participation through suffrage may not be universal—serious arbitrary exclusions may be, and have been, made. Restraints on government periodically may break down; personal freedom may be curtailed, sometimes in the name of democracy. The party system may tend toward monopoly rather than competitiveness. Elected delegates may prove unscrupulous and self-interested. The electorate may not be as rational, informed, or interested as the traditional theorists suggest is desirable. Majority rule may be frustrated in Congress or the Supreme Court. The whole cumbersome process of democracy may limit the government's effectiveness or leave it open to manipulation.

Some see the failure of democracy because it permits vast inequalities in wealth and power. [5, 12] They claim that so-called democratic institutions of government are merely devices to defend the propertied classes and to exploit the working man. Others who believe in the justice of democracy feel that political reforms will pave the way for social and economic leveling. The New Deal rested on a belief that government powers should be extended to benefit the common man by providing him with more opportunities to better himself. [7, 10]

The conclusion to be drawn is neither that traditional democratic theory is invalid nor that our society today is not democratic because its practice fails to meet the demands of the ideal. Rather, it may be concluded that when properly examined and understood, the system we know is properly termed democratic: the insights and data available to us make it possible to re-evaluate, restate, and revitalize our notions of what democracy is. Building upon the contributions of traditional democratic theory we may better understand the nature of American democracy today.

One of the most important elements influencing the operation of democratic institutions is the degree of basic agreement (consensus) about institutions and policies. Some minimum degree of agreement is necessary for democratic processes to operate. When agreement declines beyond this imprecise but vital limit, democracy disintegrates into instability, civil war, dictatorship, secession or some other rupture of the existing political system. The United States has enjoyed a relatively broad consensus on its basic constitutional processes, despite great sectional, ethnic, religious, and economic diversity.

THE IDEAL AND THE REAL IN DEMOCRATIC SOCIETY

Now let us change our focus and our technique. What follows is an exercise in theory, not just a specification of what has been developed in theory but an examination of one of the most difficult and important theoretical concerns facing democrats of the twentieth century, the problem of the conflict between the ideal and the real and the disillusionment of democratic man with the democratic ideal. It is hoped that the following discussion will help to eliminate the confusion involved in the statement, "That may be all right in theory, but in practice it doesn't work that way." Theory is the explication of reality, the attempt to explain that which is (or might be, or ought to be) given the nature of things. It is not wild hypothesizing, nor is it idle speculation about a dream world. There is no inherent conflict between theory and practice, though the former may deal, and probably most often does when at its best, with realms of being, with reality, *beyond* the realm of practice or experience.

THE DISILLUSIONED AND LONELY DEMOCRAT

Today, once-assumed truths are on trial before the analytical eyes and mind of modern man, [1] the result being a re-evaluation of our democratic aspirations and the implied values. [12] The virtues of democracy as espoused by the seventeenth- and eighteenth-century liberals gave incentive to a powerful, optimistic faith in man's capacity for goodness. This faith has been repeatedly challenged by two world wars, a devastating depression, and the near-permanent tensions of the nuclear age. Jeffersonian assumptions concerning agrarian man's benevolence if given his natural rights of life, liberty, and property have been called into question by industrialization and its psychological and physical conflicts.

The conflict between the philosophy of materialism, which has been more influential in American history than we usually admit, and the natural-rights philosophy, which was the basis of the traditional theorists' democratic credo, has become especially pronounced today. We have undergone a materialistic—scientific and technological—revolution which has had world-wide impact. Science, scientific research, and "things" have become near-dominant values of the United States in the twentieth century. Mastering the challenges of the material world of the Newtons, Bacons, Edisons and Freuds is necessary if we are to protect our "otherworldly" values, such as human rights, upon which our democratic credo has placed so much emphasis. But can the classical philosophy of democracy, including faith in the natural rights and dignity of man, stand concurrently with an opposing faith in an "earthly reality" which assumes the ability to manipulate the material world? [13]

Much of the despair which so characterizes our age might be simply lack of nerve. It is the authors' conviction that Americans have been unwilling or unable to face up to certain realities of human life and history, realities which have been ignored or denied as un-American. A strong neo-Platonic tradition pervades our culture and its philosophy. Much of the liberal tradition has insisted that we are steadily progressing, under the guidance of reason and hard work, toward a democratic ideal where everyone will live in earthly bliss. Historically, the fulfillment of the Platonic ideal has been associated with a very real material progress. For a while it seemed that the ideal might be actualized. Industry grew by leaps and bounds and with it the general prosperity of all, and science and democratic ideals seemed reconciled.

Yet, economic exploitation, civil war, and political corruption continued to pinch the consciousness of hopeful idealism. It seemed that, although material progress continued, man had not advanced far enough to solve concomitant social problems. Then World War I confronted democratic idealists, and a "lost generation"—Hemingway, E. E. Cummings, Eliot, Dos Passos and others —left the ranks of the hopeful. [3] Idealists had not yet recovered when a devastating depression, climaxed by World War II, seemed to expose the American messianic vision as a fraud.

The result is a vacuum or near-vacuum of belief and a lack of commitment of Americans to any ideal way of life. Anxious, many have attempted escape from earthly problems in evangelical fanaticism, the protecting organization, the mass culture, or other kinds of group conformity which give security by denying individual freedom and responsibility. The damage to the basic values of democracy have been of little concern save to the philosopher.

DEMOCRATIC MAN'S SEARCH FOR AUTHORITY

The modern American is lonely in the great crowd of modern society. [18] Not knowing who he is, he does not know where to go or what to believe. In the wake of his disillusionment and insecurity, and his anxiety for stability, have come serious threats to the American democratic philosophy. Their external forms in the twentieth century have been Nazism and Communism, yet these are not the real threats to American democracy. The challenge is internal—internal to the country, internal to the man. Both the USSR today and Nazi Germany yesterday represented totalitarian power and a conforming credo which claimed absolute truth. To some in America, conformity to absolute truth is highly attractive, whether such truth takes the form of extreme nationalism or communism.

Perhaps Erich Fromm is correct when he says that modern man wishes to escape from freedom. Fromm points out that man has an inner desire for submission as well as freedom.[4] Twentieth-century man was not prepared for the evil he found and innocently refused to examine himself. He falsely believed that since he was free from political and ecclesiastical restraints he was really free, free to express himself autonomously.

Fromm turns to Freud to examine man's antisocial needs. In general, Freud's analysis of the human psyche points out the irrationality of the self. The drive of self-preservation and fear of self-destruction cause the individual to disassociate from parents, friends, and groups. To preserve the self from dangerous threats to its identity requires this isolation. Yet, coexistent with the will to live is the desire to be identified with something permanent. In its extreme form this is the death wish, the ultimate attempt to deal with the anxiety of aloneness.

According to Fromm, one historical answer to the death wish or desire for an identity outside of the self has been authoritarianism. On the one hand, man fears his isolation, his death, and the possibility of making a wrong choice; thus, he attempts to submit to an authority or a belief that cannot be challenged. On the other hand, man has a need for individuality, to remain free from attachments to people and institutions that pose possible threats to his being, his unique identity. The results of the interaction of these two forces in a sublimated form is human history.

Fromm sees modern man as becoming self-reliant, critical, and independent of ecclesiastical and secular authorities. But freedom from external authority has not established what man will be free to do. One result of man's political and economic freedom has been an intense need for a new authority and submission to its demands.

The age of enlightenment only temporarily compensated for man's isolation and anxious independence by telling him that he was the center of the universe and the source of goodness. Then the concepts of natural law and rational man were seriously questioned by the realities of the industrial revolution, which pointed out that reason and freedom could do evil as well as good. Freud's discoveries of the subconscious and Kierkegaard's philosophical criticisms began to challenge the myth of natural man and his rational progress toward a benevolent state of being.

A natural aristocracy of virtuous, reasonable men did not develop as

---

[4] For further consideration of Fromm's contributions, see Erich Fromm, *Escape from Freedom* (New York: Rinehart & Co., 1941), especially pp. 170–90 and 270–76; and Fromm, *The Sane Society* (New York: Rinehart & Co., 1955).

Jefferson and the liberals had hoped. [23] Nor have we progressed spiritually as the Darwinians [8] had prophecied. Disillusioned in his failure to reach the neo-Platonic ideal, man has turned cynic, embittered and guilty for his failure. Identified with no cause, no teleology, he has been atomized by the hugeness of corporational, recreational, governmental, and military organizations. The anxious American joins a multitude of groups and clubs—the union, bridge club, church, political organization—but still feels no real sense of identity or belonging.

As such he is a victim of the Madison Avenue psychologists who manipulate the consumer by appealing to his insecurity and selfishness, his need for identification and fellowship. Soap ads promise to give youth to the aged, playing on the theme that only the young and physically active are "real Americans." "You owe it to yourself" slogans urge more self-indulgence to an over-indulgent people. Automobiles are advertised as the cars that "everyone is buying"; you will be out of step with the crowd if you buy the wrong make. [14]

From the standpoint of traditional democratic theory, a working political democracy and its imperative, a rational and educated citizenry, are also threatened. The voter is confronted with mammoth parties and incomprehensible "issues." Candidates no longer represent his particular interests but many conflicting interests. The result has often been "Golden Kazoo"[5] politics: political candidates are offered as demigods who mutter chauvanistic and religious platitudes, promising to amend all evil. The mass man, helpless as an individual in the face of the complexity of modern politics, disillusioned with his theoretical expectations, identifies with the demigod leader and retires from political involvement.

Yet the tragic truth is that the complex organization of government and business is necessary to meet present economic, political, and military challenges. Both the USSR and the United States have immense power. They, therefore, are the hope and yet the fear of the world for its survival. The fact that the two nations are ideologically opposed intensifies the power conflict. But "if we believe in the free society hard enough to keep on fighting for it, we are pledged to a permanent crisis which will test the moral, political and possibly the military strength of each side."[6] We are concerned with the moral problem, not Sunday-school morality, but the fundamental principles upon which our government and ethics are based—the dignity and unique value of the individual, his right to free expression, and to reasonable economic and legal security.

The biggest threat to American democracy lies within its borders. In order to wage an ideological battle with a modern totalitarian state, will we discard the fundamental values of human freedom and dignity as inefficient and replace them with a totalitarianism of our own? The pyschological appeal of the demagogue is strong for the anxious individual with the heavy responsibility of free choice. He seeks the heaven of submission where he is not responsible for his choice because he has no choice. Marx promised this heaven, and

---

[5] John G. Schneider, *The Golden Kazoo* (New York: Dell Publishing Co., 1956). One of the first political novels dealing with the theme of "merchandising" a candidate.
[6] Arthur Schlesinger, Jr., *The Vital Center* (Boston: Houghton Mifflin Co., 1949), p. 9.

millions today have accepted his promise. The real Communist threat to America is that it offers an escape valve for the anxious, the lonely.

Some would face the problem of anxiety by making a religion out of democracy. The thesis is that America has, in democracy, the real revolution, which is applicable to all mankind. It is possible, therefore, to educate mankind to respond to our ideals to face the Communists with a renewed vigor. But democracy is not a fighting faith; it is by nature disseminating rather than concentrating in its moral force. It leans toward compromise, tolerance, and diversity in society.[20] The plea for a new democratic idealism to cure the problems of the modern world is based on false absolutes and overestimates the moral virtue of the American democracy. There is no natural man who will be virtuous and rational simply because he is free.

Nor will Fromm's "loving man" be a final solution, for he is not naturally produced no matter what process of education one uses, nor does he inevitably progress toward the fulfillment of his loving nature. Nevertheless, democracy, although it will never be heaven, is worth the struggle. We must become more self-conscious of our shortcomings if we are to maintain faith in democracy in the light of failures. Realizing our limits may be an answer to the dilemma of the ideal versus the real if we wish to salvage what we already have. If so, the modern authoritarians may not be correct in their prophecies of American moral collapse. Perhaps we can visualize the American dream as just that—a dream—and at the same time accept the realities of a working democracy.

NIEBUHRIAN APPROACH

Another way to view this problem is through the approach of Reinhold Niebuhr.[7] The question which inevitably presents itself in reading Niebuhr is how can a man who seems to accept the Calvinist doctrine of human damnation actively support constitutional democracy, a philosophy which traditional theorists hold necessitates belief in human reason and benevolence as a means of solution to social problems? Niebuhr's thesis is that the assumptions of natural benevolence, natural reason and inevitable progress, as opposed to unnatural tyranny, stupidity, and reactionary power struggles, are illusory. His ideas differ from the Calvinist doctrine of human depravity in believing that man realizes his limitations, good and evil, through self-consciousness, "for man, unlike other creatures, is gifted and cursed with an imagination which extends his appetites beyond the requirements of subsistence."[8] So man needs to love, to create, to philosophize, to find meaning in life, all of which needs have a religious character since they are outside of the finite self, reaching for the external. Yet man can never deny his finite self completely. He must establish morality by which to live, ethics by which to judge. This often results in the establishment of false absolutes due to his need for self-assertion and self-

[7] The discussion which follows is drawn from the following of Reinhold Niebuhr's books: *The Nature and Destiny of Man* (New York: Charles Scribner's Sons, 1941); *Moral Man And Immoral Society* (New York: Charles Scribner's Sons, 1932); *The Irony of American History* (New York: Charles Scribner's Sons, 1954); and *Faith and History* (New York: Charles Scribner's Sons, 1949).

[8] Niebuhr, *Moral Man and Immoral Society, op. cit.,* p. 1.

preservation. This is the paradox of freedom: political freedom is not a good in itself, since man is not always virtuous when he is free.

If this is the nature of man, what is the political order which Niebuhr favors? The answer is the free society, not because it is natural, in accordance with rational law or Christian law, but because it is necessary. Although man tends to establish false absolutes and, in religious terminology, becomes a competitor with God, he is capable of achieving some sort of objectivity in his treatment of social injustices, and responding to them.

Recognizing, as many have not in the past, that social conflict and coercion cannot be escaped, Niebuhr believes that we must work with the coercion that seems reasonably compatible with the moral and rational factors in human society, and discriminate between the purposes and ends for which coercion is used. Niebuhr favors an educated, morally-concerned society which will place a greater emphasis on the purposes and ends for which coercion is used than on schemes to eliminate coercion and conflict.

Niebuhr favors something akin to a balance of power of interests in a political society where no one group can achieve dominance over another. Indeed, he sees Western democracy arising largely from the multiplicity of religious sects as a result of the Reformation in England. Out of this religious and secular pluralism came a need for compromise, tolerance and representative government. Democracy gives each group an opportunity to defend its interest by civil law and enfranchisement. Thus, self-assertion of an interest group in political society allows for an approximate social redemption. Yet, he warns, "a too consistent political realism would seem to consign society to perpetual warfare."[9]

So a system of democracy is the most feasible political order to avoid the two options of tyranny or anarchy. Since it is very difficult to judge individual motives in political and social affairs, it is natural that, from a morally-concerned exterior perspective, the social consequences of an action or policy should be regarded as more adequate tests of its morality than the hidden motives. Niebuhr writes:

When viewing a historic situation all moralists become pragmatists and utilitarians. Each action is measured in reference to the ultimate goal and the greatest good for the greatest number. . . . The choice of instruments and immediate objectives which fall between motive and ultimate objectives, raises issues which are pragmatic to such a degree that they may be more political than they are ethical. The realm of politics is a twilight zone where ethical and technical issues meet. A political policy cannot be intrinsically evil if it can be proved to be an efficacious instrument for the achievement of a morally approved end. Neither can it be said to be wholly good merely because it seems to make for ultimately good consequences. Immediate consequences must be weighed against the ultimate consequences.[10]

Niebuhr also recognizes the danger of an "ends justifies the means" doctrine.

Moral reason must learn how to make coercion (and pragmatism) its ally without running the risk of a Pyrrhic victory in which the ally exploits and negates the tri-

[9] *Ibid.*, p. 1.
[10] *Ibid.*, pp. 170–71.

umph. . . . The most obvious rational check which can be placed on the use of co-ercion is to submit it to the control of an impartial tribunal which will not be tempted to use it for selfish ends. Thus society claims the right to use coercion but denies the same right to individuals. The police power of nations is a universally approved func-tion of government. The supposition is that the government is impartial in reference to any disputes arising between citizens and will therefore, be able to use its powers for moral ends.[11]

Of course, even a democratic government is never an impartial trib-une, but constitutional democracy that is responsible to a wide variety of interest groups is by political necessity somewhat impartial to all for fear of alienating any. Furthermore, the democratic credo, realizing the egotism of men, establishes constitutional laws and courts which are momentarily out of the reach of the majority. For Niebuhr, democracy becomes necessary because of human egotism; it becomes possible because of man's capacity for justice. As his classic dictum puts it, "Democracy is a method of finding proximate solu-tions for insolvable problems."[12] Niebuhr agrees with Charles Frankel,[13] one of his severest critics, that the ideal of perfect justice must be believed, regard-less of its absurdity. Yet, Niebuhr also insists on a political realism that recog-nizes the impossibility, at least for the present, of perfect justice.

If we accept the fact that the gap between the "should be" and reality is not going to close, what will happen to the faith in progress so central to traditional democratic thought? Can the mass of mankind accept the Niebuhrian concepts of absurd idealism and reasonable realism at the same time? Crane Brinton puts it this way:

The mass of mankind, even in the West, have never been able to take the tragic view of history without the help of a personal religion, a religion hitherto always transcending, supernatural, other worldy. Somehow, democracy, if it is not to return wholeheartedly to Christianity (which many today would have it do), must take on the cure of souls.[14]

There are signs that people can accept such a realistic attitude. After a relatively innocent isolationism the United States entered World War II with a very mature attitude. It was no war to make the world safe for democracy! While it may be true that we would like to reject the burdens of responsibility in the postwar period, there is some hope that our material abundance might condition us to a more responsive attitude toward the present problems of society, even though the American people seem to be able to respond to scar-city in a more mature fashion than they respond to plenty.

Still, to quote Brinton again,

A realistic, pessimistic democracy—a democracy in which ordinary citizens approach morals and politics with the willingness to cope with imperfection that characterizes the good farmer, the good physician, the good holder of the cure of souls, be he priest, clergyman, counselor, or psychiatrist—such a democracy would demand more of its

---

[11] *Ibid.*, p. 238.

[12] Reinhold Niebuhr, *The Children of Light and The Children of Darkness* (New York: Charles Scribner's Sons, 1944), p. 118.

[13] Charles Frankel, *The Case for Modern Man* (New York: Harper & Brothers, 1955). See chapter VI for his criticism of Niebuhr.

[14] Crane Brinton, *Ideas and Men* (Englewood Cliffs, New Jersey: Prentice-Hall, Inc., © 1950), p. 543.

citizens than any human culture has ever demanded. Were its demands met, it might well be the most successful of cultures.[15]

The three selections reprinted below represent three different elaborations of current and recent American political theory. Riemer ("The Revival of Democratic Theory in the United States") offers a defense against what he refers to as the shotgun attack on political theory which fails to distinguish between liberal-democratic and radical-totalitarian theory. Riemer suggests that there *is* room for a sane and meaningful democratic theory. Hacker ("Liberal Democracy and Social Control") discusses the politics and bases of liberal democracy in America with particular emphasis on the new men of power in our emerging society who have replaced the older ruling classes. It is this new group, the human engineers, which constitutes the key to our total current existence. Aiken ("The Revolt Against Ideology") argues forcefully for the need for political philosophy.

[15] *Ibid.,* p. 550.

The Revival of Democratic Theory in the United States

NEAL RIEMER

Neal Riemer is professor of political science at The University of Wisconsin–Milwaukee. He is the author of The Revival of Democratic Theory *(1962), co-author of* World Affairs: Problems and Prospects *(1958), and author-editor of* Problems of American Government *(1952). He was a Fulbright Professor of American Studies at the University of Innsbruck, Austria, 1961–62, and held a Rockefeller Fellowship in Political Philosophy, 1958–59.*

There is, I believe, a clear and urgent need in the United States for a political theory which can provide theoretical illumination and practical guidance for those who are concerned with the preservation and advancement of worthy values.[1] This need is felt by both liberals and conservatives, although they do not respond to this need in the same way. The need is seen in our painful efforts to live by the light of divinity in a cruelly disturbed world. Two cataclysmic world wars within a single generation, the sickening evils of totalitarianism, the explosive revolution of rising expectations in Asia, Africa, and Latin America, the momentous responsibility of the United States as a bulwark against totalitarian aggression, the fearful prospect of the thermonuclear destruction of mankind—these emphatically underline the need for a wise, sane, and helpful democratic theory. To these challenges in world affairs, we must add nagging problems on the domestic scene, for example, the problem of race relations, the problem of pockets of poverty in a supposedly affluent society, the problem of harmonizing individual freedom and social welfare, the problem of reconciling excellence and consent.

Reprinted from *The Annals of the American Academy of Political and Social Science,* 344 (November 1962), 34–43, by permission of the publisher and author.

[1] The fuller statement of this position will be found in Neal Riemer, *The Revival of Democratic Theory* (New York: Appleton-Century-Crofts, 1962).

WHAT KIND OF GUIDANCE?

The big question dividing liberals and conservatives is whether a liberal-democratic theory can provide guidance of the right kind. And whose liberal-democratic theory? And what kind of guidance? And can this guidance be of help not only to academicians but to statesmen, politicians, administrators, newspaper editors, business, farm, and labor leaders? And can it be meaningful to the public at large?

Can a modern democratic theory get beyond vague, pious, and platitudinous expressions of what ought to be done? Are these "oughts" the right ones? Is democratic theory doomed to an allegedly amoral and indifferently scientific description of what is? Is an operational democratic theory—one capable of functioning in the real political world—limited to a cynical Machiavellian strategy of what can be? Can the democratic theorist meet the objections of those who maintain that a modern democratic theory is immature or dangerous or vain or impossible?

MISCONCEPTIONS OF DEMOCRATIC THEORY

A number of misconceptions make it particularly difficult for many of us to understand the democratic political theorist, his problems, and the relevance of political theory to public life. To the man-on-the-street, for example, the democratic theorist is often considered an idealist preoccupied with a Good and Beautiful World that has no meaningful relationship to life. To the public servant or statesman, he is an academician out of touch with the practical problems of administration or the harsh realities of power. And, to the academician himself, the democratic theorist may be suspect as a dangerous or naive or foolish or ponderous purveyor of ideas.

His life is not made happier by the fact that he is attacked both from without and from within the democratic camp. For example, as a liberal-democratic theorist, he is assailed by the Communists who view him as a lackey of the capitalists. His job, as the revolutionary Marxists see it, is to defend a reactionary bourgeois regime in which the capitalists deceive and oppress the poor workingman. On the other hand, many advocates of the *status quo* or the *status quo ante* within the democratic camp look upon the democratic theorist as the advance agent of collectivism. He is the fellow, they often argue, whose preachments on behalf of the welfare state prepare the way for totalitarianism. His abstract democratic dogmas, divorced from the nation's historical tradition, lead straight to *Animal Farm,* to *1984,* or to *Brave New World.* Or so, at least, we are told by the more reflective conservatives who oppose doctrines which allegedly lead to the brutal attempt to cut or stretch man until he fits the Procrustean bed of a utopian never-never land.

THE UNHAPPY DEMOCRATIC CONSCIOUSNESS

In the academic world, we find not only such conservative critics whose voices —often transformed and distorted—are heard in the market place, but also a number of other diverse critics whose refined lectures are coarsely echoed in the pulpit, press, or privy. These diverse critics may share only one thing in common: the unhappy consciousness that modern democratic theory is deaf or dumb or blind, or sick or impotent or dead.[2] They may existentially bemoan or scientifically observe the lack of faith that today makes democratic theory impossible in their judgment. Many in this group are skeptics, nihilists, or pseudosophisticated intellectuals who find it incredible that other modern men can believe—can believe in certain religious truths, can believe in the rational arguments of certain great philosophers, can believe in the prescriptive validity of certain democratic ideals.

Other critics may assert that we have gotten away from the classical model which alone can lead to the recovery of political philosophy. Here the argument is that we moderns have lost respect for virtue—that is, excellence—and will not recover from our modern ills until we are prepared to take the classical medicine of

[2] For analysis of and reply to "the unhappy democratic consciousness," see *ibid.,* pp. 33–42.

a Plato or an Aristotle. How this medicine, compounded before the advent of popular democracy, the American presidency, the American federal system, the rise of totalitarianism, the atomic bomb, sputnik, the world-wide revolution of rising expectations, can indeed cure our ills is unfortunately not made too clear.

Still other critics—attacking from yet another vantage point—may contend that political theory is unfeasible because true political science, after the model of the physical sciences, is still a mere babe in the scientific woods! Here the assumption is that political theory will not get anywhere until political theorists have amassed much more information, organized it in accordance with the methodology of the physical sciences, and are prepared to predict behavior more reliably than at present.[3] Finally, there are those who maintain that the theorist misinterprets the function of political theory when he asserts that we can, in fact, uncover the universal political truths that do exist and can wisely guide us. These critics argue that there are no such political truths and no such certain guidance.

HAVE WE BEEN TOO EASILY INTIMIDATED?

These misconceptions of and critical attacks on the nature and tasks of political theory within the democratic camp lead

[3] See here my criticism under the heading "Big Brother Science Is Watching You," ibid., pp. 26–33.

to a nerve-shattering conclusion. These views, if accepted, lead to the conclusion that a comprehensive democratic theory is politically dangerous, psychologically impossible, philosophically putrefying, scientifically suspect, or logically misconceived. Now, it is certainly no easy task to run the gantlet of such criticisms. Yet, may it not be that we have been too easily intimidated by those who wield the weapons in this ordeal by intellect? May it not be that we can run this gantlet and emerge, if not completely unscathed, at least on our feet, toughened, and therefore strengthened by the ordeal? May we not emerge, moreover, with a democratic theory whose values are sound, whose empirical propositions are realistic, and whose policy recommendations are wise?

In this article, I should like to focus attention primarily upon some conservative critics of the kind of political theory essential, in my judgment, to the revival of democratic theory in the United States.[4] Let me, then, first, state the tasks of such a modern democratic theory; second, indicate why these critics believe such tasks are dangerous and vain; and, third, reply briefly to these conservative attacks in the interest of the revival of democratic theory in the United States.

[4] Primary attention will be devoted to the following conservative critics: Daniel Boorstin, *The Genius of American Politics* (Chicago: University of Chicago Press, 1953); Russell Kirk, *The Conservative Mind* (Chicago: Henry Regnery, 1953); Michael Oakeshott, "Political Education," in Peter Laslett (ed.), *Philosophy, Politics and Society* (Oxford: Basil Blackwell, 1956), pp. 1–21.

THE FIVE TASKS

The revival of democratic theory requires the performance of five tasks.[5] The democratic political theorist must, first, seek a unifying conceptual scheme which can harmoniously integrate the political values, factual generalizations, and public policies of a democratic society. Second, he must more fully and deeply explore, identify, project, and justify the values

[5] For the more complete statement, see Riemer, *op cit.,* chap. 1, "Political Theory in the Dog-House," pp. 1–17.

that sane and civilized men ought to, do, and can live by. Third, he must provide us with a theoretical explanation of the way a democratic society actually conducts its business—how in fact it authoritatively allocates values in relationship to the actual functioning of political institutions, forces, and actors, how it actually umpires the struggle for power in accord with its own operative ideals. We need here a keener awareness of the gap between actual democratic aspiration and actual democratic behavior. Fourth, the democratic theorist must concern himself with the relationship of political theory to concrete issues of public policy. He must concern himself with the fundamental problems that beset democratic men and nations as they seek to advance the good life, to umpire the struggle for power, and to meet the challenges that ideology and science thrust upon them. In brief, he must attempt to provide for democratic men and nations a prudent guide to action. Here political theory must function to guide us prudently in working out public policies, designed in the light of the limitations and possibilities of empirical reality, to advance consciously conceived values. Fifth, the democratic theorist must call attention to areas of normative, empirical, and prudential research—research concerned with what ought to be, with what is, and with what can be—which is needed to deepen our ethical wisdom, advance our empirical knowledge, and increase the soundness of our public policies. Most importantly, such research may involve, for example, the future of the democratic revolution. This is the future that calls into question the possibility of achieving equality of consideration in race relations, of reconciling excellence and consent, of avoiding being either "Red" or "dead," of enhancing the unity and strength of the West, of successfully harnessing the revolution of rising expectations. The research may include reexamination of old values in the light of new conditions. It may embrace strictly empirical research. It may concern problems of administration, domestic policy, or international strategy. Unquestionably, this research will touch such diverse domestic fields as civil liberties, employment, education, health, housing, and public responsibility in the arts and sciences. Similarly, the recalculation of democracy's risks in the Cold War will demand research into the problems of genuine coexistence with the Soviet Union and Red China, of western European unity, of the perilous transition of the less-developed nations of the world.

THE SIN OF PROCRUSTES

One major obstacle to the fulfillment of these tasks is our dread of the sin of Procrustes. This is the sin of stretching or multilating political reality in order to make the world conform exactly to our radical theory. This dread is a legitimate reaction against totalitarian political theories which have sought to destroy much of the best in our civilized heritage. But, unfortunately, this dread has sometimes led to an indiscriminate attack on political theory in general and to a shotgun attack on all radical theories which are opposed to the wisdom of the prescriptive constitution, the historic, duly established way of attending to the business of the political community. In these attacks, the distinction between a liberal-democratic political theory—firmly committed to civil liberties for all, a decent livelihood for all, and the creative development of each man to the best of his ability—and a totalitarian political theory is often blurred. Similarly, these attacks often ignore the sane, sagacious, preservative features of liberal democracy. And, frequently, the attackers restrict our choice to one between conservatism à la Burke or radicalism à la Marx-Comte-Bentham-Rousseau-Condorcet. Consequently, disturbed by the sin of Procrustes, the democratic theorist holds back from a vigorous performance of the tasks of democratic theory.

SHOTGUN ATTACK ON RADICAL THEORIES

The upshot of the dread of the sin of Procrustes is a hostile reaction against the five major tasks of democratic theory. Initially the conservative thinkers who best express this reaction reject political theory as an architectonic scheme which should or can harmoniously integrate the normative, empirical, and prudential components of democratic political life. These are the components, recall, that deal respectively with what ought to be, with what is, and with what can be. The Communist attempt to blend a vision of a good society with laws of historical development and with a strategy of revolutionary action is held before us as a warning of the danger of an embracing and unifying formula. These conservatives thus oppose the effort to make theory explicit and comprehensive. With Burke, they argue that "one sure symptom of an ill-conducted state is the propensity of . . . people to resort" to political theories. Our best reliance is "the accumulated wisdom of tradition and institutions," a wisdom which makes an explicit theory superfluous.[6]

Second, these conservative thinkers reject radical probing or articulation of values. Political philosophy "will not help us to distinguish between good and bad political projects. . . " There is "no model laid up in heaven to which we should approximate our behavior. . . ." We need not search for values and incorporate them into a political theory. Our values have already been given to us and automatically defined for us by certain facts of geography and history peculiar to the American scene. Moreover, radical probing often leads to such evils as meliorism, contempt for tradition, political and economic leveling, and a rejection of the state as a "divinely ordained moral essence, a spiritual union of the dead, the living, and those unborn." It may also lead to other radical heresies: to a belief in the "perfectibility of man and the illimitable progress of society," to the conviction that "education, positive legislation, and alteration of environment can produce men like gods," to the denial "that humanity has a natural proclivity toward violence and evil," to the condemnation of "order and privilege," to an endorsement of total democracy, "centralization and consolidation," to an attack on private property.[7]

Third, they reject as dangerous the search for the empirical laws of politics. Political theory cannot provide us with an adequate understanding of politics. It only distorts political reality and denies the complexity of political life. Fortunately, we are told, Americans "have [at least

up to now] been more interested in the way it [politics] works than in the theory behind it." Here, then, we see a fear of alleged empirical laws which, when believed in and acted upon, serve only to oppress.[8]

FEAR OF EXTRAVAGANT AND PRESUMPTUOUS SPECULATIONS

Fourth, they reject the possibility that political theory can function as a prudent guide to action. Theory is dismissed as extravagant and presumptuous speculation. We should beware of using a theory as a blueprint for remaking society. We should not make "our society into the graven image of any man's political philosophy." Political theory, conceived either as political ideology or political philosophy, cannot provide us with right guidance. Such theories not only deny the complexity but also repudiate the wisdom and upset the functioning of the prescriptive historical tradition. It is false to think that a "political ideology . . . is able to determine and guide" us in political life. When a political ideology takes the "place of a tradition of political behavior" and becomes the normative pattern which society is then cut to fit, we have a "false and misconceived guide." It is so because a theory is only a part of political reality —and an exaggerated and distorted part at that! Political philosophy, which can help us "in removing some of the crookedness from our thinking," cannot be expected to increase our ability to be successful in political activity. It will not help us to distinguish between good and bad political projects; it has no power to guide or direct us in the enterprise of pursuing the intimations of our tradition. There is no "steady, unchanging, independent guide to which a society might resort to meet a serious political crisis." There are no guides of "superhuman wisdom and skill."[9]

Fifth, they reject—at least implicitly— a broader role for research. Presumably, research is to be limited primarily to the

[6] See, particularly, Boorstin, *op. cit.,* pp. 3, 8–9, 170–171.
[7] See Oakeshott, *op. cit.,* pp. 16 and 20; Boorstin, *op. cit.,* pp. 8–9; Kirk, *op. cit.,* p. 9.

[8] See Oakeshott, *op. cit.,* p. 14; Boorstin, *op. cit.,* p. 2.
[9] See Boorstin, *op. cit.,* p. 3; Oakeshott, *op. cit.,* pp. 7–8, 14, 20, 15, 16.

accumulated wisdom of our tradition and our going institutions.

Here, then, is one major reason for the lack of interest and of will in the performance of a democratic theory's five tasks. What critique of this position can be offered which can at once accept the legitimate warnings raised about the sin of Procrustes and yet free democratic theory to perform its essential tasks? The main criticism to be made, I believe, is that this essentially conservative position is too narrow, too misleading, and too restrictive. It concentrates much too heavily on the *status quo* and the *status quo ante*. Its view of the nature and role of political theory results in the absence of a fair hearing or a just verdict for a differently conceived democratic political theory.

DANGERS OF UNDUE RELIANCE UPON TRADITION

If there are real dangers in a totalitarian political theory, we must also appreciate that there can also be dangers in too heavy a reliance upon a country's tradition of political behavior, all of its historical institutions, and every feature of its prescriptive constitution. Such reliance can take our attention away from unfulfilled goals which we legitimately strive toward even though we recognize that they may be unfulfillable. It can destroy the tension between what ought to be and what is. It can place too high a premium on the going system and not enough on a searching re-examination of the *status quo* to see if the *status quo* is or is not in harmony with our consciously conceived values. It can result in a deadening of political vision and a loss of that vitality so essential to the advancement of democratic values.

We must, of course, *start* with a given tradition. We have no other realistic choice. But we need not *stop* with tradition, certainly not with a dominant tradition which, however salutary in so many respects, may still harbor the most virulent of political cancers affecting our vision, our vitality, our courage, and our integrity.

This is by no means the best of all possible worlds! And everything in it is not a necessary evil! [10] There is no reason why we cannot go beyond considering what resources our political tradition offers for dealing with certain situations. Indeed, survival itself may call upon us, in important instances, to break with tradition. The emphasis on the prescriptive constitution, interpreted in the fashion of Edmund Burke and the late eighteenth century, may be out of tune with the more rapid rate of change called for by modern life in the very interest, ironically, of some of the values that conservatives in the Burkean tradition hold. It may be out of tune with some radical changes essential to a United States still interested in preserving the great prescriptive values enshrined in the Preamble.

These changes involve, for example, the improved status of the Negro in American life, the higher priority that must be afforded excellence in all aspects of life, a heightened sense of communal responsibility for education, health, the arts, and our natural resources. It seems difficult to see how these objectives can be achieved pursuant to a conservative philosophy which is so deeply suspicious of reason, a faster rate of change, a less structured class system, social equality, and a larger role for the state in political, economic, and social matters. One may strongly doubt that such a conservative philosophy is capable of coping with the powerful democratic ferment in modern America, let alone the modern world. In brief, then, too great an emphasis on tradition and the going order may weaken the tension of democratic aspiration, paralyze prophetic vision, and nullify the constant striving to fulfill the conditions of the good life.

A SANE LIBERAL-DEMOCRATIC THEORY

If there are real dangers in a totalitarian political theory, there are also real dangers in reducing the alternatives facing us to a choice between a totalitarian or radical political theory and that conservative understanding based upon the prescriptive constitution. Such a choice leaves

[10] Compare Oakeshott, *op. cit.,* p. 21: " 'The world is the best of all possible worlds, and *everything* in it is a necessary evil.' "

no room for a sane and more accurate liberal-democratic theory.

There can be no doubt that certain political theories have been, and can be, highly dangerous. But there is no "iron law" that I know of that says that all political theories must be guilty of the sins of communism or fascism or of other extravagant and presumptuous speculations. To shrink from an articulate, comprehensive, and activistic political theory because Marx, Lenin, Stalin, Mussolini, and Hitler have committed the sin of Procrustes is shortsighted and suicidal. It is shortsighted because it represents an unmerited surrender. It is suicidal because it leaves the field of battle open to those who have declared they will bury us.

Political theorizing, we must appreciate, need not imply the construction of blueprints for remaking society or the idolatrous enforcement of uniformity pursuant to abstract and dogmatic theories derived from Reason. Whether a theory is dangerous or not will depend upon the kind of theory involved and upon the men who interpret it. There are, in brief, theories and theories. There are "Procrustean" (or totalitarian) theories whose practitioners mold men ruthlessly to fit the theory. And there are also what we might call "chameleon" theories whose adherents opportunistically adapt to any set of circumstances. But there are also theories which possess character. A theory with "character" is like a man with character. It is a theory which embodies a thought-out pattern of values and recommended behavior. It is neither dogmatic nor wishy-washy. It is, however, a theory whose proponents are respectful of the traditions of civility, are aware of the evil as well as the good in man, and are conscious of the double-edged sword that is political power. It is, above all, a theory whose interpreters appreciate the need to square values with the facts of life and to address themselves creatively to the changes and problems of the good political life.

It is indeed regrettable that Plato, Marx, and Hitler have so dominated our thinking about either political ideology or political philosophy or political science that we are unable to conceive of political theory as a guide to action differently from the way they conceived it. There is, of course, always the danger that a given political theory is a distorted abstract or imperfect abridgement of a given political tradition.[11] But all political theories need not be. Certainly, a wise democratic theory will seek to remedy its imperfections and correct its distortions. Like any guide-map, a political theory must, I grant, not pretend to do more or tell more than it can. Furthermore, its dependence on the reality which gives it sense must always thoroughly be appreciated. A good guide-map, constantly revised and intelligently employed, is a tremendous asset. It fails not necessarily because of its inevitable exaggerations and emphases but because of ours. We may misinterpret it, attempt to use it for unexplored terrain and unmapped ocean, neglect to bring it up to date. We may, in brief, place too great a reliance upon it and not enough upon our own creative role in exercising judgment.

The political sea is indeed deep and frequently stormy. However, if we have no scientifically established starting place or destination in God's universal history, we can certainly ascertain our present position on the social geographer's ocean and seek, if not final haven, at least more favorable voyages. Perfect guidance may not be man's earthly lot, but what sane democratic theorist would expect it in the first place?[12]

CREATIVE ROLE OF DEMOCRATIC THEORY

In making room for a sane liberal-democratic theory between assorted "radical" and "conservative" theories, it is important to stress that the values involved in a theory come from men, not from "landscapes."[13] The social "landscape" obviously influences the values that we believe in, but it is men in history who impregnate the social "landscape"

[11] See Oakeshott, op. cit., pp. 8, 9, 10, 12, 14, 21.
[12] See Oakeshott, op. cit., p. 15: "In political activity, then, men sail a boundless and bottomless sea; there is neither harbour for shelter nor floor for anchorage, neither starting-place nor appointed destination." For Oakeshott's defense of his position see his footnote 1, p. 15.
[13] See Boorstin, op. cit., for the use of this word.

with values and who have the ability to accept or reject the "given" values of a nation's tradition. We were born free, not because democracy alone was compatible with the frontier, but because of our inherited, debated, revised religious, political, economic, and social ideas. We have remained free, not necessarily because of the gift of abundant land and resources, but because Americans have ever debated and revised their inheritance to make reality square better with re-examined ethical norms. To make this point is not to maintain that political theory, properly conceived, displaces "history by philosophy," or makes us contemptuous of our past, or flouts the wisdom of our institutions.[14] Obviously, political theory must, to some extent, reflect history and institutions. But it must do so in a creative, selective, and critical way.

[14] *Ibid.*, p. 170.

It is as dangerous to abandon values, unwittingly, to history as to allow mad theorists—like a Stalin or a Hitler—to make history conform to the theorists' insane conception of what reality should be. In *both* instances, the dominant forces in the older tradition or the dominant forces in the revolutionary or reactionary tradition may not be affecting that prudent compromise between "ought" and "is" which is the essence of sensible politics. Certainly it is no sin to attempt comprehensively to bring our programs of action into accord with the values we ought to live by and the facts that condition our prudent efforts to advance our values. There may be no absolutely perfect independent guide in this world, and there may be many mischievous utopian guides, but there certainly is the possibility of a guide which provides limited and modest and prudent help.

CONCLUSION

We must, then, clearly recognize that the sin of Procrustes is not the inevitable concomitant of the messianic tradition of Western democratic political theory. A democratic political theory may preserve the tension between ought and is—which is so characteristic of Western thought—without succumbing to totalitarianism. The development of a democratic political theory to guide us does not mean that we employ Procrustean techniques to make political reality fit an ideological bed. Respect for the prescriptive tradition is not incompatible with the creative theoretical response often called for if men are sanely to understand and prudently to manage their changing world.

Once, then, we have accepted the tasks of democratic political theory as difficult but not inescapably dangerous, as urgent and not inevitably vain, we can begin to explore with a firmer will and a keener vision the concepts of a reformulated democratic theory and their more precise relationship to our present problems in the United States.

Liberal Democracy and Social Control

ANDREW HACKER

Andrew Hacker is professor of political science at Cornell University. His special field of interest is political theory.

Liberal democrats, like all those who elect to paddle in the placid waters of liberalism, show a charming imperviousness to the existence of power. It is the ingenuousness which permitted the ideology of individualism to flourish for well over a century in the Western world. But all chickens—political as well as others—eventually come home to roost; and the failure to imbibe the home truths set

Reprinted from *The American Political Science Review*, 51 (December 1957), 1009–1026, by permission of the publisher and author.

down by such ungentlemanly characters as Thrasymachus, Machiavelli, and Pareto now accounts for the dilemmas, reconsiderations, and tortured defenses of liberal democracy which we see abounding on all sides.

Liberal democracy—that uneasy compromise which was never a compromise at all—is, from the moral standpoint, the worthiest of political creeds.[1] It can arouse the enthusiasm of the humane, the heretical, and the responsible: in short, of all men of good will. But the tenets of liberal democracy can only be a guide for governors and governed in a community if there exists a halcyon situation in which the traditional status system is placidly taken for granted by all in the community. Only in this way can attention be focussed on the preservation of liberties and the encouragement of individual development. For social arrangements set the stage for the allocation of power, interests, and status. As long as these arrangements are not questioned in their fundamentals, then the conditions for promoting the liberal democratic ethic are possible of attainment. It goes without saying that any community must maintain a consensus if it is to survive. The question to be explored continually, then, is what propositions must be agreed upon. The startling fact of our time is that there are fundamental propositions about the allocation of power which were sublimely taken for granted heretofore and which are now being called to the bar to defend themselves. That they have no ultimate defense is the tragedy of liberal democracy in the modern world.

Liberal democracy in America never had a politics. It was essentially an upper-middle-class and upper-class creed. Unable, through ignorance—or unwilling, because of sensibility—to make explicit its class basis, its proponents persuaded themselves that the ideology was accepted on its merits. In point of fact, it was the class and not the ideology which was accepted. Liberal democracy, the creed of that class, was the received ideology simply because the men who promulgated it were the men who had deference automatically and unquestioningly accorded to them. The liberal democratic tradition in America has had an infinitely smaller constituency than we prefer to believe. The man in the street accepted political, economic, and social arrangements the basis for which he did not in the least perceive or comprehend. If he occasionally rebelled at them, it was not for the purpose of furthering individual liberty in the liberal democratic sense; it was rather status or interest revolt in the name of popular or direct democracy. For if liberal democracy never had a politics it never had to have one either. The classes, which supplied the personnel for the positions of power and prestige, had the built-in means of control which exist in any stratified society. In short, the basis of power of liberal democracy has traditionally been deference to a ruling class.

[1] "Liberal democracy," for present purposes, must be defined briefly and arbitrarily. It describes both an ideology and an institutional system; and its appeal is to those who claim to be fearful alike of the consequences of elite rule and of direct democracy. Both ideology and institutions, therefore, postulate a dynamic equilibrium between two values: (1) majority rule and human equality, *i.e.,* that each shall count for one in political arrangements and that self-government, with the majority decision prevailing, is the best government; and (2) individual rights and constitutional guarantees, *i.e.,* that there shall be an optimum area in which neither government nor society shall interfere with the individual in his pursuit of activities he thinks good. Both these values, Liberal Democrats postulate, are crucial: neither must be allowed to overwhelm the other. The means by which a majority is to be brought to respect minorities, and the areas in which individuals are to be left unhindered, as well as the methods for ensuring that in "proper" cases a majority shall have its way—these questions are open to constant discussion, compromise, and accommodation. This creed seems to be the received doctrine among academic political scientists; and the juxtaposition of majority rule and individual liberty is the alpha and omega of most introductory courses and textbooks. For the definitive exposition, see J. Roland Pennock, *Liberal Democracy: Its Merits and Prospects* (New York, 1950).

THE CLASS BASIS OF LIBERAL DEMOCRACY

Whether we like to admit it or not, a society which encourages the full flowering of individual liberty is, and can only be, a stratified society. Such encouragement requires a strong measure of tolerance on the part of those with power. The man in the street, as John Stuart Mill never ceased repeating, is fearful of the unusual and the idiosyncratic. It is only a secure class which can afford to set down the conditions which allow for non-conformist behavior. This means that social controls must exist which, on one side of the coin, will allow a ruling class to exercise the significant power without having to worry about the emotional insecurities of the mass of men; and, on the other, will divert the mass of men from questioning the fact that a small class has arrogated to itself the privilege of deciding what forms of behavior are to be tolerated.

For almost a century and a half, America had just such an unquestioned class. It ruled the country without having to worry about public opinion or popular emotion. And the social control which permitted this class to hold informal sway was the very traditional one of deference. Deference here is not to be thought of as an Old World retainer tugging at his forelock as the lord of the manor drives by. It means more simply that the bulk of the community defers to a small section and does not think to question that this class will hold the important positions and make the vital decisions. America has had such a class, and to it has been delegated national power in its economic, political, and social aspects. These "old" Americans possess, for the most part, some common characteristics. First of all, they are "WASPs"—in the cocktail party jargon of the sociologists. That is, they are white, they are Anglo-Saxon in origin, and they are Protestant (and disproportionately Episcopalian). To their Waspishness should be added the tendency to be located on the Eastern seaboard or around San Francisco, to be prep school and Ivy League educated, and to be possessed of inherited wealth. Talcott Parsons has generalized about such a group:

There is a continuing tendency for earlier economic developments to leave a 'precipitate' of upper groups, the positions of whose members are founded in the achievements of their ancestors, in this case relatively recent ones. By historical necessity these groups are strongest in the older parts of the country. Hence the cit-

ies of the Eastern seaboard have tended to develop groups that are the closest approach we have—though still very different from their European equivalent—to an aristocracy. They have generally originated in business interests, but have taken on a form somewhat similar to the mercantile aristocracies of some earlier European societies, such as the Hanseatic cities.[2]

There is no point in belaboring the definitional question of whether or not this group or groups constitutes a "class." What is being said is simply that it was these people who, without serious question on anyone's part, entered, *au naturel,* the positions of power in the political and economic worlds. They provided the presidential candidates, the diplomatic personnel, the cabinet officers, the judges and influential lawyers, and the heads of the important banks, investment houses, commercial interests, and the boards of directors of many of the great corporations. They also, of course, dominated the churches and the institutions of higher learning. In short, it was this group which exercised national power. Of course, immigrants gained access to seats of municipal power quite soon; and on the frontiers of the economy trails were blazed by men who, if of old American stock, did not spring from the ruling class. But the power of the city politician was localized, and the Robber Baron was too busy on the industrial front to worry much about national politics and social arrangements. At all events, we must not overestimate the national power of the city boss or the entrepreneur, despite their flamboyant behavior and the publicity which attended it.[3] In reality, it was members of the tra-

[2] "Social Strains in America," in Daniel Bell, ed., *The New American Right* (New York, 1955), p. 125.

[3] The American mythology, of course, is that most nineteenth-century businessmen were shrewd, ill-tutored freewheelers like Jay Gould and Daniel Drew. In fact, studies in entrepreneurial history show that, for the most part, the men who headed the great enterprises were from a privileged background. See Mabel Newcomer, *The Big Business Executive* (New York, 1955), and W. Lloyd Warner and James C. Abegglen, *Big Business Leaders in America* (New York, 1955). For an evaluation and comparison of these studies, see Morroe Berger, "The Business Elite: Then and Now," *Commentary,* Vol. 22 (October, 1956), pp. 367–74.

ditional ruling group who made the decisions which set the tone and atmosphere in which American politics was to be conducted. It is, of course, true that this pool of the privileged was not a caste. Failure to possess any one of the requisites mentioned above did not debar a potential entrant. Certainly, inherited wealth did not have to go back further than one generation. Analogy with the European aristocracies is, as Parsons points out, misleading. A better comparison would be with what has been referred to in contemporary Britain as "The Establishment." [4] The basis of this group is partly family, education, and social standing; but it is also to be defined in terms of a set of position-holders, or role-players. As long as people from a narrow and specified background have virtually automatic access to the seats of power, then we are speaking of a "ruling class." When recruitment for these positions is based primarily on talent, the power inherent in the roles does not necessarily diminish, but it would be more proper to refer to an "elite." However, one of the "talents" demanded for ascendency may often be possession of the manners and attitudes acquired only through the breeding and education gained by virtue of membership in the dominant class.

At all events, nothing is lost if we refer to an old ruling class in American life. This group did not possess the corporate self-awareness of the British aristocracy. Furthermore, it would be idle to accuse its members of any conspiratorial designs. If there were common objectives and common outlooks among this ruling class, it was simply because those who belonged to it were pretty much the same kind of people. Through constant contacts in clubs, churches, boards of directors, governmental bodies, and in each others' homes, they informed one another of what was going on. But again it must be stressed that such transmission, consultation, and concert can hardly be construed as "a plot against the people." Rather it was a spontaneous—and oftentimes child-like—effort to perform the tasks and du-

ties they sincerely believed to be theirs by right.

The spontaneous character of this activity ought to be apparent if we consider it in its ideological aspect. The promotion of liberal democracy was one of the chief endeavors of the old ruling class. This was not for the sake of that ideology's own intrinsic beauty, nor was it for the purpose of giving the mass of the community an opportunity to develop their potentialities. Rather, the idea of a limited government was for their own class benefit. The reasons for this, on the economic side, are quite clear. But in the process, this class came to defend the Bill of Rights, the common law, and the whole idea of decency, civility, and fair play—in short, the framework of liberal democracy. The judges and lawyers who came from this class were willing to interpret the Constitution in such a way that dissenters would be allowed free rein to express their thoughts. This tolerance, however, came not from any abstract love for civil liberties.[5] It is simply that the ruling class itself counted *among its own members* individuals who possessed radi-

[4] See Henry Fairlie, "Political Commentary," *Spectator*, Vol. 195 (September 23, 1955), pp. 379–81; and (October 21, 1955), pp. 516–17.

[5] This point has been well made by John Roche in his "Communication" in this RE-VIEW, Vol. 51 (June, 1957), pp. 484–88. Roche also discusses the lack of a libertarian strand in the American tradition in his excellent articles, "We've Never Had More Freedom," *New Republic* Vol. 134 (January 23, 1956), pp. 12–15; (January 30, 1956), pp. 13–16; and (February 6, 1956), pp. 13–15. If it seems outrageous to suggest that a ruling class was only concerned with keeping its own children out of trouble, a recent example may bring this unwelcome truth home. Contrast, for a moment, the reaction of the upper-middle-class liberal to the indictment, trial, and conviction of Alger Hiss, on the one hand, and of the Rosenbergs, on the other. In terms of the overall record, there may be equal reason to wonder at the justice of both convictions. Yet the good people who were (and still are) much aroused about the treatment of Hiss seem to find it difficult to worry about the Rosenbergs, or Morton Sobell. Would it be too much to suggest that this is because Hiss was one of the "right people"—in terms of stock, education, manner, etc.,—whereas the Rosenbergs were not? There are, of course, all sorts of complicating factors which bedevil a comparison of the two cases. Yet in light of the contemporary liberal reaction—or lack of it—to the plight of the Rosenbergs, perhaps the limited civil liberties vistas of the old ruling class become more plausible.

cal views and who tended to display idiosyncratic behavior. In order to protect its own kind, it was prepared to give strength to the law by ensuring that the Bill of Rights was a living doctrine. Tolerance, therefore, was an internalized class tolerance. The Harvard atheist of good family, the transcendental rebel with manners and breeding, the Utopian socialist who paid heed to the rules of gentlemanly intercourse—these were, after all, "our kind of people" and had to be safeguarded from the coercive power both of the state and of society in general.

The whole rationale of the liberal democratic scheme—incorporating the ideas of individual liberty and limited government—was that it could work as long as it had only to protect a particular section of the community. It takes power to guarantee freedom. And the power of the ruling class was exercised only to carve out an area of freedom for its own members. On the one hand, it shaped the law so that property rights and freedom of expression would be sanctioned; on the other, it kept the emotions of the majority at bay. It is vital to take note of this because there are many who believe that the protection of the Bill of Rights ought to be extended to cover *all* men and not simply a privileged few. In abstract terms this, of course, is a worthy belief. But what must be confronted is the question of *who*, if there is no established ruling class, is to defend the liberties of the larger constituency of citizens which has developed. It must not be thought that their fellow-citizens, or the state, or even the courts are in a position to protect *any* dissident whatsoever. Certainly, in the past, the nonconformist, if he was simply an average citizen, was not so protected. This privilege was reserved for a few.

For the Constitutional gentlemen who acted as the guardians of the common law and the Bill of Rights were traditionally in a position where they could well form a bulwark around those in need of such a hedge. If the Overseers of Harvard College or the Justices of the Supreme Court wished to condone an unpopular act, the deference they commanded stood between them and the breath of popular criticism. And even if at times, the deference showed a tendency

to wear thin, the established position of these lawyers, judges, educators, and businessmen in the social and economic structure gave them the ability to ignore the clamorings of the ordinary man. The ruling class, then, combined civility and power. Educated in a humane tradition, conscious of the value of free expression, and willing to protect their own sort, they shaped the instruments of law and social institutions so that at least the civil liberties of a few were protected.[6] The man on the street might well wonder at the wisdom of tolerating such behavior. But he did not consider it his province to question his exclusion from participating in making these mysterious judgments.

Furthermore, it must be stressed that the ruling class was quite conscious of the limitations on its power. It made no effort to educate the population to the *merits* of liberal democracy. Nor did it seek to protect those outside its own membership. The civil liberties of the trade union organizer in Colorado, of the Negro in Alabama, of the disabled factory worker in Pennsylvania or of the nonconformist professor of economics in a small Midwestern college—these persons were not considered proper materials for defense. Had the ruling class sought, say, to put its power behind the radicals of the I.W.W. it would have so endangered its foundation of deference that the existence of the class itself would come into question. Courts, universities, boards of directors all drew a firm line as to who would merit their help. This could not be otherwise. The dynamics of American growth let the ruling class know in no un-

[6] For a good statement of the tone and propriety which developed under the aegis of gentlemanly politics, see Edward Shils' chapter entitled, significantly, "The Deformation of Civility," in his *Torment of Secrecy* (Glencoe, Illinois, 1956), pp. 153–175: "As long as the political ruling classes were recruited from the aristocracy or from the classes whose conduct was guided by an aristocratic ideal of life, there was an inevitable diffuseness in their range of interest and in their attitude towards their major tasks. The aristocrat was expected to act like a gentleman, to be interested in the administration of his estate, to be interested in sports and proficient in military skills, and he was naturally expected to take his place in the government of the country, locally and nationally" (p. 156).

certain terms that its power had perceptible limitations.

It is proper, therefore, when speaking of the defense of liberal democracy to ask just *who* the defenders are. In the first century of our Republic's existence, one could readily point to these guardians: the old ruling class. Through the deference accorded to them and by virtue of their established economic power, they

were able to carry the shield for those they chose to protect. The existence of these people cannot be taken for granted. Liberal democracy would have had no meaning without their intervention and interpretation. And if this class was needed to give meaning to the idea of freedom, then one has to ask how long liberal democracy can last without the presence of its protectors.

THE NEW MEN

It is common knowledge that the power of the old American ruling class has diminished over the past fifty years. There are at least two major reasons for the toppling of the traditional hegemony and the rise of new men of power. These are the Americanization of the immigrant and the expansion of the economy.

The deference which was accorded to the old ruling class was founded on the premise that our doors would always be open to new arrivals from Europe.[7] For this flood of immigration ensured the continued existence of a large mass of people who were, in reality, second-class citizens. To be sure, in municipal politics they might sell their votes to the machine. But above this level they would not—nor would their party bosses—think to question national leadership. This proletariat for a generation provided an acquiescent base for the old family rulers. The process is made clear in the party of the immigrant: the Democrats. Ed Flynn might

boss the Bronx, but he would defer to Franklin D. Roosevelt (of Harvard); Carmine De Sapio rides behind Averill Harriman (of Yale); and Jake Arvey cleared the way for Adlai Stevenson (of Princeton). The seeming inconsonance of the fact that the party of the immigrant accepted old-stock patricians as its leaders is good evidence of the deference that was paid to the *ancien regime*. And as long as this unquestioning attitude was bolstered by the arrival of boatloads of new immigrants the old families stood secure.

More important, in many ways, was the fantastic expansion of the economy. For with tremendous expansion could go tremendous waste. There is little doubt that the old ruling class produced many brilliant leaders. But it also produced its fair share of uninspired mediocrities. A man who went effortlessly to Groton, Harvard College, and Harvard Law School then went on, without strain, to a Wall Street law firm and perhaps to a Cabinet post in time. If he had ability, it was strictly a matter of genetic probability. Yet success was not hard to achieve, for his only competition was from members of his own class. And the rules which governed this competition were those of gentlemen. The talented Harvard "poor boy," even if Protestant and Anglo-Saxon, was not urged to enter this race which was not a race. And the application of the brilliant Fordham Law School graduate was not even considered. Such an imperviousness to talent could be afforded. The rate of expansion and innovation in our economy was such that the casual, the amateur, and even the stupid in high places were cushioned by auto-

[7] There has been surprisingly little written by political scientists on the political implications of the Americanization process. The task appears to have been left to journalists and members of other academic disciplines. Samuel Lubell's *The Future of American Politics* (New York, 1952) and *The Revolt of the Moderates* (New York, 1956) are good essays in casual empiricism. William S. White's " 'Consensus American': A Portrait" in *The New York Times Magazine* (November 25, 1956) is an interesting attempt at a theory. Perhaps the best analyses (brilliant when read individually and chaotic when read at one sitting) are the papers by Peter Viereck, David Riesman, Richard Hofstadter, Seymour Lipset, Nathan Glazer, Talcott Parsons, and Daniel Bell in *The New American Right, op. cit.* While this book is a discussion of the McCarthyite-nativist fringe, much of the analysis can be applied to a far larger segment of the American population.

matic profits and prestige. It was possible, and thought preferable, to have the "right" man rather than the best men. The law, for example, was conducted among gentlemen in a leisurely way. There was no imperative that the Cravath firm had to have the best tax man. Taxes, like everything else, were far simpler in those days; and at all events, it was better to preserve traditions of civility by associating with people of one's own kind. The price of tolerating mediocrity was not high; and organizational life was sufficiently cushioned so that efficiency did not have to be the chief value.

These conditions allowed the ruling class to rule, and to rule according to its own standards of what constituted meritorious leadership. As a result, these rulers were ill-instructed in the grammar of power. It is altogether explainable that we never produced a Machiavelli or a Burke to set down the rudimentary facts of political life. From Henry Adams to Woodrow Wilson to Dean Acheson, the old-stock leaders have assumed that they stood or fell on their intelligence, honesty, or administrative skill. Never did they ask the forbidden question: "*Why* should men follow me? *Me* of all people?" It took an Edmund Burke, who was always on the fringes of Britain's Establishment to see that deference to a ruling class can be maintained only by consciously fostering the sentiments of habit, custom, and prejudice. The opium of religion, and the myth of the natural superiority of prescriptive rulers, Burke said quite frankly, must be maintained in the minds and hearts of the common people if it is to be assured that they will continue to defer to their betters. Yet the American ruling class had to do without the superstitious—and feudal—basis of its European counterparts.[8] This meant that its power could last only as long as the patterns of deference held up of their own strength. And just as unrestricted immigration and an exuberantly expanding economy were its mainstays, so changes in these areas led to the decline of the old ruling class.

For once the barriers to new Americans were closed, our second-class citizenry be-gan to disappear. With the closing off of immigration it was soon evident that a race of "pure" Americans, without benefit of hyphens, would develop. The last generations to come in during the decades before the gate clanged shut would, for a time, remain humble and deferential. But they would be the last. From then on, their children and grandchildren would become full blooded and first-class citizens. This new citizenry would be able to take at face value the rhetoric of equality. The son of the Irish truck-driver and the grandson of the Italian shoemaker can find no compelling reason to think of themselves as other than Americans. Already the Scandinavians and the Germans have lost their ethnic identity. The Slavs and Jews are well on the way to assimilation. In a brief span, only the Negroes, Mexican-Americans, and Puerto Ricans will stand outside the pale.[9]

By all traditional lights, these new Americans are arrogant.[10] It was arrogant of the Boston Irish to want one of their own—a Curley—as their mayor rather than a Beacon Hill Brahmin. This new arrogance is coming into its own; and it is now beyond the bounds of control. No longer can deference be counted on as a means of political and social control. The old families have had to join combat with the new. No one can be sure whether it was the Secretary of the Army or the Wisconsin Senator who won the televised battle several years ago, but it is certain that for all his New England heritage,

---

[8] Louis Hartz, *The Liberal Tradition in America* (New York, 1955).

[9] Even the assimilation pattern of Jews—long thought a special case—is going according to form. See Oscar Handlin, "What Will U.S. Jewry Be Like in 2000?", *The National Jewish Monthly*, Vol. 71, No. 9 (May, 1957), pp. 5, 32–33. And for a glimpse of the way middle-class Negroes are preparing themselves for the immersion, see E. Franklin Frazier, *Black Bourgeoisie* (Glencoe, Illinois, 1957).

[10] "Arrogance" is certainly the word which comes immediately to mind when one reads, say, Peter Viereck's *The Unadjusted Man* (Boston, 1956), or Walter Lippman's *The Public Philosophy* (Boston, 1955). It is the view of both "conservative" and "liberal" liberal democrats that humility ought to be the most noticeable characteristic of the man in the street. However, Viereck's flaming indictment of direct democracy ends up being not so much clarion as pathetic. Down deep, Viereck must know that the ruling class he so respects will never again command the deference of the American public.

Stevens was not the hands-down victor. The point is not that the *ancien regime* had had its day. Centuries of prestige are not dashed in an hour. Rather the old regime must now face the competition of classes which once knew their proper station. It can no longer count on automatic respect—or automatic anything at all.

Furthermore, our economy has reached a stage of complexity and consolidation where talent is needed and talent is rewarded. The American dream of open opportunity has extended to areas—important areas—never available before to large sections of the population. In an earlier day, as was pointed out, the Wall Street law firm did not suffer if it had something less than the best tax man. Today, however, talent is at a premium in the upper ranks of business and the professions, while sixteen years of full employment have forced employers to abandon many discriminatory bars in order to secure sufficient qualified help in respectable lower rank occupations—which may in turn afford entry to the upper ranks. And so citadels once closed to the child of the immigrant are now opening. It is vital to remind ourselves that it is only since 1940 that banks, investment houses, the diplomatic service, and established industries and universities have opened their positions of power and responsibility to others than those of old American stock. Twenty years ago Americans of Irish, Italian, Slav, and Jewish antecedents were simply not recruited, admitted, or welcomed.

All this is changing. New men, of both immigrant and old stock, are being admitted with greater frequency. Our society and our economy are more complex, more competitive, and more sophisticated. To stand the pace brought on by the complexity of the tasks we must perform, fewer and fewer organizations can afford to keep on those of mediocre competence. In fields ranging from medicine to advertising, from accounting to personnel, from educational administration to the ministry, from the foreign service to journalism— in all of these, skills are required. Even old family firms and partnerships must let in new men (hopefully a son-in-law, but usually not). For without these hands, the ship will surely founder in highly competitive waters. The new men are energetic. They have to be, and they have had to be. But the expenditure of this energy is at a price. The psychic cost is high. For the man who has had to run, to push, and to fight develops an outlook towards himself and towards society quite at variance from that of the man who has easily had power and responsibility thrust upon him.

The *ancien regime* was a leisure class. To be sure, many of its members toiled mightily in the vineyard. But their upbringing and even their adult years were devoid of the pressures imposed on the new men of today. That leisure enabled them to study—not necessarily in a formal, but often in a disciplined, way—the responsibilities and obligations which were to be theirs. The lawyer had, of course, to serve his client. But he was able to serve the common law and the Constitution at the same time. The educational administrator took seriously the claims of "useless" scholarship as well as those of useful preparation for life. In short, men of leisure were able to regard their power as an instrument for transmitting traditional values as well as an instrument for performing particular tasks at hand.[11] These values were sustained by a class

[11] To be sure, there were free-wheeling entrepreneurs, who lived on the frontiers of our economy in the nineteenth century, and who had no sense of responsibility to society or to posterity in the prescriptive sense. And no one expected them to. But we must not overestimate their numbers (see the references above, note 3); and we must also recall that many of them, like Rockefeller and Harriman, founded family dynasties. Thus a John D. Rockefeller, Jr. was put in a position where he could serve his fellow men in conservationist and philanthropic endeavors. And the five grandsons have carried on the "tradition" from Latin America to Winrock, Arkansas. The family character of nineteenth century and early twentieth century enterprise made it possible for these families to develop responsible second and third generations. Today's men of power have little opportunity to do this for their sons. This means that each successive industrial ruler is, in a real sense, a self-made man. Each one has made the climb himself and in doing this has not had the leisure or security to develop a sense of *noblesse oblige* which, some might wish, would inform his exercise of power. See Daniel Bell, "The Break-Up of Family Capitalism," *Partisan Review,* Vol. 24 (Spring, 1957), pp. 317–20.

which could ignore the demands of career-building and organizational competition. For it is plain enough that there is all too frequently a conflict between, let us say, defending the Bill of Rights and earning a dollar or winning a vote. Simple exhortation is not enough to lead a man to strike a blow for the one at the risk of losing the other. He must first be sure that he is in a position to make a short-run sacrifice for the long-term good.

The new men are not cushioned either by status or by private incomes. If we ask the newly arrived man—who, let it be said, is never completely sure that he has arrived—to take a stand on fundamental liberties, we are asking too much of him. One may, with good reason, demand that a Senator from an old Cincinnati family or a Boston lawyer of wealth and standing stake a claim in defense of the First Amendment. But to ask this of a bright young politician from California or an engineer who has risen through the ranks of an automobile company is asking the impossible. The distinction is not one of character or personality. What distinguishes a Taft from a Nixon is what separates the old from the new men. As Shils points out, the new

American elites in business, politics, publicity and learning tend to come great geographical distances from the places of their birth to the places where they work and achieve. The great size of the country makes the loss of local ties in the leadership of the country a common phenomenon. Moreover, the cultures, the professional and social milieu into which the newly ascended leaders come, do not ordinarily possess powerful traditions which impose themselves firmly on most new-comers. There is no aristocratic or gentry pattern of life to which newcomers can clearly aspire and which they can definitely assimilate.[12]

The new men have neither family nor wealth nor geographical ties to support them. They have only their talent. And the talent must be a "marketable" one: it must accommodate itself to the demands of customers, voters, and colleagues. The *ancien regime* did not have to worry about the market. Either the customer-voter would docilely take what was offered; or, if he had the presumption to refuse the offering, he could be ignored with impunity.

The objective needs of the man in the street have not changed over the years. It is doubtful if he is more tolerant of the unusual or unknown than was his grandfather. What has changed is the fact that more and more of our men of power *must* be directed in their actions by these popular demands, whims, and caprices. We are entering a more perfect democracy in that the customer-voter is now, more than ever before, "always right." The new lawyer, for instance, is not so secure that he can ignore the wishes of his clients. Neither is the new broker or corporation president or university professor. And the stark fact is that a larger and larger proportion of market demands, be they economic or social or political, are in conflict with the traditional values of liberal democracy. The law has ceased to be a profession and has become an arm of our corporate economy. The chief reason for this transformation is to be found in the new lawyers, who know full well that they have no personal choice other than to serve their clients. The modern university

[12] *Op. cit.,* p. 79. A number of recent novels juxtapose the new and the old men quite neatly. Louis Auchincloss's *The Great World and Timothy Colt* (Boston, 1956) shows how a Wall Street law firm undergoes this transition in its leading personnel. The senior partner, a venerable figure on the style of Oliver Wendell Holmes, is forced to admit to partnership a Fordham Law School graduate. The latter has not one iota of feeling for the legal profession's prescriptive responsibilities (we can just imagine what *his* response would be if he were asked to defend a Communist under a Smith Act indictment); but he is highly skilled in bringing in the kind of business a large firm needs to survive. When the patrician dies, it is inevitable that the new man will take over complete charge. The firm will be successful; but success will be judged by an entirely different standard. The legal ethic of the old regime will be looked on as a curiosity; perhaps a worthy relic, but hardly attuned to modern needs. On the other side of the street, Cameron Hawley's *Cash McCall* (Boston, 1955) shows just how the new manipulator is capable of meeting problems which are totally incomprehensible to the old-style businessman. It is significant that when the editors of *Business Week* gave this book to several top executives to read and asked them to discuss the "moral problem" raised by the existence of Cash, most of them saw nothing unusual in his activites—but if there was, it could be remedied by changing the current tax laws! No. 1372 (December 17, 1955), pp. 104–114.

cannot be expected to hold up the flag of liberal education against the cries of students—and their future employers—for vocational or pre-professional training. The few institutions which hold out for the traditional values can do so because they are so prestigious and so financially cushioned that they can ignore market demands. But to think that the small New England college will set the future standard for the new campuses of state universities being created in the middle and far west is wishful thinking. While many professors at such campuses might like to follow such a lead, their institution cannot afford to. More and more they will be forced to imitate, and with success, the pattern set by a Michigan State University. What the defenders of liberal education fail to concern themselves with are the structural conditions under which such education—and institutions imparting such education—can flourish. The first condition is internal strength: and power to do the right is hardly bestowed by exhortation. For strength is the strength to ignore the market. Is there not a high positive correlation between size of endowment and whether or not a private institution kept on a professor who pleaded the Fifth Amendment? Today neither the institutions, nor the professors, nor the students, are in a position to tell the consuming public to go to the devil.

America, then, is more democratic than ever before. Careers are open to the talents, and not by virtue of an Horatio Alger-like break. But the new men of power have, in their climb, had no time to develop a sense of responsibility toward what have been our traditional standards —our liberal democratic values. Furthermore, these new men are always personally insecure. They cannot rely on traditional patterns of deference to maintain their power. For they have no family ties or inherited wealth to bolster their careers. But what is more crucial is that deference to the old ruling class has all but ceased to exist in the popular mind. Indeed, just as the new men show small respect for the family connections of those they have joined, so this attitude is spreading throughout society.[13] Despite the

fact that we live in a period of prosperity, there is a slackening indulgence of the old rich. Those who are admired are those on their way up. Talent—especially talent in "human relations"—is what is held up as the noteworthy achievement.

But if the new men are admired, they are admired only for the duration of the popular appeal which they evoke for their personal performances. As individuals, the new men cannot be said to command deference in the traditional sense of that word. This means, as will be seen, that they must seek other forms of control. The members of the *ancien regime,* who were habitually deferred to simply because of their class connection, never had to concern themselves with control. They ruled; they were obeyed. Their interest was in administration and the pursuit of the right as they saw it. The new men, on the other hand, have been given the instrument of power without a built-in form of control. It is not guaranteed to them that habitual deference will be accorded by those over whom they must exercise power. This potentially anarchic situation necessitates the calling forth of a set of political arrangements far different from those found in traditional societies. The theories of John Locke and John Stuart Mill are not of much use here. What must be called forth is the Machiavellian prescription, as old as Thrasymachus and as new as the latest

---

[13] That traditional American class relationships have little meaning not only to the man-in-the-street, but also to his wife in the split-level house, is brought out by Elizabeth Janeway in her review of Diana Barrymore's *Too Much, Too Soon* in *The New York Times Book Review,* April 7, 1957. Miss Janeway was commenting on what is wanted in novel-reading today: "Today's mass audience finds fiction hard going. Very few people, I think, really read for escape; most readers are anxious to learn about the world and their place in it. But the old mythology of class and social relationship on which the novel has relied for the last two hundred years is neither interesting nor pertinent to the mass audience, for the mass audience stands outside that crumbling structure. . . . The ordinary members of 'the lonely crowd' need stories which will help them understand and control their lives, they need signposts to behavior and meaning as much as men always have. And a new mythology is consequently being created for them. Like all mythologies in the beginning, it is based on particular events. When the reader asks, 'Did this really happen?' it is able to reply, 'Oh yes, it did. I really knew this Unforgettable Character. This is a direct quote from Marilyn Monroe.' "

public relations handbook. For the new men are only able to rule because of what they *do*—not because of what they *are*. The new men are not anything as individuals. All they possess is their wits.

For this reason they must think constantly of ways in which to achieve not the deference of the man in the street, for that is impossible to acquire in our age, but simply his obedience.

FROM DEFERENCE TO MANIPULATION

It is the constant effort at gaining consent which explains the importance of public relations and the use of communications media in modern politics. No longer can a would-be leader or his organization assume continual deference on the part of the public. Control cannot be taken for granted, it must be engineered at every juncture. What we have, then, is the replacement of social control by means of deference with social control by manipulation. Whereas in the past, the man in the street habitually followed those situated above him in the social structure, today, because the barriers of the old structure have crumbled, our men of power must consciously and premeditatedly condition those who fall beneath them.[14]

The rise of professional public relations and the development of sophisticated communication techniques, while fascinating as subjects of study in and for themselves, must be viewed in perspective. The "engineering of consent" is necessary on

the part of the new men simply because the obedience of the man in the street cannot be taken for granted, nor even less left to chance. The managers of a great corporation, for example, cannot assume that the public will feel that what is good for the corporation will be good for the country. Instead, the managers will have to work overtime conditioning underlying attitudes so that the community will not bring itself to the point where it might question the mode of operation, or even the very existence, of the company. The same is true of trade, professional, and other powerful organizations. The chief aim of public relations is throw sand in the public's eyes. Talk about scientific progress rather than profits. Talk about ownership by millions of stockholders rather than the power of a few managers. Talk about the success stories of the fortunate few rather than the thwarted ambitions of those left behind. And, most important, talk of the institution as if the decision of its managers contained no element of power, but rather were the natural and rational outcome of an overriding desire to serve consumers. The principal technique of public relations, then, is never to discuss a case on its own merits. In fact, the highest desideratum is to persuade the public that the organization has no power whatsoever. The body in question is to be viewed purely as a service entity: rather like a national Lion's Club. It should be known by its immediate products—the dashing style of the automobile, the polite voice of the telephone operator—and not by its power as a social institution.

That the public is susceptible to manipulation such as this ought not to be surprising. There is no good reason to suppose that the average American citizen of our time is any more able to withstand such organized powers of persuasion than any other average person in history has

---

[14] See, for example, Stanley Kelley, *Professional Public Relations and Political Power* (Baltimore, 1956) and Vance Packard, *The Hidden Persuaders* (New York, 1957). Both of these studies show that when expert technicians work from a basis of power, persuasion can be effectively engineered on a mass scale. The elements of manufactured obedience are well outlined in Edward Bernays, ed., *The Engineering of Consent* (Norman, Oklahoma, 1955). However, it is a big mistake to overestimate the extent to which people can be influenced from a long distance. Penetration can be deeper, and hence more lasting and effective, if it is conducted on the individual or small-group level. For there the processes of persuasion can be especially tailored to the needs of the individual person who is the object of attack. Certainly, the small-group approach is the basis of the "human relations" techniques in industry and the effectiveness of psychotherapy rests on its person-to-person relationship. For a discussion of the latter, see my "A Political Scientist Looks at Psychotherapy," *The International Journal of Social Psychiatry*, Vol. 2 (Summer, 1956), pp. 23–33.

been able to exempt himself from the exercise of concerted manipulative power. Nor does the practice of manipulation render this country any less a democracy. Democracy describes a system based on the free consent of the governed. If this consent is engineered, it certainly does not make it any the less consent. And it is doubtful if it is any the less free for its being the produce of manipulation. To be sure, there is a difference between liberal democracy and what is coming to be called "mass" democracy. But inasmuch as the former variety is dependent on the unquestioned authority of the old ruling class we have discussed, it ought to be clear that as an ideology it is increasingly anachronistic. What must concern us, therefore, is the consequences to liberal democracy inherent in the coming mass democracy.[15]

First of all, it must be noted that there has not been any widening or deepening of the basis of power in America. Rather, power has been transferred from one group to another. That is, with the descent from exclusive power of the old ruling class, and the concomitant necessity of sharing their power with the new elite,

it cannot be argued that the public at large has gained anything in the process. All that can be said is that where once, because of ingrained habit and custom, he consented to arrangements by reason of deference, now, because of conscious and premeditated conditioning, he consents to arrangements by reason of manipulation. The factors operating on him are different. But his powerlessness remains constant. The average American of our day gives his consent not to prescription and the works of men long dead, but to a system of power which is controlled by men who are alive and among us. Both deference and manipulation are similar in that they are control. Both permit a few men to rule many men.

The American public, then, is kept content with congenial work, a feeling of participation, a high pattern of consumption, and the general belief that they live in the best of all possible societies. Such a public can be led to a state of satisfaction with its other-directed—non-economic, non-political—existence.[16] This public is composed of those who have neither the talent nor the will to compete for positions of control. They remain where they are, not because they are discriminated against, but because they prefer the easy life. These are, in short, the organization men. And they are not much

[15] The changing character of democracy in our century has been the chief concern of such writers as E. H. Carr and C. Wright Mills. Carr is concerned with the shift in ideological underpinning which has accompanied the transition from "individualism" to "mass democracy," *The New Society* (London, 1951), ch. 4; and Mills, in what is certainly the most important chapter of his much misunderstood *The Power Elite* (New York, 1956), discusses the differences between a "public" and a "mass" as the human raw materials for a democratic society. For liberal democracy required, as a citizenry, a "public." But as mass characteristics infuse this public, so a liberal democracy is transformed into a mass democracy. The citizen of the latter society must be managed by his rulers rather than be led by his leaders. Hence there arises the need for a "power elite" which comes into being not because of the lust for power on the part of its individual members, but because such a group is ready to perform certain functions which society requires (ch. 13). Neither Mills nor Carr goes into the dynamics which transform a public into a mass. A good analysis of this process, in economic and psychological terms, is to be found in Erich Fromm's *The Sane Society* (New York, 1955). See, in particular, his discussion of alienation, at pp. 120–52.

[16] The starkest fact—for students of politics—in the spate of sociological essays now appearing, is the acquiescent *powerlessness* of the people who inhabit the emerging middle-class. For the members of the lonely crowd, politics is a spectator sport; for the organization men, patterns of life and work are determined by an amoral institution; for the exurbanite, participation is social or civic, rather than partisan; and for all, the fruits of a surfeit of honey are sufficient exchange for removal from the decision-making process. See David Riesman, *The Lonely Crowd* (New Haven, 1950); William H. Whyte, Jr., *The Organization Man* (New York, 1956); A. C. Spectorsky, *The Exurbanites* (Philadelphia, 1955); Russell Lynes, *A Surfeit of Honey* (New York, 1957). To be sure, these people have power in the very special sense that they compel decision-makers to frame policies in such a way that they will be acceptable to the "market" (be it economic, political, or social). But the consequence is that decision-makers strive to *anticipate* reactions rather than waiting for the political-economic "customer" to make his wishes known.

different from the little men who have populated the streets of a thousand lands since the dawn of history.[17]

Of more concern to us are the exceptions—the new men of power—who rise above the happy and placid life of the engineered existence. The new men who should command our attention are not the run of the mill organization men.[18] Rather, they are the engineers. The new engineer is not simply a modern Henry Ford, a wizard with an assembly line and a part-time tinkerer with watches. Rather, he applies the principles of his calling—and he probably does not regard them as principles—to the order of human as well as material resources. Ever pragmatic, he is willing to learn and develop new techniques the better to accomplish the job at hand. Human engineering, therefore, becomes his major consideration. Not simply the workers at the bench, but higher managers must be treated like fragile mechanisms: their egos must be pampered lest the workings of the whole machine go awry. The feeling of participation, the feeling of being consulted, the feeling of self-esteem—all of these must be nurtured if the optimum output is to be achieved.[19] The science of committee procedure, the catalyst of modern management, is the skill most demanded of the human engineer. All must be allowed to believe that they are part of the team, be it the informal-turned-formal group on the factory floor, or the board of directors itself. These principles, too, are applied to the areas of community relations and public relations. People must be managed. They are not intractable; but their pliability must not be approached too facilely. Human resources can be controlled. However it is a full-time task and few if any of its aspects can be taken for granted.

[17] If we claim that the average man of our time is content with the amenities of his placid, middle-class existence, we must also go on to insist that he is, in point of fact, soft. He has little in the way of internal strength and he possesses few resources—either material or psychic—of his own. The fact that these people are willing to allow themselves to be carried is made clear in an episode in Sloan Wilson's *The Man in the Grey Flannel Suit* (New York, 1955). Hopkins, the ulcerous network president, finally states an unpleasant fact of life to Tom Rath, the nice young man who wants to take it easy: " 'Somebody has to do the big jobs! This world was built by men like me! To really do a job, you have to live it body and soul! You people who just give half your mind to your work are riding on our backs!' "

[18] Standing out like a sore thumb in *The Organization Man* is the chapter called "The Executive: Non-Well-Rounded Man." (ch. 11) Here we are allowed a glimpse of the top three men in the nation's 300 largest corporations. Their lives and personalities present a sharp contrast to those of the middle-managment men depicted in the remainder of the book. One wonders if, in fact, the well-adjusted organization men will be recruited into the highest echelon at all.

[19] The classic statement is Russell Davenport, "The Greatest Opportunity on Earth," *Fortune,* Vol. 40 (October, 1949), pp. 65ff. See also Alpheus T. Mason's analysis of this trend, "Business Organized as Power," this REVIEW, Vol. 44 (June, 1950), pp. 323–42.

CONCLUSION

The new engineers are the focus of power in the emerging American society. They are the ones who have replaced the old ruling class. They are not a class in the old sense, although they are developing into an "Establishment" along a number of significant lines. The new men stand, furthermore, in stark contrast to the tens of thousands of well-rounded, well-adjusted people in middle-management. We know a little about how they differ from their immediate subordinates in terms of personality characteristics. We know a little about how they, rather than others, are recruited for the top echelons. But by and large we must rest content with saying that, as in all ages, they take the leading positions because they are best able to deal with the particular problems at hand. Foxes rather than lions, to use Pareto's distinction, they can meet the imperatives of a time which calls for the sophisticated manipulation of men's attitudes and sensibilities.[20] This minority is the key to American politics

[20] For an elaboration, see my "Utopia, Inc.," *The Commonweal,* Vol. 65 (February 8, 1957), pp. 479–81.

and society. Its members are not so much typical as prototypical of the new men who are found not only in industry, but in politics and the military. They are aware of the need for, and familiar with the ways to achieve, control. Controllers rather than controlled, they find their own satisfactions in their careers and in providing the happiness of others. Unlike David Riesman's egoistic "saving remnant," this group does not flee from responsibility.[21] It dimly understands that its role is the important one. The new men must forfeit their own happiness and serve the happiness of a public which cannot and will not plan its own existence. The new men work overtime at their job; they develop ulcers and nervous tensions; they neglect their families, outside interests, and the pursuit of culture. But they do their task with imagination and vigor. It is no understatement to say that they are carrying the rest of us on their backs.

The new men are our new rulers. They are intelligent, but not cultured. They are tolerant in informal social relations, but they have no compassion for those who are subject to political injustice. The American tradition, for them, probably began in 1945. Values are judged not by their place in the prescriptive scheme of things, but by their current utility. For the new men it would be suicide to regard individuals as ends in themselves: they must always be viewed as resources to be managed. Liberty deals not with freedom of expression or with protection from tyranny by the state: rather it is the complex of conditions under which organizational ends can be pursued and organizational order maintained. And truth becomes an image of the world which ordinary men are capable of comprehending without too much strain on their imaginations.

These definitions obviously appear anomalous. But this is simply because the words are the vocabulary of liberal democracy and their content is not. With the rise of the new men the conditions necessary for liberal democracy have seen their day. This means that we must turn to a new set of prescriptions. The focus must be on control and the controllers.[22] The "Legend of the Grand Inquisitor"— *with* its stress on responsibility—has more meaning in prescriptive terms than the legend of the town meeting. The controllers are not men without souls. They are not philistines by nature. And there is good reason to believe that, in time, they can be civilized. But at this point they are simply busy. And if, in their furious activity, they are unknowingly breaking the idols of liberal democracy, we ought to think twice before we complain. For the new men are the products of equality of opportunity. If we *really* believe that careers ought to be open to the talents, regardless of background or adherence to traditional values, then we must accept the new ascendency with a good grace.

[21] This is the title of an essay in *Individualism Reconsidered* (Glencoe, Illinois, 1954), pp. 99–120. Riesman tells the would-be autonomous or self-directed man to find his satisfactions in highly personalized activities. Indeed, it is rather difficult to discover the difference between "autonomy," which Riesman thinks good, and "marginal differentiation," which Riesman implies is rather hollow. The solution-via-abdication is illustrated in Ernst Pawel's novel, *The Dark Tower* (New York, 1957), where the hero concludes that he cannot meet the standard of success in his corporation or the standard of good citizenship in his suburb, and hence packs up his family and finds a country-editor job for himself in the Rockies. The point about the new men is that, unlike Pawel's hero, they find their brand of autonomy by attaining the heights where they can exercise power within the framework of the organization. The climb may, in one sense, appear to be morally and intellectually debilitating. But in another it can be viewed as the only road to freedom in today's society.

[22] A fascinating attempt to evolve a new set of prescriptions for a new society and a new citizenry is to be found in the work of B. F. Skinner. The whole of his philosophy is in his Utopian novel, *Walden Two,* (New York, 1948). A briefer statement is his "Freedom and Control of Man" in *The American Scholar,* Vol. 25 (Winter, 1955–56), pp. 47–65. Also of value is a two-man symposium between Skinner and Carl R. Rogers, in which Skinner defends his ideas against a variety of criticisms: "Some Issues Concerning the Control of Human Behavior," *Science,* Vol. 124 (November 30, 1956), pp. 1057–66.

The Revolt Against Ideology

HENRY DAVID AIKEN

Henry David Aiken is professor of philosophy at Harvard University. He is the author of Reason and Conduct *and co-editor (with William Barrett) of* Philosophy in the Twentieth Century. *The present selection was adapted from a major study currently in preparation on contemporary attitudes toward ideology.*

Can it any longer be doubted that, on all sides of the Iron Curtain, the age of Leviathan is upon us? And for serious men does there remain any significant form of activity that is politically indifferent? We still profess loyalty to the ideal of "free inquiry," but the fact is that, directly or indirectly, governments supply the major resources, and politics most of the incentives, for our scientific research. And if some fortunate scientists of eminence are still encouraged to do "pure" or "basic" research, according to their interest, the primary reason is not that such studies exemplify one of man's essential intrinsic goods, but that the state cannot survive without them. Indeed, our universities and governments, along with our great industrial complexes, look increasingly like the interlocking arms of a great, if also headless, political establishment. Free enterprise (who doubts it?) is everywhere a dead issue save in the mythology of fundamentalist Republicanism, and whether our political leaders favor state capitalism or corporate socialism, the welfare state is accepted by all as an irremovable reality. Politics provide the primary themes of our literature, and when the critics charge a novelist or poet with "retreating from life," what they mean by "life" does not need to be construed. "Aesthetics" signifies merely enfeeblement and irrelevance; the "pure" artist, like the pure scientist, is a dying species, and none will mourn him save perhaps a few old "new critics" who, be

it added, well understood the political meaning of their own dandified aestheticism. Our most exigent moral perplexities are overwhelmingly political, and our gods, such as they are, seem wholly preoccupied with affairs of state.

I must admit, however, that there still exists one quiet place where a man may go if he is nauseated by problems of politics and hence of power, and one course of study which he may still pursue without fear of political encroachment: he may go, that is, to the graduate school of any great university and take up the subject known there as "philosophy." Among the intellectuals, to my knowledge, we philosophers alone are politically inert. The meaning of the concept of political obligation fascinates some few of my colleagues, but I have rarely heard them, in congress assembled, discuss their political obligations. And if any were asked to offer their opinions concerning the ends, or limits, of government they would probably either decline to answer or regard the question as philosophically improper.

In order to prove the rule, there remain a few notorious exceptions such as Bertrand Russell, Jean-Paul Sartre, and Professor Sidney Hook. But we have Russell's own word for it that his politics, like his ethics, and his philosophy have nothing in common except that both were hatched under the same head of hair, and both Sartre and Hook are frequently dismissed by their more academic colleagues as publicists who have deserted philosophy for careers as ideologists and politicians. Recalling the greatest names in the history of philosophy from Socrates to Aquinas and from Hobbes to Mill, one may wonder momentarily how such a state of affairs could have come to pass. But when one remembers what men have done, and in many parts of the world are still prepared to do, in the name of a political philosophy, the answer seems evident: from a "pragmatic" point of view, political philosophy is a monster, and wherever it has been taken seriously, the consequence, almost invariably, has been revolution, war, and eventually, the police state. Russell himself once wrote an essay entitled, "The Harm that Good Men Do." Many would regard this as an appropriate subtitle for any honest and realistic history of political philosophy. With Socrates, political philosophy became a gadfly; in Plato, a monstrous dream; in Rousseau, Fichte, Hegel, Marx, and the rest, it has become a scourge and an obscenity.

Such is the prevailing view. And if Peter Laslett, the editor of a recent volume of essays on political philosophy, is correct in saying that "for the moment, anyway, political philosophy is dead," then none mourn its passing less than the philosophers themselves. Those few who, as philosophers, still suppose that they have a useful political role to play, discover it to be only that of unmasking the pretensions of other political philosophers.

Just what is wrong with political philosophy as a genre nonetheless remains obscure. Of course many political philosophies from Plato to Aquinas, and from Hobbes and Rousseau to Hegel and Marx, have been tied to the kites of theological or metaphysical systems. And for some, no doubt, this fact suffices to put them beyond the pale. But roundhouse objections to "metaphysics" are less fashionable than they were some years ago. In fact, under pressure from the philosophers of ordinary language, philosophical analysts are increasingly reluctant to proscribe as meaningless any established form of discourse on principle, as the positivists used to do with the propositions, not only of metaphysics and theology, but also of ethics. In this respect, recent analytical philosophy has steadily moved in the direction of prag-

matism or, I had better say, the direction in which pragmatism has tended to move since the days of William James. Any form of utterance, so it is now argued, is to be interpreted and judged only in the light of its own characteristic "practical bearings." Thus, for example, if political philosophers in their own terms are given to general moral evaluations of political activities and institutions, the question is only whether such appraisals, all things considered, are acceptable as value judgments: that is to say, do they express commitments to which, on sober second thought and in view of the historical record, we should be ready to give our own conscientious assent? Do the lines of social action which they commend appear on the whole to be worth the trouble it would take to realize them? Above all, would we in conscience be able to give our blessings to the sort of "representative man" who might emerge if such lines of action were resolutely pursued?

Questions of this sort, which I take more seriously, have produced another round of objections which, although they do not rule out political philosophy on supposedly semantical or logical grounds, do nonetheless seem to condemn it virtually as a genre. These objections are all the more telling and all the more significant since they come from a quarter in which there has been no general animus against metaphysics and no self-denying ordinance which would exclude from the purview of philosophy any problem that is not purely a conceptual problem about the "logic" of expressions.

To my knowledge the most powerful attack upon political philosophy from this quarter (which for convenience may be called "existentialist") is to be found in Albert Camus's arresting work, *The Rebel.* Camus's indictment is easily misunderstood. To be sure, it is profoundly anti-rationalistic, but it is by no means based upon a romantic or nihilistic disillusionment with human reason or with the value of its exercise. Quite the contrary, reasonableness, in the more classical sense of the term, is Camus's forte. What he condemns, rather, are the crimes incited by the political philosophers in the name of Reason or of Reason's God. All men, say the philosophers, are created equal; *ergo,* let them be restored at once to their pristine estate, whatever the cost. All men are by nature free, yet everywhere they are in chains; *ergo,* Reason demands that they immediately be released, though ten thousand jailers perish in the process. Man is, above all, the rational animal, but because of the blinders which the ancient regime places before his mind, he cannot freely exercise his reason; then destroy the regime, let reason, or its self-appointed representatives, reign, and the devil take those who stand in the way. No doubt the political philosophers never meant to be quite so simple or so brutal as these caricatures suggest. But what of their followers, those who take them, or try to take them, at their word? Can the political philosophers altogether disclaim responsibility for their crimes? Is there not an ingrained metaphysical or moral pride, a fatal lack of continence in the very attempt of political philosophers to set forth, whether in the name of reason or of nature or of humanity, the absolute ends of government and the supposedly invariant forms of the just society?

But Camus's criticisms are by no means directed exclusively to the 18th-century *philosophes* and their descendants. They are extended also to the Hegelians and the Marxists who attempt to formulate a universal law, or dialectic, of historical development which is then made to double in brass as an immanent principle of justification for their own incitive prophecies about man's social destiny. Whether such prophecies proclaim a future of unlimited freedom, of absolute justice and equality, or of perpetual peace, in each case they too represent that criminal pride of reason which destroys the sense of limitation which for Camus is the beginning of political, as of every other form of, wisdom.

From these remarks it would be easy enough to conclude that Camus's indictment of traditional political philosophy is actually an indictment of philosophy itself. And so in a way it is, at least as philosophy has been conceived and executed in the dominant Western tradition. Yet Camus is not just another literary counter-philosopher. Nor is his indictment of rationalistic political philosophy a condemnation of political philosophy *per se.* For it is plain that, as Sir Herbert Read points out in his discerning preface to the English translation of *The Rebel,* Camus himself has a philosophy of politics. But it is, at any rate, a philosophy of politics radically different from those of his predecessors. For Camus makes no attempt to define *the* function or the end of government or to state *the* rightful basis of political authority. Nor does he propose any universal principle of political action save one of self-limitation or restraint. It is also characteristic of Camus that although he repudiates any and all form; of unlimited revolution, he accepts the necessity, on occasion, of rebellion or civil disobedience.

Despite many differences both in philosophical background and in literary style, there are striking parallels between Camus's existentialist critique of modern political philosophy and those to be found in the writings of the pragmatist, John Dewey. In Dewey one finds the same hatred of essentialism and apriorism, the same antipathy to utopianism, and the same distrust both of radical individualism and of radical collectivism. There is a similar emphasis upon the concrete "problematic situations" (as Dewey calls them) which alone he takes it to be the business of "creative intelligence" to resolve. And there is the same underlying humanism which opposes the sacrifice of living men to principles and to ideals realizable, if at all, only in an abstract and indefinite future. For obvious reasons, Dewey was more confident than Camus of the efficacy of democratic procedures, at least in "developed" societies. Yet he was by no means prepared to demand the immediate institution of such procedures in all countries and circumstances; nor did he, like more romantic majoritarians, regard the will of the many as an absolute source of rightful political authority. Democracy for Dewey is a method rather than an end. Or if, in certain writings, democracy also tends to become an end, then it is in a looser sense of the term which now begins to take on meanings more strictly associated with the concepts of community, fraternity, and social equality.

Dewey's pragmatic criticisms of earlier political philosophy are usually regarded as methodological rather than moral—although in his case, as in that of all pragmatists, it is always a question where problems of method leave off and problems of ethics (and politics) begin. Thus, whereas Camus ascribes the primordial fault of the political philosophers to their incontinent passion for absolute transcendence of the finite conditions of man's historical social existence, Dewey ascribes it to the illusory "quest for certainty" which, according to his reading, dominated virtually the whole history of philosophy before the 20th century. Yet in Dewey's case also, one senses that the more radical evil lies not in the illusion itself but in its attendant waste and destructiveness. The quest for certainty begins in hope and ends in skepticism and despair. In promising us an unlimited intellectual and moral security, it brings us by stages to the war of all against all. Dewey's more unfriendly critics have often charged him with advocacy of the gospel of human perfectibility. No criticism could be more perverse. Man, as Dewey conceives him, is, once for all, a mortal creature who lives and has his being within the orders of nature and of history. Indeed, this is the governing metaphysical principle underlying his logic, his theory of knowledge, and his moral philosophy. Uncertainty, and hence imperfection, are ingrained in the very texture of human existence. And no method, including the methods of science, can extricate us from them.

In other spheres, philosophical forgetfulness of this fact has been unfortunate; in politics, as in ethics, it has proved a calamity. This is not to deny that Dewey has a philosophy of politics, but like Camus's it is of a sort quite different from the major political philosophies of the tradition. He is sometimes criticized for offering us no explicit general theory of governmental authority, no principled statement of the grounds or proper limits of political obligation—above all, no settled position toward the most vexatious of modern political problems, namely, revolution. But Dewey's vagueness on these scores is quite intentional. In politics as in ethics, Dewey repudiates any and all fixed principles for the institution of the good society or for the establishment and maintenance of good government. His preoccupation as a political philosopher is solely with the controlling attitudes which men bring to their political deliberations.

MARXISM AND IDEOLOGY: THE FIRST REVOLT

Impressive as they are, the foregoing criticisms of political philosophy are largely matters of individual judgment. And if the professional philosophers now decline to do political philosophy, it may be argued that this is owing to their own disillusionment with the achievements of their predecessors rather than to any inherent fault in political philosophy as a genre. It remains to ask whether there may be, after all, some deep-lying confusion of mind, some pervasive logical fault or category mistake, which really does afflict political philosophy as a form of discourse.

As a way of confronting this question, it may prove useful to examine certain aspects of the widespread attack against the modern offspring of and successor to political philosophy, namely, ideology.

Most of the "anti-ideologists," as I shall call them, share certain attitudes in common with the existentialists; indeed, it is my impression that some of them owe more to the latter, and particularly to Camus, than they have as yet acknowledged. They owe something also to the pragmatists; in fact, most American anti-ideologists fancy their own point of view as essentially "pragmatic." But (generally speaking) they go beyond the existentialists and the pragmatists in contending that ideological thinking is the function of certain features of the social situation in which intellectuals as a group find themselves in an era of exact science, advanced technology, and the welfare state. In predicting the end of ideology, they thus imply that the social and intellectual conditions which have been conducive to ideological thinking are now disappearing. Their own role, in effect, is to make certain that the prediction will come true.

Now the primary target of our contemporary Western anti-ideologists is, of course, Marxism. And in prophesying the end of ideology, it is the end of Marxism of which they mainly dream. It is worth remembering, therefore, that: (a) Marx was the first great critic of political philosophy; and (b) he was also the first great prophet of the end of the ideological age.

According to Marx, ideology always involves a conception of reality which systematically "inverts" the whole relation of thought to being.[1] As a form of thought, therefore, ideology is inherently confused; it stands to science, in Marx's words, as an inverted image in a "camera obscura" stands to a veridical perception. This inversion, of which Hegel's "objective" idealism is a prime philosophical example, results directly or indirectly from that process of "alienation" whereby human artifacts, including "ideas," are invested with a power and a reality that are supposedly independent both of their producers and of the material conditions and operations involved in their production. Such an investment, which philosophers call "reification," is also necessarily accompanied by "mystification," i.e., by an obscuring of the interests and relationships that actually determine social behavior. For example, in imputing an independent reality and power to their reified ideas and principles, their rights

and duties, their ends and "reasons," men thereby conceal from themselves the fact that it is they, the creators of such entities, whose underlying actions and whose work alone give them whatever significance they may have.

Except for genuinely empirical science, the whole cultural "superstructure" of hitherto existing societies is permeated by the same process of alienation and ideological inversion. For this reason it would be a radical mistake to conceive of ideology as limited to political philosophy; on the contrary, ideology also includes, among other things, religion, ethics, art, metaphysics, and the "dismal science" of economics. Properly understood, political philosophies are merely special applications of far-flung ideological patterns that invest them with their own magical "authority" and "justification." Furthermore, since alienation is a social process, ideologies, whether as wholes or as parts, are to be understood as expressions, not of the interests of isolated individuals, but of the conflicting concerns—or better, tendencies—of social classes. It is thus only by relating political ideologies to their objective social conditions and causes that we can begin to interpret their true objective meaning (i.e., what they signify or portend within the order of nature), and hence, by stages, to correct the inverted images of reality which they present to the ideologists themselves. One of the primary functions of Marxism, in fact, is precisely to provide the intellectual, including the social-theoretical, tools for such interpretations and corrections, and thus for the first time to enable us, in principle, to demythologize ideology.

But it is one thing to explain ideology and another to overcome it. Mankind as a whole can permanently overcome ideological thought (and action) not by any process of purely conceptual analysis on the part of individual philosophers, but only by removing the material causes of alienation which, according to Marx, are rooted in the institution of private property. And it is for this reason, and this reason alone, that Marx's historical prophecy of the coming of world socialism amounts at the same time to a prophecy of the end of the ideological ages.

[1] In this section I have been aided by Stanley W. Moore's *The Critique of Capitalist Democracy, An Introduction to the Theory of the State in Marx, Engels, and Lenin,* Paine-Whitman Publishers, New York, 1957. Moore's fourth chapter, "Ideology and Alienation," pp. 114–137, is highly compressed and schematic, but I know of no other discussion of the subject which, within its limits, is so clear and so accurate. I have also benefited from Norman Birnbaum's *The Sociological Study of Ideology (1940–60), Current Sociology,* Vol. IX, No. 2, 1960, Basil Blackwell, Oxford, England. Birnbaum's essay, which he subtitles "A Trend Report," is a masterly survey of current literature on the subject of ideology, including Marxist ideological theory. It also contains an invaluable critical bibliography.

DISILLUSIONMENT IN THE WEST: THE SECOND REVOLT AGAINST IDEOLOGY

Marx's view of ideology underlies the thinking of most of our own anti-ideologists. However, they go beyond Marx in extending the pejorative associations of the term to the role of ideology in ordering human attitudes. Thus, they not only regard ideological doctrines as wrongheaded; they also object to their employment as vehicles for the formation, guidance, and control of social behavior. But they go Marx one better in another way, for they also regard Marxism itself as a prime example of ideology.

The first non-Marxist writer, so far as I know, explicitly to inquire whether we might be approaching the end of the ideological age was Raymond Aron in his book, *The Opium of the Intellectuals*. The prevailing temper of Aron's book is not unlike that of Camus's *The Rebel*. There are also a number of striking parallels between Aron's point of view and that of Karl Popper, as developed in the latter's *The Open Society and its Enemies*. For example, there is the same constitutional distrust of large-scale social planning, the same insistence upon the impossibility of large-scale historical predictions of social behavior, and the same celebration of the virtues of "the open society." Above all, there is the same castigation of any attempt to determine the drift and meaning of human history as a whole and hence of the attempt to formulate universal and necessary laws of historical development.

"The last great ideology," says Aron, "was born of the combination of three elements: the vision of a future consistent with human aspiration, the link between this future and a particular social class, and trust in human values above and beyond the victory of the working class, thanks to planning and collective ownership." Aron believes that at the present time the hope aroused by that ideology is gone beyond peradventure. One main reason for this disillusionment, so he argues, is that "Confidence in the virtues of a socio-technique has begun to wane." Furthermore, on this side of the Iron Curtain, no one believes any longer in the reality of a social class that will carry us, under the leadership of the socio-economic engineers, to the frontiers of the classless society. Like Camus and Popper, Aron cannot bring himself flatly to renounce the values of the Enlightenment; but in practice he is no more able than they to take them with absolute seriousness as governing ideals for the reconstruction of society in the 20th century. In his own terms, he no longer fully believes in the vision of a future consistent with "human aspirations." And it is this fact perhaps that accounts for the vein of pessimism and the self-division which run through his writing.

In any case, it is plain that for Aron the approaching end of the age of ideology represents also a crisis of faith and of hope for mankind. On the penultimate page of his book, Aron asks, "Does the rejection of fanaticism encourage a reasonable faith, or merely skepticism?" His analogical answer is that "one does not cease to love God when one gives up converting pagans or the Jews and no longer reiterates 'No salvation outside the Church.'" Coming as late as it does in Aron's book, this has something like the effect of an unprepared major cadence at the end of a funeral march. What is its basis? No matter how personal one's religion may be, it is hard to see how it could fail to be attenuated by a radical renunciation of one's belief that it should prevail. If one really gives up trying to convert the "pagans," does this not entail reservations about the value as well as the possibility of converting them? If so, does this not also suggest that one has ceased completely to love God or else that only a gesture toward the love of Him remains? Making due allowance for the analogy, I cannot, as a pragmatist, see how one can be said actively to seek a less cruel lot for humanity if one can trust no technique and no plan for its amelioration. To will the end is to will the means, and to reject the means is, in practice, to renounce the end. Like Peirce in another connection, one is minded to say to the political as well as to the epistemological moralists: "Dismiss make-believe!" This means also, so far as I can see, "Dismiss professions of 'reasonable faith' if you do not believe in the *power* of reason; and do not talk about abolishing 'fanaticism,' unless you believe that there is a way (or 'technique') of abolishing it." Like all anti-ideologists, Aron is opposed to the expectation of "miraculous changes" either from a revolution or an economic plan. Very well. The question is whether he gives us any reason to expect unmiraculous changes from any sort of concerted human action. "If tolerance is born of doubt, let us teach everyone to doubt all the models and utopias, to challenge all the prophets of redemption and the heralds of catastrophe." And, "If they alone can abolish fanaticism, let us pray for the advent of the skeptics." The rhetoric is appealing. But it smacks of ideology, in Aron's own sense. For toleration is also a principle and a method. And it too has its dangers.

These comments are not made in a spirit of mockery. My purpose is rather to make clear what may be implied in the prophecy that we are living at the end of the ideological age, the age, in Mr. Aron's own apt words, in which men still actively search "for a purpose, for communion with the people, for something controlled by *an idea and a will*" (my italics). As he points out, we Westerners have suffered an increasing fragmentation of our universe; our poetry becomes more and more obscure and diffuse, and our poets are isolated from one another as well as from "the big public" which "in their heart of hearts, they long to serve"; our scientists have ideas aplenty but no control over their use or indeed any consistent belief in the possibility of their control; our scholars control limited areas of specialized knowledge, but present-day science "seems to leave . . . [them] as ignorant of the answers to

the ultimate questions as a child awakening to consciousness"; and our economists and sociologists, for all their facts and statistics, their jargon and their lore, have not the vaguest notion whether "humanity is progressing toward an atomic holocaust or Utopian peace." This process of fragmentation and dissociation, moreover, is not new; it has been going on at an ever more rapid pace, at least since the Renaissance. But here precisely, as Aron admits, "is where ideology comes in. . . ." For ideology represents the insistent demand for a coherent *way* of individual and social life, an orientation toward the world and toward the human predicament, controlled as he says both by an idea and by a will, or, rather, by a will infused with an idea and an idea animated by will. Ideology, as Aron tacitly acknowledges, is a creature of alienation; but it represents also a passion to reduce alienation, to bring it down to bearable human proportions. It also represents the belief that alienation may be reduced through collective human endeavors. Thus, by his own account, an end to the age of ideology would amount to this extent to a virtual skepticism about the possibility of reducing alienation through corporate planning and action (ideas infused with will). And this means that man has no choice but to live with alienation. Here, however, one faces precisely one of those metaphysical and historical "necessities" against which the anti-ideologists themselves rail when they find them in the writings of other ideologists. Here, too, it seems, we are faced with a "simplified" idea of man's fate which, as in the case of the Stoicism it is plainly a variant of, forms the basis of still another ideology, an idea that in this instance is, if I may say so, fused with inaction.

THE SOCIOLOGICAL CRITIQUE OF IDEOLOGY

Aron's analysis of ideology, although suggestive, does not take us very far. Let us therefore cross the ocean to the heartland of contemporary anti-ideology. In the United States perhaps the leading anti-ideologist is the sociologist and social critic, Professor Daniel Bell. Bell, who knows his Marx, is also a good strategist.

Already in the introduction to his book, *The End of Ideology*, he moves beyond Aron, for, unlike the latter, he proposes to make a positive virtue of alienation. "Alienation," he tells us flatly, "is not nihilism but a positive role, a detachment, which guards one against being submerged in any case, or accepting any particular embodiment of community as final. Nor is alienation deracination, a denial of one's roots or country." This persuasive definition has its points. It is also an interesting instance of the notion of an idea fused with will which Bell, like Aron, tends to identify with ideology.

As befits a sociologist, Bell is concerned not just with the content of ideas but with their social origins, causes, and roles. Thus, in an attempt to locate the sources of ideological thinking, he begins his analysis with a characterological division of the intelligentsia into two main types: (a) the "scholars"; and (b) the "intellectuals." The scholar, as Bell conceives him, "has a bounded field of knowledge, a tradition, and seeks to find his place in it, adding to the accumulated, tested knowledge of the past as to a mosaic." He is, so to say, a "pro" for whom "the show must go on," however and whatever he himself may feel about it. Accepting the scholarly tradition within which he has found a place, he is able to judge himself, or at least his scholarly performance, by impersonal and objective standards. And if he performs with a modicum of efficiency and does not stray beyond the limits of his scholarly "competence," he is entitled to a modicum of self-respect. Indeed, his self-respect, like his role-governed conception of himself, is a function of his assurance of the respect of his peers and, more indirectly, of the society of which his discipline is an established part.

The intellectual, on the other hand, has no such responsibility or security. Lacking a scholarly discipline, perhaps lacking the talent for achievement within such a discipline, which can hold him continuously responsible to "objective" methods and to "facts" wholly independent of himself, his only recourse is an endless dialectic and critique of general ideas. And because he is without a legitimate social role to play within society, he perforce finds himself alienated from its institutions and is left to manipulate his "ideas" in a mood of unrequited and unfocused resentment. He doesn't so much think with his ideas as feel through them. In the discourses of an intellectual, therefore, the thing to look to is not his argument, which, where it exists, is merely a

vehicle for his resentments, but rather to the effect which it is meant to induce. He presents his readers not with information but with a goad and with an outlet for their own repressed emotions of estrangement of violence. He may, in the process, tell them something, but it is doing something to them that is his real, if unavowed, aim. For him, the beginning and end of a process of reflection is not a specific problem about objective processes and events; as Professor Bell charges, he begins always with "*his* experience, *his* perceptions of the world, his privileges and deprivations, and judges the world by these sensibilities." For him, the "world" is not a thing in itself, but rather his will and his idea, and if there is something *there,* in itself, then he acknowledges it only as something which he is up against and which exists only in so far as he is up against it. His business, in Marx's words, is not to understand the world, but to change, or better, to overcome it. And if he can't change it in any other way, he may at least reject it, and thus, by an obvious inversion, still show his superiority to it.

In this way, every statement and every discussion becomes for the intellectual an implicitly political move in an endless game of power. Of course he fancies his own moves really to be in the interest (*n. b.*) of "justice" or "freedom," while those of his "opponents," whether they invoke the names of "legitimacy" or of "law and order," are actually made in the interest of business as usual which it is the function of the established order to protect and to promote. The sad fact remains, however, that the intellectual's power *is* severely limited by the existing system. Hence, in order to maintain the illusion of his freedom or of his power to realize it, he is obliged, as Bell puts it, to embark "upon what William James called 'the faith ladder,' which in its vision of the future cannot distinguish possibilities from probabilities, and converts the latter into certainties."

What is the nature of the conceptual tools with which the "free-floating" and unscholarly intellectual does his work? In order to answer this question, Bell is obliged to move from sociology to logic and semantics. Thus he speaks repeatedly, in terms which I find merely more explicit than Aron's, of ideology as being somehow a "fusion" of thought with emotion or passion which at one and the same time does the trick of "simplify-[ing] ideas, establish[ing] a claim to truth, and, in the union of the two, demand[ing] a commitment to action." The result—and it is this which Bell most seriously objects to—is not just a "transformation" of ideas, but also a transformation of people. The typical effect of any ideological argument is, then, a kind of conversion. The road by which the ideologist comes to Damascus doesn't matter; what matters is that he is made to see the light. Says Bell: "Ideology is the conversion of ideas into social levers. Without irony, Max Lerner once entitled a book 'Ideas Are Weapons.' This is the language of ideology. It is the commitment to the consequences of ideas."

Bell is rarely more analytical than this, but toward the end of his study he does say one further thing which is at least symptomatic of the point of view which he represents: "If the end of ideology has any meaning, it[sic]is to ask for the end of rhetoric, and rhetoricians, of 'revolution,' of the day when the young French anarchist Vaillant tossed a bomb into the Chamber of Deputies, and the literary critic Laurent Tailhade declared in his defense: 'What do a few human lives matter; it was a *beau geste.*'" The general idea that concerns us here is not the tacit identification of ideology with revolutionary activity, especially of the more bizarre and feckless sort, but rather its identification with rhetoric.

If by "rhetoric" Bell means the use of language in order to persuade or influence others—and many things he says suggest that this is his meaning—then his vision of the end of ideology as an end to rhetoric is a utopian fantasy. Worse, it is an evil fantasy, for it implies a conception of human relations which would deprive us of the right to address one another except for the purpose of comparing notes about matters of fact. Consider what would happen were such a fantasy to come true. In any ordinary sense, it would mean a virtual end to discourse, to communication, and to argument. For it would mean an end to any speech-act

addressed to others with a view to their guidance, their instruction, their edification, or their pleasure, with a view, in short, to changing their minds. Indeed, the image of man implicit in Bell's dream of the end of ideology is precisely one of an academic grind or functionary to which he himself, as a counter-ideologist and counter-rhetorician, is fortunately unable to conform.[2]

The American anti-ideologists, Bell included, regard themselves as pragmatists. However, we should remind ourselves that it is the great pragmatists who have insisted, time out of mind, that ideas have consequences and that, indeed, their operative meaning can only be construed in

[2] What Bell does not sufficiently emphasize is that the intellectuals' "faith ladders" have indeed converted possibilities into certainties. Otherwise it is hard to see why he and his fellow anti-ideologists make such a hullabaloo about ideology and why they are enthralled with the thought that we have reached the end of the age of ideology. The simple fact is that ever since the French Revolution the intellectuals, with the help of their ideologies, have been moving mountains. And if *their* ideologies are exhausted, as Bell contends, this does not necessarily entail the end of ideology as such. No doubt the old ideologies of the right and the left have lost much of their power to persuade, and no doubt, all over the world, radicalism and intellectualism in our time must inevitably take new forms. But they will persist, by Bell's own analysis, until every intellectual has become a scholar (or worker) and until every scholar becomes a scholar (or worker) merely; that is, until there are no full- or part-time "out-groups" (to employ a fashionable term of sociological analysis) and no general ideas for them to think with. At this point one begins to have visions of an academic utopia within which there are no "free-floating" intellectuals, no alienated, critical minds, such as Professor Bell's, that are not wholly committed to their vocations and that possess an over-plus of energy and passions that is not expended in the conduct of their own "researches." In such a utopia (if I may speak metaphorically) there would be no New York and no Concord, but only a series of semi-urban centers for semi-advanced study for semi-advanced scholars who would sternly deny themselves the use of any concept or the affirmation of any statement whose "practical bearings" cannot be shown to lie wholly within the range of their legitimate scholarly activity or work. Such a utopia, I fancy, would have no place even for counter-ideologists like Professor Bell whose own "restless vanity" (the phrase is his) is evidently not sated by the rewards that accrue from the performance of his scholarly labors.

consequential terms. Rhetoric, from this point of view, it is not necessarily a bad or degenerate form of expression; rather it is a dimension of any form of speech which is addressed to others. Furthermore, pragmatism is also a normative theory which asks us to evaluate any form of speech, and hence of rhetoric, in terms of its consequences. The question, therefore, is not whether a discourse persuades or influences other minds and other hearts, but how it does so and with what effect. Not every rhetorician is a demagogue. Plato's Socrates professed to despise the Sophists because they were rhetoricians, and this Socrates, I surmise, is the grandfather of all the countless anti-rhetoricians and anti-ideologists from his day to Bell's. But it should not be forgotten that Socrates himself was a master rhetorician and that his admirers ignore the fact because they believe his cause was just. Moreover, Socrates was not only a lover of truth; he was also, politically, a reactionary whose hatred of the Sophists was directed not only to their rhetoric but also to their liberal, democratic, and plebeian political and social attitudes. In saying this, I do not mean to attack our latter-day anti-ideologists by innuendo. I do mean to say that the plain effect of *their* rhetoric is to reinforce acceptance of our own institutional status quo and to declass those "intellectuals" who seek to modify in any radical way the fundamental structures of "Western" political life.

There remains a secondary sense of the term "rhetoric" which Bell may also have in mind. In this sense, rhetoric means eloquence. So conceived, the demand for an end to rhetoric is tantamount to a request for plain talk and, so to say, for an age of prose. So far so good. But there may be more to it than this. Elsewhere Bell harps upon the theme that "Throughout their history, Americans have had an extraordinary talent for compromise in politics and extremism in morality." It is plain that Bell is repelled by "this moralism," though, I gather, not so much because it is hypocritical but rather because, as moral, it is uncompromising. "The saving grace, so to speak, of American politics, was that all sorts of groups were tolerated, and the system of the 'deal'

became the pragmatic counterpart of the philosophic principle of toleration. But in matters of manners, morals, and conduct —particularly in the small towns—there has been a ferocity of blue-nosed attitudes unmatched by other countries." And again, "It has been one of the glories of the United States that politics has always been a pragmatic give-and-take rather than a series of wars-to-the-death." Of course this last is *not* true. Among our national "glories" have been a war for independence and a civil war, both of them (among other things) wars of principle. Our periods of "give-and-take" have usually also been periods of drift and complacency which have ended in orgies of political corruption and degradation. In one domain, however, Bell believes that our underlying political "postures" have not been "pragmatic." "One of the unique aspects of American politics is that . . . foreign policy has always been phrased in moralistic terms. Perhaps the very nature of our emergence as an independent country forced us to constantly adopt a moral posture in regard to the rest of the world; perhaps being distant from the real centers of interest conflict allowed us to employ pieties, rather than face realities. But since foreign policy has usually been within the frame of moral rather than pragmatic discourse, the debate in the fifties became centered in moral terms."

These passages are typical. In asking for an end to rhetoric, what Bell appears to be calling for is, among other things, an end to *moral* discourse and a beginning of consistent "pragmatic discourse" in every sphere of political life. What does this mean? So far as I can make out, it means an end to judgment and to principle, to praise and to blame, in the political domain and a beginning of plain, unvarnished "politicking" in the name of our "realistic" national, social, or individual "interests." It means, in effect, that in political discourse two and only *two* forms of expression are to be regarded as legitimate: (a) realistic, verifiable statements of fact; and (b) bald, undisguised expressions of first-personal (singular or plural) interest. On such a view, one would be permitted to say, "I don't like segregation and I will try—without, however, upsetting the apple cart—to do what I can to limit segregationalist practices," but not "Segregation is an affront to the humanity of the Negro people," or, "Those who practice segregation are unfair and unjust." What is wrong with moral, as distinct from "pragmatic," discourse? It is not to be doubted that moral discourse is more eloquent and more incitive, and in this sense more rhetorical, than the "pragmatic" forms of speech which Bell prefers. But what is wrong with eloquence *per se?* No doubt it should not be used to cloud an issue, to obscure relevant facts, or to promote unreason. But this is no more a necessary consequence of moral discourse than of any other form of eloquence. Without eloquence, especially in times of crisis, few great political movements would succeed. In fact, eloquence, including the eloquence of moral judgment, is native to the language of politics, and particularly so, as Bell himself admits, in democratic societies where persuasion of the great masses is a condition of success. Thus to put an end to eloquence would be to put an end, not only to "moralism" (which is usually nothing more than the morality of those with whom we disagree) and to "ideology," but also to any form of politics in which great issues are stated or argued in terms of human rights and responsibilities and in which it is essential to gain the approval of the people, or their representatives, before any fundamental change in governmental policy is made. Perhaps a tightly knit, self-interested, and all-powerful elite might get along (among its members) with "pragmatic discourse" alone. But despite Bell, democratic politics does not just mean "bargaining between legitimate groups and the search for consensus." It means also a form of politics in which men are governed by, and hence with reference to, principles and ideals—in a word, to morals and to ideology.

But now a word of caution: It is no part of my intention to suggest, much less admit, that ideology and morality *are* rhetoric; the equation is Bell's, not mine. I contend only that if, as is true, ideological discourses are full of rhetoric (in the above senses), there is no reason to deplore the fact. Quite the contrary.

Webster also mentions a third sense (or senses) of "rhetoric" which for our purposes is perhaps the most interesting of all. In this sense, "rhetoric" means "ostentatious or artificial speech." That some ideologists and moralists are ostentatious need not be denied. My own impression, however, is that academic scholars, particularly in some of the more immature sciences of man, are at least as prone to ostentatious speech (and thought) as other intellectuals. Sociology, indeed, might almost be defined as the ostentatious science. But except in beautiful women, ostentation is surely a minor vice, and only a fool would write off a whole field of study or an entire form of expression because some of its practitioners, like Molière's learned ladies, tend to give themselves airs.

Artificiality is another matter, which will repay closer scrutiny. Now "artificiality" often connotes a way of doing things which, although not necessarily ostentatious, is mannered, contrived, studied, and "unnatural." On occasion, a rhetoric which is artificial in this sense can be very powerful, as for example, in the poetry of Milton or in the prose of Burke and Macaulay. Among moralists and men of letters one associates it with the conservative wits of the 18th century and with the elaborate courtesy and the elegant banter of Matthew Arnold and his disciples. For obvious reasons, it is not a rhetoric characteristic of revolutionary ideologists. In our own time one runs into it only occasionally among writers of the right or the right-center. In England, Michael Oakeshott employs it with some effect; as (in another way) do T. S. Eliot and his followers. In this country, some of the so-called southern agrarians, such as Allen Tate, are minor masters of this rhetoric. But I fancy that Tate, at least, is well aware that he is fighting in a lost cause, and his style, like a ruffled cuff, is intended to give us a heightened sense of the fact. To my unaccustomed ears, the Encyclicals of Leo XIII, which are among the modern masterpieces of Catholic ideology, are also effective examples of a rhetoric of this sort. Indeed, it is precisely the impervious, anachronistic artificiality of Leo's prose which makes one realize how remote, for better or worse, is the concessive modernity of his social thought from the radical liberalism of a Bentham or a Mill.

But "artificiality" has another connotation in this context that is more central to our theme. In this sense, I take it, rhetoric is to be contrasted with literal statement. Here I must limit my remarks mainly to political ideology, but what will be said holds also of all ideologies, including those we normally think of as religious or metaphysical. Now political ideology is nothing but political discourse (as distinct from political science) on its most general formative level. It is, that is to say, political discourse insofar as the latter addresses itself, not just to specific, piecemeal reforms, but to the guiding principles, practices, and aspirations by which politically organized societies, absolutely or else in certain typical situations, ought to be governed. This being so, political ideologies inevitably include, among their leading articles, statements of general principle or method and expressions of basic attitude, orientation, and concern which, as they stand, are so highly abstract as to appear to many minds preoccupied with day-to-day problems of "practical politics" virtually meaningless. Such statements are of course habitually formulated in terms like "general welfare," "common good," "justice," "equality," "democracy," "security," and the rest.

But these very terms, so natural or even essential, when one is defining and appraising political practices or systems, also tend through over-use to become mere counters which elicit from us the tired, stock response that leaves us, and hence the practices themselves, unchanged. Or worse, because our responses are dull and routine, and hence *practically* of no political importance, we may conclude that all general philosophical discussions of politics are pointless and that one political ideology is just as good —or bad—as any other. What does matter, so we feel, is not what we say or think about "the system," but only what we do within it. And so, by stages, we are led to the conservative conclusion that political manifestoes, declarations of independence, and constitutions (with their embarrassing ideological preambles) make no difference to society as a going concern. In short, so far as we are concerned, ideology is useless verbiage. On the other side, unfortunately, we discover to our dismay that other peoples, politically and intellectually less "advanced" than ourselves, are enflamed, sometimes to the point of revolution, by ideological discourses, fresher and more affecting, in part because less literal and less abstract, than those to which we are accustomed. And to our contempt for our own ineffectual ideological abstractions we now add a positive hatred (or fear) of an ideological rhetoric which suddenly endows those same abstractions with a new life that disturbs our own.

It should be observed, however, that our very hatred is itself a backhanded tribute to the power of ideology. And if, out of a misplaced loyalty to "reason," we merely limit ourselves to "exposing" it, we stand in danger of losing our world. Most of us, realizing that the world is *never* well lost, find ourselves drawn back inescapably into the ideological struggle which, if we are to win it for ends that are right and just, requires that we produce a counter-rhetoric more imaginative, more distinguished, and more durable than that of our opponents. But if, as literalists of the imagination, we still decline to go the whole hog, resorting now only to formal reaffirmation of the old abstract "principles" which no later than yesterday we professed to find meaningless, who will believe us? Why should they? They have heard the same golden words mouthed a thousand times on the party platforms by hacks who have no notion of their meaning. And, if it comes to that, what *do* they mean?

In science it normally suffices to state a fact, and one man may do this as well and as accurately as another. But in the sphere of conduct much more is involved. For here we have to do with matters of attitude and intention and with problems of authenticity, legitimacy, and authority. Here words must not only predict what will be but determine what shall be; they must not only inform but also prepare and initiate lines of action. And what *is* it that is being determined, prepared, and initiated? This, so I contend, can be fully revealed only through the "poetry" which the ideologist may afford us.

Since Plato, rationalists have ever been afraid of poetry. And even those who profess not to be so worry lest "the people" confuse the true poet with the counterfeit. But just as true poetry, known and loved, is the only real protection against the malefactions of pseudo-poets, so also its ideological analogue is the only guarantee against the factitious "myths" of a Rosenberg, a Hitler, or a Mussolini. Our worry, in America, should be not that the false rhetoric of "foreign" ideologies may divert our people from their loyalties to our establishment, but that we do so little to replenish the fund of ideological poetry with which the founding fathers, along with Lincoln and a few others, have provided us. Our contemporary ideology is, or seems to be, all ghost-written. The voice sounds as reedy and hollow as are the men who contrive it. But if we should lose the power both to create and passionately to respond to a great ideological rhetoric, we would also lose the power to tell the difference between the phony and the real thing.

Further, figurative and hence rhetorical language enables, or compels, men to perform in advance of experience those crucial symbolic actions and imaginative experiments upon which, as Dewey has persuasively argued, genuinely rational judgments of practice and of value entirely depend. Know the truth, and the truth will set you free: how dangerous and how misleading is this half-truth. How, in a moral and practical sense, *are* we to know it? I can assent to the proposition that on the first day of an atomic war every major city in the United States would be destroyed, without in the least *realizing,* in human terms, what the statement really means. In order that I may even remotely grasp such an idea, in absence of the event, I must somehow try symbolically to live through the horror and the agony of such a calamity. But this is precisely what the cold, literal, objective statement of fact does not require me to do. To this end, therefore, it is essential that I find a way of thinking and talking about the fact which will make me realize from a practical, and even, if you please, from a metaphysical point of view, what it comes to. For most of us,

this can be done only through the artificial linguistic devices, known to every reader of fiction and of poetry, which enable us to perform "in imagination," as we say, those symbolic actions in which alone the "reality" of *literary* art exists. To disdain "rhetoric," therefore, is to disdain the very condition through which full practical understanding and judgment is possible. And to deny oneself its use is not to guarantee the preservation of scientific "objectivity" but to preclude the possibility of really being objective in trying to decide, in political terms, what one's way of life is to be.

It remains to say a word about "simplism," that final bogey of the anti-ideological mentality. Through rhetoric, according to Bell, ideology infuses ideas with passion, thus, as might be expected, winning friends and influencing people. But the principal underhanded intellectual (or is it, too, rhetorical?) trick of the ideologists is to "simplify ideas." It therefore seems necessary to remind the anti-ideologist that simplification, so far from being a fault peculiar to ideology, is, as William James well knew, a large part of the saving virtue of rationality itself. To oppose simplism on principle, in politics as in every other sphere of activity, is not to make a legitimate demand for recognition of the complexities and diversities of political life, but, in effect, to ask for an abandonment of policy and a fatal acquiescence in the drift of events. For simplification is an essential feature of any rational initiation of action. To refuse to simplify when one confronts a problem is in effect to reject the obligation to reach a solution; it is to make a game of possibilities and hence to move automatically outside the context of agency and choice. Every procedure that helps us to make decisions does so precisely by reducing the range of possibilities which we may reasonably be expected to consider. And every method, in setting a limit to the considerations that ought to be taken into account, thereby secures our deliberations against an endless spread of doubts.

On the score particularly, Professor Bell seems merely disingenuous when he tells us—incidentally letting a fair-sized ideological cat out of his own elastic bag —that although "There is now more than ever some need for utopia, in the sense that men need—as they have always needed—some vision of their potential, some manner of fusing passion with intelligence. . . . The ladder to the City of Heaven can no longer be a 'faith ladder,' but an empirical one; a utopia has to specify *where* one wants to go, *how* to get there, the costs of the enterprise, and some realization of, and justification for the determination of *who* is to pay." There is a rather terrible irony in the fact that Bell, who in other contexts is so prone to rail against those who think in terms of all or none, should find it so hard at this point to think in terms of degree. Were one seriously to try, in detail and at the outset, to meet all his requirements for a "good" utopia, the magnitude and complexity of the task would paralyze thought. The "good" utopian, like the unholy ideologist, must settle for considerably less if he is ever to bring his deliberations to a conclusion. And if he eventually does reach a conclusion, then no matter how long he reflects and however precise his calculations, it will have been conceived in sin. For it will always reflect a radical simplification of the possibilities and the alternatives which a more scrupulous utopian would think it obligatory to consider.

But Bell's advocacy of even his "good" utopias is, at best, half-hearted. For he really has no faith in any long-range scheme aimed at the amelioration of society as a whole. "Ideology," he tells us, "makes it unnecessary for people to confront individual issues on their individual merits." But in one sense this is true of any rule, any procedure, and any plan, including the plans of piecemeal social engineers like Bell and Popper. What would be the point of any such scheme, however limited in its scope, unless it relieved us of the necessity of confronting every blessed individual issue on its (otherwise) individual merits? And if it comes to that, what is an "individual issue," and what is it to confront one on its "individual merits"? Is the issue of desegregation, for example, one such issue or is it many? Indeed, is the issue of desegregating one individual classroom in one individual school in one God-forsaken county of the state of Mississippi an in-

dividual issue? And if it is, what, pray, are *its* individual merits? How far do these extend?

One of the overwhelming advantages of a bill of human rights (which is nothing but a schedule of enforced ideological commitments), is that it drastically reduces the number of "issues" over which men in societies must continue to quarrel. In this way it reduces the terrible wear and tear of political life which, even in the best-run societies, is nearly unendurable. Bell and his allies, following Popper (and at a distance Bergson), are admirers of the "open society." But of course a completely open society, if such ever existed, would be not a society, but a chaos. If an "open society" is one in which each individual issue is decided, *ad hoc,* on its own peculiar merits, then who wants an "open society"? And if a "closed society" is one in which, owing to the presence of a prevailing ideology (or constitution), many issues are, in any practical sense, dead issues, why then let us by all means continue to have a closed society. Were we Americans seriously to invoke the principle that individual cases should be settled exclusively on their (otherwise) individual merits, we would have to repudiate our Declaration of Independence and to dismantle our whole constitutional system and the characteristic rule of law which it provides.

Is this what the anti-ideologists want? The question is by no means merely "rhetorical." Consider, for example, what that most determined and most consistent of anti-ideologists, Professor Michael Oakeshott, has to say about the Declaration of Independence. It is, he tells us, "A characteristic produce of the *saeculum rationalisticum.* It represents the politics of the felt need interpreted with the aid of an ideology. And it is not surprising that it should have become one of the sacred documents of the politics of Rationalism, and, together with the similar documents of the French Revolution, the inspiration and pattern of many later adventures in the rationalistic reconstruction of Society." Whatever else may be true of Professor Oakeshott, he at least knows an ideology when he sees one and is candid enough to say so. It would clear the air if his fellow anti-ideologists on this side of the Atlantic would speak as clearly and unequivocally.

Let us no longer mince words. Our own anti-ideological foxes are no more "empirical" and no less rhetorical than their leonine opponents; they are, on broad issues, merely more indecisive and more eclectic. As it stands, their point of view is so lacking both in consistency and in clarity that, as I have discovered at some cost, it is virtually impossible to argue with them without fear of doing them some frightful injustice. Still, out of a sophisticated but paralyzing fear of over-simplification, they have managed to fashion a kind of counter-ideology, or fetish, of complexity, difficulty, and uniqueness. They tell us that "the present belongs to the living" and that we should lift from our shoulders "the heavy hand of the future" as well as "the dead hand of the past." Yet they evidently have not the courage to say that the preamble to the American Constitution, which speaks among other things of securing the "Blessings of Liberty to ourselves *and our Posterity*," is so much wicked ideological flourish and moonshine. Their "pluralism" has become a kind of mania which, when pressed to its own counter-ideological extremes, leads inescapably (as William James long ago perceived) to anarchism and, at last, to nihilism. Were their political and social attitudes generally to prevail in the West—and it is primarily of the West that they speak in talking of the end of ideology—the result would be a pessimistic *carpe diem* philosophy which would render us helpless in the world struggle against the ideology of Communism. At home, in the political parties, in the Congress, and in the courts, it continually weakens what remains of our national commitment to the ideological principles that animate our constitutional system; in the Presidency, it provides merely the covering excuses for a spate of uncorrelated, "piecemeal" moves which, however admirable from a tactical point of view and however skillful as "pragmatic" politics, result in an ever increasing loss of basic political control and social direction. Curiously, the over-all picture is one of Hegelian "gray on gray." The only difference is that unlike our anti-ideologists Hegel knew that gray on gray is the color of barrenness, of late autumn and approaching winter.

SUGGESTED ADDITIONAL READINGS

1. Arendt, Hannah, *Between Past and Future,* New York: Viking Press, 1961, 246 pp. A difficult, searching analysis of current issues. The six essays deal with the concepts of tradition, history, authority, education, freedom, and culture.

2. Brinton, Crane, *Ideas and Men,* Englewood Cliffs, N. J.: Prentice-Hall, 1950, pp. 256–298. A short and informative definition of renaissance, reformation, and humanism and their relationship.

3. Commager, Henry Steele, *The American Mind,* New Haven: Yale University Press, 1952, pp. 247–276. Part of an interpretive study of American thought since the 1800's. Deals with the writers of protest from the days of the Populists through the 1940's.

4. Gooch, G. P., *English Democratic Ideas in the Seventeenth Century,* New York: Harper and Row, 1959, 310 pp. (paper). Though an older book (originally published in 1898), it remains one of the best. Begins with a description of the origin of modern democratic ideas; concludes with an analysis of democratic ideas throughout the seventeenth century. Also contains three interesting appendices on the impact of these ideas on other times and places.

5. Grimes, Alan P., and Horowitz, Robert H. (eds.), *Modern Political Ideologies,* New York: Oxford University Press, 1959, pp. 211–461. Contains selections on communism from Marx through Djilas and Mao Tse-tung. Also includes two sections on racial elitism (e.g., H. S. Chamberlain and Hitler), and political elitism (e.g., Nietzsche and Mussolini).

6. Herberg, Will, *Protestant-Catholic-Jew,* Garden City, N.Y.: Doubleday, 1955, 320 pp. A description of the conditions and factors which have led to a transformation of the original "melting pot" to a new "triple melting pot." As a by-product, the book gives a perspective on the religious revival of the 1950's.

7. Hofstadter, Richard, *The American Political Tradition,* New York: Vintage Books, 1957 (paper), pp. 315–352. Last chapter in a series of biographical sketches on Franklin D. Roosevelt.

8. ———, *Social Darwinism in American Thought,* Boston: Beacon Press, 1955, Rev. ed., 298 pp. (paper). Considered by many the best book on the subject. Traces the influence of Darwinism in America through some of its leading exponents and critics and on through its deterioration into racism and imperialism.

9. Latham, Earl (ed.), *The Declaration of Independence and the Constitution,* Boston: D. C. Heath, 1956, 126 pp. (paper). A heated debate among a series of political scientists and historians as to whether the Constitution was a fulfillment or rejection of the Declaration.

10. Leuchtenburg, William E., *Franklin D. Roosevelt and the New Deal,* New York: Harper and Row, 1963, 393 pp. (paper). Comparatively short and scholarly work on the New Deal; one of the best of a voluminous literature on this period.

11. Madison, Charles A., *Critics and Crusaders,* New York: Henry Holt, 1947, 572 pp. Criticism of every kind by crusaders of all shades. The author presents brief and effective biographies and summaries of the lives and ideas of a galaxy of American writers and political figures who found fault with some aspects of American life.

12. Mason, Alpheus Thomas (ed.), *Free Government in the Making,* New York: Oxford University Press, 1965, pp. 886–914. Six short selections by prominent Americans each giving expression to some form of reappraisal. Among the authors are John F. Kennedy, William Fulbright, and Walter Lippmann.

13. Matson, Floyd W., *The Broken Image,* New York: George Braziller, 1964, 355 pp. A very ambitious work which attempts to report on the encounter between the cultures of science and humanism. Of particular relevance are Chapters III ("The Manipulated Society"), VI ("The Freedom to Be Human"), and VII ("The Human Image").

14. Mayer, Milton, *Madison Avenue, U. S. A.,* New York: Harper, 1958, 332 pp. A pungent, witty description of the advertising world. No one and nothing is spared. Not merely an exposé but a solid piece of scholarship by a noted and sensitive writer.

15. Miller, John C., *Origins of the American Revolution,* Boston: Little, Brown, 1943, pp. 495–506. The closing chapter ("The American Revolution as a Democratic Movement") of a famous book; remains authentic and lucid. Author reminds us that the revolution "has not yet ended."

16. Morrall, John B., *Political Thought in Medieval Times,* New York: Harper, 1962, 152 pp. (paper). Compact size makes it an excellent reference for the new student.

17. Muller, Herbert J. *The Uses of the Past,* New York: Oxford University Press, 1952, pp. 72–199. The first of several books by the same author. Written beautifully; packs into three excellent chapters all the vital data on the legacy of Judaism, the glory of Greece, and the rise of Christianity.

18. Reisman, David, *The Lonely Crowd,* New Haven: Yale University Press, 1950, pp. 3–35; 177–209. Analyses of inner-direction, other-direction and tradition-direction, both as to what they are and their role in politics.

19. Rossiter, Clinton, *1787—The Grand Convention,* New York: Macmillan, 1966, pp. 159–335. A grandiose work describing in full detail the setting, men, and events at the Constitutional Convention. The last section deals as well with its immediate consequences. Contains some very useful documents and bibliographical material.

20. Smith, T. V., *The Ethics of Compromise,* Boston: Starr King Press, 1956, 117 pp. Summarizes almost a lifetime of work dedicated to the theory of compromise. Of special note are pp. 40–81, discussing the nature, context, and limits of compromise.

21. Troeltsch, Ernst, *The Social Teachings of the Christian Churches,* Vol. I, New York: Harper, 1960, 448 pp. (paper). Published originally in German in 1911; has come to be regarded as definitive. Starts with the foundations of the early Church and proceeds through the Medieval Catholic world. An excellent, comprehensive work.

22. Ward, Barbara, *Nationalism and Ideology,* New York: W. W. Norton, 1966, (paper), pp. 38–43. Brilliant; wastes not a word. The result of a series of lectures at Carleton University, Ottawa. The few pages cited here concern the contributions of Hellas and Jewry to Western culture.

23. Wilstach, Paul, *Correspondence of John Adams and Thomas Jefferson, 1812–1826,* Indianapolis: Bobbs-Merrill, 1925. One of the most fascinating and revealing exchanges of letters on record between these elder statesmen in the years 1812–1826. Included among their many topics of discussion was the question of what constitutes a true aristocrat.

FOR FURTHER CONSIDERATION

1. What would you suggest now are the major ingredients of classical democratic theory? Are all of these familiar to your experience? If any of these ingredients (or requirements) of democracy should prove to be unnecessary or not present in our society, what conclusion would you draw as to the existence of democracy here? Which ones seem indispensable?

2. It has been stated that "significant restraints were imposed [by the Constitution of 1789] on the democratic elements of society; guarantees against excessive popular participation were numerous." Are there still such restraints and guarantees? Do they differ more than in degree from these early ones? Can you justify the idea of such restraints on democracy? What does this suggest that might be helpful in answering the question: What is democracy? (You may want to return to this question after you have read the rest of this volume.)

3. "The foundation of freedom is creative doubt." Do you agree? What do you suggest would be the problem, if any, faced by the intellectual elite in this regard? Must one doubt his own superior intellect in order to be a democrat? Or does freedom not necessarily relate to democracy?

4. After studying this chapter what do you now mean by "theory"? Does it make sense to tell a colleague that he may be right in theory but in practice things don't work that way? Can one talk about democratic theory and not be talking about things as they are? Do questions of what *ought* to be properly belong in a political theory discussion? What do *you* mean by the term "democratic political theory"? Does theory have any value as a guide to action?

5. Do you see any evidence in our society of "democratic man's search for authority"? What is this evidence? Does this discussion of man's urge to escape freedom suggest or cast doubt on the assumption that "man is by nature free"? Could it be that government is necessary to make man free?

The Constitution and
Constitutionalism 2

The Constitution of the United States is the "centre of American government and politics. . . ." It has "acquired . . . a claim to reverence, to uncritical acceptance, that has no parallel in the world."[1] It has been seen "not merely as a frame of government, but as a means of social and political salvation."[2] The Constitution has become "sacrosanct . . . America's uncrowned king . . . above party, a common object of veneration, a living symbol of national unity."[3] However, that "Constitution is not a king who reigns but does not govern, for to the average American, the sacred text is an oracle that, properly consulted, gives an infallible answer and if the answer given by the priests of the oracle is displeasing, the explanation must lie in the intellectual or moral faults of the priesthood, not the work of the men of 1787."[4] [2]

The Constitution of the United States is one of the world's oldest operating written constitutions. It is also one of the shortest. However, the document is not complete within itself. To be understood, it must be read in conjunction with Supreme Court decisions, legislative acts, executive orders, administrative rulings, traditions and customs, and historical developments of the more than 175 years since it was adopted.

But a genuine constitution, and consequently constitutionalism, is neither dependent upon, nor synonymous with, a written document. Constitutionalism can exist without a written document and can be absent when there is a

[1] D. W. Brogan, *Politics in America* (New York: Harper, 1954), p. 2.
[2] *Ibid.,* p. 11.
[3] Alfred H. Kelly and Winifred A. Harbison, *The American Constitution,* 3rd ed., (New York: W. W. Norton, 1963), pp. 162–163.
[4] Brogan, *op. cit.,* p. 31.

written constitution. The most that can be said is that a written constitution may be useful in the establishment of a constitutional system.

Carl J. Friedrich suggests that a constitution exists when there is constitutionalism, and constitutionalism exists when there is a "system of effective restraints upon governmental action."[5]

As a political process, the constitution can be described as analogous to the rules of the game insuring fair play. This is the meaning of the word 'constitution' in its functional sense, as distinguished from its meaning in law, in history, and in medicine. The political scientist inquiring into the process of constitutionalizing a government must study the technique of establishing and maintaining effective restraints on political and governmental action.[6]

Constitutionalism exists when there are regularized restraints on government whether or not those restraints are formalized in a written document. [5] In our national experience, a system of regularized restraints on government is reflected both in the requirements of the written document and, more importantly, in a societal attitude towards the use of governmental power, in the expectation that government will function in an orderly, predictable, and restrained fashion. This is the real constitution of the United States. This constitution has to do with the spirit, the myths, the actual operative procedures, and the expectations of the people, not simply with the document per se.

The experience of other countries with constitutions, written and unwritten, supports this approach. [18] Both the United States and France operate under written constitutions, and, although they operate in significantly different fashion, both are constitutional and democratic societies. On the other hand, the Union of Soviet Socialist Republics has a written constitution, one which many observers agree compares favorably in form with our own. The difference in the experience of the United States or France and the Soviet Union is significant, however. In the former two, constitutionalism—regularized restraints on governments, an expectation that government will function in an orderly, predictable, and restrained fashion—does exist, whereas the USSR does not seem to have produced such constitutionalism. The British operate without a written constitution, although there are various landmark documents which make up a part of the British constitution. But there is no doubt that the British operate with regularized restraints on government. In the Weimar Republic in Germany after World War I a democratically conceived and constructed written document did not guarantee constitutional government. The experience of our Latin American neighbors with written constitutions, some almost verbatim reproductions of our own, has provided striking evidence that a written constitution will not guarantee a constitutional government.

THE CONSTITUTION IN HISTORICAL PERSPECTIVE

The Constitution is a product of our history. The original document need not be considered a divinely-ordained instrument nor the product of men of extraordinary brilliance and unique insights. It was the result of conflict and

---

[5] Carl J. Friedrich, *Constitutional Government and Democracy* (New York: Ginn, 1950), p. 26.
[6] *Ibid.*, p. 121.

compromise, trial and error, a pragmatic effort to solve the known problems of government in a new society by men who were privileged or burdened, as the case may be, with responsibility for participation in that society. It was an experiment based on empirical data and experience in failure. It represents the efforts to correct the causes of that failure as men tried again to institutionalize their notions of what a constitutional system should be.

The colonists brought with them an inheritance of constitutionalism, but in the New World they were faced with the concrete problems of how to constitute their own governing institutions. The Declaration of Independence declared their purposes, announced to themselves and to the world their rationalization for revolution against the British. Not only was it a revolutionary document designed as a propaganda instrument, but it was also an important treatise on government. The Declaration served its purpose well and remains today of considerable historical interest. But it is not a governing instrument, a constitution, or a part of our law today. It establishes no legal responsibilities, no rights or privileges, no solutions to constitutional questions. Its importance lies in its contribution to the developing myths about freedom, self-government, and constitutionalism.

With the end of the revolution the Articles of Confederation established a confederation (1781–1789) recognizing the independence and sovereignty of the individual colonies. The machinery of government at the national level consisted only of Congress, in which each state had a single vote. There was no real legislative power and no separate executive or judiciary. Congress was a "grand committee of the states," lacking most significant powers, including the power to tax, to enforce its sanctions, to regulate or govern the people directly, or to regulate interstate commerce, although it had "paper" powers of considerable scope in foreign relations.

The significance of the Articles of Confederation lies in its contribution to the colonists' experience in government. This government was not satisfactory, its failures were evident, and the need for new attempts at solution was recognized.

Respect for, indeed adulation of, the founding fathers may be an important ingredient of the national myth today. But the constitution is not so much the product of the brilliance and insight of the framers of the constitution as it is the result of an historical progression from recognition of a problem, to attempts at solution, through failure or only partial success, to a new attempt at solution. The Constitutional Convention of 1787 was more a gathering of repairmen than an assemblage of artists. [1, 3, 16] It had before it specific experience with a constitutional document which had demonstrated shortcomings, and it set out to correct those deficiencies.

The sovereignty of the states had thwarted the national government; in the new document, the states, though independent, were subordinated to the national government in the crucial area of national powers. Under the Articles the central government lacked significant powers; under the new arrangements the central government had specifically delegated powers, including the important powers to tax, to coin and regulate money, to regulate interstate and foreign commerce, and by implication to operate directly upon the people of the United

States rather than upon states as such. Under the Articles there was only a Congress; under the new Constitution there were three separate branches, legislative, executive, and judicial, each with significant powers within its respective jurisdiction but none able to thwart the others permanently. Under the Articles representation had been equal regardless of the size of the state; under the Constitution, a compromise had been worked out so that large and small states, and states with different economic bases, could agree to participate in the government with reasonable expectation that their interests would be protected.

The Constitution was not so much a new approach to government as a continuation of past efforts to establish an effective method of governing. And the Constitution today is the product of development through various historical periods, reflecting society's best efforts to solve its changing problems. It is an evolving, developing, living document.

THE CHANGING CONSTITUTION

How has the Constitution developed and how is it developing today? The major methods of change are formal amendment, interpretation, and custom and tradition.

The framers provided a specific means for formal amendment. The amendments are not inconsequential, but their impact on the system of government has been less than that from other means of change. In general, they have made relatively minor structural changes and have not been responsible for growth in the basic powers of government, modifications in the federal relationship, or significant economic, political, and social changes of direction. (Some, of course, such as the income tax amendment, have been quite important in these regards). They have been most important in providing the opportunity for expanding individual freedom and political participation. Although the language of some of these formal amendments—such as the "equal protection of the laws" clause or "due process" clause of the Fourteenth Amendment—has become extremely important in recent years, this has developed primarily through judicial interpretation.

The Constitution changes primarily through interpretation, through changing the meaning of language in the document and filling in the gaps where the document is silent. In passing statutes Congress is always potentially expanding the meaning of constitutional provisions. In creating, for instance, the independent regulatory commissions, such as the Interstate Commerce Commission or the Federal Trade Commission, to regulate major segments of the economy, Congress has gone far beyond the simple language granting Congress the power to regulate interstate commerce. Presidential succession, the executive departments, the size and appellate jurisdiction of the Supreme Court and all other federal courts, and matters pertaining to governing the territories have been matters for congressional elaboration.

The president and the administrative agencies also fill in and interpret meanings of the Constitution. For example, the Cabinet is not mentioned in the Constitution. Presidential interpretation established that the Union cannot be dissolved and that the presidential purchase of territory, such as the Louisiana and Alaska Purchases, is constitutional. The power of the president to remove his own appointees without obtaining the permission of the Senate was not stated in the Constitution but was established through presidential action and later tested in the Supreme Court.[7] Procedures in case of presidential inability to carry out the duties of the office have been established from time to time by presidential agreement with the vice-president. Administrative policy-making involves elaboration of constitutional procedure and principles, as the decisions made by Congress and the president filter down through the administrative hierarchy.

The Supreme Court, however, is the most important interpreter of the constitution. The Court sits as the final determiner of the constitutionality of any action of government and declares definitely the meaning of constitutional provisions.[8] For example, the Court's decision in 1954 that segregation is no longer permissible in public education[9] changed the meaning of the equal protection of the law clause, which had until then permitted "separate but equal facilities."[10] Expansion of freedom of religion and of speech and the protections given to those accused of crimes have also been primarily the work of the Court. Decisions on representation have resulted in state legislatures reapportioning both houses according to population and the modification of many congressional districts.

Custom and tradition also change the Constitution. Many of the most important political and governmental procedures are the product of nothing more formal than custom. For instance, the nomination of the president and vice-president was not mentioned in the Constitution, but the gap has been filled by a customary procedure which is as formal and regularized as any in our constitutional system. The party system, indispensable to the competitive struggle for political power which is the heart of the democratic process, has been supplied by usage. The congressional committee system, through which legislative consideration of public policy questions is conducted, is nowhere mentioned in the Constitution. The customary requirement that a member of the House of Representatives reside in the district from which he is elected is as definite as the minimum age limits specified in the Constitution. The use of executive agreements to supplement and/or avoid the necessity of formal treaties and the fact that the electoral college operates quite differently than specified in the document, are products of our "way of doing things."

The Constitution must be meaningful in terms of the problems facing society. These problems change as economic, social, and political conditions change. The constitutional language must be made to fit the needs of the day so as to provide bases for solutions without endangering the continuity and stability of the constitutional system. It is one of the great accomplishments of this system that we can in the mid-twentieth century still operate under a Constitution

[7] *Myers v. U.S.*, 272 U.S. 52 (1926); *Humphrey's Executor v. U.S.*, 295 U.S. 602 (1935); *Wiener v. U.S.*, 357 U.S. 349 (1958).
[8] Even this power of judicial review was a product of judicial interpretation. In *Marbury v. Madison*, 1 Cranch 127 (1803), the Supreme Court asserted that it had the power to review the acts of Congress and to declare them unconstitutional if they violate the Constitution.
[9] *Brown v. Board of Education*, 349 U.S. 483 (1954).
[10] *Plessy v. Ferguson*, 163 U.S. 537 (1896).

written by people whose experiences were limited to the eighteenth century. They would not recognize their handiwork; it may not sound like the same Constitution, yet it is still the basis of the same constitutional system.

One of the popular concerns of courts is with the original intent of the framers. [11] The courts quite often justify their interpretation of a constitutional provision by reference to what they assert to have been the intention of the founding fathers in adopting that provision. Antagonists of various persuasions, in commenting upon interpretations of the Constitution, frequently claim that a new interpretation is not representative of the intent of the framers. Useful as the "original intent" idea may be for the courts, popular as it may be in argument, and interesting as it may be for the students of history, the intention of the founding fathers is irrelevant to the meaning of the Constitution today. Aside from the impossibility of determining such intent with any degree of certainty,[11] it cannot be justified that a group of men whose experiences were those of the eighteenth century should forever bind a nation to their solutions and their understanding of the necessary governing arrangements. The founding fathers, for example, could not have envisioned governmental efforts to reach the moon, or governments having the power to regulate the speed of automobiles on an interstate freeway. They could not have "intended" about these simply because they could not have conceived of them. Their contribution was not providing final answers to the problems which were yet to be thought of, much less faced, but "roughing in" a framework for a genuine constitutionalism through which the solution of vexing problems in any given era can be approached.

We can admit of no final meaning to the Constitution, for when we conclude that we have reached that final, clear, unchangeable meaning, that Constitution, like many others before it, will be dead. Only so long as the Constitution grows, changes, stays alive and vital in terms of the problems of the day can it be a meaningful basis for a genuine constitutionalism and an instrument for successful government.

All of this, however, must be understood in connection with the processes for determining what the people expect of government. A change in popular expectation as to what government ought to do must be reflected institutionally in new procedures, new solutions, and new constitutional interpretations. Constitutional changes, by formal amendment, interpretation, or custom and tradition, are manifestations of changes in the demands of the people and their expectation as to the way government should operate. The Constitution of the United States cannot be separated from the political processes, for the Constitution both defines the way in which that political process will operate and is defined by it.

---

[11] It is highly doubtful that a positive intention by a collegial body, be it convention or legislature, can be assumed whenever that body acts or fails to act formally. About all that can be claimed is that the body when acting or refusing to act was willing or unwilling collectively for unspecified and probably undeterminable considerations to allow the particular business to become an official product of that particular body. The notion of a collective intent or will does not correspond to reality; there is a significant difference between the formal collective action of a collegial body and the considerations by which the individual members are moved to join together, or refrain from joining together, to form a majority in favor of that collective action. The problem is compounded in the constitution-approving and amendment-ratifying processes, which involve decision-making participation by many such collegial bodies—Congress and the ratifying conventions or state legislatures.

STRUCTURE OF GOVERNMENT

The Constitution established the basic structural arrangements by which this country has been governed since its enactment. These include (1) a representative system of government; (2) a skeleton framework of government; and (3) a federal system.

REPRESENTATIVE GOVERNMENT

The Constitution established a system of representative, as distinguished from direct, democracy. Although procedures for direct participation—the initiative, referendum, and recall—have been tried in various states, there is nothing in the Constitution suggesting any form of direct participation of the people in the business of governing. The role of the electorate is to select those who will govern and make public policy in the name of the electorate, subject only to the restraints incorporated into the Constitution or imposed by the political system itself.

Occasionally the argument arises that the Constitution established a republic, rather than a democracy, and that in the twentieth century we have been moving away from a republican form of government, an undesirable deviation from the original intent. The inappropriateness of the original intent argument has already been noted. Eighteenth-century concepts of democracy fall far short of democracy in twentieth-century terms. But the basic structure out of which that twentieth-century democratic society could grow was provided by the eighteenth-century document. It did not create an ideal democracy, but the rudimentary ingredients were there. Their evolution in the twentieth century is good evidence that the basic requisites existed.

The crucial point, however, is that the distinction between republican and democratic government is labored and contrived. Republican government is impossible to define. There is only one mention of the term in the Constitution— "the United States shall guarantee to every state in this union a republican form of government. . . ." [12] No definition was given, and the courts have refused to supply that definition, holding that it is a "political question" whether a government is republican. Consequently, if one wishes to call the system republican he may, but to oppose this to a democratic system is nonsense, theoretically and legally. The best we can do with the term republican is to specify that it is to be distinguished from monarchy or dictatorship; it connotes some kind of popularly-selected government, some kind of democratic procedure for selection and removal and control of the agents of government—in short, it is representative government.

FRAMEWORK OF GOVERNMENT

The Constitution established only a skeleton framework upon which the enormous governmental machinery of today has gradually been built. It provided for only three institutions of government: the Congress, the president, and the Supreme Court. It vested legislative power in Congress, executive power in

---

[12] Article IV, section 4.

the president, and judicial power in the Supreme Court and such inferior courts as Congress might establish. The details of that organizational structure, other than those pertaining to selection, the bicameral structure of Congress, and some congressional procedures, were not included.

THE FEDERAL SYSTEM

The heart of the Constitution is the delegation of powers, the critical feature of the federal system. A federal system exists when there is a meaningful division of powers between two or more levels of government, so that each operates relatively independently of the other within its own sphere of powers. [17] But it must be emphasized that the exercise of powers is relative. Such a view admits of the possibility of change in the relationship of levels of government, such that at times one level may be more or less powerful than another in relation to a specific set of powers. Such elasticity has been one of the marked characteristics of our experience with federalism. [4, 6, 8, 15]

The delegated powers are those specifically given to the federal government by the Constitution—the power to tax, borrow money, regulate interstate and foreign commerce, coin money and regulate its value, establish a postal system, create courts, declare war, maintain armies and a navy, assist the states in the maintenance of militia, and use the state militia to execute the laws of the land, suppress insurrections and repel invasions. Other specifically delegated powers include the power to establish a uniform rule of naturalization, legislate on bankruptcies, fix standards of weights and measures, punish counterfeiting, provide for patents and copyrights, define and punish piracies and felonies on the high seas and offenses against the law of nations, and govern the seat of government, the District of Columbia.

No such list of powers could be sufficient as social, economic, and political conditions changed. Fortunately, the Constitution did not fix government in a form of static federalism. The federal government was also authorized "to make all laws which shall be necessary and proper for carrying into execution the foregoing powers. . . ." This clause, variously referred to as the necessary and proper clause, the implied powers clause, or the elastic clause, made the delegated powers pliable, capable of application to the multitude of specific problems that would face the new government. In 1819, the Supreme Court upheld the power of Congress to charter a bank of the United States on the basis that such an act was necessary and proper to the carrying out of the delegated powers. In language as applicable today as it was in 1819, Chief Justice John Marshall declared that the implied powers provision

is made in a constitution intended to endure for ages to come, and consequently, to be adapted to the various crises of human affairs. To have prescribed the means by which government should, in all future time, execute its powers . . . would have been an unwise attempt to provide, by immutable rules, for exigencies which, if foreseen at all, must have been seen dimly, and which can be best provided for as they occur. To have declared that the best means shall not be used, but those alone without which the power given would be nugatory, would have been to deprive the legislature of the capacity to avail itself of experience, to exercise its reason, and to accommodate its legislation to circumstances.[13]

[13] *McCulloch v. Maryland,* 4 Wheat. 316, 415 (1819).

Certain powers are specifically prohibited to government. For example, neither a state government nor the federal government may pass a bill of attainder—a legislative imposition of punishment—or an ex post facto law, or grant titles of nobility. The federal government is specifically prohibited from suspending the writ of habeas corpus except in cases of rebellion or invasion where the public safety may require it, imposing any direct tax except on the basis of population (modified by the Sixteenth Amendment), imposing an export tax, or giving any preference to the ports of one state over those of another. The states are specifically prohibited from entering into any treaty, coining money, passing any law impairing the obligation of contracts, or imposing duties on imports or exports without the consent of Congress.[14] All other powers—those not specifically delegated, implied, or prohibited to the states—remain with the original repository, the states or the people. The Tenth Amendment, added by the first Congress, reiterates this relationship.

This picture of the division of powers is technically accurate but nevertheless misleading. In emphasizing the division of powers as an arbitrary system it obscures the fact that there is more an interaction than a division of powers. The federal system is one of separate governments with interacting and complementary powers. The Constitution presents a basis for a meaningful division of powers between two levels of government, not a final specification of that division. The basic problem of federalism in American experience has been and will continue to be the precise division of powers in any given case at any given time. It is precisely this relational aspect which is the key to understanding the federal system.

In our federal system the Constitution, federal laws, and treaties are the "supreme law of the land." Constitutionally, there can be no conflict between federal law and state law. The conflict will be only apparent, for the supremacy clause clearly means that the federal law will survive. This is, in sum, a system not so much of divided as shared powers, maximizing the opportunity for government at both levels to address problems and attempt to solve them, but protected from the disunity and internecine tendencies potential in federalism by the guarantee of the supremacy of the government of the whole.

Examination of the present powers of the federal government will serve to clarify this federal relationship. The three most important and extensive are the power to tax and spend, the power to regulate commerce, and the war powers.

POWER TO TAX, BORROW, AND SPEND

One of the greatest deficiencies of the Articles of Confederation was the government's inability to raise sufficient revenue. The new instrument clearly corrected the deficiency of the old. The first delegated power enumerated in the Constitution is the "power to lay and collect taxes, duties, imposts and excises," and the second is "to borrow money on the credit of the United States."

The taxing power can be used constitutionally (1) to raise revenue, (2) as a regulatory instrument, and (3) for promotional purposes. These three

[14] Article I, sections 9 and 10. There are numerous other prohibitions on federal and/or state power specifically written into the amendments, especially the first eight and the Fourteenth Amendment, and interpreted into these amendments by the Supreme Court.

uses of the taxing power result in an extremely broad grant of power, the effective limits of which are difficult to define and which rest more on general acquiescence of the people and their satisfaction with the ends being accomplished than upon rigid constitutional constructions. [12]

Subject only to the specific prohibitions of the Constitution, the power to tax in order to raise revenue is apparently unlimited. Congress cannot, for instance, impose taxes which deny "equal protection of the law," or which are direct and not apportioned according to population, or which discriminate between ports. But except for this kind of restraint, the taxing power has no easily identified bounds.

One of the oldest regulatory uses of the taxing power has been the protective tariff, by which imported goods are taxed to guarantee that they cannot be sold in this country at a price which is unduly competitive with domestic products. But the regulatory function of taxation includes the power to tax prohibitively; "the only checks upon the rate of taxation are political checks." [15] For example, a federal tax on state bank notes in 1866 was sufficiently high to drive them out of circulation. In 1902, Congress imposed a ten cent per pound tax on colored oleomargarine and a one-quarter cent per pound tax on uncolored oleomargarine, a tax clearly designed to place colored oleomargarine in an unfavorable economic position relative to butter. In 1912, Congress imposed a two cent per-one-hundred match tax on poisonous white-phosphorus matches, for the purpose of discouraging their production.

The use of the taxing power to assist the states in regulating the narcotics and gambling businesses has been extensive. Ordinarily, a nominal tax is imposed on the sale of drugs, and in order to facilitate the collection of this nominal tax the taxpayer must register his transactions and keep records, open to inspection by the Bureau of Internal Revenue. The effect on clandestine transfer of narcotics is obvious. In 1890 Congress imposed a $10 per pound tax on the sale of opium for smoking, and in 1914 increased the tax to $300 per pound, a fairly high price to pay for the privilege of selling a product.

In 1953 the Supreme Court upheld a federal tax on gamblers, requiring them to purchase a $50 tax stamp. Most states prohibit gambling, and anyone purchasing the federal tax stamp runs a considerable risk of disclosing his illegal operations to local authorities, since federal tax officials release to local law-enforcement agents the name and place of business of any person purchasing the stamp. If the gambler chooses not to purchase the federal tax stamp, in order to protect his operation from disclosure to state and local officials, he is clearly violating federal revenue laws.

A tax is not invalid which "on its face" is a tax measure even though its primary effect is regulatory or prohibitory.[16] While in some few cases the Court has been willing to invalidate a federal tax,[17] if Congress can

---

[15] Robert E. Cushman and Robert F. Cushman, *Cases in Constitutional Law* (New York: Appleton-Century-Crofts, 1958), p. 286.

[16] *McCray v. U.S.,* 195 U.S. 27 (1904).

[17] For example, a tax on products produced by child labor, a penalty tax of twenty cents per bushel on certain grains sold without submission to elaborate regulations administered by the Secretary of Agriculture, and a special excise tax of $1,000 annually upon those who carry on the liquor business in violation of state law.

make the regulation look like a tax in the statute, the Supreme Court usually will not inquire into the purposes of Congress. Thus, a $200 annual license tax on dealers in firearms and a $200 tax on each transfer of a machine gun, sawed off shotgun, or silencer was upheld by the Court because "on its face it is only a taxing measure."[18]

The promotional use of the taxing power is also important. Through use of the tax offset a state is induced to undertake certain programs in order to avoid a federal tax. In the early 1920's, the lack of uniformity in state taxes for the transfer of property after death caused considerable difficulty for those states which had inheritance taxes, since transfer of property before death to a state not having an inheritance tax was possible. Congress, in assisting the states to overcome this problem, enacted a graduated inheritance tax but provided that 80 percent of the tax would not have to be paid if the state had collected this amount in state inheritance taxes. In the Social Security Act of 1935, Congress levied a tax on certain employers but provided that 90 percent of the tax would not have to be paid if these employers were contributing to a state-administered unemployment compensation plan which met specific requirements. By this use of the taxing power Congress succeeded in inducing the states to enact inheritance tax and unemployment compensation plans.

The power to tax does not stand alone, however. Its corollaries are the power to borrow and the power to spend. The power to borrow is limited realistically only by the ability of the government to find willing lenders. The power to spend is virtually unlimited, the Constitution granting authority to Congress to levy taxes in order to "pay the debts and provide for the common defense and general welfare." It is very difficult to challenge federal spending, for an ordinary taxpayer does not have sufficient "standing" to sue to invalidate federal expenditures.[19] There have been a few cases in which the purpose for which a tax revenue was to be used was held to be beyond congressional power,[20] but the general rule is that the Tenth Amendment does not impose any limitation upon the federal government in the exercise of its delegated powers, and thus the power to spend "to provide for the . . . general welfare" is not seriously limited. It is this power to spend upon which the extensive federal grants-in-aid program has been built.

THE COMMERCE POWER

The power to regulate commerce is, like the taxing power, extremely broad.[21] There is little in our society today which does not either directly or indirectly affect interstate commerce and thus come potentially under the power of the federal government. [13]

The power to regulate commerce has been expanded to include the promotion, protection, and prohibition of commerce. It serves (in conjunction with

---

[18] *Sonzinsky v. U.S.*, 300 U.S. 506 (1937).
[19] *Massachusetts v. Mellon*, 262 U.S. 447 (1923).
[20] For example, *U.S. v. Butler*, 297 U.S. 1 (1936), held that an agriculture processing tax was void because the money raised from it was to be used to finance a system of federal regulation of agriculture, outside the delegated powers of Congress.
[21] *Gibbons v. Ogden*, 9 Wheat. 1 (1824).

the postal power) as a substitute for a national police power.[22] The federal government has prohibited the shipment of lottery tickets between states, enacted and administered pure food and drug laws, assisted the states in eliminating the "white-slave" traffic, assisted the states in controlling the automobile theft racket, provided for investigation and prosecution of kidnapping, imposed minimum wage and maximum hours legislation, and established marketing quotas for agriculture products. The government in controlling commerce regulates all forms of communication and transportation—the railroad, steamboat, telegraph, telephone, motor vehicles, radio, the airplane and television—all manufacturing, mining, lumbering and other productive enterprises in which the raw materials or finished products are carried across state lines, and the corporate and financial affairs of all kinds of business enterprise even remotely connected to interstate commerce.

WAR POWERS

Congress is given the power to declare war, to raise and support armies, to provide and maintain a navy, to regulate the land and naval forces, to call the state militia into federal service, and to organize, arm, and discipline the state militia. These grants, the president's powers as commander-in-chief of the armed forces and as representative of the nation in foreign affairs, and a generally agreed-upon inherent right of government to preserve itself, combine to give the United States the power to wage war and to wage it successfully. [14] In World War I and II the government imposed economic and personal regulations far beyond those normally exercised, including conscription, rationing, censorship, and forced relocation of citizens.

Two basic problems recur in reference to the war powers—the degree of wartime controls necessary, and their abrogation in peacetime. Fortunately, and encouragingly suggestive of genuine constitutionalism, neither one has presented serious difficulty for the United States. While there have been extremes of governmental activity during the wars—the forced relocation of American citizens of Japanese ancestry from the West Coast during World War II, for instance— these are exceptional cases and do not indicate a failure of the constitutional system. [10] Because of the nebulous nature of the post-World War II peace, there may remain vestiges of the wartime emergency powers; however, the United States has not faced serious problems in returning to the anticipated and expected controls of the Constitution.

The federal system is adaptable to the circumstances and requirements of the day. It is not an arbitrarily defined division of powers but a relationship capable of change as the requirements for governmental action change. The states and the central government work together, in cooperative federalism. This cooperative federalism involves more than constitutional language dividing powers. It requires dynamic interrelationships to enable this federal system to meet the challenges of different periods of history. Two instruments—the interstate compact and federal grants-in-aid—have been particularly important in

---

[22] The "police power" is the power to legislate for the health, happiness, and well-being of the people—a power not delegated to the federal government.

this regard. Often when there is need for action in that gray area between federal and state authority—such as in the control of crime, the promotion of regional educational aims, or the development of regional water supplies—states, with the permission of Congress, have entered into interstate compacts [19] enabling them to solve problems not otherwise possible because of their limited powers. On the other hand, federal funds have been made available through grants-in-aid [7] to assist the states to accomplish purposes beyond their limited means, at the same time avoiding the necessity of full federal involvement in the activity. The grants-in-aid program and the interstate compact have helped maintain the vitality and success of local and state governments, without centralization at the national level.

RESTRAINTS ON GOVERNMENT

The concept of constitutionalism places major emphasis on restraints on government. It is in this respect that the Constitution of the United States—both the written document and the Constitution in the broader sense—is most specific. The basic document and the amendments include a number of restraints as to procedure, structure, and activities of government. There is a general expectation that the Constitution assures a regularized governmental process and that these guarantees will be meaningful in application, not just symbolic. For instance, the role of the Supreme Court as an authoritative determiner of the extent to which government may exercise its authority and as a protector of the individual against government, although nowhere specified in the document, has become thoroughly accepted as a meaningful part of the restraint pattern. Furthermore, the restraints, both formal and traditional, are sanctioned in the political system by the competition for political power. Regardless of the language of the document, public officials must tread lightly in attempting to exercise exceptional authority, not so much because of the danger of going beyond their legal authority but because of the repercussions on their political futures. Thus, the democratic political process as a continuing open competitive struggle for power serves both to enforce and to supplement the formal constitutional restraints.

Structurally the Constitution determines the major institutions, their powers, and the relationships of these to each other. The separation of powers, through which the three major divisions—the legislative, executive, and judicial—interact in a kind of "antagonistic cooperation," is a major part of this pattern of restraint. The division of powers in the federal system is an important part of the constitutionally-imposed restraint on the various levels of government. The prohibited powers also restrain government.

The "full faith and credit clause" requires that each state recognize as valid all public acts, records, and judicial proceedings of every other state.[23] The "privileges and immunities clause" guarantees that every United States citizen will receive the privileges and immunities of his citizenship in any state he

[23] Criminal matters and divorce proceedings are two notable exceptions to the full faith and credit requirement.

enters, thus preventing states from discriminating against non-residents.[24] These two major clauses serve as important restraints on the states in their relationships to the citizens of other states and have helped to establish this nation as a union of states rather than fifty independent states.

Congress is prohibited from forming states from the territory of any state without its consent. The United States is obligated to guarantee to every state a republican form of government, and to protect the states against invasion and domestic violence upon request of the state.[25]

The amendments impose a long list of restraints. The amendments as interpreted by the Supreme Court and applied in practice provide the framework for a meaningfully restrained government vis-a-vis the individual citizen. The amendments specify that there shall be freedom from governmental interference with religion, speech, press, assembly, and the right to petition the government for redress of grievances. There is protection against unreasonable search and seizure, imprisonment without trial, repeated prosecution after once determined not guilty of an alleged violation of the law, self-incrimination, trial without counsel, excessive bail, cruel and unusual punishments, deprivation of life, liberty, or property without due process of law, and denial of the equal protection of the laws.

The application and meaning of these terms have been modified and extended through the years. Two phrases, "due process of law" and "equal protection of the laws," relatively meaningless within themselves, have become perhaps the most fertile phrases in all constitutional history for the protection of individual liberties. It is, for instance, "equal protection of the laws" that is the basis for elimination of segregated schools, as well as for restructuring state legislatures to insure that representation is based on "one man, one vote."

The Constitution further guarantees that slavery is not permissible, that no citizen may be denied the right to vote because of race or sex, and that the poll tax cannot be used as a basis for determination of the eligibility to vote in elections for federal officials.

American constitutional experience is firmly grounded on the premise that a constitution is meaningful only insofar as it establishes a regularized, restrained process of government. The specific application of these restraints, the extent to which a particular restraint is desirable or necessary, and the frustrations incident to their imposition pose serious problems at any time, but these are unavoidable and even necessary for the proper functioning of a democratic society. What is critical is that these differences arise within, and can be reconciled by, orderly government operating within a general societal expectation that the Constitution can and will work.

The Civil War stands as a reminder that no constitution is an absolute guarantor of success in governing. But our history of social, economic, and political revolution of an evolutionary and peaceful variety—such as the major

[24] Important exceptions include the privilege of entering into certain professions and business—law, medicine, barbering, etc.—and the use of the states' proprietary facilities—the state university, fish and game resources, etc. Distinctions may be made between state residents and non-residents in these areas.

[25] However, the president does not have to wait for such request when the domestic violence interferes with the carrying out of federal statutes or federal court orders.

change of direction of the New Deal in the 1930's or the civil rights revolution of the 1960's—stands as good evidence of the utility of the Constitution as an instrument of government, more viable and meaningful today than in the 1790's.

The Constitution of the United States is a living document, changing and growing to meet the needs of a changing and growing society. If there were genius in the work of the founding fathers it was not the establishment in immutable provisions of how society ought to be governed, but the lack of definition and the flexibility of the phrases incorporated within the document. These phrases—equal protection of the law, due process of law, regulation of interstate commerce, the taxing power, for example—lacking content but pregnant with possibilities, have been available for change as the conditions of society change and as the challenges to government grow. Consequently, the American people have been able to rewrite the Constitution by giving meanings to these phrases that bear on the problems of their day, while retaining the continuity and attachment to the tradition and spirit of constitutionalism of the past.

The three following selections supplement the approach to the Constitution and constitutionalism presented here. Sartori ("Constitutionalism: A Preliminary Discussion") argues that a constitution must, to be a genuine constitution, impose restraints on, guarantees against, government. Corwin ("The Constitution as Instrument and Symbol"), a dean among students of American constitutional development, in this classic article written in 1936, discusses the two distinct functions of the United States Constitution, a distinction now taken as axiomatic by students of the Constitution. Grodzins ("The Federal System") advances the thesis that all levels of government have shared in all functions of government. This thesis contrasts sharply with the traditional views of federalism.

These articles invite the reader to consider, first, the basic conceptual problem of the nature of a constitution; second, the U. S. Constitution in regard to its role as symbol and as instrument of government; and, finally, the central ingredient of the Constitution, the federal system.

Constitutionalism: A Preliminary Discussion

GIOVANNI SARTORI

Dr. Sartori is professor of sociology and political science at the University of Florence. His special fields of interest are political theory and state and local government.

In the 19th century what was meant by the term "constitution" was reasonably

Reprinted from *The American Political Science Review,* LVI, No. 4 (December 1962), 853–864, by permission of the author and the publisher.

definite and clear. Paradoxically enough, if the word retained some ambiguity, this was because of the British constitution; that is, because the mother country of modern constitutionalism appeared to have an obscure constitution, or even—

according to some of the standards that seemed very important elsewhere—no constitution at all.

I

Yet the very term "constitution" has acquired its modern meaning in English, in the course of the evolution of the English legal terminology. The Latin term *constitutio* meant the very opposite of what is now understood by "constitution." A *constitutio* was an enactment; later, after the 2d century, the plural form *constitutiones* came to mean a collection of laws enacted by the Sovereign; and subsequently the Church, too, adopted the term for canonical laws. The terms *constitutio* and *constitutiones* were not frequently used, however, by the English medieval glossators (while frequently used, as a synonym for *lex* and *edictum,* by the Italian ones). This explains why, in the course of time, the word constitution became a "vacant term"—*i.e.,* a term available for a new employment—in English (this does not necessarily mean in England), and not in those languages which had retained the Roman legal terminology.

For terminological reasons also, then, we have to refer to an English meaning of the word constitution,[1] although the United Kingdom has a difficult and *sui generis* constitution, deriving from a tortuous sedimentation of common law, acts and conventional usage, partly legal and partly extra-legal, and despite the fact that, when one reads the British constitutional lawyers, one is often reminded of what was said in a review of Stirling's book, *The Secret of Hegel:* "never has a secret been better kept."

For one thing, English constitutional lawyers appear to take a particular pleasure in pointing out to foreign jurists and political thinkers (beginning with Montesquieu) that their understanding of the English system is quite wrong. To be

sure, this has been and still is very often the case. But one remains with a feeling that the British find a special gratification in confounding alien scholars: there is an element of polemic coquetry in the emphasis they lay on the principle of the supremacy of Parliament (exhibited as being unlimited, arbitrary, omnipotent, *supra* and *contra legem,* etc.); in the somewhat provocative and bold statement that, according to the American and French meaning of the term, the United Kingdom does not have a constitution,[2] in the point that the British system is based not on the "division" but on the "fusion" of powers;[3] or in the way in which Sir Ivor Jennings puts forward that, "Since Great Britain has no written constitution, there is no special protection for 'fundamental rights'."[4] And one could quote at length.

All these statements are, to be sure, true. But they are "literally true," and one is brought to wonder why the emphasis is laid on the *letter* so much more than on the *spirit* of the law of the constitution. After all, constitutionalism has a prescriptive purpose; whereas English scholars appear more inclined to address themselves to an MP by saying "you could" rather than "you cannot."

Let us take, for instance, the principle of the supremacy of Parliament. Would it be far from the mark to say that if the principle is related to the historical circumstances of its establishment, it hardly carries with it the dangerous implications that British scholars somewhat proudly expound?[5] Parliament, in the English terminology, means the King, the Lords and the Commons acting together as the supreme governing body of the realm. Thus, if the principle of the supremacy of Parliament is translated into continental terminology, it amounts to what is otherwise

---

[1] Despite Jellinek's contrary opinion. According to Jellinek, "constitution" derives from the Latin phrase *rem publicam constituere. Cf. Allgemeine Staatslehre* (Berlin, 1914, 3d ed.), vol. III, ch. iv. However, no historical continuity appears to exist between *constituere* and "constitution" (see *infra* notes 21, 25), and this derivation is bound to give us a misleading start.

[2] *Cf., e.g.,* K. C. Wheare, *Modern constitutions* (London, Oxford University Press, 1960), p. 21.

[3] *Cf., e.g.,* W. Bagehot, *The English Constitution,* ch. ii.

[4] *The Law and the Constitution,* 5th ed. (London, University of London Press, 1959), p. 40.

[5] Bagehot is no exception when he asserts that "a new House of Commons can *despotically . . .* resolve" [my italics]. *Op. cit.,* ch. vii.

called the "sovereignty of the State." Historically speaking, moreover, the principle of the supremacy of Parliament is the counterpart of the principle of the supremacy of the Crown, and what it really meant when it was affirmed was that the King had no power *outside* of Parliament, that his prerogatives could only be exercised according to the formula of the King *in* in Parliament. If this be so, would it be very wrong to conclude, despite the contrary opinion of British scholars, that parliamentary sovereignty in England actually contradicts the idea of a "higher law" no more than any flexible constitution does, and that the conventions of the constitution hardly allow a parliamentary majority to pass *any* law whatever? [6] (The point being the "any." Let us remember that the difference between accepted political behavior and wicked Machiavellian politics is rendered by the difference between the sentence, "The end justifies the means," and "The end justifies *any* mean.")

Probably I shall be told that I am wrong. However, as I was trying recently to sort out the juridical features of present-day dictatorial systems, it occurred to me that some English constitutional textbooks would be of great help. "No higher law and limitless legislative power," "fusion of powers," "no special protection for fundamental rights," etc.—all these principles applied very nicely to dictatorships. What is more, the very definition given in Wheare's textbook, "The British constitution is the collection of legal rules and nonlegal rules which govern the government in Britain," [7] appeared to be—but for the terms, "British and "Britain"—the most fitted to describe dictatorial constitutions. (For "rules" applies to any kind of rule—including the rule of rulership—and the specification "non-legal rules" just gives the final touch of perfection to the concept of unchecked, uncontrolled and absolute exercise of power.) I have not made the experiment the other way

around, that is, using the apologetic writings on dictatorial constitutions in order to get highlights on the virtues of the English one: but my guess is that, again changing but one word (the geographic referent), the English constitution would come out in brighter colors following this procedure than it appears, *e.g.,* to the reader of Jennings' *The Law and the Constitution.* [8]

So, I may well be wrong. But something must be wrong too in the way in which many English scholars understate their constitution, seem to make a particular point of not being helpful, and leave the alien reader with the feeling that the British constitution really amounts to the fact that, in the final analysis, the British people are clever and fine people who know how to go about in politics. I am personally convinced of this. But allow me to repeat that this conclusion is not very helpful.

I have drawn attention to the British habit (and perhaps coquetry) of understatement, for unless this element is taken into account, one is likely to miss some important points. To begin with, this point: that, despite the English "mystery," in the 19th century, all over Europe as well as in the United States, a general agreement prevailed as to the basic meaning of the term "constitution." In 1830, and especially during the 1848 revolutions, it was very clear on both sides of the Channel what the people were asking for when they claimed a constitution. [9] If, in England, "constitution" meant the system of British liberties, *mutatis mutandis* the Europeans wanted exactly the same

---

[6] This is to deny that there is a substantial difference between the British and the Continental principle of parliamentary sovereignty. If the term of reference is the American Congress then, of course, there is a good deal of difference.

[7] *Op. cit.,* p. 2.

[8] A comparison between Jennings' classic text and Vishinsky's *The Law of the Soviet State* (New York, 1951), would be to the point. According to Vishinsky, Stalin's Constitution draws "ever broader masses of the people into the government of the State," constantly strengthens "the bonds between the apparatus of authority and the people"; and Soviet constitutions in general "confirm genuinely democratic rights and freedoms," "establish and emphasize material guarantees," etc. (pp. 88–89).

[9] In 1860, the formula for the Italian plebiscites said only: "Do you want to enter the constitutional monarchy of King Victor Emanuel II?" Evidently, the mere adjective "constitutional" was assumed to be understood as implying all the difference.

thing: a system of protected freedom for the individual, which—according to the American usage of the English vocabulary —they called a "constitutional system." Having to start from naught, people on the Continent (as was first achieved by the Americans) wanted a written document, a charter, which would firmly establish the overall supreme law of the land. The British too, however, had, from time to time, relied on particularly solemn written documents: the Magna Charta, the Confirmation Acts, the 1610–1628 Petition of Rights, the Habeas Corpus Act of 1679, the Bill of Rights, the Act of Settlement, etc. The circumstance that these British "supreme laws" are not collected in a single document does not really mean that England has an unwritten constitution. I would rather say that the English do not have a codified constitution, *i.e.*, that Britain has a constitution which is written only in part (or, even better, unwritten to a much greater extent than "written" constitutions are), in a piecemeal fashion, and scattered in a variety of sources.

However that may be, and if it pleases the British to emphasize the fact that they have a constitution which is not written, this question is of secondary importance. I mean that the written, complete document is only a means. What really matters is the end, the *telos*. And the purpose, the *telos,* of English, American and European constitutionalism was, from the outset, identical. If the English vocabulary had not to this day refused to import the word (another paradox!), this common purpose could be expressed and synthesized by just one word: the French (and Italian) term *garantisme*.[10] In other terms, all over the Western area people requested, or cherished, "the constitution," because this term meant to them a fundamental law, or a fundamental set of

principles, and a correlative institutional arrangement, which would restrict arbitrary power and ensure a "limited government." And during the whole of the 19th century and until World War I, "constitutions" remained, in the United States, in England, and in Europe, different means (technically speaking) which had nevertheless the same common purpose in view. That is, for almost 150 years "constitution" has been—on the whole—an unambiguous term.

II

In the 20th century, in the few decades following the first World War, this situation of over-all basic agreement has come to an end rapidly and radically. So rapidly and so radically that one must wonder why. The main reason (or, we might say, the specific agent of change) has been, I believe, the following: that legal terminology—to the extent that it affects what Rousseau would have called *droit politique,* political right—shares the same destiny as political terminology in general: that is, it tends to be abused and corrupted. And this is all the more the case in a time in which politicians have become ever more conscious of the "power of words."

In our minds, constitution is a "good word." It has favorable emotive properties, like freedom, justice or democracy. Therefore, the word is retained, or adopted, even when the association between the utterance "constitution" and the behavioral response that it elicits (*e.g.,* "The constitution must be praised, for it protects my liberties") becomes entirely baseless. More precisely, the political exploitation and manipulation of language takes advantage of the fact that the emotive properties of a word survive—at times for a surprisingly long time—despite the fact that what the word denotes, *i.e.,* the "thing," comes to be a completely different thing.[11]

---

[10] Of course the query, "What do the guarantees include?" (*e.g.,* a certain technique of allocation of power, a bill of rights, the rule of law, judicial review, etc.) receives different, complex and changing answers. This is all the more reason for adopting a general term, reminding us both of the goal, and particularly of the fact that unless we think that *somebody needs protection against somebody else,* there is no point in being concerned with constitutionalism.

[11] The extent to which political terminology is subject to this kind of abuse can be exemplified by the very term "politics." In the Middle Ages the expression *dominium politicum* meant (in contrast to *dominium regale*) government deriving from, or given consent by, the people (*i.e.,* by the *polítes,* the inhabitant of the *polis*). That is to say that *politicum,* or *police* (in French), was coined—

To be sure, the agent of change has not only been insincerity and the political debasement of language. For technical reasons of their own, jurists too have been gradually covering up the *garantiste* feature of "constitution." This technicojuridical explanation cannot be pushed too far, however. It is quite true that Continental constitutional lawyers have never been at ease when confronted with the problem of putting forward the "strictly juridical" point of view. On the other hand, the fact remains that, more or less until the 1920's, they managed to combine the requirements of "pure law" with the *telos* of constitutionalism. If one reads, for instance, the *Leçons* of a representative figure of the pre-1848 period, Pellegrino Rossi,[12] one finds both the statement that "every State has a constitution" (*ex hypothesis*), and the statement that "a constitution is the law of the free countries." Let us face it: the two statements are not consistent. Nevertheless they introduce and represent an approach which received wide acceptance in the European juridical literature for almost a century. It is interesting to realize, therefore, why the Continental constitutional lawyers took this approach, and how they found a way of giving consistency to an inconsistency.

Descriptively speaking, and having reference, *e.g.*, to the terminology of the Constitution of Pennsylvania of September 28, 1776, a constitution contains two basic elements: a "plan (or frame) of government," and a "bill of rights." For the framers of the 18th century charters it was self-evident that the two component parts could not be separated: both were needed for a constitution to be a constitution. They did not mean in the least that *any* plan of government amounted to a constitution: they meant that this was

the case only when a frame of government provided for a bill of rights and the institutional devices that would secure its observance. Continental jurists, however, were anxious to put their rationalistically trained juridical consciences at ease by finding a "universal" definitition of constitution. And for this purpose they found it expedient to separate the universal trait (the "plan of government" meaning) from the *garantiste* component. Therefore, often enough, they did come to say—*qua* pure jurists—that any "frame of government" amounted to a constitution. They said it, but—let me stress this point—they immediately denied it. For they went on to say that "it had become customary"[13] to use the term constitution in a more specific *garantiste* sense; and therefore that, according to this practice, it was improper to hold that every state was a constitutional state. *Every* state had a "constitution," but only *some* states were "constitutional."

Unquestionably, the distinction is very thin; and moreover it is hard to explain why the phrase, "It has become customary," should have been accepted by jurists as a juridical argument. The interesting fact is therefore that they did accept it. And they accepted it—among other reasons—because they fully realized that their "universal" definition had no denotative value: it indicated *everything*, not *something*. Thus, generation after generation, European public law went ahead riding simultaneously two horses: the constitution as any "State order," and constitutionalism as a specific "content" of guarantees.

It was an uneasy equilibrium, I grant. It made them vulnerable, exposed. But one can have an Achilles heel and nevertheless survive. So, despite this weakness, I believe my former assertions still hold good, namely: (i) that for almost 150 years "constitution" has been associated with *garantisme;* and (ii) that the primary agent of change cannot be located in the inner logic of development of the European juristic tradition. Continental constitutional lawyers were hardly in a position to resist change; but they did not start the change. What started the

having reference to the Greek root—as a good word. Nowadays this originally pleasant word denotes the most unpleasant reality of politics: those who are entitled to arrest us. Let us hope that "constitution" may not have a similar destiny.

[12] Pellegrino Rossi (1787–1848) was professor of law in Bologna in 1814, the framer of the 1832 project of reform of the Swiss constitution, and subsequently a celebrated professor of constitutional law at the *Collège de France* in Paris.

[13] The wording varies, but this was, in substance, the invariable gist of their argument.

new trend was the impact of the political atmosphere of the 1920's. For a new look about politics was taking shape in those years. "Feeble politics," so to speak, was giving way to "intense politics"; that is, the peaceful-legalitarian approach to political relationships was giving way to a warlike view of politics.

I have said "political atmosphere." It is fair to add that in some countries it was not only a question of atmosphere. In Italy, and in the 1930's in Germany, jurists were somehow compelled to adopt a merely formal, "organizational," neutral definition of constitution. This is not surprising, and Italian and German constitutional lawyers can hardly be blamed for this. What is surprising is that in the meantime the British, too, had come to adopt very much the same position.

Let me refer again to Wheare's definition, according to which the English constitution is "the collection of legal rules and non-legal rules which govern the government in Britain." Or allow me to quote, as another instance, Jennings' definition, according to which a constitution is "the document in which are set out the rules governing the composition, powers and methods of operation of the main institutions of government." [14] The peculiar feature of these definitions is not only the unspecified use of the term rule (even games have "rules": are they the same kind of rules?), but the silence which covers the *telos* of constitutionalism. Actually they are purely "formal" definitions, in the sense that they can be filled with any content whatever. We are thus faced, nowadays, with this puzzling situation: that the very inventors of the constitutional solution provide us with a definition which amounts to saying that any instrument of government, any "traffic rule," is a constitution. And this according to the most authoritative yardstick. It is not astonishing, therefore, if the Continental theory of constitutionalism has shown, since World War II, very little evidence of recovery. For whenever somebody claims that "constitutional dictatorships" have proved that *garantisme* remains the

core of constitutionalism, one is likely to be confronted with this reply: why should we be concerned with this problem more than the English?

My reply is—and this is the second point that I wish to stress, having reference to the English habit of understatement—that one must be very careful about importing the British constitutional textbooks. They have not been written for export. They have been written for a happy people whose constitutional system is liable to work nicely anyhow. If the alien scholar does not make explicit what often remains implicit, and does not say what is often left unsaid, the British case easily lends itself to bearing false witness.[15] Of course, English liberties remain protected even if English constitutionalists forget to mention that this is why Britain has a constitution. But the case might be very different elsewhere.

III

The foregoing *mise au point* has a bearing on what will follow, but it certainly does not alter the fact that nowadays "constitution" has become an ambiguous term, covering two very different meanings: a strict, substantive meaning (the *garantiste* meaning), and a formal, cosmic meaning. It follows from this that whereas in the 19th century a question such as, "What is the role of a constitution in a political system?", could be answered without asking first, "What is a constitution?", this is no longer the case.

It is equally clear—at least to me—that if a constitution is defined as "any way of giving form to any State whatever," then the question "What is the role of a constitution in a political system?" either cannot be answered, or can be answered only country by country, and even then in a very uninteresting and banal way. For in this case the answer is that the constitution plays no role, properly speak-

[14] Or, where no such document exists, simply "the rules determining the creation and operation of governmental institutions." *The Law and the Constitution*, pp. 33, 36.

[15] Or else to bear no witness. Thus in F. A. Hayek's *The Constitution of Liberty* (London, Routledge, 1960), the 12th chapter bears the title: "The American Contribution: Constitutionalism." To be sure, Americans have made an outstanding contribution to constitutionalism. But to say more than this is saying too much, even though Hayek's conclusion is hardly surprising if one is not cautioned against the British mood of understatement.

ing: It is only a shorthand report which may describe—assuming that the constitution in question is applied—the formalization of the power structure of the given country. (This is not to deny that the conclusion, "The constitution plays no role," may not be reached also after applying the standards of the *garantiste* type of constitution. I am simply pointing out that the query is relevant only if we consider the constitutions which are supposed to play a role.)

On both accounts, then, we have to make up our minds and to look for a convincing answer to the question, "What is a constitution?".

In the first place, we may say: "This is what I understand when I use this term." This kind of answer, however, leaves untouched a very basic point, namely: What is the truth-value of this definition? Is it only a "stipulative definition"?

Therefore, and in the second place, we may also find it necessary to say: "The term constitution *ought* to be used in this way."

In the third place, we may have recourse to a classification. We may say: given the fact that we are now using the term constitution in very different meanings and to cover altogether different referents, then let us speak specifically of this and that type of constitution.

These three lines of approach are not mutually exclusive. The contrary is true. But in most cases political scientists either follow solution number one, or solution number three, or both. At any rate, they usually bypass step number two, that is, they usually refrain from saying that the term constitution *ought* to mean this and not that. I wonder, however, whether the "ought" can really be avoided.

When general agreement prevails—as was the case with "constitution" in the 19th century—"ought-propositions" (if I may call them so) are superfluous. In this case one need not discuss whether a definition of "constitution" is merely a private convention of the stipulator (*i.e.*, a stipulative definition), or a lexical kind of definition,[16] or something more, *i.e.*, a

definition having warranted truth-value. Agreement automatically settles all these problems. But we live in a world—let me stress—of terminological cleavage in which the "war of words" plays a very important role. Our first reaction has therefore been to make some fine distinctions (*e.g.*, the one between stipulative and lexicographic definitions), and to have recourse to a classification of the various meanings and referents of the word constitution.

On second thought, however, one is bound to discover that the stipulative approach is only a fire escape (and an unsafe one at that) which actually helps the fire grow, and that classifications cannot, *per se*, solve our problems either. Classifications are only *prima facie* a neutral device. Classifications have a purpose in view, and differ according to their purpose. Therefore, classifications cannot replace definitions. They follow a definition of constitution, and imply that we have previously taken a stand *vis-à-vis* its nuclear meaning, so to speak. And this stand cannot be provided by the stipulative approach.

According to this approach, the speaker says: I propose to use the term constitution in this sense, and this is *my* definition of it. The emphasis is laid on the "my," for stipulations are an arbitrary choice. As Richard Robinson asserts in his valuable book "In stipulation we freely make any word mean anything we choose."[17] This is hardly a way out, however. Let us assume, for instance, that one meets with the following definition: a constitution is the will of the sovereign. In some cases one could hardly object that this definition is factually false. According both to the *Führer-prinzip* and to actual practice, it would be quite realistic to say that during Hitler's decade the German constitution amounted to the will of the *Führer*. And Stalin's constitution can well be resumed in similar terms. As these extreme but very relevant examples go to show, if one wishes to retort that Hitler's or Stalin's regime was not a constitutional regime, this cannot be done on the ground that the sentence, "The Soviet constitution was the

[16] See R. Robinson, *Definition* (Oxford, 1954), pp. 35–92. For an application of these criteria, see M. Cranston, *Freedom—A New Analysis* (London, 1953).

[17] Robinson, *op. cit.*, p. 65.

arbitrary will of Stalin," is factually false, but on the ground that one does not accept the meaning "will of the sovereign" as a permissible meaning of constitution: *i.e.*, because one refuses the definition.

Yet if definitions are just arbitrary and private stipulations of each speaker, on what grounds may one discuss the definitions of constitution which differ from his own stipulation? Clearly, one can write a book of 500 pages to show that Hitler's or Stalin's so-called constitution amounted to a non-constitutional system; anybody can simply dismiss it by saying: This is your stipulation, but I have mine, and that is that. How easy, and how convenient!

I cannot develop here the criticism of the conventional approach.[18] In my view definitions are not private conventions of each speaker, but (whenever they have a historical referent) storehouses of past experience shaped by former practice. We bring them up to date, but their ultimate truth-value lies in the fact that they tell us how to behave *as experienced people* in matters regarding which each generation starts by having no experience. And this is precisely the reason why we are not condemned to a solipsistic conventionalism, and why we are entitled to discuss and to look for a "true definition" (touching on a basic meaning, of course) of equality, of liberty, of law, of constitution, etc. In particular, *the* definition of constitution which has objective worth is the one that appears to be the outcome of a long and painstaking process of trial-and-error concerned with the question: How can we be governed without being oppressed?

Implicitly I have already indicated why I attach a great importance to whether the sentence "This is the meaning of the term constitution" has a normative undertone or not. For if the speaker takes the view that his definition cannot be phrased as a normative proposition—*i.e.*, in the form, "This is also what 'constitution' ought to mean"—then, no matter how unwittingly, he is surrendering to the stipulative and conventionalistic approach.

To be sure, one may not be concerned

with long-range consequences of this kind. Nevertheless, we must decide here and now the test, or the criteria, according to which we declare: This is the meaning given in this text to the word constitution. Now, are we going to ascertain what "constitution" means in the 20th century by asking the Russians, the Chinese, the Egyptians, and so forth, or by inquiring what the Italians and the Germans were taught to believe a constitutional system to be under Mussolini and Hitler? If so, then I grant that there is no "ought" about it. But otherwise (that is, if we do not believe that knowledge follows a majority principle), then the "ought" is inevitably there—no matter whether openly or not—for surely we are not speaking of what "constitution" actually means to all the people of the world in the 20th century, but of a correct meaning which we find advisable to propose for future observance.

I am acquainted with the sophisticated methodological reasons that are being brought forward to explain why the form "ought" should be expelled from the realm of science, and in particular of political science. Yet, my guess is that future historians will find a much simpler explanation for our "ought complexes." They will say that we have been unable to meet the challenge of the environment; and rightly so, I believe. For since the beginning of time the people entrusted with the development of learning have followed this very simple rule: to use the form "is" when they agreed with general usage, and the form "ought" when they did not. Yet now we refrain from saying "This is what the term constitution *ought* to mean," even though we are well aware of the fact that "constitution" no longer bears a common acceptance and even though we are in a good position to realize that a situation of ambiguity and confusion is being deliberately fostered by political double-talk and insincerity, with the precise purpose of deceiving the audience.

Let there be no misunderstanding. I am not advocating a behavioral "ought," but a terminological and logical "ought." [19] The meaning of "constitution" is neither

---

[18] For my views on the truth-value of definitions, see G. Sartori, *Democratic Theory* (Detroit, Wayne Univ. Press, 1962), ch. 10.

[19] The form "ought" is not necessarily related to ethical imperatives.

an arbitrary stipulation, nor something to be discovered in the "popular mind" of semi-literate majorities. At least, if we believe that rational discourse and an intelligible vocabulary are to be maintained, then the meaning of "constitution" has been decided by historical testing, and has to be ascertained by adequate information and sound thinking. And if these criteria bring us to a definition which no longer receives common acceptance, then it is not only right but necessary to say: This is what the term constitution *ought* to mean (for otherwise it is meaningless, or superfluous, or deceiving, or whatever). This does not imply that people are being requested to respond favorably to a certain pattern of constitution defined as the "true constitution." I am only saying that terminological clarity is a basic requirement for any science, and that political scientists in particular have to take stock of the fact that the vocabulary of politics tends to be used for the purpose of beguiling the listener. I am not advocating, therefore, the preferability of one type of constitutional *telos* in relation to another. I am simply saying that it is a scientific requirement to discuss whether it is proper to use "constitution" where, in order that the public (and even, at times, the expert) be not deceived, we should *not* use this term.

IV

The objection will be that even if we reject the stipulative approach, even then "constitution" is, by its own constitution, an ambiguous term.[20] That is, even if one agrees that constitutions have been shaped by historical experience in order to protect the freedom and the rights of the power addressees, the fact nonetheless remains that constitution has always been a Janus-faced concept, hovering as it were between the idea of "political order" on the one hand and of "limit" on the other. I would however disagree with this statement.

The history of the word in its modern meaning only begins in the 18th century.[21] Let us not confuse the noun with the con-

cept, or, we might say, the Latin *constitutio* with our "constitution," a homonymy with a homology. In its present-day conceptualization, "constitution" only emerges, perhaps, with Bolingbroke,[22] and the term really gained ground and acquired a definite connotation only in America during the years 1776–1787. (The French did not receive it directly from England, but from the Philadelphia Convention. This is not surprising for it was Paine, not Burke and the English writers in general, who gave the first explicit, complete account of the modern concept.[23])

Now, it is undeniable that the whole of the American tradition has understood "constitution" as a means for "limited government." The same is true, from the outset, for French constitutionalism (should one be reminded of article 16 of the Declaration of Rights of 1789? Or, for the following period, of Benjamin Constant?). And I have previously explained at length why I firmly hold—despite the possibility of exhibiting numberless quotations to the contrary effect—that English constitutionalism belongs entirely to the same tradition: the British advocate, and have advocated from the time of Glanville and Bracton, an "unlimited government" just as much, or, rather, just as little as the Americans.[24]

[20] I am no longer referring to the strictly juridical approach mentioned previously, but to the overall issue of constitutionalism as discussed in the history of political thought and in philosophy of law.

[21] Cicero's use, in *De Republica,* I, 45, 69, was quite casual, and left no trace in the following literature. Actually, this much-quoted Roman precedent cannot claim precedent status. This is so true that the 15th and 16th century commentators rendered Cicero's *constitutio* with the terms *status publicus* (Jean de Terre Rouge), *status Reipublicae* (Bodin), or *politicum* (Fortescue), *police* (Seyssell).

[22] I say "perhaps" on account of McIlwain's reservation: "Bolingbroke in fact is only restating views as old as the *Politicus* of Plato. . . ." *Constitutionalism: Ancient and Modern* (Ithaca, Cornell University Press, 1947), p. 3.

[23] On Paine see esp. C. H. McIlwain, *op. cit.,* pp. 8–10. In Burke "constitution" was used much more loosely as a synonym for "commonwealth" (*Thoughts on the Cause of Present Discontents*), for "engagement and pact of society" (*Reflections*), for "frame" and "pattern" (*Speech on Reform*); all in all, it meant the substantive principles deriving from the British political tradition and to be inferred from the working of the institutions.

[24] *Cf., e.g.,* Burke: "In [our] Constitution . . . I feel both that I am free, and that I am

It is not unsafe to conclude, therefore, that, with the decline of the age of Absolutism, people began to cast about for a word which would denote the techniques to be used for controlling the exercise of State power. This term turned out to be (Americans decided this issue) "constitution."[25] And "constitution" was in no way born as a Janus-faced concept. The term was re-conceived, adopted and cherished not because it merely meant "political order," but because it meant much more, because it meant "political freedom." We may put it thus: because it denoted *the distinctive political order which would protect their liberties*; or—to paraphrase Friedrich's felicitous wording—because it not only "gave form" but also because it "limited" governmental action.[26]

The idea that this specific, *garantiste*, meaning derives from a pre-existing wide, unspecified meaning, is an optical illusion, which has been suggested—I believe—by the commentators and translators of Aristotle. As is well known, Aristotle's term was *politeía*, and, surely, *politeía* is difficult to translate. So occasionally, the authors having Plato's and especially Aristotle's writings in mind, found it expedient to render it by the term constitution. This, however, happened only occasionally (the relevant example is Montesquieu)[27] until the time when "constitution" acquired a specific meaning. It was only at this stage that "constitution" came to be used consistently as the proper equivalent of *politeía*. Wrongly, to be sure. For *politeía* only conveys the idea of the way in which a polity is patterned. And if Aristotle meant by *politeía* the ethico-political system as a whole, we cannot infer from this that "constitution" has in Aristotle a loose meaning. The only correct conclusion is that Aristotle has been mistranslated. For to us "constitution" means a frame of political society, *organized through and by the law,* for the purpose of restraining arbitrary power. And surely nothing resembling his concept was in the mind of Aristotle.[28]

V

Having established the frame of reference (the historically valid "nuclear meaning" of constitution), we may now turn to the problem of how we should go about classifying the variety of present-day so-called constitutions. I shall deal swiftly with this problem, for I agree very much (in substance, even though not in terminology) with the threefold classification suggested by Loewenstein.[29]

Basically we are confronted with three possibilities: (i) *garantiste* constitution (constitution, proper); (ii) nominal constitution; (iii) façade constitution (or fake constitution).

---

not free dangerously to myself and to others. I know that no power on earth, acting as I ought to do, can touch my life, my liberty, my own property" (*Speech on Reform of Representation.*) Let it be noted that, according to the letter of the constitution, in 1782 the doctrine of the omnipotence of Parliament was already established. Was Burke wrong, then? Or should we not question, instead, the validity—for a constitution largely based on conventions—of the "literal" approach?

[25] In this connection, recall that in the years of the Commonwealth and the Protectorate (1649–1660) the English made several attempts to establish a written constitution. However, they never called these documents "constitution": they made recourse to terms such as covenant, instrument, agreement, model, paramount or fundamental law.

[26] Carl J. Friedrich, *The Philosophy of Law in Historical Perspective* (University of Chicago Press, 1958), p. 220.

[27] In the famous ch. 6, Book XI of the *Esprit des Lois* the term *constitution* appears only in the title.

[28] I grant that there are a few passages in Aristotle's *Politics* in which the term *politeía* specifically refers to the way in which the *polis* magistracies are ordained. *Cf., e.g.,* 1278 b. However, this meaning appears in passing, and it cannot be denied, I believe, that (*i*) the ethico-political all-embracing meaning of *politeía* is by far the prevalent one, and, on the other hand, (*ii*) the term never appears in Aristotle in our juridical meaning, that is, in the sense of being an institutionalized way of controlling the dynamics of political freedom. Actually, I find it quite absurd to speak of a Greek "constitutionalism." Only the Romans indirectly tackled the problem, and only from the "rule of law" angle (as Jhering and Bryce have remarked), that is, very much in the same way in which—according to Dicey—the principles of the English constitution are inductions and generalizations resulting from judicial decisions determining the rights of private persons.

[29] *Cf.* Karl Loewenstein, *Political Power and the Governmental Process* (University of Chicago Press, 1957), esp. pp. 147 ff.

I call "nominal" the constitutions that Loewenstein labels "semantic" (a difficult, and perhaps not quite appropriate labelling). Apart from this semantic divergency, I entirely underwrite his description of the specimen: "The constitution is fully applied and activated, but its ontological reality is nothing but the formalization of the existing location of political power for the exclusive benefit of the actual power holders" (p. 149). Nominal constitutions are therefore "nominal" in the very simple sense that they bear the "name" constitution. This amounts to saying that nominal constitutions are merely organizational constitutions, *i.e.*, the collection of rules which organize but do not restrain the exercise of political power in a given polity.[30] Actually, nominal constitutions do not really pretend to be "real constitutions." They frankly describe a system of limitless, unchecked power. They are not a dead letter. It is only that this letter is irrelevant to the *telos* of constitutionalism.

The façade constitutions are different from the nominal ones in that they take the appearance of "true constitutions." What makes them untrue is that they are disregarded (at least in their essential *garantiste* features). Actually they are "trap-constitutions." As far as the techniques of liberty and the rights of the power addressees are concerned, they are a dead letter.

I suppose that the labeling "façade constitution" will be criticized on the ground that it implicitly rules out the possibility of an educational purpose. But I do not think that a fake constitution has an educational *purpose*. It *may* turn out that it has an educational *effect*. But this is a very different matter. We are not historians dealing with past events and looking for their *a posteriori* justification. We are concerned with actual will and actual doings. And to credit with an "educational role" the instances that make forecasts all the more dubious (as in the

case when we are confronted with discretional power) is very much like toying with wishful thinking. Moreover, and in point of principle, education is not the purpose of constitutions. I mean, this is not a sufficient (or sufficiently pertinent) criterion for singling out a special class of "educational constitutions." [31] A constitution may contain, to be sure, statements of "aspiration," and thereby provide "incentives," even pedagogic incentives. However, this occurrence does not indicate an essential constitutional feature; it merely indicates a possible content of any type of constitution.

There is often a considerable overlapping between nominal and façade constitutions. The distinction is nevertheless basic, for the two cases are indeed very different. Nominal constitutions actually describe the working of the political system (they do not abide by the *telos* of constitutionalism, but they are sincere reports), while the façade constitutions give us no reliable information about the real governmental process. In most cases one can clearly perceive, despite the overlaps, which is the prevalent aspect: I mean, whether a constitution is basically nominal or basically a disguise. At any rate, or otherwise, the distinction is serviceable for analytical purposes, that is, for dissecting the component parts of a "mixed type" (partly nominal and partly fake) of pseudo-constitution.

The distinction is serviceable from another point of view as well, for it goes to show that if we refuse the *garantiste* qualification, then no line can be drawn between "constitution" and "constitutional government." To be sure, if a constitution is not applied, this is an instance of constitution without constitutional government. But this argument applies only to the façade constitutions. What about the other possibility? In the case of nominal constitutions we no longer have a "prerogative state" that replaces *de facto* the "legal state"; we have instead a prerogative state legitimized by the constitution. In this latter case, then, we are confronted with a government which, by

---

[30] It is often held that the mere ordering, the mere existence of a definite and stable "form," is in itself a "limit." This may well be—but not a *garantiste* kind of limit. Armies are usually well ordered, but this fact does not necessarily protect subordinates *vis-a-vis* their superiors.

[31] Car accidents may serve the purpose of improving our driving. Would this be a reason for creating the category "educational accidents"?

definition, will always govern according to the constitution. On what grounds may we maintain that this is not a "constitutional government"? Certainly not on the grounds of logical syntax. Therefore, either we adhere to *garantisme,* or the distinction between constitution and constitutional government really becomes meaningless.

Some troublesome problems arise when one focusses further attention on: (i) the *décalage* between the written and the living constitution, and on (ii) the frequent disregard of some of the constitutional provisions. In this connection the point can be made that a clear-cut distinction between real constitutions and façade constitutions is hardly realistic, since the real ones too come to differ widely, in practice, from their original formalization, or may not be fully activated (the former being usually the case with old constitutions, and the latter with recent ones).

Personally I am not dismayed by the first indictment. If a constitution is written, then, with the passing of time, the formal document and the living constitution inevitably come to be related much as the past is related to the present. (In this sense, then, written constitutions too become, in part, non-written.) However, as long as the spirit and the *telos* of the original document are maintained in the new circumstances, the *décalage* only affects the myth of a "fixed constitution"; and the American experience goes to show, if anything, that written constitutions can endure despite the anti-historical assumption upon which they have been conceived.

On the other hand, the remedy for this could hardly be found in a non-written constitution. The drawbacks and the dangers of this solution are so serious, that only the British can afford the luxury of not formalizing their constitution. And it remains questionable whether it is really true that the British constitution is unwritten. (I would be tempted to say that it is "written differently.")

The thorny point is instead the non-fulfillment of constitutional provisions not because of the time factor, because they have gradually become outdated, but with reference to norms that have never

been activated owing to the unwillingness of the executive or of the legislative body to give them life. This problem cannot be dismissed lightly, if we consider that "delinquencies in the application" of the constitution (as Loewenstein calls them) are rather frequent in most countries. It is safe to ask: "Why?". Is it because the constitutional spirit (as well as the corresponding type of the constitutional gentleman) is withering away? Or is it because of other reasons?

It is well to remind ourselves that most countries have a recent constitution, either because they have re-written their previous charters, or because they have started anew. And contemporary constitutions are, as a rule, bad constitutions—technically speaking.[32] They have come to include unrealistic promises and glamorous professions of faith on the one hand, and numberless frivolous details on the other. Some of them are by now so "democratic" that either they are no longer constitutions (for a constitution limits the "will of the people" concept of democracy just as much as it limits the will of the power holders),[33] or they make the working of the machinery of government too cumbersome for government to work, or both. Under these conditions, non-application may well be a remedy for inapplicability. I mean by this that it may also serve the purpose of saving the constitutional system as a working system.

So we should not react dramatically in all cases, but only in those in which the disregard actually has a direct bearing on the withering away of the constitutional *telos.* This implies that we can no longer partake, in all instances, of the strict juristic view that "*all* the Constitution *must* be applied at whatever cost." Personally speaking at least, I take the view that

[32] Contemporary constitutions are being said to improve on the former ones in that they are no longer "negative" but "positive." If positive means that they are also an instrument for social and economic policy then let us be happy with this positive development. Under one condition, however: that the follow-up, *i.e.,* the "economic" tail, should not eat the "political" head.

[33] Among other reasons, because a constitution cannot effectively limit the will of the power holders if they can outflank constitutional impediments by making direct appeals to the will of the people.

we should always ascertain whether the non-application affects the machinery of government in its *garantiste* aspect and the basic purposes of constitutionalism, or not. In the former case it is proper to speak of "delinquencies"; in the latter I confess that I remain quite indifferent. And if we follow this rule of thumb, the difference between "real constitutions" and "façade constitutions" remains very firm, despite the fact that even in the context of the real constitutions a number of provisions may not be activated.

VI

Summing up my line of argument, I have tentatively submitted the following theses:

(1) That the word constitution has been re-conceptualized, if I may say so, for a specific purpose, and more precisely to denote a distinctive and unprecedented "technique of liberty" (as Mirkine-Guetzévitch would have said), the features of which had already materialized clearly enough when, for instance, Montesquieu was visiting England in 1730.

(2) That this purpose has often been obscured by the complexity of the original model (the English constitution) on the one hand, and by a somewhat polemic isolationism of the British scholars on the other hand. Despite these unfortunate circumstances, however, the fact remains that the idea of limit is basic to the English prototype just as much as to the American and the French subsequent models.

(3) That the view that the *garantiste* meaning of "constitution" was preceded by a loose, formal meaning lacks historical proof, for this view actually goes back to a mistranslation, or to a casual way of referring to Aristotle's term *politeía*.

(4) That the equivalence "constitution = any state form" is therefore not the older but indeed a recent loosening up of the concept, reflecting either the juridic illusion of attaining a "purified," universal depoliticized right, or reflecting the purpose of exploiting the word constitution as a trap word.

(5) That on both accounts it should be pointed out that either the term is used in its specific *garantiste* meaning, or

it is a meaningless (and deceiving) duplicate of terms such as organization, structure, form, pattern, political system, and the like.

(6) That, according to this view, the variety of so-called "constitutions" of our time may be classified in three categories: real, nominal and facade.

(7) That the existence of nominal constitutions implies that either we abide by *garantisme*, or we can no longer draw a line between "constitution" and "constitutional government."

(8) That the political scientist, in particular, is responsible for ruling out insincere language, for two reasons: the general reason being that the language of the observer is required to improve (whenever necessary) the language of the observed; while the specific reason is that terminological housecleaning is all the more necessary whenever the political scientist is confronted with terminological distortions that are deliberately fostered with a view to deceiving the audience.

Speaking of political scientists, a final question should perhaps be raised, namely: why should we, *qua* political scientists, be concerned with the constitutional problem?

Actually, constitutionalism is not a traditional subject matter of political science. To the extent that political scientists have been concerned with it, they have either leaned on a previous legal training of the individual scholar, or they have shown a tendency to underplay the role and importance of constitutional checks as compared with social and political pluralistic checks.[34] In the first case it could be said that their treatment of the topic constitutionalism belongs to the "old" political science. In the second case it can be shown, I believe, that the "new" political science is hardly equipped to discuss the problem at all. For one thing, political science is keen about informal processes, not about formal structures. In particular, the new generation of po-

[34] This is not to deny that pluralism is a requisite condition for the proper working of constitutional systems. My own view, however, is that the relationship between societal pluralism and constitutional patterns of behavior is a two-way relationship, at least in the sense that it is very important, for pluralism, to have the constitution on its side.

litical scientists distrusts concepts having a high degree of abstraction (such as State), concentrates very much on elementary grass roots units (such as groups), and has developed a keen feeling for dynamics, for change, for "something doing," to use Bentley's telling expression. Now, clearly, from this platform constitutions appear to be: (i) the juridical counterpart and support of the abstract entity, "the State"; (ii) certainly not the "raw material" of politics; and (iii) the expression *par excellence* of a typically static view of the political process. (The foregoing are, of course, very broad and very rough generalizations.)

If these underlying premises are duly weighed, the present-day mood of skepticism toward the efficacy of constitutional devices and mechanisms was only to be expected. However, where is the error? In the purview of the observer, or in the constitutional solution? All in all, my feeling is that contemporary political science has not found, as yet, the strategic juncture in which and from which it can make a positive contribution to the understanding of constitutionalism. My own tentative suggestion is that, perhaps, this strategic point is to be found in the "role theory" approach,[35] that is, by examining the constitutional solution as a preor-

[35] I have in mind, *e.g.,* the approach devised by Heinz Eulau and associates in a related subject. *Cf.* Wahlke, Eulau, Buchanan, Ferguson, *The Legislative System—Explorations in Legislative Behavior* (New York, 1962).

dained, binding technique of *role-enforcement* (in its difference from a spontaneous role-taking.)

Within the limits of a preliminary perusal, I cannot push the argument further. I leave it as an open suggestion for discussion that the query, "What is the role of a constitution in the political system?" could perhaps be fruitfully approached from the following angle: what is the impact, or the role, of a constitution *vis-à-vis* the role-taking of the power holders? That is, does it help to enforce, and if so to what extent, a desired "role performance" upon the persons in office?

Whatever the merit of this suggestion, I do feel that political scientists should go back with a fresh look to the vital issues that constitutional lawyers have been neglecting. For the experience of the last 30–40 years has shown, particularly in Italy and in Germany, that when a political problem—and constitutionalism is, inescapably, a juridical solution of a political problem—is depoliticized, the real consequences of taking the juridical "neutral" attitude are (no matter how unwittingly) political. I mean that when the time of trial comes, one discovers that what the "pure" jurists have really been doing—under the shield of their juridical indifference to metajuridical matters—was to pave the way for allowing unscrupulous politicians to make a discretionary use of power under the camouflage of a good word. Politics cannot be taken out of politics, so to speak.

The Constitution as Instrument and as Symbol

EDWARD S. CORWIN

For more than forty years Mr. Corwin was a professor of jurisprudence and constitutional law at Princeton University. He has written prolifically and has left an indelible mark on the theory and practice of government in the United States.

On an early page of his celebrated *Constitutional Limitations,* Judge Cooley

Reprinted from *The American Political Science Review,* XXX, No. 6 (December 1936), 1071–1085, by permission of the publisher.

defines "constitution" in the following curt terms: "That body of rules and maxims in accordance with which the powers of sovereignty are habitually exercised." Returning later to the subject, he quotes with approval a more eleborate conception, couched in these words: "What is a constitution, and what are its objects? It is easier to tell what it is not than what it is. *It is not the beginning of a community, nor the origin of private rights; it is not the fountain of law, nor the incipient state of government; it is not the cause, but consequence, of personal and political freedom; it grants no rights to the people,* but is the creature of their power, the instrument of their convenience. *Designed for their protection in the enjoyment of the rights and powers which they possessed before the constitution was made, it is* but the framework of the political government, and *necessarily based upon the preëxisting condition of laws, rights, habits, and modes of thought. There is nothing primitive in it, it is all derived from a known source. It presupposes an organized society, law, order, property, personal freedom,* a love of political liberty, and enough of cultivated intelligence to know how to guard it against the encroachments of tyranny. *A written constitution is in every instance a limitation upon the powers of government in the hands of agents;* for there never was a written republican constitution which delegated to functionaries all the latent powers which lie dormant in every nation, and are boundless in extent, and incapable of definition." [1]

The first of these definitions answers to what I mean in this paper by the term "constitutional instrument"; the second approximates, particularly in the passages which I have stressed, what I have in mind when I speak of "constitutional symbol."

To the modern mind, confident in the outlook afforded by science and its achievements, the word "instrument" connotes the future and things needing to be done in the future. It assumes that man is the master of his fate, able to impart a desired shape to things and events. And regarded from this point of view a constitution is *an instrument of popular power—sovereignty,* if you will—*for the achievement of progress.*

American constitutional symbolism looks, on the other hand, to the past and links hands with conceptions which long antedate the rise of science and its belief in a predictable, manageable causation. Its consecration of an *already established order of things* harks back to primitive man's terror of a chaotic universe, and his struggle toward security and significance behind a slowly erected barrier of custom, magic, fetish, tabu. While, therefore, the constitutional instrument exists to energize and canalize *public power,* it is the function of the constitutional symbol to protect and tranquilize *private interest or advantage as against public power,* which is envisaged as inherently suspect, however necessary it may be. What has been the relation of these two conceptions in the case of the Constitution of the United States? To answer this question is the main purpose of this paper.

The aspect of the Constitution of the United States as an instrument of popular government for the achievement of the great ends of government is stamped on its opening words: "We, the people of the United States, in order to form a more perfect union, establish justice, insure domestic tranquillity, provide for the common defense, promote the general welfare, and secure the blessings of liberty to ourselves and our posterity, do ordain and establish this Constitution for the United States of America."

The aspect of the Constitution as symbol and bulwark of a previously achieved order of human rights appears most evidently in the ninth article of the Bill of Rights: "The enumeration in the Constitution of certain rights shall not be construed to deny or disparage others retained by the people." The same idea was expressed by Webster in the following words: "Written constitutions sanctify and confirm great principles, but the latter are prior in existence to the former." Or as Governor Landon put the same idea recently: "The Constitution was not framed to give us anything, but to protect inherent rights already possessed." [2]

That the attitude of the members of the Federal Convention toward their task was predominantly instrumentalist and practical is clear at a glance. They had

[1] Cooley, *Constitutional Limitations* (2nd ed., 1871), pp. 2, 38. Italics are mine.

[2] Speech at Topeka, Kansas, Jan. 29, 1936.

not gone to Philadelphia merely to ratify the past, Governor Landon to the contrary notwithstanding, but with *reform* in mind, and specifically the creation of *a strong, effective national government.* Theirs, it must be remembered, was one of the great creative periods in the history of political institutions, and they were thoroughly imbued with the faith of their epoch in the ability of the human reason, working in the light of experience, to divert the unreflective course of events into beneficial channels; and in no respect did they deem man more evidently the master of his destiny than in that of statecraft. Furthermore, most of these men had been reared in the Mercantilist tradition, and accordingly regarded governmental intervention in the field of economic activity as one of the chief reasons for the existence of government; while the importance to government in turn of engaging the self-interest of groups and individuals by its active policies was a thing constantly present to their minds. The atmosphere of the Convention was, in fact, almost scandalously secular. Despite the social preëminence of the cloth in 1787, not a clergyman was listed among its fifty-five members; and when Franklin suggested that one be recruited to open the meetings with prayer, the proposal was shelved by his obviously embarrassed associates with almost comical celerity. Nor did the Constitution as it came from their hands contain a bill of rights.

And naturally the party which brought the Constitution into existence continued to regard their work pragmatically while they elaborated a working government under it. "You have made a good Constitution," a friend remarked to Gouverneur Morris shortly following the Convention. "That," Morris replied, "depends on how it is construed"; and in his characterization of the Constitution as "an experiment," Hamilton voiced the same pragmatic point of view. The new Ship of State was quickly crowded with all the canvas of powers "implied," "resultant," "inherent," that its slender, vibrant phrasing would carry; and it is a significant fact that the constitutional validity of not a single item of the Hamiltonian program was challenged judicially, even in principle, until a generation later.

The Constitutional Instrument was the work of a limited class, comprising those whose "interests and outlook," as Woodrow Wilson put it, "transcended state lines." The Constitutional Symbol, on the other hand, *being a symbol,* was the work of the many, a creation of the *mass mind.* Indeed, prevision of the symbolic rôle of the Constitution is older than the Constitution itself. In the same number of *Common Sense* in which he urged independence, in February, 1776, Thomas Paine also urged "a Continental Conference." He said: "The conferring members being met, let their business be to frame a Continental Charter or Charter of the United Colonies (answering to what is called the Magna Charta of England), fixing the number and manner of choosing members of Congress and members of Assembly . . . and drawing the line of business and jurisdiction between them (always remembering that our strength is continental, not provincial) securing freedom and property to all men . . . with such other matters as it is necessary for a charter to contain. But where, say some, is the King of America? That we may not appear to be defective even in earthly honors, let a day be solemnly set apart for proclaiming the charter; let it be brought forth placed on the divine law, the word of God; let a crown be placed thereon, by which the world may know that so far we approve monarchy that in America the law is King."[3]

That so able a propagandist as Paine proved himself to be should have sensed the popular need for a symbol, as well as the fact, of authority is perhaps not to be wondered at. At any rate, the Constitution had not long been in operation before his prediction was fulfilled most amazingly. The outbreak of the wars of the French Revolution, by enlarging British and Continental demand for American products, brought a hazardous prosperity which minds unaccustomed to looking so far afield for causes attributed to the Constitution. Speaking on the floor of the Congress in 1794, Richard Bland Lee declared: "I will only mention the stimulus which agriculture has received. In travel-

[3] Paine, *Political Writings* (1837), I, pp. 45–46.

ling through various parts of the United States, I find fields a few years ago waste and uncultivated filled with inhabitants and covered with harvests, new habitations reared, contentment in every face, plenty on every board; confidence is restored and every man is safe under his own vine and fig tree, and there is none to make him afraid. To produce this effect was the intent of the Constitution, and it has succeeded."[4]

To be sure, there were skeptics. "It has been usual with declamatory gentlemen," complained sour old Maclay, "in their praises of the present government, to paint the state of the country under the old Congress as if neither wood grew nor water ran in America before the happy adoption of the Constitution."

Such disparagement, discreetly confided to the pages of a private journal, did not stem the course of opinion. Hardly has Holy Writ itself been more eulogized than the Constitutional Symbol presently came to be. "In the Constitution of the United States," wrote Justice William Johnson in 1823, "—the most wonderful instrument ever drawn by the hand of man—there is a comprehension and precision that is unparalleled; and I can truly say that after spending my life in studying it, I still daily find in it some new excellence."[5] And inevitably the virtues of the Framers were imputed to their handiwork, as were its virtues to them. Jefferson, ordinarily no reverent spirit, at first described the Convention as an assemblage of "demi-gods," though he later reconsidered this appraisal. On the other hand, while Hamilton's cold evaluation of the Constitution as "an experiment" was repeated by Washington in his Farewell Address eight years later, Jackson in his Farewell Address in 1837 demurred to this description as no longer suitable. Even in the midst of civil war, when the "experiment" seemed to have failed, it was apostrophized as embodying much more than "calm wisdom and lofty patriotism," as "providential," "God's saving

gift," "His creative fiat over a weltering chaos: 'Let a nation be born in a day.'"[6]

But when one says that the Constitution had become "a symbol," one has not advanced very far, for the question remains, *symbol of what?* Initially the symbol was, it would seem, hardly more than decorative—the tribute which the American people rendered their own political sagacity for ordaining such a marvelous constitution. Yet this symbol of high political achievement became in time a symbol of distrust of the political process —a symbol of democracy's fear of democracy. How explain this seeming paradox, and what have been the results?

It is no contradiction of what has been said in preceding paragraphs to point out that the *original* attitude of the American masses toward the document which came from the Philadelphia Convention was very far from being one of worship. The said masses were small farmers with slight social experience and vast social suspicions, and the latter had been given by the agitation leading to the Revolution a decided anti-government—and especially an *anti-central-government*—set. Nor, in fact, was the Constitution which its former opponents presently vied with its former champions in praising altogether the same Constitution as the one over whose merits they had originally divided. Not only had it now a bill of rights, but what was vastly more important, the authors of the Virginia and Kentucky Resolutions, squaring the logical circle, had succeeded in affixing to it, for those who chose to welcome the improvement, a gloss of the extremest states-rightism. It is true, of course, that Marshall was still to propound from the bench for more than a third of a century the original conception of the Constitution as the ever-adaptable instrument of national needs; yet only, as it were, academically, and in behalf of statutes for which the Congresses of the period were enacting few counterparts. The national sovereignty had become in truth, long before the end of Marshall's chief-justiceship, a sovereignty *in vacuo,* in no small measure.

But certain environmental factors have

---

[4] For this and the quotation in the next paragraph, see Frank I. Schechter, "The Early History of the Tradition of the Constitution," in this REVIEW, Vol. 9. pp. 707, 720 (Nov., 1915).

[5] Elkinson v. Deliesseline, 8 *Fed. Cas.* 593.

[6] Quoted by Fletcher M. Green in *Pubs. of Emery Univ.,* Vol. 22, No. 5, p. 7 (May, 1936).

been, perhaps, even more potent than intellectual currents in finally affixing to the Constitutional Symbol its distinctively negative quality. The presence to the eastward of the Atlantic Ocean, with its fair assurance against hostile invasion, discredited from the outset any plea in favor of strong government in the name of defense. The presence to the westward of endless stretches of cheap lands opened to even the humblest members of society an opportunity for self-assertion on a scale never before approached in the history of mankind. Lastly, the presence throughout this richest of continents of vast mineral and other natural resources which public policy, or rather the lack of it, threw open to private preëmption with little restriction vested the acquisition of wealth with a moral and legal sanction of its own. People were content with the answer that the country was being developed.

It is a commonplace that Constitutionalism has worked in this country to impress upon the discussion of public measures a legalistic—not to say theological—mold. By a terminology which treats *doctrines* as *facts,* the actualities which should control statesmanship have been too often kept at arm's length; while for the question of the beneficial *use* of the powers of government has been substituted the question of their *existence*. The tendency in question manifested itself at an early date. Said W. H. Crawford in a speech in the Senate in February, 1811: "Upon the most thorough examination, I am induced to believe that many of the various constructions given to the Constitution are the result of the belief that it is absolutely perfect. It has become so extremely fashionable to eulogize the Constitution, whether the object of the eulogy is the extension or contraction of the powers of the government, that whenever its eulogium is pronounced, I feel an involuntary apprehension of mischief."[7]

Crawford's words carry the significant

suggestion that there were those who looked upon the constitutionality of a measure as a positive quality, a reason by itself for the measure's enactment. Such an attitude is, in truth, a normal phase of the psychology of Constitutionalism. What better reason can there be for doing a thing than the right to do it when that was challenged in the first instance? Speaking generally, nevertheless, constitutional debate proceeds characteristically from the point of view of *negation* and treats the Constitutional Symbol as a source of *tabu;* and the "great constitutional lawyer" is one who knows how to make two constitutional restrictions grow where one grew before. Indeed, it is astonishing the extent to which the taint of constitutional obliquity has always dogged the footsteps of the American people and their representatives. The Constitution itself was unconstitutional by an argument to which Madison felt it necessary to reply in *The Federalist*. Most of Hamilton's legislative program was unconstitutional in the opinion of half of Washington's cabinet. The Louisiana Purchase was unconstitutional in the opinion of the President who accomplished it. The most important measure by which the slavery question was kept in abeyance for years was unconstitutional in the opinion of large numbers of people, and finally in the opinion of the Supreme Court. The Civil War was brought to a successful issue by resorting to measures which two out of three Americans alive at that time would have voted to be unconstitutional; and according to the Democratic *Almanac* of 1866, the Thirteenth Amendment was unconstitutional. And the enumeration might easily be prolonged to include almost every measure of scope and of somewhat novel character that the Congress of the United States has enacted within the last half-century.

Despite all which, it may be remarked of constitutional negativism, as Lord Acton remarked of liberty, that it must have remained impermanent and inefficient had it not found embodiment in an implementing institution. I refer, of course, to judicial review, and especially to the power of the Court to disallow acts of Congress on the ground of their being in conflict with the Constitution. Recently

[7] Benton, *Abridgment,* etc., IV, 266. See also his further statement (*ibid.,* 308): "The gentlemen . . . still view it [the Constitution] as a model of perfection. They are certainly at liberty still to entertain that opinion. Every man has a right to erect his idol in this land of liberty, and to fall down and worship it according to the dictates of his conscience."

there has been a renewal of the old debate as to the intentions of the Framers in this respect. Neither party, perhaps, has quite all the truth on its side. That the Framers anticipated some sort of judicial review of acts of Congress there can be little question. But it is equally without question that ideas generally current in 1787 were far from presaging the present vast rôle of the Court.

Thus, as we saw earlier, constitutional negativism exalts the Bill of Rights as the bulwark of achieved liberties. In the Virginia convention, on the other hand, which ratified the Constitution, Marshall declared of bills of rights that they were "merely recommendatory. Were it otherwise," he continued, ". . . many laws which are found convenient would be unconstitutional." The principle of the separation of powers, too, was originally thought to be "directory only," and hence as not affording a judicially applicable restriction upon legislative power. Again, the Constitution is today assumed to comprise *a closed, a completed system.* Indeed, this assumption is asserted by Cooley to be the underlying basis of judicial review. Yet in the debate on the location of the removal power in the first Congress to assemble under the Constitution the most strongly held theory was that the Constitution did not declare itself on the point, as obviously it does not, and that accordingly Congress was confronted with a *càsus omissus* which under the necessary and proper clause it was entitled to supply. And no less paradoxical by modern standards is Chief Justice Marshall's suggestion early in 1805, while the Chase impeachment was pending, that the power of impeachment ought to be surrendered by Congress in return for power to reverse such "opinions" of the Court as Congress found objectionable. In a recent discussion of this episode in the Senate, it was confidently asserted that what Marshall had in mind was an amendment to the Constitution.[8] But quite clearly this was not the case. The situation was an urgent one; Marshall was trembling not only for the safety of the Court but for the safety of his own position. What he evidently had in mind was an *ad hoc* understanding between the two branches, one that would ripen in time into a fixed custom of the Constitution.

The opinion of our Senatorial wise men confirms Professor Maitland's statement as to the tendency of the law (i.e., of the lawyers) to "antedate the emergence of modern ideas," and it may be added that they sometimes antedate other things too. How account otherwise for that door-panel of the new Supreme Court Building which pictures—or at least was originally thought to do so— Chief Justice Marshall as handing to Justice Story the former's opinion in Marbury v. Madison, although this opinion was rendered some nine years prior to Story's appointment to the Bench;[9] or for the occasionally encountered motif in court-room murals of the *signing* of Magna Carta by King John, although John probably could not write, and at any rate the great seal, affixed by the Chancellor, was thought to serve such occasions very adequately. Nor is this to mention Senator Borah's speech last February 22, in which Washington is represented as delivering the Farewell Address in the new capital named for him some four years before said capital was open for business!

Judicial review of national legislation first disclosed its potentialities seventy years after the framing of the Constitution, in the Dred Scott Case, where it is placed squarely on a symbolic basis. The Constitution, Chief Justice Taney there declares, speaks always "not only with the same words, but with the same intent" as when it came from the Framers. Thus is the miracle which is the Constitution of 1787 to be maintained and preserved by the mystery which is judicial power—its clairvoyance into the intentions of men long dead as to things which did not exist when they lived!

And by the same token, if judicial review has conserved the Constitutional Symbol, the Constitutional Symbol has conserved judicial review, by screening its operations behind the impersonal mask of the unbiased past. Even today, the notion of the judicial mouthpiece of a

[8] *Cong. Record,* June 18, 1936, p. 10013.

[9] See Mr. Benjamin Ginsburg's communication to the *Washington Evening Star,* Sept. 15, 1936; also the *New York Times* of July 5, 1936.

self-interpreting, self-enforcing law has its adherents. Listen, for instance, to this defense by a correspondent of the *New York Times* of the decision in the Rice Millers' Case, which awarded some 200 millions of dollars to people most of whom were probably not entitled to it: "For so long as the Constitution of the United States endures in its present form, it must operate with the infallibility of the laws of nature. Sound and fecund growths will be fortified by its influences. Its impact will always strip the fruit from any governmental tree which is too defective to maintain its own integrity. The office of the Supreme Court is simply to elucidate the process." [10]

Coming now to the heart of the problem here under discussion, I propose to point out briefly certain restrictions upon the national legislative power which the Court has from time to time ratified in favor, primarily, of certain minority interests, on the theory that such interests comprised an essential part of a prior order of things which it was a fundamental—*the* fundamental—purpose of the Constitution to put beyond the reach of popular majorities. Viewed from this angle, the Constitutional Symbol is seen to part company with the Constitutional Instrument very radically. *The symbol of the many becomes the instrument of the few, and all the better instrument for being such symbol.*

The two minority interests which have left the deepest imprint on our constitutional law, so far as national power is concerned, are slavery and that fairly coherent group of interests which are commonly lumped together as "Big Business." Slavery was awakened to its situation by the Tariff of 1828. But as no appeal could be taken to the Court with any hope of success so long as Marshall dominated it, Calhoun, reversing his constitutional creed almost overnight, fashioned a fantastic substitute from the Virginia and Kentucky Resolutions of thirty years previous; and by the aid of Nullification the South was presently able to force a compromise with the adherents of the American System.

Twenty years later the question of slavery in the territories was to the fore,

[10] *New York Times,* May 5, 1936.

and meantime the menacing possibility had presented itself that the rising forces of Anti-Slavery in Congress would attempt to put a stop to the interstate slave trade. Whether by dint of foresighted management or by accident, the slaveholding states had now a majority on the Court, and the drive which culminated nine years later in the Dred Scott decision, to get a judicial determination of the territorial question was launched. But what line ought the Court to take in handling questions of national power affecting slavery? Should it treat slavery as constituting a special case, a sort of enclave, withdrawn by the intention of the Framers from the constitutional powers of the national government; or should it construe these powers in such a way as to render them harmless for slavery considered simply as any proprietarian interest? In his opinion in the Passenger Cases, Justice Wayne of Georgia, the strongest nationalist on the Taney Bench, suggested the former expedient, but without success. The consequence is that the two doctrines which have proved most restrictive of the powers of Congress in recent years are directly traceable to the Taney Court. The first of these is the doctrine that the Tenth Amendment segregates to the states certain "subjects," "fields," or "interests," and hence forbids Congress to exercise any of its powers, but especially its interstate commerce and taxing powers, with the effect or intention of governing such "subjects," "fields," or "interests." The second is that the due process clause of the Fifth Amendment authorizes the Court to invalidate any act of Congress which it finds to impair property rights "unreasonably." Furthermore, from the defenders of the Dred Scott decision came the doctrine of the "finality" of the Court's interpretations of the Constitution—a doctrine which Lincoln assailed in his first inaugural as transferring to the Court the people's right of self-government.

And it is on these bases, shaky as they are in both logic and history, that the Court has chosen to rest the most outstanding of its recent decisions. There is no need to review these holdings in any detail in order to show their bearing on our subject. The climax is reached when they are considered for their impairment of the Constitutional Instrument, in the A.A.A. Case, which, when evaluated in the light of Justice Robert's's opinion, appears to assert that Congress may not legitimately employ its granted powers in order to further on a *national* scale any end which the states may legitimately attempt on a *local* scale. Others of these decisions have suddenly thrust into prominence as a restrictive principle the heretofore innocuous and unused doctrine that a legislature may not delegate its power, but without giving that doctrine coherent or understandable form. Still another decision rejects the principle of emergency power on the basis of the equivocal or erroneous assertion that the powers of the national government have proved "adequate" "both in war and peace." Still another implies a theory of judicial autonomy in relation to legislative power which represents a *vast* departure from the views of the Framers. Lastly, the American Liberty League, whose mission it is to spread the gospel of the Constitution as symbol of the "American Way," informs us that the Constitution may be amended "in harmony with its fundamental principles"—that is, may *not* be amended in disharmony therewith. Perhaps it is to be regretted that the judicial history of the Prohibition Amendment contains small assurance of this doctrine ever receiving that acceptance which would round off most conclusively and artistically the triumph of the Constitutional Symbol over the Constitutional Instrument.[11]

Considered, in short, from the point of view of the national legislative power, especially in the important fields of taxation and interstate commerce regulation, the Constitution has passed through the following phases: from (1) an instrument of national government, a source of national power, to (2) an object of popular worship, finally valued chiefly for the obstacles it interposed to the national power, to (3) a protection of certain minority interests seeking escape from national power; or, in other words, from constitutional instrument to constitutional fetish, to constitutional tabu, to constitutional instrument again, albeit the *negative* instrument of certain special interests, not the *positive* instrument of a government of the people.[12]

And with what final result for national legislative power? The question is answered admirably by Mr. Irving Brant in his recent *Storm over the Constitution:* "During this later period the United States shifted from a Constitution of *implied powers* under the express powers [of Congress] to a Constitution of *implied limitations* on the express powers. It was virtually the same thing as writing a new, and infinitely narrower, Constitution" [13]—that is, the same thing as permitting the Court to do this.

It would be easy to ascribe this conversion, partial but immensely important, of the Constitutional Instrument of the many into the Constitutional Instrument of the few to a conspiracy of the latter; or, to use Sir Thomas More's words, to a "conspiracy of rich men, procuring their own commodities under the title of commonwealth." And the truth of the matter is that the effluvia of conspiracy are never altogether absent when authority joines itself to a mystery, such as the Constitution of the United States has to many intents and purposes become today. On the other hand, the propensity of the professional exalter of the Constitutional Symbol for modern propaganda technique hardly fits the charge, inasmuch as propaganda—or so we are assured—rarely builds *de novo*, but works upon *existing* beliefs. We may therefore concede that the propagandist against the expansion of national power *thinks* that there is that in the popular mind to which he can appeal successfully; and he may be right. For, as a colleague suggests, we are today in the presence of the reverse of the situation which elicited from Mr. Dooley his famous remark anent

---

[11] It is doubtless with the Liberty League in mind that Professor Radin wrote recently: "The search for a new capitalist religion in the United States is rapidly taking the form of consecrating patriotic symbols and multiplying rituals which will inevitably be associated with the existing type of economic organization." *New York Univ. Law Quar. Rev.,* Vol. 13, p. 505.

[12] In support of the immediately preceding paragraphs, see generally my *Commerce Power versus States' Rights,* published by the Princeton University Press on August 4 last.

[13] Brant, *Storm over the Constitution,* p. 129.

the Supreme Court's following the "election returns." The question at present is, Will the election returns follow the Supreme Court?

Certain of the characteristics of popular thinking which go to explain the rise of constitutional negativism, and thereby the implementation of certain minority interests by the Constitution, were adverted to early in this paper. One, however, I have reserved for more special mention in these closing paragraphs; and it is the fundamental premise of economic individualism. I mean the assumption that economic power is *natural* and political power *artificial,* from which the conclusion is drawn that *"arbitrary"* power is characteristically *governmental* power. The latter idea clearly underlies the more significant of the Court's recent decisions. Thus, in the A.A.A. Case the Court held that in requiring agriculturists to sign contracts as a condition of receiving certain payments from the Treasury, the government "coerced" the agriculturists, who "involuntarily" accepted its terms. Yet had Mr. Henry Ford stood in the place of the government in such a transaction, who would ever have thought of using such language about it? Moreover, there are still cases in good standing which hold that a laborer is not coerced when confronted by his employer with the alternative of giving up his job or quitting his union, although it *is* coercion for government to forbid the employers to do this! Likewise, in the Alton Case the Court holds that for Congress to require a carrier to pension a superannuated employee is to deprive the carrier of liberty and property without due process of law, the "liberty" in question being the carrier's right to dismiss a superannuated employee without pensioning him.

The unreality of such thinking is hardly travestied in the following passage from Professor Arnold's witty little volume, *The Symbols of Government:* "If the American people were actually free from countless petty restrictions, it is not likely that they would build a mansion in the judicial heavens dedicated to the principle, before which we make such curious sacrifices, that there should be no such restrictions. If we were not so constantly subject to arbitrary and uncontrolled power over our very means of existence, we would not require the dramatization of the abstract ideal that no such power could exist in America, provided that the case could be properly presented to the Supreme Court of the United States. The only absolute essential of a heaven is that it be different from the everyday world." [14]

The American people are today moving rapidly toward a constitutional crisis of unpredictable gravity, a crisis due chiefly to the Court's endeavor to put "Big Business" and its methods—the "American Way"—out of reach of effective government. Thanks to the Court's excessive preoccupation with this problem, the question has even been raised whether the entire system of constitutional limitations, judicially implemented, is not incompatible with popular government. Personally, I am not convinced that this is so; but I do think that if the dilemma suggested is to be avoided, short of formal constitutional change, the Court will have to enlarge some of its conceptions, and especially will it have to enlarge its conception of public power *to include economic power.* For when this is done certain other important truths will also emerge. It will be seen that most people have to take orders from some source or other, and that therefore the problem of human liberty is not to be completely solved by the purely negative device of setting acts of Congress aside as contrary to the Constitution. Also recognition will dawn that there is no reason underlying the nature of things why acts or procedures which are regarded as unjust when they are resorted to by government are necessarily more defensible when resorted to by business management. Lastly, it will appear that unless we are to resign ourselves to economic autocracy, governmental power must be as little embarrassed by boundary lines as is economic power.

All this, however, I am conscious, is somewhat negative; and I would conclude on an affirmative note. I find it to hand in a passage from Señor Ortega's *Revolt of the Masses:* "The State is always, what-

[14] Arnold, *Symbols of Government,* p. 224.

ever be its form—primitive, ancient, medieval, modern—an invitation issued by one group of men to other human groups to carry out some enterprise in common. That enterprise, be its intermediate processes what they may, consists in the long run in the organization of a certain type of common life. State and plan of existence, programme of human activity or conduct, these are inseparable terms." And he elsewhere adds: "When there is a stoppage of that impulse towards some-

thing further on, the State automatically succumbs . . . breaks up, is dispersed." [15]

Revision of the Constitutional Symbol there must be, I submit, to bring it into conformity with the Constitutional Instrument, regarded as the instrument of a people's government and of a unified nation which has not yet lost faith in its political destiny.

[15] Ortega y Gasset, *Revolt of the Masses,* pp. 176, 183.

The Federal System

MORTON GRODZINS

Morton Grodzins was professor of political science and director of the federalism workshop at the University of Chicago. He specialized in the study of American political parties but wrote, too, on the American relocation centers for the Japanese in World War II.

Federalism is a device for dividing decisions and functions of government. As the constitutional fathers well understood, the federal structure is a means, not an end. The pages that follow are therefore not concerned with an exposition of

American federalism as a formal, legal set of relationships. The focus, rather, is on the purpose of federalism, that is to say, on the distribution of power between central and peripheral units of government.

THE SHARING OF FUNCTIONS

The American form of government is often, but erroneously, symbolized by a three-layer cake. A far more accurate image is the rainbow or marble cake, characterized by an inseparable mingling of differently colored ingredients, the colors appearing in vertical and diagonal strands and unexpected whirls. As colors

Morton Grodzins, "The Federal System," in The President's Commission on National Goals, *Goals for Americans,* by the American Assembly. © 1960. Reprinted by permission of Prentice-Hall Inc., Englewood Cliffs, N. J.

Authors' note: This paper is the product of research carried out in the Federalism Workshop of the University of Chicago. I am indebted to the workshop participants, particularly Daniel J. Elazar, Dennis Palumbo, and Kenneth E. Gray, for data they collected. I profited greatly in writing Part III of the paper from Mr. Elazar's prize-winning dissertation, "Intergovernmental Relations in Nineteenth Century American Federalism" (Chicago, 1959).

are mixed in the marble cake, so functions are mixed in the American federal system. Consider the health officer, styled "sanitarian," of a rural county in a border state. He embodies the whole idea of the marble cake of government.

The sanitarian is appointed by the state under merit standards established by the federal government. His base salary comes jointly from state and federal funds, the county provides him with an office and office amenities and pays a portion of his expenses, and the largest city in the county also contributes to his salary and office by virtue of his appointment as a city plumbing inspector. It is impossible from moment to moment to tell under which governmental hat the sanitarian operates. His work of inspecting the purity of food is carried out under federal standards; but he is enforcing state laws when inspecting commodities that have not been in interstate commerce; and somewhat perversely he also acts under state authority when inspecting milk coming into the county from producing areas across the state border. He is a federal officer when impounding impure drugs shipped from a neighboring state; a federal-state officer when distributing typhoid immunization serum; a state officer when enforcing standards of industrial hygiene; a state-local officer when inspecting the city's water supply; and (to complete the circle) a local officer when insisting that the city butchers adopt more hygienic methods of handling their garbage. But he cannot and does not think of himself as acting in these separate capacities. All business in the county that concerns public health and sanitation he considers his business. Paid largely from federal funds, he does not find it strange to attend meetings of the city council to give expert advice on matters ranging from rotten apples to rabies control. He is even deputized as a member of both the city and county police forces.

The sanitarian is an extreme case, but he accurately represents an important aspect of the whole range of governmental activities in the United States. Functions are not neatly parceled out among the many governments. They are shared functions. It is difficult to find any governmental activity which does not involve all three of the so-called "levels" of the federal system. In the most local of local functions—law enforcement or education, for example—the federal and state governments play important roles. In what, a priori, may be considered the purest central government activities—the conduct of foreign affairs, for example—the state and local governments have considerable responsibilities, directly and indirectly.

The federal grant programs are only the most obvious example of shared functions. They also most clearly exhibit how sharing serves to disperse governmental powers. The grants utilize the greater wealth-gathering abilities of the central government and establish nation-wide standards, yet they are "in aid" of functions carried out under state law, with considerable state and local discretion. The national supervision of such programs is largely a process of mutual accommodation. Leading state and local officials, acting through their professional organizations, are in considerable part responsible for the very standards that national officers try to persuade all state and local officers to accept.

Even in the absence of joint financing, federal-state-local collaboration is the characteristic mode of action. Federal expertise is available to aid in the building of a local jail (which may later be used to house federal prisoners), to improve a local water purification system, to step up building inspections, to provide standards for state and local personnel in protecting housewives against dishonest butchers' scales, to prevent gas explosions, or to produce a land use plan. States and localities, on the other hand, take important formal responsibilities in the development of national programs for atomic energy, civil defense, the regulation of commerce, and the protection of purity in foods and drugs; local political weight is always a factor in the operation of even a post office or a military establishment. From abattoirs and accounting through zoning and zoo administration, any governmental activity is almost certain to involve the influence, if not the formal administration, of all three planes of the federal system.

ATTEMPTS TO UNWIND THE FEDERAL SYSTEM

Within the past dozen years there have been four major attempts to reform or reorganize the federal system: the first (1947–49) and second (1953–55) Hoover Commissions on Executive Organization; the Kestnbaum Commission on Intergovernmental Relations (1953–55); and the Joint Federal-State Action Committee (1957–59). All four of these

groups have aimed to minimize federal activities. None of them has recognized the sharing of functions as the characteristic way American governments do things. Even when making recommendations for joint action, these official commissions take the view (as expressed in the Kestnbaum report) that "the main tradition of American federalism [is] the tradition of separateness." All four have, in varying degrees, worked to separate functions and tax sources.

The history of the Joint Federal-State Action Committee is especially instructive. The committee was established at the suggestion of President Eisenhower, who charged it, first of all, "to designate functions which the States are ready and willing to assume and finance that are now performed or financed wholly or in part by the Federal Government." He also gave the committee the task of recommending "Federal and State revenue adjustments required to enable the States to assume such functions."[1]

The committee subsequently established seemed most favorably situated to accomplish the task of functional separation. It was composed of distinguished and able men, including among its personnel three leading members of the President's cabinet, the director of the Bureau of the Budget, and ten state governors. It had the full support of the President at every point, and it worked hard and conscientiously. Excellent staff studies were supplied by the Bureau of the Budget, the While House, the Treasury Department, and, from the state side, the Council of State Governments. It had available

[1] The President's third suggestion was that the committee "identify functions and responsibilities likely to require state or federal attention in the futrue and . . . recommend the level of state effort, or federal effort, or both, that will be needed to assure effective action." The committee initially devoted little attention to this problem. Upon discovering the difficulty of making separatist recommendations, i.e., for turning over federal functions and taxes to the states, it developed a series of proposals looking to greater effectiveness in intergovernmental collaboration. The committee was succeeded by a legislatively-based, 26-member Advisory Commission on Intergovernmental Relations, established September 29, 1959.

to it a large mass of research data, including the sixteen recently completed volumes of the Kestnbaum Commission. There existed no disagreements on party lines within the committee and, of course, no constitutional impediments to its mission. The President, his cabinet members, and all the governors (with one possible exception) on the committee completely agreed on the desirability of decentralization - via - separation - of - functions - and - taxes. They were unanimous in wanting to justify the committee's name and to produce action, not just another report.

The committee worked for more than two years. It found exactly two programs to recommend for transfer from federal to state hands. One was the federal grant program for vocational education (including practical-nurse training and aid to fishery trades); the other was federal grants for municipal waste treatment plants. The programs together cost the federal government less than $80 million in 1957, slightly more than two per cent of the total federal grants for that year. To allow the states to pay for these programs, the committee recommended that they be allowed a credit against the federal tax on local telephone calls. Calculations showed that this offset device, plus an equalizing factor, would give every state at least 40 per cent more from the tax than it received from the federal government in vocational education and sewage disposal grants. Some states were "equalized" to receive twice as much.

The recommendations were modest enough, and the generous financing feature seemed calculated to gain state support. The President recommended to Congress that all points of the program be legislated. None of them was, none has been since, and none is likely to be.

A POINT OF HISTORY

The American federal system has never been a system of separated governmental activities. There has never been a time when it was possible to put neat labels on discrete "federal," "state," and "local" functions. Even before the Constitution, a statute of 1785, reinforced by the Northwest Ordinance of 1787, gave grants-inland to the states for public schools. Thus the national government was a prime force in making possible what is now taken to be the most local function of all, primary and secondary education. More important, the nation, before it was fully organized, established by this action a first principle of American federalism: the national government would use its superior resources to initiate and support national programs, principally administered by the states and localities.

The essential unity of state and federal financial systems was again recognized in the earliest constitutional days with the assumption by the federal government of the Revolutionary War debts of the states. Other points of federal-state collaboration during the Federalist period concerned the militia, law enforcement, court practices, the administration of elections, public health measures, pilot laws, and many other matters.

The nineteenth century is widely believed to have been the pre-eminent period of duality in the American system. Lord Bryce at the end of the century described (in *The American Commonwealth*) the federal and state governments as "distinct and separate in their action." The system, he said, was "like a great factory wherein two sets of machinery are at work, their revolving wheels apparently intermixed, their bands crossing one another, yet each set doing its own work without touching or hampering the other." Great works may contain gross errors. Bryce was wrong. The nineteenth century, like the early days of the republic, was a period principally characterized by intergovernmental collaboration.

Decisions of the Supreme Court are often cited as evidence of nineteenth century duality. In the early part of the century the Court, heavily weighted with Federalists, was intent upon enlarging the sphere of national authority; in the later years (and to the 1930's) its actions were in the direction of paring down national powers and indeed all governmental authority. Decisions referred to "areas of exclusive competence" exercised by the federal government and the states; to their powers being "separate and distinct;" and to neither being able "to intrude within the jurisdiction of the other."

Judicial rhetoric is not always consistent with judicial action, and the Court did not always adhere to separatist doctrine. Indeed, its rhetoric sometimes indicated a positive view of cooperation. In any case, the Court was rarely, if ever,

directly confronted with the issue of cooperation *vs.* separation as such. Rather it was concerned with defining permissible areas of action for the central government and the states; or with saying with respect to a point at issue whether any government could take action. The Marshall Court contributed to intergovernmental cooperation by the very act of permitting federal operations where they had not existed before. Furthermore, even Marshall was willing to allow interstate commerce to be affected by the states in their use of the police power. Later courts also upheld state laws that had an impact on interstate commerce, just as they approved the expansion of the national commerce power, as in statutes providing for the control of telegraphic communication or prohibiting the interstate transportation of lotteries, impure foods and drugs, and prostitutes. Similar room for cooperation was found outside the commerce field, notably in the Court's refusal to interfere with federal grants in land or cash to the states. Although research to clinch the point has not been completed, it is probably true that the Supreme Court from 1800 to 1936 allowed far more federal-state collaboration than it blocked.

Political behavior and administrative action of the nineteenth century provide positive evidence that, throughout the entire era of so-called dual federalism, the many governments in the American federal system continued the close administrative and fiscal collaboration of the earlier period. Governmental activities were not extensive. But relative to what governments did, intergovernmental cooperation during the last century was comparable with that existing today.

Occasional presidential vetoes (from Madison to Buchanan) of cash and land grants are evidence of constitutional and ideological apprehensions about the extensive expansion of federal activities which produced widespread intergovernmental collaboration. In perspective, however, the vetoes are a more important evidence of the continuous search, not least by state officials, for ways and means to involve the central government in a wide variety of joint programs. The search was successful.

Grants-in-land and grants-in-services from the national government were of first importance in virtually all the principal functions undertaken by the states and their local subsidiaries. Land grants were made to the states for, among other purposes, elementary schools, colleges, and special educational institutions; roads, canals, rivers, harbors, and railroads; reclamation of desert and swamp lands; and veterans' welfare. In fact whatever was at the focus of state attention became the recipient of national grants. (Then, as today, national grants established state emphasis as well as followed it.) If Connecticut wished to establish a program for the care and education of the deaf and dumb, federal money in the form of a land grant was found to aid that program. If higher education relating to agriculture became a pressing need, Congress could dip into the public domain and make appropriate grants to states. If the need for swamp drainage and flood control appeared, the federal government could supply both grants-in-land and, from the Army's Corps of Engineers, the services of the only trained engineers then available.

Aid also went in the other direction. The federal government, theoretically in exclusive control of the Indian population, relied continuously (and not always wisely) on the experience and resources of state and local governments. State militias were an all-important ingredient in the nation's armed forces. State governments became unofficial but real partners in federal programs for homesteading, reclamation, tree culture, law enforcement, inland waterways, the nation's internal communications system (including highway and railroad routes), and veterans' aid of various sorts. Administrative contacts were voluminous, and the whole process of interaction was lubricated, then as today, by constituent-conscious members of Congress.

The essential continuity of the collaborative system is best demonstrated by the history of the grants. The land grant tended to become a cash grant based on the calculated disposable value of the land, and the cash grant tended to become an annual grant based upon the national government's superior tax powers. In 1887, only three years before the frontier was officially closed, thus signalizing the end of the disposable public domain, Congress enacted the first continuing cash grants.

A long, extensive, and continuous experience is therefore the foundation of the present system of shared functions characteristic of the American federal system, what we have called the marble cake of government. It is a misjudgment of our history and our present situation to believe that a neat separation of governmental functions could take place without drastic alterations in our society and system of government.

DYNAMICS OF SHARING: THE POLITICS OF THE FEDERAL SYSTEM

Many causes contribute to dispersed power in the federal system. One is the simple historical fact that the states existed before the nation. A second is in the form of creed, the traditional opinion of Americans that expresses distrust of centralized power and places great value in the strength and vitality of local units of government. Another is pride in locality and state, nurtured by the nation's size and by variations of regional and state history. Still a fourth cause of decentralization is the sheer wealth of the nation. It allows all groups, including state and local governments, to partake of the central government's largesse, supplies room for experimentation and even waste, and makes unnecessary the tight organization of political power that must follow when the support of one program necessarily means the deprivation of another.

In one important respect, the Constitution no longer operates to impede centralized government. The Supreme Court since 1937 has given Congress a relatively free hand. The federal government can build substantive programs in many areas on the taxation and commerce powers. Limitations of such central programs based on the argument, "it's unconstitutional," are no longer possible as long as Congress (in the Court's view) acts reasonably in the interest of the whole nation. The Court is unlikely to reverse this permissive view in the foreseeable future.

Nevertheless, some constitutional restraints on centralization continue to operate. The strong constitutional position of the states—for example, the assignment of two senators to each state, the role given the states in administering even national elections, and the relatively few limitations on their law-making powers—establish the geographical units as natural centers of administrative and political strength. Many clauses of the Constitution are not subject to the same latitude of interpretation as the commerce and tax clauses. The simple, clearly stated, unambiguous phrases—for example, the President "shall hold his office during the term of four years"—are subject to change only through the formal amendment process. Similar provisions exist with respect to the terms of senators and congressmen and the amendment process. All of them have the effect of retarding or restraining centralizing action of the federal government. The fixed terms of the President and members of Congress, for example, greatly impede the development of nation-wide, disciplined political parties that almost certainly would have to precede continuous large-scale expansion of federal functions.

The constitutional restraints on the expansion of national authority are less important and less direct today than they were in 1879 or in 1936. But to say that they are less important is not to say that they are unimportant.

The nation's politics reflect these decentralizing causes and add some of their own. The political parties of the United States are unique. They seldom perform the function that parties traditionally perform in other countries, the function of gathering together diverse strands of power and welding them into one. Except during the period of nominating and electing a president and for the essential but non-substantive business of organizing the houses of Congress, the American parties rarely coalesce power at all. Characteristically they do the reverse, serving as a canopy under which special and local interests are represented with little regard for anything that can be called a party program. National leaders are elected on a party ticket, but in Congress they must seek cross-party support if their leadership is to be effective. It is a rare president during rare periods who can produce legislation without facing the defection of substantial numbers of his own party. (Wilson could do this in the first session of the sixty-third Congress; but Franklin D. Roosevelt could not, even during the famous hundred days of 1933.) Presidents whose parties form the majority of the congressional houses must still count heavily on support from the other party.

The parties provide the pivot on which the entire governmental system swings. Party operations, first of all, produce in legislation the basic division of functions between the federal government, on the one hand, and state and local governments, on the other. The Supreme Court's permissiveness with respect to the expansion of national powers has not in fact produced any considerable extension of exclusive federal functions. The body of federal law in all fields has remained, in the words of Henry M. Hart, Jr. and Herbert Wechsler, "interstitial in its nature," limited in objective and resting upon the principal body of legal relationships defined by state law. It is difficult to find any area of federal legislation that is not significantly affected by state law.

In areas of new or enlarged federal activity, legislation characteristically provides important roles for state and local governments. This is as true of Democratic as of Republican administrations and true even of functions for which arguments of efficiency would produce exclusive federal responsibility. Thus the unemployment compensation program of the New Deal and the airport program of President Truman's administration both provided important responsibilities for state governments. In both cases attempts to eliminate state participation were defeated by a cross-party coalition of pro-state votes and influence. A large fraction of the Senate is usually made up of ex-governors, and the membership of both houses is composed of men who know that their re-election depends less upon national leaders or national party organization than upon support from their home constituencies. State and local officials are key members of these constituencies, often central figures in selecting candidates and in turning out the vote. Under such circumstances, national legislation taking state and local views heavily into account is inevitable.

Second, the undisciplined parties affect the character of the federal system as a result of senatorial and congressional interference in federal administrative programs on behalf of local interests. Many aspects of the legislative involvement in administrative affairs are formalized. The Legislative Reorganization Act of 1946, to take only one example, provided that each of the standing committees "shall exercise continuous watchfulness" over administration of laws within its jurisdiction. But the formal system of controls, extensive as it is, does not compare in importance with the informal and extra-legal network of relationships in producing continuous legislative involvement in administrative affairs.

Senators and congressmen spend a major fraction of their time representing problems of their constituents before administrative agencies. An even larger fraction of congressional staff time is devoted to the same task. The total magnitude of such "case work" operations is great. In one five-month period of 1943 the Office of Price Administration received a weekly average of 842 letters from members of Congress. If phone calls and personal contacts are added, each member of Congress on the average presented the OPA with a problem involving one of his constituents twice a day in each five-day work week. Data for less vulnerable agencies during less intensive periods are also impressive. In 1958, to take only one example, the Department of Agriculture estimated (and underestimated) that it received an average of 159 congressional letters per working day. Special congressional liaison staffs have been created to service this mass of business, though all higher officials meet it in one form or another. The

Air Force in 1958 had, under the command of a major general, 137 people (55 officers and 82 civilians) working in its liaison office.

The widespread, consistent, and in many ways unpredictable character of legislative interference in administrative affairs has many consequences for the tone and character of American administrative behavior. From the perspective of this paper, the important consequence is the comprehensive, day-to-day, even hour-by-hour, impact of local views on national programs. No point of substance or procedure is immune from congressional scrutiny. A substantial portion of the entire weight of this impact is on behalf of the state and local governments. It is a weight that can alter procedures for screening immigration applications, divert the course of a national highway, change the tone of an international negotiation, and amend a social security law to accommodate local practices or fulfill local desires.

The party system compels administrators to take a political role. This is a third way in which the parties function to decentralize the American system. The administrator must play politics for the same reason that the politician is able to play in administration: the parties are without program and without discipline.

In response to the unprotected position in which the party situation places him, the administrator is forced to seek support where he can find it. One ever-present task is to nurse the Congress of the United States, that crucial constituency which ultimately controls his agency's budget and program. From the administrator's view, a sympathetic consideration of congressional requests (if not downright submission to them) is the surest way to build the political support without which the administrative job could not continue. Even the completely task-oriented administrator must be sensitive to the need for congressional support and to the relationship between case work requests, on one side, and budgetary and legislative support, on the other. "You do a good job handling the personal problems and requests of a Congressman," a White House officer said, "and you have an easier time convincing him to back your program." Thus there is an important link between the nursing of congressional requests, requests that largely concern local matters, and the most comprehensive national programs. The administrator must accommodate to the former as a price of gaining support for the latter.

One result of administrative politics is that the administrative agency may become the captive of the nation-wide interest group it serves or presumably regulates. In such cases no government may come out with effective authority: the winners are the interest groups themselves. But in a very large number of cases, states and localities also win influence. The politics of administration is a process of making peace with legislators who for the most part consider themselves the guardians of local interests. The political role of administrators therefore contributes to the power of states and localities in national programs.

Finally, the way the party system operates gives American politics their overall distinctive tone. The lack of party discipline produces an openness in the system that allows individuals, groups, and institutions (including state and local governments) to attempt to influence national policy at every step of the legislative-administrative process. This is the "multiple-crack" attribute of the American government. "Crack" has two meanings. It means not only many fissures or access points; it also means, less statically, opportunities for wallops or smacks at government.

If the parties were more disciplined, the result would not be a cessation of the process by which individuals and groups impinge themselves upon the central government. But the present state of the parties clearly allows for a far greater operation of the multiple crack than would be possible under the conditions of centralized party control. American interest groups exploit literally uncountable access points in the legislative-administrative process. If legislative lobbying, from committee stages to the conference committee, does not produce results, a cabinet secretary is called. His immediate associates are petitioned. Bureau chiefs and their aides are hit. Field officers are put under pressure. Campaigns are instituted by which friends of the agency apply a secondary influence on behalf of the interested party. A conference with the President may be urged.

To these multiple points for bringing influence must be added the multiple voices of the influencers. Consider, for example, those in a small town who wish to have a federal action taken. The easy merging of public and private interest at the local level means that the influence attempt is made in the name of the whole community, thus removing it from political partisanship. The Rotary Club as well as the City Council, the Chamber of Commerce and the mayor, eminent citizens and political bosses—all are readily enlisted. If a conference in a senator's office will expedite matters, someone on the local scene can be found to make such a conference possible and effective. If technical information is needed, technicians will supply it. State or national professional organizations of local officials, individual congressmen and senators, and not infrequently whole state delegations will make the local cause their own. Federal field officers, who service localities, often assume local views. So may elected and appointed state officers. Friendships are exploited, and political mortgages called due. Under these circumstances, national policies are molded by local action.

In summary, then, the party system functions to devolve power. The American parties, unlike any other, are highly responsive when directives move from the bottom to the top, highly unresponsive from top to bottom. Congressmen and senators can rarely ignore concerted demands from their home constituencies; but no party leader can expect the same kind of response from those below, whether he be a President asking for congressional support or a congressman seeking aid from local or state leaders.

Any tightening of the party apparatus would have the effect of strengthening the central government. The four characteristics of the system, discussed above, would become less important. If control from the top were strictly applied, these hallmarks of American decentralization might entirely disappear. To be specific, if disciplined and program-oriented parties were achieved: (1) It would make far less likely legislation that takes heavily into account the desires and prejudices of the highly decentralized power groups and institutions of the country, including the state and local governments. (2) It would to a large extent prevent legislators, individually and collectively, from intruding themselves on behalf of non-national interests in national administrative programs. (3) It would put an end to the administrator's search for his own political support, a search that often results in fostering state, local, and other non-national powers. (4) It would dampen the process by which individuals and groups, including state and local political leaders, take advantage of multiple cracks to steer national legislation and administration in ways congenial to them and the institutions they represent.

Alterations of this sort could only accompany basic changes in the organization and style of politics which, in turn, presuppose fundamental changes at the parties' social base. The sharing of functions is, in fact, the sharing of power. To end this sharing process would mean the destruction of whatever measure of decentralization exists in the United States today.

GOALS FOR THE SYSTEM OF SHARING

THE GOAL OF UNDERSTANDING

Our structure of government is complex, and the politics operating that structure are mildly chaotic. Circumstances are ever-changing. Old institutions mask intricate procedures. The nation's history can be read with alternative glosses, and what is nearest at hand may be furthest from comprehension. Simply to understand the federal system is therefore a difficult task. Yet without understanding there is little possibility of producing desired changes in the system. Social structures and processes are relatively impervious to purposeful change. They also exhibit intricate interrelationships so that change induced at point "A" often produces unanticipated results at point "Z." Changes introduced into an imperfectly understood system are as likely to produce reverse consequences as the desired ones.

This is counsel of neither futility nor conservatism for those who seek to make our government a better servant of the people. It is only to say that the first goal for those setting goals with respect to the federal system is that of understanding it.

TWO KINDS OF DECENTRALIZATION

The recent major efforts to reform the federal system have in large part been aimed at separating functions and tax sources, at dividing them between the federal government and the states. All of these attempts have failed. We can now add that their success would be undesirable.

It is easy to specify the conditions under which an ordered separation of functions could take place. What is principally needed is a majority political party, under firm leadership, in control of both Presidency and Congress, and, ideally but not necessarily, also in control of a number of states. The political discontinuities, or the absence of party links, (1) between the governors and their state legislatures, (2) between the President and the governors, and (3) between the President and Congress clearly account for both the picayune recommendations of the Federal-State Action Committee and for the failure of even those recommendations in Congress. If the President had been in control of Congress (that is, consistently able to direct a majority of House and Senate votes), this alone would have made possible some genuine separation and devolution of functions. The failure to decentralize by order is a measure of the decentralization of power in the political parties.

Stated positively, party centralization must precede governmental decentralization by order. But this is a slender reed on which to hang decentralization. It implies the power to centralize. A majority party powerful enough to bring about ordered decentralization is far more likely to choose in favor of order centralization. And a society that produced centralized national parties would, by that very fact, be a society prepared to accept centralized government.

Decentralization by order must be contrasted with the different kind of decentralization that exists today in the United States. It may be called the decentralization of mild chaos. It exists because of the existence of dispersed power centers. This form of decentralization is less visible and less neat. It rests on no discretion of central authorities. It produces at times specific acts that many citizens may consider undesirable or evil. But power sometimes wielded even for evil ends may be desirable power. To those who find value in the dispersion of power, decentralization by mild chaos is infinitely more desirable than decentralization by order. The preservation of mild chaos is an important goal for the American federal system.

OILING THE SQUEAK POINTS

In a governmental system of genuinely shared responsibilities, disagreements inevitably occur. Opinions clash over proximate ends, particular ways of doing things become the subject of public debate, innovations are contested. These are not basic defects in the system. Rather, they are the system's energy-reflecting life blood. There can be no permanent "solutions" short of changing the system itself by elevating one partner to absolute supremacy. What can be done is to attempt to produce conditions in which conflict will not fester but be turned to constructive solutions and particular problems.

A long list of specific points of difficulty in the federal system can be easily identified. No adequate congressional or administrative mechanism exists to review the patchwork of grants in terms of national needs. There is no procedure by which to judge, for example, whether the national government is justified in spending so much more for highways than for education. The working force in some states is inadequate for the effective performance of some nation-wide programs, while honest and not-so-honest graft frustrates efficiency in others. Some federal aid programs distort state budgets, and some are so closely supervised as to impede state action in meeting local needs. Grants are given for programs too narrowly defined, and over-all programs at the state level consequently suffer. Administrative, accounting and auditing difficulties are the consequence of the multiplicity of grant programs. City officials complain that the states are intrusive fifth wheels in housing, urban redevelopment, and airport building programs.

Some differences are so basic that only a demonstration of strength on one side or another can solve them. School desegregation illustrates such an issue. It also illustrates the correct solution (although not the most desirable method of reaching it): in policy conflicts of fundamental importance, touching the nature of democracy itself, the view of the whole nation must prevail. Such basic ends, however, are rarely at issue, and sides are rarely taken with such passion that loggerheads are reached. Modes of settlement can usually be found to lubricate the squeak points of the system.

A pressing and permanent state problem, general in its impact, is the difficulty of raising sufficient revenue without putting local industries at a competitive disadvantage or without an expansion of sales taxes that press hardest on the least wealthy. A possible way of meeting this problem is to establish a state-levied income tax that could be used as an offset for federal taxes. The maximum level of the tax which could be offset would be fixed by federal law. When levied by a state, the state collection would be deducted from federal taxes. But if a state did not levy the tax, the federal government would. An additional fraction of the total tax imposed by the states would be collected directly by the federal government and used as an equalization fund, that is, distributed among the less wealthy states. Such a tax would almost certainly be imposed by all states since not to levy it would give neither political advantage to its public leaders nor financial advantage to its citizens. The net effect would be an increase in the total personal and corporate income tax.

The offset has great promise for strengthening state governments. It would help produce a more economic distribution of industry. It would have obvious financial advantages for the vast majority of states. Since a large fraction of all state income is used to aid political subdivisions, the local governments would also profit, though not equally as long as cities are under-represented in state legislatures. On the other hand, such a scheme will appear disadvantageous to some low-tax states which profit from the in-migration of industry (though it would by no means end all state-by-state tax differentials). It will probably excite the opposition of those concerned over governmental centralization, and they will not be assuaged by methods that suggest themselves for making both state and central governments bear the psychological impact of the tax. Although the offset would probably produce an across-the-board tax increase, wealthier persons, who are affected more by an income tax than by other levies, can be expected to join forces with those whose fear is centralization. (This is a common alliance and, in the nature of things, the philosophical issue rather than financial advantage is kept foremost.)

Those opposing such a tax would gain additional ammunition from the certain knowledge that federal participation in the scheme would lead to some federal standards governing the use of the funds. Yet the political strength of the states would keep these from becoming onerous. Indeed, inauguration of the tax offset as a means of providing funds to the states might be an occasion for dropping some of the specifications for existing federal grants. One federal standard, however, might be possible because of the greater representation of urban areas in the constituency of Congress and the President than in the constituency of state legislatures: Congress might make a state's participation in the offset scheme dependent upon a periodic reapportionment of state legislatures.

The income tax offset is only one of many ideas that can be generated to meet serious problems of closely meshed governments. The fate of all such schemes ultimately rests, as it should, with the politics of a free people. But much can be done if the primary technical effort of those concerned with improving the federal system were directed not at separating its intrerelated parts but at making them work together more effectively. Temporary commissions are relatively inefficient in this effort, though they may be useful for making general assessments and for generating new ideas. The professional organizations of government workers do part of the job of continuously scrutinizing programs and ways and means of improving them. A permanent staff, established in the President's office and working closely with state and local officials, could also perform a useful and perhaps important role.

THE STRENGTH OF THE PARTS

Whatever governmental "strength" or "vitality" may be, it does not consist of independent decision-making in legislation and administration. Federal-state interpenetration here is extensive. Indeed, a judgment of the relative domestic strength of the two planes must take heavily into account the influence of one on the other's decisions. In such an analysis the strength of the states (and localities) does not weigh lightly. The nature of the nation's politics makes federal functions more vulnerable to state influence than state offices are to federal influence. Many states, as the Kestnbaum Commission noted, live with "self-imposed constitutional limitations" that make it difficult for them to "perform all of the services that their citizens require." If this has the result of adding to federal responsibilities, the states' importance in shaping and administering federal programs eliminates much of the sting.

The geography of state boundaries, as well as many aspects of state internal organization, are the products of history and cannot be justified on any grounds of rational efficiency. Who, today, would create major governmental subdivisions the size of Maryland, Delaware, New Jersey, or Rhode Island? Who would write into Oklahoma's fundamental law an absolute state debt limit of $500,000? Who would design (to cite only the most extreme cases) Georgia's and Florida's gross under-representation of urban areas in both houses of the legislature?

A complete catalogue of state political and administrative horrors would fill a sizeable volume. Yet exhortations to erase them have roughly the same effect as similar exhortations to erase sin. Some of the worst inanities—for example, the boundaries of the states, themselves—are fixed in the national constitution and defy alteration for all foreseeable time. Others, such as urban under-representation in state legislatures, serve the over-represented groups, including some urban ones, and the effective political organization of the deprived groups must precede reform.

Despite deficiencies of politics and organizations that are unchangeable or slowly changing, it is an error to look at the states as static anachronisms. Some of them—New York, Minnesota, and California, to take three examples spanning the country—have administrative organizations that compare favorably in many ways with the national establishment. Many more in recent years have moved rapidly towards integrated administrative departments, state-wide budgeting, and central leadership. The others have models-in-existence to follow, and active professional organizations (led by the Council of State Governments) promoting their development. Slow as this change may be, the states move in the direction of greater internal effectiveness.

The pace toward more effective performance at the state level is likely to increase. Urban leaders, who generally feel themselves disadvantaged in state affairs, and suburban and rural spokesmen, who are most concerned about national centralization, have a common interest in this task. The urban dwellers want greater equality in state affairs, including a more equitable share of state financial aid; non-urban dwellers are concerned that city dissatisfactions should not be met by exclusive federal, or federal-local, programs. Antagonistic, rather than amiable, cooperation may be the consequence. But it is a cooperation that can be turned to politically effective measures for a desirable upgrading of state institutions.

If one looks closely, there is scant evidence for the fear of the federal octopus, the fear that expansion of central programs and influence threatens to reduce the states and localities to compliant administrative arms of the central government. In fact, state and local governments are touching a larger proportion of the people in more ways than ever before; and they are spending a higher fraction of the total national product than ever before. Federal programs have increased, rather than diminished, the importance of the governors; stimulated professionalism in state agencies; increased citizen interest and participation in government; and, generally, enlarged and made more effective the scope of state action.[2] It may no longer be true in any significant sense that the states and localities are "closer" than the federal government to the people. It is true that the smaller governments remain active and powerful members of the federal system.

CENTRAL LEADERSHIP: THE NEED FOR BALANCE

The chaos of party processes makes difficult the task of presidential leadership. It deprives the President of ready-made congressional majorities. It may produce, as in the chairmen of legislative committees, power-holders relatively hidden from public scrutiny and relatively protected from presidential direction. It allows the growth of administrative agencies which sometimes escape control by central officials. These are prices paid for a wide dispersion of political power. The cost is tolerable because the total results of dispersed power are themselves desirable and because, where clear national supremacy is essential, in foreign policy and military affairs, it is easiest to secure.

Moreover, in the balance of strength between the central and peripheral governments, the central government has on its side the whole secular drift towards the concentration of power. It has on its side technical developments that make central decisions easy and sometimes mandatory. It has on its side potent purse

[2] See the valuable report, *The Impact of Federal Grants-in-Aid on the Structure and Functions of State and Local Governments,* submitted to the Commission on Intergovernmental Relations by the Governmental Affairs Institute (Washington, 1955).

powers, the result of superior tax-gathering resources. It has potentially on its side the national leadership capacities of the presidential office. The last factor is the controlling one, and national strength in the federal system has shifted with the leadership desires and capacities of the chief executive. As these have varied, so there has been an almost rhythmic pattern: periods of central strength put to use alternating with periods of central strength dormant.

Following a high point of federal influence during the early and middle years of the New Deal, the post-war years have been, in the weighing of central-peripheral strength, a period of light federal activity. Excepting the Supreme Court's action in favor of school desegregation, national influence by design or default has not been strong in domestic affairs. The danger now is that the central government is doing too little rather than too much. National deficiencies in education and health require the renewed attention of the national government. Steepening population and urbanization trend lines have produced metropolitan area problems that can be effectively attacked only with the aid of federal resources. New definitions of old programs in housing and urban redevelopment, and new programs to deal with air pollution, water supply, and mass transportation are necessary. The federal government's essential role in the federal system is that of organizing, and helping to finance, such nation-wide programs.

The American federal system exhibits many evidences of the dispersion of power not only because of formal federalism but more importantly because our politics reflect and reinforce the nation's diversities-within-unity. Those who value the virtues of decentralization, which writ large are virtues of freedom, need not scruple at recognizing the defects of those virtues. The defects are principally the danger that parochial and private interests may not coincide with, or give way to, the nation's interest. The necessary cure for these defects is effective national leadership.

The centrifugal force of domestic politics needs to be balanced by the centripetal force of strong presidential leadership. Simultaneous strength at center and periphery exhibits the American system at its best, if also at its noisiest. The interests of both find effective spokesmen. States and localities (and private interest groups) do not lose their influence opportunities, but national policy becomes more than the simple consequence of successful, momentary concentrations of non-national pressures: it is guided by national leaders.[3]

[3] Messrs. Perkins and Redford state:
Professor Grodzins has made a significant contribution. The federal system has contributed to a "mild chaos" both administratively and financially. He accurately assesses the several quite futile attempts to disentangle the administrative and fiscal relationships of the states and the national government.

At this juncture, however, it should be remembered that the present system of shared responsibility confuses rather than fixes responsibility. Ascertainable responsibility for policy, administrative performance, and financing is an essential feature of effective self-government. The possibility of achieving it needs to be explored.

A reduction of the sharing of power would to some degree cause greater centralization of responsibility in the federal government. It would not necessarily result in loss of appropriate administrative decentralization and the loss of influence by the ordinary citizen over the activities of government. This is illustrated by what Mr. Grodzins himself says concerning the influence of the localized party structure on administration of centralized national functions.

The chaos of party processes itself impairs leadership for national functions and national aims. Mr. Grodzins' conclusion that the costs of this chaos are tolerable may be drawn too easily. Whether the centrifugal pulls of party decentralization are so strong as to seriously threaten national leadership and responsibility in our government deserves careful assessment.

Decentralization is an essential goal of American policy. So also are responsibility and leadership. Public concern needs to manifest itself about both of these goals.

SUGGESTED ADDITIONAL READINGS

1. Beard, Charles A., *An Economic Interpretation of the Constitution of the United States,* New York: Macmillan, 1913. A classic, arguing that the Consti-

tution was the product of the efforts of the propertied and well-to-do to protect their interests and to check democratic majorities. One of the essential books for an understanding of the Constitution in historical perspective.

2. Brogan, D. W., *Politics in America,* Chap. 1, "The Character of the American Polity," New York: Harper, 1954, (also available in paper, Anchor Books, Doubleday and Company, New York: 1960). An incisive discussion of the central role the Constutution plays in American experience, by one of the best of contemporary foreign observers. Provides valuable historical background for an understanding of the development of constitutionalism in America.

3. Brown, Robert E., *Charles Beard and the Constitution: A Critical Analysis of 'An Economic Interpretation of the Constitution,'* New York: W. W. Norton, 1965, 219 pp. (paper). Reviews and critiques Beard's theses, dissecting the Beard volume chapter by chapter; surveys the literature relative to Beard's volume; suggests fourteen substitute propositions for Beard's conclusions.

4. Corwin, Edward S., "The Passing of Dual Federalism," 36 *Virginia Law Review* (1950), 1. Historical review of the process of change in American federalism, posing the question "whether the Constituent States of the System can be saved for any useful purpose, and thereby saved as the vital cells that they have been heretofore of democratic sentiment, impulse, and action."

5. Friedrich, Carl J., *Constitutional Government and Democracy,* Chap. I, "A Historical Sketch of Modern Constitutionalism in Theory and Practice," and Chap. VII, "The Making of a Constitution as a Political Process," Boston: Ginn, Rev. ed., 1950. Advances the concept of constitutionalism as effective regularized restraint on government. Provides excellent background, theoretical and historical, for an understanding of the nature of a constitution.

6. Goldwin, Robert A. (ed.), *A Nation of States: Essays on the American Federal System,* Chicago: Rand McNally, 1963, 148 pp. (paper). Seven essays by leading students of American federalism, representing differing and sometimes conflicting views. Although the essays vary in significance and sophistication, the volume serves as an excellent reference on federalism in the U. S. The essays include: Morton Grodzins, "Centralization and Decentralization in the American Federal System"; Martin Diamond, "What the Framers Meant By Federalism"; Russell Kirk, "The Prospects For Territorial Democracy in America"; Herbert J. Storing, "The Problem of Big Government"; James Jackson Kilpatrick, "The Case For 'States' Rights' "; Harry V. Jaffa, "The Case For a Stronger National Government"; and Walter Berns, "The Meaning of the Tenth Amendment."

7. Hamilton, Howard D., "The Commission on Intergovernmental Relations and Grants-In-Aid in the United States," *Public Finance,* Vol. 9, No. 2 (1954), pp. 140–156. Defense of grants-in-aid as a means of strengthening the federal system. Analyzes the arguments against grants, specifying five basic myths upon which the opposition is based. Statistics are dated, but the analysis is useful.

8. Hutchins, Robert M., *Two Faces of Federalism: An Outline of an Argument About Pluralism, Unity and Law,* Santa Barbara, Calif: Center for Study of Democratic Institutions, 1961, pp. 5–24.

9. Kilpatrick, James Jackson, "The Case For 'States' Rights,' " in Robert A. Goldman, ed., *A Nation of States: Essays on the American Federal System,* Chicago: Rand McNally, 1963, pp. 88–105. An articulate statement by a leading exponent of "states' rights" today, which contrasts sharply with the view of federalism expressed in this chapter.

10. *Korematsu v. United States,* 323 U. S. 214 (1944). Supreme Court decision upholding the presidential executive order of 1942 under which Japanese-Americans were evacuated from the West Coast. Indispensable for understanding the complexity of the war powers and the questions of constitutionality.

11. McCloskey, Robert G., *Essays in Constitutional Law,* Chap. 1, "Judicial Review and 'the Intent of the Framers,'" New York: Alfred A. Knopf, 1957. Utilizing an article by Charles A. Beard, ("The Supreme Court—Usurper or Grantee," *Political Science Quarterly,* 27 (1912), 1), the author focuses on the question of intent relative to the central question of judicial review. Although the Beard article takes a different approach to that suggested in the commentary, it serves well to demonstrate the dedication and faith with which many have approached the task of determining "original intent."

12. Mason, Alpheus T., and William M. Beaney, *The Supreme Court in a Free Society,* Chap. 6, "National Taxing and Spending," Englewood Cliffs, N. J.: Prentice-Hall, 1959. Factual and readable survey of the development of the power to tax and spend, including summaries of the major judicial decisions. Provides the non-specialist a very satisfactory basic understanding of the extent of these powers. Volume includes useful selected bibliography.

13. ———, *The Supreme Court in a Free Society,* Chap. 7, "Governing Under the Commerce Power," pp. 151–173. Surveys the development of the power to regulate commerce. Useful selected bibliography included.

14. Pritchett, C. Herman, *American Constitutional Issues,* Chap. 16, "War Powers," New York: McGraw-Hill, 1962. A brief but thorough survey of the substance of the war powers and the major judicial decisions relating to them. Includes a useful list of selected references.

15. Riker, William H., *Federalism: Origin, Operation, Significance,* Boston: Little, Brown, 1963, 169 pp. (paper). A comprehensive consideration of federalism, especially in the U. S., utilizing comparative, theoretical and empirical tools. Sharply critical of federalism, particularly in its frustration of majorities.

16. Roche, John P., "The Founding Fathers: A Reform Caucus in Action," *American Political Science Review,* Vol. LV, No. 4 (December 1961), 799–816. Describes the framers of the Constitution as *"political men*—not metaphysicians, disembodied conservatives, or Agents of History . . ." who "[hammered] out a pragmatic compromise . . ." Advances the argument that the Constitution "was not an apotheosis of 'constitutionalism,' a triumph of architectonic genius; it was a patchwork sewn together under the pressure of both time and events . . ."

17. Wheare, K. C., *Federal Government,* Part I, "What Federal Government Is," London: Oxford University Press, 3rd ed., 1953. A well-regarded but somewhat mechanistic examination of the nature of federalism, useful as a background on the mechanical arrangements generally identified with federalism. Concentrates on U. S. experience, but considers comparative cases also.

18. ———, *Modern Constitutions,* London: Oxford University Press, 1951, 216 pp. A useful, though somewhat pedestrian, survey of constitutions in general with specific references to many existing conditions.

19. Zimmerman, Frederick L., and Mitchell Wendell, *The Interstate Compact Since 1925,* Chicago: Council of State Governments, 1951. Basic, detailed information on the use of the interstate compact. Demonstrates the utility of this instrument in interstate cooperation.

FOR FURTHER CONSIDERATION

1. How would you now respond to the charge by a "strict constructionist" that a given governmental program (say, Medicare, or federal grants to parochial schools) is (or would be) unconstitutional because it violates the intent of the framers? Be specific. Cite your evidence. Support your argument. Now—how

confident do you feel that he will be convinced? Why? Does this suggest anything to you about the difficulty involved in explaining the nature of a constitution?

2. "Constitutionalism exists when there are regularized restraints on government. . . . In our experience . . . [such restraints are] reflected both in the requirements of the written document and, more importantly, in a societal attitude towards the use of governmental power, in the expectation that government will function in an orderly, predictable, and restrained fashion." What evidence can you suggest that such a societal attitude exists? Upon what could you base the conclusion that there is an "expectation that government will function in an orderly, predictable, and restrained fashion?" Do *you* expect government to function in this way? If not, how would you explain the nature of constitutionalism in the U. S.?

3. "The Constitution says . . ." What is your understanding of the meaning of this statement? How would you explain just what the Constitution does say about any particular problem (say, the rights of a religious group to distribute pamphlets or the limits of the power of Congress to regulate commerce)? What assurance could you have that your answer would be correct? Or does the Constitution not really answer the question? If so, consider the implications. What do you do when someone contends *he* knows what the Constitution really says and his explanation differs from your understanding? Family, if the Constitution is so vague as to make its meaning unclear, of what value is it?

4. What justification is there for continuance of a federal arrangement today? Is it necessary? What might be suggested as a new arrangement? Could such changes be made constitutionally? What do you think are the chances of such changes being made? Explain.

5. Do you think we could expect to produce a written constitution from a national convention today which would be as good as that produced in 1789? Why or why not? What problems would you suggest we would face in (a) trying to set up such a convention, (b) trying to write a new constitution, and (c) trying to put it into operation? Would they be different in kind from those facing the nation in 1789? How would you place this hypothetical new constitution (or the effort to write one) in historical perspective?

The Political Process

3

Democracy in the United States has been challenged both externally and internally. Notwithstanding the mid-twentieth century ideological and military-economic struggle against the Soviet Union and China, the most important and continuing challenges to democracy come from those who reject its premises or are disillusioned with its practices. Much of this disillusionment rests in the inability of the process in action to meet the expectations generated by the process in theory. Political alienation, non-participation, and skepticism reflect not so much pathology in practice as pathology in theory of democracy. As Schattschneider says,

We become cynical about democracy because the public does not act the way the simplistic definition of democracy says it should act, or we try to whip the public into doing things it does not want to do, is unable to do and has too much sense to do. The crisis here is not a crisis in democracy but a crisis in theory.[1]

Or, as Murray Levin, puts it:

Although most scholars who have advanced these theories point out that democratic theory as it was developed in the seventeenth and eighteenth centuries is archaic, the elementary and secondary schools continue to teach and the students continue to believe that it is eminently workable. The latter tend to place the blame for political apathy and frustration on the improper functioning of democratic institutions, particularly corruption. . . .
In effect, democratic theory is one of the sources of political alienation. Feelings of political alienation will arise when the political role that an individual expects to play and believes is rightfully his cannot be realized. . . .

[1] E. E. Schattschneider, *The Semisovereign People* (New York: Holt, Rinehart and Winston, 1960), p. 134.

Feelings of alienation will arise in individuals who accept the classical democratic theory because it demands more of the individual citizen than he can realistically fulfill and promises more than can be delivered[2]

This chapter examines the realities of politics in the United States democracy today. [12] An understanding of the realities of the political process will help us to avoid the frustration and alienation so often resulting from an awareness that many of the expectations of traditional democratic theory are not verifiable in experience. Many of the "perversions" of democracy are in fact normal parts of an operable democratic process, often identified as pathological because they do not conform to the prescriptions of classical democratic theory. If the democratic political process does not operate as reflected in the traditional theory, it is not because there is something wrong with democracy but because our theoretical model is inaccurate. [4, 7, 15, 19]

The following discussion will concentrate on (1) the nature of the democratic political process, (2) the role of elections and the electorate in the process, and (3) the role of political parties and interest groups. [5]

THE NATURE OF THE DEMOCRATIC POLITICAL PROCESS

Probably the most difficult task in any political system is to solve the problem of the legitimacy of political power. How to decide who governs and how to effect transfer of power in an orderly and politically acceptable fashion is the central problem, and the answer may well distinguish democratic and non-democratic systems.

The democratic political process may be described as an open competitive struggle for political power. [14] The locus of political power is not easily identified, and the wielders of power—those who make public policy—are numerous. Normally, however, those who make public policy in this society are privileged to do so because they have won the struggle against others who seek the privilege of making that policy.

The open competition for political power is the distinguishing characteristic of democratic politics. The crucial question is not who governs but how those in power achieve their positions. If they get into power by virtue of inheritance, physical force, superior economic standing, membership in an elite group, or any process other than open competition for the approval of the people at large, they are not democratically-selected policymakers. This does not mean, of course, that all policymakers must be personally involved in elections, for many policy positions in the United States are filled by appointment. Nevertheless, those who are appointed get into office as a result of the open competition for political power engaged in by those who appoint them. That is, those who win the competitive struggle are privileged to select appointees for the great number of offices to be filled by this method. (To the extent that civil service fills appointive positions largely without regard to who wins the compet-

[2] Murray B. Levin, *The Alienated Voter* (New York: Holt, Rinehart and Winston, 1960), pp. 72–73.

itive struggle for political power, the political victor is not able to shape the civil service system, but it is well established in theory and practice that these civil-service employees are then responsible to the elected representative and obliged to function according to his wishes.)

There is no conflict between this analysis of the nature of the democratic process and the classic democratic theorists' argument about the sovereign people as the source of government and the grantors of power. [20] So long as political power depends upon victory in an open competitive struggle in which the people at large make the final choice between the competitors, political power is dependent upon those people, and governors become governors by their action. The basis for the participation of the people in the governing process is competition for their approval. Power flows to those who win in the competition for the votes of the electorate. As E. E. Schattschneider says,

. . . *[T]he people are powerless if the political enterprise is not competitive.* It is the competition of political organizations that provides the people with the opportunity to make a choice. Without this opportunity popular sovereignty amounts to nothing.[3]

REGULARIZED TRANSFER OF POWER

Democratic politics requires first a regularized procedure for an effective periodic transfer of power, a procedure for the participation of the electorate as the final determiners of the legitimacy of victory. As suggested in Chapter 2, this operative procedure must reflect a verifiable expectation on the part of the people that they can periodically transfer power from one set of officials to another. "Paper" provisions will not suffice; experience must show that those in power get there and stay there as a result of an open competition for the favor of the people.

Some type of election, then, is assumed. The exact nature and form of the election may vary, but an election which actually determines the victors after an open competition for the voters approval is a prerequisite of the political process in a democracy. So well recognized is this that even non-democratic regimes have labored to give the impression that their officials are selected by the people in open elections. The Soviet Union, for example, has an elaborate set of procedures for elections. However, in such non-democratic systems the election is not the final stage of an open competition for the approval of the people nor do the people in the election make a genuine choice between competitors for the privilege of governing. [13]

UNRESTRICTED PARTICIPATION AND FREEDOM TO COMPETE

A second requirement for the political process to be genuinely competitive is unrestricted participation and freedom to organize, criticize, and differ. The process of competition must be institutionalized, that is, the ability to compete must be protected by guarantees that all who wish to compete may do so with a meaningful chance of being able to win. This presumes that no potential

---

[3] Schattschneider, *op cit.,* p. 140.

competitors will be told before the competition that they are not allowed to compete. Insofar as they are prohibited from competing the question of who would win has been begged, the competitive struggle has been foreclosed to some, and the outcome has been partially predetermined. To this extent it is a non-competitive or at least restricted competitive system, differing only in degree from the closed systems in which some elite group—the party, the church, the privileged class, the favored race—reserves to itself the guarantee of success.

No such rigid exclusions are operative in the American democratic process today, but we have had our experience with restriction of the field of participation. Excluding Negroes from registering and/or voting, prohibiting communists from appearing on the ballot, setting property or literacy qualifications for voting are all prior restraints on the openness of participation. Persons in these proscribed groups are thus prevented from any chance of gaining political power because they are excluded from the competitive system. Regardless of the justifications suggested for such restrictions, they nonetheless stand as qualifications to the open and unrestricted participation presumed in a democratic political process.

The corollary of unrestricted participation is the freedom to organize, criticize, and differ. The classical democratic theorists' interest in freedom and liberty has its most important application to the competitive struggle for power, for freedom and liberty to speak, advocate, criticize, organize, and act in a political fashion, are not just desirable, ethical, or normative goals but indispensable ingredients in the democratic political process. Competition cannot be meaningful unless it is based on a genuine freedom of speech and action.

ACQUIESCENCE OF THE LOSERS

Third, the democratic political process as a competition for power requires the acquiescence of the losers. Once the electorate has spoken, once a winner has emerged, those who did not win must accept their at least momentary defeat and allow the winners to govern. There is no room for revolution, suspension of the Constitution, assassination of the opponent, or withdrawal from the political arena in the democratic political process. Those who do not gain office, furthermore, are not really losers, for all they have lost is the momentary grasp of power. This is never a final defeat, and the momentary losers are institutionally guaranteed the privilege, and indeed have the responsibility, of continuing the competition for power. They cannot and may not prevent the winners from governing, but they are privileged to continue to oppose, both within and without the government, to continue to campaign, educate, criticize, and propose alternate policies, and to stand ready to challenge the incumbents each step of the way in the process of policy formation and implementation.

Thus, there is a continuous competition for power. When an election ends and the victors take up their positions of power, those who are not in office join together with those of their same political position who are still in office to carry out the important function of continuous criticism and challenge to the government.

FACTORS NOT REQUIRED

We may become so familiar with certain factors in our own experience that we assume they are necessary or inherent to democracy. Some of these, however, are not required. For example, the democratic political process does not require any particular set of institutional arrangements. We do not have to have a presidential (as opposed to a parliamentary) system, separation of powers, a system of checks and balances, federalism, a written constitution, or judicial review.

Nor does democracy require a superior level of intelligence or morality of its political members. Democratic competition for power is dependent on the people, but this is possible without their possession of superior intelligence. Education and higher intelligence, and the more sophisticated understanding of reality which possibly result, may make democracy easier and the means of competition more sophisticated. But the process can be competitive even in the absence of widespread education and high intelligence.

Democracy does not require any particular economic system. We must not confuse socialism, capitalism, and democracy. While the exact boundaries of economic systems and political systems are hard to identify, a society may be both democratic and socialist. While capitalism and democracy do seem to have been historically coincident, it is doubtful that they are interdependent. What is important to the existence of democracy is not the content of economic policies but the way in which they are adopted; that is, they must be determined by policymakers who hold office as the result of an open competitive struggle over the question (among a host of other questions) of what the content of the policies should be.

Finally, democracy does not require, and cannot tolerate, conformity or uniformity in the body politic. What has been called democratic consensus may indeed be necessary, if it is understood to mean a general understanding and acceptance of the belief that democracy can work and is worth the effort. [2, 16] Acquiescence in the "rules of the game," although difficult and at times impossible to prove, would also seem to be necessary. But conformity to a single standard, unwillingness or inability to differ on values, uniformity of belief as to programs, all point to a diminution of conflicts of interests (as opposed to a rationalization and accommodation of them) and thus to a low level of meaning of the political struggle. It is highly doubtful that there can be real competition for political power if there are not differences that matter, so that it becomes necessary for people to struggle to gain power in order to assure that their ideas, values, and interests are maximized. Competition will be most meaningful when it is based on basic differences in values and interests rather than simply a mutually-shared will to power.

Political competition in American experience is not necessarily ideal. It has never been fully open for all potential wielders of power, and perhaps it never will be. Questions of the degree of competition, the willingness to allow competition, and the availability of the means of competition are important, and there is no guarantee that the answers coming from the political process will be correct ones or that the power holders will be good governors. But the democratic process offers us a working chance to make these governors representative and responsible. If there are problems in the system, they can be more easily overcome by increasing the opportunity for competition than by restricting it. The answers to the problems of democracy do not seem to lie in denial of the procedures of democracy but in further extension of them.

THE ROLE OF ELECTIONS AND THE ELECTORATE

Traditional democratic theory has regarded elections as the way the general will could be expressed on major policy questions. This is not an accurate portrayal of reality. Policy-making by the electorate is not the rationale for elections; elections cannot accomplish this goal, and the electorate is not equipped to function in this fashion. [3, 20] Criticism of traditional theory has grown increasingly through the years as the empirical evidence has become more persuasive. [7, 15, 19] For instance, a quarter of a century ago Joseph A. Schumpeter suggested:

. . . [O]ur chief troubles about the classical theory centered in the proposition that "the people" hold a definite and rational opinion about every individual question and that they give effect to this opinion—in a democracy—by choosing "representatives" who will see to it that that opinion is carried out. Thus the selection of the representatives is made secondary to the primary purpose of the democratic arrangement which is to vest the power of deciding political issues in the electorate. Suppose we reverse the roles of these two elements and make the deciding of issues by the electorate secondary to the election of the men who are to do the deciding . . . We now take the view that the role of the people is to produce a government, or else an intermediate body which in turn will produce a national executive or government. And we define: the democratic method is that institutional arrangement for arriving at political decisions in which individuals acquire the power to decide by means of a competitive struggle for the people's vote.[4]

Elections serve as an integral part of the competition for political power. Their primary function is to allow the electorate to participate in the competitive struggle. The election is the culmination of the concentrated campaign, the most public and open phase of the continuing competition for power. The election does not decide what government shall do but who will decide what government shall do.

The election, of course, has serious implications for public policy. Who wins obviously will affect the kind of policy developed. Yet the difference between the winners and losers is seldom great enough to distinguish clear alternatives that might have occurred had the other competitors won. The process of election demands that the competitors appeal to a broad cross section of society in the interest of maximizing their votes, with the result that the election seldom if ever clearly indicates critical differences in programmatic orientation. Explanations of the results of a national election as a mandate for a particular policy or a series of policy decisions may be a useful technique in politics but is less than precise as an analytic statement. Elections do not produce mandates; elections produce governors. Serious competitors for political power, knowing

[4] Joseph A. Schumpeter, *Capitalism, Socialism, and Democracy* (New York: Harper, 1942), p. 269.

that they must maximize their vote in an election, do not ordinarily deviate far from the well-recognized mean in terms of policy, seldom advocating radical or extreme measures, since such appeals would not be calculated to win an election. In this sense, the necessity of competing for the electorate's vote does set the outer limits of policy proposals.

Several years ago, Angus Campbell reviewed the evidence for the adequacy of normative democratic theory on the functioning of elections. [1] A brief summary of that discussion is pertinent here.[5] Campbell suggested that normative democratic theory generally assumes two facts about the role of the election as a means by which the acts of government can be brought under the control of the governed. First, the theory assumes that the public is aware of policy goals and has the ability to decide which policies can best attain these goals so that it can make a rational choice between alternatives. Secondly, the election is assumed to present the electorate with recognizable policy alternatives that have attracted partisan commitment in such a way that the electorate can make a definite choice between these different policies.

Campbell observed that there is much evidence that the electorate lacks policy awareness. Individually, the voter does not know the issues, does not understand the alternatives, and generally, when aware, is oriented only to the general problem, not the specifics or the implications of the policy. Collectively, the electorate displays no coherent pattern of beliefs relative to policy on the major questions, such as welfare legislation, foreign policy, economic policy, or civil liberties. There is almost no evidence of ideological commitment (liberal—conservative), only programmatic preferences. Furthermore, there is little evidence that the electorate is certain as to what specific policies one party or the other would effect; that is, party alternatives in terms of policy alternatives are not generally recognized.

Campbell concludes that this gives us a portrait of the electorate as almost wholly without any detailed information about decision-making in government, knowing little about what government has done as a result of previous elections or what government will do as a result of any specific electorate choices in the present election, and unable to appraise its goals or the appropriateness of the means chosen to meet these goals. As a result, realistic appraisal suggests that the electoral decision will be ambiguous as to specific government acts and will leave those who frame government policy real freedom in the policy-making process. Elections will bring ·little pressure from the electorate on the policy makers; public pressure almost always comes from specific groups with specific interests, not, as the classical democratic theory assumes, from the great mass of the body politic.

What then is the importance of elections? Campbell suggests that the election defines the broad goals of governmental action and the very generalized means of reaching those goals, not specific goals and means. The electoral decision expresses the comparison of total images of one of the candidate-party alternatives with that of the other, and these images reflect certain differences

[5] See Angus Campbell, *The American Voter* (New York: John Wiley and Sons, Inc., 1960), pp. 541–548.

of generalized goals and means. Hence, the electoral decision process sets the limits of acceptable policy discussion, that is, sets the limits to the appeals to be made in the competition for votes. This does not suggest that the electorate is insignificant nor that its decisions are unimportant. Indeed, this limited but realistic role of the electorate marks the significant difference between our democratic political scheme and those where the electoral decision is manipulated and the competition for votes is not genuinely open.

Morris Janowitz and Dwaine Marvick investigated the prerequisites for a democratic election, that is, an election that reflected a "process of consent" rather than a "process of manipulation."[6] [9] They suggested three requirements. First, a democratic election requires competition between opposing candidates which pervades the entire constituency. Second, it requires both parties to engage in efforts to maintain established voting blocs, to recruit independent voters, and to gain converts from the opposite party. Third, it requires that both parties be engaged vigorously in attempting to win the current election and also in attempting long-run advancement of their chances to succeed in the next and subsequent elections.

In order for the electoral competition to make for consent rather than manipulation of the electorate, Janowitz and Marvick suggest that five ingredients must be present. First, the election must produce high levels of citizen participation among all social groupings. Second, participation must be based upon political self-confidence as well as self-interest. Third, the competition must stimulate effective political deliberation as a basis for the electoral decision. Fourth, there must be no monopoly of the mass media. And fifth, interpersonal pressures must operate independently of the influence of the mass media. If these criteria are met, elections will be genuinely competitive, and the electorate will be able to perform its primary function of selecting governors in a fashion promoting the process of consent.

All this suggests, then, that while the basic purpose of an election is to make the electorate the final determiner of who wins the competitive struggle for political power and is thus authorized to govern, the process of competition may involve some degree of manipulation of the electorate. The less manipulative the election, that is, the more sophisticated the tools of competition in order to get the approval of the voter, the more desirable the outcome of the election is apt to be. Nonetheless, in any given election all the electorate can do is to choose between the alternatives presented to it by the competitors. In the long run, the alternative candidates or programs which are presented to the electorate will reflect the level of sophistication of the electorate. Each competitor for office, each party, will tend to compete for the electorate's vote at the level necessary to maximize support for their candidates. If one competitor more correctly calculates the appropriate kind of appeals, he will win the election.

Traditional democratic theory, as the article by Bernard Berelson re-

---

[6] See Morris Janowitz and Dwaine Marvick, *Competitive Pressure and Democratic Consent* (Institute of Public Administration, University of Michigan, 1956). A summarization is reprinted in Heinz Eulau, Samuel J. Eldersveld, and Morris Janowitz, *Political Behavior: A Reader in Theory and Research* (Glencoe, Ill.: The Free Press, 1956), pp. 275–286.

printed here indicates, has set up requirements for the components of electoral decisions and the characteristics of the electorate. For instance, it has been assumed that the electorate decision must be the result of full information and knowledge on the part of the voters and that the electorate must possess political principle or moral standards. Furthermore, the electorate is required to observe and perceive political reality accurately, to be able to communicate and discuss, and to reflect rational judgment in political decisions. Finally, the electorate is supposed to react in consideration of the common good or community interest rather than in self-interest.

These normative requirements for the electorate, however, are not necessary to the operation of a genuinely competitive electoral process. Electorate knowledge, principle, rationality, involvement, interest, etc., may make the competitors for the vote of the electorate raise more significant questions. [10] But the crucial factor is still whether or not those who govern are privileged to do so as a result of getting the vote of the people, even though those people may not be the "democratic types" required by normative democratic theory.

This is a tremendously important point to understand. What a democratic society must promote is genuine competition for the vote of the electorate at large as a means of achieving political power. Appeals to normative democratic expectations often lead to the incorrect identification of ills in the body politic. For instance, many voters are ignorant, irrational, and biased, yet nonetheless are not pathological constituents of the body politic. Many voters do not know what the issues are, yet can and do participate in the process of conferring of power. Issues in an election are not so much the major questions of public policy as they are instruments of competition, and since the election does not determine public policy but those who will make public policy, the lack of issue orientation on the part of the population is not destructive.

Electoral competition has its own built-in control on the techniques used. Those techniques which succeed will probably be used again, but the fact that others are competing against the user of these techniques serves to set limits on the selection of techniques. Abstract morality or electorate intelligence are not in themselves restraints on the selection of techniques. Empirical calculations as to the anticipated success or failure resulting from the use of selected techniques is a far more effective control. [11]

In summary, then, consider the following statement by Murray Levin on the problem of alienation in politics and its relationship to democratic theory:

> Most citizens do not and cannot play an active role or display the sustained interest in politics required of them by the [classical democratic] theory. The majority do not engage in true discussion, are not well informed or motivated, and do not vote on the basis of principles. . . . The theory also fails to account for the necessary roles of leadership and exaggerates the active role of the masses. Those who do lead are therefore regarded as potential usurpers of what rightfully belongs to the electorate. The theory also leads its followers to believe that the bargaining and compromising, which is so essential to democratic politics, is necessarily evil. In short, the roles as defined by eighteenth-century democratic theory are too demanding and the political structure designed to implement them cannot be what it is supposed to be. . . . If individuals continue to believe in the classical view, they will feel politically alienated. [7]

---

[7] Levin, op. cit., p. 73–74.

THE ROLE OF POLITICAL PARTIES AND INTEREST GROUPS

The primary role of political parties [8, 12, 17, 18] is to serve as instruments of the competitive struggle for political power. As Clinton Rossiter says,

> The primary function of a political party in a democracy such as ours is to control and direct the struggle for power. From this function all others derive naturally. . . .
> It is one of the aspirations of democracy to bring this struggle as much as possible into the open. It is the great purpose of political parties, the handmaidens of democracy, to bring the struggle under control: to institutionalize it with organization, to channel it through nominations and elections, to publicize it by means of platforms and appeals, above all to stabilize it in the form of that traditional quadrille in which the Ins and the Outs change places from time to time on a signal from the voters.[8]

Political parties have no functions independent of this primary role. They do many other things, such as enlighten and educate, but these are subsidiary to the primary function. Thus, many of the failures of American political parties identified by various observers from time to time are not failures at all; setting arbitrary requirements as to what parties are supposed to do and then judging them deficient because they do not do these things is not realistic. What parties must do is rationalize the process of competition for the voters' approval; judgments as to their success must be made in terms of their effectiveness in winning elections. [13]

American political parties tend to gravitate towards the moderate or middle-of-the road stand on issues and are not readily identified on an ideological conservative-liberal spectrum. This is the norm and not a deviation. What the parties must do is to maximize the vote for their set of candidates; the parties are not established to distinguish between ideological positions, acceptable or otherwise, and knowledgeable politicians know this.

The 1964 presidential election is a case in point. The Republican Party was moved to differentiate itself from the Democratic party in a futile effort to give the voter "a choice for a change." To the extent that the party did this—differentiated its positions from those which had been appealing successfully to the American electorate increasingly over the last half century—that party did not compete effectively for the votes of the electorate. The 1964 presidential election was, then, only formally competitive, in that the Democratic nominee was not forced by the other party seriously to defend, challenge, or otherwise compete.

In this process, in which the political party serves as the chief instrument of organization and conduct of competition for power, many other things are accomplished. Parties select the candidates, sorting out from all potential candidates those who will maximize the possibilities of winning. [6] Furthermore, parties serve to single out individuals for participation, both in the conduct of a campaign and in government, either as members of the winning side (the Administration) or as members of the opposition inside government. Parties also articulate positions upon public policy questions both during and after election campaigns, both as government and opposition. They provide identification and continuity for the involvement of individuals and groups in the political

---

[8] Clinton Rossiter, *Parties and Politics in America* (Ithaca, N.Y.: Cornell University Press, 1960), p. 39.

process. They serve as instruments of responsibility of public officials to the electorate. They serve as organizers and conductors of public policy and as institutionalized means of challenge to that policy. [17, 18] These other activities follow directly from their primary responsibility for serving as a basic means of competition for political power.

Once the election is over, the party becomes a means of continuation of the competition for political power. For those who won and are in policy-making positions, the party is an instrument of government; for those who lost, the party is an instrument of opposition. In both cases, however, the role of party does not essentially change, although its techniques do. It is still to maximize the possibility of that party's victory in future elections.

The parties do differ; the records of the parties as to electoral appeal, success, and policy commitment are not beyond specification. [18] Party adherence is a major source of the data available in analyzing the results of elections. Policy orientation is also important. But these are results of, not reasons for, the existence of the political parties and reflect differences in the techniques of the parties in carrying out their primary function as instruments of competition.

Elections and political parties cannot represent policies and issues in any specific detail. They tend to fuse issues and policy questions into easily manipulated generalizations, rather than to break them down into specific, manageable parts. They tend to frame policy questions in terms of such symbols as peace, prosperity, honesty, efficiency, high standard of living, democracy, rather than concrete questions of the interests involved and the effect on these interests. This is as it must be, since issues and policies are, for political parties, mainly tools or techniques of competition.

Political parties are organizations created for the purpose of winning political power through the electoral process and maintaining it once it is obtained. Political interest groups, while interested in influencing those who wield power toward maximization of their aims in public policy, do not normally seek to hold political office. While political parties are obliged to seek as broad a base of support from as many divergent groups in society as possible, political interest groups are organized to represent a particular and limited clientele. Consequently, political interest groups are not structured so as to maximize their possibilities to win in competitive elections; their importance lies in their being major potential support groups which must be competed for by the parties, both during electoral campaigns and while in office.

Political interest groups are important adjuncts to the formal processes of representation. Since elections cannot give specific answers to the multitude of questions upon which the innumerable decisions must be made by those in power, the policymakers must have communication with the major interests in the society which have a stake in particular issues. Public policy is the outgrowth of the process of accommodating various interests. Politics is the business of representing the conflicting, sometimes overlapping, often diametrically opposed interests of various groups in society. While the election determines who wins the privilege of making public policy, the political interest groups feed the information to the policymakers upon which they base both the decisions as to policy and their calculations of the impact of these decisions upon their chances of staying in office. We no longer need to posit, as did the classical theorists, the existence of a general will or public opinion representative of what the people of the country want. What we now recognize as public interest grows out of the conflict of the wills of special interests and is a product of the rationalization, compromise, and accommodation of these interests.

The democratic political process is by no means perfect, and efforts to improve it are both germane and desirable. We can have the best of both the norms and values of classical democratic theory and the operative procedures of contemporary democracy. There is basically no conflict between them. Although classical democratic theory seems to set requirements for the electorate and goals for the electoral process which are both unrealistic and unattainable, if we avoid concluding that because they are unattained there is something wrong with democracy, we may yet understand that the value of classical democratic theory may be precisely the high norms it sets. The electorate does not meet the requirements of classical democratic theory, but if it did—if it were as motivated, active, interested, rational, informed, and unselfish as many have assumed it must be—we might have an even more effective competition for political power. The problem with classical democratic theory arises when one or both of two things occur: first, when we assume that the classical model is correct and thus fail to understand our own democracy; or second, when we designate as pathological those normal components of the democratic process which do not conform to the classical model. A realistic understanding of democracy as it does operate, however, will lead one to conclude that while it is by no means a perfect system, and while it does not give any guarantee of success either in terms of excellence or avoidance of crises, it does maximize the attainment of democratic values.

In conclusion, the following statement by Robert A. Dahl is pertinent:

. . . [E]lections are a crucial device for controlling leaders and . . . are quite ineffective as indicators of majority preference. These statements are really not in contradiction. A good deal of traditional democratic theory leads us to expect more from national elections than they can possibly provide. We expect elections to reveal the "will" or the preferences of a majority on a set of issues. This is one thing elections rarely do, except in an almost trivial fashion. Despite this limitation the election process is one of two fundamental methods of social control which, operating together, make governmental leaders so responsive to non-leaders that the distinction between democracy and dictatorship still makes sense. The other method of social control is continuous political competition among individuals, parties, or both. Elections and political competition do not make for government by majorities in any very significant way, but they vastly increase the size, number, and variety of minorities whose preferences must be taken into account by leaders in making policy choices. . . .

If the majority rarely rules on matters of specific policy, nevertheless the specific policies selected by a process of 'minorities' rule' probably lie most of the time within the bounds of consensus set by important values of the politically active members of the society, of whom the voters are a key group. . . . For politicians subject to election must operate within the limits set both by their own values, as indoctrinated members of the society, and by their expectations about what policies they can adopt and still be reelected.[9]

The three readings reprinted below are representative of the kinds of materials upon which the foregoing analysis of the democratic political process is

[9] Robert A. Dahl, *A Preface to Democratic Theory* (Chicago: University of Chicago Press. 1956), pp. 131–132.

based. Berelson ("Democratic Theory and Public Opinion") restates the fundamental requirements of normative theory of political democracy and indicates
how public opinion research has helped us evaluate those requirements and may
help to bring "democratic practice more and more into harmony with the requirements and the assumptions—that is with the ideals—of democratic theory."
Schattschneider ("The Semisovereign People") argues for a restatement of
democratic theory to reflect the fact that "the role of the people in the political
system is determined largely by the conflict system, for it is conflict that involves
the people in politics and the nature of conflict determines the nature of public
involvement." Banfield ("In Defense of The American Party System") considers
the four main criticisms leveled against the American party system by those
who feel that the structure and operation of the parties do not accord with
the theory of democracy. He suggests that changes in the system would bring
undesirable results, that the American party system as it operates is entirely defensible, and that "there is . . . a danger that reform will chip away the foundations of power upon which the society rests."

Democratic Liberty
and Public Opiinon

BERNARD BERELSON

*Professor of library science and of social science at the University of Chi-
cago, Mr. Berelson is also vice-president of the Population Council and is
best known for his participation as co-author of a large number of voting
studies.*

The field of public opinion research has
had a number of intellectual godparents.
Psychologists have contributed their experience with attitude and intelligence
tests and measurements, as well as substantive concepts and propositions. Sociologists have provided experience with field
and community studies and ideas about
social structure and the place of opinion
within it. Market research has developed
new techniques and furnished a variety of
practical problems on which to try them.
The statisticians have worked on such
problems as sampling and scaling. But
my subject is the claim of political theory
to contribute to the character of public
opinion research.

Reprinted from *Public Opinion Quarterly*,
Vol. 16 (Fall 1952), 313–330, by permission of the publisher.

It would be too much to say that it has
played no role thus far. For a good many
years the political scientists have been
discussing the nature of public opinion
and the role it plays in the political
process. But somehow, in recent years, we
have tended to overlook the related facts
that there is a political content in what
we call public opinion; that there exists
a long and elegant intellectual tradition
(in the form of the political theory of
democracy) for dealing with opinion
problems; and that this theory provides a
helpful framework for the organization
and conduct of opinion studies. The
normative theory of political democracy
makes certain requirements of the citizen
and certain assumptions about his capacity to meet them. The tools of social
research have made it possible, for the

first time, to determine with reasonable precision and objectivity the extent to which the practice of politics by the citizens of a democratic state conforms to the requirements and the assumptions of the theory of democratic politics (insofar as it refers to decisions by the electorate). The closer collaboration of political theorists and opinion researchers should contribute new problems, new categories, and greater refinement and elaboration to both sides.

The theorists tell us how a democratic electorate is supposed to behave and we public opinion researchers claim to know something about how the democratic electorate in this country actually does behave. The task I have taken on myself is figuratively to confront the one with the other. Such an analysis should be useful not only in organizing the results of opinion studies in terms of an important body of theory, but also in revealing neglected and promising areas for further investigation. I bespeak the interest of both theorists and researchers in extending, refining, and, in general, improving this formulation. For even on the basis of my preliminary exploration, I am convinced that each side has a good deal to learn from the other and that joint work

on this common problem can be valuable both for social science and for public policy.

Such collaboration, like most cross-disciplinary work, is not easy, but it is necessary since neither side can solve the problem alone. In this connection, the deficiencies of the present formulation on the theoretical side will be particularly clear to the political theorist; I can only hope that the representation of theory, drawn as it is from a variety of sources, has not been caricatured, and that the theorists will themselves undertake the indicated corrections.

What, then, does democratic political theory assume or require of the democratic citizen, and to what extent are the assumptions or requirements realized? There are a number of ways of identifying and classifying the requirements, depending upon which political philosophers are given primary consideration. It has seemed most appropriate in this preliminary analysis to present a composite set of requirements, even though they may overlap at various points and thus not present a coherent system. While not all of them may be required in any single political theory of democracy, all of them are mentioned in one or another theory.

THE PREREQUISITES OF ELECTORATE DECISIONS

There appear to be two requirements in democratic theory which refer primarily to characteristics demanded of the electorate as it initially comes to make a political decision. These are the preconditions for electorate decisions.

The first is the possession of a suitable *personality structure:* within a range of variations, the electorate is required to possess the types of character which can operate effectively, if not efficiently, in a free society. Certain kinds of personality structures are not congenial to a democratic society, could not operate successfully within it, and would be destructive of democratic values. Others are more compatible with or even disposed toward the effective performance of the various roles which make up the democratic political system. Among the characteristics

required—and this is not intended as anything more than an illustrative list— are a capacity for involvement in situations remote from one's face-to-face experience; a capacity to accept moral responsibility for choices; a capacity to accept frustration in political affairs with equanimity; self-control and self-restraint as reins upon the gross operations of self-interest; a nice balance between submissiveness and assertiveness; a reasonable amount of freedom from anxiety so that political affairs can be attended to; a healthy and critical attitude toward authority; a capacity for fairly broad and comprehensive identifications; a fairly good measure of self-esteem; and a sense of potency.

The distribution of such personality characteristics in the population, let alone their relationship to political behavior, is not known. What is more or less known is only a beginning of the problem. We know, for example, that contrary to common belief the incidence of psychosis has not increased in this country over the past century (Goldhamer and Marshall); on this score, at least, we are not less capable than past generations of governing ourselves. We know that the authoritarian personality is associated with social prejudice and restrictive politics (the Berkeley study of Adorno, Frenkel-Brunswick, *et al.*); that neuroticism limits attention to political matters (Elmira study); that a wide discrepancy between aspiration and achievement leads some persons to overaggressive acts against the political environment and lowers their respect for political leaders (Bettelheim and Janowitz); that the "democratic character" is more flexible and adaptable than the authoritarian character (Lewin and Lippitt).

There is a great deal of work to be done on this problem; and it is here particularly that the psychologists can make an important contribution to the study of political behavior. The influence of character on political democracy has been perceived in general terms by a number of theorists, and some psychologists and sociologists have begun to work on the topic. The dependence of democratic processes upon the "democratic character" seems clear in general, but the nature of this relationship has been only slightly documented in the literature. Without doubt, a sympathetic and imaginative study of the literature of democratic theory will generate many important hypotheses for empirical investigation.

The second requirement is not only a prerequisite but also an outcome of electorate decisions. This is the factor of *interest and participation;*[1] the electorate is required to possess a certain degree of involvement in the process of political decision, to take an appropriate share of responsibility. Political democracy requires a fairly strong and fairly continuous level of interest from a minority, and from a larger body of the citizenry a moderate-to-mild and discontinuous interest but with a stable readiness to respond in critical political situations. Political disinterest or apathy is not permitted, or at least not approved.

Here the descriptive documentation provided by opinion studies is relatively good. The amount of political interest in the community, its fluctuations through time, its incidence among various population groups, its causes and its consequences—on all these topics we have reasonably systematic data. Less than one-third of the electorate is "really interested" in politics, and that group is by no means a cross-section of the total electorate. The more interested people are more likely to affect others and thus to exercise a greater influence upon the outcome of elections. The decreasing political interest in the population, viewed with alarm by some people who are distressed by the fact that a smaller proportion of eligible people vote now than did fifty years ago, is to some extent due to the increasing feeling people have that they are impotent to affect political matters in the face of the complexity and magnitude of the issues. Participation in the actual election is not only segmental but also partial; if everybody eligible to vote actually did vote, the distribution of support in recent national elections would have been measurably different. Finally, interest is not a simple unidimensional factor. A recent analysis identified three kinds of interest: spectator interest (regarding the campaign as a dramatic spectacle); citizen interest (deciding how to vote); and partisan interest (securing the election of one's own candidate). Of these, only the second is "pure" interest according to some theorists.

The major question raised by this requirement, both for political theory and for opinion research, is the fundamental one of its universality and intensity. People have always argued whether the vote is a duty or a privilege, and there have always been advocates of an unlimited

---

[1] Included here is acceptance of the political sphere as one of the legitimate elements of social life. In a democratic society the political sphere must not be widely viewed as unclean or degraded or corrupt. Opinion studies have produced some data on the image of politics and of politicians among the citizenry.

and continuous requirement of interest. As early as the Athenian democracy it was said that "we regard a man who takes no interest in public affairs not as a harmless but as a useless character." But is he really so useless to the operation of democracy? Some recent theorists and studies have suggested that a sizable group of less interested citizens is desirable as a "cushion" to absorb the intense action of highly motivated partisans. For the fact is that the highly interested are the most partisan and the least change-able. If everyone in the community were highly and continuously interested, the possibilities of compromise and of gradual solution of political problems might well be lessened to the point of danger. It is an historical axiom that democracy requires a middle class for its proper operation. Perhaps what it really requires is a body of moderately and discontinuously interested citizens within and across social classes, whose approval of or at least acquiescence in political policies must be secured.

THE COMPONENTS OF ELECTORATE DECISIONS

The political theory of democracy also makes requirements regarding the components of electorate decisions; that is, the content of the decision.

The first requirement of electorate decisions is the possession of *information and knowledge;* the electorate must be informed about the matters under consideration. Information refers to isolated facts and knowledge to general propositions; both of them provide reliable insight into the consequences of the decision. This is a requirement nearly everyone sets down for a democratic electorate; politicians and statesmen, adult educators, journalists, professors of political science—all of them pay deference to the need for "enlightened public opinion."

This is another factor on which opinion researchers have assembled a good deal of data. What do they show? One persistent conclusion is that the public is not particularly well informed about the specific issues of the day. A recent survey of the current status of American public opinion states that "tests of information invariably show at least twenty per cent of the public totally uninformed (and usually the figure is closer to forty per cent)." And at that, most of the studies have been based upon simple and isolated questions of fact (i.e., information) and only seldom, if at all, upon the historical and general propositions (i.e., knowledge) which underlie political decisions. Perhaps the proportion of the knowledgeable would be even lower than the proportion of the informed. At the same time, it must be recognized that there is a significant middle ground—a kind of vaguely perceived impression which reveals to the possessor certain relationships which are very "real" to him, which form "reasonable" bases for his decision, yet which cannot be explicitly articulated by him in any detail. An obvious example is the difference between the Republican and Democratic parties, a difference visible to many partisans of both.

Thus it often appears that people express opinions on issues when they seem to know very little about them. Lack of information may be a bar to the holding of an opinion in the minds of the theorists but it does not seem to be among the electorate (where, of course, it is not experienced as lack of information at all). In most campaigns, whether political or informational, the people best informed on the issue are the ones least likely to change their minds. Much of this represents attitudinal stability; some of it may represent rigidity.

Information and knowledge are required of the electorate on the assumption that they contribute to the wisdom of the decision; informed citizens make wiser decisions. In this country it is clear that the better-educated people are the best informed and most knowledgeable, yet it is also clear that other variables are involved in the development of wise decisions, e.g., flexibility of predispositions, a wide range of identifications, a low level of aggressiveness, etc. Finally, it appears from most studies that information and knowledge are sought and used more often as rationalization and reinforcer than as data to be used in making what might be called a free decision.

The requirement thus does not seem to be met in any direct way. But this is really an oversimplified statement of the requirement. How can an electorate be expected to be informed on the wide range of issues which confront the modern public? For example, the front page of *The New York Times* for one day alone recently contained stories on the following events, in each of which is embedded an issue on which the public might be expected to inform itself: price ceilings, the Korean war and the British position in it, the American defense build-up, Communist riots in France, the Berlin crisis, a new disarmament proposal, American military aid to France, official Soviet spies in this country, and the Mutual Security Aid Bill. Clearly there is too little time for simply getting the relevant information, let alone digesting it into a generalized system of political opinions. Actually the major decisions the ordinary citizen is called upon to make in a modern representative democracy involve basic simplifications which need not rest upon a wide range of information so long as they are based upon a certain amount of crucial information, reasonably interpreted. After all, the voter's effective choice is limited; he can vote Republican, he can vote Democratic, or he can refrain from voting, and becoming informed on a number of minor issues usually does not tip the scales against the weight of the few things that really matter—employment, social security, the cost of living, peace.

If the theoretical requirement is "full" information and knowledge, then democratic practice does not conform. But for some theorists the requirement is more differentiated than that. Representative government with large-scale political organization does not require that everyone be equally informed on everything all the time. To such a differentiated standard, actual practice may conform reasonably well. Opinion studies should not only document this requirement, but also refine their inquiries into the actual ways in which information and knowledge are held and used by the citizen in his vote decision. At the same time, theorists should differentiate and elaborate their conceptions of the intellectual requirements for a democratic citizenry.

The second component required of decisions is the possession of *principle;* the electorate is required to possess a body of stable political principle or moral standards, in contrast with fluctuating impulses or whims, to which topical questions can be referred for evaluation and decision.

Such principles are of two kinds. In the first place, there are the principles which refer to democratic procedures (as distinguished from the content of democratic decisions) and on them there must be consensus. Everyone, or nearly everyone, must agree on the rules of the political game and accept them in advance of the controversy so that they will obtain even in defeat. Among such principles are the rules that violence must not be involved in the making of electoral decisions; that the majority decision must be accepted as final in any particular instance, until legitimately appealed to a court, a legislative body, or the citizenry; that the citizen must have due respect for constituted authority; that the citizen must share respect with other parts of the community and thus be ready for political compromise. Few data on such questions have been collected in opinion studies, perhaps because their wide observance seems so obvious. It would be instructive to describe more precisely the citizenry's image of desirable and actual processes of democracy and to analyze the factors responsible for it.

The other kind of principle refers to the substantive bases of political decisions —the underlying moral or political ends in terms of which particular issues are determined at particular times. Just what they are for different parts of the population is difficult to say in the absence of more systematic research devoted to this purpose. At this time, however, it would seem at least likely that the *same* avowed principles underlie political positions at every point on the continuum from left to right. Full employment, a high standard of living, freedom, a better life for one's children, peace—these are the types of answers we have now, and we get them from persons of every political persuasion. Now this is not so empty as it sounds. Democratic theorists have pointed out what is often overlooked because too visible, namely, that an effective democracy must rest upon a body of political and moral consensus. If splits in the population are too sharp or too great, democratic processes cannot be maintained because of actual, threatened, or suspected conflict among partisans. In this circumstance, a seeming consensus which is accepted at its face value is far better than no consensus—and a seeming consensus is sometimes reflected in loyalty to the same symbols even though they carry different meanings. A sense of homogeneity is often an efficient substitute for the fact of homogeneity. Thus it is not an empty assertion to say that the role of substantive principles—like that of some information—is both to rationalize and to guide the choice simultaneously. Rationalization has a social function, too. What this means, then, is that the selection of means to reach agreed-upon ends is more likely to divide the electorate than the selection of the ends themselves.

At the same time, however, the principles must be applicable to current political life. Political decisions made today in the light of principles which support or oppose the major social reforms identified as the "New Deal" or the "welfare state" are relevant. But decisions made *simply* in conformity to an historical regional loyalty or to a primary group loyalty are of dubious relevance; and those made *only* in conformity to an ancestral loyalty or a religious loyalty are of no relevance at all. When theorists insist that public decisions in a democracy must be based upon principle and doctrine, they mean principle and doctrine which can confront and cope with the major problems of the age. Yet the studies show that a large proportion of the party vote today is by this test unprincipled.

If it is nothing more, then, the requirement of principle or doctrine means that the electorate must genuinely accept the procedures and rules involved in democratic processes, that it must at least share the symbols describing the substantive ends to which political action is directed and in terms of which it is justified, and that it must make political decisions on the basis of relevant standards. The first two requirements are met to a greater extent than the third.

THE PROCESS OF ELECTORATE DECISION

The third set of essentials in democratic theory refers to the process by which decisions are made. Here there seem to be three requirements.

The first of the requirement relates to the process of perception of which information and knowledge are the end products. This is the requirement of *accurate observation;* the electorate is required to perceive political realities clearly and objectively, with an absence or only a small amount of subjective distortion. It is difficult indeed to see life steadily and see it whole, and in politics clarity of perception is made doubly hard on the one hand by the predispositional strength which the citizen brings to the matter and, on the other, by the deliberate and in many cases inevitable ambiguity which the political leader brings there.

There is no need to labor this point. Walter Lippmann made a reputation for himself thirty years ago by elaborating the differences between the "world outside and the pictures in our heads." For the most part, he said, "we do not first see and then define, we define first and then see." Recent studies provide some documentation which refines this general observation. According to data from the Elmira study, not only is the citizen's image of the candidate and the campaign subject to the influence of preconception, but so is his view of group support for the candidates and even of the candidates' stand on political issues. Given just a minimum of ambiguity to work with— and that is usually available—people tend to think their candidate agrees with them, or at least they manage not to know where he stands on the particular issue when they stand on the other side. The stronger the party affiliation, the greater the misperception.

The consequences of such misperception are interesting to speculate about. It seems to decrease the tension within the individual since it enables him to bring his opinions into an internal consistency without disturbing his basic position. At the same time, it increases the internal solidarity of the parties and thus increases political tension within the community by seeming to sharpen the differences between the parties, particularly under the stress of a political campaign. Thus political perception is by no means simply a matter of concrete observation; it also involves protective coloration from a total position. And hence, that democratic theory which assumes clarity and objectivity of political perception must be qualified at the outset.

The second important requirement of democratic process is *communication and discussion;* the electorate is required to engage in discussion and communication on political affairs. Democratic decision-making requires free examination of political ideas, and this means discussion. Democratic citizens are supposed to listen to their political leaders arguing with one another, to listen to them when they speak directly to the electorate, to talk back to them, and to discuss among themselves the public issues of the day. According to many modern theorists, this requirement stands at the heart of the democratic process. "Above all, if it is to be true to its own peculiar nature, democracy must enlist the effective thought of the whole community in the operation of discussion."

Now here again, as in the case of information, public opinion researchers have assembled a sizable body of data, not only on the amount and kind of communication and discussion within the community but also on the conditions under which it takes place. The overall picture presented by the opinion studies looks something like this: There is a 20 per cent nucleus of people who are active and regular political discussants, another group of 25 per cent who engage in political discussion on occasion, another 25

per cent who are activated into discussion only by dramatic political events, and a residual group of 25 or 30 per cent who do not engage in political discussion at all. Furthermore, it is particular groups within the community that give most attention to politics: the better-educated, the men, the "joiners"—in short, those groups most subject to social pressure translated into expectations of how "our kind of people" should behave in this respect. And the people who read and listen to political content in the mass media also talk and listen to other people, and thus the concentration of political communication and discussion is carried one step further.

To complete the picture we need to ask two other questions which together bring into consideration another aspect of this requirement. Democratic citizens are required not simply to discuss politics, but to discuss political alternatives in a genuine effort to clarify and refine public policy. The first question is, "Who talks to whom?", and the answer is that people mostly discuss politics with other people like themselves—"like" in such characteristics as social position, occupation, and attitude. Mainly this goes on inside the family, but even outside it there is a clear tendency for political discussions to be carried out intra- rather than inter-social groups. The second question is, "What do they see and hear and talk about?" The broad answer is, "What pleases them"; i.e., what is congenial to their own point of view. People usually read and listen to their own side. In person-to-person discussion of politics, about a third or more of the talk centers upon topics not directly involving political preferences—for example, predictions of and arguments about who will win an election —and the remainder consists overwhelmingly of exchange of mutually agreeable remarks. What this all means—and this is clearly documented—is that the people who do the most reading and listening and talking are the people who change their minds the least. Lowell did not say it first but he said it well: "To a great extent, people hear what they want to hear and see what they want to see. They associate by preference with people who think as they do, enter freely into conversation with them, and avoid with others topics that are controversial, irritating or unpleasant. This is not less true of what they read. To most people, that which runs counter to their ideas is disagreeable, and sought only from a sense of duty."

In summary, then, genuine political discussion—-not acrimonious argumentation on the one hand or mutual admiration for right thinking on the other, but free and open discussion devoted to finding a solution to a problem through the clarification and modification of views —this is not marked by its magnitude. Perhaps it is naive to point this out once more; perhaps it is naive to require it in the first place. We cannot inquire here into what the requirement of discussion can really mean in a modern democracy; whether self-interested argument is improper, whether genuine discussion goes on a different level in the political process. But certainly democratic practice does not conform fully to the requirements of some theorists: "The person or party formulating political principles or policies in advance of discussion, and refusing to compromise under any circumstances; or settling such principles or policies before the process of discussion is completed and refusing to compromise further; renders discussion a farce in the first place, and in the second, limits its usefulness."

The third requirement under process is *rationality;* the electorate is required to exercise rational judgment in political decisions.

Philosophers and economists still talk professionally about "rational behavior," but sociologists never really used the concept, psychologists have given it up, and political scientists seem to be in process of doing so. The problem of giving the term a clear meaning acceptable to others is partly responsible for this state of affairs. The term, says a recent writer on rational conduct, "has enjoyed a long history which has bequeathed to it a legacy of ambiguity and confusion. . . . And man may be excused when he is puzzled by the question how he ought to use the word and in particular how he ought to use it in relation to human conduct and to politics."

The difficulty, of course, is not that there is no reasonably clear definition for the term but that there are several definitions describing several different kinds of rationality. And the conformity of democratic practice varies with each definition. Let us review a few major meanings and their relationship to democratic practice. In the first place, we may distinguish between the rational decision as outcome and the rational decision as process. In the former case we speak of rationality as equivalent to a "right" decision. This assumes that there is one right answer to every problem, and that the power of reason can arrive at truths of policy which should be evident to all— all, that is, except those ruled by prejudice or emotion. When this is not simply a euphemism for describing decisions of which we approve, it presumably refers to a decision taken in conformity with an estimate of desirable ends (it thus assumes a valid analysis of whose interest lies where) and also in conformity with a correct estimate of which means will achieve the given ends. If we leave determination of self-interest up to the individual involved, then virtually all electorate decisions are rational by this definition; if we leave it up to the "objective observer" then the proportion will vary arbitrarily with his estimate of the present situation and the future. Even in philosophy, this meaning appears to be so ambiguous that it is difficult to see how we can design empirical research to test the extent of its observance by the electorate.

If we take rationality as referring to the process of decision—a more likely definition—then various possibilities are available. One meaning requires a certain independence of the rational process from the influence of predispositions broadly defined. Here rationality becomes the "free decision"—free from coercive imposition; free from blinding institutional loyalties; free from personal position (such as class or race); free from passions and impulses; free, in short, from any distorting or distracting pressures which prevent clear observation and calm, sober reflection. Here the term refers to logical, syllogistic ratiocination. But this seems to be an impractical, untenable, undesirable, and quite unreasonable definition; it takes the content heart out of politics and leaves the voter with no real basis on which to evaluate political proposals. By this standard, at least in its extreme version, there are almost no rational voters. As a social philosopher says, "individuals who on their own initiative form or change their fundamental beliefs through genuine critical reflection are so rare that they may be classed as abnormal."

A second meaning of rationality is close to, if not identical with, our requirement of information and knowledge: the voter should be aware of the correct state of public affairs at the present and of the "reasonable" consequences of alternative proposals for action. By this definition someone who made up his political mind on the basis of ends for which there are no present means of attainment would be making a non-rational decision, and so would the person whose estimates of the present situation or of the future were wrong. Also by this meaning the voter should be capable of indicating some relevant grounds for his decision, and most voters can cite such grounds. Here we meet the difficult question of rationalization, as against rationality, but we can suggest a partial answer. Rationality is limited by the individual's incapacity to deal with the real world in all its complexity, so it must allow for the legitimacy of dealing with simplified models of reality. In politics, the voters may "really" decide on the basis of one or two issues which are dominant for him (for example, peace or the New Deal) and use other issues as reinforcing rationalizations (for example, the military background of a candidate or corruption in the Federal administration).

A third definition requires the presence of convincibility or open-mindedness in consideration of political issues. This does not require the citizen to change his mind but only to be genuinely open to a change of mind. Here the time involved seems crucial. If this means, for example, that the citizen should be open-minded between June and November of an election year, then probably fewer than half the electorate is rational, and very few indeed in the South and parts of New England. If it includes the four years of a

presidential administration or the "natural history" of a major political issue, from birth in controversy to death in near-unanimity, then the figure would become quite higher. It is hard for the researcher to be more specific because of the difficulty of determining just when "genuine consideration," as against rationalization, goes on.

Still another meaning of rationality as process requires that the decision be made in a state of low psychic tension; that is, that the decision not be an emotional one but be marked by a certain amount of detachment and freedom from passion. This poses a nice democratic dilemma; the people most rational by this definition are the people least interested in the political process and least involved in its outcome. The more interested people are the more emotional, in this sense, and the least detached; they are the ones who ascribe important consequences to the outcome of the decision and thus find enough psychic energy to be active about the matter. Here the rational voter is the independent voter, that is, the one without sufficient interest or investment in the election to get excited about it.

Still other meanings are available. There is the meaning in which rationality refers to the presence of deliberately directed behavior to consciously formulated purposes. Here again, almost all voters could qualify. There is the meaning in which rationality refers to a choice of behavior that is optimal in some sense, and this definition can be readily satisfied on the grounds of a subjective optimum if nothing more. There is the meaning in which a rational decision is a self-consistent decision. There are undoubtedly other meanings.

If it is not easy to say what is meant by a rational decision, it is somewhat easier to say what is not meant by it. A rational decision is not a capricious decision, or an impulsive one, or an unprincipled one, or a decision guided by custom or habit or tradition or sentiment alone. But the central problem is to relate the demand of rationality to the analysis of decision-making in terms of such sociopsychological concepts as the reference group; that is, to see the "rational decision" as imbedded in a social context which limits it at the same time that it gives it political meaning. While the types of rationality are not easy to define and while they are certainly never present in a pure or extreme form, they can be isolated empirically, clarified, and investigated as to their frequency, their functions, and their preconditions.

THE OUTCOME OF ELECTORATE DECISIONS

Finally, there is one basic requirement which might be included under the need for principle but which seems to deserve independent treatment in view of its central importance with reference to the outcome of the decision. This is the requirement of *community interest;* the electorate is supposed to come to political decisions on consideration of the common good rather than, or in addition to, self-interest.

In several formulations of democratic theory, the electorate is required to devote thought to what is good for the community as a whole instead of relying exclusively upon calculation of what is good for oneself or one's own group. The classical formulation comes from John Stuart Mill: "In any political election . . . the voter is under an absolute moral obligation to consider the interests of the public, not his private advantage, and give his vote, to the best of his judgment, exactly as he would be bound to do if he were the sole voter, and the election depended upon him alone."

Now here again the problem of definition is a central one. How is the researcher to distinguish between honest conclusion and forced rationalization, as in the slogan, "What's good for me is good for the country"? How distinguish the "immediate and apparent interest" from the "ultimate and real interest"? Does self-interest refer only to the criterion of direct self-gain or to that of benefit to one's group or class, and over what period of time? Does community interest refer to agreement on procedures, or to an outside criterion (and if so, what), or to the residual decision after the various self-interests have balanced themselves out, or to genuine concern for other groups, or to restraint upon self-interest, or to deviation from the predominant vote of one's group? The more one looks into the matter, the more it appears that one man's self-interest is another man's community interest, and that many people sincerely identify the one with the other. Nor have the theorists overlooked this. "Men come easily to believe that arrangements agreeable to themselves are beneficial to others," said Dicey. "A man's interest gives a bias to his judgment far oftener than it corrupts his heart." And from Schumpeter: "To different individuals and groups the common good is bound to mean different things. This fact, hidden from the utilitarian by the narrowness of his outlook on the world of human valuations, will introduce rifts on questions of principle which cannot be reconciled by rational argument."

In a current study of opinion formation (the Elmira study), we concluded that it is more satisfactory to analyze this question in terms of the forces making for political cleavage and political consensus within the community. The health of a democratic order depends on achieving a nice balance between them: enough cleavage to stimulate debate and action, enough consensus to hold the society together even under strain. Political parties in a democracy should disagree—but not too much, too sharply, nor too fundamentally. The evidences of cleavage are clear to everyone. Cleavage along class and religious and regional lines in addition to direct attitudinal differences on basis issues of foreign and domestic policy—these are so familiar as to require no elaboration. At the same time there are important evidences of consensus, of political cohesion, which deserve more attention than they usually get. In the first place, there is the basic fact that group memberships and identifications overlap political choices; sizable political minorities are found in various social groups and this provides a kind of glue to hold the community together. In addition, even at the height of a presidential campaign there are sizable attitudinal minorities within each party and each social group on political issues, and thus sizable attitudinal agreements across party and group lines. Such overlappings link various groups together and prevent their further estrangement. All of this means that democratic politics in this country is happily not total politics—a situation where politics is the single or central selector and rejector, where other social differences are drawn on top of political lines. Cross-pressures in political allegiances, based upon a pluralistic sys-tem of values, are thus highly important to the society.

So the question of self and community interest may best be seen as the question of cleavage and consensus. The multiplicity and the heterogeneity of identifications and associations in the great society develop an overlapping, pluralistic social organization which both sharpens and softens the impact and the consequences of political activity.

CONCLUSION

The political theory of democracy, then, requires that the electorate possess appropriate personality structures, that it be interested and participate in public affairs, that it be informed, that it be principled, that it correctly perceive political realities, that it engage in discussion, that it judge rationally, and that it consider the community interest.

Now this combination of requirements sets a high—an ideal—standard for the political process. And since this is a composite list, from a variety of sources, it is not necessarily a matter for disillusionment or even disappointment that the democratic electorate does not conform to every requirement in the full degree. There is always an appropriate observation from Lord Bryce:

Orthodox political theory assumes that every citizen has, or ought to have, thought out for himself certain opinions, for example, ought to have a definite view, defensible by arguments, of what the country needs, what principles ought to be applied in governing it, of the men to whose hands the government ought to be entrusted. There are persons who talk, though certainly very few who act, as if they believed this theory, which may be compared to the theory of some ultra-Protestants that every good Christian has or ought to have, by the strength of his own reason, worked out for himself from the Bible a system of theology.

Opinion studies in recent years have done much to fill in the picture of what actually happens in democratic decision-making. As is evident even from this brief survey, they have done so in three ways: first, by documenting the theoretical assumptions with facts about actual political behavior; second, by clarifying the concepts and assumptions of democratic theory, if in no other way simply by insisting upon researchable formulations; and third, by differentiating and reformulating the general theoretical propositions in more exact terms. Further systematic exploration of this subject within a sharper, more valid, and more sophisticated framework of political theory should make a rich contribution to each side. The difficulties of collaboration between political theorists on the one hand and opinion researchers on the other must not be allowed to stand in the way of joint work, for the theorists can provide a systematic statement in terms of which public opinion studies can be meaningfully organized, and the empirical researchers can document the theoretical requirements. The theorists can suggest new concepts and hypotheses to the researcher, and the researcher can force the theorists to sharpen and differentiate —yes, and quantify—their formulations.

Of course there are problems but they should be negotiated or overcome. For example, the theorists tend to use descriptive categories (e.g., rationality) and the researchers prefer predictive categories (e.g., group memberships) in "explaining" political preferences. Hard and joint thinking on such problems should bring returns.

The investigation of the realities of democratic processes at the level of the electorate is a useful service and it should be carried forward. Opinion studies can help a democracy not only to know itself in a topical and immediate way but also to evaluate its achievement and its progress in more general terms. In this framework, the study of public opinion can make a telling contribution in the basic, continuous struggle to bring democratic practice more and more into harmony with the requirements and the assumptions—that is, with the ideals—of democratic theory.

The Semisovereign People

E. E. SCHATTSCHNEIDER

Emeritus professor of government at Wesleyan University, and a leading contributor to the literature of American political parties, E. E. Schattschneider is best known for two works, Party Government *and* The Semi-sovereign People.

The role of the people in the political system is determined largely by the conflict system, for it is conflict that involves the people in politics and the nature of conflict determines the nature of the public involvement.

The idea that the people are involved in politics by the contagion of conflict does not resemble the classical definition of democracy as "government by the people." The difference between the idea of popular "involvement" in conflict and the idea that people acutally "govern" is great enough to invite a re-examination of the classical theory of democracy. Does the consideration of the place of conflict in a free political system open up the way for a redefinition of democracy in modern terms?

Whether we know it or not all speculation about American politics rests on some image of democracy. The literature on the subject has been so permeated by democratic and pseudodemocratic ideas that it is impossible to understand what we are talking about unless we isolate and identify these ideas and try to distinguish between the democratic and antidemocratic elements in them.

The devotion of the American public to the democratic ideal is so overwhelming that we test everything by it. It is surprising to find, therefore, that political philosophers have had remarkable difficulty in defining the word *democracy*. As a matter of fact, the failure to produce a good working definition of democracy is responsible for a great part of the confusion in the literature of politics. An examination of the problem might be worth while, therefore.

The classical definition of democracy as government by the people is predemocratic in its origins, based on notions about democracy developed by philosophers who never had an opportunity to see an operating democratic system. Predemocratic theorists assumed that the people would take over the conduct of public affairs in a democracy and administer the government to their own advantage as simply as landowners administer their property for their own profit. Under the historical circumstances this oversimplification is easy to understand. There is less excuse for the failure of modern scholars to re-examine the traditional definition critically in the light of modern experience.[1]

One consequence of our reliance on old

[1] What the Greek philosophers had to say about Athens, a city-state having a population of thirty thousand, three-fourths of whom were slaves, has very little to do with democracy in a nation of 175 million.

definitions is that the modern American does not look at democracy before he defines it; he defines it first and then is confused by what he sees. In spite of the fact that the ancients made some astonishing miscalculations about democracy as an operating system, their authority is so great that the traditional definition is perpetuated in the textbooks and governs our thinking in the entire area.

The confusion of ideas about democracy looks like a job for the political scientists. What we need is a modern definition of democracy explaining the facts of life of the operating political system, a definition that distinguishes between the democratic and antidemocratic elements in the developing contemporary political situation. The great deficiency of American democracy is intellectual, the lack of a good, usable definition. A good definition might shed a flood of light on modern politics; it might clarify a thousand muddy concepts and might help us to understand where we are going and what we want. It might even help us get rid of the impossible imperatives that haunt the literature of the subject and give everyone a sense of guilt. We need to reexamine the chasm between theory and practice because it is at least as likely that the ideal is wrong as it is that the reality is bad. Certainly our chances of getting democracy and keeping it would be better if we made up our minds about what it is.[2]

Perhaps as good a point as any at which to test our ideas about democracy is in the general area of public opinion research. This research is based on the assumption that public opinion plays a great role in a democracy. Lurking in the background is the notion that the people actually do govern.

What image of democracy leads us to assign a central place in political theory

to public opinion? The question is: Can we define the role of public opinion in a democracy before we make up our minds about what democracy is? Before we invest the energies of a generation of political scientists in public opinion research, would it not be wise to make an attempt to *test* the validity of the underlying propositions about the relations of public opinion to what is happening in the world about us?[3]

It requires no research to demonstrate that it is difficult to relate the copybook maxims about democracy to the operating political system. If we start with the common definition of democracy (as government by the people), it is hard to avoid some extremely pessimistic conclusions about the feasibility of democracy in the modern world, for it is impossible to reconcile traditional concepts of what ought to happen in a democracy with the fact that an amazingly large number of people do not seem to know very much about what is going on. The significance of this kind of popular ignorance depends on what we think democracy is.

Research might have enlightened us much more than it has if the researchers had taken the time to formulate an operating democratic theory. It is hard to see how anyone can formulate a satisfactory theory of public opinion without meeting this problem head on. What is the function of the public in a modern democracy? What does the public have to know? The failure to understand how the public intervenes in the political process, what the public can be expected to do, what it cannot do, how questions get referred to the public has led to quantities of remarkably pointless speculation. How do we find out what we are looking for?

[2] There have been many attempts to define democracy. This is not the place to make a compilation of these definitions. The attack here is on the most pervasive and widely accepted common definition of democracy as "government by the people." At the same time that we have defined democracy as something unattainable, we have made democracy one of the most emotion-charged words in our civilization. This is the impossible imperative which threatens to entrap all of us.

[3] See Bernard Berelson, "Democratic Theory and Public Opinion," pp. 107 ff., in Eulau, Eldersveld and Janowitz, *Political Behavior*, Free Press, Glencoe, Illinois, 1956, for a good statement of what seems to be the concept of democracy prevailing among students of public opinion; it illustrates very well how much students of public opinion have been influenced by the common definition of democracy.

See also Burdick's criticism of Berelson's ideas in Burdick and Brodbeck, *American Voting Behavior*, Free Press, 1959, pp. 136 ff.

The reader can make a test of the basic proposition for himself by spending some time examining the massive compilation of polls in *Public Opinion, 1935–1946* made by Hadley Cantril and Mildred Strunk.[4] While this compilation, twelve hundred pages of it, is no longer fully representative of the work done by scholars today, it has one incomparable advantage to students of politics—*the polls were taken at least thirteen years ago.* After a lapse of several years we are in a position to ask: How nearly do the data turned up in these polls correspond with what actually happened? For some reason when one now looks at this body of data, it seems to lack reality. If the assumption is that public opinion is important because it determines public policy, a comparison of the polls and the history of the decade raises a flood of doubts. How much difference did the opinions measured in these polls actually make?

It is necessary only to look at the polls on birth control, the budget, capital punishment, divorce, employee representation schemes, the excess profits tax, free speech, income limitation, industrial and labor relations, small business, socialized medicine, race relations, government ownership of public utilities, neutrality and the territorial expansion of the United States to realize that public opinion about specific issues does not necessarily govern the course of public policy.

The point of this discussion is that political research is never better than the theory of politics on which it is based. The theory of the polls is essentially simplistic, based on a tremendously exaggerated notion of the immediacy and urgency of the connection of public opinion and events. The result is that sometimes we seem to be interviewing the fish in the sea to find out what the birds in the heavens are doing.

What would it be worth to students of politics if by some miracle they could know precisely what everybody in the country was thinking at twelve noon last Friday? Probably very little. We are in trouble because we are confused about what is supposed to happen in a democracy.

[4] Princeton University Press, 1951.

The image implicit in the schoolbook definition of democracy is that of a mass of people who think about politics the way a United States senator might think about it. In this image public opinion has great consequences; what the people think has a compulsive impact on what the government does. It follows that the scholar ought to begin his studies at the grass roots.

The great difficulty here is theoretical, not technical; it concerns the assumptions made about the role of the people in a democracy. The unstated premise in a multitude of polls is that the people really do decide what the government does on something like a day-to-day basis. This assumption implies a definition of democracy. How can we get hold of the subject if we do not deal with this definition?

A hundred million voters have a staggering number of opinions about an incredible number of subjects. Under what circumstances do these opinions become important?

The problem is one of definition. What is the role of the public in a democracy? What have we a right to expect of the public? Is it possible to reformulate the question in terms of democratic concepts other than the primitive notions derived from the ancients?

Apparently the attitude of the public is far more permissive than the hortatory, high-pressure, special-interest school of theorists thinks it ought to be. The tendency of the literature of politics is to place a tremendous premium on the role of the interested and to treat indifference as a mortal sin, but the reluctance of the public to press its opinions on the government concerning a great multitude of issues is really not as bad a thing as we may have been led to think; it is a mark of reasonableness and common sense. The public is far too sensible to attempt to play the preposterous role assigned to it by the theorists. We have tended to undervalue this attitude because we have labored under an illusion about democracy.

We become cynical about democracy because the public does not act the way the simplistic definition of democracy says that it should act, or we try to whip the public into doing things it does not want to do, is unable to do and has too much sense to do. The crisis here is not a crisis in democracy but a crisis in theory.

The importance of democratic theory is demonstrated by the way in which students of public opinion have neglected what is perhaps their most important discovery, the discovery of the "don't knows," the very large category of people who are willing to confess that they do not seem to know very much about what is going on in the government. The tendency has been to ignore this discovery because it does not fit very conveniently into our preconceptions about democracy and the democratic process. The "don't knows" are treated as unfortunate exceptions to the democratic proposition about whom we prefer not to think. This is remarkable because ignorance is an ancient condition of the human race. The significance of this widespread ignorance about public affairs depends largely on what we think democracy is.

One implication of public opinion studies ought to be resisted by all friends of freedom and democracy; the implication that democracy is a failure because the people are too ignorant to answer intelligently all the questions asked by the pollsters. This is a professorial invention for imposing professorial standards on the political system and deserves to be treated with extreme suspicion. Only a pedagogue would suppose that the people must pass some kind of examination to qualify for participation in a democracy. Who, after all, are these self-appointed censors who assume that they are in a position to flunk the whole human race? Their attitude would be less presumptuous if they could come up with a list of things that people must know. Who can say what the man on the street must know about public affairs? The whole theory of knowledge underlying these assumptions is pedantic. Democracy was made for the people, not the people for democracy. Democracy is something for ordinary people, a political system designed to be sensitive to the needs of ordinary people regardless of whether or not the pedants approve of them.

It is an outrage to attribute the failures of American democracy to the ignorance and stupidity of the masses. The most disastrous shortcomings of the system have been those of the intellectuals whose concepts of democracy have been amazingly rigid and uninventive. The failure of the intellectuals is dangerous because it creates confusion in high places. Unless the intellectuals can produce a better theory of politics than they have, it is possible that we shall abolish democracy before we have found out what it is!

The intellectuals have done very little to get us out of the theoretical trap created by the disparity between the demands made on the public by the common definition of democracy and the capacity of the public to meet these demands.[5] The embarrassment results from the reluctance of intellectuals to develop a definition that describes what really happens in a democracy.

The whole mass of illusions discussed in the foregoing paragraph arises from a confusion of ideas about what people need to know, what the role of the public in a democracy is, how the public functions in a democracy.

If we assume that the people "govern," it follows that the governing majority ought to know more than any majority has ever known or ever could know. This is the *reductio ad absurdum* of democratic theory. We cannot get out of the dilemma by (1) making a great effort to educate everyone to the point where they know enough to make these decisions nor (2) by restricting participation to the people who do know all about these matters. The first is impossible. The second is absurd because *no one* knows enough to govern by this standard. The trouble is that we have defined democracy in

[5] So highly respected a modern theorist as Francis W. Coker deals with this subject in one short paragraph and disposes of the matter by quoting Bryce's definition of democracy as "majority rule." *Recent Political Thought*, New York, 1934, p. 291.

Among the textbook writers Carr, Morrison, Bernstein and Snyder, *American Democracy in Theory and Practice*, New York, 1951, p. 24, say, "As a political system it is the mechanism through which the people govern themselves." Examples could be multiplied indefinitely. The trouble with these definitions is that they leave us deep in a bottomless pit.

such a way that we are in danger of putting ourselves out of business.

There is no escape from the problem of ignorance, because *nobody knows enough to run the government*. Presidents, senators, governors, judges, professors, doctors of philosophy, editors and the like are only a little **less ignorant** than the rest of us. Even **an expert is a** person who chooses to be ignorant about many things so that he may know all about one.

The whole theory of knowledge underlying these concepts of democracy is false—it proves too much. It proves not only that democracy is impossible; it proves equally that life itself is impossible. Everybody has to accommodate himself to the fact that he deals daily with an incredible number of matters about which he knows very little. This is true of all aspects of life, not merely of politics.

The compulsion to know everything is the road to insanity.

People are able to survive in the modern world by learning to distinguish between what they must know and what they do not need to know. We get a clue to the solution of the problem when we begin to realize that it is not necessary to be an automotive engineer to buy an automobile or to be an obstetrician in order to have a baby. Our survival depends on our ability to judge things by their results and our ability to establish relations of confidence and responsibility so that we can take advantage of what other people know. We could not live in modern society if we did not place confidence daily in a thousand ways in pharmacists, surgeons, pilots, bank clerks, engineers, plumbers, technicians, lawyers, civil servants, accountants, courts, telephone operators, craftsmen and a host of others. We pass judgment on the most complex mechanisms on the basis of the *results* they produce. Economists, trying to explain the operation of the economy, use a political expression when they speak of the "sovereignty of the consumer," precisely because they realize that it is not necessary to know how to *make* a television set in order to buy one intelligently. Democracy is like nearly everything else we do; it is a form of collaboration of ignorant people and experts.

Primitive democratic theorists never tire of telling us that democracy was designed to work in New England town meetings, not in a modern national state. The analysis is fatuous. We might as well attempt to return to a handicraft economy. The crisis is a purely theoretical one because operating democratic political systems have in fact already accomplished what is theoretically impossible and are doing it every day. It is only the theory that has broken down. The problem of modern democracy is the problem of learning to live in the modern world.

We can find our way through the maze if we learn to distinguish between different kinds of knowledge, between what amateurs know and what professionals know, between what generalists know and what specialists know. The problem is not how 180 million Aristotles can run a democracy, but how we can organize a political community of 180 million ordinary people so that it remains sensitive to their needs. This is a problem of *leadership, organization, alternatives and systems of responsibility and confidence*. The emphasis is on the role of leadership and organization in a democracy, not on the spontaneous generation of something at the grass roots. If we approach the problem from this side, it does not look impossible. The achievements of the American regime are tremendous, but they have been brought about in spite of the theoretical illusions under which we have labored.

The people are involved in public affairs by the conflict system. Conflicts open up questions for public intervention. Out of conflict the alternatives of public policy arise. Conflict is the occasion for political organization and leadership. In a free political system it is difficult to avoid public involvement in conflict; the ordinary, regular operations of the government give rise to controversy, and controversy is catching.

The beginning of wisdom in democratic theory is to distinguish between the things the people can do and the things the people cannot do. The worst possible disservice that can be done to the democratic cause is to attribute to the people a mystical, magical omnipotence which takes no cognizance of what very large numbers of people cannot do by the sheer weight of numbers. At this point the common definition of democracy has invited us to make fools of ourselves.

What 180 million people can do spontaneously, on their own initiative, is not much more than a locomotive can do without rails. The public is like a very rich man who is unable to supervise closely all of his enterprise. His problem is to learn how to compel his agents to define his options.

What we are saying is that conflict, competition, leadership, and organization are the essence of democratic politics. Inherent in the operations of a democracy are special conditions which permit large numbers of people to function.

The problem is how to organize the political system so as to make the best possible use of the power of the public in view of its limitations. A popular decision bringing into focus the force of public support requires a tremendous effort to define the alternatives, to organize the discussion and mobilize opinion. The government and the political organizations are in the business of manufacturing this kind of alternatives.

What has been said here has not been said to belittle the power of the people but to shed some light on what it is. The power of the people is not made less by the fact that it cannot be used for trivial matters. The whole world can be run on the basis of a remarkably small number of decisions. The power of the people in a democracy depends on the *importance* of the decisions made by the electorate, not on the *number* of decisions they make. Since the adoption of the Constitution the party in power has been turned out by the opposition party fourteen times, and in about six of these instances the consequences have been so great that we could not understand American history without taking account of them.

The most important thing about any democratic regime is the *way* in which it *uses* and exploits popular sovereignty, what questions it refers to the public for decision or guidance, how it refers them to the public, how the alternatives are defined and how it respects the limitations of the public. A good democratic system protects the public against the demand that it do impossible things. The unforgivable sin of democratic politics is to dissipate the power of the public by putting it to trivial uses. What we need is a movement for the conservation of the political resources of the American people.

Above everything, *the people are powerless if the political enterprise is not competitive.* It is the competition of political organizations that provides the people with the opportunity to make a choice. Without this opportunity popular sovereignty amounts to nothing.

The common definition of democracy may be harmless if it is properly understood, but the fact is that it is very commonly misunderstood. It would be more imaginative to say that some things we now are actually doing are democratic even though they do not fit the traditional definition. Definitions of democracy since the time of Aristotle have been made on the assumption that the "many" in a democracy do the same things that the "one" does in a monarchy and the "few" do in an aristocracy. But obviously the shift from the "one" to the "many" is more than a change in the number of people participating in power but *a change in the way the power is exercised.* The 180 million cannot do what a single ruler can do. This is not because the 180 million are stupid or ignorant but because it is physically impossible for 180 million to act the way one acts. In the interests of clarity and the survival of the political system we need a definition of democracy that recognizes the limitations that nature imposes on large numbers.

A working definition must capitalize on the limitations of the people as well as their powers. We do this when we say that liberty and leadership are the greatest of democratic concepts. *Democracy is a competitive political system in which competing leaders and organizations define the alternatives of public policy in such a way that the public can participate in the decision-making process.* The initiative in this political system is to be found largely in the government or in the opposition. The people profit by this system, but they cannot, by themselves, do the work of the system. We have already had a great deal of experience with this kind of system. Is it not about time that we begin to recognize its democratic implications?

Conflict, competition, organization, leadership and responsibility are the ingredients of a working definition of democracy. Democracy is a political system in which the people have a choice among the alternatives created by competing political organizations and leaders. The advantage of this definition over the traditional definition is that it is *opera-* *tional*, it describes something that actually happens. It describes something feasible. It does not make impossible demands on the public. Moreover, it describes a going democratic concern whose achievements are tremendous.

The involvement of the public in politics is a natural outgrowth of the kind of conflict that almost inevitably arises in a free society. The exploitation of this situation by responsible political leaders and organizations is the essence of democracy; the socialization of conflict is the essential democratic process.

In Defense of the American Party System

EDWARD C. BANFIELD

Henry Lee Shattuck professor of urban government at Harvard University, Edward C. Banfield is also a member of the Joint Center for Urban Studies of MIT and Harvard. In addition to his writing in urban studies he has also contributed to the literature on underdeveloped areas.

The American party system has been criticized on four main grounds: (1) The parties do not offer the electorate a choice in terms of fundamental principles; their platforms are very similar and mean next to nothing; (2) they cannot discipline those whom they elect, and therefore they cannot carry their platforms into effect; (3) they are held together and motivated less by political principle than by desire for personal, often material, gain, and by sectional and ethnic loyalties; consequently party politics is personal and parochial; and (4) their structure is such that they cannot correctly represent the opinion of the electorate; in much of the country there is in effect only one party, and everywhere large contributors and special interests exercise undue influence within the party.[1]

Reprinted from *Political Parties, U. S. A.,* ed. Robert A. Goldwin (Chicago: Rand McNally, 1964). Copyright © 1961, 1964 by the Public Affairs Conference Center, The University of Chicago. All Rights Reserved.

These criticisms may be summarized by saying that the structure and operation of the parties do not accord with the theory of democracy or, more precisely, with that theory of it which says

[1] These criticisms are made, for example, by the French political scientist, Maurice Duverger, in *Political Parties* (New York: Wiley, 1954). For similar criticisms by Americans, see especially Committee on Political Parties of the American Political Science Association, *Toward a More Responsible Two-Party System* (New York: Rinehart, 1950), and E. E. Schattschneider, *Party Government* (New York: Farrar & Rinehart, 1942). Criticisms of American parties are summarized and analyzed in Austin Ranney, *The Doctrine of Responsible Party Government* (Urbana: University of Illinois Press, 1954). Defenses of the American party system include A. Lawrence Lowell, *Essays on Government* (Boston: Houghton Mifflin, 1889), Chs. I, II; Arthur N. Holcombe, *The Political Parties of Today* (New York: Harper, 1925); and *Our More Perfect Union* (Cambridge: Harvard University Press, 1950); Pendleton Herring, *The Politics of Democracy* (New York: Norton, 1940); and Herbert Agar, *The Price of Union* (Boston: Houghton Mifflin, 1950).

that everyone should have a vote, that every vote should be given exactly the same weight, and that the majority should rule.

"It is a serious matter," says Maurice Duverger, a French political scientist who considers American party organization "archaic" and "undemocratic," "that the greatest nation in the world, which is assuming responsibilities on a world-wide scale, should be based on a party system entirely directed towards very narrow local horizons."[2] He and other ciritics of the American party system do not, however, base their criticisms on the performance of the American government. They are concerned about procedures, not results. They ask whether the structure and operation of the parties is consistent with the logic of democracy, not whether the party system produces— and maintains—a good society, meaning, among other things, one in which desirable human types flourish, the rights of individuals are respected, and matters affecting the common good are decided, as nearly as possible, by reasonable discussion.[3]

If they were to evaluate the party system on the basis of results, they would have to conclude that on the whole it is a good one. It has played an important part (no one can say how important, of course, for innumerable causal forces have been at work along with it; in the production of a society which, despite all its faults, is as near to being a good one as any and nearer by far than most; it has provided governments which, by

the standards appropriate to apply to governments, have been humane and, in some crises, bold and enterprising; it has done relatively little to impede economic growth and in some ways has facilitated it; except for the Civil War, when it was, as Henry Jones Ford said, "the last bond of union to give way,"[4] it has tended to check violence, moderate conflict, and narrow the cleavages within the society; it has never produced, or very seriously threatened to produce, either mob rule or tyranny, and it has shown a marvelous ability to adapt to changing circumstances.

Not only has the American party system produced good results, it has produced better ones than have been produced almost anywhere else by other systems. Anyone who reflects on recent history must be struck by the following paradox: those party systems that have been most democratic in structure and procedure have proved least able to maintain democracy; those that have been most undemocratic in structure and procedure—conspicuously those of the United States and Britain—have proved to be the bulwarks of democracy and of civilization.

This paper explores this paradox. It maintains that there is an inherent antagonism between "democracy of procedure" and "production of, and maintenance of, a good society"; that some defects of procedure are indispensable conditions of success from the standpoint of results, and that what the critics call the "archaic" character of the American party system is a very small price to pay for government that can be relied upon to balance satisfactorily the several conflicting ends that must be served.

[2] Op. cit., p. 53.
[3] The report of the Committee on Parties of the American Political Science Association, cited above, discusses the "effectiveness" of parties entirely in terms of procedure. Duverger does the same.

[4] Henry Jones Ford, The Rise and Growth of American Politics (New York: Macmillan, 1900), p. 303.

DIFFICULTIES IN PLANNING CHANGE

Before entering into these matters, it may be well to remind the reader how difficult is the problem of planning social change.

Social relationships constitute systems: they are mutually related in such a manner that a change in one tends to produce

changes in all of the others. If we change the party system in one respect, even a seemingly trivial one, we are likely to set in motion a succession of changes which will not come to an end until the whole system has been changed. The party system, moreover, is an element of a larger political system and of a social system. A small change in the structure or operation of parties may have important consequences for, say, the family, religion, or the business firm.

The changes that we intend when making a reform, if they occur at all, are always accompanied by others that we do not intend. These others may occur at points in the system far removed from the one where the change was initiated and be apparently unrelated to it. Commonly changes produced indirectly and unintentionally turn out to be much more important than the ones that were sought. This is a fact that is seldom fully taken into account. Those who support a particular reform are often indifferent to its consequences for values that they either do not share or consider subordinate. Even those who feel obliged to take a wide range of values into account do not usually try very hard to anticipate the indirect consequences of reforms—often for a very good reason: the complexity of the social system makes the attempt implausible. Usually we take it on faith that the consequences we get by intention justify the risk we take of incurring others that we do not intend or want. Since these others are seldom recognized as consequences of our action at all (they either go unnoticed or seem to have "just happened"), the basis of our faith is not called into question.

No doubt it is a great help to the practical reformer to have tunnel vision. But those who are concerned with the welfare of society as a whole must take the widest perspective possible. They must try to identify all of the consequences that will follow from a reform—the unintended ones no less than the intended, the remote, contingent, and imponderable no less than the immediate, certain, the specifiable. And they must evaluate all of these consequences in the light of a comprehensive system of values.

Those who devise "improvements" to a social system can rarely hope to attain all of their ends; usually they must be prepared to sacrifice some of them to achieve other. This is so because resources are usually limited and also because there are often incompatibilities among ends such that a gain in terms of some neces-

sarily involves a loss in terms of others. The reformer must therefore economize. He must be able to assign priorities to all ends in such a way that he can tell how much of each to sacrifice for how much of others, on various assumptions as to "supply."

The critics of the party system tend to value democratic procedure for its own sake, that is, apart from the results it produces. There is no reason why they should not do so. But they are in error when they do not recognize that other values of equal or greater importance are often in conflict with democratic procedure, and that when they are, some sacrifice of it is essential in order to serve the other values adequately. If they faced up to the necessity of assigning priorities among all of the relevant ends, they would not, it is safe to say, put "democratic procedure" first. Probably they, and most Americans, would order the ends as follows:

1. The party system must above all else provide governments having the will and capacity to preserve the society and to protect its members. Any sacrifice in other ends ought to be accepted if it is indispensable to securing this end.

2. The party system must insure periodic opportunity to change the government by free elections. Any sacrifice of other ends (except the one above) ought to be accepted if it is indispensable to securing this one.

3. The party system should promote the welfare of the people. By "welfare" is meant some combination of two kinds of values: "principles," what is thought to be good for the society, described in rather general terms, and "interests," the ends individuals and groups seek to attain for their own good, as distinguished from that of the society. The party system should produce governments that assert the supremacy of principles over interests in some matters; in others it should allow interests to prevail and should facilitate the competitive exercise of influence.

4. The party system should moderate and restrain such conflict as would threaten the good health of the society. Other conflict it should not discourage.

5. The party system should promote and exemplify democracy, meaning reasonable

discussion of matters affecting the common good in which every voice is heard.

These ends have been listed in what most Americans would probably consider a descending order of importance. In devising a party system, we ought not to try to serve fully each higher end before serving the one below it at all. The first two ends are exceptions to this rule, however: each of them must be attained even if the others are not served at all. With respect to the remaining three, the problem is to achieve a proper balance—one such that no reallocation from one end to another would add to the sum of value.

Finally, we must realize that we can rarely make important social changes by intention. The most we can do is to make such minor changes as may be consistent with, and more or less implied by, the fixed features of the situation in which we are placed. Even to make minor changes in an institution like a political party requires influence of a kind and amount that no group of reformers is likely to have or to be able to acquire. It is idle to propose reforms that are merely desirable. There must also be some possibility of showing, if only in a rough and conjectural way, that they might be carried into effect.

With respect to the American party system, it seems obvious that the crucial features of the situation are all fixed. The size of our country, the class and cultural heterogeneity of our people, the number and variety of their interests, the constitutionally-given fragmentation of formal authority, the wide distribution of power which follows from it, the inveterate taste of Americans for participation in the day-to-day conduct of government when their interests are directly at stake —these are all unalterable features of the situation. Taken together, they mean that the party system can be reformed only within very narrow limits.

A MODEL PARTY SYSTEM

Let us imagine a system free of the alleged defects of ours. In this model system, every citizen is motivated—highly so—by political principles, not subsidiary ones, but ones having to do with the very basis of the society. (In France and Italy, Duverger says approvingly, political warfare "is not concerned with subsidiary principles but with the very foundations of the state and the nature of the regime." [5]) The electoral system, moreover, is such as to give every side on every issue exactly the weight that its numbers in the population warrant; no group or interest is over- or underrepresented ("One's thoughts turn," Duverger says, "to the possibility of a truly scientific democracy, in which parliament would be made up of a true sample of the citizens reproducing on a reduced scale the exact composition of the nation, made up, that is, according to the very methods that are used as a basis for public opinion surveys like the Gallup polls." [6])

[5] *Op. cit.*, p. 419.
[6] *Ibid.*, p. 158.

Assuming that the society is divided by the usual number of cleavages (e.g., haves versus have-nots, segregationists versus anti-segregationists, isolationists versus internationalists, etc.), the following would result:

1. There would be a great many parties, for no citizen would support a party with which he did not agree fully.

2. The parties would tend to be single-issue ones. If logically unrelated issues (for instance, segregation and isolationism) were linked together in a party program, only those voters would support the party who chanced to be on the same side of all of the linked issues. The number of these voters would decrease as the number of issues so linked increased.

3. Parties would be short-lived. They would come into and pass out of existence with the single issues they were organized to fight.

4. In their election campaigns and propaganda, parties would emphasize their single defining principles. This would tend to widen the cleavages along which the parties were formed.

5. Ideological issues, not practical

problems, would constitute the substance of politics.[7]

6. The number of such issues pressing for settlement at any one time (but being incapable of settlement because of their ideological character) would always be more than the system could accommodate.[8]

7. Coalitions of parties would seldom form, and such as did form would be highly unstable. Party leaders would find compromise almost impossible because it would lead to loss of highly principled supporters.

8. Coalitions of parties being unstable, governments would also be unstable and therefore lacking in power and decision.

9. Those selected for positions of political leadership would tend to be ideologues skilled in party dialectics and symbolizing the party and its positions. Practical men, especially those with a talent for compromise and those symbolizing qualities common to the whole society, would be excluded from politics.

10. Matters having no ideological significance (a category that includes most local issues) would either be endowed with a spurious one or else would be left outside the sphere of politics altogether.[9]

These points should suffice to show that a system with a perfectly democratic structure would not produce results acceptable in terms of the criteria listed above.

Now let us introduce into the model system one of the alleged defects which the critics find most objectionable in the American party system. Let us suppose that at least half of the electorate is prevailed upon to exchange its vote in matters of fundamental principle for advantages that have nothing to do with principle, especially private profit, sectional gain, and nationality "recognition."

One effect of this would be to reduce greatly the intensity of ideological conflict and to make political life more stable and conservative. This, in fact, seems to be what happened when American parties first came into being. John Adams tells in his diary how in 1794 "ten thousand people in the streets of Philadelphia, day after day, threatened to drag Washington out of his house and effect a revolution in the government, or compel it to declare war in favor of the French Revolution and against England."[10] After parties had been organized, however, patronage took the place of ideological fervor. "The clubs of the social revolutionists which had sprung up in the cities, blazing with incendiary ideas caught from the French Revolution," Henry Jones Ford says, "were converted into party workers, and their behavior was moderated by considerations of party interest."[11]

Another effect would be to encourage the formation of a few (probably two) stable parties. These might begin as alliances among the profit-minded, the sectional-minded, and the nationality-minded, but to attract support from principled voters the parties would have to seem to stand for something—indeed, for anything and everything. Since no faction of them could hope to win an election by itself, principled voters would attach themselves to those parties that they found least objectionable. The parties would develop corporate identities and mystiques; principled voters would then subordinate their differences out of "loyalty" to the party and in response to its demands for "regularity." Competition for middle-of-the-road support would cause the parties to offer very similar programs. This competition might lead to there being only two parties, but this result would

---

[7] In France, according to Siegfried, "every argument becomes a matter of principle; the practical results are relegated to second place." André Siegfried, "Stable Instability in France," *Foreign Affairs,* XXXIV (April 1956), 395.

[8] According to Siegfried: "The difficulty is that too many questions of fundamental importance on which the various parties have cause to disagree have come up for decision at one time." *Ibid.,* p. 399.

[9] In France, Luethy says, "politics," which deals with ideological matters, and the "state," i.e., the bureaucracy, which deals with practical ones, function "in watertight compartments" with the consequence that French democracy is an amalgam of absolutist administration on the one hand and of anarchy, tumultuous or latent, on the other. Herbert Luethy, *France Against Herself* (New York: Meridian Books, 1957), p. 61. On this see also Siegfried, *op. cit.,* p. 399.

[10] Quoted by Henry Jones Ford, *op. cit.,* p. 125.

[11] *Ibid.,* p. 144.

probably be insured by introducing another supposed defect into the system: a principle of representation (single-member districts and plurality voting) which, by letting the winner take all, would force small parties to join large ones in order to have some chance of winning.

In one way or another, the "defects" of the system would tend to produce these consequences—consequences which have in fact been produced in the United States:

1. A strong and stable government would be possible. The country would be governed by the party that won the election, or (given the particular complexities of the American system) by two closely similar parties engaged in give-and-take and, therefore, in a sense constituting one party under two names.

2. There would be a high degree of continuity between administrations elected from different parties. Elections would not shake the nation to its foundations because the competing parties would be fundamentally in agreement. Agreement would be so built in by countless compromises within the parties (each of which would be under the necessity of attracting middle-of-the-road support) that a change of party would seldom entail complete reversal of policy in an important matter.

3. There would exist many substructures of power that would be largely or wholly impervious to the influence of political principle or ideology. "Machines"—party organizations of the profit-minded, the sectional-minded, and the nationality-minded—would not be inclined to offer pie in the sky or to stir the emotions of the masses because they could count upon getting their votes in other ways. These essentially apolitical centers of power would therefore exert a stabilizing and conservative influence throughout the political system. By making businesslike deals with the leaders of the "machines," the President could sometimes buy freedom to do as he thought best in matters of principle.

4. The diversity of the principles and the multiplicity of the interests within the party would be another source of strength to the leader elected from it. He could afford to offend some elements of the party on any particular question because there would be enough other elements unaffected (or even gratified) to assure his position. The more fragmented his party, the less attention he would have to pay to any one fragment of it.

5. The assertion of interests (as distinguished from principles) would be encouraged. The profit-minded, the sectional-minded, and the nationality-minded would in effect give up representation on matters of principle in order to get it on matters involving their interests. Thus two different systems of representation would work simultaneously. The party leader would act as a trustee, disregarding interests in favor of principles ("Congress represents locality, the President represents the nation," Ford wrote in 1898.[12]) Meanwhile legislators dependent on machines and, in general, on profit-minded, sectional-minded, and nationality-minded voters would act as agents of interests. The trustee of principles (the President) and the agents of interests (Congressmen) would of necessity bargain with each other; by allowing the agents of interests some successes—but only in this way—the trustee of principles could win their support in the matters he considered most important. Thus, there would be achieved that balancing of interests and of interests against principles (the most important principles usually being vindicated) that a good party system should produce.

6. The formation of deep cleavages would nevertheless be discouraged. The competition of the parties for the middle-of-the-road vote; their tendency to select practical men of wide popular appeal, rather than idealogues, for positions of leadership; and the definition of the politicians' task as being that of finding the terms on which people who disagree will work together, rather than that of sharpening ideological points—these would all be unifying tendencies.

Some critics of the American party system have attributed its alleged defects

[12] *Ibid.,* p. 187. For a recent brilliant account of how the two systems of representation work, see Willmoore Kendall, "The Two Majorities," *Midwest Journal of Political Science,* IV, No. 4 (November 1960), 317–345.

to the absence of class consciousness in our society. No doubt there is some truth in this. But causality may run the other way also. We may be lacking in class consciousness because our politicians are prevented by the nature of the party system from popularizing the rhetoric of the class struggle; the party system actually induces the voter to forego the allurements of principle and ideology by offering him things he values more: e.g., personal profit, sectional advantage, and nationality "recognition." [13]

In those countries where the voter expresses at the polls his ideology rather than his interests, he may do so not from choice but because the party system leaves him no alternative. In such countries, class warfare may be the principal subject-matter of politics simply because matters of greater importance to the voters are not at stake.

Experience in the underdeveloped areas seems to bear out the claim that certain "defects" in a party system may be essential to good government. The transplanted "defects" of the American party system are among the factors that have made the Philippines the most

[13] ". . . in coordinating the various elements of the populations for political purposes," Ford says, "party organization tends at the same time to fuse them into one mass of citizenship, pervaded by a common order of ideas and sentiments, and actuated by the same class of motives. This is probably the secret of the powerful solvent influence which American civilization exerts upon the enormous deposits of alien population thrown upon this country by the torrent of emigration. Racial and religious antipathies, which present the most threatening problems to countries governed upon parliamentary principles, melt with amazing rapidity in the warm flow of a party spirit which is constantly demanding, and is able to reward the subordination of local and particular interests to national purposes." (*Op. cit.*, pp. 306–307.)

democratic country in Southeast Asia. According to Professor Lucian W. Pye:

. . . the image of leadership that evolved in the Philipines was clearly that of the politician who looked after the particular interests of voters. Elsewhere the pattern of the Western impact under colonialism gave emphasis to the role of the rational administrator who apparently operated according to the principles of efficiency and who was not supposed to be influenced by political pressures within the society. Consequently, when the politicians emerged in these societies, they tended to become the champions of nationalistic ideologies and even the enemies of the rational administrators.[14]

In the Philippines, as at home, our party system has had the defects of its virtues—and the virtues of its defects. On the one hand, Pye says, the Philippines have never had an efficient administrative machinery, and the demand for higher standards of personal integrity among their public officials is reminiscent of the muckraking era of American politics; on the other hand, "the Philippine electorate seems to recognize that the most fundamental question in politics is who is going to control the government, and thus, while the parties have not had to expend much effort in trying to distinguish themselves ideologically from each other, the expenditures of money on political campaigns in the Philippines are probably the highest in proportion to per capita income of any country in the world." [15]

[14] Lucian W. Pye, "The Politics of Southeast Asia," in G. Almond and J. Coleman (eds.), *The Politics of the Developing Areas* (Princeton, N. J.: Princeton University Press, 1960), p. 97. Copyright © 1960 by Princeton University Press.

[15] *Ibid.*, pp. 123 and 126.

MAKING PARTIES "RESPONSIBLE"

Some think that the American party system can be reformed without changing its nature essentially. Several years ago, a Committee on Parties of the American Political Science Association proposed making certain "readjustments" in the

structure and operation of the party system to eliminate its "defects." These readjustments, the Committee said, would give the electorate "a proper range of choice between alternatives" in the form of programs to which the parties would be committed and which they would have sufficient internal cohesion to carry into effect. Thus, the two-party system would be made more "responsible." [16]

What this means is not at all clear. "Responsibility" here seems to be a synonym for accountability, that is, the condition of being subject to being called to account and made to take corrective action in response to criticism. In the case of a party, this can mean nothing except going before an electorate, and in this sense all parties are by definition responsible. "Reponsibility" can have no other meaning in this context; as William Graham Sumner remarked, "a party is an abstraction; it cannot be held responsible or punished; if it is deprived of power it fades into thin air and the men who composed it, especially those who did the mischief and needed discipline, quickly reappear in the new majority.[17]

Leaving aside both the question of what "responsibility" means when applied to a party and the more important one of whether as a matter of practical politics such "readjustments" could be made, let us consider how the political system would probably be affected by the changes proposed.

The hope that the two-party system might be made to offer a choice between distinct alternatives is illusory for at least two reasons. One is that a party which does not move to the middle of the road to compete for votes condemns itself to defeat and eventually, if it does not change its ways, to destruction. But even if this were not the case, the parties could not present the electorate with what reformers think of as "a valid choice." The reason is that the issues in our national life are such that there does not exist any one grand principle by which the electorate could be divided into two camps such that every voter in each camp would be on the "same" side of all issues. The idea of "left" and "right" is as close as we come to having such a grand principle, and it has little or no ap-

plication to many issues.[18] The logic of "left" and "right" does not, for example, imply opposite or even different positions on (for example) foreign policy, civil liberties, or farm subsidies. Without a grand principle which will make unities —opposed unities—of the party programs, the electorate cannot be offered "a valid choice." A choice between two market baskets, each of which contains an assortment of unrelated items, some of which are liked and some of which are disliked, is not a "valid" choice in the same sense that a choice between two market baskets, each of which contains items that "belong together" is a "valid" one. In the American party system, most items are logically unrelated. This being so, "valid" choice would become possible only if the number of parties was increased to allow each party to stand for items that *were* logically related, if one issue became important to the exclusion of all of the others, or if, by the elaboration of myth and ideology, pseudological relations were established among items.

The hope that the parties might commit themselves to carry out their programs is also illusory. A party could do this only if its leaders were able to tell the President and the party members in Congress what to do, and could discipline them if they failed to do it. Therefore, unless, like the Russians, we were to have two sets of national leaders, one in governmental office and another much more important one in party office, it would be necessary for our elected leaders—in effect, the President, since only he and the Vice President are elected by the whole nation —to control the Congressmen and Senators of their party. This would be possible only if the President could deny reelection to members of Congress who did not support the party program. Thus, instead of merely bringing forward and

---

[16] See the Committee Report, *op. cit.,* pp. 1 and 85.

[17] William Graham Sumner, *The Challenge of Facts* (New Haven, Conn.: Yale University Press, 1914), pp. 271–272.

[18] One can imagine a set of symbols connected with a diffuse ideology dividing the society into two camps, and to a certain extent this exists. But it is hard to see in what sense this would present the electorate with "a valid choice." In other words, the existence of a body of nonsense which is treated as if it were a grand principle ought not to be regarded by reasonable critics of the party system as equivalent to the grand principle itself.

electing candidates, as they do now, "responsible" parties would have to govern the country. We would have a parliamentary system with the President in a position somewhat like that of the British Prime Minister, except (a very important difference) that, not being a part of the legislature, he could not use it as a vehicle through which to exert his leadership.[19] The legislature would in fact have no function at all.

This great shift of power to the President would remedy another "defect" in the party system: its receptivity to the demands of interest groups.[20] With the President in full control of Congress, logrolling would cease or virtually cease. It would do so because no one could any longer make the President pay a price for assistance in getting legislation passed; the traders who now sell their bits and pieces of power to the highest bidders would have to lower their prices and would probably go out of business. With their opportunities for exercising influence vastly reduced, interest groups would be less enterprising both in their efforts to anticipate the effects of governmental action and in bringing their views to the attention of the policy makers.

The making of policy would thus pass largely into the hands of technical experts within the majority party, the White House, and the executive departments. These would be mindful of principles and impatient of interests. They would endeavor to make "coherent" policies, meaning, presumably, policies not based on compromise.[21] In all important matters, however, "the public interest" would prove an insufficient guide; the experts, when confronted with the necessity of choosing between alternatives that were equally in the public interest—that is, when no authoritative, ultimate criterion of choice existed for them to apply —would by the very necessities of the case have to balance the competing values as best they could, which means that they would have to fall back upon their personal tastes or professional biases.[22] Thus they would do badly (but in the game of "impartial administration") what is now done reasonably well by the political process.

The destruction of political traders and of local centers of power would mean also that the President's power would derive from somewhat different sources than at present. Instead of relying upon logrolling and patronage to get the votes he would need in Congress, he would have to rely upon direct appeals to the electorate. To some extent he might manipulate the electorate by charm and personality; TV and the arts of Madison Avenue would become more important in politics. But in order to get elected he would have to depend also, and to a greater extent, upon appeals to political principle or ideology. Whereas the political trader maintains his control by giving and withholding favors to individuals (a circumstance which makes his control both dependable in its operation and cheap), the President would have to maintain *his* by the uncertain and costly expedient of offering to whole classes of people—the farmer, the aged, the home owner, and so on—advantages that they would have only at each other's expense. If charm and the promise of "something for everybody" did not yield the amount of power he required to govern the country, the President might find it necessary to exploit whatever antagonisms within the society might be made to yield more power. Class and ethnic differences might in this event serve somewhat the same function as logrolling and patronage do now. Mayor LaGuardia, for example, depended for power upon direct, personal appeal to the voters rather than upon

[19] The Prime Minister is the leader of his party outside as well as inside Parliament. Party leaders who are not also members of Parliament take no part in the running of the government, as the late Professor Harold Laski discovered when, as a leader of the Labour Party, he presumed to give advice to Prime Minister Attlee. The party leaders discipline their followers by threatening to deprive them of renomination; accordingly most members of the House are "backbenchers" who participate in its affairs only as audience, and the function of the House as a whole is to criticize and advise the leaders of the majority party.

[20] Cf. Report of the Committee on Parties, *op. cit.,* pp. 19–20.

[21] *Ibid.,* p. 19.

[22] This argument is developed in E. C. Banfield, *Political Influence* (Glencoe, Ill.: Free Press, 1961), Ch. 12.

organization. His charm and his support of "liberal" programs are well remembered. But it should not be forgotten that he depended also upon exploitation of ethnic loyalties and antipathies. According to Robert Moses,

It must be admitted that in exploiting racial and religious prejudices La Guardia could run circles around the bosses he despised and derided. When it came to raking ashes of Old World hates, warming ancient grudges, waving the bloody shirt, tuning the ear to ancestral voices, he could easily out-demagogue the demagogues. And for what purpose? To redress old wrongs abroad? To combat foreign levy or malice domestic? To produce peace on the Danube, the Nile, the Jordan? Not on your tintype. Fiorello La Guardia knew better. He knew that the aim of the rabble rousers is simply to shoo into office for entirely extraneous, illogical and even silly reasons the municipal officials who clean city streets, teach in schools, protect, house and keep healthy, strong and happy millions of people crowded together here.[23]

That a President might rely more upon appeals to political principle does not at all mean that better judgments or results would follow. For the discussion of principles would probably not be *serious;* it would be for the purpose of securing popular interest and consent, not of finding a wise or right course of action. As

[23] Robert Moses, *LaGuardia: A Salute and a Memoir* (New York: Simon & Schuster, 1957), pp. 37–38. Copyright © 1957 by Simon & Schuster.

long ago as 1886, Sir Henry Sumner Maine observed that democracy was tending toward government by salesmanship. Party and corruption had in the past always been relied upon to bring men under civil discipline, he said, but now a third expedient had been discovered:

This is generalization, the trick of rapidly framing, and confidently uttering, general propositions on political subjects. . . . General formulas, which can be seen on examination to have been arrived at by attending only to particulars few, trivial or irrelevant, are turned out in as much profusion as if they dropped from an intellectual machine; and debates in the House of Commons may be constantly read, which consisted wholly in the exchange of weak generalities and strong personalities. On a pure Democracy this class of general formulas has a prodigious effect. Crowds of men can be got to assent to general statements, clothed in striking language, but unverified and perhaps incapable of verification; and thus there is formed a sort of sham and pretence of concurrent opinion. There has been a loose acquiescence in a vague proposition, and then the People, whose voice is the voice of God, is assumed to have spoken.[24]

Efforts to create "levity of assent," as Maine called it, will become more important in our politics to the extent that other means of bringing men under civil discipline are given up or lost.

[24] Sir Henry Sumner Maine, *Popular Government* (New York: Henry Holt, 1886), pp. 106–108.

THE DANGER OF MEDDLING

A political system is an accident. It is an accumulation of habits, customs, prejudices, and principles that have survived a long process of trial and error and of ceaseless response to changing circumstance. If the system works well on the whole, it is a lucky accident—the luckiest, indeed, that can befall a society, for all of the institutions of the society, and thus its entire character and that of the human types formed within it, depend ultimately upon the government and the political order.

To meddle with the structure and operation of a successful political system is therefore the greatest foolishness that men are capable of. Because the system is intricate beyond comprehension, the chance of improving it in the ways intended is slight, whereas the danger of disturbing its working and of setting off a succession of unwanted effects that will extend throughout the whole society is great.

Democracy must always meddle, however. An immanent logic impels it to self-reform, and if other forces do not prevent, it must sooner or later reform itself out of existence.[25]

The logic of this is as follows. The ideal of democracy legitimates only such power as arises out of reasonable discussion about the common good in which all participate. Power that comes into being in any other way (e.g., by corruption, logrolling, appeals to sentiment or prejudice, the exercise of charm or charisma, "hasty generalization," terror, etc.) is radically undemocratic, and people inspired by the democratic ideal will therefore endeavor to eliminate it by destroying, or reforming, whatever practices or institutions give rise to it.

No society, however, can be governed *solely* by reasonable discussion about the common good; even in a society of angels there might be disagreement about what the common good requires in the concrete case.[26] In most societies, far more power is needed to maintain civil discipline and protect the society from its enemies than can be got simply by reasonable discussion about the common good. Therefore the logical culmination of democratic reform, viz., the elimination of all undemocratic sources of power, would render government—and therefore the preservation of the society—impossible. Democratic reform can never reach this point, of course, because, before reaching it, democracy itself would be destroyed and the impetus to further reform removed.

So far as it does succeed, however, the tendency of democratic reform is to reduce the power available for government. Such loss of power as occurs from the elimination of undemocratic sources of it will seldom be offset by increases in power of the kind that arises from reasonable discussion about the common good. Since there is a point beyond which no increase in democratic power is possible (the capacity of a society to engage in reasonable discussion about the common good being limited), reform, if carried far enough, must finally reduce the quantity of power.

There is, then, a danger that reform will chip away the foundations of power upon which the society rests. But this is not the only danger. A greater one, probably, is that in making some forms of undemocratic power less plentiful, reform may make others more plentiful, and by so doing set off changes that will ramify throughout the political system, changing its character completely. If, for example, politicians cannot get power by the methods of the machine (corruption, favor-giving, and patronage), they may get it by other methods, such as charm, salesmanship, and "hasty generalization." The new methods may be better than the old by most standards (they cannot, of course, be better by the standard of democracy, according to which *all* power not arising from reasonable discussion about the common good is absolutely illegitimate); but even if they are better, the new methods may not serve as well as the old, or may not serve at all, in maintaining an effective political system and a good society.

Reform is, of course, far from being the only force at work. Compared to the other forces, some of which tend to produce competing changes and others of which tend to check all change, reform may be of slight effect. This is certainly true in general of such reform as is sought through formal organizations by people called "reformers." It is much less true of reform in the broader sense of the general view and disposition of "the great body of right-thinking people." This kind of reform is likely to be of pervasive importance in the long run, although its effects are seldom what anyone intended.

Jefferson may have been right in saying that democracy cannot exist without a wide diffusion of knowledge throughout the society. But it may be right also to say that it cannot exist *with* it. For as we become a better and more democratic society, our very goodness and democracy may lead us to destroy goodness and democracy in the effort to increase and perfect them.

[25] For data and analysis pertinent to the discussion that follows, see James Q. Wilson, *The Amateur Democrat* (Chicago: University of Chicago Press, 1962).

[26] See Yves R. Simon, *The Philosophy of Democratic Government* (Chicago: University of Chicago Press, 1951), Ch. 1.

SUGGESTED ADDITIONAL READINGS

1. Campbell, Angus, *et al.*, *The American Voter,* New York: John Wiley, 1960, pp. 541–548, (also in paper). Reviews the empirical evidence for the adequacy of normative democratic theory to explain the functioning of elections, particularly with reference to policy determination.

2. ————, Gerald Gurin, and Warren E. Miller, *The Voter Decides,* Appendix A, "Sense of Political Efficacy," Evanston: Row, Peterson, 1954, pp. 187–194. Concludes that "citizens who feel that public officials are responsive and responsible to the electorate, who think that political activity is worth while and capable of influencing public policy, and who see that the private citizen's channels of access to governmental decision-makers are not confined to the ballot box, are much more likely to be politically active than those citizens who feel largely overwhelmed by the political process."

3. Dahl, Robert A., *A Preface to Democratic Theory,* Chicago: University of Chicago Press, 1956, 154 pp. (paper). Critical examination of democratic theories with suggestions for revision. Concluding chapter suggests seven propositions bearing on the "American hybrid": (1) on matters of specific policy the majority rarely rules; (2) while elections are ineffective in indicating majority preferences they are a crucial device for controlling leaders; (3) specific policies selected by the process of "minorities rule" probably lie most of the time within the bounds of consensus set by the important values of the politically active; (4) majority tyranny, like majority rule, is mostly a myth; (5) protection against deprivation by one group of freedom of another is not discovered in constitutional forms, but, if at all, in extra-constitutional factors, particularly polyarchy; (6) constitutional rules are significant because they help to determine what particular groups are to be given advantages or handicaps in the political struggle; and (7) a central development has been the evolution of a political system in which all active and legitimate groups can make themselves heard at some crucial stage in the process of decision.

4. ————, "Hierarchy, Democracy, and Bargaining in Politics and Economics," in Stephan K. Bailey, ed., *Research Frontiers in Politics and Government,* Washington, D. C.: Brookings Institute, 1955, pp. 47–66. Reprinted in Heinz Eulau, Samuel J. Eldersveld, and Morris Janowitz, *Political Behavior: A Reader in Theory and Research,* Glencoe: Free Press, 1956, pp. 83–90. Extracted in Oliver P. Williams and Charles Press, *Democracy in Urban America,* Chicago: Rand McNally, 1961, pp. 406–410. Consideration of the "full-blown contrast [which] has arisen between the assumptions of many of the older democratic theorists and what now appear to be the actual facts of political life." Examines the requirement of full participation and concludes that, "Earlier assumptions about the amount of participation required for democracy seem to have been faulty, and more realistic assumptions give rise to questions about democracy, hierarchy, and bargaining that have not yet been answered."

5. ————, *Modern Political Analysis,* Englewood Cliffs, N. J.: Prentice-Hall, 1963, 118 pp. (paper). Incisive overview of political analysis reflecting the best of modern scholarship. Aims "to equip you with a small number of basic concepts, ideas, and analytical tools—ancient or recent, whichever seem the better—so that you can proceed afterward with more competence toward what should be, in a democracy, a life-long vocation: the analysis of politics." Essential reading.

6. David, Paul T., Ralph M. Goldman, and Richard C. Bain, *The Politics of National Party Conventions,* Washington, D. C.: Brookings Institute, 1960, 274 pp. (paper). Condensation of the original study by the same authors. A thorough presentation of all aspects of conventions and their roles; also includes a wealth of materials and data on the parties.

7. Davis, Lane, "The Cost of Realism: Contemporary Restatements of Democracy," *The Western Political Quarterly,* Vol. XVII, No. 1 (March 1964), pp. 37–46. Critical evaluation of efforts toward restatement of democratic theory. Excellent review of the literature of contemporary "realist" theory. Useful both for summary of the restatement efforts and for a counter view to that presented here. Bibliographical references are extensive and can be used profitably for further study on the subject matter of this chapter.

8. Goldwin, Robert A. (ed.), *Political Parties, U. S. A.,* Chicago: Rand McNally, 1964, 158 pp. (paper). Series of essays by leading scholars: Stephen K. Bailey, "Our National Political Parties"; Edward C. Banfield, "In Defense of the American Party System"; Walter Berns, "Reform of the American Party System"; Harry V. Jaffa, "The Nature and Origin of the American Party System"; Charles M. Hardin, "Emergent Defects in the American Constitutional System"; Morton Grodzins, "Party and Government in the United States"; and Herbert J. Storing, "Political Parties and the Bureaucracy."

9. Janowitz, Morris, and Dwaine Marvick, *Competitive Pressure and Democratic Consent,* Institute of Public Administration, University of Michigan, 1956; summarized in Heinz Eulau, Samuel J. Eldersveld, and Morris Janowitz, *Political Behavior: A Reader in Theory and Research,* Glencoe, Ill.: Free Press, 1956, pp. 275–286. Discussion of the prerequisites for a democratic election.

10. Kelley, Stanley, *Political Campaigning: Problems in Creating an Informed Electorate,* Washington, D. C.: Brookings Institute, 1960, 163 pp. "[M]uch of the dissatisfaction with the character of our campaigns is eminently justified if one basic assumption is granted: that campaign discussion should help voters make rational voting decisions." An important book for an understanding of the problem of the role of campaigns and the role of the voter.

11. ———, *Professional Public Relations and Political Power,* New York: Johns Hopkins Press, 1956. An important study of the role of professional public relations firms as directors of political campaigns.

12. Key, V. O., Jr., *Politics, Parties, and Pressure Groups,* New York: Thomas Y. Crowell, 5th ed., 1964, 738 pp. Probably the leading textbook on parties and politics; encyclopedic, but indispensable for a wealth of detail.

13. ———, *Southern Politics in State and Nation,* New York: Alfred A. Knopf, 1949, pp. 298–311. Discussion of the nature and consequences of factionalism in one-party states in the South in the absence of competition from another party.

14. Lasswell, Harold D., *Power and Personality,* New York: W. W. Norton, 1948, pp. 9–58. Examines the meaning of power conceived as "sanctioned expectations" of deprivation of value. A highly sophisticated discussion of power in relation to political roles and types, the bases of power, and the political personality.

15. Levin, Murray B., *The Alienated Voter: Politics in Boston,* New York: Holt, Rinehart and Winston, 1960, 84 pp. (paper). A case study of political alienation in Boston. Suggests democratic theory is one of the sources of alienation. Chapter 4, "Political Alienation," is a particularly useful analysis of the theoretical implications of alienation and democratic theory.

16. McClosky, Herbert, "Consensus and Ideology in American Politics," *The American Political Science Review,* Vol. LVIII, No. 2 (June 1964), 361–382. Examination of the relationship between consensus and democracy. Discusses the evidence which demonstrates that the belief that consensus is a prerequisite of democracy is not entirely accurate.

17. McDonald, Neil A., *The Study of Political Parties,* Garden City, N.Y.: Doubleday and Random House, 1955, 97 pp. (paper). Reviews the literature on party

functions and roles; recapitulates the evidence on party make-up; considers party influence on the electorate and officialdom. A useful overview.

18. Rossiter, Clinton, *Parties and Politics in America,* Ithaca, N. Y.: Cornell University Press, 1960, 205 pp. (paper). Thorough and readable examination of the party system: the pattern of American politics (Chap. 1), the functions of parties (Chap. 2), distinctions between the Republican and Democratic party in adherents and policy (Chaps. 3 and 4).

19. Schattschneider, E. E., *The Semisovereign People: A Realist's View of Democracy in America,* New York: Holt, Rinehart and Winston, 1960, 147 pp. (paper). Provocative examination of the political process, based on "the assumption . . . that the nature of political organization depends on the conflicts exploited in the political system, which ultimately is what politics is about. The thesis is that we shall never understand politics unless we know what the struggle is about." Suggests re-examination of the classical definition of democracy as "government by the people."

20. Schumpeter, Joseph A., *Capitalism, Socialism, and Democracy,* Part IV, "The Classical Theory of Democracy," and "Another Theory of Democracy," New York: Harper, 1942. Examines classical democratic theory and suggests a restatement in which the selection of those who will govern, not the deciding of issues, is made the primary role of the electorate.

FOR FURTHER CONSIDERATION

1. "If the democratic political process does not operate as reflected in the traditional theory, it is not because there is something wrong with democracy but because our theoretical model is inaccurate." In what respects would you suggest restatement of democratic theory? Does this quotation suggest there can be nothing pathological in the operative democratic process? Can you identify any such factors? Do they really indicate a malfunctioning of democracy or is the democratic theory model you are applying inaccurate?

2. "It is the open competitive struggle for political power that is the distinguishing characteristic of democratic politics. The crucial question is not who governs but how those in power get into power." Does this mean that competence, ability, experience, knowledge are therefore of no consequence in the process of selecting those who will govern? What is the significance of these factors, then, in the democratic electoral process? What chance is there that we will elevate competent men to office? Does the system promote or discourage this?

3. What rules can you suggest as a guide to determining what individuals or groups should be excluded from "any chance of winning or participating in the winning of political power . . ."? Apply your rules to selected cases: communists, Negroes, socialists, nudists, atheists, Presbyterians, etc. Are you sure that your rules are not just a convenient mechanism for justification of your own prejudiced or otherwise preconceived preferences as to the kind of people, groups, ideas you would prefer to have win, or not win? Under your rules would the competition for political power be genuinely open? Can we reconcile the idea of an open competition for power as a necessary ingredient of a democratic process with any prior restraints on the opportunity to compete?

4. "Issues in an election are not so much the major questions of public policy as they are instruments of competition." Consider this statement in reference to the most recent election of which you have knowledge. Did the candidates and parties seem to be operating in conformity to this statement? Why do you think so? Now, do you think that a vote for a particular candidate really relates to the issues? What of conflicting issue positions? Do issues sort themselves out so

that when the voter votes for a given candidate he really expresses an affirmative choice on *all* issues? If issues are more than tools, how do you explain the fact that the two major parties must appeal to the "great middle" in order to win? Is this compatible with clear-cut issue differences between the parties? Can the parties really differ on basic issues or approaches and hope to compete meaningfully?

5. Consider yourself the campaign advisor to a candidate for a partisan political office. Specify your considerations in deciding how to conduct the campaign. What issues should he use? What techniques? Are there moral questions involved? What would you advise if your candidate finds he cannot, for moral or intellectual reasons, do something which you consider necessary to maximize his vote? Would you advise him to attempt to educate his electorate on the inadequacy of traditional theory as discussed in this chapter? Why? Would he be a better candidate if he did not know of this inadequacy? What are the benefits of his knowing and/or the costs of his not knowing?

States, Cities, and Metropolitan Areas 4

Both history and tradition assign an important role to state and local government. Historically, the states pre-existed the national government. They were the repositories of all governing power. Traditionally, we have accepted the notion that democratic government works best at the "grass-roots" level, that smallness is somehow equated with legitimacy in the exercise of governmental power.

This traditional inheritance, however, contrasts sharply with the real world of the twentieth century. The fact that the growth of national powers and activities has been accelerated and is still accelerating has clashed sharply with traditional faith in localism.

Some years ago it became popular to predict the demise of state and local government. In the 1960's some still forecast the imminent withering away of these levels of government in the shadow of the colossus of national power. But the facts belie such predictions. Government below the national level has never done so many important things, spent so much money, employed so many people—in short, has never been as active and vital in the governing of this society as it is at the present time. By any index, state and local governments are today viable and dynamic partners in government. Government has been getting bigger at all levels, including the state and local levels.

The purpose of this chapter is to place the states, cities, and metropolitan areas within the context of the theory and practice of democratic government in the United States, to examine some of the conceptions and misconceptions concerning these levels of government, and to examine some of the major problems and their implications for the future of our democratic processes. The chapter will be concerned primarily with (1) the relationships between state, local, and federal governments; (2) a re-evaluation of the role of localism in democratic theory; (3) demographic considerations and their implications; (4) some problems of structure and function of local governments; and (5) some important aspects of politics at the local level.

STATE, LOCAL, AND NATIONAL GOVERNMENT RELATIONSHIPS

Whereas the states pre-existed the federal union and the national government was created through a specific act of delegation of powers, all local governments—city, county, and special district—were created by the state and are subunits of the state. They have no inherent powers, and they received no delegation of powers. The state-local relationship is clearly a unitary one, in which all power resides with the central government and local units of government exercise such powers as the state government finds it convenient to have them exercise.

Local governments are agents of the state. They exercise state power and are subject to the control of state authority. The extent to which state controls are exercised, however, may vary. In some states, state control of local government is quite rigid. Notwithstanding provisions in most state constitutions prohibiting "special legislation" (legislative acts designed to apply to a specific city or local area and often discriminatory towards that area), some state legislatures sit as a kind of supercity council. In others, various degrees of local self-government have been extended, ranging from fairly restrictive optional charter provisions (in which a city or county selects one of several proffered charters) to rather extensive home-rule provisions (through which the local community is free to govern itself within the areas specified). Yet even these relatively self-governing home-rule areas receive their permission to be self-governing from the state, through action of the state legislature or by amendment to the state constitution. With varying degrees of difficulty, these provisions can be modified by the granting authority. Home-rule cities or counties, thus, are allowed to exercise independence of state interference primarily because it suits the convenience of the state for them to do so. They are not sovereign or independent in any sense comparable to the state in its relationship to the national government.

Cities generally come into existence as the result of the concentration of population in a limited geographic area and the need for solutions to the problems incident to such concentration. Counties, on the other hand, have come into existence in most states almost entirely as the result of arbitrary lines being drawn on a map somewhere in the early stages of the organization of the state. Counties represent in most instances arbitrary and convenient subdivisions of the state, designed primarily for the carrying out of administrative activities of state government through machinery dispersed throughout the state. They have not been, in most states, major governing units (although there are notable exceptions, such as California) but rather administrative subunits of the state.

Special districts—governing units established to deal with a single function or a group of closely related functions—are sometimes set up by the state legislature and sometimes by the local governing authority. In both cases they tend to be largely independent of existing governing units—state, city, and county—with their own powers and sources of revenue. They remain, however, as legally subordinate units of the state government. The major problem created by special districts is the confusion of responsibility resulting from the multiplying of levels of government and the possibility of overlapping or conflicting jurisdictions.

While the United States Constitution does not mention local governments, recent years have seen an increasing tendency for local governments to deal with the national government, sometimes directly without state government involvement, particularly in the receipt of federal grants-in-aid. While the cities and other local governments are the offspring of the state, they have been drawn closer to the federal government in mutual recognition of the need to solve the grave problems of the cities and metropolitan areas. Thus, intergovernmental relationships now involve not only a flexible federalism between state and national government and a traditional legal relationship of subordination of local to state government but also a new and increasingly direct relationship between national and local governments.

DEMOCRATIC THEORY AND LOCAL GOVERNMENT

The myth of the superiority of small-town democracy is one of the most persistent in American tradition. Whether used to defend the small town, to condemn the tendency toward nationalism, or to promote the virtues of state and local government generally as opposed to the national government, this grass-roots democratic theory holds that democracy works best at the lowest governmental level, that the prerequisites for democratic government exist most clearly at the local level, and that the benefits of democratic involvement are realized in inverse relationship to size. It is a cliché of political discourse that the growth of the size of government diminishes the chances of democracy.

The faith in grass-roots democracy has little to support it. There is no evidence that democracy works better in small communities than in large, that the characteristics of government and community at the local level are such that democratic procedures are encouraged. Indeed, the evidence points in exactly the opposite direction. The open competition for political power, essential to a democratic political process, is difficult if not impossible in most local communities. While large size is no guarantee of a democratic political process, the conditions promoting competition are not maximized in the largely homogeneous fraternity of the small town. The alleged virtues of small towns— community of interest, lack of divisive elements, the intimacy of face-to-face relations, interdependence, common goals and values, shared beliefs and customs—in short, as Robert C. Wood terms it, fraternity—are precisely the characteristics which make a democratic process highly unlikely if not impossible. Small towns are not usually noted for their ability to generate, and certainly not their willingness to tolerate, the kind of social-political climate in which genuinely open competition for power can flourish. Furthermore, corruption, crime, malfeasance in office, graft, and a multitude of political if not moral sins have been far more prevalent at the city and county level than at the state or national level. In fact, it appears that problems of this character increase as the size of the political community decreases. Compared to the amount of corruption in city politics, the national scene has been a fount of virtue. Democracy and localism in politics are not conterminous. Although it is useful for politicians in attempting to justify or condemn a particular policy or procedure, the myth which identifies democracy with localism contributes little to an understanding of the way democracy operates in our society. [25]

POPULATION MOVEMENTS AND THEIR EFFECTS

In view of the population trends of the last half century, it is fortunate that the grass-roots myth is not an accurate portrayal of the requirements of democracy. If it were, the future of democracy in the United States would be dim, for we have not fit the small-town model for the better part of the century.

There is one overriding demographic fact: the population of the United States is now predominantly urban. [3, 17] Over 70 percent of the population lives in cities, and the decline in the rural population has become absolute as well as relative. With over two out of every three persons in the United States living in urban areas, no state is less than 35 percent urban, and at least eighteen states are more than 70 percent urban. Only eleven of the fifty states in 1960 were less than 50 percent urban. In a predominantly urban nation, problems of government are primarily those relating to an urban population complicated, but neither shaped nor overshadowed, by the concerns of the remaining part of the population.

A corollary to the increase of urban population is the growth of the suburbs. [33] While the urban population is steadily increasing, most of the growth is in suburban areas surrounding the central cities. In fact, almost all of the central cities of our metropolitan areas have been growing, if at all, at a significantly slower pace than their surrounding suburbs. In the decade prior to 1960, central cities increased approximately 7 percent in population while the metropolitan suburbs increased over 50 percent. At the same time all but one (Los Angeles) of the ten largest cities were losing population.

The general population movement is not from rural areas to suburbs but primarily from rural areas to the central cities of the metropolitan areas, and from there to the suburbs. While the large core cities are the recipients of the large numbers of people who come seeking services, these same cities have witnessed an accelerating exodus to the suburbs of the more affluent residents. The core cities are left with an increasingly large proportion of their population in the lower income brackets, demanding and needing additional governmental services, while the more affluent, those most capable of owning property and thus supporting through the property tax the needed governmental services, are leaving the city and taking up residence in suburban areas. This discrepancy between yield of the property tax and increased demand for services, compounded by an almost universal deterioration of the central cities, poses one of the most serious problems facing the nation today. [15]

A further corollary of this tendency toward urbanism is the growth of metropolitanism. A metropolitan area is usually defined as the population area around a central city of at least 50,000 people plus all predominantly urban contiguous counties. By 1960, two-thirds of the people in the United States lived within the 212 metropolitan areas, and half of the total population lived in the fifteen largest of these metropolitan areas. The number of metropolitan areas is increasing steadily. Not only is this an urban nation, it is now distinctly a metropolitan nation.

Some metropolitan areas are growing together to form what may be called a "megalopolis," or super-metropolitan complex. [31] The most advanced of these multi-metropolitan giants is that running over 600 miles down the eastern coast from New Hampshire to Virginia, including parts of ten states and thirty-two metropolitan areas. Within this vast megalopolis are the metropolitan areas of Boston, New York, Philadelphia, Baltimore, and Washington, D.C. Over thirty-two million people—almost one out of every six people in the United States—live within this continuous urban area. Across the continent on the West Coast, Los Angeles is fast combining with San Diego, over one-hundred miles south, and three contiguous metropolitan areas (comprising most of the counties of Los Angeles, Orange, and San Bernardino) to include nearly 50 percent of the total population of the state of California.

Some megalopoli, and many of the metropolitan areas themselves, spill across the boundaries of two or more states. When this is the case there are not only metropolitan-wide problems without metropolitan-wide government but also problem areas which fall within the gray zone between state authority and federal jurisdiction.

These population trends—movement to the cities, the growth of suburban areas, and the development of metropolitanism and super-metropolitanism—are of prime influence on the political life of this country today. [13] No other single phenomenon is as critical to an understanding of what is going on in the United States in the 1960's. Urban demands, urban interests, and urban political power are the stuff of politics in the 1960's and the major concern of government. It is suggested later that government is essentially a set of institutionalized arrangements for arriving at politically acceptable answers to politically important questions. Those questions which are politically important are increasingly defined by the two-thirds of the population living in urban and metropolitan areas.

The political power of the cities is increased by the fact that large metropolitan complexes tend to be located in the highly populated states, making the city vote crucial in the accumulation of sufficient electoral votes in a presidential election. The creation of a cabinet-level Department of Housing and Urban Development in 1965 and presidential proposal of a new Department of Transportation underscores the fact of urban political power.

Further, the changes in state legislative apportionment coming about as a result of the Supreme Court's decisions in the reapportionment cases will change the relative strength of the cities and rural areas in the state legislatures of all states, with predictable political consequences. [19, 29] In California, for instance, a reapportionment act adopted in 1965 shifted the predominance of representation in the state legislature to metropolitan Southern California, giving Los Angeles County fourteen and one-half senators in place of its former single senator. Eight Southern California counties now have forty-six of the eighty lower house (assembly) seats and twenty-two of the forty senate seats. The competition for political power will be increasingly a competition for support of the city.

STRUCTURAL-FUNCTIONAL PROBLEMS OF LOCAL GOVERNMENT

Concern for the structural-functional aspects of state and local government concentrates primarily on the local level, principally because it is at that level that the problem of population concentration and structural deficiency converge so dramatically and, potentially, disastrously. Structural problems at the local level are state problems, however, for local government is a subunit of the state government and exists for the purpose of governing a smaller unit of the state. Perhaps this state-local relationship is at the heart of the problem. The relationship, both legally and practically, has not changed significantly in most states since the creation of subunits of government. Yet the realities of population location and the types of concerns which have become politically significant as a result have changed enormously during the last one hundred years. As a result, in our states we are essentially trying to govern a mid-twentieth-century society with eighteenth-century governmental arrangements. [27]

Although we adhere to the legal formality that the state is the parent and the local areas are the children, often the state is not an appropriate agency, either because of inability or unwillingness, for the solution of many of the problems facing the metropolitan areas. The metropolitan areas increasingly are turning directly to the federal government for assistance because the state is structurally, politically, or financially incapable of carrying out its paternalistic responsibilities. [9] In fact, most of the children have long since outgrown the parent; yet both law and myth require us to act as if the state were the basic governing unit.

But there are other structural-functional problems of local government. Perhaps the most important is the disparity between problem area and jurisdiction. Many of the most important problems facing the United States domestically involve metropolitan areas. Yet governmental jurisdiction is still defined largely as it was 150 years ago. In most states, a city ordinarily cannot operate beyond the limits of its own legally defined boundaries. Yet obviously the problems in our metropolitan areas do not respect city boundary lines. Pressing metropolitan problems—crime, health, public welfare assistance, slums, air pollution, sewage disposal, water supply, transportation—cannot be either defined or solved within the jurisdictional boundaries of existing cities. They are metropolitan-wide problems and require metropolitan-wide solution. [2, 11, 13, 18, 32] And to further complicate the situation, as noted above, many problems spread across state lines as metropolitan areas spread across state lines.

Counties have not proved effective in governing or administering metropolitan areas, for they are, on the whole, the most antiquated and archaic of

American governing institutions.[1] Counties almost universally lack an effective executive, being governed by collegial bodies. That they cannot be modified so as to become effective units has not been established, but the fact that they have not often been so modified is a matter of record.[2] They are essentially rural administrative agencies, peculiarly unsuited to the demands of the age of metropolitanism. [20, 30]

Most states, recognizing the disparity between jurisdiction and problem area, have created additional units and levels of government in a hit-or-miss effort to cope with specific problems. As a consequence, American local government today is characterized by fragmentation of government responsibility and multiplicity of governing units, which have hampered the solution of the problems of a metropolitan society. [8]

The 212 metropolitan areas in 1962 contained 18,442 separate governmental units. At the extreme were the 1,112 units of government in the New York-Northeastern New Jersey metropolitan area and the 1,170 in the Chicago-Northwestern Indiana area. It is not unusual for a metropolitan area to include parts of two states, two or more counties, scores of cities, and hundreds of special districts.

Special districts are a popular means of overcoming the rigidity of corporate boundary lines and the consequent inability of governing units to attack area-wide problems satisfactorily. [7] There are special districts for almost every conceivable purpose, including the most popular, schools, as well as street lighting, sidewalk construction, irrigation, air pollution control, transportation, and cemetery maintenance. These districts are superimposed on existing governmental structures, and the jurisdiction of a given special district may extend, for example, over more than one municipality, over both city and county territory, or may be limited to a small part of a municipality. Special districts may and frequently do overlap each other, so that a resident of a given city may be subject to the governmental authority at the local level of the county, a municipality, a school district, and several other special purpose districts, such as water district, street lighting district, flood abatement district, air pollution control district, and rapid transit district.

The reasons for this multiplicity of governing units at the local level are not hard to identify. Probably the most important reason has already been mentioned—the inappropriateness of the traditional county-municipality structure for the solution of problems which cannot be contained within the jurisdictional boundaries of existing governing units. Often there is no existing government at the local level, city or county, which has the legal authority to tackle a specific problem, such as air pollution, or the problem may be such that the exercise of authority by the existing units is largely ineffective, as in the case of widespread crime. Sometimes the existing governments have inadequate financial resources,

---

[1] Not all students of local government agree, however. See, for instance, George S. Blair, *American Local Government,* (New York: Harper & Row, 1964), especially pp. 193–195, where the trends in county government suggest a considerably brighter picture.

[2] Perhaps the most encouraging modification in county government has been the institution in some counties of either a county-manager or a chief administrative officer system, which has helped to provide the county with an effective executive. However, only a relatively small number of counties have adopted this kind of plan.

for most cities have rigid limits on their power to tax and borrow, limits imposed upon them by the state legislature or the state constitution. Sometimes, as in the case of school districts, the rationale for the creation of a special district is to free the activity from the actual or potential political control of the city government. Whatever the reasons for the creation of new levels of government, the results usually involve a less than adequate overall accomplishment of major governmental services, considerable duplication and overlapping, unevenness and gaps in services, multiple levels of taxation, and confusion of the citizenry as to who is responsible governmentally. In fact, many citizens are not even aware of the existence of the multiple levels of governing authorities to which they are presumably responsible.

A great deal of attention has been given over the years to the question of which forms of government at the local level are best. Emphasis has shifted gradually from consideration of the three basic forms of city government— mayor-council, commission, and city-manager forms [12]—to a more general concern for metropolitan organization—city-county merger, county-wide metropolitan government, city-county separation, for example. [2, 18, 22, 32] While such concern is necessary, much of the discourse fails to recognize that forms of government are not solutions in themselves but only means towards solutions. Affection for a particular institutional arrangement, be it at the local level or the national, should not lead one into the error of assuming that the adoption of that particular structure will guarantee success in the solution of the problems facing the society. However, careful consideration of alternate forms may indicate that some of them can be expected to hinder while others may be expected to promote satisfactory approaches to solution of the problems facing the governed area.

POLITICS AT THE LOCAL LEVEL

In the United States all politics is ultimately local. There is no national politics; our political parties are not national parties; and, in the aftermath of periodic cooperative efforts geared to the winning of national elections, the parties tend to devolve into their independent and widely-varying units. These units are not even usually state parties. The significant ongoing political involvement is at the lower levels—county, city, and precinct.

This characteristic political particularism justifies consideration of politics at the local level, but our concern here is more specific. Since most of the population of the United States lives in urban areas, and in fact in a few highly concentrated metropolitan complexes, the day-to-day political struggles which affect local government are apt to be most important to the day-to-day life of the citizen.

Paradoxically, however, for over half a century much of the literature and a great deal of the activity at the local community level have been preoccupied with eliminating politics from local government. To understand both the way government and democracy operate at the local level and how this experience fits, or fails to fit, overall American experience with democracy requires awareness of this paradox—that the politics of democracy is the politics of conflict largely at the local level, yet a good part of the past century has been spent in efforts to depoliticize American communities. Perhaps our best avenue towards such understanding is an examination of the municipal reform movement, its purposes and aims, the situation out of which it grew, and the "nonpolitical" institutions, especially nonpartisan elections, which have been its most notable legacies.

THE MUNICIPAL REFORMERS

Municipal reform, principally intended to rid the cities of the evils of political corruption, has been a dominant theme in most states since the turn of the century. [14, 5] It has not been an organized movement, but its advocates have made a loose identification with certain general philosophical positions. Although there have been notable persons identified as municipal reformers, there has been no continuing leadership or organization. Most reformers have been middle-class businessmen, academicians, and morally indignant and civic-minded women. Underlying the interest in reform has been a commendable concern for making government and democracy workable at the local level. Unfortunately, many of the reformers have given evidence that they understand little about democracy and even less about politics and its role in a democratic system. The two basic assumptions of municipal reformers have been that politics and politicians are at best necessary evils, not to be trusted, and not genuinely identified with the public good, and that good government would be best attained through application of good business principles. The slogan "economy, efficiency, and morality" sums up the general concerns of the reformers.

Even a catalogue of the major reforms advocated and in some cases adopted by the reformers will demonstrate this basic orientation. They include elimination of political parties, election by nonpartisan ballot, substitution of the collegial commission form of government for the more avowedly political mayor-council form, substitution of a professional administrator (city manager) for a politically elected mayor, proportional representation, the initiative, referendum, and recall (to give the average citizen direct participation and means of control of the politicians), improved procedures for budgeting, accounting, and fiscal controls, and a variety of other institutional and mechanical arrangements.

Since its heyday in the first twenty years of this century, the reform movement has declined, but many of its proposals have remained as valuable contributions to government at the local level. In this category might be listed, for example, improved budgeting, accounting, and other fiscal procedures, and increased concern for professionalism and administrative competence. On the other hand, the adoption of nonpartisanship at the local level, although widespread, has not been free of costs.

Approximately 60 percent of all cities in the United States have nonpartisan elections, that is, candidates for public office are not openly identified with a political party. [1] Nonpartisanship in city government stands as one of the most sacred of the sacred cows. It would be virtual political suicide in many communities for a politician to suggest its abolition, and academicians who question its value invite indignant condemnation from citizen and politician alike. Even seasoned politicians who have spent most of a lifetime in the combat of political wars find it expedient to toot the horn of local nonpartisanship.

Coupled closely with the aim of ridding the city of the evil of politics through nonpartisan elections has been the adoption of non-political city government forms. With the mayor-council form closely identified with strong political bosses in American cities, [12, 26, 16] the substitution of the commission form,[3] in which there is a collegial body and no single executive, and the city manager form [6, 23], in which the executive is an administrative expert hired by the city council, promised to fulfill the demands for a government free of the evils of politics. To the extent that these innovations have increased expertise and administrative competence *without* eliminating politics, they have been valuable improvements. But they have succeeded in giving some communities local government without the dynamics of political control or, which is much more frequently the case, politics has been hidden beneath an aura of respectability called nonpartisanship. They have contributed also to the reinforcement of the myth of the undesirability of politics and political involvement. They have contributed to a kind of schizophrenia in the body politic in which the prime necessity of a democratic system—open, deliberate conflict for power—is viewed by many as a perversion of the democratic process.

Few big cities have adopted nonpartisan elections or non-political forms of government. [4] The main reason has been that such solutions are inappropriate to the political realities of the big city. [16] Although nonpartisanship and its institutional corollaries do work in many cities, it can still be concluded that the premises upon which these reforms are based, the analysis of the requirements of political democracy from which they follow, lead to the untenable proposition that democracy can work best when politics, and the political struggle, are defined as alien to good government and satisfactory policy. It is precisely politics—the open competition for political power—which is at the heart of the democratic process, which promotes (though by no means guarantees) government and public policy reflecting the articulated demands of the people.

In recent years we have learned a lot about politics at the local level. The literature now demonstrates convincingly that to understand the politics of the local community one must be able to identify the power structure. [10, 21, 24, 28] There are many in the community who wield power, influence public policy, affect the business of governing, who do not hold public office and are not politicians in the traditional sense. The political arena, correctly viewed, includes not only the politicians in office, those who run for office, and those who are their confidents, but also businessmen, academicians, civic leaders, newspaper editors, ministers, labor leaders, and perhaps, to their chagrin, the municipal reformers themselves. The effort to eliminate politics or control politicians through de-politicizing elections and structuring government so as to elevate the expert, misses the crucial point that politics at the local level is inherent to the

[3] Commission government, after some flurry of enthusiasm among reformers, gradually began to fade, and can no longer be considered as a major form of local government. See Charles R. Adrian, *Governing Urban America* (New York: McGraw-Hill, 1961), pp. 214–218, for a brief summary of the commission plan.

democratic process. There can be, in short, no really nonpartisan or non-political democratic government.

In the readings that follow, Collins and Freeman ("The States"), both former governors, focus on state government as it relates today to both its own subordinate units of local government and the federal government. Wood ("The Miniature Re-examined") examines the small-town democracy myth in relation to a realistic democratic theory. Freedgood ("New Strength in City Hall") discusses big city government with particular emphasis on the need for politics in city government. Together these readings will serve to introduce the reader to many of the provocative problems facing democratic government in the states, cities, and metropolitan areas.

The States

LEROY COLLINS

Mr. Collins was formerly the governor of Florida. He is at present Undersecretary of Commerce.

In these comments on our changing federal-state system of government, I have been assured that I am not expected—because I am from the South— to start off with a rebel yell and wind up with an impassioned defense of states' rights! For the truth is, the South has never enjoyed any monopoly in championing the sovereignty of states. Bruce Catton tells this mordant anecdote to illustrate the point:

General Thomas, the phlegmatic Union commander, rode to the rescue of the Yankee troops at Chickamauga, and finally carried the day after some of the heaviest casualties of the war. After the battle, he went out, according to custom, with his quarter-master to pick the burying ground for the Yankee dead.

"Shall we do it the way we always do, General?" the quartermaster inquired. "Put the Illinois men together over there, and the Iowa men next, and the New York men over yonder . . . ?"

"No," the General replied. "Mix 'em all up. I'm getting pretty damned sick of states' rights."

Reprinted from *The Mazes of Modern Government,* Center for the Study of Democratic Institutions, 1964, by permission of the Fund for the Republic.

I have no wish to leave the states defenseless, but I would strongly emphasize that the more pertinent issue is states' abilities rather than states' rights.

In the first place, states never have had rights in this country, not even during their heyday under the Articles of Confederation. It has always been the people who have had the rights, who have held the ultimate sovereignty. This has always been at the heart of our American form of government. The people have given nothing of their sovereignty away. All they have done is to authorize appropriate levels of government to exercise certain powers for them and in their name.

This course was set when the "divine right of kings" was rejected through the force of such documents as the Magna Carta, the Declaration of Independence, and the Constitution, with their avowal of the inalienable rights of individual human beings. We have tossed onto the junkheap of history the notion about governments, as such, holding sovereignty.

Nowhere in its recitation of various rights does the Constitution mention any rights as belonging to the states—or to the federal government, for that matter. In the Constitution, rights pertain only to people. The Tenth Amendment, which is regarded as the ark of the covenant of states' rights, speaks, only in terms of "powers" reserved to the states, not "rights" vested in them. To many the difference may seem to be one of semantics, but there is more to it than that.

As James Madison stated in the *Federalist:* "The ultimate authority resides with the people alone, and it will not depend on the comparative ambition of the different governments, whether either, or which of them, will be able to enlarge its sphere of jurisdiction at the expense of the other."

Throughout American history and the states' rights argument has been put repeatedly to test. But most people have wanted a "more perfect union" and a less disjointed one, and have said so emphatically, time and time again—by ballot and by bayonet.

Many states'-righters contend that state and local governments are being hog-tied by swiftly growing encroachments of the federal government into what heretofore were constitutionally reserved functions of state and local governments. On the other hand, detractors of the states argue that state governments are useless relics of a bygone era and that the only answer is to throw the full weight of the federal government into providing the entire cafeteria of services once left to the state and local governments. I do not find myself in harmony with either position.

The states' rights banner has been waved so often in our history that we tend to forget it has been most generally used essentially as a political weapon—first by one group and then by another, as it seemed to suit their various purposes. In American political life it has been an expression of protest or a defensive tactic, far more than a sincere call for constructive effort.

This has been true from the beginning of our federal republic. Thomas Jefferson, in the early part of his career, had no more love for strong state governments than he had for a strong national government. James Madison, at the Constitutional Convention, actually sought to give the federal Congress the power to nullify any enactment of a state legislature. Yet both exploited the states' rights issue as a means of driving the Federalists out of power, and in the process they became the real fathers of the "interposition" doctrine, although this could not have been more inconsistent with Madison's basic philosophy or with Jefferson's subsequent actions as President. The Federalists, on the other hand, responded with a defense of their New England commercial interests under the banner of states' rights, and even very seriously considered secession.

Even Calhoun's position on states' rights was somewhat flexible. As that perceptive southern scholar and author, James McBride Dabbs, has pointed out: "Calhoun's brilliant theory [the independence of states] was motivated by his devotion to the southern situation. The South opposed states' rights when that seemed profitable, as in its bitter condemnation of certain northern states which refused, on the ground of states' rights, to return fugitive slaves."

Just after the turn of the century, Congress was faced with a strong plea to grant home rule to the voteless District of Columbia, which has been committed to its care by the Constitution. Fearing a heavy Negro-voter registration, many Congressmen, from the North as well as from the South, strong champions of states' rights back home, argued that the "federal interest" in the District of Columbia could not be jeopardized by local self-government.

States' rights always have been a favorite haven of refuge for special interests in fear of government regulation.

In the latter part of the nineteenth century the states' rights argument played a prominent part in the debates over social legislation and economic regulation. Then, railroads and their political spokesmen first vigorously denied the power of states to regulate interstate railroads. To prevent the states from regulating them, they strongly argued that this was a job for the federal government. But when the U. S. Supreme Court finally agreed with them, they quickly lost interest in federal regulation.

State legislators often scream for "local rights" in opposition to the exercise of powers of state government on behalf of human rights and needs, and frequently it turns out that they are advancing the same special interests whose cause governors and congressmen and senators espouse when they call for "states' rights" in opposition to the exercise of federal authority on behalf of the same human rights and needs. Often it really is not the "rights" of county or state or federal or any other government about which these people are primarily concerned. Rather, it is the "right"—or, more precisely, the preferential advantage—of the particular special interests they seek to serve.

Minimum wages are a good example. Those economic interests which have opposed—in the name of states' rights—every single effort at the federal level to provide American citizens assurance of decent minimum wages have not encouraged the state governments to provide such. It is not really the "federal encroachment" they oppose: it is minimum wages. Lost somewhere in all of this are the human rights and needs involved.

Much of the change and shifting in government power has come about through the fault of no one, including local, state, and federal governments. Rather, it has been attributable directly to the national character of the growth and change taking place in the economy and in the society.

Initially, both the federal and state levels of government performed a minimum of functions—in keeping with the needs of a predominantly agricultural society in which each family could provide, more or less independently, for its own sustenance and security. But that society changed rapidly in the nineteenth century. The industrial and scientific revolutions were beginning. In the last quarter of that century state governments began to enact laws establishing the eight-hour workday, regulating working conditions of women and children, requiring safety and sanitary facilities in factories, and creating local boards of health and public welfare.

Yet the great revolution in American government had scarcely begun to take place. And when the depression of the late 1920's and early 1930's struck, it was national, and, therefore, most of the remedy had to be national in character. One result was Social Security, which obviously could be created and administered only on a national scale by a national government.

A state government still possesses complete and exclusive authority over any railroad that is entirely within its territory and that handles no significant amount of traffic originating in other states. The states still have the regulatory power, but the railroads which fit that description are now virtually non-existent. With the nationwide evolution of transportation, commerce, and communication, the regulation of industries serving the public in these categories clearly could not be left exclusively in the hands of state governments. More recently we have learned that through-highways linking the nation's major population centers, essential to the national convenience and defense, could not be left to the initiative and exclusive control of dozens of different state governments.

These examples can be multiplied many times, as the growth of the nation and its technology and the interdependence of the states have dictated that the country must become more united, more truly national, in many of its characteristics.

In many cases, however, it is not the evolution of our society that has made the exercise of greater federal power necessary but the lack of will and the limited abilities of the states. State failures and mounting national concern about them have invited and encouraged the federal government to move in.

As governor, I served on a joint federal-state commission, created by President Eisenhower in cooperation with the Council of State Governments. The commission set out bravely to examine the whole field of federal-state relations and to identify functions that should be returned to state jurisdiction. It turned out to be an exercise in futility. We found that, notwithstanding all . the return-to-states'-rights talk, there were no substantial federal functions that the states really wanted back.

The reason was simple: "'New" functions that the federal government had undertaken were, by and large, serving important needs of national scope and characteristics. There was widespread unwillingness or inability by the states to provide such services. The states needed all their revenues for other purposes. For example, no state wanted the federal government to stop its assistance to hospital construction within the states or to stop making it possible for states to build collage dormitories with long-term federal loans or to discontinue its stimulative grants for improved health and education services, and so on.

Now, every state in the union had the power, the legal authority, to undertake such services. But state governments lacked either the desire to make the try or the ability to do so in terms of facilities, funds, and the extent of geographical jurisdiction.

The whole blame for this cannot reasonably be visited upon state officials. The people who have elected them too often have insisted upon or encouraged commitments of "no additional taxes"; they have cheered the ringing promises of candidates to get the "federal government off our back"; they have lighted up with hope and expectation for pension increases and countless new services—all at the same time.

Another very strong reason for increasing federal power has developed in the area of national civil rights. The protection and advancement of the individual rights of American citizens should be the primary aim of all government. To the degree that a government fails to serve this fundamental purpose, to that extent it fails as a government. Much foundering by the states can be measured directly from this standard.

The sad truth is that the states have allowed their own prominence to be lowered, their own effectiveness to be impaired, their own stature to be tarnished, by their failure to serve that fundamental purpose of meeting the clear needs of their citizens. In this last half of the twentieth century, the world has grown too small and the times too perilous for us, for the nation, to be divisible into fifty different concepts of our central rights of American citizenship.

While I was governor of Florida, our legislature joined several other southern legislatures in adopting a resolution of "interposition," which, on the face of it, declared void the U.S. Supreme Court school desegregation ruling and sought to "interpose" the doctrine of states' rights. I had no veto power over it, for it was a simple expression of the legislature's viewpoint, but I publicly branded it as a fraud and hoax. Further, I could not let it pass my desk without in some way registering my disapproval, and so I picked up my pen and wrote a little message on the face of the original recorded resolution before it went into the state archives.

In that message I stated that if this resolution "declaring decisions of the Court to be 'null and void' is to be taken seriously, it is anarchy and rebellion against the nation which must remain 'indivisible under God' if it is to survive." And I said if history was to judge me wrong in this regard, there would be proof of where I stood.

I have always felt rather good about having done that. But I also wrote something else—another sentence in which I stated that in my opinion the U.S. Supreme Court had improperly usurped powers reserved to the states under the Constitution, but that the state should seek only legal means of avoidance.

I wish I had not written that last part. I do not feel that way now. But since I did, and feel differently now, I think I should say so. Looking at the desegregation decision of the Court in the light of a longer perspective, with the benefit of experience and reflection that the passage of time has brought, I do not now feel that there was any usurpation of the powers of a state.

Granted that the Constitution reserves to the states the power to provide for the education of their residents, it does not reserve to the states the power to provide adequate educational opportunities to some American citizens living within other boundaries and not to others. Indeed, there is an overriding obligation on the federal government to see to it that the rights of all Americans as citizens of the United States are not abridged by actions or by defaults of state governments. I am now convinced that the Court was acting entirely within its authority in taking that step to assure the full rights of American citizenship for all American citizens. It is just unfortunate that long failure of state government made federal action necessary.

There simply can be no state right to default on a national duty.

As a state legislator and state senator and as a governor in a state which had the most malapportioned legislature of all the fifty states, I used to feel that substantial reapportionment could be obtained from within the legislature itself —not on the first try, but certainly in stages. That is the way it should come, through the legislative bodies themselves. After six years of trying and failing, and trying and failing, I learned by bitter experience that this was impossible. I did not want to see reapportionment come through coercion by the federal government. But now that I am convinced this is the only way it can come, I welcome the recent entry of the federal courts into this field. Our whole system would be in serious peril if such a glaring fault in government should be without a remedy.

What is more, I am pleased to note the grounds upon which that federal judicial entry has been made—the federal protection of a federally assured right, the right to equal protection of the laws. There is no question in my mind that the courts are entirely within their proper jurisdiction in this instance, that citizens living in the more heavily populated section of persistently malapportioned states are, without question, being denied equal protection of the laws. And in this historic decision the highest court in the land may well have saved the state governments from being wrecked by those who profess to be their strongest defenders.

It is ironic indeed that many of those who scream loudest against this effort to assure all the people the equal protection of the laws in legislative representation are the first to insist upon the federal protection of their property rights—such as keeping inviolate contract obligations and making private property safe from confiscation—all guaranteed under the same organic provisions. Rather than an improper invasion or smothering of the prerogatives of the states, I regard the action by the federal judiciary in this field as the greatest liberating force for

restoration of the effectiveness and prestige of the states in a long, lone time.

The day will come—as come it must— when state government, freed of the highly favored predilections of malapportioned legislatures, will be championing the cause of those in the society who are not adequately represented under the existing arrangement. When that happens, state governments will be in position to command the respect and stir the enthusiasm of greater numbers of their citizens. There will be a much wider range of opportunities for state governments to exercise their powers which now are too often in atrophy.

State government is not dead; it is not dying; if it is sick, the disease is curable.

As a system, its greatest fault is that too often and in too many places it has been dominated by, and made to serve the advantages of, a whole band of special interests which have no intention of voluntarily yielding more control of the ship of state to the people.

While many states have moved effectively, it seems that in many others it is going to be necessary for the federal government—in this instance, the federal judiciary—to follow up the shot it has fired across the bow and actually clear the decks of malapportioned legislatures.

It should not be concluded from what I have said that states have been idle, leaving the whole job up to the federal government. In 1962, federal expenditures—not counting what was spent for defense and foreign aid, for veterans' affairs, for interest on the national debt and for Social Security payments—were less than $35 billion. State and local governments, on the other hand, spent in 1962 a total of more than $81 billion. Total federal aid to the states was less than $7 billion in 1962—a very small fraction of the total expenditures of state and local government. And the direct federal contributions to our local governments were less than $800 million.

What has actually happened is that as our nation has grown, so have the needs of its people. And government—federal, state, and local—simply has been slow to serve these human needs as they have developed.

Instead of demeaning the importance

of states, the increased need for human services should increase the importance of states, for it calls upon them to become more and more effective in terms of service to their citizens.

In every state in the union there is a crying need for stronger efforts by the state governments to advance programs that will enrich and safeguard the lives of people—in such fields as expanded public education, public health and hospitalization, slum clearance and urban renewal, industrial development, rehabilitation programs, juvenile deliquency and the whole gamut of services for children, air-land-water pollution control, conservation of natural resources, civil rights and public defenders, consumer protection—all the things that bear on the welfare and happiness of people.

There is need for more uniform laws of state-wide application to provide higher standards in such areas as zoning and planning, building codes, fair tax assessment, traffic control, law enforcement—the list seems almost endless. Anyone with any doubts about this should just take a look at the figures showing future population projections.

And in none of these areas is there any lack of state authority.

Once the federal courts are able to break the legislative apportionment deadlock, I predict that we will see a real resurgence of progressive, human-need-oriented legislation from legislative halls in state after state. When this happens, state government will become a far more exciting and vital force in American life, opening up new vistas for serving the need of all our people. Once they get moving with greater effectiveness in this direction, the state governments are quite capable of making the federal efforts appear pallid in contrast.

We may be seeing the beginning, rather than the end, of the golden age of state government in America. We may stand at the threshold of a period in which state governments will be able to demonstrate all of their inherent flexibility, all of the great potential they actually have, to make the adjustments and provide the services required by a future which will be marked by increasingly rapid social, economic, and political change.

In 1960, almost seven out of every ten Americans lived in urban areas, on only 1 per cent of the land area of our country. If our state governments should fail to respond to the need and attitudes of this increasingly urban America, they could become the unnecessary middleman and cease to contribute any meaningful political vitality in our system, forcing a larger and larger degree of local home rule and stronger and stronger ties with a national government more responsive to their needs.

However, if state governments can excel in the quality of their service, they can become, perhaps for the first time, what the founding fathers thought they would be: the best guardians of the individual liberties of our people and the best servants and ministers of their needs.

I want to see us prepare for that day now, and hasten its coming. I would like to see the development of an *annual national federal-state conference,* called by the President of the United States and in cooperation with the Council of State Governments. Representing the federal government would be the President and key executive department personnel designated by him, and senators and representatives selected by their respective houses of Congress. Representing the states would be governors and top state executive department personnel designated by the governors, and key members of the state legislatures.

The purpose of the conference would be threefold:

1) To generate a better understanding—within the federal government and among the American people—of unmet needs within the states, of what the states are doing to meet those needs, and of what the federal government might properly do to help the states meet such needs.

2) To generate a better understanding—within the state governments and among the American people—of the role being performed by the federal government, of what it proposes to do in meeting national needs, and of how the states may be actively helpful in these efforts.

3) To arrive, if possible, at some common understanding as to what programs will be undertaken—and by whom—to meet the needs of modern America.

I recognize immediately many inherent difficulties, such as the possibility of the conference degenerating into tawdry, self-serving political grandstanding. But this presupposes human failures that I believe we could rise above.

I cannot help feeling that—if projected with the full power and restige of both federal and state leadership behind it—such an annual conference would provide an opportunity for injecting some fresh breezes into the stale fog which now closes in on too much of our federal-state relationships. A meeting like this well could serve as a catalyst for sound common understanding and common action.

Vast new horizons beckon to this nation and its people. It is a time to fashion some fresh approaches. Those who persist in trying to sail state governments into the backwaters of sectionalism and special-interest service, and who visualize a prime role of the states to be the detractor and antagonist of the union, some day will discover they are at the tiller of a ghost ship.

I hope this never happens. It will not happen if our hearts and efforts are with the people and their rights. It is with them that we must take our stand and do our fighting. We have run out of time for anything less.

The States

ORVILLE L. FREEMAN

Mr. Freeman is currently the Secretary of Agriculture in the President's Cabinet. Prior to his original appointment by President John F. Kennedy he served three terms as governor of Minnesota.

Perhaps a former governor, who has struggled with the shackles of a state constitution that is far too precise and far too literal, can appreciate most fully the genius of those who wrote the federal Constitution. Their inspiration was not alone in the structure of government that they designed for us but in the tone and spirit of the words they chose. Those words are specific enough to give direction, yet general enough to permit their interpretation and reinterpretation in each generation by living legislators and judges moved by the circumstances of new times.

This does not mean, however, that the Constitution has always adapted itself rapidly enough to prevent hardship and suffering, or rapidly enough to promote maximum progress. Always, over our system, hangs the threat of breakdown, because the founding fathers, in their re-

Reprinted from *The Mazes of Modern Government,* Center for the Study of Democratic Institutions, 1964, by permission of the Fund for the Republic.

action against tyranny, bequeathed us a structure of government with powers that are dispersed and scattered—between the branches of the federal government and between the federal government and the states. In times of crisis, foreign and domestic, these powers have to be reassembled so that they can be used.

What saves us is that people know this to be true. Instinctively, they recognize that a weakness does exist in the structure of their government that in time of crisis must be overcome. The great, unifying force is the office of the Presidency, and, when it is vital to do so, the people, the Congress, and the governors of the states do rally behind the President. We have witnessed such periods of rallying—in the great depression and during war. We have just seen another such period of rallying.

Perhaps there is no better area in which to illustrate how the American people instinctively move to correct the weakness in our system than in the division of authority between the federal union and the states. Initially divided, the powers of the federal government and the states *have* been reassembled so that they can be used. I use the word "instinctively" rather than "consciously" or "deliberately," because all the time the reassembly of divided powers was going on, the public and the politicians alike still theoretically accepted the premise that the Constitution intended a clean-cut division of powers between federal and state government—each level with its own set of functions and authorities, to be administered without "interference" from any other level.

Every politician bows to what Galbraith would call the "conventional wisdom" on these matters. Nobody ever campaigned for the Presidency on a platform denouncing "state sovereignty" or "states' rights." For that matter, nobody ever campaigned for governor on a platform denouncing local autonomy and local rights.

I believe Morton Grodzins first used the metaphor that government in the United States is not, if it ever was, a three-layer cake; it has to be, and has become, a marble cake, with chocolate strands of governmental functions intertwined through it from top to bottom.

Today's new pattern of federal-state relations was not conceived full-blown in anybody's brain. It was evolved piece by piece by pragmatists who had no patience with constitutional absolutes and asked instead, "What works?" But those who did this were, I suggest, completely faithful to the founding fathers. Those young men who struck down the divine right of kings, who risked their lives and property in support of a new political and social relationship they had not yet even defined, were surely pragmatists.

Let us accept their mandate. Let us look around us at what is, instead of what has been, and examine our federal-state relationships against the test of what works instead of against a mythology of absolutes.

The literature of federal-state relationships is replete with myths that need to be demolished. One of them is the layer-cake absolute that calls for neat division between federal and state governments. This myth ought to have been demolished by decades of repudiation in practice, but there is still a widespread wistful notion that all this is temporary and that one of these days, when we just put our minds to it, we will sort out the functions of government and put the cake back into the proper layers.

The notion has an amazing longevity; indeed, there are always candidates who seek to attract a substantial following by suggesting that, if elected, they would restore the states to their rightful position in the scheme of things. President Eisenhower came to power after a campaign in which he, too, explicitly contended that the federal government was over-grown, had usurped too many state functions, and spent too much money. Yet, when he left office, the federal government was bigger, had undertaken more functions while giving up none, and was spending considerably more money.

Mr. Eisenhower should be given full credit, however, for putting the issue to a thorough test. Two months after his election he asked the Congress to authorize the appointment of a commission to study how to develop what he called "sounder" relationships among federal, state, and local governments. The Congress in setting up the commission swallowed the layer-cake myth without even gulping. It directed the commission to define "the proper roles" of the federal government and the states "to the end that these relations may be clearly defined and the functions concerned may be allocated to their proper jurisdiction."

The Commission on Inter-Governmental Relations, which came to be known as the Kestnbaum Commission, acknowledged two years later that functions could not be neatly allocated among layers of government, but it still contended that "duties" could. With considerable sophistication, it laid out general principles to guide the reallocation of duties, placing much and appropriate emphasis, incidentally, on strengthening the state governments so that they could assume their greater role. But, then, in the second half of the report, when the commission began to deal with individual areas of government activity, the members found not a single area in which they were willing to recommend any drastic decentralization. They apologized for the dichotomy between their theory and their pragmatism.

That might have been the end of that. But it wasn't. In 1957 President Eisenhower laid down a challenge to the Governors' Conference to set up a joint Federal-State Action Committee to identify functions of government, as well as revenue sources, that could be shifted from the federal government to the states. Governor Collins has described this in his paper. After a year of labor the committee identified four functions that they proposed to shift in whole or in part, along with one revenue source. The most important function that they proposed the federal government abandon was aid for the building of sewage treatment plants. Some of us minority governors felt that a more unlikely place to begin the dismantling process could hardly have been conceived, since few things are more interstate by nature than a river carrying sewage across state lines. The recommendations of the task force were greeted with no enthusiasm, and the whole undertaking quietly ended.

Still, myths die hard. We can already hear this one in the campaign rhetoric of 1964.

There are some other myths that also die hard. I select just three:

The myth that the level of government that administers a function should raise the money to pay for it, and vice versa.

This precept is violated in every grant-in-aid program that exists, yet it is still used as an argument against every new one that is proposed. In spite of the successful operation of federal aid for vocational education for nearly half a century, new, important programs for federal aid to education have been killed largely by this myth—by the slogan, "Federal aid means federal control." But experience has shown that federal control does not follow federal aid unless we decide, as pragmatic legislators, that it should. And I know of no legislator who wants federal control of education.

The fact is that a higher level of government may have superior tax resources, but a lower level may have superior administrative resources. If that is the case —and in the field of education it clearly

is—then federal aid without federal control may be the right solution. Those who are familiar with the vocational education program, for one example, know that such a relationship can be established and maintained. In other circumstances, where uniformity of policy or administration is important, federal control should accompany federal aid. But the question is, in a given case, what works best? There is no absolute.

The myth that local government is more democratic, and, thus, functions administered by governmental units close to the people are administered best.

This myth has come to take such an extreme form these days that the federal government is sometimes portrayed as a kind of alien monster set loose to prey upon the people's liberties. Yet I have watched at close range the legislative bodies of a city, a state, and the nation, and I would not contend that the United States Congress is any less responsive to the people's will than either a state legislature or a city council. Nor am I any less mindful of public opinion in my present post as a federal executive official than I was as a state governor.

At its best, local government may be more democratic and responsive simply because it is more accessible. But this depends on the existence of free and contested elections and a well-informed electorate. The pressure that forces a government to be responsive to the people is the pressure of the next election, when the consent of the governed is given or withdrawn. Every Presidential election is a hotly contested two-party race, as are most state elections. It is at the local level that we are most likely to find one-party rule, without effective political competition.

Indeed, it can be easily documented that the nearest thing to dictatorship in America has been the petty tyrannies of local political bosses, some of which have survived for decades during which control of state and national governments has changed hands over and over again. It is far easier for a citizen to be intimidated by the local power structure than by those who rule in far-off state capitals and in Washington. And we know, of course, as one example, that in a few localities in this country the vote is permitted to only a minority of citizens.

As for efficiency, the most monumental examples of waste and corruption, in relation to the size of budgets, have been in local governments, particularly those under the domination of bosses who are outside popular control.

The myth that the federal government is collecting and spending an increasing share of the nation's tax resources, at the expense of the states and localities.

Quite the opposite is true. In the postwar period through 1961 (which is the last year for which complete figures are available) state and local budgets rose more than twice as fast as the federal budget. Specifically, while the federal budget receipts about doubled during this period, state and local revenues more than quadrupled. As for the national debt, it rose during this same period by less than 10 per cent, while state and local debt rose 400 per cent. Total *private* debt, incidentally, increased by 230 per cent— or twenty-three times as much as the national debt.

The myth of federal profligacy, as against state and local frugality, dies hard too. But it should have been buried long ago.

Those who decry the marble cake of federal-state relationships like to assert that federal action stifles local initiative. But the fact is that federal aid has added to—not subtracted from—the vitality of public life in the states, the counties, and the cities. Programs of federal aid have made it possible to share scarce technological knowledge over wide areas and have provided a technique for sharing with local and state governments the revenue resources of the federal government.

There are many cities in America where the federal program known as "urban renewal" has brought a renaissance in civic spirit. The availability of federal help has inspired communities to organize, to plan, to initiate, to re-house their slum dwellers, to rehabilitate blight, to replace dreariness with shining newness. Not only the economic base of downtown areas but the morale of whole communities has been uplifted. Yet, if there is such a thing as a local governmental function, which in no way crosses city boundaries, surely urban renewal is that function. So why don't the cities just go ahead and renew, without demanding federal help? The reason can be given in a word: Urban renewal requires an infusion of public financial resources beyond those which local communities can tap. And, so, before there was a federal urban renewal program, there were only a handful of local projects of this type; today there are many hundreds; and if the federal law were repealed, there would again be but a handful.

When we look at the comparable problems of rural America, the issue comes into even clearer focus. For half a century population has been drained out of the American countryside, pulled on the one hand by the economic opportunity of the cities and pushed on the other by advancing technology that has released manpower out of agriculture. Small towns and villages almost everywhere in our land outside the orbit of metropolitan areas have been drying up. One bank may survive where four flourished a generation ago; Main Street is spotted with vacant and decaying stores. More than half the counties of America lost population during the decade of the 1950's, and almost all of them were rural.

Thus, a vicious circle has come into being. The inherent limitations of the property tax are now compounded by a decline in taxable resources. Many local governmental jurisdictions in rural areas simply lack the means to support an acceptable level of public services. Few have the resources necessary for the self-generation of new growth.

In the Department of Agriculture we have been searching for devices and programs that will give to rural America the incentive and the means for revival that urban renewal and corresponding urban programs have provided to our cities. We are fully aware of the fact that the principle factors underlying the plight of rural America are the technological revolution in farming and the economic consequences that result. We know that agricultural programs designed to improve income from the production of agricultural commodities are not, in themselves, enough to bring to many of our rural areas the economic progress they need. Rather, these areas need help in making the most of both human and natural resources. They need help to enable both the young and the mature who cannot earn a decent living in farming to find and qualify for other economic opportunities. They need help to transform land resources that are no longer needed to produce crops into resources for timber, for grazing, or for recreation. And so we are developing a broad range of programs that we call Rural Areas Development.

The federal government has so many programs of community assistance that no local official can be expected even to know of all the agencies, much less all the individual programs. The Area Redevelopment Administration, the Small Business Administration, the Community Facilities Administration, the Farmers Home Administration, the Soil Conservation Service, the Agricultural Stabilization and Conservation Service, and other agencies of the Department of Agriculture and other departments can provide loans where private credit is not available, technical assistance, and in some circumstances even grants. The Department of Health, Education, and Welfare offers assistance for vocational education and retraining, for hospital construction, for waste treatment plants, and various welfare services, channeled mainly through state agencies. States can occasionally offer some financial aid and coordinate their own programs, such as highways, with the development plans, but they are perhaps most important as sources of leadership and expert counseling, the latter provided mainly by their universities and colleges.

The objectives of Rural Areas Development are to provide a means of communication through this complex array of federal and state help for community effort, so that local leaders can know of the aids that are available; to encourage their use; and to identify the deficiencies in the combined federal-state-local effort, with a view to further legislation or appropriations where they may be needed.

Federal assistance, far from stifling local initiative, releases it from the confines of inadequate resources. Federal aid makes it possible for community energies to be rewarded. It enables people who want to do things, and who otherwise could not, to do those things. In our marble-cake relationship, the public life of rural America as well as urban America is being revitalized. By the pragmatic test, the system works.

But it may be asked whether the states would not do the job of leading their communities if the federal government stepped out. The record tells us, no. The Kestnbaum Commission emphasized the handicaps of antiquated state constitutions and outmoded state governmental structures, and these are truly serious handicaps. In my experience, however, the most serious drawback to state and local action is the lack of financial resources.

Ours is a *national* economy. Wealth and income are highly concentrated—and highly mobile. If we are to tap wealth and income for public purposes where they exist—and do so with any approach to equity—we must rely heavily on the corporate and individual income taxes. No single state can afford to step far beyond its neighbors in taxing corporations without being subjected to the blackmail of tax competition. To cite a single example: The governor of a state, some years ago, proposed a new corporation tax to help pay the costs of education. The next day a giant corporation headquartered in the state announced that if the tax were passed it would locate no more plants in that area. And on the day after that, some other major corporations in the state's leading industry announced that their policy would be the same. No governor or legislature can take the political heat of being charged with the responsibility for driving industry out of their state. So the tax was dropped, and education continued to suffer.

The federal government now taxes corporate and individual wealth and income uniformly, wherever they exist, in whatever state. These taxes cannot be escaped, except by fleeing the confines of the country. It is ludicrous to suggest that this tax system be dismantled because of some supposed constitutional absolute that the states should take on more responsibility. Particularly is this true when the states can be allowed to spend money—through further extension of our federal-state grant systems. In short, the system of federal-state-local relationships that has evolved does work. It gets results. Indeed, because of the inherent nature of the different tax systems, it has proved to be the only way we have been able to get such results.

For these reasons one of the most pernicious features of our national life is the current virulent anti-federal government crusade. The streams of propaganda that pour forth in the organs of conventional wisdom, day after day, year after year, portraying the federal government as some kind of ogre have had their effect throughout America. It is a dangerous state of affairs when citizens are indoctrinated to regard their own government as though it were a dangerous alien power. Of course, federal bureaucracy has its faults. But it is these that should be attacked, not the institution itself. And it is the latter that is being undermined.

What is the motivation for all this? Are those who so violently defend states' rights and attack the federal government really concerned with constitutional principles? Some are, of course. They are bemused by the myths that I enumerated earlier. But I am sure that deeply involved in this crusade are the less worthy motives of economic self-interest. Too many times I have observed that the same organizations that oppose federal expenditures for, say, education are the same groups that, at the state level, also oppose state expenditures for the same purpose. And then, when one looks at what goes on at the local level, they are in the ranks of the opposition there as well. Far too many of those who use the club of "states' rights" to beat the federal government over the head turn out to be against the expansion of government services at any level.

They recognize what we all know— that government at all levels involves some contest between the "haves" and the "have-nots," and taxation always results in some redistribution of the wealth. Those who are opulent enough to have no need for public welfare, or public clinics, or public recreation, or public housing, or public education simply consider it in their self-interest to starve these functions.

But even for those who are ideologically consistent, who support state programs while opposing federal programs, the motive of self-interest may not be wholly missing, for the basic fact is that the federal tax structure is progressive, and state and local tax systems tend to be regressive. The federal tax load is carried heavily by corporations and their stockholders; the sales and property taxes of state and local governments fall lightly on corporations and usually do not touch at all those forms of property which are locked in safety deposit vaults. Thus, any redistribution of financial responsibility from the federal government to the states would be a shift of the tax burden downward on the income scale. And any expansion of federal aid, in lieu of state taxation, would be a redistribution of the burden upward.

This is not a case of myopia. Those who stand to gain from the redistribution of taxation can see the situation very well. And this explains, I am sure, why the propaganda campaign against the federal government is so lavishly financed.

The federal government will continue —and should continue—to have a growing role in the affairs of our communities. We cannot retreat to the day of self-contained local governmental units any more than we can restore an economy of frontier subsistence farms.

We must have done with semantic absolutes about our federal system. We must stop chasing the will-of-the-wisp of governmental stratification. Then we can get on with the job of making the tangled skein of federal-state-local relationships work better and more effectively in meeting the needs of today and the years ahead.

Our government has always been able to adapt itself, by evolution instead of revolution, to meet the needs of our people under changing conditions. The severity of the test it faces today arises out of the accelerated rate of change. Our challenge today is to accelerate our rate of progress in the field of social engineering. The barriers and roadblocks most seriously impeding that progress are tied less to the structural characteristics of our government than to the degree of vision and understanding on the part of our people. If we can dispel the myths that cloud people's minds with regard to government, if we can bring about a clear understanding of the problems and potential of the years ahead, we will be able to demonstrate to ourselves—and prove to the world—that democracy *is* the wave of the future, and that under democratic institutions we can achieve the abundance that science and technology now offer to mankind.

The Miniature Re-examined

ROBERT C. WOOD

Robert C. Wood is a former professor of political science at MIT and a leading contributor to the literature dealing with suburbia. He is now Undersecretary of the Department of Housing and Urban Development.

DEFENDERS OF THE FAITH

The values of the small government and the small town are not usually considered proper subjects for debate in America. As Roscoe Martin observes, "the Grassroots concept is invoked with confidence in support of manifold causes . . . treated almost universally with a respect bordering on reverence . . . one who rejects or ignores a grassroot incantation does so at his peril, for the public mind does not entertain the alternative of grassroots fallibility. *In hoc signo vinces* was not devised for the grassroots talisman, but it might have been. . . ."

The question is universal and timeless, and, simply put, it is: why believe that the small community produces the best life, and more especially, the best government?

Since antiquity the answers to this question have been overwhelmingly on the side of the ideology and, as Martin indicates, the consensus is so great that any criticism begins with poor prospects of success. . . .

In the modern world, the small town still appears to provide an opportunity for people to participate in public affairs, to have a "sense of personal competence to

Reprinted from Robert C. Wood, *Suburbia: Its People and Their Politics* (Boston: Houghton Mifflin Company, 1958), pp. 259–291, by permission of the author.

make a difference," to make mistakes and not bear catastrophe as a consequence. For the most part, technology and the disparate elements of industrial life appear to confirm rather than destroy the ideology. To many scholars the job of modern political thought is to preserve the intimate contact of the neighborhood, to reconcile large-scale operations with small-scale independence and to make the small community a living one for twentieth century man.

Of course, those who see human relations essentially as a matter of deliberate contrivance differ importantly from those of the body politic school of thought in the values they ascribe to small government. Especially in the United States, we have not accepted the Greek concept of a society of order, class and structural balance. Our sense of community emphasizes individual equality, and, since the begining, Americans have been "held together not by the knowledge that they were different parts of a corporate whole, but by the knowledge that they were similar participants in a uniform way of life." Where Plato and Aristotle sought civilization as the supreme objective of the self-sufficient community, where Burke appealed to the continuity of history, the philosophy of reason emphasizes individual freedom and democratic participation as more important end-products.

Nevertheless, whether man arrives pure and undefiled on the political scene or finds his true birthright only in political association; whether he is rational in the eighteenth century sense or psychologically encircled by twentieth century emotions; whether there is a natural law or the expressions of Locke are only fiction, there has always been, in every general scheme, a place for the small community and the small government. Its origins may be utilitarian or ordained by supernatural prescription, individualistic or pluralistic, but the result is almost always a recognition of the locality and a reaffirmation of its right to separate existence, wherever possible. The construct of community remains the highest purpose of political science, and though the Great Society may offer more security and wealth, few have argued that it is as happy or as kindly as the small. In the final judgments the great thinkers concerned with the problem of legitimate government unite in defense of the grassroots ideal.

THE LOGIC OF THE FAITH

Testimonials—the conclusions of important philosophers—are one way to defend the small community; logical argument is another. To buttress the case in the modern world, the insights and judgments of every age can be put together into a simple, apparently commonsense chain of reasoning that runs essentially like this: Small towns offer certain indigneous qualities which, taken collectively, create a milieu in which the American aims of equality and liberty are best secured. They promise the development of individual initiative, operate as a bulwark against concentrated political power, provide the most effective union of the collective and private disposition of mankind that we can hope to find. Destroy these qualities, embrace completely the gargantuan world in which we live, and the traditional goals of American society are also in peril.

But what specifically do the qualities of small town life contribute to a harmonious relation of man to man and to good government? In the logic of the faith, each characteristic has its own beneficial effect which can be recognized and defended. Whether found in the small town of other centuries or in the modern suburb, propinquity, interdependence, common beliefs and backgrounds, some measure of leisure time are thought to encourage political activity which almost guarantees effective democratic government. And when their separate contributions are added together, the case for the small locality seems sturdy indeed.

Propinquity, for example, apparently provides the familiarity and experience, the intimacy of personal relations, that Plato and Aristotle stressed so heavily and that helps ensure the sense of integration so sought after today. In a small town, individual identity is never a problem; people can know whomever it is important to know. There are fewer secrets and fewer idols than in the large cities; flaws and strengths of character are quickly recognized; the good are separated from the bad. In the small government, the public program and the official who carries it out are known, judged, understood directly; they can be experienced, they are visible. Life does not impose impossible demands on rationality and character; community organization is attuned to the reality of human nature. The situation is of manageable proportions, and, because the boundaries are fixed, it can stay within manageable proportions.

To the concreteness of life that propinquity provides, the condition of interdependence is thought to add a healthy motive of good will. Men want to cooperate in the small town; they cannot tolerate the troublemaker, for his existence threatens the existence of all. Since they are bound together in their common fortunes, the solution to communal problems affects directly each man's personal future. Since total resources are limited, all members are encouraged to pull together, to be good neighbors. Sickness, adversity, natural disaster visited on one member are known to all, and since all recognize that an act of God may come again, the urge to help is reinforced by the knowledge that everyone "is in the same boat."

The bonds of fellowship that propinquity and interdependence encourage seem further strengthened by the common goals and common values inherent in the equality of a small town. The locality may be, relatively speaking, better off or less fortunate than its neighbors, or than similar communities elsewhere, but its very size fixes limits on the extremes within its own social order. There can be, it is argued, only a few who live on the Hill, if there is only one hill in town; only a few who are socially unacceptable if there is only one shanty town. Opposing values, different ambitions, sharply divergent beliefs are rarities in such a situation.

Even where differences in wealth and position exist, the variation seems acceptable. The successful succeed not through any mystique, but by working harder or being more excellent in the pursuits in which the majority are engaged. In these circumstances it is difficult to infect recognition of ability with envy and spite, for the means of accomplishment are open to all. Sharp dealings, to be countenanced, must be the established rules of the game, part of the mores of the entire community. A vast common ground of shared beliefs and customs makes cooperation comfortable and intimacy pleasurable.

Under these conditions, so the rationale runs, each member is likely to participate fully and freely in public affairs. A citizen speaks his piece in the small town first of all because what goes on is vital to his own ambitions. It concerns property, education, and the provision of utilities basic to existence. Wars, diplomacy, the fluctuations of the national economy, these matters are both difficult for the average man to understand and difficult for him to influence, but the land use of his neighborhood, the proper recording of his property, zoning, water rights, the protection of his person, the education of

his children, the construction of a new highway at the right place and at the right time, affect his everyday life. Whether or not they are provided, how they are provided, the use made of the limited resources to which the citizen contributes directly and not by the accounting sleight-of-hand of the withholding tax, are matters he understands and cares deeply about.

And even if a small town resident did not care, if his stake were slight and his status low in the narrow scale of the social order, he would still participate in public affairs, for that participation expresses, asserts, and guarantees his political equality. Only the eccentric, the hermit, the deviate, remains aloof; the proof of citizenship is by association with your neighbor, and a man establishes himself when he stands up and is counted.

In such a context, the defenders of the small town insist, leadership partakes of special qualities, at once removed from the patrician and the rabble-rouser. A leader in the small community supposedly can be neither, for in an equal society he can neither assume that his fellows are inferior nor can he raise the standard of the underdog and cannily set slave against master. The leader expresses the sense of the community and he helps formulate and crystallize it. But he can never "deliver" the majority opinion and he cannot be above it. Bounded by the conditions of equality and participation, known intimately by his fellows, the leader cannot rely on oratory or adulation, nor can he exhibit only driving ambition. Typically, he operates almost invisibly, knotting together one personal association with another until he has secured sufficient respect and support to put his measures through.

The respect may be misplaced; the leader may simply have cultivated a familiarity which his neighbors mistake for fellowship. On the other hand, he may have a genuine, lively interest in the work which must be done, and a willingness to accept responsibility. But, regardless of motives, his leadership is never flamboyant. Small town leadership is in town moderator style, unassuming, calm, equitable and knowledgeable, without frills or airs. Accessibility is the key condition, whether the leader operates as a petty tyrant or a devoted trustee to the community spirit, and being accessible, his success depends on his own sensitivity to the moods and aspirations of his fellows.

Finally, it is argued, the activities of the small community are likely to take place in an atmosphere of leisure, in the sense that vocation does not consume all time and all attention. There is a limit to the number of things that must be done, and a limit to the number of events that demand attention. Each day or each week may bring a major problem to the fore, but it is likely that the problem is the only one for that period. The question of *choosing* the event is rarely an issue, for in the small town there is usually but one church social, one fire, one scandal, one television program, one public emergency at a time, and men shift attention successively from one event to another and are not—indeed cannot be —confused by competing spectacles.

So advocates of the ideology point out that there is time for reflection, for contemplation, for second thoughts, for deliberation, for the cooling of emotions, for rational appraisals, which permit a sense of direction and rational decisions. To many, this quality of time is the most precious blessing the small community can offer. More than propinquity, equality, the opportunity for active participation and passive leadership, the slower rhythm ensures the manageability of the small community. It encourages the ex-

pression of the communal nature of man in an orderly, regular fashion; it removes the tensions of self-seeking and provides the requisites for sensible common action.

The elaboration and description of these qualities, collectively and individually, is the reasoned argument that supports the authority of the philosopher and the instinct of the laymen who defend the small government. Its appeal seems universal, because the traits seem common to all men of all times. Good will, neighborliness, courage, fair play, tolerance, patience, open-minded inquiry—since Plato, these are the human qualities that are to be idealized. And they can exist, if one follows the logic, only in small settings. They are not, in Arthur Morgan's words, "the fruits of civilization, but rather its roots." Since they can apparently be found only on a small scale, great civilization paradoxically can be constructed only from small societies where government and neighborhood commingle and political and social reality become one.

It is little wonder that men wax sentimental when they write of the grassroots, speak of "plain citizens and humble leaders," and find poetry in the Town Meeting. The spirit of communion affects each quality observed, and reason confirms instinct in approving the Miniature. Individuality tempered by neighborliness, equality used to promote cooperation, community which tolerates eccentricity— this would seem to represent the best of America.

PROBING THE LINES

A faith so long established, so closely reasoned and so universally acclaimed has the aspect of a phalanx on the battlefield of philosophy. Yet the very unanimity of opinion is suspicious, for the two broad schools of though that collectively supply the arguments for the small community have contradictory basic assumptions and seek widely divergent ends. Given this fact, evidently one of them is mistaken when it embraces the faith. Either the men who view society and politics as principally corporate affairs with collective goals beyond those of the

individuals err when they applaud the ideology, or those who regard the state as a contrivance serving only private purposes are deceived. If the desirability of the Miniature is the issue, one question to ask is which philosophy was right and which wrong when it sided with the small town?

The most accurate answer to this question is that both of the philosophical camps we have been describing deluded themselves. The ultimate aim of those who see man essentially as a social animal is to create a body politic of such dimensions that the richness and variety of human experience can be encompassed. Their vision is a mosaic of intricate design, in which each individual makes his contribution to a purpose higher than his own aims, and the grandeur of that vision is used to justify the gradations in rank and status, the obligations of duty and discipline, the array of mutual responsibilities and social controls that are required to product the splendid work of art.

But the small community, in and of itself, never realizes that end—it never comprehends the variety of life; at best, it can serve only as an intermediate grouping within the greater whole. In Greece, the golden age was not associated with the city-state; it arrived with the Athenian Empire. The medieval city had meaning only within the Kingdom of God; Burke's parish was but a connection between the family and the commonwealth. In short, civilization has never existed within village boundaries, and the small community is nothing more than a segment in the larger pattern, expressive of only one element in the universe, and by itself quite meaningless.

Yet if corporate philosophers can use the small community only as a stepping stone for its greater purpose, the advocates of individualism have even greater difficulty in fitting it into their scheme of values. Particularly, the American version of the ideology, with its emphasis on equality as a means for liberating the individual, errs grievously when it embraces the small community. Participation in communal affairs is a simple matter in the small towns, but this expression of equality does not lead necessarily to freedom in the personal sense. More often than not, the common standard of the small community, its proudly displayed principle of equality, its suspicion of "social airs," operates in a profoundly anti-individualistic way. In Louis Hartz's words, "The man who is as good as his neighbors is in a tough spot when he confronts all his neighbors combined."

Precisely because the small town represents the most radical application of the democratic theory, it raises the greatest problem for individualism. Here is the extreme expression of popular sovereignty against which Madison strove: popular control unchecked by a notion of minority rights; a principle derived from natural rights which destroys natural rights, with all the ethical and impersonal inconsistencies and deficiencies that Robert Dahl has detailed. Here is no conscious agreement freely developed through debate and discussion but rather passive acquiescence, an irrational expression of uniformity of attitude and outlook, a certainty of the rightness of the majority which amounts to compulsion.

It may be true, as Dahl suggests, that theoretically the respective roles of majority and minority are never neatly balanced in the search for freedom, but certainly, in the small communities, the scale is weighed heavily in favor of the majority. "You have to go on living with people," Sherwood Anderson reflects, "day after day, week after week. You can't just ignore your brother-in-law, forget him as you might in a city. Tomorrow you will meet him in the street. You will be meeting him in the stores and in the post-office. Better make it up, start over again." Equality of this kind liberates only when the individual is part of the majority. When he dissents, equality is as likely to display as intolerant a disdain for private opinion as does an autocratic state.

When the lines are probed far enough the small community stands as representative of the worst of both philosophies: the requirement that man subordinate his individual aims to that of the group, without the group possessing any quality of greatness; the prescription that a man begins on the basis of equality with his neighbor, with no guarantee that he can go forward on his own. The respectable values that both interpretations hold out as perennially valid, the insights into human nature that they contribute, are lost. What is left over are the dregs of their speculation, the flaws of their grand analysis, the unacceptable portions of their doctrine. Order without purpose; equality without liberty; these become the hallmarks of the ideology.

The essence of this residue can be summed up in a single concept: fraternity. Grassroots life is "the test of man's ability to adjust himself. It tells the story of his skill in living with others."

This is the heart of the small town, the reason it is acclaimed and the reason why it may be defective. It is not surprising that the descriptions of "democracy at work," town meeting style, become invariably anecdotal: instance after instance of informality, good will, the triumph of personality over procedure, the potency of the wisecrack at the proper time, the decision tailored to the person involved, the horseback judgment overriding the expert opinion. In the rosy glow of the fellowship which propinquity and equality produce, the pattern dissolves into a series of character sketches, each actor classified and typed, each reading his lines in the comfortable assurance that the script has been agreed upon by all.

Quite certainly, fraternity is a persistent inclination of mankind; it fills some needs of human nature. It promises security in a group of like persuasion; it bolsters faltering egoes, it banishes an awful sense of loneliness, it fosters togetherness and belongingness. To the degree that these qualities reinforce the individual, soothe nerves, banish discord, promote harmony, they are doubtless useful. Lodges, clubs, fraternities have their function, for when a man is free to choose his associates the choice can be both a bulwark against the world and an expression of himself. No one doubts the beneficial values of neighborhood, where the lessons of getting along with the outsiders are first learned in the company of friends, where a knowledge of the common traits of human nature is gained, and where the drift of affairs is, above all, predictable. In these circumstances, the uses of fraternity are sometimes admirable.

At other times, however, fraternity may be less than admirable, with overtones of exclusiveness, narrowness, provinciality and clannishness. Privacy cannot be countenanced in a brotherhood; personal ambitions bow necessarily to group aims; unanimity becomes essential, for how else can a fraternity survive? When the fraternal order is the only order of life, it seems unsatisfactory as a way of organizing society-at-large or establishing a government. When neighborhoods are equipped with political boundary lines, when the fraternal club becomes not an informal part of life but instead its formal expression, when individual purposes can be achieved only through the fraternal process, then the less attractive elements of conformity—compulsion and suspicion—come to the fore.

Yet the concept of fraternity as *the* way of life is, of course, the inescapable implication of grassroots autonomy: an ideal of a self-contained whole to which all members belong and from which none can exit without a violent wrench, a vision of a government which "institutionalizes the neighborliness of the village." But this neighborliness is no universal brotherhood with a higher purpose of a greater civilization, nor is it a voluntary brotherhood, where the common bounds of every man are freely recognized and freely defined. The fraternity of the small community is a union without ambition and without competition. It may be comfortable; it may be forgiving; but it cannot promise the excellence that civilization itself or the individual alone can possibly achieve. "It is," in Sherwood Anderson's words, "a case of love," justified because "Life can never be intimate enough."

CHECKLIST OF OPERATIVE DEMOCRACY

1. THE RULE OF LAW

The conflict between democracy and fraternity can be set forth in abstract terms; it can also be documented specifically. Once the spirit of the small community is equated with the spirit of fraternity, the violence the suburban image wreaks upon other operative ideals of American society becomes clear in three important ways. A nation committed essentially to the concept of contractual relations as the legitimate method to order human associations has embraced a doctrine of personal relations. A nation that has constructed sophisticated and highly complex restrictions on popular participation in the actual operation of government has accepted the doctrine of direct democracy in its most extreme form. A nation that establishes individuality as the prime goal for its society has deprived itself on the local level of the means to secure that end.

The inconsistency most immediately apparent is between the concept of fraternity and the theory of contractual relations. American life is built on the Lockian proposition of "the reality of atomistic social freedom," a view of the state as an association of free men and an insistence that there be a clear distinction between society and government. The classical expression of this view of legitimate government has always been constitutionalism—the application of systematic regularized restraints on the political power, the guarantee that certain aspects of living are beyond the reach of organized community power, that the government is both something less than, and different from, society.

As Carl Friedrich describes the constitutional process, it rests fundamentally on law—on rules that organize a government, limit the exercise of its authority, and provide the means by which the community and its political organization are distinguished. Government, restrained in action by a bill of rights, by the separation or geographical division of powers, by judicial review, remains apart from the community it governs, and the supreme power of the community comes into play only when the political process fails to function.

There is, of course, no place for such a systematic distinction between the social and political spheres within the meaning of fraternity. Although men are bound together in the American small town not as a hierarchy but as a brotherhood, their bonds remain tightly drawn. They are simply members of a larger family, and intimacy and intercourse are so inevitable that public and private affairs are difficult to separate. The proud boast so often repeated that "the town meeting *is* the town" is true, and the entire community is the government, not on the rare occasions of catastrophe but whenever public affairs are carried out.

One result, of course, is the special environment in which local government tries to carry out its duties. A public agency operates not so much according to law or under the collective supervision of the community assembled formally as its governing body; instead, it functions under the constant, haphazard, and sometimes suffocating scrutiny of whichever members of the town decide to busy themselves with the agency's affairs. The outstanding example is the public school, for here the line between public function and social institution becomes almost impossible to draw. Lane Lancaster captured the blending of the professional obligations and personal characteristics of the small town teacher in a memorable passage when he wrote: "Not only does the teacher live under the constant espionage of her charges, but she is seldom free from the feeling of utter dependence upon the community which controls her 'job.' From the moment she arrives in the community her goings and comings become matters of general interest and in every real sense her life ceases to be her own. Where she shall 'board and room,' do her banking, attend church, seek diversion and recreation, the charities she supports, the books she reads, where she will make her personal purchases, the choice of her associates and her clothes, the use of her weekends —all these are matters for gossip in the village which has 'hired' her and which exacts a rigid conformity to the lowest common denominator of village mores."

More serious, perhaps, is the intrusion government can make upon society under these circumstances. The concept of constitutionalism, of law, of impersonal relations between the individual and the group, becomes difficult to maintain. The notion of systematic, regularized restraints filters down from higher levels of government; statutes, regulations, Robert's rules of order become the departure point for public action. But the most significant feature of small town politics is the frequency with which legal and procedural requirements are overlooked and ignored. They are always to be adjusted according to the "common sense, down-to-earth judgment" of the participants, to take account of unique conditions and provincial pecularities. Tickets can be fixed, favors granted, contracts awarded, not because these irregularities will remain hidden but because they are acceptable on the basis of personal esteem. The successful town moderator is the one who moderates between the rules of the game and the disposition of the meeting. Government indistiguishable from society, when no country gentry is permitted, no lord of the manor allowed, is personalized government. Men come to take on, as Granville Nicks notes, a profound cynicism toward the law. "Every predatory pioneer instinct goes into operation when the average native is confronted with his government—town, state or federal. Governmental bodies apparently exist to be cheated and regulations were made to be evaded."

Personalized government can be both effective and beneficial. It can adjust abstract legal generalizations to the actual state of affairs, make regulations tolerable, and bring them into line with informal mores and customs. But it can also be offensive, as were the personalized duchies which Huey Long created out of the Louisiana parishes, the tight dominions of courthouse gangs, the one-man sovereigns of the rural county whose rule was no less arbitrary because it was accepted.

It is no accident that the folk hero of local America is the law-enforcement agent who interprets the law according to his own lights. The archetype of the Western sheriff substitutes his concept of justice for the statute book; he does his duty, as in *High Noon,* and then grinds his badge underfoot; he operates as often as a vigilante outside the law as within it. And he is applauded, approved, even today, because his concept of justice seems so direct, without frills, legalism, or delays. In short, his law ignored the processes of restraint and orderly procedure on which order is built.

So in the small community, power depends on personal qualities, on the "fit" of the individual to his neighbor, whether or not the official and the citizen are on good terms. Tocqueville identified this grassroots tendency precisely when he wrote, "In general, the American functionaries are far more independent than

the French civil officers within the sphere which is prescribed to them. Sometimes, even, they are allowed by the popular authority to exceed those bounds; and as they are protected by the opinion, and backed by the cooperation, of the majority, they venture upon such manifestations of their power as astonish a European. By this means habits are formed in the heart of a free country which may someday prove fatal to its liberties."

Grassroots government may or may not be good government then; it is difficult to say. It depends on whether the town is good or not. The smaller the town, the more justice is a matter of personal opinion in the community itself, rarely formalized, rarely examined, rarely permanently established, depending on the sentiment of the moment. It is little wonder that the local justice of the peace is the laughing-stock of the legal profession. Even if he knows his duties, how can he possibly impartially administer justice in an atmosphere of overwhelming intimacy?

In this way personalized government, the only form acceptable to fraternity, moves counter to the tradition of law and constitutionalism, confident that familiarity makes it possible to rule by direct knowledge of the neighborhood in place of abstract principle. In such a context, the notion of contractual relations is replaced by the reality of personal relations, who belongs and who does not. The individual depends on the sanction of the group and remains uncertain of his rights and prerogatives. In the end, he has no fixed standard to indicate how he stands in the face and the eyes of his neighbors.

2. THE ROLE OF CONTROVERSY

An innate tendency toward personalized government is one way in which the small community goes against the grain of the broader American creed. An undiluted acceptance of the principle of direct democracy is another. Woven into the institutions and procedures of the nation and the states is an array of formal and informal provisions designed to limit direct popular participation in government, to check and to balance it. Partly, of course, these strictures arose as necessities for managing a popular government over a wide expanse of territory. Partly, they result from prejudices of the founding fathers, long since abandoned. But in good measure, these complicated arrangements are the product of considered judgment and experience as to how a popularly supported government can work effectively. They are rooted in both a realistic view of human nature and a thoughtful appraisal of the limits of popular sovereignty if left to function on its own.

The fundamental premise of American democratic politics, as of Western politics generally, is that men view the public good in different ways, from different perspectives. Factions and parties are regarded as part of the political process, however regretfully men may have accepted their existence and hesitated to sanction their operation. Given this recognition of conflicting opinions and judgments, it has followed, in the logic of constitutional government, that a public policy is hammered out in an arena of discussion and debate until some acceptable compromise develops. It follows also that in order to make the discussion meaningful and reasonably effective, "opposition," in V. O. Key's words, "should be institutionalized"; in short, that it be expected in the normal course of affairs.

In a sense, this expectation of disagreement provides the saving grace of humility to stand against the inherent arrogance of a belief in popular sovereignty and righteousness. The normal democratic political process becomes not a gilt-edge guarantee of responsible, able government, but instead, as Dahl explains, "one in which there is a high probability that an active and legitimate group in the population can make itself heard effectively at some crucial state in the process of decision." A pair of competing party hierarchies, a polyarchal political structure in which many minorities participate, a pattern of interest groups and pressure politics appear as the most effective ways in which modern democracies can operate.

By these standards, the small community is singularly ill-equipped to construct a working democratic process. Its spirit of fraternity proceeds on an assumption quite contrary to disagreement and opposition: it expects essential unanimity. This unanimity is not just an agreement on fundamentals, a consensus about profound beliefs; it is a characteristic supposedly operative on every major public problem. The ideal of the town-meeting citizen is a man capable of divining the public good as a thing apart from his personal attitudes, prejudices, and beliefs. It is a notion of public discussion that has all the aspects of a conference, not a debate. Provide the facts, set forth the problem, and all right-thinking men will arrive at the same decision; or, in the rationale of suburban nonpartisanship today, "there is no Republican or Democratic way to pave a street, all the citizens want is 'good' government."

It is no accident that Madison, perhaps the most realistic of the early American statesmen, after his statement on the inevitability of divisions within the body politic, looked sourly on the direct democracy of the small town. To him, "The smaller the society, the fewer probably will be the distinct parties and interests composing it; the fewer the distinct parties and interests the more frequently will a majority be found of the same party; and the smaller the number of individuals composing a majority, and the smaller the compass within which they are placed, the more easily will they concert and execute their plans of expression." Madison saw clearly that the grassroots ideology had no expectation of serious divisions within its constituency and consequently made no effective provision for the protection of the minority. Instead, it embraced the principle of popular sovereignty to its limits, certain that the majority would always be right.

It is not the possible deprivation of the theoretical natural rights of a minority that is the central issue, however. It is doubtful whether a convincing case for natural rights, demonstrably defined by God, can be established in modern times. In any event, the popular sovereignty of small town and suburb will seldom produce persecution, or even the conditions of oppression that Madison hypothesized. The personalized aspect of local government, rather than its majority principle, is more likely to be the villain in this respect.

What is significant, however, in the direct democracy of the idealized small town is its ineffectiveness in providing a practical operating popular government. The highly optimistic conviction that reason will prevail fails to provide contrasting poles of opinion for meaningful discussion, and most of all, for effective opposition. Here is no spectacle of competing minorities, of parties appealing to the voters while always sensitive to the strategy of the opposition, of organizations sophisticated in political strategy, of seasoned leaders, of professional politicians ready to play the broker between the governed and the governing. Here is only the annual town meeting, the occasional popular referendum, the mass of citizens face to face with the complex public problem, expected to operate always at the peak of civic virtue. It is quite natural that Carl Friedrich, for all his sympathetic concern and respect for the grassroots tradition, could warn of the danger of the manipulation of mass psychology, and point out that too strong a dose of direct democracy destroys the balance of constitutional government. An excessive reliance on direct popular action can lead, as the discussion of suburban politics has suggested, to no popular action at all with the citizen baffled and perplexed and the expert and the small clique in charge.

Tested against the working standards of modern democratic theory, the small town version, with its reliance on citizens instead of institutions, thus operates under major handicaps. To begin with, its very scale makes it unlikely that a reasonable variety of attitudes and opinions will be brought to bear on a problem and that the process of discussion will provide information, knowledge and understanding. A minority that is hopelessly outnumbered can be forgiven for declining to make its case with vigor and completeness. In this way the prime function of minority rights—to provide an opportunity to persuade, to enlighten, to require the majority to defend its position more adequately, to amend and qualify—often goes by default. Sensible

men hesitate to stick their necks out when the prospects of success are dim.

Even given a determined minority, however, the opportunity for that minority to organize itself and to operate as a going concern runs into severe institutional handicaps in an atmosphere of nonpartisanship and direct participation. The town meeting is not an effective arena for continuing debate or persuasive argument; it may "ventilate grievances" but it rarely settles them. A dissenter may make a noise, but he rarely can make the kind of noise Dahl defines as an effective voice: one that officials not only listen to "but expect to suffer [from] in some significant way if they do not placate the group, its leaders or its most vociferous members." No wonder Lancaster discovered "New England querulousness institutionalized in the Town Meeting." An opposition, despairing of being effective and accustomed to unrelieved defeat, has a right to be peevish. Rousseau's judgment was even more succinct: "So perfect a government does not suit human beings."

3. THE QUEST FOR FREEDOM

The final defect in the grassroots model, and its most fundamental one when judged by operative democratic standards, is the limitations it places on individual development, or, more directly, on freedom. The most obvious of these restrictions applies to the isolated minority and arises out of the internal contradiction in the notion of equality when applied in too intimate circumstances. This limitation, as we have seen, is the fatal inconsistency in the liberal philosophical argument for the small democratic unit, the theoretical flaw in the doctrine of majority rule that has never been erased.

Yet, even if the individual in a small town belongs to the majority, believes in its values, and plays the part of a favored son, a second limitation comes to bear. Unless one believes "the local is the ultimate universal, and as near an absolute as exists," unless the outside world is only an endless repetition of experiences found within the village, then small size diminishes the prospects for individualism.

Individualism can only be defined as the special way a man responds to an elemental and recurrent cycle of experiences—birth, courtship, marriage, family and death; spring, summer, fall, and winter. A spectacle arises of man inexorably facing the rhythm of nature, testing himself against a fixed number of temptations and a fixed number of challenges.

Ideologically, Americans have, of course, never accepted this view of individualism, in spite of the fact that in the context of the small town it is a true one. Opportunity, limitless, boundless, unfettered, has been the key concept—the notion that one could never tell what one would become, what experiences and what adventures one might have. The almost moral obligation of an individual to rise, to get up in the world, has been a fixed constant in our faith. "Energy, self-reliance, and independence, a strong conviction that a man's fate should depend upon his own character and conduct, are qualities without which no nation can be great."

This type of individualism has had its crass side, of course, in the roughshod climb of an Horatio Alger scrambling for undreamed-of heights. And it has its idealistically optimistic side, the dream of perfectibility, as each generation moves another step along the road of progress. Its essence remains, however, a conviction that on his own initiative, a man selects from a number of alternatives instead of simply reacting to one; that growth is unlimited, and that as the number of alternatives expands, freedom expands as well.

The spirit of fraternity directly contradicts this American concept. It cannot rise above the commonness of experience. In place of a promise of progress, of many rainbows and many pots of gold, there is only the routine of the provincial life: the work week, the Saturday night revelry, the schooldays, the church service, the hours spent on the bench on the courthouse square. The village never stirs itself; it is moved only by exits and entrances from the outside world. And so, in place of incentive, of growth, of development, are the characteristics of parochialism: somnolence, lethargy and resignation, "the buried life," "cornpone opinions," the "mill-bound world." Or as R. A. Woods has described it, "The country village is made up of those who are out of the fight because they never tried. Life runs in a narrow circuit; there is little to stir the blood or stimulate the imagination."

Of course, under modern circumstances, the issue of individuality is cast in a different context. When suburbia becomes the carrier of the grassroots image, there is no physical isolation between the town and the city, and the variety among suburbs presents a spectacle of many ways or living. Thus Edward C. Banfield and Morton Grodzins see the existence of suburbs in the metropolitan area as enhancing the prospects for individuality when defined as a choice among alternatives. They liken the small town suburbanite to a consumer faced with an array of cultural islands, each representing a special brand of homogeneity. The individual can live in the area that best represents the social status he desires, and "spheres of free choice for individuals and community groups" are maintained. "Wide options, including the option to be exclusive and expensive, prevail," and, in modern suburbia, "the consumer is in a position to know what combination of goods and services—trees and sidewalks as against food and clothing, for example—will give him the greatest satisfaction."

Two comments are in order about the individualism fostered by the modern suburb. First, though a system which ensures "that the widest possible range of choice will be open to the consumer" is clearly within the American tradition, it is doubtful that it represents the best of that tradition. As the ideal of equality can result in conformity, so the ideal of personal enterprise can border on selfishness. The analogy of the "consumer" used by Banfield and Grodzins is revealing, for the individuality the modern suburb offers is of the laissez-faire variety. The man who chooses his community in the metropolitan free market in the same way in which he buys his car has embraced the theory of contractual relations in its most extreme form. Self-interest, unmitigated even by the notion of obligations freely entered into, becomes the definition of freedom, and issues of equity and humanitarianism are muted. The sense of responsibility of free men to one another and the recognition of common purposes that constitute a persuasive part of the American creed are lost, and the spectacle ensues of a simple scramble to the top for the best market baskets of local government services.

A second observation to make about the streamlined suburban version of the small town is that the rampant individualism it exposes by no means dampens the spirit of fraternity. Paradoxically, an attempt to rediscover fraternity becomes the overriding goal of suburban free choice. Freedom is sought in order to return to some facsimile of the elemental world; men struggle to succeed for the purpose of residing in a community peopled exclusively by their own kind. The growing homogeneity of these cultural islands, and the restrictive practices that bar the unsuitable, become little more than a reassertion of the fraternal spirit.

In this context, modern observers sometimes speak approvingly of the reappearance of clusters of suburban small towns as a means "for the effective management of conflict, especially of conflict arising from the growing cleavages of race and class." Yet, even the desire to "manage" conflict, to promote harmony by the ghetto system of society, remains basically a fraternal drive—and an anti-individualistic one. An individual exercises options among a series of fraternities but once he makes his choice, he reenters a world where individuality is suspect. Discussion, debate, disagreement thus have no role either in building a community on the basis of recognizing common interest, or in the expression and articulation of individuality. A man is freed to follow his immediate desires but forfeits his individuality by the very process.

Meanwhile, the carefully preserved boundary lines, the meticulously drawn building regulations, the informally applied restrictive practices, ensure that the fraternal spirit predominates; that harmony, once natural in the small town, is now contrived; that conflict, out of which understanding and individual growth conceivably could come, is carefully avoided. Unless one reconciles himself to a series of moves as his values grow and change, freedom of choice is exercised only once or twice. As an everyday proposition, it becomes unworkable.

OTHER ROADS

What emerges from a comparison of grassroots values and democratic values is a single major conclusion: in this vision of the "good American" life, there has always been a fundamental confusion between the concepts of fraternity and of democracy. It cannot be said too often that the fraternal spirit has a crucial role to play in the organization of human affairs. Neighborhoods, clubs, associations are the means by which men come to recognize that they have common traits and common goals. The happy savage, Eden before redemption, are perhaps indications of man's potentiality, but they are far from accurate descriptions of the reality of human nature.

Yet it also cannot be said too often that democracy, as commonly understood, is something much more than and much different from fraternity. It must begin with an understanding of things men hold in common, but it must proceed to a recognition of their uncommon qualities as well. The trademark of democracy is a process by which men decide and accept responsibility for the interests they hold in common while retaining the option to exercise individual choices. And in that process, in the American tradition, the recognition of "things in common" does not appear automatically or easily but is painfully put together by compromise, by adjustments, by trial and error. It is an aggregate of a series of choices by a series of minorities temporarily coming together. To move in an opposite direction, as the modern suburb now does, to identify the uncommon qualities, segregate them, and place them with their own kind, is an effort to avoid the process of democracy entirely.

Beyond this basic misapprehension of the requirements of democracy, still another factor makes the suburban renaissance less than laudable. The small town ideal not only embodies basic flaws within its own dominion, but it mirrors with peculiar intensity the deficiencies of the larger American system. The pressures for conformity represented by super-Americanism on the national scene stem from the same excessive application of equality that reveals itself in the suburban drive for unanimity. The extreme individualism (almost indistinguishable from sheer exploitation) that marred the rise of American capitalism is identical with the suburban consumer's "shopping" for his exclusive home. It is ironical, in the exact sense of the word, that the ideology most revered in the United States is the one that does the greatest disservice to our broader vision. In the grassroots world, our vices stand the most completely exposed; our virtues are almost totally ignored.

Perhaps an even deeper irony in the suburban attachment to the old dream is that it is no longer necessary today. The historical confusion between democracy and fraternity in the United States is understandable because there was, in the beginning, no alternative to small town life. Men were forced to live with the internal contradictions of equality and individualism at the grassroots level. In the mid-twentieth century, this necessity no longer exists; the technology that has given us the wealth to reconstruct the republic in miniature has also given us other choices. We are free to choose; we can accept other ways for organizing metropolitan life, if we will. . . .

New Strength in City Hall

.SEYMOUR FREEDGOOD

Seymour Freedgood, formerly an associate editor of Fortune, *is currently on the staff of* Time-Life Books. *He has been a staff writer on* The New York Times *and* Time *and was a staff writer for the Department of State from 1949–53.*

At the troubled core of the big city stands City Hall, a block-square, granite citadel heavily encrusted with myth. It was a half-century ago that Lincoln Steffens described the "shame of the cities"—the bosses, the boodlers, the job sellers, and the hopeless inefficiency of the city's housekeeping. The image persists. Most people are aware that the machines have fallen on parlous times— but they're not sure that what's left is much better. The dramatic corruption may have gone but the belief that the big city's government is a mess remains. When people look for models of munic-

Reprinted from Editors of Fortune, *The Exploding Metropolis* (Garden City, New York: Doubleday & Company, Inc., Anchor Books, 1958), pp. 62–91.

ipal efficiency, it is outward, to the hinterland, that they are apt to turn; here, where "grass roots" are more visible, are the slumless smaller cities and the towns with city managers, and it is to them that most of the accolades for municipal success are directed.

The emphasis is misplaced. Where the problems are the toughest—in the big, crowded, noisy city—government has virtally transformed itself. Today the big city must rank as one of the most skillfully managed of American organizations —indeed, considering the problems it has to face, it is better managed than many U. S. corporations.

The suburbanization of the countryside has plunged America's big cities—specifically the twenty-three cities with population of 500,000 and over—into a time of crisis. Hemmed in by their hostile, booming suburbs, worried about the flight of their middle class, and hard pressed to maintain essential services for their own populations, they need, if they are to hold their own, let alone grow, top-notch leadership.

They have it. Since the 1930's, and at an accelerating rate after the second world war, the electorate in city after city has put into office as competent, hard-driving, and skillful a chief executive as ever sat in the high-backed chair behind the broad mahogany desk. At the same time they have strengthened the power of the office.

This has not been a victory for "good government." To most people, good government is primarily honest and efficient administration, and they believe that the sure way for the city to get it is to tighten civil service, eliminate patronage, and accept all the other artifacts of "scientific" government, including the council-city-manager plan. But today's big-city mayor is not a good-government man, at least in these terms, and if he ever was, he got over it a long time ago. He is a tough-minded, soft-spoken politician who often outrages good-government people, or, as the politicians have called them, the Goo-Goos.

One of the biggest threats to his leadership, indeed, is too much "good government." The big problem at City Hall is no longer honesty, or even simple efficiency. The fight for these virtues is a continuous one, of course, and Lucifer is always lurking in the hall, but most big-city governments have become reasonably honest and efficient. Today, the big problem is not good housekeeping: it is whether the mayor can provide the aggressive leadership and the positive programs without which no big city has a prayer. What is to get priority? Industrial redevelopment? More housing? (And for whom?) There is only so much

money, and if hard policy decisions are not made, the city's energies will be diffused in programs "broad" but not bold.

The mayor is hemmed in. As he strives to exercise policy leadership, his power is challenged on all sides. In his own house the staff experts and the civil-service bureaucrats threaten to nibble him to death in their efforts to increase their own authority. Then there are the public "authorities." Some are single-purpose authorities—like the city housing authorities, and the sewer districts; some, like the Port of New York Authority, handle a whole range of functions. They are eminently useful institutions, but however efficient they may be, they are virtually laws unto themselves and they have severely limited the mayor's ability to rule in his own house and, more important, his ability to plan for long-range development.

The power struggle also goes on between the mayor and the state legislature, which has a controlling voice in the city's fiscal affairs, but whose membership is apportioned in favor of the rural areas. It is the rare mayor who need not make frequent trips to the state capital for additional funds, and the legislature is usually unsympathetic. Colorado's, for example, gives Denver a niggardly $2,300,-000 a year in state aid for a school system of 90,000 children; right next to it, semi-rural Jefferson County, with 18,000 pupils, gets $2,400,000.

There is the continuing struggle between the mayor and the suburbs, whose people, the big city firmly believes, are welshing on their obligations to the city. The mayor must win the cooperation of his suburban counterparts if he is to do anything at all about the city's most pressing problems—e.g., the traffic mess—and the going is grim. No one is against "saving our cities," but in this seemingly antiseptic cause there are fierce conflicts of interests and the power struggle is getting more intense.

WHAT CITIZENS WANT: MORE

There has been a change in City Hall because there has been a change in the city itself. For the better part of a cen-

tury, the core of big-city life was its immigrants—waves and waves of them, many illiterate, few English-speaking, all poor. Their grinding misery kept the machine in power at the hall. The machine fed on the immigrants, but it also helped them—with jobs, with welfare services and personal favors, with Christmas baskets and dippers of coal—and the immigrants, in turn, were generous with their votes. The 1924 Immigration Act put an end to this cycle. Reduced immigration gave the city time to absorb the earlier newcomers, reduce the language barriers, educate them and their children, and raise many of them into the middle class. This, along with federal social security and unemployment insurance, reduced the dependence of the big-city masses on the political machines. After World War II came the huge influx of southern Negroes and Puerto Ricans, but by this time the machine was beyond a real comeback.

A half-century's work by the National Municipal League, the Institute of Public Administration, and other government research groups was a big factor. They fought and in many places won the hard fight for the short ballot, which eliminates "blind" voting, and for better city charters, better budgeting, and more efficient management methods.

Better-qualified people came into government. During the unemployment of the 1930's governments could recruit talent they couldn't before. Most of the bright young men went off to Washington, but many of them went into city government too. Some now man its top administrative posts, and they have done much to raise civil-service standards.

Most important, the public began asking for more. It now demands as a natural right better-administered services—police and fire protection, water, sewerage, and all the rest—and it judges its public officials on how well they are able to satisfy this demand. It also demands services—psychiatric clinics, youth boards, air-pollution control—it never had before. City government, as a result, has been transformed into an enormous service machine, infinitely complicated to run.

THE MANAGEMENT MEN

To many an aspirant who wouldn't have thought of city politics a generation ago, the mayorality is now eminently worth his mettle. This has been particularly true in cities where long-standing sloth and corruption had created the possibility of a dramatic reversal; in these places an able and ambitious man might well conclude that his opportunities for spectacular, visible achievement outran those of a governor or senator. But the new mayors are more than opportunists. They come from widely different social and economic backgrounds, and they differ as widely in temperament, but all share a sense of mission: while it also happens to be good politics, they feel deeply that they should make their decisions in terms of the community-wide interest rather than the interest of any one group.

The profile of today's big-city mayor—with one difference—is quite similar to that of the chief executive of a large corporation. Typically, the mayor is a college graduate, usually with a legal or business background, and is now in his late fifties. He puts in hard, grinding hours at his desk, sometimes six or seven days a week, and his wife suffers as much as his golf game. The difference is in salary: he usually makes $20,000 to $25,000. There is also a chauffeur-driven limousine and, in some cities, an expense allowance, ranging from $2,000 (Milwaukee) to $55,000 (Chicago).

"Public relations" take a big chunk of his time. He is aggressively press-conscious, holds frequent news conferences, often appears on TV-radio with his "Report to the People"; and from his office flows a flood of releases on civic improvements. About five nights a week there are civic receptions, banquets, policy meetings, and visits with neighborhood civic groups. In between he may serve as a labor negotiator, or a member of the Civil Defense Board.

The mayor is also seeing a lot more of the city's business leaders, whose interest in urban renewal is growing steadily. Despite the fact that His Honor is likely to be a Democrat, he gets along very well with the businessmen, though he is apt to feel that they have a lot to learn about political decision-making. A City Hall man recently summed up the feelings of his fellows: "These business-men like everything to be nice and orderly—and nonpolitical. They're getting hot now on metropolitan planning. They think it's not political! Throw them into shifting situations where there are a lot of conflicts and no firm leadership and they're completely buffaloed. It's painful to watch them trying to operate. But once there's a firm program lined up and they've bought it, they're very effective."

Above all the mayor is a politician. True, he may have risen to office on the back of a reform movement. But he is not, as happened too often in the past, a "non-political" civic leader who rallies the do-gooders, drives the rascals out of City Hall, serves for an undistinguished term or two, and then withdraws—or gets driven out—leaving the city to another cycle of corruption. Instead, he fits the qualifications of the mayors whom Lincoln Steffens called on the public to elect: "politicians working for the reform of the city with the methods of politics." His main interest is in government, not abstract virtue, and he knows that the art of government is politics.

DeLesseps Morrison of New Orleans is a notable example of a political leader who leaped into office on a reform ticket, then used the methods of politics to put his programs across. In the years since insurgents elected Mayor Morrison over opposition from the long-entrenched regulars who had run the town wide open, he has done more than demonstrate that hard-working and efficient manage-ment can change the face of a city. Morrison has consolidated the gains—in large part by his ability to turn the loose organization that first supported him into a thoroughly professional political or-ganization, which regularly helps elect friendly councilmen. The Morrison or-ganization, not surprisingly, is anathema to the old Democratic machine.

In Philadelphia, Richardson Dilworth and his predecessor, Mayor (now Sena-tor) Joseph Clark, have followed the Morrison pattern up to a point. In 1952 Philadelphia civic groups wrested control of City Hall from a corrupt and con-tented Republican machine, and the Clark and Dilworth administrations have given the city vigorous and honest gov-ernment ever since. Mayor Dilworth, in office since 1956, is making considerable headway with his programs; unlike Mor-rison, however, he has not yet chosen to organize his followers into a political organization that can regularly get out the vote on election day. The old-line Democrats and Republicans, as a result, have been increasingly successful in elect-ing their own men to the council. . . .

The new mayor, of course, does not need a dragon to fight. Indeed, some of today's best mayors are in cities that have enjoyed reasonably honest government for quite some time. Detroit's late aggressive Mayor Albert Cobo was one of these. He believed that government should be run like a business: during his eight years in office he overhauled the city's govern-ment, department by department, replac-ing the old, wasteful ways of doing things with machines and management systems that would do credit to any corporation.

St. Louis, Cincinnati, and Milwaukee, all with long traditions of honest govern-ment, have a remarkable trio of mayors: each wears a distinctively scholarly air, and is a pretty good politician to boot. St. Louis, once an ailing city, has found one of the ablest leaders in its history in an engineering professor, Raymond Tucker. Enthusiastically backed by the city's business leaders and the St. Louis press, Mayor Tucker has persuaded the voters to approve new taxes and public-improvement bond issues with which he has pulled the city out of the red and away from the blight. Milwaukee, a well-governed city since 1910, now has pro-fessorial, mild-mannered Frank P. Zeidler as its mayor. He too has stimulated a con-servative, frugal citizenry into approving needed physical improvements. Cincin-nati, under council-city-manager govern-ment since 1926, has Charles Taft, a top mayor who has given the city's urban-renewal and highway programs a power-ful boost.

BRIDGING THE GAP

The mayors of Pittsburgh and Chicago bridge the gap between the traditional machine-boss mayor and today's management-man mayor. Pittsburgh's David Lawrence and Chicago's Richard Daley are both powerful Democratic organization leaders as well as strong mayors: each has given his city increasingly good government—and a big push forward in meeting its problems—while at the same time maintaining his organization in viable if declining power. Of the two, Daley has been the bigger surprise. When he was elected many people believed he would sell City Hall to Cicero without a qualm. Instead, Daley went along to a remarkable extent in putting into effect reform legislation that tightened and improved the structure of Chicago's city government. Chicago, Senator Paul Douglas once observed, is a city with a Queen Anne front and a Mary Ann rear. That may still be the case with its government: it undoubtedly has much to do before its rear is as respectable as its front. But Daley, a man who has been known to do odd things with the queen's English, seems determined to close the gap. "We will go on," he once announced at a town-and-gown dinner of the city and the University of Chicago, "to a new high platitude of success."

THE STRONG MAYOR

In his drive for more power, the big-city mayor is in direct conflict with a strong trend in municipal government. This is the council-city-manager plan, which is the fastest spreading form of government among cities of 25,000 to 100,000. To many do-gooders, it is the ideal form of government for the American city, big or small. Basically, it is government by a board of directors: an elected committee decides on city policies, and the hired manager and his experts carry them out.

The system has been most successful in smaller cities—e.g., Watertown, New York (population, 35,000), whose inhabitants are for the most part homogeneous and native born, where ethnic and economic tensions are low, and where the future holds no big threats. Cities like Watertown may thrive under such government; most big cities cannot.

Their electorates seem to sense this. When asked to vote on a new city charter, they have usually settled on one providing for a strong mayor rather than committee leadership. As a result, the trend to the strong chief executive, long evident in the federal government and the urban state capitals, is now running high in the cities. Of the twenty-three largest, fourteen have adopted some kind of "strong-mayor" charter, five still vest most power in the council, and four use the council-manager plan.

Philadelphia, which is symbolic of so much of the best and worst that can happen to a city, has indicated why the major cities are choosing the strong-mayor-council rather than the council-city-manager form of government. In 1949, civic dissatisfaction with the machine was picking up so much steam that Mayor Bernard Samuel consented to the appointment of a fifteen-man bipartisan commission to draft a charter for the better government of the city. After months of study, the commissioners arrived at these alternatives:

New York: Under the 1938 charter, drafted by a commission appointed by Mayor La Guardia, New York's mayors were given strong statutory powers, and the city council, then called the board of aldermen—and sometimes the Boodle Board or the Forty Thieves—was cut in both size and authority. The charter gave the mayor two prime tools of the strong chief executive: the right (1) to hire and fire his key department heads and (2) to make his operating budget, which the council may cut but not increase. He may also veto council ordinances, and a two-thirds vote is needed to override him. But the mayor's fiscal powers were shackled from another direction: the city's "upper house," the board of estimate, may do almost as it pleases with his budget and the mayor has no veto there.

Cincinnati: In 1924, civic reformers, now called the Charter party, swept out the corrupt administration of the Boss Rud K. Hynica and adopted a package of related reforms—the city-manager plan with a nine-man council elected at large on a nonpartisan ballot by proportional representation. Under the plan, the council elects the mayor, who, with the council's approval, appoints the city manager and the city's boards and commissions. The manager, in turn, picks his department heads and is responsible for administration.

The Philadelphia commissioners, at least half sold on the beauties of the council-manager plan, decided to visit Cincinnati to take a firsthand look at a successful city-manager city. They spent a day in the city, and consulted closely with Charles Taft and other Cincinnati officials. Finally, the Philadelphians asked Taft if he would recommend the manager plan for a city of two million people—i.e., as large as Philadelphia. "No," he said flatly.

"When the Lord himself said he didn't want those ten commandments spread elsewhere," an ex-commissioner observes, "that was the death knell."

One reason the manager plan has worked admirably in Cincinnati is that the Charter party—which first sponsored the system—is a fairly well-organized political party, and it has been helped considerably at the polls by proportional representation. The Charterites, a fusion of independent Republicans and Democrats, have been able to beat off the regular Republican machine at election time and thus maintain a majority—or at least a strong minority—on the council. (The city, although technically nonpartisan in municipal elections, has local political parties, and the voters generally know who the parties' candidates are.)

In other cities, however, the council-manager form of government revealed a significant flaw: it failed to produce political leadership on which responsibility for the city government could be pinned. The very large cities, with all their complex needs and challenges, require an elected chief executive to serve as the center of political leadership and responsibility, and to provide policy guidance and planning.

The new Philadelphia charter, overwhelmingly approved in 1951, incorporated the elements of New York's "strong mayor" plan with the significant omission of the board of estimate and with some very important additions. Most notably, the mayor's office was strengthened by permitting him to appoint a managing director, who, with the mayor's approval, appoints most of the city's department heads and is responsible to the mayor for over-all administration. The idea was to relieve the chief executive of routine administrative chores, and thus give him more time for the important job of hammering out policy.

BUILT-IN BUREAUCRATS

Presumably, the professionalization of his staff is a great help to the mayor in his efforts to provide leadership for the city. Increasingly, his appointed department heads are top specialists in their fields. The public-health commissioner, in vivid contrast even to twenty years ago, is a Doctor of Public Health, or at least an M.D. The public-works and sanitary commissioners are graduate engineers. Almost always, the men serving as division and bureau chiefs under the executive staff are career civil-service officers. The trend to professionalism is at high tide in Dallas, San Antonio, Cincinnati, and Kansas City—all manager cities. But it is also far advanced in the very big cities, where the need for expertise is great. Mayor Wagner's first city administrator (New York's version of the general-manager idea) was Luther Gulick, perhaps the country's foremost specialist in municipal affairs. In Chicago, reformers were incredulous when Richard Daley announced on taking office: "I'm going to listen to the professors." He has done so, and he has also hired some of them. His city controller and guard of its moneybags, for example, is Carl Chatters, one-time executive director of the Municipal Finance Officers Association, and a distinguished public servant.

Almost everywhere, in fact, only one big soft spot seems to remain—the police department. There are some exceptions. One is Cincinnati. Another is Milwaukee: its police department is one of the few in the country where organized crime has never acquired a foothold, and the city's policemen, long free from political taint, are professional from the top down. But in most big cities the gambling fix is still a problem, and corruption appears to be endemic—in spite of many top-notch police commissioners.

On the whole, however, the mayor—and the city—has profited from this administration by specialists. To many a big-city government, hard pressed to find money to maintain essential services, much less to provide new ones, the presence of a band of top professional at City Hall has probably meant the difference between success and failure in operating the big service machine.

CURBING THE SPECIALISTS

But this aspect of "good government" has its draw-backs too. "The next big concern for the big city electorates," says Columbia University political scientist Wallace Sayre, "is how to curb the bureaucrats, how to keep the experts under control, how to keep them from making all the decisions."

The mayor can hire and fire his appointed experts. Controlling the civil servants beneath them, however, is something else again. In Newark, Mayor Leo Carlin was recently confronted with a typical case of a bureaucracy trying to extend its control over a city government. Carlin, under his city's "strong mayor" charter, adopted in 1954, has the right to hire and fire his aides with the council's consent. The New Jersey Civil Service Commission, which gives the examinations for and acts as the guardian of all "classiffed" city employees, challenged the mayor's right in the case of his deputy: it attempted to bring the deputy mayor's job under civil service, claiming the post was within its juridiction under the wording of the state law. The city rejected the claim, and the commission sseems to have backed down. If the civil service is able to extend its authority to city officials as well as employees, many people feel, it will be able to hamper, if not control, city government and policy making in the same way that the French civil service controls much of the government of France.

TOO "TIGHT" A SYSTEM?

The municipal civil-service system, ordinarily, is administered by a semi-independent commision whose members are appointed for fixed terms. Once in office, they have wide latitude in running their show. In addition to setting up and conducting the examinations, they see to it that employees are dismissed only for "cause," usually after trial by the commission. The system, as a result, is fairly "tight" in most big cities—i.e., the vast majority of city employees are hired through civil-service channels and enjoy full job security. But tightness, whatever merit it once had in discouraging politically motivated hirings and firings, can make for considerable inefficiency. The entrenched bureaucrats, protected by tenure, tend to develop a clique feeling among themselves, and the clique is opposed to all change—except in the direction of greater rigidity.

The mayor may try to solve this problem by exerting greater executive control over the civil-service commission, and by raising wage scales to attract higher-caliber civil servants. Each course is difficult, the first perhaps more than the second. The commissions were originally set up as semi-autonomous agencies to "take them out of politics." The do-gooders feared—with great justification a half-century ago, with much less justification now—that if the commission was made directly responsible to the chief executive, he might use his influence over the commissioners to get patronage jobs for his followers, and the fear persists. For the mayor intent on providing aggressive, efficient government, the net effect is to put him at a competitive disadvantage in hiring new, better-qualified people, and at an institutional disadvantage if he wishes to clear some of the tenured deadwood out of the hall.

"OUTSIDE OF POLITICS"

As the mayor struggles to enlarge his freedom of action in dealing with his own bureaucracy, his ability to exercise policy and planning leadership for the city is being challenged by a growing external bureaucracy. The challenger is the public corporation or "authority," a legal device created by the state with power to raise money, hire specialists, and administer a bothersome facility, whatever it is, from managing the port to providing water. Today the authority is the fastest-growing division of local government in the U.S., but its increasing use has alarmed many political scientists.

Robert Moses, no mean authority himself (he holds ten jobs in New York City and State, among them the chairmanship of two authorities), disclosed the great attraction of the authoritarian device, and the major argument against it, in a recent issue of the New York Sunday *Times*. "The nearest thing to business in government is the public authority, which is business with private capital under public auspices, established only when both private enterprise and routine government have failed to meet an urgent need, and this device is often attacked because it is too independent of daily pressures, too unreachable by the boys and therefore essentially undemocratic."

The authority, indeed, has many attractions, not the least of which is its right to incur debt outside the limits imposed on the city by the state. It has performed notable service, especially by its ability to handle bistate problems, as in the case of the Port of New York Authority, and area-wide problems, as in the case of the Metropolitan Water District of Southern California. But the device also had major disadvantages. All too often, the new authority is created to do something more than evade a debt limit or handle an area-wide function. Under pressure from the interested specialists— the sewer and water engineers, the transit experts—it is created to remove an undertaking from "politics," and hence from democratic controls. The result, as Moses indicated, is "independent" government, which may or may not be beneficent government. But in neither case will it be self-government.

The New York Port Authority is a classic example of the independent authority at work. Its officers, appointed for six-year terms by the Governors of New York and New Jersey, are far removed from public or political pressures, on either the state or local level. In part as a result, the N.Y.P.A. is perhaps the most efficiently run public-works agency in the world. It has performed unequaled services for the bistate port area: it has built tunnels and bridges, and it has taken over the airports. But the N.Y.P.A., its critics charge, does not make its decisions to build another tunnel, or to expand an airport instead of investing in mass-transit facilities, in terms of the whole public, or of the interest of the whole area, including the needs of New York City. It makes its decisions in terms of its own, more limited public— i.e., the auto driver who keeps it going with his tolls, and the bond market. The N.Y.P.A., set up to handle a bistate problem, and, like many another authority, ostensibly "nonpolitical," has developed a politics of its own, a politics of specialists who may or may not be responsive to the public interest.

DIVIDING THE HOUSE

His Honor may have no choice in the matter. Until a more democratic way of managing interstate or area-wide functions is invented, he must live with what he has. But the mayor has another charge against him, and for this one he alone is accountable. He has encouraged the rash of authorities and independent boards that have emerged—not in the area of city-suburb or interstate relations but within the framework of the city government itself—and their growth has put him in an exceedingly odd spot. These are the municipal authorities—the housing, airports, and redevelopment authorities, the special transit, sewer, parking, recreational and park districts, and all the rest.

For even the strongest mayor, the temptation to create a muncipal authority to build and manage the airport of the city's parking lots—and thus relieve his own departments of new burdens—can be most compelling. The municipal authority, too, allows the city to get around its debt limit. Like its interjurisdictional sisters, the municipal authority usually has "tax" powers of its own: it pays for its revenue bonds by exacting a user's fee, rather than by calling on the city treasury for tax money. The authority has other advantages, and the mayor who is sold on the device—like Pittsburgh's David Lawrence—is particularly warm about one of them. In naming members to the boards, he is likely to choose the city's leading citizens, and he usually does so on a nonpartisan basis. Thus, as he enjoys pointing out, investors are more willing to buy bonds to finance the city's comeback. As for the charge that the authority, in effect, is a separate government divorced from the formal government, the mayor replies: "I do the appointing."

TOO MUCH AUTHORITY

The mayor may do the appointing; it is much more difficult for him, however, to reverse the process. Except in cases of dishonesty, he may not be able to get rid of a board member who is bucking his policies. As in the case of the older, semi-independent civil-service commissions, the over-all result is still another core of bureaucrats within the city government—but fairly well insulated from it, and as often as not indifferent or hostile to the chief executive and his plans for the city. A strong mayor, of course, will be able to bring about some coordination between the authorities—both area-wide and municipal—and the city government. But their very existence severely limits his policy-making role, for no one body—and certainly not the mayor's office—is responsible for over-all planning. The public authority, as municipal specialist William A. Robson has pointed out, may solve the particular problem that has been assigned to it, and sometimes solve it very well, "but only at the cost of weakening the general structure of local government in the great city and its environs, whereas the real need is to strengthen it."

CHILD OF THE STATE

The big test of the mayor as policy leader is whether he can provide the city with vigorous programs of development and expansion—if possible, within an organized plan. The problem is awesome, and much of it boils down to money—money for capital development, and money to meet the rising costs of city services, including services to suburbanites who don't want to pay for them. The city's own tax revenues are rarely enough to pay for all its needs, and to raise taxes much higher would simply drive more people to the suburbs. For a solution of his money problem, the mayor must rely on governments other than his own. He must look to the encircling suburban governments, and to the state legislature. When he looks, he may be excused for blanching.

The arena in which the big-city mayor wages this fiscal struggle is the state legislature, and the struggle can be rough. The city, as a municipal corporation, is the child of the state, and the state legislature or constitution usually limits its power to levy taxes or borrow money. City dwellers, moreover, pay a wide variety of state taxes, but the big city, as likely as not, gets a disproportionate share of the return. Pennsylvania, for example, pays every nonsectarian hospital $8 a day for care of indigent patients —except Philadelphia's city-owned General Hospital. The revenue loss to the city is almost $2,500,000 a year.

LOW ON THE TOTEM POLE

Chicago's Daley has summed up the consistent lament of most big-city mayors: "I think there's too much local money going to the state capitals and Washington. It's ridiculous for us to be sending them money and asking for it back. I don't think the cities should have to go hat in hand when they need money for improvements. We're going to have to clarify the role of the locality in relation to state and national governments. The cities and metropolitan areas are the important areas of the country today, but they're still on the low part of the totem pole."

Chicago isn't starving for money: its maximum property-tax rate is not set by law, and Daley recently won an additional privilege—although at a price. He got a bill through the state legislature giving him a ½ per cent sales tax, which the state collects and returns to the city, minus 6 per cent for its bother. A number of other cities, among them New York, Los Angeles, and New Orleans, are in fairly good financial shape, in part because they have been authorized by the state to levy special taxes in addition to the basic property tax. They and others—among them Pittsburgh and Dallas —have also been helped by their building booms, expanding the property-tax base. But some of the rest are in trouble, and the trouble can be bad. Boston, perhaps, is in the worst shape of all. It has had a legacy of inefficient government; both its population and its property-tax base are shrinking, and the state government, itself strapped for funds, won't help the city with its problems.

WANTED: SUPERCITIES?

The mayor's big problem with the suburban and state governments arises from his need to plan ahead for the physical development of the city. But here he is besieged with troubles. No big city, for example, has yet approached its transportation problem in such a way as to come out with an integrated plan of street systems, parking, mass surface transportation, and railroads. The failure is not the result of simple negligence. The city itself is not the master of its transportation fate. Such problems are area-wide, not city-wide, and their solution, if there is to be a solution, will require cooperation between the city government and all the other governments in the metropolitan area—those of the satellite towns and cities—and the cooperation of the state and federal governments as well.

One solution to the metropolitan problem that is being talked about a lot is the creation of a supergovernment; it would absorb all the duties and functions of the local governments in the metropolitan area, and would reign as a single unit over the new supercity. But such a supergovernment, in most cases, is a political impossibility: for one thing, the big cities, by and large, are Democratic and the suburbs are Republican, and neither are willing to relinquish their sovereignty to a new layer of government where these differences are likely to be intensified or, what may be worse, blurred. And even if supergovernment were feasible, there is doubt that it would be desirable. Government so big would be remote from the particular needs of the localities. And bigness and remoteness, in turn, would accelerate the trend to rule by specialists.

Many big cities have sought to solve their suburban problem by wide-scale annexations, but some of them have come to realize that the cost of providing services for the newly annexed suburbs outweighed the anticipated tax return and the other advantages of consolidation, including the over-all planning advantage, and the movement seems to have subsided. The suburbs, moreover, have fought back in many places by incorporating themselves as municipalities to prevent annexation. In 1956 only two large cities, Houston and Dallas, sought and obtained the authority to annex large surrounding areas.

Since neither supergovernment nor annexation seems feasible, the big cities are considering other ways to coexist with their booming suburbs. The Metropolitan Toronto plan is a significant approach. Under it, a federated government was established for Toronto and twelve surrounding municipalities to provide

area-wide services for all of them, leaving the local governments their control over local services. There are similar approaches in the U. S.—notably in Dade County, Florida, which includes Miami and twenty-five smaller communities. Dade County recently accepted a plan strengthening the county government, and giving it powers to provide for such county-wide needs and services as sanitation, arterial highways, water supply, and comprehensive planning. Many students of municipal government, most notably the University of California's Victor Jones, maintain that no attempt at metropolitan government can work well unless, as in Miami, it is based on the "federal" principle—that is, a system that will render unto the central authorities only those matters that cannot be dealt with locally.

THE FEDERATED REGION

Seattle's Metro Plan, for which Mayor Gordon Clinton has helped win legislative sanction, is another example. Metro will allow Seattle and some 175 towns, special districts, and other units in the Lake Washington area to work as a single unit in sewage and garbage disposal, water supply, mass transportation, parks, and planning.

Even without a formal arrangement cities can do a great deal. Dallas, for example, works closely with its outlying communities on specific issues—water supply, zoning—and Mayor Thornton has helped set up the Dallas County League of Municipalities, whch includes all the incorporated towns in the area, to

act as a frame for working out mutual problems on an area-wide basis.

Notably against all these devices is Milwaukee's government, which sells water to the suburbs. "This city," snaps Mayor Zeidler, "consults with suburban governments, but we do not believe they have a reason for existing." Zeidler, who loathes the suburbs and takes every opportunity to say so, wants no functional federation with their governments. He believes that if they want to use Milwaukee's costly water-distribution system they should consolidate with the city in all things. Milwaukee, however, is an exception: most cities have lost their appetite for the suburbs.

TACTICS VS. STRATEGY

In dealing with the how-to problems of government, the mayor is making considerable progress. At another task, however, he is failing. In his preoccupation with means, he is in danger of neglecting ends. He is not doing a good job of planning the city's future. When he is asked for his ideas on what the city should be like in twenty years, he is apt to reel off

a long list of particular improvements—a new expressway here, a new superblock of housing there. Sometimes he will point to a spanking marble-and-glass civic center built in the downtown business district to increase property values and to act as "a center of decision making."

But the projects, however worthy, are too often unconnected: the mayor doesn't really seem to have a general plan for the city's development. His pragmatism, of course, is not to be scorned, and a static, all-embracing master plan would never really work. But while any plan must be revised time and again, without a continuing effort to look ahead—far ahead—many basic policy questions will be left unasked. Everybody, for example, enthuses about redevelopment. But redevelopment for *whom?* Is it to be redevelopment for the middle-income groups? Or should the city woo first the upper-income groups? If so, is the accepted super-block design the way to do it?

Poked off in a corner of most city halls are a couple of rooms housing the city planning commission. The unit is topped by a board of prominent citizens and it has a staff: a full-time director, professional planners, architects, engineers, draftsmen. They prepare, with more or less foresight, the capital budget. They may also be at work on a general plan for the physical development of the city. As defined by the 1954 Housing Act, which requires that a city have in hand some kind of broad community plan as a condition for receiving federal urban-renewal funds, the general plan should include and consolidate the city's renewal projects with its zoning and land-use plans, and its thoroughfare and public-improvements programs. Most large cities are now preparing or claim to have completed such over-all plans. But with a few exceptions—notably Detroit and Cincinnati—few major cities are using their plans as genuine guides for decision making.

Expert as professional planners may be, planning is ultimately a line rather than a staff function. To be effective, it requires the mayor's active support and coordination. It is here more than anywhere else that he is required to serve as a center of leadership and responsibility:

if he is unwilling to mesh planning and execution, no one else can. In too many cities the mayor has abdicated this responsibility, and when he has, planning becomes an exercise in futility. Even in cities where planning and management are meshed, there remain many obstacles to effective planning. In New York, for example, where Mayor Wagner has made planning a genuine arm of the administration, he and his planning commissioners still have to sweat to establish some connection between the city's projects, the authorities' projects, and what often seem to be the personal projects of Mr. Moses.

On the other end of the scale is Houston, the only major city still without a zoning ordinance, where Mayor Oscar Holcombe recently turned down a suggestion that he adopt capital budgeting over five-year periods, as do most other big cities. Mayor Holcombe frowns on budgeting—which is the area in which plans are transformed into policy decisions and programs—beyond the term of the administration that is in power at the time. Pittsburgh's Lawrence, who countenances both planning and fragmentation, may have been speaking for the middle ground when he said recently: "My effort must go not into architectural and planning critiques, but into the limited, tedious, persevering work of making things happen."

The mayors, indeed, have made things happen—and this is prerequisite. But it is not enough. Long-range strategy for *what* is to happen is as badly needed. If the city is to reassert itself as a vital center in American life and, not so incidentally, if it is to help the federal and state governments prevent the rest of the country from turning into a suburban mess—the mayors must take the lead. The omens are promising.

SUGGESTED ADDITIONAL READINGS

1. Adrian, Charles R., "Some General Characteristics of Nonpartisan Elections," *American Political Science Review,* XLVI, No. 3 (September 1952), 766–776. Suggests eleven propositions characteristic of nonpartisanship, including: weakening of political parties; restriction of channels of recruitment for office; restriction of fund-raising opportunities; avoidance of policy issues in campaigns; frustration of protest voting; lack of collective responsibility.

2. Advisory Commission on Intergovernmental Relations, *Alternative Approaches to Governmental Reorganization in Metropolitan Areas,* Washington, D.C.; U. S. Government Printing Office, 1962, pp. 20–25. Discussion of use of extra-territorial powers to enable a city to provide services or attempt to regulate activity beyond its legal boundaries.

3. Baker, Benjamin, *Urban Government,* Chap. 1, "The Changing City," pp. 3–19, and Chap. 2, "The Growth of the City," pp. 20–33, New York: D. Van Nostrand, 1957. Survey of the growth of the city, its causes and consequences.

4. Banfield, Edward C., *Big City Politics,* New York: Random House, 1965, 149 pp., (paper). Readable description of the government and politics of Atlanta, Boston, Detroit, El Paso, Los Angeles, Miami, Philadelphia, St. Louis, and Seattle.

5. ———, and James Q. Wilson, *City Politics,* Chap. 11, "Reform," pp. 138–150, Cambridge: Harvard Univ. Press and M.I.T., 1963. Brief but thorough discussion of municipal reform, the reform ideal, program, strategies, and significance.

6. ———, *City Politics,* Chap. 13, "The Council-Manager Form," pp. 168–186, Cambridge: Harvard Univ. Press and M.I.T., 1963. Surveys the council-manager form—development, functioning, case studies, and evaluation.

7. Bollens, John C., *Special District Government in the United States,* Berkeley: University of California Press, 1957. The basic reference on the structure and powers of special districts.

8. ———, and Henry J. Schmandt, *The Metropolis: Its People, Politics, and Economic Life,* Chap. 6, "Government in the Metropolis," pp. 141–182, New York: Harper & Row, 1965. Clear, concise, and readable discussion of the structural-functional problems of government in metropolitan areas; useful as a general source and reference.

9. Connery, Robert H., and Richard H. Leach, *The Federal Government and Metropolitan Areas,* Cambridge: Harvard University Press, 1960, especially pp. 225–230. Probably the most thorough examination of the relationship between the federal government and metropolitan areas. Not entirely favorable toward federal involvement as it has developed, but a very useful discussion of this relationship and problems relating to it.

10. Dahl, Robert A., *Who Governs?,* New Haven: Yale University Press, 1961, 355 pp., (paper). Community power study of New Haven which found not a single pyramidal power structure (*cf.* Hunter), but numerous power centers dependent on political resources—experience, money, friends—held by each elite. Various combinations of these resources help explain variations in power in different situations.

11. Fiser, Webb S., *Mastery of the Metropolis,* Chap. 6, "Governmental Reorganization," pp. 108–130, Englewood Cliffs, N. J.: Prentice-Hall, 1962, (paper). Discusses the role of the federal and state governments in solving metropolitan problems. Considers leading attempts at metropolitan reorganization, including the Toronto, Dade County, and Detroit experiments.

12. Grant, Daniel R., and H. C. Nixon, *State and Local Government in America,* pp. 312–322, Boston: Allyn and Bacon, 1963. Textbook discussion of three basic forms of city government. Adequate for background information and convenient comparison.

13. Greer, Scott, *Governing the Metropolis,* New York: John Wiley, 1962, 153 pp., (paper). A short but indispensable book on the problems of governing the metropolis. Pertinent, useful, and comprehensive in approach.

14. ———, *Metropolitics,* New York: John Wiley, 1963, 207 pp. A thorough study of reform campaigns, using empirical data from St. Louis, Miami, and Cleve-

land. Considers who the reformers are, where they come from, what they strive for, and what they accomplish.

15. Grodzins, Morton, *The Metropolitan Area as a Racial Problem,* Pittsburgh: University of Pittsburgh Press, 1959, pp. 8–15, reprinted in Friedrick T. Tietze and James E. McKeown, *The Changing Metropolis,* Boston: Houghton Mifflin, 1964, pp. 118–123. Consideration of the consequences of urban-suburban population distribution—racial, economic, and political.

16. Flynn, Edward J., *You're the Boss,* New York: Collier Books, 1962, 255 pp., (paper). Former "boss" of the Bronx for twenty-five years tells his story of how a big-city political machine and its boss operates. His conclusion is that although bosses are inevitable, bad bosses are not.

17. *Guiding Metropolitan Growth,* New York: Committee for Economic Development, 1960, 47 pp., (paper). A concise survey of the problems of metropolitanism; pp. 13–18 review the population trends relative to urban growth, translating complex census data into easily understood text.

18. Gulick, Luther, "Metropolitan Organization," *The Annals of the American Academy of Political and Social Science,* 314 (November 1957), 57–65. Suggests four "political inventions" to improve metropolitan area government: creation of a state department of local affairs with a "metropolitan desk"; reconstruction of metropolitan counties; creation of "open-ended" metropolitan service agencies; creation of new level of regional government, the metropolitan council.

19. Hamilton, Howard D., *Legislative Apportionment: Key to Power,* New York: Harper & Row, 1964, 181 pp., (paper). Readings and sources on the problem of state legislative apportionment. The editor "regards representation as a question perhaps pre-eminent among those timeless issues involved in the attempt to govern men democratically."

20. Hillenbrand, Bernard F., "County Government Is Reborn," *Public Administration Survey,* University, Miss.: Bureau of Public Administration, May 1960, pp. 1–8. An optimistic assessment of the revitalization of county government.

21. Hunter, Floyd, *Community Power Structure: A Study of Decision-Makers,* Chapel Hill: University of North Carolina Press, 1953, 294 pp. Probably the classic study of the community power structure. See especially Chapter 4, in which Hunter explains his methodology for determining the community power structure. Hunter discovered in his case city a single pyramidal power structure of some thirty businessmen who were key decision-makers.

22. Jacobs, Jane, "Metropolitan Government," *Architectural Forum,* CVII (August 1957), 124–127, 204–205. Informative and concise survey of major approaches to metropolitan government. Considers metropolitan consolidation impossible, but examines three possible approaches: extension of *ad hoc* devices (special districts, authorities, contracts); greater dependence on the federal government; and federated metropolitan government.

23. Kammerer, Gladys M., *et al., The Urban Political Community: Profiles in Town Politics,* Boston: Houghton Mifflin, 1963, 216 pp., (paper). Eight case studies in the working of city-manager government in Florida cities, and general conclusions.

24. Kaufman, Herbert, and Victor Jones, "The Mystery of Power," *Public Administration Review,* XIV (Summer 1954), 205–212. Critical consideration of Hunter's *Community Power Structure,* especially the methodology and the "conspiracy theory" which seemed to be implied.

25. Martin, Roscoe C., *Grass Roots,* University, Ala.: University of Alabama Press, 1957, 103 pp. Short but incisive consideration of the grass-roots concept, its history, characteristics, and application. Seriously questions the identification of

democracy with rural government, and suggests "there is credible authority for the proposition that democracy and local government are mutually antagonistic."

26. Meyerson, Martin, and Edward C. Banfield, *Politics, Planning, and the Public Interest,* Glencoe: Free Press, 1955, pp. 64–75. Description of machine politics in Chicago in the 1950's.

27. Minar, David W., and Scott Greer, "The Metropolis and Its Problems," in *1963–1964 American Government Annual,* ed. Jack W. Peltason, New York: Holt, Rinehart and Winston, 1963, pp. 106–130. Concise summary of the problems relating to metropolitanism. Considers the growth of metropolitanism, the political framework of the metropolitan area, the structures of government and their consequences, and legal relationships.

28. Rossi, Peter H., "Power and Community Structure," *Midwest Journal of Political Science,* IV (November 1960), 390–401. Discussion of four types of community power structures: pyramidal, caucus rule, polylith, and amorphous.

29. Schubert, Glendon, *Reapportionment,* Part II, "State Legislatures," New York: Scribner's, 1965. A thorough research anthology, including articles and sources covering every aspect of reapportionment. Part II reprints twenty-two sources on reapportionment of state legislatures.

30. Snider, Clyde F., "American County Government: A Mid-Century Review," *American Political Science Review,* XLVI, No. 1 (March 1952), 66–80. Surveys county government to determine the "extent to which the backward institution of the early 1900's has since been modernized . . ." Considers all major aspects of county government, and argues that county reform is still in its infancy.

31. Von Eckardt, Wolf, *The Challenge of Megalopolis,* Macmillan, 1964, 126 pp., (paper). Condensed version of the original 810-page report: Jean Gottmann, *Megalopolis: The Urbanized Northeastern Seaboard of the United States,* The Twentieth Century Fund, (1961).

32. Will, Arthur G., "Another Look at Lakewood," in *Readings in State and Local Government,* ed. Joseph F. Zimmerman, New York: Holt, Rinehart and Winston, 1964, pp. 328–336. Considers the Lakewood plan for city contracts with the county to provide necessary services. Concludes that the plan can solve most interjurisdictional problems without the necessity of changing the basic city-county organization or powers.

33. Wood, Robert C., *Suburbia: Its People and Their Politics,* Boston: Houghton Mufflin, 1958, 340 pp., (paper). Indispensable reading for an understanding of suburbanism and its problems. The thirty-two pages of notes are an invaluable guide to additional sources.

FOR FURTHER CONSIDERATION

1. Does the traditional legal relationship between state and local governments satisfy the needs of this country today? What bearing does the population movement have on this question? Are states really necessary? Are they adequate to the tasks? Can you suggest any changes in governmental relationships (state-local-national) which you feel might make government more effective? Or can you suggest ways of improving effectiveness within the present legal relationships?

2. How would you begin to restate democratic theory so as to overcome the problems involved in the grass-roots or small-town democracy myth? What is the relationship, if any, of size to democracy? Is the growth of "Big Government" dangerous to democracy? Or can democracy work as well, or better, as size and complexity increase? Of what value, or danger, is the grass-roots myth?

3. "These population trends—movement to the cities, the growth of suburban areas, and the development of metropolitanism and supermetropolitanism—must be considered as prime characteristics of the political life of this country today." What advice would you give to the two major political parties based on your understanding of population trends? How do the trends affect local, state, and national politics? What implications for the Democratic party do they suggest? For the Republican party?

4. How would you go about deciding whether your particular city has governmental structural arrangements which hinder or promote satisfactory solution of problems facing the city? What factors would you consider in proposing new arrangements? In what sense, if any, can one say that there is a best form of city government?

5. What are the evils of local politics? Are they inherent? If so, what can be done about them? Does their existence suggest democracy really is not workable at the local level? If they are not inherent, how do we eliminate them? Can they be eliminated without eliminating politics? What would suggest is a legitimate and useful role for municipal reformers?

The Dynamics of
Policy Formation 5

Any American student knows that there are three branches of American government: the legislative, the judicial, and the executive. He knows that Congress makes the law, the president executes the law, and the Supreme Court interprets the law. He knows that the system of checks and balances insures that the powers of no one of the branches encroaches upon any other. He may remember that there are 435 permanent members of the House of Representatives, that the justices of the Supreme Court are appointed by the president for life, and that the president can veto bills passed by Congress. It is hoped that he will know much more than this, and the more he knows about these institutional arrangements the better.

As he grows up, however, his understanding of the democratic process must grow also. It would be inaccurate if he saw the Congress, the president, and the Supreme Court as agencies with differing roles set in an antagonistic relationship to each other. He will understand more about these institutions and the roles they play if he comes to view them not as separate institutions but as interrelated aspects of the democratic process.

In this chapter the focus is not on the institutions per se but on these institutions as producers of public policy. Government will be considered as a set of institutionalized arrangements for arriving at answers to a series of questions: Who will determine public policy? How will we decide between competitors for power? What problems will be open for solution by government? By what procedures will such policy be made? Different societies develop different answers to these questions and thus different institutions of government. But each society deals with the problem of how to determine the subject of public policy, who will make the decisions about public policy, and by what procedures those decisions shall be made.

Public policy-making cannot be considered synonymous with law-making. Law-making, defined as the passing of statutes by a legislative body, is simply one manifestation of public policy. Other expressions of public policy, some having the force of law while others are simply expressions of publicly declared purposes or aims, include presidential policy statements, executive orders, administrative rules, adjudications made by administrative hearing boards, and decisions of federal courts. All of these represent determinations of what government should or should not do about certain public problems.

Public policy emanates from the executive and judicial branches as well as the legislative branch. Some agencies, such as the Congress, are engaged extensively and continuously in the process of developing policy relative to a wide spectrum of problem areas. Others, such as the numerous administrative agencies (Interstate Commerce Commission, Veterans Administration, and Securities Exchange Commission, for example) make policy pronouncements in comparatively limited spheres but which may have broad implications and effects. Still others, such as federal courts, make infrequent policy pronouncements which are almost always incidental to carrying out non-policy-making activities. All, however, are pronouncing, modifying, or implementing policy.

Governmental institutions are engaged in translating public demands into public policy. [17] The effort may be imperfect, and the policy pronounced may not reflect accurately the demands of the various publics, either because the demands of the various publics defy rationalization in an articulate policy, or because the procedures for determining the demands of the publics and for translating those demands into policy are defective. Nonetheless, public policy in a democratic society is the nearest possible approximation of what the people want as expressed through imperfect mechanisms for representing their demands.

We have seen that democracy is characterized by a competitive struggle for political power. In fact, democracy is not possible in the absence of a genuinely competitive struggle for power among those who wish to become policy-makers, with the winner being determined by the people at large. Those that have competed and "won" (in the sense that they are now in policy-making positions) are empowered to determine public policy. They cannot, however, ignore the wishes, demands, and policy alternatives suggested by their political competitors if they are to compete successfully in future elections. Also, among those who have won the competition continues, for there are differences of approach to public policy. In Congress, for instance, the "winners" include many who differ widely on major policy questions. The making of public policy is carried on within a continuing struggle for political power between elections, and the policy pronounced is the subject matter of the struggle. Those who won may set the stage favorably for their own victory in the next election, and those who lost may compete by establishing the incompetence of the policy.

Government, then, provides institutionalized means to arrive at politically acceptable solutions to politically important problems. This does not necessarily result in correct solutions or solutions to all problems. Indeed, many significant questions are politically unimportant, in that they are not easily translated into the competitive struggle for political power. The question of the rights of the Negro, for instance, was for the better part of a century not politically significant, although of undeniable moral importance. However, in the last few years, with increasing evidence of the political strength of the Negro, the rights question has become very much a part of the competition for political power. Politically unimportant problems have to be solved, if they are to be solved at all, by means other than governmental activity. Recognition of realistic limitations of the process may help avoid frustration, disillusionment, or error in assuming there is something wrong with the process itself because it produces no answers or incorrect answers to what one considers critical questions.

SEPARATION OF POWERS AND POLICY-MAKING

Our hypothetical student should also be well-versed in the classic notion of the separation of powers. [8] As popularly understood, there is a deliberate and rational division of powers at the national level between the three branches of government. The Congress makes the law; the president and the administrative branch administer the law; and the courts enforce and interpret the law. Checks and balances are written into the Constitution to insure the effectiveness of this separation. Through these checks and balances no one branch is able to monopolize power. Each branch has the constitutional power to check the other branches when there is danger of misuse of power.

Congress can pass statutes, but the approval of the president is required before they become law. However, even this check is counter-checked. If the President vetoes the bill, Congress can pass it over his veto by a two-thirds vote in each house.[1]

The president, as the chief spokesman for the United States in international relations, negotiates all treaties. His treaty-making power, however, is checked by the requirement that no treaty becomes effective until consented to by two-thirds of the Senate. Likewise, while the president has an extensive power to appoint, his appointments are subject to the approval of the Senate. The Supreme Court, which has firmly established its power to declare acts of Congress unconstitutional, relies upon Congress for the determination of its appellate jurisdiction under which most of the cases the Court hears come to it. Finally, Congress has the power of impeachment.

This picture of the separation of powers is accurate but not complete. It tends to obscure the fact that there is more of a separation of structures than of powers. The federal government is composed of separate structures performing cooperative, interacting, complementary activities. While no one of these agencies may monopolize the policy-making activity, no one may uncompromisingly block all others. The critical point is that this system of separate structures with interacting powers is a guarantee of the vitality of the policy-making process, insuring the continuance of competitive interaction among the various participants. Separa-

---

[1] If, however, the president fails to sign the bill or veto it within ten days, the bill becomes law without his signature. If in this ten-day period Congress has adjourned the president may "pocket veto" the bill by simply failing to sign it.

tion of powers is really a system of "antagonistic cooperation" in the making of public policy.

Statutes are not necessarily original expressions of public policy. In many cases Congress is not so much establishing new policy as formalizing and regularizing policy developed somewhere in the executive or administrative process. The fact that Congress finally considers a bill is usually evidence that there has already been a considerable amount of political involvement by interests anxious to see the policy adopted. Much of this activity may have been directed toward influencing administrative policymakers. In many instances—some notable, such as the lend-lease agreements entered into by the president in World War II and later formalized by congressional action—the policy has already been established by non-legislative agencies.

The president and administrative officials do not legislate, but they make policy decisions, act upon them, and cause others to act upon them. In foreign policy the president is the official voice of the government. Although he may not formally commit the United States to a treaty without the consent of the Senate, the mere fact that he has undertaken negotiations on a prospective treaty may well commit the United States to positions that Congress may find it impossible to modify. Beyond this, the president may negotiate informal agreements with the heads of state of other nations which do not require ratification by the Senate. Presidents Truman, Eisenhower, Kennedy, and Johnson each committed this nation to international engagements having tremendous impact on the future of this country. Korea, Lebanon, Cuba, the Dominican Republic, and South Vietnam stand as good evidence of the power of the president to commit the country to particular courses of action in foreign affairs. On the domestic scene the president also makes policy. President Truman, for example, instituted by executive order in 1947 a security program for federal employees which, continued in effect (though modified) through the administrations of Eisenhower, Kennedy, and Johnson, has shaped the character of the federal service, affected the lives of its members, and has had significant repercussions on the character of the political process.

The administrative branch, an extension of the arm of the president, is involved in policy-making both before and after congressional action. Statutes generally can establish only broad policy, leaving to administrative determination the application to specific cases. In making such applications, administrators may elaborate the broad general policy. Often administrative officials are faced with the necessity of making decisions in the absence of a clear-cut answer in the statutes, and in applying their own judgment they establish the policy of the agency. Later these administratively determined policy directives may be formalized in statutes.

Administrative decisions about how to implement a legislatively determined policy may have the most immediate and direct effect on the citizen, whose contact with the government is largely administrative. Examples of administrative policy-making range from the informally declared and largely clerically pronounced answers to procedural questions, to decisions by the Bureau of Internal Revenue on permissible tax deductions, and determination by the Bureau of the Budget that certain funds shall not be expended even though Congress appropriated them for a specific purpose.

The regulatory commissions, though largely independent of presidential influence, operate as quasi-legislative-judicial agencies in the regulation of some of the most complex and significant areas of the American economy. [20] Congress has determined the broad outline of economic policy relative to commerce, for example, but the Interstate Commerce Commission operates as a supplemental policy-making body as it applies general statutory policy to the numerous individual cases that come before it.

No fiction is more firmly established in American governmental folklore than that the courts are non-political, that they do not make law or policy—they simply interpret the law. This is not a realistic portrayal of the role of the courts in the American political system. [14] Much of the work of federal courts is adjudication of conflicts arising over the specific applications of legal requirements, but this involves the judicial elaboration of the meaning of a statute or other policy pronouncement. Statutory interpretation involves definition or redefinition of public policy. In the realm of constitutional interpretation the Supreme Court and often lower federal courts are determining the definitive meaning of constitutional provisions and thus establishing the framework in which other policymakers will have to operate.

Illustrations of policy-making by the courts are not hard to find. When in 1896 the Supreme Court held that "equal protection of the law" required by the Fourteenth Amendment did not prohibit the maintenance of "separate but equal" facilities for Negroes,[2] it had determined the meaning of constitutional language and predetermined the acceptability of a half-century of segregation. The court declared new public policy when in 1954 it held that the "separate but equal facilities" rule was no longer good constitutional law and that the equal protection of the law clause of the Fourteenth Amendment would no longer permit racially segregated public educational institutions.[3]

In 1962 the Court decided that the question of apportionment of the lower house of a state legislature was no longer a "political question" and consequently was open to judicial consideration.[4] Two years later the Court ruled that malapportionment of congressional districts involves infringement of the right to vote.[5] In another decision that year the Court held that "one man one vote" is a constitutional requirement for representation in state legislatures, thus necessitating major changes in the upper legislative houses in all states.[6] The effects of these decisions on the political system and upon the panorama of public policy decisions made by legislative bodies is incalculable. They may prove as important in their impact upon society as any policy decisions of the president or of Congress.

Two central aspects of the policy-making process now require attention. The first is the question of representativeness. To what extent is each of the policy-making institutions representative, and how do they complement each other as

[2] *Plessy v. Ferguson,* 163 U. S. 537 (1896).
[3] *Brown v. Board of Education,* 347 U. S. 483 (1954).
[4] *Baker v. Carr,* 369 U. S. 186 (1962).
[5] *Wesberry v. Sanders,* 376 U. S. 1 (1964).
[6] *Reynolds v. Sims,* 377 U. S. 355 (1964).

agencies of representation? And second, how do these institutions differ procedurally in policy-making, and what might the procedural differences tell us about the nature of policy-making in our democracy?

REPRESENTATION AND PUBLIC POLICY FORMATION

Our hypothetical student knows well the importance of "taxation without representation" in American history and the idea that no government can be democratic unless it is representative of the people. This idea is essentially correct, and problems arise only when we fail to recognize the real nature of representation. [6, 7] Is a governmental institution representative of the people only when is selected by popular election? Can a court, for instance, be representative even though it is not elected and not subject to removal except by extraordinary procedures?

The major agencies of public policy formation differ significantly in the methods by which they are selected, their availability to those interested in affecting public policy, and the procedures and instruments for holding them accountable. These three factors—selection, access, and responsibility—are central to the nature of representation in the policy-making process.

SELECTION

Congress, the president, administrative agencies, and courts differ markedly as formal channels of representation. Congress and the president are elected; administrative agencies and courts are appointed.

Even though both Congress and the president are elected, they represent different constituencies. Congress, made up of two houses with different terms of office, does not represent a national constituency but numerous local constituencies. The House is elected anew every two years, and one-third of the Senate is elected every two years. At no time does the entire Congress change because of the result of a given election. Members of Congress are elected from relatively small territorial constituencies. A senator's electoral district is a state, and, except in the extraordinary circumstances of at-large election, the congressman's electoral district is considerably smaller than a state. Individual members of Congress may demonstrate attitudes which transcend electoral provincialism, but they have usually been elected on the basis of local not national interests. [11]

Representation in Congress has been disproportionate in favor of small states and rural areas and interests. In the Senate each state, regardless of population, elects two senators. In 1965 two senators represented almost eighteen million people in California but only slightly over a quarter of a million in Alaska. The apportionment of seats in the House of Representatives, though not as disproportionate as in the Senate, has always resulted in some areas having more than their mathematically due representation. Congressional districts are created by state legislatures, themselves usually over-representative of rural and small town areas. Some congressmen have represented four times as many people as other congressmen from the same state, and many states have had some districts three times as populous as others.[7] With a national population over 70 percent urban, nearly 60 percent of the House membership has been from rural districts. [4, 5, 26]

Of greater importance, however, is the seniority rule under which those representatives who stay in Congress the longest move into the most influential positions as members or chairmen of the most important committees. In safe districts (such as in the Southern states, which are also less urbanized) the members have a long tenure and thus have disproportionate influence on the activities of Congress.

This basis of representation has led to another characteristic of the Congress—its conservatism. Congress historically has been slow to adopt new or radical programs. Partly this may be due to its collegial nature, its lack of an aggressive leadership closely attuned to the demands of a wide electorate, and the narrow scope of the demands placed on congressmen by their mostly rural constituents.

The president, on the other hand, must compete for office on a national basis. His is a national constituency; his electorate is a composite of the electorates of all the members of Congress. Though certain states and regions are more important in terms of their electoral strength, the president must align himself with national concerns and interests. The president is the only elected official in the United States, other than the vice-president, [31] who has a national constituency.[8]

The president can operate nationally far better than any other elected or appointed official. He has the power to appoint a legion of federal officials in every section of the country. He also speaks as the advocate of programs which are national in scope but also coincide with the concerns of the electorate for which he competes. [15, 25]

The administrative branch is an adjunct of the executive branch, and the administrators are subordinates of the president. None of them is elected. All come into office as employees; many are appointed by the president with the consent of the Senate; most are a part of the permanent civil service. The lack of electoral support makes the representative role of administrative officials considerably different from that of the president or Congress. It would be incorrect, however, to assume that because the president appoints a large proportion of the administrative officials he is always able to make them serve his own policy-making inclinations. The extensive civil service, the professionalism of many of the administrators, and the size of the administrative structure all tend to modulate direct presidential influence. These factors make possible and encourage administrative policy-making.

Many state courts have elected members, but all federal courts are appointed by the president with consent of the senate. [13] The members of the federal courts have no elective constituency, they do not have to campaign for office, they do not have to satisfy electorate demands, and they do not lose office because of a change in voter sentiment. Although the justices are to this extent insulated from politics, they get into office by an extension of the political

---

[7] U.S. Department of Commerce, Bureau of the Census, *Congressional District Data Book,* 1961.

[8] The vice-presidential candidate represents a regional constituency more than does the president, in that he traditionally is selected as a running mate for the presidential candidate largely for his ability to supply electoral strength from a region in which the presidential candidate would run weakest.

process of election, through appointment and approval by elected officials whose political careers may be seriously affected by the appointments they make. Even more than the president's appointments to the administrative agencies, his appointments to the courts, and particularly to the Supreme Court, may weigh heavily on the possibility of his re-election.

ACCESS

The ease with which those who have special interests can gain access to the policymakers is an important indicator of the representativeness of the policymakers. The average citizen, the individual who has something on his mind, can be heard—through letters to Congress, visits to the office of an administrative agency, letters to the editor, and the like—but the major influencers of public policy are the organized political interest groups, sometimes referred to as pressure groups. There are thousands of such groups, active at all levels of government, expressing the interests of those they represent to those who make public policy. Name a social, political, or economic interest in the United States and we can probably find a group representing it before government agencies. [16, 28]

The older term, pressure group, is misleading, as it connotes a kind of political arm-twisting. This evaluation of political interest group representatives, often called lobbyists for their traditional operations in the lobby of Congress, fails to recognize their positive role in representation. Rather than being a perversion of a democratic representative process, political interest groups are an indispensable adjunct to the formal process of representation. They transmit to the policymakers the demands of the various publics, providing firsthand information of their constituents' views on specific matters. They provide detailed background material for proposed legislation. They also provide evaluations as to the effect of various proposals on the welfare of the interest group, the broader welfare of society, and the political welfare of the policymaker himself.

Political interest groups are very much concerned with the outcome of elections; if people who favor their interests are elected, their chances of success in influencing public policy will be enhanced. However, political interest groups normally do not concentrate on electing people to office or attempt to gain public office themselves; rather they attempt to influence those who hold public office. In this role the political interest group represents the most highly articulated and organized extra-governmental agency for influencing public policy. Access to the legislative process by these groups insures that policy-making in Congress will involve a continuous adjustment of conflicting interests, an important addition to the formal processes of representation through election.

Political interest groups also have access to administrative policy makers. Since administrators often formulate policy proposals which are later presented to Congress for formalization into law, political interest groups seek access to this pre-legislative policy determination stage. They also seek access in the post-legislative stage, when the administrators are implementing the broad policy determinations of Congress.

Political interest groups attempt to influence executive and administrative decisions in a variety of ways. Many interest groups are vitally concerned with presidential decisions on appointments, for if they can influence the composition of an agency they may more easily influence the policy determinations of the agency. Some administrative agencies are virtually governmentally instituted interest groups. [10] The Veterans Administration, for instance, seems to operate both as a federal administrative agency carrying out national policy affecting veterans and also as the most important exponent of veterans' policy. Access to the Army Corps of Engineers is important to those interested in promoting government construction of dams, bridges, and other public works. The value of contact with the Department of Labor for the AFL–CIO and other labor interests, with the Department of the Interior for those concerned with conservation and wildlife, and with the Department of Health, Education, and Welfare for a whole host of interests is not hard to see. Executive creation of advisory committees on a multitude of problems provides opportunity for representatives of interested groups to serve in quasi-official positions, thereby combining their functions as interest group representatives and government policy advisors.

Access to judicial policymakers is further evidence of the complexity and pluralism of the representative system. Political interest groups often find it desirable, sometimes because of inability to compete effectively in the legislative, executive, and electoral arenas, to transfer their efforts to the courts in attempting to modify public policy in their own interests. [29] Access can be attained, however, only through the professionals—lawyers—who alone are authorized to appear before federal courts. Political interest group representatives do not themselves directly attempt to "lobby" the courts.

The most effective mechanism for access to the judiciary is the test case, through which those interested in challenging an established public policy seek to have the courts invalidate it or modify it to maximize the interests of the group bringing the case. The National Association for the Advancement of Colored People, for example, has through most of its history concentrated on challenging legislative and administrative actions in the courts, with the result that public policy relevant to Negroes' rights has been developed mainly through judicial action. [30] The Jehovah's Witnesses, a politically powerless religious sect, have, through the courts, greatly expanded both their own religious freedom and the meaning of the First Amendment. [19]

The litigants are often joined by *amicus curiae*, a "friend of the court" who, interested in the outcome of the case, files a brief in support of one of the litigants. Frequent users of this means of access include the NAACP, the American Jewish Congress, the AFL–CIO, the American Bar Association, and the American Legion.

Access to the courts is not limited to the large and highly financed interest groups. Even an individual can sometimes bring about change of public policy through the courts. For instance, Clarence Earl Gideon, a fifty-one-year-old penniless prisoner in Florida, who had been in and out of prisons most of his life, succeeded in obtaining from the Supreme Court of the United States, in an *in forma pauperis* case,[9] a monumental ruling declaring the constitutional right of a defendant to counsel. As Anthony Lewis in *Gideon's Trumpet* said:

---

[9] Federal statutes provide that a litigant unable to pay the regular costs and provide the usual forms may proceed *in forma pauperis*—in the manner of a pauper—without paying these fees or filing the required forms. Even handwritten applications for review are accepted under the Supreme Court's rules.

The Supreme Court indeed often provides a forum for those—the despised and rejected—who have no effective voice in the legislative chamber. . . . Enlightened opinion holds, without sentimentality, that treating criminal defendants in a decent way serves the interest of a civilized society. Yet legislatures, feeling no demand from the voters, will rarely do anything about unfairness in the administration of the criminal law except under pressure from the courts—or until the courts, especially the Supreme Court, generate a broad moral concern. The criminal-law decisions of the Supreme Court have awakened significant forces in society to the moral considerations, and the result has been a fruitful interplay between courts and legislatures. Certainly the concern shown for the right to counsel in 1963 by the Kennedy Administration, Congress, the Ford Foundation and the many bar groups grew in large part out of the Supreme Court's decisions on the issue over three decades.[10]

RESPONSIBILITY

In what ways are the institutional means of representation comparable as to responsibility? What are the procedures and instruments for holding them accountable? Are there procedures through which the system guarantees, or tends to promote, restraint and control of policymakers? [9, 2]

Here again we refer to the key role played by competition for political power in the democratic process. There is no evidence that an election is an appropriate instrument for making rational evaluations of the effectiveness of policymakers. However, the necessity of competing for public office, through elections in which the winner is empowered for a specific length of time to make public policy, provides the institutional arrangements whereby policymakers may be held politically responsible. The various policymakers, however, are related in different ways to the competitive electoral process.

Congress and the president are responsible directly through the electoral process. Every act by a member of Congress or the president may affect his chances of re-election and the political future of himself and his associates. He must participate in policymaking with one eye on the election returns, past and prospective. He may and often does influence the voters (some would say educate) to respond favorably to his point of view, but he is forced to recognize that his competitors for power can influence as well. As long as he depends on votes for his right to office he must act responsibly—that is, well within the limits of tolerance of his constituents.

On the other hand, federal administrators and courts are not elected. They do not depend directly on the favor of the electorate for office and the consequent authority to make policy decisions. But are they thus non-responsible? Here we must recognize the indirect responsibility imposed upon appointive officials through the elected officials. The president is politically responsible for all that his administrative branch does or does not do. The civil service system and the independent regulatory commissions restrict the president's authority over administrative matters by largely removing these administrators from his political control. But the president must compete for public office at least partly on the record of the administrators in making and implementing public policy. A congressman may maximize his chance for re-election through his success in controlling the administrators through vigorous challenge, investigation, personal contact, and the whole range of mechanisms available to the Congress for review of administrative

[10] Anthony Lewis, *Gideon's Trumpet* (New York: Random House, 1964), pp. 211–212.

action. [27] Similarly, the courts are responsible indirectly through the president and Congress. Both the president and Congress share political responsibility for the acceptability (in terms of future electorate response) of those selected to sit on the courts. Thus, for example, the race question and the electorate's views of it may affect the kind of judges appointed to federal courts in the South. And Congress can curtail the activities of the courts by modifying the appellate jurisdiction of the courts to remove certain kinds of policy-affecting cases from their jurisdiction.

There is no easy explanation of the way American institutions operate to insure representativeness in public policy formation. He who would understand the policy-making process must first understand the differences that exist between the three major policy-making institutions—differences in selection, in access, and in responsibility.

PROCEDURAL ASPECTS OF POLICY FORMATION

Our second major concern is this: how do policy-making institutions differ procedurally, and what do these procedural differences tell us about the nature of policy-making in our democracy?

LEGISLATIVE PROCEDURES

Congress can be considered an institutionalized arena for conflict over policy. Legislative procedures are attempts to rationalize and order this conflict. Their purpose is not to eliminate conflict but to facilitate it. The procedures are designed to permit maximum conflict over policy with minimum danger to the body politic.

Congress is in the business of accommodating conflicting interests—of making it possible for conflicting interests to be maximized. Total victory is rare; compromise is almost always the result of the legislative battle well fought. Inevitably there will be interests represented which are uncompromisable or are thought to be uncompromisable by those who hold them. If the purpose of a legislature were simply to count heads to decide what the majority wants, these interests which cannot bend the majority would be left with no alternative but to withdraw. This is not what happens in the Congress of the United States. Congress makes public policy for all the people and all the interests, and its procedures do not allow those who form a majority to require all others to acquiesce or withdraw.

Looking at Congress this way will help explain certain procedural machinery. Central to congressional procedures are the House Rules Committee, the seniority system, and unlimited debate in the Senate. Criticism of these three procedural mechanisms has been extensive and varied, and mainly express the judgment that through their exercise the will of the majority may be frustrated. [3, 4]

The House has twenty and the Senate sixteen standing committees. These committees perform most of the legislative business—holding hearings, considering proposed legislation, proposing amendments to bills, recommending passage or defeat of measures. While the committees are not miniature reproductions of their respective houses, they are bipartisan and reflect to a considerable degree the configuration of power in the chamber.

The Rules Committee of the House of Representatives is one of the permanent committees. [23] It serves essentially as a "traffic cop," deciding which bills will be considered by the whole house and under what circumstances. Every bill except taxation and appropriation bills must go to the Rules Committee after it is reported from one of the legislative subject-matter committees. The Rules Committee decides when it will be debated on the floor, what provisions will be made for length of debate, and the conditions for amendment. On occasion, the Rules Committee simply refuses to give a bill a "rule," effectively bottling up any bill its majority does not favor.

The record is clear that the Rules Committee has operated to frustrate efforts to pass legislation generally considered liberal. Proposals for federal aid to education, increased use of the social security system for health benefits, and civil rights legislation have been blocked or delayed. But in spite of condemnation by scholars, impassioned challenges by members of the House, and efforts by at least three presidents, the Rules Committee continues to watch over conflict in the House and to frustrate prevailing and/or momentary majorities. The majority can be prevented from legislating until it has tempered its proposals to accommodate the interests of the minority. If the interests of the minority or minorities are basic,[11] if they are in fact or are thought to be uncompromisable, the Rules Committee often can insure that the majority cannot pass the legislation. The majority can use a discharge petition of 218 signatures to move the bill to the floor, but the members of the House have been reluctant to utilize this procedure.

Basic to the committee system, and thus to the operation of Congress, is the seniority system. [12] Appointments to committees are made on the basis of length of service in the respective house. Those who come from safe districts (those in which the incumbent normally is re-elected with little or no opposition) are insured eventually of becoming members and often chairmen of the most important committees. Thus, senators and representatives from the least competitive electoral districts usually gravitate to the most powerful positions in Congress.

The seniority system has been severely criticized, and the case against it is a strong one. Power in Congress is not so much the result of ability and experience as the result of good fortune in coming from a safe district. Junior members of Congress, regardless of competence, are subordinate to those who have been there the longest, although many of these senior members have rarely if ever had to compete in a genuine electoral struggle. In this respect the leaders of Congress are often those who are least representative of new and changing public attitudes and demands, since they come from electoral districts in which effective competition at the polls is exceptional. When the Democratic party controls the Congress, Southern Democrats predominate as committee chairmen. When the Republicans control the Congress, representatives of Midwestern rural areas gain in chairmanships. The seniority system is most strongly opposed by organized labor, civil rights groups, and urban interests. The seniority system maximizes the ability of the conservatives to frustrate the liberal majority, thus requiring the dominant majority to compromise with the outvoted minority.

[11] In referring to minorities and their uncompromisable interests we are not referring to transitory or momentary interests of those who oppose a particular policy proposal but to the basic, long-range interests of prevailing minorities, such as may be included within the terms conservative or liberal, Southerner or Easterner, laborer or capitalist, etc.

The seniority system, however, solves one of the basic problems of any arena of competition—how legitimacy will be conferred. As an automatic process for filling positions of power inside the Congress, it serves to rationalize the process of conflict, concentrating conflict on policy alternatives rather than on questions of who should hold these positions of importance.

The Senate is procedurally dedicated to unlimited debate. Ordinarily any senator may speak as long as he wishes without fear of being cut off by his colleagues. The filibuster has become a familiar part of the working of the Senate. [24] The filibuster can prevent an overwhelming majority from passing legislation until the wishes of the minority are recognized. For instance, after the Civil Rights Act of 1875,[12] Congress did not enact any civil rights legislation[13] until 1957. Although at many times the majority of the Senate was ready to pass legislation on civil rights, the filibuster repeatedly enabled a small minority from the South to frustrate the aims of the majority. This can be condemned as an undemocratic procedure, but only if one accepts the premise that in a democracy the majority must have its way regardless of the consequences to the interests of the minority. On the other hand, regardless of the validity of their position, a Southern minority which was uncompromisingly opposed to congressional action on civil rights was enabled to continue to act in Congress, to continue to represent their constituents in the policy-making process, albeit at the expense of the majority. In recent years, however, Congress has been comparatively aggressive in adopting civil rights legislation. An anti-poll tax amendment to the Constitution has been adopted, and passage of civil rights acts has become almost routine. Yet the representatives of the Southern states are still participating in the policy-making process. The political strength of the Negro now makes it necessary for Southern congressmen to allow public policy enactments relevant to the advancement of the Negro in his civil and political rights.

It is not suggested that these procedures be accepted uncritically. They cannot be evaluated, however, by simply deciding a priori what is right and what is wrong, or by positing that a democracy requires that the majority have its way. Democracy does not require that the majority have its way. What it does require is that all those who have an interest in public policy have an institutionalized procedure whereby they may compete with others for the privilege of making public policy. It requires that this competition be open and genuine, but that the participants who lose—who do not succeed in defeating policy proposals which they feel are adverse to their own interests—not be so inconvenienced or damaged by the new policy that they can no longer participate.[14] It requires that the interests of the minorities not be dismissed by the process of counting heads alone. (The minorities, of course, in practice include only those who are enfranchised and are otherwise politically significant. Disenfranchised Negroes and Indians have

[12] This Act was declared invalid in *The Civil Rights Cases,* 109 U.S. 3 (1883).

[13] The section of the Interstate Commerce Act of 1887 prohibiting discrimination between individuals in interstate commerce was not really a civil rights provision, although its subsequent use and interpretation has made it an important instrument against segregation on interstate carriers.

[14] For example, the majority lost repeatedly in not being able to enact civil rights bills, but they were still able to continue to compete. The Negro minority lost at the same time, but they, too, have prevailed; civil rights legislation is now possible, and increasingly so. The process is slow, but it is preferable to revolution.

not been accommodated historically, nor have American Communists done very well in this regard.) In this sense, Congress can be understood as an institutionalized arena for the carrying on of conflict over policy, in which the procedures guarantee that the conflict shall continue even at the expense of failure to make policy that is clearly favored by a numerical majority, at least until the majority has recognized and accommodated the minimum demands of the minorities necessary for them to continue to play the game.

EXECUTIVE AND ADMINISTRATIVE PROCEDURES

The following are the major roles the president plays in American government: he is chief of state, chief executive, commander-in-chief of the armed forces of the United States, chief diplomat in relations with other nations, chief legislator, chief of his political party, the voice of the people and "the leading formulator and expounder of public opinion," the protector of the peace, the manager of prosperity, and a world leader.[15] Simply listing the roles is sufficient to demonstrate the almost impossible burden placed on the president. No one man can perform all these functions; the President, is, in a real sense, the composite of thousands of agencies and officials who operate within the executive branch.

The enormous size and complexity of the job to be done by the president and those who function in his name suggests the impossibility of any simple explanation of the policy-making process in the executive branch. Although ultimately the president is responsible for all the decisions made by those in the executive branch ("the buck passes up"), most of the decisions are made by his subordinates, some very far down in the hierarchy. Whereas Congress operates in a physically limited area, for a specific amount of time, and through highly structured and defined procedures and rules, the executive branch is dispersed throughout the United States and many other countries, it operates continuously, and is made up of a multitude of persons and agencies dealing with the minute and technical as well as the high policy aspects of government. Thus to speak of a policy-making process in the executive branch is to stretch the use of that term past the point of utility.

The American president is the world's most powerful executive. At the same time, he may be one of the world's most constitutionally restricted executives. Although in the field of international relations he can commit the United States to actions which may change the future of this country and the world, on the domestic scene he is not nearly so powerful. Many of the president's important proposals may run into serious difficulty in Congress. The president's decision-making powers are both unlimited and restrained, and failure to comprehend this admixture of power and disability means failure to comprehend the nature of the president as a maker of public policy.

Since most executive decisions are made by subordinates to the president, the character of the executive bureaucracy is important. "Big Government" is a fact today, and the bigness is largely administrative. Among the reasons for this bureaucratic expansion are the growth of population from 75 million in 1900 to 190 million in 1966; increased urbanization; the growth of science and technology;

[15] Clinton Rossiter, *The American Presidency* (New York: Harcourt, Brace, 1960), pp. 15–23.

wars and their aftermath; economic crises; nationalization of the economy; increased international involvement; and the demands of the people for increased services.

The federal bureaucracy has been created by Congress, which must appropriate funds and grant statutory authority for agencies to operate. The administrative structure is characterized by geographic dispersion. Only a very small part of it is in Washington, D.C.; most of the agencies are in regional, field, and local offices scattered throughout the fifty states and many other nations of the world. Most of those working in federal administrative positions are local people living in local communities throughout the country; they are not really "feds" at all except in receipt of their paychecks. The picture of a horde of bureaucratic administrators centered in Washington (the hypothetical "they" who some find to be the explanation for all those things they do not like) is neither accurate nor constructive in explaining the role of the administrators in public policy-making.

The federal bureaucracy is characterized by a predominance of war and defense employees. More than half of the employees of the federal government are civilian employees of the Army, Navy, Air Force, and other defense agencies. About three-fourths of all federal employees are connected with the fighting of past, present, or future wars. Only about 10 percent work for welfare agencies. And the independent regulatory agencies, which govern so much of the economic life of the country, employ an even smaller percentage of federal employees.

If administrative bureaucracy is an essential part of the policy-making process, attention should be given to some of its major problems. How do we obtain competent administrators, at the lower levels as well as the upper levels of scientists, accountants, and specialists of all kinds, in competition with the private sector? What standards of competence do we apply? Are the standards the same for employment in the administrative agencies of government as they are in the private sector? What of loyalty? How do we determine loyalty, and what kind of loyalty is required before one can do a competent job in government? How do we keep the administrator politically responsible but not politically subservient? How do we insure that we do not develop bureaucracy that becomes indispensable to the wielding of political power by politicians? Is the civil service system the answer? Or do we destroy political responsibility as we increase administrative isolation from politics? What of the "built-in conservatism" of bureaucracy? Can the bureaucracy change direction when a new master is elected? Are administrators a dependent class—dependent on government for their livelihood and professional standing and therefore tending to support the government of the day? [10]

In administrative policy-making, the bureaucracy must be (1) competent, and (2) responsive to political influences and thus popular demands, yet (3) protected so that it is not the "army of the establishment." The bureaucracy does not belong to the bureaucrats. The competitive struggle for power, influence, and advantage must and does affect the administrative branch. In fact, the administrative branch is very much the product of that competitive struggle. So long as this is true, the administrative bureaucracy functions within the mainstream of the democratic policy-making process.

At the apex of the administrative pyramid stands the president. While Congress is zealous in its efforts to review and control administrators—through

appropriations reviews, hearings, investigations, revisions of enabling acts, etc.—
the president also must be able to exercise supervision. At the very least there
must be ways to insure that he is informed and consulted, that the proposals of
administrators can be evaluated for him, and that he is able to influence their
decision-making. The instruments for executive control are mainly political and
derive from his position as the leader of his party. [22] But he also has broad
powers of appointment and removal, and the Bureau of the Budget is at his right
hand to aid in controlling the fiscal affairs of the administrative branch.

The most ill-defined yet potentially dangerous problem of executive procedure can be stated as follows: In a world in which the potentiality for mass
destruction is a reality, and in a day when the decision to use such power must be
made almost instantaneously, what procedures have we developed to guarantee
that a momentary breakdown of the president could not commit the United States
to irrevocable actions which have consequences terrifying beyond the grasp of the
average mind? This problem—how to reconcile the necessity for decision with
the possibility of error—has yet to be mastered. [18]

JUDICIAL PROCEDURES

The courts' procedures are couched in the language of the law rather than
politics. They hear litigants, not political interest group representatives. They consider cases, not programs. They write decisions, not statutes or policy statements.

But the courts are really another arena for the continuation of the battle
over public policy. [14] After Congress has declared broad general policy, and
the administrative branch has attempted to implement the policy by applying it
to the specific case, those affected may turn to the courts for determination of the
appropriateness of the congressional policy or the correctness of the administrative
application. [29] These political interest group representatives, like their counterparts in the administrative and legislative arenas, attempt to obtain determinations
from the courts favorable to their interests. They no longer discuss electoral implications and economic and social repercussions but rather constitutionalism,
justice, common law, reasonableness, and due process. But the game is still the
same. What is now being fought over is whether the particular policy shall be
applied to a particular person or group in a particular way so as to produce
particular results. Those policies which are clear beyond doubt, or which cause
little or no hardship to important segments of the society, rarely if ever are the
subject of litigation. Those conflicts of interests which have not been resolved by
legislative and administrative action eventually come to the courts.[16] As a result,
when the court does settle a conflict by handing down a legal decision, more
heated reaction may be generated than by the policy pronouncements of other
agencies of government.

The courts are extremely restricted in their policy-making functions. The
form of consideration the courts use is the antagonistic proceeding between interested parties, one of which claims that he has been adversely affected by the
action of the other. This form of consideration seriously limits those who may

---

[16] Not all lawsuits involve matters of public policy, of course, but consideration of the
courts is here limited to their role in public policy making, ignoring the whole realm of private law, the role of the courts in settling individual conflicts between citizens.

operate within the judicial arena. The courts, furthermore, have their jurisdiction defined largely by the Congress. Consequently, the kinds of cases which can be heard by the courts is controlled by political considerations reflected in Congress. Congress can, as noted above, restrict the appellate jurisdiction of the Supreme Court so as to remove an entire area of cases from its jurisdiction, and the jurisdiction of lower federal courts is entirely determined by Congress. (Several proposed constitutional amendments have been introduced in Congress to remove questions relating to state legislative apportionment from the jurisdiction of federal courts, as an aftermath of *Baker v. Carr* and *Reynolds v. Sims*.) The courts impose upon themselves a set of restraints, under which they will not entertain certain kinds of cases. [1] For instance, the Supreme Court will not hear "political questions," which it adjudges are appropriate for consideration by political agencies, not by courts.

The courts are not only insulated from the politics of election but also from the more obvious forms of political conflict. No political interest group representatives would directly approach a federal judge to try to influence him in his decision; he would probably find himself held in contempt of court, perhaps disbarred, at least unwelcome before that court in the future. His influence on the court must be made effective through the prescribed forms and procedures peculiar to law courts. His legal counsel may file briefs, and even engage in oral arguments, but there will be no open debate, no extensive give-and-take in committee hearings, and no invitation for compromise and "horse-trading" as in a legislative chamber.

We know far less about court procedures than about legislative procedures. The decision-making process in the courts is little studied primarily because scholars are not welcomed into the inner sanctum. What goes on in the offices and conferences of the Supreme Court is known in general outline through the occasional revelations of the justices and their law clerks, but no student of the Court has been privileged to sit in to observe or to conduct systematic research. State courts have been, in some instances, more open to study, but the inner workings of federal courts are still largely unexplored. Most of what is known about the courts has been gleaned from a study of court decisions. This "insulation from inspection" may be the most significant characteristic of the courts in regard to the procedures by which the courts operate, and out of which comes policy-affecting decisions.

The courts may enter the policy-making process at almost any point. They may find legislative acts unconstitutional, invalidate administrative decisions, determine the winner of contested elections, and set in motion legal requirements obligating other government agencies to act. But most policy pronouncements by courts will tend to be remedial, in the nature of review of already established policy. The effect, however, may be prescriptive of future policy, such as in the desegregation and reapportionment cases.

The courts, then, differ significantly from the other policy-making agencies. They are more politically insulated, less open to scrutiny by interested citizens, more restricted procedurally, and less openly involved in political decision-making. They function, however, as an integral part of what has been called here the system of "antagonistic cooperation" in the making of public policy.

The four selections reprinted below deal with the dynamics of public policy-making. Gilbert ("Operative Doctrines of Representation") examines the major doctrines of representation which have figured in democratic theory and their significance for policy research. The article will serve to introduce the student to a broad range of theoretical problems relating to the nature of representation, which will be useful in considering the representativeness of the various participants in policy-making in the United States. Gable ("Interest Groups as Policy Shapers") discusses the role of political interest groups in shaping public policy in all three branches of government, and the factors which limit their access.

Cleveland ("The Executive and the Public Interest") considers the role played by the president and the administrative agencies in translating the public interest into policy. He explores the relationship of these agencies with Congress and examines many of the problems identified in the preceding commentary. Dahl's ("Decision-Making in a Democracy: The Role of the Supreme Court as a National Policy-Maker") is the classic discussion of the policy-making role of the Supreme Court. He considers the Court as "a political institution, an institution . . . for arriving at decisions on controversial questions of national policy."

Together these four selections serve as a balanced introduction to the realities of policy-making in American democracy.

Operative Doctrines of Representation

CHARLES E. GILBERT

Charles E. Gilbert is a professor of political science at Swarthmore College. He specializes in the areas of public administration and local and comparative governments.

The main point of this article is to identify some traditions of American thought that figure in analysis of the distinctively democratic aspects of government. The discussion is centered on doctrines of "representation." While that term has a generally understood meaning, its application in specific contexts depends upon values and expectations closely related to other largely procedural aspects of politics; and together these per-

Reprinted from the *American Political Science Review*, LVII No. 3 (September 1963), 604–618, by permission of the author and the publisher.

Author's note: I wish to acknowledge especially the contributions to this paper by David G. Smith, and the helpful criticism of my colleagues J. Roland Pennock and Kenneth N. Waltz (Political Science) and Monroe Beardsley (Philosophy).

spectives figure in appraisals and decisions of policy.

The "distinctively democratic aspects of government" have broadly to do, I think, with relations between public officials and the population. These can be conceptualized and described in terms of institutions, influence, identification, or exchange, and are so treated in various positive or empirical approaches. At the points where normative critique and empirical description join, the literature of American political science seems to have converged on several broad concerns that tend to organize and orient discussion—e.g., representation, responsibility, rationality, and lately, the "public interest," of which "representation" surely has the clearest empirical reference. These are overlapping or intersecting concerns. They emphasize different aspects of government and different blends of calculation and control (or intellectual *versus* institutional elements); but they do not refer to distinct phenomena, and they relate to common normative traditions.[1] Such terms are often, I think, of dubious utility because they tend to obscure the more detailed values at stake in action or discussion and perhaps thereby to discourage more pointed empirical inquiry relevant to those values. However that may be, the interrelatedness of these concerns and the broad relevance of "representation" can be briefly indicated.

There is a school of thought that would distinguish "representative government" from democratic government; but the term representation itself surely stands for a basic democratic relation. It may be regarded as expressive (symbolic) or instrumental, in the language of Parsons.[2] It may be virtual or actual (sanctioned). It may concern likeness of a wide range of characteristics of elected officials and constituents or it may relate merely to agreement on stated issues of policy; it may be a matter of psychological "identification" or of correspondence respecting explicit issues or interests.[3] Elections apart, proponents of "representative bureaucracy" have argued the actual or potential reflection in administration of broad socio-economic strata, or a balance of concrete interests, or of basic constitutional traditions. All discussions of the subject deal, at least implicitly, with two of its aspects: *what* is represented, and *how;* with the identification and evaluation of interests, and with the norms and sanctions affecting official behavior.[4]

Both "rationality" and "responsibility" chiefly relate to the *how* of representation. The critique and defense of the classical model of rational choice in administration have largely to do with the institutions in which ends are defined, the organization of search for alternatives and selection of relevant interests, the validity of abstract or *ex ante* expressions of popular wants, the superiority of long-run governmental leadership to short-run responsiveness.[5] The connotations of "responsibility" vary with the context: accountability, rationality, or effectiveness, or all these may be involved.[6] The classical, Benthamite democratic model emphasized *ex post* accountability through elections, assuming a simple governmental structure and a politics about limited, concrete, discrete concerns; once these assumptions are outmoded or relaxed we face the problem of appropriate indices of governmental performance beside simple and clearly sanctioned "accountability" and including norms relating to "rationality" and "representation." Finally, as "control" suggests the problem of responsibility, "calculation" points to the "public interest" issue. As the simple accountability model breaks down in, say, Anthony Downs's analysis and requires reliance on broad indices of governmental performance, so on, say, Kenneth Arrow's demonstration the problem of mapping individual preferences onto a social welfare function cannot be solved, given his conditions, except under special assumptions about how interests are to be identified and related by political processes; and with these assumptions we are back to doctrines of representation.[7]

The interrelation of these concerns will be apparent in the discussion of separate

---

[1] On "calculation" and "control," see R. Dahl and C. E. Lindblom, *Politics, Economics, and Welfare* (New York, 1953).

[2] Talcott Parsons, *The Social System* (Glencoe, Ill., 1951), p. 400 ff.

[3] Harold F. Gosnell, *Democracy: The Threshold of Freedom* (New York, 1948), ch. 8.

[4] *Cf.* the discussions in A. L. Lowell, *Public Opinion and Popular Government* (New York, 1914), ch. 9; and H. Eulau, *et al.,* "The Role of the Representative . . . ," this REVIEW, Vol. 53 (1959), p. 742.

[5] *Cf.* Norton E. Long, "Public Policy and Administration: The Goals of Rationality and Responsibility," *Public Administration Review,* Vol. 14 (1954), p. 22; C. E. Lindblom, "The Science of Muddling Through," *Ibid,* Vol. 19 (1959), pp. 79–88, and "Policy Analysis," *American Economic Review,* Vol. 48 (1958), p. 298–312; Jas. March and Herbert Simon, *Organizations* (New York, 1958), ch. 6.

[6] J. R. Pennock, "Responsiveness, Responsibility, and Majority Rule," this REVIEW, Vol. 46 (1952), pp. 790–807.

[7] See Anthony Downs, *An Economic Theory of Democracy* (New York, 1957); and Kenneth Arrow, *Social Choice and Individual Values* (New York, 1951).

traditions that follows.[8] The traditions are primarily academic rather than popular. Some are rather distinct philosophical positions; but others are not. Despite the danger of ambiguity or misunderstanding it will be convenient to title the traditions: idealist, utilitarian, formalist, pragmatic, participatory, populist. These categories, it will be seen as the discussion proceeds, are not always mutually exclusive.

I

The distinctive element of *idealism* appears to be that important values attach to the community and polity as wholes, or as complexes of institutions. Short of the entire community, high value inheres in organizations and institutions in which individuals cultivate common and usually non-material interests. The interests or goods preferred in idealism may be collective (inhering in groups) rather than common (reflecting agreement); but reducing this distinction is an important idealist objective; and the interests normally emphasized are the kinds of "goodness" that can be predicted *of* the community rather than located *in* the community.[9] They are ethical conceptions, better described as values than as interests.

Such values need social definition. If the logical method of idealism is dialectic, its preferred social expression is dialogue which, as a practical matter, requires some mix of political leadership and mutual discussion. The larger the society the more crucial the functions of leadership—not only the conduct of discussion and articulation of aspirations and agreements; but the conservation of authority by stressing collective purposes, obviating conflict by prompt action, or

attending to interests not served by decentralized "social choice" processes. In such processes the electoral sanction helps encourage responsiveness and sensitivity in officials and participation by publics; but the direct or exact reflection of interests is impossible for the most important interests.

Where explanation is concerned, idealism bears on the fact of political obligation and the forms of political institutions rather than particular policy outcomes. Often its method is functionalism: it emphasizes "system values"; and its seeming tautologies sometimes refer to cumulative social processes. Popular aspirations are partially shaped by leadership; but leadership rests on authority, and authority depends upon faithful reflection of popular aspirations. The ambiguity of these aspirations requires ample official discretion. The important effects of social choice processes are those on the political system itself.

A somewhat more specific way of viewing the idealist tradition is to envisage the American President as Chester Barnard's executive presiding over an economy of incentives and contributions which, however, he can largely define and redefine by moral leadership.[10] This kind of organization theory also lends itself to utilitarian analysis, depending on the nature of the incentives and contributions. But the idealist can argue that, where moral leadership is heavily emphasized and accepted by all concerned, and where "identification" with either the "organization" or broad purposes is widespread, then executive discretion in defining purposes (values and obligations) tends to maximize both "efficiency" and "effectiveness" in Barnard's terms.

Another characteristic of idealism is its emphasis on "expressive" representation —on "style" rather than procedure or accountability to concrete interests or defined constituencies. This will be important if representatives are to have the latitude that the idealist accords them; then people can presumably look to such attributes as energy, decisiveness, or indicia from oratory or social position for assurance that candidates or officials share

[8] Thus, there will be some affinities with such discussions of these concerns as Alfred de Grazia, *Public and Republic* (New York, 1951); M. Meyerson and E. Banfield, *Politics, Planning, and the Public Interest* (Glencoe, Ill., 1954); Appendix by Banfield; Glendon Schubert, *The Public Interest* (Glencoe, Ill., 1959); and C. J. Friedrich (ed.), *Responsibility* (Cambridge, Mass., 1960); and it will be convenient to refer to these.

[9] The distinction seems due to McTaggert; see C. D. Broad, *Five Types of Ethical Theory* (New York and London, 1930), p. 249 ff.

[10] *The Functions of the Executive* (Cambridge, Mass., 1938).

the proper image of the community as well as for clues to likely concrete choices. The importance of the idealist position here, I think, is its attempt to deal with those aspects of the political process where interests, ends, or values lack specificity; its valuing of representation in its non-sanctioned sense; and its recognition that representation must be virtual rather than actual in some degree. Generally, idealists want to enlarge those areas of politics whereas other traditions do not; but one suggestion of idealism for social science would be to try to identify the elements of "style" that figure in policy and electoral decisions.

I think the idealist tradition is not generally well thought of today. We tend to mistrust its ambiguity about leadership and responsiveness, to doubt that the same subtle dialogue and ethical argument are possible in the great society and in the small group and to emphasize, therefore, the electoral sanction and the specifics of instrumental representation rather than the diffuseness of expressive representation; we set more store by substance and procedure than by style; we suspect that unitary claims often mask sinister interests.

There is nonetheless an American idealist tradition, native or transplanted. De Grazia has described the effects of transcendentalism on the notion of "enlightened individualism" as a doctrine of representation; and the effects of German idealism on early American political scientists and their philosophical contemporaries is reflected in John Dewey's beginnings. Woodrow Wilson's encomium of the presidency seems an implicit expression of the idealist tradition with respect to representation, and Glendon Schubert has described some outcroppings of the tradition in modern writing on public administration.[11]

A strong modern statement is that of Joseph Tussman: the analysis begins with the "body politic" and turns on the relation between it and its members, between members and authoritative agents.[12] Membership implies in part a "recognition of some *common* or shared concern"

[11] *The Public Interest, op. cit.*
[12] *Obligation and the Body Politic* (New York, 1960).

as well as "that one's own interest constitutes only a subordinate part of a broader system of interests;" it also involves some minimum moral commitment to the body politic (commitment to the moral beliefs of the body politic?), and some modicum of active participation to make authority acceptable. Agency (authority) involves "a task related to some aspect of the public good and . . . a measure of discretion." Government— authority and obligation—is the outcome of implied agreement: "only by dint of ceaseless devotion to the task of keeping the delicate structure of consent, participation, and authority in good repair can we save the claim of self-government from being a bitter mockery."

II

The implications of the *utilitarian* tradition for modern democratic government are ambiguous, as chroniclers of British thought have often pointed out. At least three strains of utilitarianism appear to affect democratic theory today. Arbitrarily, I shall treat one of these as my "utilitarian" tradition, on the ground that the others are now largely merged in other traditions to be reviewed below.

All three versions have in common the definition of interests in "individualistic" terms. In one, the emphasis is placed on the primacy of the individual's preferences (as they have been represented since marginalism entered the utilitarian tradition), on the incommensurability and noncomparability of personal utilities, and on the inadequacy of any but the simplest and most perspicuous political processes and laissez faire governments for representing and aggregating individual wants. In this school of thought there is a strong presumption against governmental intervention and political action; its adherents are often styled "conservative" today although, historically, "liberal" is more apt. This is the view I shall term "utilitarian"; but two other versions should be distinguished from it. One can be called the populist aspect of the utilitarian tradition, which has emphasized the radical, reforming, and especially majoritarian doctrine of Bentham and James Mill.[13] Though stressing individualistic

[13] *Cf.* A. V. Dicey, *Law and Opinion in*

definitions of interest and "direct" representation, the emphasis on *equality* in this school evidently covered an assumption of sufficient agreement to enable majority rule to work. The final version of utilitarianism appears to stress central decision rather more than direct representation. This version is reflected in some of Bentham's writings on governmental reform and, in a sense, in the nineteenth century British administrative reforms. Interests are defined in terms of individuals; but the "greatest good of the greatest number" can be discovered by administrative management and central decision and the overview these afford. This is the notion of the "service state," and it would seem to assume substantial agreement on the needs to be met and the services to be rendered—on the scope and ends of state activity. Grant this assumption, together with governmental consolidation and electoral reform (enlargement of civic and official perspective, abatement of "vested" interests, and enhancement of competition and participation), and the identification of interests, including "externalities," by central administrators may be admissible; and it might be more accurate than majority voting alone because of its attention to externalities and intensities.[14] It seems to me that *both* the populist and, let's say, the "centralist" versions of utilitarianism assume substantial, if implicit, agreement in the population on the ends and means of public policy (or on ends, with means of secondary importance); they are at the opposite extreme from idealism in discounting the problems of disagreement

of dissensus and the need for elaborate political processes for the integration of interests. "Representation" is simple and direct and uninteresting; politics is at a minimum.

The distrust of complex political or representative processes is common to all three versions of utilitarianism; but with the critical difference that the first version is mistrustful of state activity as well. (This view may sometimes reflect ethical egoism rather than strict ethical utilitarianism, or an implicit or explicit analogizing from economic to political contexts.) Public action entails sanctions and "pains;" private interests belie the easy majoritarian assumption of agreement on ends and means. If implicit agreement or a simple felicific calculus won't work, then individual differences and social disagreement become crucial and *coercion* becomes highly probable in collective decisions. The concern with coercion is, I think, the central concern of utilitarianism as here defined; "liberty" is treated in negative terms as the absence of coercion, "equality" as the integrity and noncomparability of individual preferences—and it is these that are to be maximized. *All* representative or political processes, and thus *all* state activity, threaten these values, which can also be expressed as rationality and impersonality in governmental action (concerns close to the "rationalist" tradition below).

The modern centers of this utilitarian approach have been Vienna and Chicago; its chief exponents have been economists. It is, I think, most thoroughly set out in the writings of von Mises, Hayek, Henry Simons, and Frank Knight; and Knight will here be taken as its protagonist.[15] Four recurrent propositions in Knight's writings are characteristic of utilitarianism and illustrate the points made above; these are: (1) that even persuasion and salesmanship amount to coercion in their violation of the integrity

---

England in the Nineteenth Century (London, 1905), on the "collectivist" trend in British thought; Samuel Beer, "The Representation of Interests in British Government: Historical Background," this REVIEW, Vol. 51 (1957), pp. 613–650, eps. 635 ff. on the "Radical" model of representation; and Joseph Hamburger, "James Mill on Universal Suffrage and the Middle Class," *Journal of Politics,* Vol. 24 (1962), pp. 167–190, esp. 187 on the "populist" outcome of philosophical radicalism.

[14] This brand of utilitarianism has probably been of some importance in the public administration movement in the U. S.—*cf.* the doctrine on authorities and special districts, on hierarchy and executive accountability, and on consolidation and enlargement of governmental units.

[15] *E.g.* F. von Mises, *Bureaucracy* (New Haven, 1944); F. von Hayek, *Individualism and Economic Order* (Chicago, 1948); H. Simons, *Economic Policy for a Free Society* (Chicago, 1948); Frank Knight, *The Ethics of Competition* (New York, 1936); *Freedom and Reform* (New York, 1947); *Intelligence and Democratic Action* (Cambridge, Mass., 1960).

of individual preferences;[16] (2) that the representative relation of "agency" can *never* be clearly defined politically and always gives rise to substantial discretion;[17] (3) that the proper condition of state activity is maximum agreement or consensus, which is *not* reflected or supported by the direct political or administrative action advocated by other versions of utilitarianism;[18] and (4) that heavy procedural safeguards, as well as high agreement, should accompany governmental action.[19] Knight's problem in all his recent writing has been to define the kinds or processes that will yield agreement with least "coercion;" no definite solution appears, but the discussion verges on idealism and shares the vagueness of that tradition while deemphasizing the role of leadership and representative processes that idealists often emphasize.

In politics, indeed, Knight turns out to be something of a Kantian: the integrity of personal preferences implies Kantian standards of conduct. The primary political problems are defined in largely Kantian terms: how to get agreement on ends; how to maximize the role of intelligence and rationality in defining collective ends and means; how to minimize coercion, including the manipulations of other's fields of choice.[20] The role of government turns out to be a hindering of hindrances; order and law are synonymous, ideally, with maximum freedom the first end of the state. Freedom and order are best reconciled through government by discussion in which, however, order rests heavily on habit and tradition, and in which the case for change must develop from rational discussion and demonstration; not from central decision or a simple aggregation of given preferences. The discussion is highly abstract and uninstitutional.

Utilitarianism offers a definite position on the identification of interests, but has little to say about aggregation in any political or institutional sense. The original Benthamite view, characteristically ambiguous as to egoism *versus* universalism, was that:

each voter acts as a trustee for himself and for all the rest of the community in his exercise of the suffrage. Now if he is precluded from the possibility of promoting his own particular interest to the prejudice of the remainder of the universal interest by the manner in which his vote is cast (as by ballot), then the only interest of his which he has any prospect of promoting by his vote is his share of the universal interest. And for doing this, he sees before him no other possible means except voting for the candidate who is likely to render the most service to the universal interest.[21]

Early utilitarianism implied simple and centralized institutions and concrete, definable interests. Implicit in this is an emphasis on governmental *economy* and deemphasis of the public sector (explicit in Bentham and Mill) that would improve pure accountability because the presumption against public expenditures would narrow the alternatives for public decision. This thread in utilitarianism is emphasized in the tradition outlined above,

[16] "Human nature is also averse to the mental effort of critically considering the possibilities and costs of change, especially the labor of appraising alternatives and reaching intelligent agreement on what is desirable. There is an almost instinctive appeal to force, including persuasion, one of its most insidious and dangerous forms." *Intelligence and Democratic Action,* p. 34.

[17] "The mystery is not that representative institutions were discredited but that any other result could have been expected. The agency relation presents a problem for which there is no mechanical or intellectual solution, while direct democracy, on any considerable scale and with positive functions, is out of the question. . . . To substitute competitive politics for competitive business is to jump out of the frying pan into the fire. No possible 'machinery' will preserve responsibility without actual crowd rule, or will give political guidance . . . in the absence of moral leadership accepted as such by the masses." *Freedom and Reform,* pp. 29–31; and cf. *Intelligence and Democratic Action,* pp. 127–8.

[18] *Cf.* the quotation above. "It follows that the ultimate task of *society as a whole,* as of government . . . is to create such individuals in such a total culture situation, that agreement on right ideals will be possible, and will be achieved by non-political processes." *Freedom and Reform,* p. 204.

[19] *Ibid.* ch. 12, esp. pp. 355–6. *Cf.* von Mises, *Bureaucracy, op. cit.*

[20] *Intelligence and Democratic Action,* pp. 124–5.

[21] *Handbook of Political Fallacies,* ed. Harold A. Larrabee (Baltimore, the Johns Hopkins Press, 1952), p. 184.

which argues that intelligent electoral appraisal (either public interested or egoistic) and an accountable officialdom are *only* maximized as public action and alternatives are minimized.

The tradition dealt with here has had its major applications in public finance, where it has stressed the condition of individuals rather than collective benefits, together with governmental economy and the rationality and integrity of individual preferences. The other major elements of utilitarianism seem to have merged in other American traditions, and to have been dissipated in the process. The innovating thrust of the tradition shows up most sharply in pragmatism (below)—though the hedonistic point of it is qualified. The centralizing and synoptic strain has been largely assimilated to rationalism (below). The populist development will be dealt with separately.

III

Idealism and utilitarianism can perhaps be regarded as the two basic traditions with respect to the definition of interests —one aspect of representation.[22] Nonetheless, I think two other traditions can be distinguished on this point; these are rationalism and pragmatism.

What I shall term the *rationalist* tradition is difficult to define and distinguish. This is partly because it is so widespread; probably it was the dominant tradition in American political science until recently, and perhaps, in a normative sense, it still is. It is less distinctive philosophically than the other major traditions, and it is not easy to identify in a word; in the following discussion the terms "formalism" and "rationalism" will be used interchangeably.[23] An important aspect of this tradition is its alliance with

public law; a related aspect is its reliance on certain analytical concepts—such as "state," "sovereignty," political "authority"—from which it is difficult to eliminate the normative content. Formality is highly valued in governmental institutions because certain broad end values are in some degree "built in" and protected against perversion through interpersonal interaction. The tradition thus has in it a good deal of the "formalism" against with pragmatism revolted.[24] In its normative and analytic concerns, rationalism is more-or-less equivalent to "constitutionalism."

The formalism and formality in the tradition would seem to result from the way in which interests are defined. In Banfield's terms, the rationalist persuasion is "qualified individualistic;" that is, the ends of the polity are in the first instance those of individuals, but are selected from certain "appropriate" classes of ends.[25] In practice, these ends or classes of ends are hard to define and give rise to some of the classical problems of political theory—*e.g.*, the meaning of "liberty." In theory, the ends or interests have often been designated "rights:" indeed, one characteristic of the rationalist tradition is its historical tendency to define interests as rights or "natural rights." In modern theory these "rights" have often become "ends of the state"—*e.g.*, security, liberty, justice, welfare, order— but these are ends *of individuals,* or imputed to individuals, satisfied through state action or inaction.[26] The shift of emphasis from individual "rights" to common "ends" has helped to reconcile state

[22] *Cf.* Banfield, *op. cit.*

[23] The most germane philosophical tradition seems to me to be the Lockean one described by Louis Hartz, *The Liberal Tradition in America* (New York, 1955). No single term occurs to me that does justice to what is described below: "liberalism" and "constitutionalism" are a good deal too broad and "proceduralism" somewhat too narrow. Since Schubert's writing on the "public interest" was referred to above I should point out that I don't use the word "rationalism" as he does; and this discussion should not be equated with his.

[24] Morton White, *Social Thought in America: The Revolt Against Formalism* (Beacon Press Edition: Boston, 1957).

[25] Banfield, *op. cit.* and *cf.* R. Brandt, *Ethical Theory* (New York, 1959), ch. 15, on "extended rule utilitarianism." Since the ends in these appropriate classes are often imputed to everyone, or denominated "ends of the state," the line between rationalism and idealism is often a thin one in theory as well as in practice. Woodrow Wilson's discussion of the representative role of the American president was cited above as an illustration of idealism; yet Wilson as political scientist seems to belong to the formalist tradition, as will be argued below.

[26] The five "ends" listed are those of Charles E. Merriam, *Systematic Politics* (Chicago, 1945), esp. ch. 2.

action with the liberal tradition and to obviate or obscure the difficult question of rights. Thus it has tended to separate the formalist tradition from the variant of utilitarianism emphasized above, and to relate it more closely to the other trends of utilitarianism.

This kind of definition of interests—one root of the rationalist tradition—raises several issues. One, of philosophical interest, concerns the intellectual bases of the tradition. I think these mainly lie in natural law theory which, while sometimes "naturalistic" in the metaethical sense, also emphasized a rational faculty by which ultimate ends are apprehended and applied. Formalism as here defined has close affinities with formalism in normative ethics though it does not imply such a position. Thus the rationalist tradition has inherited one important and distinctive orientation to the study of politics: a means-ends approach in which "rights" or "ends" are the starting point for the analysis of institutions; an important method of explaining or understanding "the state" or its elements is in terms of the ends of the state.[27] This approach entails the emphasis on formality and procedure already remarked, not only in a normative sense but also in empirical inquiry. Empirically, the purposive, means-ends approach suggests an emphasis on institutions, constructs and procedures that are often defined by their relation to general and abstract ends; normatively, attention is centered on this relation and the refinement and illumination of ends in terms of institutional means and conversely. The same goes for certain key concepts. Hence the traditional distinction between "power" and "authority" in which authority is tested ultimately by general, abstract ends and immediately by procedures reflecting these ends (historically, "rights" and "authority" were the main considerations in a more contractual view of political obligation). Hence, also, the distinctive concern of the rationalist tradition to segregate *public* and *private* ends in political

action and to maintain the state-society distinction by formality and publicity. The distinction helps guarantee that the leverage of "authoritative" institutions will not be lent to private purposes, and that governmental action will—in part by publicity—be limited to areas of general agreement.[28] Hence, further, the rationalist emphasis upon clear definition and separation of institutional functions, upon separation of powers thinking and especially the policy (politics)—administration distinction drawn by Goodnow, Lowell, and Wilson. In part, the point of the distinction is to further synoptic and "rational" decision making through hierarchy; in part, I think, to see to it that certain institutions are clearly charged with the protection or promotion of certain set "ends;" and primarily to protect rights by checks and balances. A final consideration: often the rationalist tradition appears to place high value on a large measure of agreement or consensus. The reason for this is not obvious. It may be that sharp dissensus, or even a highly pluralistic politics, calls in question imputations of common ends or common understandings about procedures; the result is particularism in assertions of ends, and resort to "power" in political action at the expense of rights or ends assumed to be common.

It was mentioned above that the formalist tradition probably constitutes the mainstream of American political science; for many purposes it would be too broad and indiscriminate a characterization, but I do not think it is for the present purpose.[29] Indeed, on the normative side, this tradition certainly remains important; but, among other reasons, the difficulties it presents to distinguishing normative and positive inquiry have led to its repudiation by some as political *science*. The early "greats" of American political science were predominantly in

[27] An important way, but not necessarily *the* way. The rationalist tradition may not be at odds with, say, "behaviorism;" *cf.* Merriam's writing.

[28] *Cf.* the doctrine of "public purpose" in our public law and in the period of "revival of natural law theories," the "public" ends of the police power and the doctrine of "business affected with a public interest."

[29] It is interesting that the tradition has been less dominant in English political thought, where both idealism and utilitarianism have been stronger.

this tradition: note Woodrow Wilson's emphasis on the constitutional "ends" of representative government; A. L. Lowell's insistence on substantial consensus as the condition of a "really public" public opinion; and Frank Goodnow's implicit concern with formality and procedure and explicit attention to publicity in politics and impartiality in administration.[30] Historically and *ad hominem* it is tempting to interpret the political science of these eastern academicians as a Brahminical endeavor to protect middle class, Anglo-Saxon amenity against the new political pluralism arising from late nineteenth century immigration, industrialization and urbanization; but Wilson, Goodnow, and Lowell did not invent the rationalist tradition: before them were the Founding Fathers. Turning to a recent and influential political scientist, much of Charles E. Merriam's writing can be construed as an attack on the empirical side of the formalist tradition; but only as an adjustment or adaptation of the normative side; certain problems generated by that tradition (*e.g.,* the public-private distinction and the definition of institutional ends or functions) were crucial to him, and some of the classical concepts (*e.g.,* state and sovereignty) remained at the center of his thought.[31]

To come at last to the question of "representation," I think it can be argued that this relation derives much of its status as a concept—or, more simply, as a concern and object of inquiry—from the rationalist tradition. This is probably because representation in the rationalist tradition is not direct; it is acknowledged that there is no permanent or mechanical solution of the problem of agency, and it appears in this tradition that a modicum of discretion is desirable. As Banfield

points out, the "qualified individualist" position requires some latitude in the selection of ends by those in responsible positions; the abstract nature of the "ends" favored in the rationalist tradition requires a balancing of more parochial interests in concrete situations. Discretion, in turn, raises the problems of "responsibility" alluded to above, and it is in this connection that the rationalist emphasis on formality and publicity—on the distinction between public and private —is important. In summary, "representation" presents interesting questions of organization because of the twin necessities of discretion and control that are entailed in the rationalist tradition and the procedural and intellectual values that must therefore be balanced.

The large role of representation in rationalist thinking is evident in the opening pages of Woodrow Wilson's *Constitutional Government:* the history of constitutional government is the history of "political liberty," and political liberty is "the right of those who are governed to adjust government to their own needs and interests." [32] In changing circumstances this calls for constant adjustment between "the power of government and the privileges of the individual . . . :

And so the growth of constitutional government has been the growth of institutions, of practices, of methods of performing the delicate business of maintaining an understanding between those who conduct the government and those who submit to it. The object of constitutional government is to bring the active, planning will of each part of the government into accord with the prevailing popular thought and need, and thus make it an impartial instrument of symmetrical national development; and to give the operation of the government thus shaped under the influence of opinion and adjusted to the general interest both stability and an incorruptible efficacy." [33]

This statement expresses aspects of rationalism already discussed: formality and impartiality in government; common understandings and ends in the population.

---

[30] Woodrow Wilson, *Constitutional Government in the United States* (New York, 1908); A. Lawrence Lowell, *Public Opinion and Popular Government* (New York, 1914); and Frank Goodnow, *Politics and Administration* (New York, 1900).

[31] See esp. *Systematic Politics, op. cit.; On the Agenda of Democracy* (Cambridge, Mass., 1941); *Public and Private Government* (New Haven, 1944); and *The Role of Politics and Social Change* (New York, 1936).

[32] *Constitutional Government,* p. 4.
[33] *Ibid,* p. 14.

To these are added Wilson's characteristic concern with leadership, energy, and efficacy as official attributes and national perspectives on policy, to which are related his well known views on the roles of president and parties. For Wilson, as well as for Lowell and Goodnow, "responsible" government implied rationality (means-ends, central, synoptic decisions), effectiveness (given agreement on ends and impartial administration of means), and adjustment between "opinion" and the "general interest." This adjustment is the job of political representation and implies discretion rather than direct reflection; responsible government means more than merely representative government.

The rationalist tradition approximates idealism at times in its emphasis on common ends, official discretion, and the practical importance of political obligation. The crucial differences are that ends are more specific in the rationalist tradition; that they are more clearly attached to individuals and are thus plainly common rather than collective; that more detailed attention is given to the organization and institutions of representation so that discretion, while necessary, is relatively narrow and clearly reviewable. Policy is penultimately referred to procedural standards. In order to foster an overview of common ends and to enforce "public" concerns where some private interests are leveraged, rationalism today usually leans toward more centralized and synoptic decision making, though this is a matter of context.

IV

The *pragmatic* tradition is a recent but extremely influential one. Historically, the philosophical tradition—the revolt against "formalism" or, in political science, against rationalism—may be seen as most influential; or it may be argued that the pragmatic tradition in political science, with its emphasis on group interests, was mainly a recognition and attempt at explanation of an altered political structure in the twentieth century. Probably both developments were important: it seems plausible to argue that American politics developed a pronounced economic pluralism with the rapid capitalization and industrial growth of the late nineteenth century and a more pronounced cultural particularism and class consciousness a bit later in the wake of the "rise of the city." If some rationalist writing can be construed as an effort to reverse or mitigate the resultant political tendencies, then the pragmatic tradition can probably be interpreted as an attempt to work with them rather than against them. Two other socio-political tendencies may have encouraged pragmatism: one is the increased importance of education and communication with urbanization; another the growth of governmental regulation and social service and the consequent concern to relate the specialist or expert to the public. Together these are the "problems" of *The Public and its Problems;* they call in question the rationalist model of agreed-upon ends, central and synoptic decisions, understood procedures, all consistent with the ready adjustment of government to popular preferences. On the other hand, the philosophical and intellectual history of pragmatism seem to have an independent importance in two respects: a change in *what* is valued accompanied by emphasis on "experimental" ethics and politics; and the beginnings of the "group approach" to politics in the development of "symbolic interactionism" in philosophy, psychology, and sociology.[34] Thus, both the *what* and the *how* of representation were reoriented in the pragmatic tradition.

The discussion that follows is focused on John Dewey; but I do not mean to limit the pragmatic tradition to philosophy or philosophers. I think the tradition has been strong in political science, including much of what Glendon Schubert has recently called the "realist" position on the public interest and, in terms of empirical work, the pervasive "group approach" to politics. The characteristic outlooks on concerns relevant to "representation" seem, however, to be most clear in the

[34] By "symbolic interactionism" I mean the common emphasis on socialization and communication in the work of, *e.g.,* James, Dewey, Mead and Cooley in the disciplines mentioned above. *Cf.* Fay Karpf, *American Social Psychology* (New York, 1932) for a summary discussion relating these developments.

writings of John Dewey—in particular in *The Public and Its Problems.*[35]

Dewey's work is certainly a rejection of rationalism; its relation to idealism and utilitarianism is less clear; but I think it can be taken as a combination and a qualification of both. Briefly and broadly, Dewey's central problem is to explain and justify (or, explain-and-justify) the emergence of "publics" and the incidence of state action. There are two lines of explanation: one runs in terms of "externalities" (the third-party effects of private transactions), and is cast in the utilitarian tradition; the other relies on communication and socialization (symbolic interaction), and largely belongs to the idealist tradition. Since Dewey's philosophical self-consciousness about both these traditions is a matter of record, his ambivalent approach is not surprising.[36] The general proposition suggests itself that Dewey was a utilitarian respecting the identification of interests and an idealist with respect to their aggregation; but it is not clear that he himself would have admitted the distinction, since it implies given interests independent of or exogenous to political interaction. As a political method, pragmatism appears to call for minimizing the role of *a priori* interests and maximizing the effects of political processes, so long as they are properly organized.

Dewey is generally felt to have been an especially ambiguous philosopher. His ambiguity about utilitarianism and idealism is especially important. The "first causes" of political action appear to be utilitarian.[37] But three symbolic interactionist modifications are crucial: one is the significance accorded to social determination of interests;[38] a second is the primacy and reality of groups in the study and understanding of politics;[39] and a third is the role of communication in defining and creating common interests.[40] When Dewey approaches these problems in terms of conventional philosophy the result is a doctrine of consciousness which, while akin to that of James, was heavily influenced by idealism and is highly social in nature.[41]

Pragmatism is thus distinct from utilitarianism and idealism, emphasizing neither concrete, parametric interests nor abstract, emergent ideals. Dewey argued that interests are changed by interaction which cannot be labeled "coercive," that ideals are only meaningful for *individuals* in *action,* and that general "ends" cannot properly be imputed to societies by philosophers—thus rejecting our three previous traditions. *The* political problem is not the guarantee and adjustment of

[35] New York, 1927. While the influence of this book is necessarily problematical, judging from internal evidence as well as from citation it was of enormous influence on political scientists trained in the 1930s and thus on the "group approach" to politics. Bentley's *Process,* of course, was published long before and is, indeed, a very different kind of book, despite some philosophical affinities between the two authors. I think it is arguable that Dewey's work has been the more influential in political science; but I do not know just how to argue the point here.

[36] *Cf. German Philosophy and Politics* (New York, 1915); *Creative Intelligence* (New York, 1917); Morton White, *The Origins of Dewey's Instrumentalism* (New York, 1943); and White's discussion in *Social Thought in America, op. cit.*

[37] "Conjoint . . . action is a universal trait. . . . Such action has results. Some of the results are taken account of. Then there arise purposes, plans, measures and means to secure consequences which are liked and eliminate those which are found obnoxious. Thus perception generates a common interest. . . . Consequences have to be taken care of, looked out for. This supervision and regulation cannot be effected by the primary groupings themselves. . . . Only the exigencies of a preconceived theory would confuse the state with that texture of friendships and attachments which is the chief bond in any community, or would insist that the former depends upon the latter for existence." *The Public and its Problems,* pp. 34–5; 27; 26.

[38] "The underlying and generative conditions of concrete behavior are social as well as organic: much more social than organic as far as the *differential* wants, purposes, and methods of operation are concerned. . . . The desires, aims and standards of satisfaction which the dogma of 'natural' economic processes and laws assumes are themselves socially conditioned phenomena." *Ibid,* 103–4.

[39] See esp. *ibid,* 19–27; 39–47.

[40] *Ibid,* ch. 5; and esp. pp. 141–159.

[41] *Cf. Human Nature and Conduct* (New York, 1922: Modern Library Ed.). p. 62 ff., and the closing chapter.

"rights" nor the maintenance of authority and obligation nor the maximization of net pleasure; but is more nearly defined in utilitarian than any other terms as the progressive adjustment of interests that will afford maximum opportunity for individual expression and choice. Thus the main point is to improve political organization and communication so as to promote easy access, broad participation, and an adequate range and accuracy of information. Like a market, the political process facilitates trading and thus reflects intensities; unlike a market it should promote common social values at least to relieve externalities and perhaps for their own sake as well.

Three other aspects of Dewey's position are worth brief notice: the implications of "instrumentalism" for political science; his outlook on the public-private distinction; and his emphasis on process rather than structure.

Talk of "problem-solving" runs through Dewey's discourse and figures in the title of his most relevant book. The point is that questions of public policy are treated as discrete and immediate issues requiring adjustment rather than challenges to "rational" decision wherein choices must be made among complex programs in light of ultimate ends of the rationalist type. The issue here is not quite Weldon's "problems" *versus* "difficulties;" the point of instrumentalism is to obviate the formal fact-value problem by foreshortening means-ends chains, by depicting purposeful choice as a scanning of immanent consequences only, and by emphasizing an experimental or conditional approach to choice. It is a "scientific" approach to social choice in Dewey's sense of science as control (rather then prediction); it discards governmental divisions of labor in which some officials decide on "ends" while others deal in "means;" and its relevance to some current conceptions of "incrementalism" and "representative bureaucracy" is evident.

The erosion of the public-private distinction follows from instrumentalism: if abstract ends or endemic rights are discounted, then the rationalist reasons for distinguishing the two spheres are less important. "Publics" are formed when the "lasting, extensive, and serious consequences of associated activity" are perceived. They differ only in degree (of duration, extensiveness, and intensity of consequences) from "groups." *The* public differs only in degree in the opposite direction: it consists in a broader perception of consequences; it progresses from "society" to "community" through fuller communication and firmer understandings.[42] Nonetheless, the point of *The Public and its Problems* is to argue that the public-private distinction is important; to redefine it in more realistic, less rationalistic terms; and to reverse the "eclipse" of the public in a pluralistic society. The question of *criteria* for the adjustment of interests is implicit in Dewey's statement of "problems" in terms of "externalities;" but his solution is to try to obviate serious problems by organization, communication, and interaction. If the political process works freely and reflects interests fully, it will sufficiently narrow the expert's discretion.

The shift of attention from structure to process stems from symbolic interactionism: individual interests and attitudes are principally shaped by interpersonal interaction in primary groups; shared interests or groups are created and maintained in the same fashion; "publics" and the political system also depend on these basic processes. Here again, Dewey can be understood to argue that secondary and political groupings simply reflect a balance of common and complementary over competing interests to which economic analysis would be most appropriate; but in the main he is concerned with the processes of interaction by which interests are altered and adjusted and these are primarily social-psychological in nature. A crucial consideration is that of constant change in interests. Formal institutions admittedly reflect more enduring interests or purposes; but they need not be represented as abstract or ultimate "ends," and are more realistically regarded as subject to redefinition and revaluation as as result of new transactions and inter-

---

[42] *The Public and its Problems,* esp. p. 146. Dewey relied heavily on the type of community-society distinction stressed by Tönnies and Weber.

actions.[43] For political science, the most important result of the emphasis on "process" has probably been to encourage reliance on social psychological and small group models for characterizing key points in "representation."

From all this it would seem to follow that, for Dewey and pragmatism, formal, arm's length institutions of representation will not be favored. It does appear that *any* government is in some degree a "representative" institution:

A public, articulated and acting through representative officers is the state; there is no state without a government, but there is also none without a public. . . . By our hypothesis all governments are representative in that they purport to stand for the interests which a public has in the behavior of individuals and groups. . . . Rarely can a person sink himself in his political function; the best which most men attain to is the domination by the public weal of their other desires. What is meant by 'representative' government is that the public is definitely organized with the intent to secure this dominance. The dual capacity of every officer of the public leads to conflict in individuals between their genuinely political aims and acts and those which they possess in their non-political roles. When the public adopts special measures to see to it that the conflict is minimized and that the representative function overrides the private one, political institutions are termed representative.[44]

Both aspects of "representation" are here —the identification of interests, and the definition of "responsibility"—but the emphasis is on the "public interest" rather than the "responsibility" aspect. The "representative function" is to relieve or forestall externalities; the role of the representative for Dewey today would seem to be to signal the affectation of some by the activities of others, probably to reflect intensities of interest, and to effect satisfactory adjustments of interest. For the pragmatist, *the* political problem consists in the conflict of interests; the solution is twofold: "expertise," and creation of a "public" or "community" through improvement of communication and understanding. No *standards* for decision—either substantive or procedural—are proposed.

In construing interests as changeable and profoundly affected by social organization pragmatism has tended to press political analysis back to psychology and sociology and to discount political forms and their finality as norms. The tradition thus has little to say about procedure and "responsibility" because it mistrusts categorization and institutionalization of adjective or procedural values. On the instrumentalist view the values relevant to a particular problem are only developed, ordered, and clarified in the process of decision. Thus, the test of policy is necessarily more procedural than substantive, indirect rather than direct: maximize access, communication, participation so that individual choice is frequent, informed, influential, and broadly affected by the choices of others. Like instrumentalism in ethics, this tradition tends to view policy problems in specific social contexts over the short run, arguing that, under the foregoing conditions, free experiment will produce "appropriate" (for "correct") solutions. For the decision maker the implication is: consult; look to intensities and breadth of affectation; let the process and the private parties carry most of the weight of decision.

V

Two traditions remain to be described; but the descriptions will be brief. One tradition will be termed the participatory; I have in mind theorists who emphasize the importance for democratic government of individual participation in groups and localities to the near exclusion of any

[43] "The very fact that the public depends upon consequences of acts and perception of consequences, while its organization into a state depends upon the ability to invent and employ special instrumentalities, shows how and why publics and political institutions differ widely from epoch to epoch and place to place. To suppose that an *a priori* conception of the intrinsic nature and limits of the individual on one side and the state on the other will yield good results once for all is absurd." The Public and its Problems, p. 65. Cf. Reconstruction in Philosophy (New York, 1920; Beacon Press Ed., Boston, 1948), p. xiii.

[44] The Public and its Problems, p. 76.

attempt to represent a public at large. As a doctrine about *what* is to be represented this tradition sometimes reduces to pluralism, syndicalism, or a functionalist or producers' ethic, as it has in Europe. More often in America it has been a doctrine about the *how* of representation, asserting that compatible interests are only created through participation and interaction, and that arm's length representation and formalistic political processes frustrate integration and the continuing revaluation of interests by freezing certain interests in institutions. "The evaluation of interests involves the psychological development of an interacting people." [45]

Probably Mary Parker Follett is the foremost American exponent of this point of view and the most thoroughgoing.[46] In Follett the revolt against formalism is far more thoroughgoing than in Dewey; the fact-value distinction is expressly discarded, and publics are to be built up entirely out of face-to-face interactions rather than by the apparatus and officials of the "state." Consensus on the intellectual level is specious, arrived at "by virtue of the prestige of verbal argument which arrests the activity of your mind . . . the only real consensus is that which arises on the motor level." [47]

The same considerations apply to consent as to consensus:

The theory of consent rests on the wholly intellectualistic fallacy that thought and action can be separated . . . that we think with our 'minds' and we don't. . . . Thus the fullest freedom is passing on policies is not self-government, because the participation has to take place further back, in the activity from which the policies emerge. . . . We cannot really carry out the will of another, for we can only use our own behavior patterns. . . . The 'will of the people' then is found exactly where our own will is found, in our concrete existence.[48]

Party as an agent and geographical constituencies as subjects of "representation" are out; they lead to "domination" or "compromise," but not to "integration." No parametric ends or interests are to be imputed to individuals or embodied in institutional forms; interests are at once created and expressed in interpersonal interaction, and abstract statements of ends and interests are either misleading of self-serving or both. There is no utilitarianism at all in Mary Parker Follett, but there is a strong affinity for idealism.[49]

Follett's is the most systematic and celebrated statement of the participatory approach; in her writing it is extended to the overall organization of "the state," whereas in other expressions it is usually limited to particular programs or aspects of government. In any case, the intent of this tradition is to minimize "representation" in the sense of the reflection of pre-existing interests and to maximize participation in processes by which interests are to be simultaneously created and expressed. The general result of this approach would be thoroughgoing decentralization of decision making to those immediately concerned; the question of how to deal with the third party effects of these decisions is postponed or ignored.

VI

Finally, the populist tradition on representation may be briefly described. Readers are referred to Dahl's *Preface to Democratic Theory* for a rigorous and critical exposition.[50] For present purposes, its principal elements are its emphasis upon political equality and majority rule, and its insistence on direct translation of majority preferences into public policy. These two elements tend to reduce "representation" to a negligible role—as close to strict "agency" as possible. Values of procedure and style in governmental action are minimized; so is protection of any substantive or distributive values

[45] Mary Parker Follett, *Creative Experience* (New York, 1924), p. 35.

[46] See *The New State* (New York, 1918), *Creative Experience* (New York, 1924), and *Dynamic Administration* (eds., Metcalf and Urwick, New York, 1942). *Cf.* Henry S. Kariel, "The New Order of Mary Parker Follett," *Western Political Quarterly*, Vol. 8 (1955), pp. 425–440.

[47] *Creative Experience*, p. 198.

[48] *Ibid*, pp. 198–99.

[49] This is recognized in Bosanquet's *Philosophical Theory of the State* (London, 4th ed. 1953), Introduction and Preface to the Third Edition.

[50] Chicago, 1956.

against majority action. Intensities, as Dahl points out, are not to count. The political process should be reduced, so far as practicable, to a series of electoral mandates; and it is to be hoped that politics and government can be so organized that the mandate will be clear and categorical. Neither political leadership nor responsiveness are especially valued, since both involve some discretion on the part of the "representative." If the participatory tradition is said to seek to minimize pre-existing interests and to emphasize interaction, the populist tradition may be said to do the opposite: it emphasizes the "given" interests of individuals and seeks to minimize aggregative processes. It has often been pointed out that this is an unrealistic position on at least two grounds: that some kind of political process and some alteration of interests is necessary in order to create majorities in a modern, pluralistic society; and that, in such a society, most people will not be willing to trust the concrete interests they indulge with high intensity to the disposition of majorities—people at large are not consistently majoritarians.

Indeed, there seems to be more of disembodied ideal and less of accurate description in the populist and participatory traditions than in any of the other views outlined above. As the populist tradition ignores the stubborn facts of pluralism, intensities, and the effects of interaction revealed by all our empirical work, so the participatory view seems unduly to discount the "externalities" of interaction and the demand for a modicum of foresight, integration, and protection of certain substantive interests by formal, procedural surrogates that makes at least the fiction of an overall "public" and a "sovereign" meaningful in a pluralistic society.

The populist and participatory traditions have something else in common which, I think, can best be described as an insistence on the "popularness" of political decisions, or what Ranney and Kendall have called "popular consultation." Often, when the strict majoritarian principles of populism or the functional premises of the participatory school are relaxed, the two traditions tend to converge. Both then emphasize governmental responsiveness to publics, or they emphasize leadership in behalf of a putative common public or "people." Then problems of "representation" reappear; but then our other traditions are also involved, and populism and participation are merely emphases.

VII

What has so far been said seems to me to lead to several suggestions about "representation" and the broader relevance of the several traditions to inquiry.

1. The meaning of "representation" is not clear; otherwise the problems surrounding it would *probably* not receive such different treatment in the six traditions just discussed. I argued above that problems that are often discussed in terms of "rationality", "responsibility" and the "public interest" substantially overlap with those of "representation," and representation was there left undefined. If the term has a distinct meaning the core of it must be, as is often pointed out, in the literal sense of "present again;" but there are issues concealed in this. One issue is *what* is represented— whether abstract and ideal values referred to the community, ends presumptively common to all (or most) individuals, personal characteristics and tastes in infinite detail, or concrete wants and material interests. Closely related to what is represented is the question of *how,* in which a basic ambiguity is involved. Two kinds of processes figure in it: on the one hand those suggested by "identification" or "responsiveness;" on the other those intended by "control" or "accountability." In either case the representative relation may involve reflection of interests or characteristics in great detail or with broad discretion; but in one the interests are not thought of as concrete or clearly definable and in the other case they are; in one the relation is thought of as primarily psychological (intellectual or emotional) and in the other as physically sanctioned, ultimately. We often speak of the processes involved as informal or formal. Finally, with respect to either method of representation, there is the question of degree of discretion of the representative which, as Banfield has pointed out, also depends on what is represented.

Two aspects of what has been said require brief comment. One is that formal, electoral accountability may be employed to encourage closer "identification;" but it might also be argued that emphasis on electoral accountability discourages "genuine" identification. Second, one *might* feel more or better represented as a result of enlarged official discretion; this might be so (as idealists have argued) when concrete interests conflict but discretion allows officials to emphasize more abstract aspirations referred to the community; or where (as rationalists have argued) short-run claims can be resisted by officials until there has been time for deliberation and reflection.

Probably the basic ambiguity in the term itself has to do with the *how* of representation: in one view the method is virtual (resting on identification or responsiveness); in the other it is actual (entailed by physical control or formal accountability). Both are operative, necessarily in democratic political systems, and give rise to contrasting understandings of "representation." There is, however, a difficulty beside that of ambiguity, viz., that the detailed *reflection* of interests in policy is impossible when interests conflict. Thus the root notion of representation ignores the problem of aggregating interests, and the basic processes and relations of democratic government certainly cannot be characterized as, literally, matters of "representation." What *can* safely be said is that people are often concerned about the "representativeness" of governments and officials; that this (ambiguous) value figures in popular appraisal and thus the legitimacy and effectiveness of institutions; but the nature of this concern can't be pressed beyond the literal meaning of "represent." [51] It probably depends in part upon circum-

stances, including *what* is sought to be represented.

2. The issue between "representative government" and "popular government" seems to be largely a false issue today; surely Bentley and subsequent group theorists have been right in pointing out that democratic government is a congeries of controls, and representation, as Garceau has said, a continuum of interactions and decisions.[52] Probably the most important problems of representation today arise within groups rather than government and involve the adequate definition of "group interests" and control of discretion where there is little political competition and few standards for official conduct.

3. Two of the traditions outlined above are *primarily* concerned with "representation" in the root meanings just discussed. These are the participatory and populist traditions: the first strongly influenced by idealism (in the version treated here) and the second by utilitarianism in the ways in which they deal with the characteristic problems of the representative relation.[53] Both traditions tend to assimilate problems of aggregation to those of representation, or to discount or obscure the difficulties involved in aggregating interests. They thus appear to be the least realistic of the six traditions so far as the full range of democratic political problems is concerned; it was briefly argued above that they contribute less to explanation or understanding than the other traditions, although they express influential normative ideas or ideologies.

4. The question what is meant by the term "representation" seems of much less importance, given its ambiguity, than the question how it figures in one's approach to broader normative problems of politics. That is really the point of this sur-

---

[51] The term "representative government" doesn't help us in construing "representation." Representative government sometimes simply refers to government by officials chosen in generally competitive elections; but it frequently further implies distance and discretion for representatives and is contrasted to "popular" government. On this interpretation, to be concerned for the "representativeness" of government is not necessarily equivalent to concern for "representative government."

[52] Garceau, "Research in the Political Process," this REVIEW, Vol. 45 (1951), p. 69. Bentley's summary discussion of this point is in *The Process of Government,* pp. 455-6.

[53] There is considerable overlap here: some versions of populism appear to stem from the rationalist or even idealist tradition, simply placing greater stress on political *equality;* and the participatory tradition has, in some thinkers, close affinities with pragmatism.

vey. The first four traditions dealt with seem to me to be important types of political theory and, provisionally, to be the viewpoints of most general application to government and policy, though I mean this only for American politics. I say "types of political theory," since they are not straight applications of ethical theories to political decisions but involve different "models" of democratic government and political processes.

One difference has to do with *what* is represented or embodied in policy. It is possible to distinguish between "values" on the one hand and "preferences" or "interests" on the other. In general, the idealist and rationalist traditions regard this distinction as important and argue that it is legitimate to postulate broad agreement on "values" of rather high abstraction as standards for appraising governmental policy and performance. The utilitarian tradition has emphasized preferences or interests; and the pragmatic tradition stresses the contingent and contextual nature of values which are thus discounted relative to immediate and tangible interests.

Another difference relates to the *how* of representation. Democratic politics can be conceived of as the identification and discrimination of interests, the communication of interests, the measurement of interests, the creation of generation of interests, the direct reflection of interests. One may also find room for the critical evaluation, enlightenment or enlargement of preferences or interests. Surely all these figure in politics; and they receive differing emphases in our "traditions." Some traditions are more relevant to some policies or political problems than to others. Their relevance seems likely to depend on such considerations as: whether discrete, concrete, or individual interests are clearly identifiable; the importance of intensities and of externalities; on whether enduring . community ethical values are at stake, and how directly; whether ends are defined with sufficient clarity and agreement to permit a means-ends approach to policy; the opportunity for political favoritism; the availability of understood or expected procedures; the extent to which a traditional "right" is at issue; the threat to public "authority" from either dissensus or ineffective action; whether leadership seems essential if anything is to happen and the seeming importance to society of action; the importance of science, technology, or technique; whether affected interests can effectively compete for access or recognition; whether symbolic or "style" components of politics seem to be of popular importance; the risk of perversion of widely accepted ends to private purposes in the absence of safeguards; whether an "emergent" policy area is involved where wants are evident but inchoate—and so on.

5. While the traditions, as here defined, are primarily normative, they also offer contrasting descriptions of politics. Louis Hartz has written that the "images" of democracy have never squared well with reality; that, by a sort of dialectic, democratic traditions tend to deny what is right under their noses.[54] The traditions dealt with here are all "ideal" or at least hyperbolic statements about important relationships in democratic government, and are often attempts to correct or correct for unwanted or unwonted aspects of modern politics. There seem nonetheless to be some affinities between these traditions and some of our modern types of empirical inquiry about politics, which can be briefly suggested in conclusion. The point is not that normative and positive questions can't be distinguished—but only that certain normative concerns may predispose one to certain empirical approaches; and that a given empirical approach may yield research of more significance for some normative concerns than for others.

One positive approach to inquiry is cast in terms of simple "exchange" on the model of economic (price) theory, with no assumptions about the desiderata or counters of politics—except that the model works best where these are relatively concrete and discrete. Another prominent approach emphasizes "influence" in which sanctions—threats and deprivations—figure importantly. Both

[54] Louis Hartz, "Democracy: Image and Reality," in W. N. Chamber and R. H. Salisbury (eds.), *Democracy in the Mid-twentieth Century: Problems and Prospects* (St. Louis, 1960).

these models seem to have close relations to the utilitarian tradition. Another is the "group" approach, in which social psychological models and mechanisms of interpersonal interaction and "identification" are often basic, and which has close affinities with the pragmatic tradition. A final approach can simply be termed "institutional," though the term covers a lot of ground. Here inquiry is concerned to account not only for particular policy outcomes, or for characteristic outcomes, but for overall change or stability in the political system itself. Functional analysis is often part of this approach. In any event, in relating values to institutions it has to recognize official discretion, to describe the traditions that confine it and explain it, or which confirm or explain "authority." This general approach seems more closely connected with idealism and rationalism than with the other normative traditions, in that it finds more room for the factors and phenomena emphasized in those traditions.

A good deal of our empirical political science has come to emphasize the "influence" and "group" models either explicitly or implicitly. They are closely related to one another and to the economic model; exchange, threat, or identification (mutuality of interest) may figure as the fundamental processes in either.[55] Generally, however, these approaches would seem to have most to say about the concerns of utilitarianism and pragmatism; while approaches emphasizing norms and institutions throw more light on idealist and formalist interests.

The main point of this paper was to identify some important intellectual traditions; these necessarily brief and general suggestions about their relevance for policy and empirical research may, however, be worth further development in democratic theory. As to policy, most of the "traditions," and especially the first four, apply to problems of government other than representation and indicate that different institutional arrangements may be appropriate to different spheres of action or decision. As to research: since "representation," despite its important role in democratic philosophies and practices, is unlikely ever to meet with common understanding as a concept, the empirical study of representative processes seems likely to be affected by commitments to these traditions; and their critical examination should therefore help to clarify research.

[55] Cf. George C. Homans, *Social Life: Its Elementary Forms* (Boston, 1961).

Political Interest Groups as Policy Shapers

RICHARD W. GABLE

Now a professor at the University of California at Davis, Richard W. Gable was, for many years, on the faculty of the School of Public Administration at the University of Southern California.

The heart of government is public policy and its life blood is the policy-making process. A public policy is a decision or set of decisions that establishes a purpose, creates a precedent, or lays down a

Reprinted from *The Annals of the American Academy of Political and Social Science*, Vol. 319 (September 1958), 84–93, by permission of the author and the publisher.

course of action. The decision itself is a conclusion drawn from a set of premises.

Policy originates and results from the actions of interested groups inside or outside of government which desire to influence the basic premises underlying policy decisions or the conclusions drawn from those premises. The interested group may be a legislative group, political party, administrative agency, foreign government, or private interest group. However, policy almost never originates solely within the legislature, and political parties have largely ceased to be centers of policy creation. Foreign governments assume importance in policy making only in very special cases. Administrative agencies and private interest groups have come to be the principal originators of policy, while legislative groups, along with administrative and private groups, are the major shapers of public policy.

Contrary to a common myth, public policy does not result from any generalized feeling or opinion that exists in the "public." There is, in fact, no single public in the community. What is often referred to as the "public" consists of a number of publics which, on specific issues, have particular opinions but which, on other issues, may have no opinion or divergent opinions. This is not to say that the opinions of the various publics are unimportant. Moreover, since interest groups cannot always identify the publics which are relevant to their interests, they may direct their campaigns to manipulate public opinion at the public in general.

The role of private groups in shaping public policy depends upon the cultural setting within which they operate and the nature of the policy-making process. Brief attention will be given to these topics before analyzing the general role of private groups in the formulation of public policy. No effort will be made to catalogue all of the points at which private groups might exert pressure or to describe the myriad of techniques which have been employed. The intention is to sketch a generalized picture of pressure group functioning and to indicate some of the factors which contribute to a group's success in shaping public policy.

THE CULTURAL ENVIRONMENT

Government is an aspect of society. The political process in which political interest groups figure most directly is but an aspect of the broader social processes in which general interest groups play a role. Interest groups originate whenever an identity of interests is recognized by a group of people who are willing to organize or act in concert to promote and defend their interests; they become political interest groups when their objectives are sought by attempting to shape public policy.

The nature and functioning of political interest groups are dependent upon the social and political environment within which they operate. Properly the entire cultural milieu should be understood to appreciate fully the role and influence of interest groups in society. As cultural factors such as attitudes, status, and symbols vary, the nature and function of pressure groups may vary. Social attitudes establish expectations about the role of pressure groups in society. Some groups, like the doctors and lawyers in the United States, may have more status than others. The predominant cultural symbols may favor some groups over others also. Since ours is a business civilization, groups which utilize the symbols of private property, free enterprise, and the like enjoy an advantage.

Any analysis of the role and influence of political interest groups in shaping public policy must take into account the cultural environment within which they operate. It would be impossible to indicate here all of the factors which might have to be considered to present a realistic picture. A random listing suggests some of the more important cultural elements which condition the political activity of interest groups: the history of a people, the predominant values and myths of the culture, the structure of society, the class system, the nature of the edutional system, the influence of religion, the media of communications, the nature of the economy and the state of economic development, the role of government in relation to the economy, the constitutional separation and distribution of powers of government, the electoral system, the party system, the nature of the civil service—its organization and control—and the level of efficiency in the management of the affairs of government.

THE POLICY-MAKING PROCESS

Almost never does a public policy serve the interests of or result from the action of a single group. The more complex and controversial the decision, the more likely that a great number and variety of contending groups have participated in some way in the shaping of the policy.

The formulation of public policy pervades government in all its branches and at all its levels. It is a continuous process which intersects and overlaps the three branches of government and includes the activities of political parties and political interest groups. Public policy is made by all the processes and procedures which operate in government. It may be a legislative enactment which takes the form of law, or it may be a high leval executive decision. Policy determination also occurs in the process of administration quite as much as does policy execution. An administrative rule or regulation, internal in effect, highly specific and limited in scope, is still an aspect of public policy. Furthermore, the decisions of the courts constitute policy and have consequences for other centers of policy making.

In order to assert their will, political interest groups seek access to the key points where decisions are made. An important characteristic of the process in the United States is the multiplicity of points of decision and hence points of access. To be successful a pressure group must conduct its campaign along a series of fronts—individual legislators, legislative committees, legislative leaders, party leaders, the executive, the bureaucracy, the courts, opinion leaders in the community, and so forth.

A brief, oversimplified description of the process by which public policy in the field of natural gas regulation has evolved may be helpful in illustrating the number of contact points at which interest groups, in this case oil and gas interests and consumer groups, may direct pressure. It also dramatizes the continuous nature of the political process as a policy question gravitates between the courts, Congress, the President, and the bureaucracy.[1]

A series of Supreme Court decisions over a period of twenty-five years left a broad segment of the natural gas industry unregulated. At the production end of the industry the states imposed controls to conserve natural resources. At the other end, retail sales were subject to state regulation because the business of serving the consumer was held to be affected with a public interest. However, the rates charged by interstate pipe-line companies were found to be beyond the jurisdiction of the states because of the constitutional restraints which prevent state regulation from burdening interstate commerce.

Congress enacted the Natural Gas Act in 1938 to fill this gap. The jurisdiction of the Federal Power Commission was specified as applying to the transportation of natural gas in interstate commerce and to the sale of natural gas in interstate commerce. Production and gathering of natural gas and local distribution were specifically exempted from FPC jurisdiction. Unfortunately, the law did not make clear whether the prices charged by the producers and gatherers of natural gas, so-called field prices, were sales in interstate commerce and hence subject to FPC regulation, or whether they were a part of production and gathering and hence exempt. A review of the legislative history of the law provided no help.

In several cases the FPC denied that it had jurisdiction. Then, in 1943, the Commission handed down a ruling sustained by the courts which was interpreted as implying that the FPC did have jurisdiction over field prices. This decision triggered a campaign in Congress to amend the Natural Gas Act exempting field prices from federal regulation. When Congress failed to pass any amendatory legislation the FPC issued an order in which it announced that field prices were not subject to Commission jurisdiction.

In the next session of Congress a renewed effort to exempt field prices was

[1] For a more complete description, see the author's article, "The Jurisdiction of the Federal Power Commission over the Field Prices of Natural Gas," *Land Economics*, Vol. 32 (February 1956), pp. 39–56.

successful although the FPC, with the addition of a new member, now opposed the amendment. Congressional hostility to the members of the Commission who opposed the exemption reached such a pitch that when the reappointment of Leland Olds, the Chairman of the FPC, was submitted to the Senate for confirmation, Olds was denied the reappointment.[2] Nevertheless, Olds' replacement joined the majority of the Commission in urging a Presidential veto which was forthcoming. The Commission immediately rescinded its rule exempting field prices. Then, just a year later in the most important in a long series of cases, the FPC refused to assume jurisdiction over the field prices of the Phillips Petroleum Company. The Supreme Court reversed the Commission, asserting it did have jurisdiction over field prices under the original law. (As an aftermath of the Phillips case, the Senate refused to confirm the reappointment of another Com-

missioner, who was the sole dissenter to the Commission's denial of jurisdiction in the Phillips case.)

Again, another campaign was launched to amend the Act. It was successful in Congress and would have undoubtedly received Presidential approval if some of the pressure exerted on certain Congressmen had not been so blatant. When it was made public that money had been passed in an attempt to gain support, the President vetoed the measure.

The "Washington Symphony of Natural Gas" was played in counterpoint. The theme was set by Congress. Contrapuntal melodies were devised in the hearing rooms of the Federal Power Commission and the courts, but the harmony was sometimes discordant. Congress responded with efforts to introduce variations on the original theme, while the musicians whose brass notes were too loud were dropped from the orchestra. E. Pendleton Herring's comment on our political system is appropriate here although the metaphor becomes mixed. We believe, he said, that "power must be handled like a loving cup and passed around lest one of the company grow drunk."

[2] For a fascinating account, see Joseph P. Harris, "The Senatorial Rejection of Leland Olds: A Case Study," *American Political Science Review,* Vol. 45 (September 1951), pp. 674–92.

ROLE AND INFLUENCE OF POLITICAL INTEREST GROUPS

Political interest groups constantly endeavor to shape public policy. An interest group may succeed in shaping public policy when it is able to identify its conception of the needs of the moment with the prevailing or predominant attitudes of a number of prominent publics and when it has access to the major centers of policy decision in government.

Attention is usually given to the amount of access which an interest group has, whereas access may be the least important way by which a group gains its end. Certainly, access does not mean influence. Many groups have had extensive access, but have had little influence. After the Wagner Act was passed the National Association of Manufacturers and other employers' associations had ac-

cess to Congress and its committees, but the law was not amended for twelve years, not until there was a significant shift in the climate of opinion in the nation. Labor has had almost continual access to Congress since the Taft-Hartley Act was enacted, but it has failed to have the law repealed or modified.

The degree to which a group is able to associate itself and its objectives with relevant publics is often the crucial factor. Any decision involves the selection of certain values or premises over others. The choice of one set of values over another would result in entirely different public policy. The values or premises must be made acceptable at the place where a policy decision will be made before access can be exploited.

Identification of the interests of a group with those of relevant publics may be accomplished in several ways. A group may manipulate public attitudes so that they approximate those of the interest group or, at least, so that the relevant publics are neutral or indifferent to the group's objectives. On the other hand, the group might adjust its attitudes so that they more closely conform to public attitudes. More commonly the group will attempt to manipulate public attitudes at the same time that it modifies or adjusts its own attitudes.

For example, the NAM carried on intensive and expensive public-relations and propaganda programs designed to influence Congress to modify the Wagner Act. These programs had both strategic and tactical objectives. The strategic goal was the creation of a climate of opinion within which the NAM's conception of individualism, free enterprise, and laissez-faire would be habitually accepted as values of positive good and alternatives to it would be rejected. The tactical campaign sought a favorable response to the particular proposals the Association submitted as solutions to current labor problems.

At the same time the NAM adjusted its policies somewhat to conform to public attitudes. Between 1933 and 1945 the NAM's conception of social needs did not keep pace with rapidly changing conditions. Rather than reply any longer on the futile attempt solely to manipulate public attitudes to conform to its values, the NAM underwent a metamorphosis. Prior to 1937 the NAM strenuously opposed government guarantee of the rights to organize, bargain collectively, and engage in concerted action. Not immediately but gradually after the Jones-Laughlin decision upheld the constitutionality of the Wagner Act, the NAM came to the conclusion that these rights actually contributed to the welfare of both industry and labor—if circumscribed by certain regulations. Thus, the NAM accepted the necessity of government action and intervention in labor relations in place of industrial self-rule and laissez-faire; but it demanded that the intervention be on behalf of employers. After modifying its basic system of values the NAM had con-siderably more success in its public-relations and propaganda efforts.[3]

PROPAGANDA: DEGREE OF SUCCESS

Much money and effort are spent by political interest groups in their unending campaigns to maintain the friendship of their supporters, woo the potentially sympathetic, sway the neutral and the indifferent, and convert the actively hostile. However, it is a mistake to assume that wide use of the various media of communications, broad coverage of the various audiences, and ingeniously prepared material are indicators of sure success. The propaganda effort might fail for any of several reasons. The target population might not perceive the group's message at the time and in the way the interest group intended it to be perceived, the group's message might fail to arouse the expected attitudes, or the propaganda might not produce the particular action sought.[4]

Furthermore, many factors involved in manipulating attitudes are external to the group and to a large extent are not subject to its control regardless of how well prepared the campaign. Generally, these factors are basic aspects of the culture which condition or limit the influence of particular interest groups in the political process. For example, the ability of a group to create a favorable climate of opinion depends upon the current political and economic conditions in the community and the values and expectations which are predominant at the time, the status and prestige of the group and its members in society and of competitive groups, and so forth. Professional groups, like doctors or lawyers, or business groups in general, as examples, enjoy a propaganda advantage because of the prestige and status factor.

Even if the group succeeds in bringing about the desired alignment of attitudes, the desired public policy might not result. The NAM was successful in convinc-

[3] See the author's article, "NAM: Influential Lobby or Kiss of Death?" *Journal of Politics,* Vol. 15 (May 1953), pp. 254–73.

[4] David B. Truman, *The Governmental Process* (New York: Alfred A. Kopf, 1951), pp. 245–61.

ing a number of employer publics of the need to change the Wagner Act, but these groups were unable to exert sufficient influence at key points in policy determination to gain their ends. In other words, the propaganda campaign may have been successful, but the publics who responded to it were not able to gain access to centers of policy formulation or to exploit that access to their advantage.

Ultimately, to gain its end a political interest group must gain access to the centers of policy making in government while at the same time it attempts to prevent or limit competing groups from gaining a similar advantage.[5] The ability of a group to gain or exploit access is limited by certain factors external to the group which, to a large extent, are not subject to its control. It is dependent upon the structure of government, the organization and procedures of the legislature and administrative offices, the party structure and degree of party responsibility, as well as the status of the group under the existing values of society.

Access involves not only the act of communicating with legislators and administrators, but the skill with which the position of accessibility is exploited and the willingness, for various reasons, of a legislator or administrator to make decisions that accord with the proposals of the group. Again, a group does not enjoy complete control over these activities. The skill with which a group can exploit its position is dependent upon the structure of government, legislative organization and procedures, party structure and responsibility, and so forth. The willingness of a legislator or administrator to decide in a way that suits an interest group may result from no action of the group itself.

[5] The concept of "access" is developed at length in Truman, *ibid.*, pp. 321–51. The effectiveness of a group's efforts to gain and exploit access, as well as to identify itself with relevant publics, is related to certain internal factors which are primarily within the control of the interest group and dependent upon its activities. These internal factors, which are beyond the scope of this paper, include: the size of the group; the alliances it can make with other groups; its structure, organization, and policy-making procedures; the quality of its leadership; its financing; and its cohesion.

In the past some political interest groups gained access to government using the techniques of what E. Pendleton Herring called the "old lobby." The stains of political corruption, underhanded methods, and payment of election expenses characterized the "old lobby." In contrast, the "new lobbies" have learned to work in the open; they have nothing to hide; they know what they want and how to get it. The "new lobbyist" offers advice, assistance, and his services to willing legislators and administrators. Modern interest groups often have access to more facts than do legislators or administrators. They have extensive staffs of highly qualified persons and the financial resources with which to do research. They can open new channels of communication between government and private groups. Legislators and administrators have actually come to rely upon them.

AREAS OF INFLUENCE

Political interest groups exert influence on the policy-making process along several fronts. They attempt to elect government officials favorable to their position and defeat those unfavorable, influence party platforms and other policy utterances of the political parties, and influence the legislative and administrative process at every phase where access is available or influence may be exerted.

The first front is the well-understood activity of nominations and elections. As the political parties decline in importance as centers for the origination of policy, the need to influence party policy positions becomes less. However, the many interest groups still put in an appearance before the Resolutions Committee of the major parties when they are drafting party platforms.

Both indirect and direct influence is exerted on legislatures and administrative agencies. Indirect influence is exerted when a group encourages members, affiliates, and other publics to engage in political activities themselves. Direct influence occurs when a group communicates with legislators and administrators through letters, by appearances before legislative committees and other fact-finding agencies, by personal visits to legislators and administrators, and the like.

In some cases, political interest groups are actually invited to participate in the processes of government. Administrative agencies may use advisory groups consisting of interest group representatives, popular referenda of interest-group opinions may be held, or representatives of interest groups may be incorporated into an agency. In certain instances, as in the case of professional licensing boards, the authority to make public policy may be delegated to private groups.

While it is true that the most important factor in the success of any interest group is achieving a situation in which individual legislators and administrators are in agreement with the group's proposals, these individuals are not mere chips on a sea of pressures, subject to shifting winds and the ebb and flow of tidal changes. They are individuals possessing attitudes, values, and frames of reference which render them more receptive to some proposals than to others. They are more likely to be receptive to proposals that stem from sources comparable to those from which their own attitudes and values have been derived.[6]

The fact that the judiciary is a political institution is sometimes overlooked. The pattern of judicial action is so well established and the form and procedures of the courts are so well known and accepted that pressure group activity is much less. Yet, the judiciary is a principal holder of public power favorably situated so that it can influence the balance among the shifting interests in society. Moreover, if the courts operate markedly contrary to the expectations of significant segments of the community or if its role is attacked, the political character of the judiciary becomes apparent.

The attacks on the Supreme Court after the decision concerning segregation in schools and cases involving loyalty-security matters illustrate this point. The role of the judiciary in economic regulation provides another example. Before 1937, business groups joined with the courts to defeat a number of acts of social legislation. The Supreme Court came under attack from liberal economic forces in the country which were allied with the President. The Court modified its position toward social legislation in a decision involving the Wagner Act which has been aptly referred to as "the switch in time that saved nine."

After 1937, a new alliance was formed between certain economic interests and powerful groups within Congress which could no longer rely on the Supreme Court for support. In fact, experiencing decisions that were adverse to their interests, they proceeded to overrule the Court by legislative action and were successful in a number of instances. The Congressional effort to overturn the Court's ruling in the natural gas controversy was balked by a Presidential veto, as was the attempt to amend the antitrust law to allow businesses to absorb shipping costs in order to quote uniform delivered prices throughout the country after the Supreme Court had declared the basing-point system illegal. Successful were the tidelands oil legislation reversing the position of the Court that offshore oil lands were subject to federal jurisdiction, the McCarran Act exempting insurance companies from federal antitrust regulation, and the McGuire Act exempting nonsigner-resale-price-maintenance agreements from the antitrust laws after the Court ruled that the original exempting legislation did not include nonsigner agreements.

The impression that the decisions of the Supreme Court are final and binding is no longer accurate. The Supreme Court is properly viewed as one more level, not necessarily the final one, of official compromise and decision in the never-ending interplay between interest groups, the legislature, the executive, administrative agencies, and political parties.

[6] See Truman, *ibid.*, pp. 338–39.

INTEREST GROUPS IN DEMOCRATIC GOVERNMENT

An understanding of the cultural factors which condition the role played by interest groups in our society might provide insight into a fundamental paradox. Interest groups are necessary and essential elements in our policy-making process, but at the same time they can impair the effective operation of representative democracy. Moreover, we expect interest groups to exert influence on government, and we condone such action. Yet, we do not expect our officials of government to submit to such influence, and we condemn the fact that they do.

The activity and influence of pressure groups can be expected to increase. Interest groups beget interest groups and pressure begets pressure. The success of one group stimulates the opposition to more vigorous activity. The locus of decision for many problems is moved from the private to the public arena. As an illustration, the Wagner Act used federal power to prevent long established practices which interfered with the efforts of workers to organize and encouraged the practice of collective bargaining. However, the Act did not attempt a detailed regulation of employer-employee relations. Instead, it left the details of this relationship to be worked out by the parties in the labor negotiations.

In time business and industrial groups succeeded in modifying this law which they saw as weighing the balance too heavily on the side of labor. Groups, like the NAM, which had been vigorous opponents of labor's rights to organize and bargain collectively and of the principle of government involvement in the economy reconstructed their basic philosophy. Under the Taft-Hartley Act government was brought into labor relations more than it had been before, this time on the side of management. What was once regarded as a matter for private negotiations between interested parties is now subject to government direction. Important areas of negotiation have shifted from the bargaining table to Washington. Political power is substituted for economic power, and private problems are made public problems. Modification of basic elements in employer-employee relations now appears to require another act of Congress instead of a new contract between union and management.

There has been frequent comment on the alleged danger from pressure groups. One of the most serious charges is that they threaten the public interest. Such a criticism presumes that the public interest can be identified. One is forced to agree with Frank Sorauf who, after a detailed analysis of the various definitions of the public interest, concludes that "the term 'public interest' has no genuinely valid intellectual definition, and that it suffers as well from a multiplicity of inadequate definitions." However, he adds, "Americans do embrace a public interest or value in another sense. They are agreed upon a governmental process that reconciles divergent interests according to established rules and processes."[7] We accept the method of democracy, even though we may share no common policy goals, and, in fact, regardless of the policies it may produce. The wisdom or reasonableness of the democratic process does not lie in any specific policy, but in the process by which decisions are reached.

By focusing on the processes of government in operation rather than on the substance of policies, the effect of political interest groups on the public interest can be more objectively evaluated. The question, then, is not whether a public policy is undesirable, piecemeal, less rational, a partial solution, or lacking in comprehensive planning. Rather, the question is whether the process of formulating policy has been perverted by pressure-group activity.

From this point of view, an evaluation of pressure groups must consider procedure rather than the policy which results. Are the media of communications available to all groups? Are there effective mechanisms for the articulation of political demands? Do unorganized interests have the opportunity to organize? Does money, power, or prestige give undue advantage to certain groups? Is the procedure employed indirect and obscure? Can responsibility be fixed? Do the groups actually represent the members for whom they claim to speak? Can the members of groups maintain accountability? On questions like these does the final appraisal of the role of pressure groups in a democracy turn.

---

[7] "The Public Interest Reconsidered," *Journal of Politics*, Vol. 19 (November 1957), pp. 630–31, 633.

The Executive
and the Public Interest

HARLAN CLEVELAND

Harlan Cleveland is currently United States Ambassador to the North Atlantic Treaty Organization and European Regional Organization, Paris. He has held many governmental positions and has also been active in the academic and journalistic worlds. In the former he served as dean of the Maxwell Graduate School of Citizenship and Public Affairs and in the latter he was, for a while, publisher of The Reporter *magazine.*

About eleven years ago, I was sitting against the wall of a Senate committee room, watching two political executives sell a lend-lease appropriation to the greatest, or at least the most deliberative, body in the world. My capacity on this occasion was as a briefcase carrier—one of those anonymous civil servants who sit behind government witnesses at these affairs, handing them scribbled calculations and bits of advice on bits of paper. The witnesses were Leo Crowley, the Wisconsin politician who headed the Foreign Economic Administration, and his deputy Oscar Cox, who as one of the New Deal's brightest lawyers had drafted that extraordinary piece of legislation, the Lend-Lease Act.

The scene was a study in contrast. Crowley seemed more senatorial than the Senators, a languid, paunchy man with a mane of white hair, a florid complexion, and a deceptively benign expression. Cox was thin and efficient, his jerky gestures matching his crisp and factual eloquence.

He was easy to carry a briefcase for: he already knew its contents by heart.

Most of the questions were taken by Cox. Before a Senator had finished asking his question, Cox was way ahead of him, guessing what was on his mind and starting to reply in impressive, uncompromising detail. Crowley leaned back, utterly relaxed, sometimes putting in a comment or telling a joke to keep things moving. Finally a Senator asked Crowley a question about one of the most intricate features of the lend-lease program, and I learned an important lesson.

"Well, I'll tell you, Senator," Crowley said in his Middle Western accent, "I've always wondered how that works too. Let's see if Oscar can explain it to us."

Soon the hearing was over, the lesson complete. Two or three of the Senators were clapping Crowley on the back, saying what a fine-presentation he had made. Cox, who had made it, was alone at the other end of the room, stuffing his papers back into his efficient-looking briefcase.

ADMINISTRATION AND POLITICS

A discussion of that political animal, the government executive, should start with some picture of the jungle in which he lives and works and, if he is fit enough, survives. From the requirements of survival in this jungle, the talents needed

Reprinted from *The Annals of the American Academy of Political and Social Science,* Vol. 307 (September 1956), 37–54, by permission of the author and the publisher.

by the top political executives can readily be deduced. Beyond this we need to consider the civil servant as a political executive.

Let us start with the proposition that government is a mixture of politics and administration, accommodation and logic, consent and decisions—a blend, in short, of Crowley and Cox.

We instinctively demand that our Presidents be "double firsts"—that they be great politicians and great administrators too. Of course they usually do not succeed on both counts. Franklin Roosevelt, who is possibly unsurpassed in this century as a builder of consent in war and peace, was as casual an administrator as ever hit Washington. Harry Truman, whose reputation and training were in politics, proved himself an able and orderly administrator, but when it came to building consent for a government program he can hardly be rated better than fair. President Eisenhower, whose forte was military administration, has combined a remarkable talent for evoking consent with an equally remarkable tendency to appoint as administrators of his policies men who disagree with them.

Yet if we seldom or never get quite the perfect Presidential blend, we continue to pine for that rare amalgam— the man who can run the executive branch and still get along with most of the other Americans, in and out of Congress, who think *they* are anointed to run the government too.

What is not so clear in much of the literature of public administration is the fact that *every* official of the executive branch must in some measure combine the two qualities we look for in a President, the ability to manage and the talent to build political support for what is managed. In my own limited experience and observation, I have yet to encounter a government official with any responsibility at all who did not have this dual function. Mark this proposition well: it is bedrock to everything I have to say on this subject. Government is a mixture of administration and politics all the way up and down the line, *not* merely at something called the political level where people called political executives get jobs by a process called political appointment. As Peter Odegard puts it, "Policy and administration are the Siamese twins of politics and are associated at virtually all levels of the administrative structure."[1] Or, as Paul Appleby wrote back in 1945, "So long as the people vote and have unrestrained the right to complain, the whole process of administration is in a sense political on every level."[2]

Does this seem obvious? Does it go without saying that, in a free society, government is politics? I shall be glad if you agree so quickly. But I should give fair warning: if you take seriously what I have just said, you will, I think, have to disagree with much of what the second Hoover Commission on Organization of the Executive Branch of the Government has said in its 1955 Report on Personnel and Civil Service.

[1] Peter H. Odegard, "Toward a Responsible Bureaucracy," THE ANNALS, Vol. 292 (March 1954), pp. 25–26.
[2] Paul H. Appleby, *Big Democracy* (New York: Alfred A. Knopf, 1945), p. 123.

THE DIFFUSION OF POWERS

What is it about our government that makes it so political a jungle? The standard explanation is the constitutional separation of powers, the built-in checks and balances, the fact that everybody is in every act but nobody seems to be in charge of the performance.

Woodrow Wilson called this "administration by semi-independent executive agents who obey the dictation of a legislature to which they are not responsible." He was sure that Congress ran the show, described legislation as "the originating force," and complained that the "blind processes" resulting from the division of power made that power irresponsible.[3]

But Wilson was too pessimistic about the ability of the government to function in spite of this division of power and purposes—or better, perhaps, because of it. He was certainly overimpressed with the power of the legislature in his academic days, though as President he later underestimated its veto power when it came to getting the League of Nations ratified. The legislature is power and can do a massive wrecking job, as we know from our own recent history. But the men who

[3] Woodrow Wilson, *Congressional Government* (Boston: Houghton, Mifflin and Company, 1885), pp. xvi, 273, 280.

wrote our Constitution were clear about the "dangers from legislative usurpations." "One hundred and seventy-three despots would surely be as oppressive as one," Madison said in one of the Federalist papers; ". . . an elective despotism was not the government we fought for."[4]

Despite the periodic flurries of legislative usurpation, we do not have an elective despotism. But we do have a Congress that participates with appalling vigor in the task of running the executive branch of the government. We have, indeed, a system that not only separates the general constitutional powers but diffuses the power of decision on quite specific matters. One of the very first things I ever had to do in Washington, as an "intern" in the office of Senator "Young Bob" La Follette, was to stand in for the Senator at a hearing in the Veterans Administration on a compensation case. I recall being struck at the time by the distortion of functions thus dramatized: here I was, a legislative bureau-

crat horning in on the efforts of executive bureaucrats to perform a judicial function.

Each official in each branch of the government has a chance to exercise two (and occasionally even three) of the constitutional powers at once; and by the same token, each of the three branches sooner or later gets a crack at nearly every major public issue.

The result of this diffusion of power is not merely, as Peter Odegard says, that "Congress has . . . found ways and means for interposing itself between the President and his executive subordinates and thus confusing the clear line of bureaucratic responsibility."[5] Each executive official, whether politically appointed or not, has to spend an unconscionable amount of his time and energy telling Congress what he is doing, and why. In my last year with the Mutual Security Agency, I spent the equivalent of six months out of the twelve preparing and presenting on Capitol Hill the detailed exposition of the program I was supposed to be helping "administer."

[4] The Federalist (Modern Library Edition), No. 48 (1778), p. 322.

[5] Odegard, op. cit. (note 1 supra), p. 20.

CONGRESSIONAL COALITIONS

Nor is it enough for an administrator to defend a program from political attack. He finds himself actively promoting a political coalition in its support. For our Congress, which I have heard described to a group of visiting Frenchmen as a model of party discipline, is of course as choice an example of coalition government as the notorious French Assembly.

If there is any doubt that Congress is managed by complex, ad hoc coalitions which shift with every issue, look for a moment at the record of the Eighty-third Congress. In this supposedly Republican Congress, the fluctuating balance of power swung against the administration on foreign aid and public housing, but supported the President on farm price supports and (by one vote) the Bricker Amendment. A coalition majority could be put together for confirming the New Deal, reducing taxes, cutting slightly the funds for defense, continuing the 1950 version of United States foreign policy,

and allowing some of its committees to trample on Executive toes. On hardly any of these issues could one party get its way solely with the votes it could deliver from its own side of the aisle.[6]

We see the same pattern operating in the Eighty-fourth Congress, which is theoretically led by the Democrats. There was an excellent example in the Senate last spring, when thirty-one Republicans and twenty-two Democrats beat twenty-four Democrats and fourteen Republicans and sent the natural-gas bill to Thomasville, Georgia, to be vetoed by a Republican President.

Because Congress is the way it is, every executive must help splice together the particular coalition that will pass his appropriation and protect his program and his reputation from damage. (His coalition may be very different from an-

[6] See "The Eighty-third Congress—Government by Coalition," The Reporter, September 14, 1954, p. 24.

other one being fashioned for a different purpose by a colleague in the next office.) If every executive has congressional relations as an important segment of his duties—even though he may not himself carry a bulging briefcase up Pennsylvania Avenue to "the Hill"—every executive has to have some of the instincts of a politician. In this sense, the "political executives" in the government are not just the holders of those seven to eight hundred "noncareer executive" posts to which the Hoover Commission Report refers.[7] The number of officials who are involved in this kind of politics is actually well up in the thousands. Under our constitutional diffusion of powers, the federal government would hardly operate at all if they were fewer.

[7] Commission on Organization of the Executive Branch of the Government *Personnel and Civil Service: A Report to the Congress* (February 1955), p. 34. Hereafter cited as "Hoover Commission Report."

THE INSIDE TRACK

Many distinguished writers have pondered whether the American Congress adequately represents the American people, but this is an academic question about which I have never been able to get excited. For the American people do not limit their representation in Washington to electing half a thousand Congressmen. The people are directly represented in the executive branch, too.

When I say "the people," I mean what David Riesman intends by the phrase "veto groups." In *The Lonely Crowd,* Riesman observed that political leadership has passed from businessmen as a class to

. . . a series of groups, each of which has struggled for and finally attained a power to stop things conceivably inimical to its interests and, within far narrower limits, to start things. . . . Among the veto groups competition is monopolistic; rules of fairness and fellowship dictate how far one can go.[8]

The tidelands group refrained from going too far; the natural-gas lobby, consisting of some of the same people, so outraged the public conscience that a President thought to be favorable to its objectives had to turn against the natural-gas bill. The farm group's effective power is enormous; the smaller effectiveness of the labor group may be traced, at least in part, to the fact that it overplayed its hand during the New Deal.

[8] David Riesman, with Nathan Glazer and Reuel Denney, *The Lonely Crowd* (abridged version, Doubleday Anchor Books, 1955), p. 247.

What Riesman did not mention is the fact that the power of these new-style lobbies can be roughly measured by the strength of their surrogates within the executive branch of the government. The Department of Agriculture has long been regarded, by both the farm organizations and the rest of the government, as a farmers' defense league inside the federal bureaucracy. Organized labor, particularly the Congress of Industrial Organizations, substantially controlled the National Labor Relations Board during the period (in the 1930's) when the Board was clearing the way for the rapid expansion of the CIO. The housing program, created by the New Deal for the purpose of getting houses built, placed itself in the hands of the speculative builders and the savings and loan associations to such an extent that moral corruption shaded over into pecuniary corruption. The organized veterans have their own preserve in the Veterans Administration. The Commerce Department has for some years had a Business Advisory Council whose function, in effect, is to bring to bear on internal government decisions an organized business opinion. Defense contracts are habitually given out by men recruited from the businesses that are getting the business, and regulations are drafted by surrogates of the industries to which they apply. The National Recovery Act was declared unconstitutional early in the New Deal, but "self-government of industry" is an established practice with a venerable tradition behind it.

During the Korean War, John Corson has said,

. . . the Office of Price Stabilization official in charge of price regulations for the apparel industry (in 1951) was borrowed from a leading firm in this industry. His aide, who specializes in women's woven underwear, is "on loan" from Barbizon, one of the principal competing manufacturers in this field. A succession of five or more chiefs of the Iron and Steel Division in the National Production Authority have been loaned by their companies, the major companies in the steel industry. The acting director of the Equipment and Materials Division of the Defense Transport Administration for most of 1951 was on loan from the American Car and Foundry Company. He actively promoted, for the Defense Transport Administrator, a plea that the NPA make available sufficient steel to build ten thousand freight cars a quarter; his firm meanwhile is engaged in the production of freight cars.[9]

From time to time this sort of thing gets out of bounds, as in the recent cases of Air Force Secretary Talbott and Chairman Hugh Cross of the Interstate Commerce Commission, both of whom admitted error in using their official positions to advance their private interests.[10] Much more often, there is no formal "conflict of interest." It is considered normal and natural for a steel man to lubricate with government contracts the growth of steel production; for a housing man to get more housing built by having the government absorb a good part of the risk; for a farmers' representative to promote aid for farmers from inside the Department of Agriculture; for a labor organizer temporarily in the government to promote the right of labor to organize. We have institutionalized the inside track.

OUTSIDE INTERESTS AND THE PUBLIC INTEREST

The political executive consequently has to do more than run his shop and

deal with Congress. He has to maintain a complex network of horizontal relations with the veto groups whose interests his actions may affect, with others who think their interests might be affected, and with the surrogates of these groups in *both* the executive and legislative branches of the government.

I am trying hard not to pass any moral judgment on this system, but merely to describe how it seems to work. Given the nature of our society, it is almost bound to work this way. The government is, after all, the least bureaucratic of the major interest groups with which it has to deal. Turnover of government personnel is high, especially at the top.[11] Even if this were not true for other reasons, we make sure of it by having reasonably frequent elections. The same is not true of the major aggregations of veto power outside: in business, labor, agriculture, and a good many other categories, elections are merely a façade for maintaining the same leadership from year to year and even from decade to decade. If you do not like the President of the United States, you can vote against him every four years. If you do not like the President of General Motors or the head of a labor union, you can only wait for him to die.

This difference in tenure between government and outside interest groups is critical. If the outside leaders know more about the subject than their opposite numbers inside the government, if they are providing key experts, advisers, and sometimes even the political executives themselves, the views of the regulated are likely to be pretty influential with the regulators. In the United States, the road to the riskless society that Europeans call socialism is paved with the incestuous intention of nearly every major economic interest to bring the government into its affairs as the risk-taking partner.

Where, in this picture, does the "public interest" appear? Not, certainly, through the organized political parties, which inflate like balloons at election time and are of small consequence in governmental decision making the rest of the time. No, the defense of the public interest

---

[9] John Corson, *Executives for the Federal Service* (New York: Columbia University Press, 1952), p. 50.

[10] *Annual Report of the Committee on Government Operations Made by Its Permanent Subcommittee on Investigations,* 84th Congress, 2d Session, Senate Report N. 1444 (January 25, 1956), pp. 16–24, 28–34.

[11] See Hoover Commission Report, p. 26.

rests in the hands of the people as a whole, who cannot do anything much about it, and of the President they elect, who can.

THE BUCK PASSES UP

Whether, under our system, the government ultimately serves the public interest or merely obliges the private and sectional Trojan horses encamped inside the walls of the federal bureaucracy, depends on the President to an extraordinary and alarming degree. He is the chief mediator among the veto groups, the one political executive whose whole job is to consider the situation as a whole. He is the one remaining safety man available to stop a specialized interest which breaks through the normal line of checks and balances and threatens to gain too much yardage at the expense of other groups.

In a revealing passage of his autobiography, Mr. Truman regarded it as quite natural that nobody should consider the public interest but the President:

I was always aware of the fact that not all my advisers looked at the problem in the same manner I did. This was nothing unusual, of course. It is the job of the military planners to consider all matters first and always in the light of military considerations. The diplomat's approach is—or in any case should be—determined by considerations of our relations to other nations. The Secretary of the Treasury thinks in terms of budget and taxes. Except for the members of his personal staff, each Presidential adviser has and should have a departmental outlook.[12]

Though we sometimes make gods or supermen of our Presidents, they have not generally been more moral than most of us. The difference is that in the White House they are compelled to stand a little higher on the mountain than anybody else, and they consequently see farther at the horizon. It is this unique and lonely vantage point that lends grandeur to the American Presidency.

NOT MORE DECISIONS

Yet the President's high rank does not necessarily mean that he makes more "decisions" than other political executives below. Indeed it is arguable that in our government the higher one's rank the fewer decisions one makes. The man who buys paper clips makes a number of unreviewed decisions without consultation— what size and shape of paper clip, from whom to buy, at what price. As you go up the ladder of authority each official is beset with more committees, more horizontal clearances, more veto groups and political personalities whose views must be reconciled or discounted before the "final decision" is reached.

I once tried to get this important idea across to a very bright businessman who had just been appointed a division director and had promptly started to operate as if he were solely responsible for the program co-ordinated by that division. One day, months after he had taken office, I knew he would survive the transition to becoming a public servant, for he came to me and said: "I'm director of this program, but that doesn't mean I direct anybody, does it? I mean I don't make any *decisions*. I'm really a sort of broker, I guess." [13]

[12] Harry S. Truman, "Years of Trial and Hope," Installment 9, *New York Times*, January 31, 1956, p. 18.

[13] Compare what Paul Appleby said shortly after completing twelve years of government service:

"The danger that our liberties are being lost because Federal executives possess too much power and because they can use it arbitrarily exists almost entirely in the imagination of persons without perspective. It is my observation that no one in Washington, not even the President, is impressed with his own power. Rather the contrary: the average 'high official' is so conscious of the restraints and limitations under which he is obliged to function that his strongest impression is likely to be that of a very restricted power. Indeed, this sense of a lack of power is what drives people out of Washington. To have to 'think of everything in terms of everything else' causes many men to think that they are so hedged about by restrictions that they 'can't do anything,' with the result that, after a while, they simply give up with a feeling that they might as well go back home. The orders and statutes in our big democracy do not invest persons with power; they invest organizations with responsibility."—*Op. cit.* (note 2 *supra*), p. 38.

The President's role as chief broker makes possible a certain order in the bureaucratic jungle. It is no accident that matters which frequently get to the White House are so often better handled than matters that do not. The Housing Agency worked off in a corner by itself for years, dealing direct with the housing industry and hardly ever creating a crisis requiring Presidential attention. As a result corrupt practices like "mortgaging out" under Section 608 came to be regarded by some as the natural order of things until Congress finally made a political scandal of it. The foreign aid program, on the other hand, has spent more than fifty billion dollars since World War II, with hardly a trace of scandal. Why? Could it be because so many departments and agencies were always fighting for the right to manage foreign aid that the program was a matter of monthly, even weekly, concern to the President himself?

The saving grace of our executive bureaucracy, then, is that nearly everybody in it works for the President. To be sure, each political executive is also responsible horizontally to four or five congressional committees; he has to deal with several outside interest groups whose leaders feel the executive is answerable to *them;* and within the executive branch he is constantly evading his own responsibility by burying it in collective decisions by interdepartmental committees. But when the chips are down on any one issue, all political executives are accountable to the President—which is another way of saying that if they get into a tight spot, they can generally pass the buck to him.[14]

[14] "Not the least of the heavy burdens the President must bear is political responsibility for the conduct and misconduct of the executive establishment. Insolence, inefficiency, incompetence, and corruption in any executive official or agency are properly chargeable to him. He ought not to escape this responsibility, as Grant and Harding, and others too, have sought to escape, by talk of 'betrayal' by 'faithless men in high places.' These men are his agents and for better or worse their deeds are his."—Odegard, *op. cit.* (note 1 *supra*), p. 21.

THE KING CAN DO NO WRONG

The buck passes *up:* many of the most serious crises in our government's operations come from temporary lapses in following this first law of the jungle. Many elements of the present federal security system—a major subject in itself when it comes to considering why it is so hard to get and keep good political executives—are a travesty of this principle. For the system legitimizes the downward passing of the buck, and even prepares ahead of time an endless file of scapegoats for administrative error and sacrificial lambs for periodic congressional slaughter. It encourages a reversion to the old English principle that the King can do no wrong: if the government errs, it must be some spy in the ointment. One lesson of our recent madness is clear—legislative usurpation generally takes the form of trying to find the disloyal official down the line on whom the blame for bad policy can be laid. The depth of the Army-McCarthy crisis was revealed when it became clear that Secretary Stevens, Counsel John Adams, and General Zwicker were to be left standing out in the rain without the umbrella of Presidential backing. The natural-law reply to that insistent question, "Who promoted Peress?" was always plain: "The President did. Want to make something of it?"

Perhaps the Hoover Commission Task Force had this in mind when it declared: "Public servants who are unfairly attacked deserve to be defended, and the public interest also requires it. . . . Defense is the corollary of discipline. Both are essential."[15] Government is politics, but the executive branch has to be run by executives. And in government as in other hierarchies, the buck can travel in one direction only—up.

[15] Quotation is from the Hoover Commission Report, p. 78, summarizing a larger section in *Report on Personnel and Civil Service,* prepared for the Commission on Organization of the Executive Branch of the Government by the Task Force on Personnel and Civil Service (February 1955), pp. 117–19. The latter publication is hereafter cited as "Task Force Report."

QUALITIES OF LEADERSHIP

The habitat of both political executive and civil servant is thus a political government. To be successful every government official needs to be aware of outside considerations, available to the concerned committees of the Congress, willing to work in a goldfish bowl, earnest in cultivating his public relations—because his personal public relations are the relations between the people and their government. He must be adept—increasingly so as he rises in rank and responsibility—in helping to build the coalition of outside forces which will provide a "political base" for the program in his charge. He must therefore not be afraid to advocate new policies if he thinks the old ones are worn out, nor can he flinch from becoming identified with the administration of which he is a part and defending his program in public. Since every government executive is something of a political executive, these are to some extent the conditions of work for bureaucrats at every level. They are the *main* conditions of work for an executive near the top of the heap, whether he is appointed from the outside or lifted out of the civil service from within.

In this jungle of close decisions, openly arrived at, the political executive must have certain natural talents and certain acquired tastes. Everybody who has given any thought to public administration has his pet list of these qualities. Here is mine.

IMBUED WITH THE PUBLIC INTEREST

First, he must be imbued with the public interest.

When I was a child, I was told to ask myself three questions before opening my mouth to say anything: "Is it kind? Is it true? Is it necessary?" If I had remembered this advice very often, silence would nearly always have overtaken speech.

Whenever a political executive says, does, or decides anything, he also needs to ask himself a question: Where does the public interest lie? The public interest cannot of course be defined in general. But in our society we have a pretty fair index ready to hand, if we approach each action or decision with the following query in mind: Would this decision—and the procedure by which it was made—stand the test of detailed public scrutiny?

Asking this question must be second nature, automatic, instinctive. It was not automatic, perhaps it was not asked at all, in many a famous political scandal. In our own time General Vaughan did not have it on his mind during the deep-freeze affair. The men who tried to slip Dixon-Yates in through the back door (when they could have carried out the Eisenhower power policy by less circuitous and more durable means) must surely have forgotten to ask themselves what would happen if somebody wanted to know what was going on.

There are, of course, a few public officials who never do get the word, even when forcibly reminded. Several days after resigning as Secretary of the Air Force under a conflict-of-interest cloud, Harold E. Talbott turned up at a Southampton, Long Island, hotel in an Air Force vehicle and was helped in with his baggage by two or three Air Force officers.[16] The action raised the question whether Mr. Talbott had any idea at all what had hit him in Washington.

General Matthew B. Ridgway, in a recent article in the *Saturday Evening Post,* revealed a different kind of fuzziness.

As Chief of Staff [he wrote] I quickly learned that though my own recommendations were made on a purely military basis, the decisions of the Defense Department were based on considerations other than clear-cut military needs. They were based on budgetary considerations, political considerations, on the advantage to be gained in the field of domestic politicis by a drastic reduction in military expenditures. . . .[17]

[16] According to an eye witness report—by a Democrat, of course.

[17] "My Battles in War and Peace," Part I, *The Saturday Evening Post,* January 21, 1956, p. 46.

How does one get to be a four-star general without learning that at the government level there is no such thing as a decision which is "purely military" or purely anything else, whether the public official making the decision is in or out of uniform?

The retort of President Eisenhower, who had one more star and a little civilian experience to guide him, was right to the point:

His responsibility for national defense is, you might say, a special one, or, in a sense, parochial. He does not have the over-all responsibility that is borne by the Commander in Chief, and by him alone, when it comes down to making the recommendations to the Congress.[18]

LEADER OF MEN

Second, the political executive must be a leader of men, with a "sense of action."[19] The very size of the government, and the complexity of the horizontal clearances required to make anything happen, create the temptation to assume that somebody else has the initiative, that it is the other fellow's move. For the effective bureaucrat, it is always his own move.

Chester Barnard has written that a leader needs five qualities: vitality and endurance, decisiveness, persuasiveness, a sense of responsibility, and intellectual capacity in that order of importance. He points out that only the last, intellectual capacity, can be increased by training. For the rest,

. . . there is no substitute for the experience of recognizing and seizing opportunities, or for making one's own place unaided and against interference and obstacles; for these kind of ability are precisely those that followers expect in leaders.[20]

I suspect that Mr. Barnard would agree that for the political executive intellectual capacity should rank higher on his list than last place. A political executive, unlike a business executive, cannot possibly delegate his thinking to a vice-president for ideas. It is a condition of survival in the jungle that he do his own homework and be in intellectual command of the subject matter of the program for which he is responsible. When a congressional committee or an important "veto group" wants to know the story and asks embarrassing questions, no understudy with a mimeographed statement will fill the bill.

HIS OWN PUBLIC RELATIONS MAN

Third, it is obvious from our earlier survey of the jungle that the political executive must be his own public relations man. One reason businessmen get into trouble in government is that many of them are accustomed to delegating to others the task of dealing with the public. In January 1953, toward the end of two long days of senatorial hearings on his General Motors stock holdings, Charles E. Wilson revealed how much he had learned about public relations at the age of sixty-two.

The thing that perhaps I overlooked myself [he mused] was that not only did I have to operate honestly and fairly without prejudice, but all the people should also think that that was the way I was operating, and that part of it I did not quite appraise.[21]

Where had he been? Presumably producing cars and trucks while somebody else worried about what the public would think.

The constrasting case is of course that of Paul Hoffman. By handling his own public relations from the start, he sold the Marshall Plan and himself in the same package: to millions of people in the early days of that singular project, he *was* the Marshall Plan. And his ideas about public relations permeated the organization he built to administer the European recovery program. I remember

[18] "Transcript of President's Press Conference," *New York Times,* February 3, 1955.
[19] Paul Appleby's phrase in *Big Democracy.*
[20] Chester I. Barnard, *Organization and Management* (Cambridge, Mass.: Harvard University Press, 1948), p. 106, and *supra.*

[21] "Excerpts from Two Wilson Hearings Before Senate Committees on Defense Appointments," *New York Times,* January 24, 1955, p. 8.

his telling us once in a staff meeting that we should answer every letter the day it came in, even if all we could say was that we would reply in detail later on. "When I ran a filling station," he went on, "I found that a man wouldn't wait for gas more than two or three minutes if nobody paid any attention to him. But if you gave him a big hello and explained that there were several cars ahead of him, he would sit there quite happily for a quarter of an hour!"

A MIXED CAREER

Fourth, the political executive should, preferably, have a mixed career. It has often been a mistake to bring into the government, especially in very high posts, men who have never before worked with or in a public bureaucracy, who have never had to live with the "public interest" from day to day. But it is also true that a lifetime public servant lacks something if he never leaves the bureaucracy; he loses track of the concerns which most of the people think about most of the time. Indeed, the very experience of dealing, year in and year out, with matters of great scale and moment can be a narrowing one; I am sure I am not the only ex-government person to whom the thousands looked like millions for a few months after leaving Washington.

It is beyond my scope in this paper—and probably beyond my powers anyway—to set forth a neat procedure to make sure that prospective political executives in the civil service get some private experience and budding Assistant

Secretaries now in private business or universities or foundations try the bureaucracy for a while. But I would be willing to bet that an objective study of political executives over the last generation would reveal that men with mixed careers behind them had been more effective and lasted longer in their jobs than those less favored by variety in their lives.

A RARE COMBINATION

That is the list. Our political executive must be imbued with the public interest; he must be a leader of men; he must do his own thinking and be his own public relations man; and he should preferably have had some public and some private experience. As the Hoover Commission's Task Force noted:

The combination of abilities is relatively rare. . . . His foresight must equal the hindsight of a host of critics, both amateur and professional, who are free to be as narrow in their point of view and time perspective as they care to be. The rules of the game of national politics allow no margin for error. . . . To lead the life of a political executive of high rank amidst the asperities of American politics is a test of toughness, of intelligence, and of devotion to the public interest.

"Such talents," the Task Force concluded with classic understatement, "are valuable to the Nation but hard to find." [22]

[22] Task Force Report (cited note 15 *supra*), p. 40.

"DRAWING A LINE"

How far down from the President should political appointment and political expendability be the rule? On this, the perennial question in discussions of civil service reform, the Hoover Commission and its Task Force were very clear: A sharp line must be drawn between political and administrative functions.[23] And

[23] Hoover Commission Report, p. 30; Task Force Report, pp. 1–38.

when they draw it, what a curious boundary it turns out to be!

The second Hoover Commission must be seen as a recession in the seventy-year drive to have civil servants take over the government. From Wilson's professorial days until a few years ago, the general idea has been to reduce to a minimum the number of jobs with a tinge of politics. Wilson himself was not sure, when he published *Congressional Government* in 1885, whether the Secretaries in the Cabinet should be regarded as political or nonpolitical officers. The idea of a strong civil service has been so powerful in this country—even if the prestige of the actual civil service has not—that as late as December 1952 a National Planning Association report seriously suggested that most or all of the President's own staff should be drawn from the career service.[24]

But the reformers overshot their mark. More and more people, especially those who had to run the executive branch of the government, became concerned about the short supply of political executives good enough and knowledgeable enough to manage the government of our big democracy. The second Hoover Commission therefore kept its enthusiasm for civil service reform within bounds, and sought to enlarge the number of political executives, now about seven or eight hundred by Hoover Commission count— though it prudently did not say how many more political executives there should be.[25] Then it added a proposal for a senior civil service of 1,500 to 3,000 individuals, a special tribe of career men and women who have demonstrated their ability to survive and advance in the bureaucracy and are rewarded with personal rank and the permission to serve in any agency that will hire them.[26]

TASK FORCE DEFINITIONS

The Task Force wisely abandoned the traditional idea that you can distinguish between two kinds of people, those who determine policies and those who carry

them out. But firm in their resolve to separate the political transients from the permanent boarders, the experts laid out a more complicated boundary line, more appropriate to the uneven terrain. Political executives should, they said, be appointed to:

(a) All positions filled by Presidential appointment, with or without confirmation by the Senate;

(b) All positions having vested in them statutory authority or executive delegations of authority requiring the incumbents to make final decisions in the establishment of governing policies, programs, objectives, and in the enunciation of principles which will control the action of subordinates in the implementation of the foregoing;

(c) All positions, the duties of which require the incumbents to act publicly in advocating new policies and in justifying or defending the governing policies or the basic principles or philosophy which controls their department or agency policies. Such duties would include direct participation with, or representation of noncareer executives in public debate, evaluative discussions, and justifications of departmental policies, programs, or activities.

(d) Most positions of a personal and confidential nature, such as personal aides, confidential secretaries, and personal chauffeurs . . . .[27]

ARTICLE OF FAITH

I confess that all this enthusiasm for drawing a sharp line between politicos and careerists leaves me very cold. It is, I know, an article of passionate faith that pervades the literature on this subject. Hardly a month goes by without a scholarly admonition about the "rigid protection of bureau chiefs from political connections and duties";[28] or a civil service advocate making the misleading analogy between a lawyer's advice to his client and a civil servant's advice to his politically appointed boss; or an expert viewing with alarm the fact that government, the product of politics, is political. In a recent book, Dr. Leonard D.

[24] Bradley D. Nash, *Staffing the Presidency* (NPA Planning Pamphlet No. 80, December 1952), p. 45 But see the dissent on this point by James Rowe, Jr., on page xiii: "I must disagree wholeheartedly with Mr. Nash's suggestion that the President's office be staffed with career men instead of non-career expendable individuals. This disagreement certainly includes the top men and should, with some technical exceptions, include most of the staff. When the country wants a new policy, it picks a new President. It is hard enough to change governmental policy when he brings into the Office of the President his own men. It is impossible if he is surrounded by career men."

[25] Hoover Commission Report, p. 34; Task Force Report, pp. 39–48.

[26] Hoover Commission Report, pp. 37–44; Task Force Report, pp. 49–58.

[27] Hoover Commission Report, Recommendation No. 2, pp. 31–32.

[28] Leonard D. White, "The Senior Civil Service," *Public Administration Review,* Autumn 1955, p. 239.

White argues the point so vigorously that in one passage about the making of decisions he draws a rather unattractive picture of a civil servant:

At the highest levels, only the confidence that comes from an inner conviction of the "rightness" of a course of action and the moral support that comes from the representative capacity of the man who must act can sustain the strength to decide. The career service does not normally breed this type. Its decisions are based primarily on the logic of efficiency rather than on the calculated risks of an uncertain future.[29]

HOW GOVERNMENT WORKS

Of course a line does have to be drawn, in the sense that you have to distinguish which jobs are going to be filled by political appointment and vacated by political action, and which jobs are going to be filled by civil servants and vacated under Civil Service safeguards. For this purpose the Hoover boundary is as good as any. What I object to is the Commission's quite unrealistic picture of what will be going on below that line: the

[29] *Introduction to the Study of Public Administration* (New York: The Macmillan Company, 1955), pp. 197–98.

image of an executive branch with a few political chiefs making policy and publicly defending it, while the drones below are carefully screened off from the ugly realities of the world of politics. But is this truly the way the government works, or the way a government under our Constitution can possibly work?

The Hoover group draws its line between "departmental management" and "bureau management." Thus in the New Deal Department of Agriculture, the heads of the Agricultural Adjustment Administration, the Farm Security Administration, and the policy-making Bureau of Agricultural Economics, all of whom ran highly controversial programs, would have been career men. Could Congress be kept from summoning such men as witnesses to explain their actions? Should such men as these be protected from the effort to explain to farm groups and business groups and labor groups and the press why they think their innovations are in the public interest? If a ranking bureaucrat cannot help build public support for the segment of the government's work for which he is responsible, is he even the right man for the job? Is there really this clear distinction between "factual material" and the policies which rest on them, between diagnosis and prescription, between "government" and "politics"?

SOURCES OF CONFUSION

The Commission's vision of how the government should work "below the line" strikes me as so exotic that I have tried very hard to think how this dreamworld came into being. There are, I think, three sources of confusion. One may be a misreading of British experience. Another source of confusion is the idea that the erection of defenses against the spoils system is still the cardinal item on the good-government agenda. And a third derangement stems from a concept of "political neutrality" which confuses party politics with the politics of national policy. We might look briefly at each of these confusions in turn.

THE FALSE BRITISH ANALOGY

It is easy for a student of American

government to be dazzled by the eminence and prestige of British civil servants compared to the low opinion generally expressed about our own bureaucrats in Washington. It is, none the less, faintly ridiculous to make the British model our own. In Britain the Civil Service has an aristocratic tradition; it was the preserve of an upper class. Moreover, the political character of Cabinet Ministers and their immediate staffs was clearer from the outset; since they had to be politicians to get into the House of Commons to begin with, no British scholar is recorded as having asked, as Wilson did about American Cabinet officers, "Are the Secretaries political or non-political officers?"

Apart from their class origin, from what comes the prestige of a British permanent under secretary? Surely not from any system that divorces him from formulating policy or becoming identified with a policy in the public mind. The reverse is true. Indeed, I would suggest that nowadays British civil servants derive much of their prestige from the general knowledge that the civil servants run the government and the political Ministers are left with little room for political deviation from the "nonpolitical" advice they get from their permanent staffs. In many Ministries an independent study would I think reveal that almost the only function performed by the political Minister is the rather specialized task of explaining to his fellow parliamentarians what the civil servants are doing in his Ministry, and why they say they are doing it.

When Hugh Gaitskell gave way to R. A. Butler as Chancellor of the Exchequer several years ago, I was privileged to watch the civil servants in the Treasury put on a routine demonstration of their power. Shortly after the Conservatives took over, Mr. Butler went to a North Atlantic Treaty Organization Council meeting and publicly agreed with the American Secretary of the Treasury, John Snyder, about the need for early convertibility of sterling—a policy which his predecessor Mr. Gaitskell had been resisting with the enthusiastic backing of the Treasury staff. I was in London not long afterwards, and I vividly remember the quiet strength with which the Treasury civil servants assured me, "Don't worry about it, the Minister will be taking a different line in a few months, after he learns the facts." And indeed, after he learned the facts which the civil servants gave him to learn, nothing more was heard from the Chancellor's office about making sterling convertible with the dollar as soon as possible. It is, in fact, not convertible yet. Either the facts or the civil servants—or possibly both—have produced an impressive continuity of policy.

The British model is not for us. Our Constitution does not exactly encourage the legislature to lie down and be walked on by an executive of its choice, an oversimplified but not too inaccurate description of British politics. Congress does not choose our President, and it therefore

is not beholden to him and cannot be bullied by him. The separation of powers forces us to have the open government which is natural for our open society. With us, civil servants have to be not only responsible to the public interest but responsive to Congress, a myriad of popular organizations, and the press. In our political government there is no room for a bureaucratic manager who is "above politics."

CIVIL SERVICE: STIFLED BY REFORMERS?

Because every program has a political origin, and every public manager must also be something of a politician, the spoils system seemed the natural way to run our national government a hundred years ago. A hard fight has long since reversed Senator William L. Marcy's famous dictum, "To the victors belong the spoils of the enemy." Yet the descendants of the original civil service reformers are still fighting the battle to protect and enlarge the place of the civil service in the scheme of things. In the process they may stifle the growth of the service itself.

Why do I say this? Because I think back to the days when I first joined the government, fresh out of school. In those days there were a good many examples of "government people" reaching high positions in the government. Daniel Bell, a civil servant who became Under Secretary of the Treasury, was held up to us as a model. Joseph Grew, a senior Ambassador and an Under Secretary of State, similarly has served as a symbol of the summit for young Foreign Service Officers. Now, sixteen years later, I find the Hoover Commission telling me that civil servants should not aspire to any post in which they make final decisions, enunciate principles, publicly advocate new policies, justify or defend existing policies, basic principles, or philosophy, or participate in something called "evaluative discussions." That sounds to me like retrogression in the kind of top position a junior civil servant can aspire to.

For purposes of comparison, consider the State Department. Of its ten statutory Assistant Secretaries today, seven are for practical purposes career men who also served under Democrats. There are 75 Chiefs of Mission (72 Ambassadors, 3 Ministers); of these posts 43 are held by career and 32 by noncareer people. Of the most important ambassadorial posts, four—Moscow, Tokyo, Buenos Aires, and Rio de Janeiro—are held by career Ministers. A Foreign Service Officer or departmental official can, therefore, get to be an Assistant Secretary and an Ambassador—perhaps a Chief of Mission in several different countries in turn—before he completes a distinguished career.[30]

The best civil servants should be able to look forward to comparable rewards of rank and prestige. They cannot do so today, by and large, and they will never be able to aspire beyond the Bureau level if the Hoover Commission prevails.

But, it will be said, let them become political executives and you make them expendable. This may not necessarily be so; it does not always work that way even in the State Department, which is surely as politically sensitive an agency as we are ever likely to have in the United States government. But even if it be true that the road to glory is strewn with turnover statistics, all is not lost. At this level a senior government official can often find an equally useful job outside the government; it is my impression that the political executives had nothing like the difficulty getting relocated that civil servants had in the 1953 exodus from Washington.

To get the best young people into the civil service, civil servants need to be encouraged to cap their careers by becoming political executives, with the glory as well as the risks that choice entails. I see no other course that will enable the government to compete successfully for the very best talent coming out of college.

PARTY POLITICS AND POLICY POLITICS

The Hoover Commission's passion to separate politics from administration takes its most extraordinary form when

[30] Basic information from U. S. State Department.

the Commission gets to talking about "political neutrality." When I first read the Commission's report I could not believe that a body predominantly composed of practicing politicians could possibly have meant what the Report said. For the Commission has built into its remarks on this subject an appalling confusion between party politics and policy politics.

Most of the policy questions which come up in the executive branch of the government, of course, have little to do with party politics. They are nevertheless highly political. As we have seen, each high administrator uses up a good part of his time and energy building and maintaining a political base to support the program for which he is responsible. In the early days of the Marshall Plan, Paul Hoffman spent nearly all his time successfully promoting the plan, in the United States and in Europe as well. Douglas McKay, until recently Secretary of the Interior, spent a good part of his time defending the Eisenhower administration's electric power and conservation policies, and the defense of his farm views seems to be almost a full-time job for Secretary of Agriculture Ezra Taft Benson. The higher one goes in the executive hierarchy, the less time there is for internal decision making, the more effort goes into the politics of getting outside groups (including other agencies of the government) to support the segment of the government for which one is responsible.

Policy politics of this kind is not at all the same thing as party politics, though there is of course some overlap. The party in office has to run generally on the issue of what it thinks and what it is doing. But the campaign issues are often very different from the real issues, because the campaign oratory generally has to do with what may be done rather than what is being done. And sometimes, as in the case of Secretary Benson at this moment, the demands of policy politics may run counter to the short-run interests of party politics. Chairman Leonard Hall of the Republican National Committee would probably settle for a little less rigorous honesty in looking at the farmer's plight; certainly the Democrats, veterans of their own many confusions between party and policy, are making the most of this one.

A "NEUTRALIST" SERVICE?

Bearing in mind this distinction between the two meanings of the word "political," I invite your attention to the Hoover Commission's description of the neutrality required of senior civil servants:

They should keep clear of all political activity, preserve their neutrality in matters of politics. . . .
. . . This means that they must avoid such emotional attachment to the policies of any administration that they cannot accept change and work in harmony with new leaders. Senior civil servants would necessarily refrain from all political activities that would affect adversely their ability to perform their official duties fairly, or that would tend to identify them personally with a political party or its policies. . . .
The senior civil servant should make no public or private statements to the press except of a purely factual nature. He should make no public speeches of a political or controversial character. . . .[31]

The civil servants described in these quotations unquestionably exist. But few of them reach, and none of them should reach, the seniority and rank which would otherwise qualify them for membership in the Hoover Commssion's senior civil service.

How can a senior government official, whose touchstone is the public interest, be expected to be "neutral" in dealing with a Senator who is plugging for some private interest that happens to be important in his state? Reading the Hoover Commission Report, I tried to picture myself, during the time when I was presenting the Mutual Security program to the Congress, being "neutral" about the reactions of Congressman John Taber, or about whether the bipartisan coalition which always wanted to cut foreign aid would have its way that year. Far from being "neutral" and avoiding emotional attachment, a bureaucrat in that position has the responsibility—not just the obligation to his administrative superior but

[31] Hoover Commission Report, pp. 39, 41.

the duty to his own concept of the public interest—to be very active in the effort to build a congressional coalition in support of his program.

AVOID EMOTIONAL ATTACHMENT?

And how on earth can a senior government official "avoid emotional attachment to the policies of any administration"? To begin with he has to help make them. Correction: he "provides facts and background data." But by a curious coincidence he usually provides just those facts and background data that support the adoption of what becomes the administration's policy. Even if he had nothing to do with establishing the policy, the Hoover Commission wants him to be "neutral" and to "avoid emotional attachment" on such questions as these:

Whether the federal government or the Idaho Power Company should preempt the Hell's Canyon power site.

Whether the federal government should aid schools in states that have not complied with the Supreme Court's desegregation decision.

Whether the federal government has any responsibility to assure a supply of polio vaccine for every child.

Whether the farmers need more subsidies or more competition.

Whether accused subordinates should be allowed to face their accusers and know the charges against them.

Whether we should or should not aid the Nationalist Chinese on Formosa.

Whether we need to be ahead of the Russians in the production of guided missiles.

Whether, in a particular situation, we should or should not go to war.

In the case of each of these issues, and dozens more, there are political executives and senior civil servants working side by side to develop the policy and sell it to the Congress and the public at large. For grown men working on matters like these, the avoidance of emotional attachment is nonsense.[32]

[32] The sharpest comment I have seen on the question of political neutrality was made by Herman Miles Somers in a recent article about the senior civil service: "It is easy [he said] to disapprove of 'emotional attach-

Certainly a man who is protected in his job should avoid party work. There are plenty of examples even of top political executives who have operated on that basis. Republicans Robert A. Lovett and William C. Foster ran the Defense Department without getting into politics in the party sense of the word, and General George Marshall, who stayed clear of party politics in spite of extreme pro-

ment.' But how about 'intellectual attachment' or 'professional attachment' or perhaps even 'moral attachment'? Are these also bad for a civil servant? Such a picture of a proper civil servant is rather lacking in charm as well as of dubious validity. To identify 'good management' in the civil service with indifference to the objects of management and unconcern with the social consequences of policies is to make of public administration a barren, if not nihilistic, affair which seems unlikely to attract the kind of imaginative competence which the Report hopes for."—Herman Miles Somers, "Some Reservations about the Senior Civil Service," *Personnel Administration,* January–February 1956, p. 11.

vocation, furnishes another notable example. But the Hoover Commission's ban on controversy and emotion goes far beyond party politics into the politics of national policy.

A senior civil service that took literally what the Hoover Commission has said about "political neutrality" would be a pool of eunuchs, a special breed of Americans who stay out of trouble by staying out of sight. No political executive in his right mind would want one of them assigned to his office. A government staffed with people who "avoided emotional attachment" would be like a hospital full of doctors and nurses who did not care whether their patients lived or died, just so the proper professional procedures were followed.

As anyone knows who has worked in Washington, it is not "neutrality" but vigorous advocacy that overcomes inertia in our big bureaucracy. Too much emphasis on neutrality would shift the whole government into neutral.

Decision-Making in a Democracy: The Supreme Court as a National Policy-Maker

ROBERT A. DAHL

Sterling Professor of political science at Yale University, Robert A. Dahl was winner of the Woodrow Wilson Foundation Award for 1962 and has written extensively in the areas of legislative politics and popular sovereignty.

To consider the Supreme Court of the United States strictly as a legal institution is to underestimate its significance in the American political system. For it is also a political institution, an institution, that is to say, for arriving at decisions on controversial questions of national policy. As a political institution, the Court is highly unusual, not least because Americans are

Reprinted from *The Journal of Public Law,* Vol. 6 (1957), 279–295, by permission of the author and the publisher.

not quite willing to accept the fact that it *is* a political institution and not quite capable of denying it; so that frequently we take both positions at once. This is confusing to foreigners, amusing to logicians, and rewarding to ordinary Americans who thus manage to retain the best of both worlds.

I

A policy decision might be defined as an effective choice among alternatives about which there is, at least initially, some uncertainty. This uncertainty may arise because of inadequate information as to (a) the alternatives that are thought to be "open"; (b) the consequences that will probably ensue from choosing a given alternative; (c) the level of probability that these consequences will actually ensue; and (d) the relative value of the different alternatives, that is, an ordering of the alternatives from most preferable to least preferable, given the expected consequences and the expected probability of the consequences actually occurring. An *effective* choice is a selection of the most preferable alternative accompanied by measures to insure that the alternative selected will be acted upon.

No one, I imagine, will quarrel with the proposition that the Supreme Court, or indeed any court, must make and does make policy decisions in this sense. But such a proposition is not really useful to the question before us. What is critical is the extent to which a court can and does make policy decisions by going outside established "legal" criteria found in precedent, statute, and constitution. Now in this respect the Supreme Court occupies a most peculiar position, for it is an essential characteristic of the institution that from time to time its members decide cases where legal criteria are not in any realistic sense adequate to the task. A distinguished associate justice of the present Court has recently described the business of the Supreme Court in these words:

It is essentially accurate to say that the Court's preoccupation today is with the application of rather fundamental aspirations and what Judge Learned Hand calls "moods," embodied in provisions like the due process clauses, which were designed not to be precise and positive directions for rules of action. The judicial process in applying them involves a judgment. . . . that is, on the views of the direct representatives of the people in meeting the needs of society, on the views of Presidents and Governors, and by their construction of the will of legislatures the Court breathes life, feeble or strong, into the inert pages of the Constitution and the statute books.[1]

Very often, then, the cases before the Court involve alternatives about which there is severe disagreement in the society, as in the case of segregation or economic regulation; that is, the setting of the case is "political" Moreover, they are usually cases where competent students of constitutional law, including the learned justices of the Supreme Court themselves, disagree; where the words of the Constitution are general, vague, ambiguous, or not clearly applicable; where precedent may be found on both sides; and where experts differ in predicting the consequences of the various alternatives or the degree of probability that the possible consequences will actually ensue. Typically, in other words, although there may be considerable agreement as to the alternatives thought to be open [(a)], there is very serious disagreement as to questions of fact bearing on consequences and probabilities [(b) and (c)], and as to questions of value, or the way in which different alternatives are to be ordered according to criteria establishing relative preferability [(d)].

If the Court were assumed to be a "political" institution, no particular problems would arise, for it would be taken for granted that the members of the Court would resolve questions of fact and value by introducing assumptions derived from their own predispositions or those of influential clienteles and constituents. But, since much of the legitimacy of the Court's decisions rests upon the fiction that it is not a political institution but exclusively a legal one, to accept the Court as a political institution would solve one set of problems at the price of creating another. Nonetheless, if it is true that the nature of the cases arriving before the Court is sometimes of the kind I have described, then the Court cannot act strictly as a legal institution. It must, that is to say, choose among controversial alternatives of public policy by appealing to at least some criteria of acceptability on questions of fact and value that cannot be found in or deduced from precedent, statute, and Constitution. It is in this sense that the Court is a national policy-maker, and it is this role that gives rise to the problem of the Court's exist-

[1] Frankfurter, The Supreme Court in the Mirror of Justices, 105 U. of Pa. L. Rev. 781, 793 (1957).

ence in a political system ordinarily held to be democratic.

Now I take it that except for differences in emphasis and presentation, what I have said so far is today widely accepted by almost all American political scientists and by most lawyers. To anyone who believes that the Court is not, in at least some of its activities, a policy-making institution, the discussion that follows may seem irrelevant. But to anyone who holds that at least one role of the Court is as a policy-making institution in cases where strictly legal criteria are inadequate, then a serious and much debated question arises, to wit: Who gets what and why? Or in less elegant language: What groups are benefited or handicapped by the Court and how does the allocation by the Court of these rewards and penalties fit into our presumably democratic political system?

II

In determining and appraising the role of the Court, two different and conflicting criteria are sometimes employed. These are the majority criterion and the criterion of Right or Justice.

Every policy dispute can be tested, at least in principle, by the majority criterion, because (again, in principle) the dispute can be analyzed according to the numbers of people for and against the various alternatives at issue, and therefore according to the proportions of the citizens or eligible members who are for and against the alternatives. Logically speaking, except for a trivial case, every conflict within a given society must be a dispute between a majority of those eligible to participate and a minority or minorities; or else it must be a dispute between or among minorities only.[2] Within certain limits, both possibilities are independent of the number of policy alternatives at issue, and since the argument is not significantly affected by the number of alternatives, it is convenient to assume that each policy dispute represents only two alternatives.[3]

If everyone prefers one of two alternatives, then no significant problem arises. But a case will hardly come before the Supreme Court unless at least one person prefers an alternative that is opposed by another person. Strictly speaking, then, no matter how the Court acts in determining the legality or constitutionality of one alternative or the other, the outcome of the Court's decision must either (1) accord with the preferences of a minority of citizens and run counter to the preferences of a majority; (2) accord with the preferences of a majority and run counter to the preferences of a minority; or (3) accord with the preferences of one minority and run counter to the preferences of another minority, the rest being indifferent.

In a democratic system with a more or less representative legislature, it is unnecessary to maintain a special court to secure the second class of outcomes. A case might be made out that the Court protects the rights of national majorities against local interests in federal questions, but so far as I am aware, the role of the Court as a policy-maker is not usually defended in this fashion; in what

[2] Provided that the total membership of the society is an even number, it is technically possible for a dispute to occur that divides the membership into two equal parts, neither of which can be said to be either a majority or minority of the total membership. But even in the instances where the number of members is even (which should occur on the average only half the time), the probability of an exactly even split, in any group of more than a few thousand people, is so small that it may be ignored.

[3] Suppose the number of citizens, or members eligible to participate in collective decisions, is n. Let each member indicate his "most preferred alternative." Then it is obvious that the maximum number of most preferred alternatives is n. It is equally obvious that if the number of most preferred alternatives is more than or equal to $n/2$, then no majority is possible. But for all practical purposes those formal limitations can be ignored, for we are dealing with a large society where the number of alternatives at issue before the Supreme Court is invariably quite small. If the number of alternatives is greater than two, it is theoretically possible for preferences to be distributed so that no outcome is consistent with the majority criterion, even where all members can rank all the alternatives and where there is perfect information as to their preferences; but this difficulty does not bear on the subsequent discussion, and it is disregarded. For an examination of this problem, consult Arrow, Social Choice and Individual Values (1951).

follows, therefore, I propose to pass over the ticklish question of federalism and deal only with "national" majorities and minorities. The third kind of outcome, although relevant according to other criteria, is hardly relevant to the majority criterion, and may also be passed over for the moment.

One influential view of the Court, however, is that it stands in some special way as a protection of minorities against tyranny by majorities. In the course of its 167 years, in seventy-eight cases, the Court has struck down eighty-six different provisions of federal law as unconstitutional,[4] and by interpretation it has modified a good many more. It might be argued, then, that in all or in a very large number of these cases the Court was, in fact, defending the rights of some minority against a "tyrannical" majority. There are, however, some exceedingly serious difficulties with this interpretation of the Court's activities.

III

One problem, which is essentially ideological in character, is the difficulty of reconciling such an interpretation with the existence of a democratic polity, for it is not at all difficult to show by appeals

to authorities as various and imposing as Aristotle, Locke, Rousseau, Jefferson, and Lincoln that the term democracy means, among other things, that the power to rule resides in popular majorities and their representatives. Moreover, from entirely reasonable and traditional definitions of popular sovereignty and political equality, the principle of majority rule can be shown to follow by logical necessity.[5] Thus to affirm that the Court supports minority preferences against majorities is to deny that popular sovereignty and political equality, at least in the traditional sense, exist in the United States; and to affirm that the Court *ought* to act in this way is to deny that popular sovereignty and political equality *ought* to prevail in this country. In a country that glories in its democratic tradition, this is not a happy state of affairs for the Court's defenders; and it is no wonder that a great deal of effort has gone into the enterprise of proving that, even if the Court consistently defends minorities against majorities, nonetheless it is a thoroughly "democratic" institution. But no amount of tampering with democratic theory can conceal the fact that a system in which the policy preferences of minorities prevail over majorities is at odds with the traditional criteria for distinguishing a democracy from other political systems.[6]

Fortunately, however, we do not need to traverse this well-worn ground; for the view of the Court as a protector of the liberties of minorities against the tyranny of majorities is beset with other difficulties that are not so much ideological as matters of fact and logic. If one wishes to be at all rigorous about the question, it is probably impossible to demonstrate that any particular Court decisions have or have not been at odds with the preferences of a "national majority." It is clear that unless one makes *some* assumptions as to the kind of evidence one will require for the existence of a set of minority and majority preferences in the general population, the view under consideration is incapable of being

---

[4] Actually, the matter is somewhat ambiguous. There appear to have been seventy-eight cases in which the Court has held provisions of federal law unconstitutional. Sixty-four different acts in the technical sense have been construed, and eighty-six different provisions in law have been in some respects invalidated. I rely here on the figures and the table given in Library of Congress, Legislative Reference Service, Provisions of Federal Law Held Unconstitutional By the Supreme Court of the United States 95, 141–47 (1936), to which I have added United States v. Lovett, 328 U.S. 303 (1946), and United States ex rel. Toth v. Quarles, 350 U. S. 11 (1955). There are some minor discrepancies in totals (not attributable to the differences in publication dates) between this volume and Acts of Congress Held Unconstitutional in Whole or in Part by the Supreme Court of the United States, in Library of Congress, Legislative Reference Service, The Constitution of the United States of America, Analysis and Interpretation (Corwin ed., 1953). The difference is a result of classification. The latter document lists seventy-three acts held unconstitutional (to which Toth v. Quarles, supra, should be added) but different sections of the same act are sometimes counted separately.

[5] Dahl, A Preface to Democratic Theory, c. 2 (1956).

[6] Compare Commager, Majority Rule and Minority Rights (1943).

proved at all. In any strict sense, no ade-quate evidence exists, for scientific opin-ion polls are of relatively recent origin, and national elections are little more than an indication of the first preferences of a number of citizens—in the United States the number ranges between about forty and sixty per cent of the adult population—for certain candidates for public office. I do not mean to say that there is no relation between preferences among candidates and preferences among alternative public policies, but the con-nection is a highly tenuous one, and on the basis of an election it is almost never possible to adduce whether a majority does or does not support one of two or more policy alternatives about which members of the political elite are divided. For the greater part of the Court's his-tory, then, there is simply no way of establishing with any high degree of con-fidence whether a given alternative was or was not supported by a majority or a minority of adults or even of voters.

In the absence of relatively direct in-formation, we are thrown back on in-direct tests. The eighty-six provisions of federal law that have been declared un-constitutional were, of course, initially passed by majorities of those voting in the Senate and in the House. They also had the president's formal approval. We could, therefore, speak of a majority of those voting in the House and Senate, to-gether with the president, as a "lawmak-ing majority." It is not easy to determine whether any such constellation of forces within the political elites actually coin-cides with the preferences of a majority of American adults or even with the preferences of a majority of that half of the adult population which, on the aver-age, votes in congressional elections. Such evidence as we have from opinion polls suggests that Congress is not markedly out of line with public opinion, or at any rate with such public opinion as there is after one discards the answers of people who fall into the category, of-ten large, labelled "no response" or "don't know." If we may, on these somewhat uncertain grounds, take a "lawmaking majority" as equivalent to a "national majority," then it is possible to test the hypothesis that the Supreme Court is

shield and buckler for minorities against national majorities.

Under any reasonable assumptions about the nature of the political process, it would appear to be somewhat naive to assume that the Supreme Court either would or could play the role of Galahad. Over the whole history of the Court, on the average one new justice has been appointed every twenty-two months. Thus a president can expect to appoint about two new justices during one term of office; and if this were not enough to tip the balance on a normally divided Court, he is almost certain to succeed in two terms. Thus, Hoover had three ap-pointments; Roosevelt, nine; Truman, four; and Eisenhower, so far, has had four. Presidents are not famous for ap-pointing justices hostile to their own views on public policy nor could they expect to secure confirmation of a man whose stance on key questions was fla-grantly at odds with that of the dominant majority in the Senate. Justices are typi-cally men who, prior to appointment, have engaged in public life and have committed themselves publicly on the great questions of the day. As Mr. Justice Frankfurter has recently reminded us, a surprisingly large proportion of the jus-tices, particularly of the great justices who have left their stamp upon the de-cisions of the Court, have had little or no prior judicial experience.[7] Nor have the justices—certainly not the great jus-tices—been timid men with a passion for anonymity. Indeed, it is not too much to say that if justices were appointed pri-marily for their "judicial" qualities with-out regard to their basic attitudes on fundamental questions of public policy, the Court could not play the influential role in the American political system that it does in reality play.

The fact is, then, that the policy views dominant on the Court are never for long out of line with the policy views dominant among the lawmaking majori-ties of the United States. Consequently it would be most unrealistic to suppose that the Court would, for more than a few years at most, stand against any major alternatives sought by a lawmaking ma-

[7] Frankfurter, op. cit. supra note 1, at 782–84.

jority. The judicial agonies of the New Deal will, of course, quickly come to mind; but Mr. Roosevelt's difficulties with the Court were truly exceptional. Generalizing over the whole history of the Court, the chances are about one out of five that a president will make one appointment to the Court in less than a year, better than one out of two that he will make one within two years, and three out of four that he will make one within three years. Mr. Roosevelt had unusually bad luck: he had to wait four years for his first appointment; the odds against this long an interval are four to one. With average luck, the battle with the Court would never have occurred; even as it was, although the "court-

TABLE 1. The Interval Between Appointments to the Supreme Court.

Interval in Years	Per Cent of Total Appointments	Cumulative Per Cent
Less than 1	21	21
1	34	55
2	18	73
3	9	82
4	8	90
5	7	97
6	2	99
12	1	100
Total	100	100

Note: The table excludes the six appointments made in 1789. Except for the four most recent appointments, it is based on data in the Encyclopedia of American History 461–62 (Morris ed., 1953). It may be slightly inaccurate because the source shows only the year of appointment, not the month. The twelve-year interval was from 1811 to 1823.

packing" proposal did formally fail, by the end of his second term Mr. Roosevelt had appointed five new justices and by 1941 Mr. Justice Roberts was the only remaining holdover from the Hoover era.

It is to be expected, then, that the Court is least likely to be successful in blocking a determined and persistent lawmaking majority on a major policy and most likely to succeed against a "weak" majority; e.g., a dead one, a transient one, a fragile one, or one weakly united upon a policy of subordinate importance.

IV

An examination of the cases in which the Court has held federal legislation unconstitutional confirms, on the whole, our expectations. Over the whole history of the Court, about half the decisions have been rendered more than four years after the legislation was passed.

TABLE 2. Percentages of Cases Held Unconstitutional Arranged by Time Intervals Between Legislation and Decision.

Number of Years	New Deal Legislation %	Other %	All Legislation %
2 or Less	92	19	30
3 - 4	8	19	18
5 - 8	0	28	24
9 - 12	0	13	11
13 - 16	0	8	6
17 - 20	0	1	1
21 or More	0	12	10
Total	100	100	100

Of the twenty-four laws held unconstitutional within two years, eleven were measures enacted in the early years of the New Deal. Indeed, New Deal measures comprise nearly a third of all the legislation that has ever been declared unconstitutional within four years after enactment.

TABLE 3. Cases Holding Legislation Unconstitutional Within Four Years After Enactment.

Interval in Years	New Deal		Other		Total	
	No.	%	No.	%	No.	%
2 or Less	11	29	13	34	24	63
3 to 4	1	3	13	34	14	37
Total	12	32	26	68	38	100

It is illuminating to examine the cases where the Court has acted on legislation within four years after enactment—where the presumption is, that is to say, that the lawmaking majority is not necessarily a dead one. Of the twelve New Deal cases, two were, from a policy point of view, trivial; and two, although perhaps not trivial, were of minor importance to the New Deal program.[8] A fifth [9] involved the NRA, which was to expire within three weeks of the decision. Insofar as the unconstitutional provisions allowed "codes of fair competition" to be established by industrial groups, it is fair to say that President Roosevelt and his advisers were relieved by the Court's decision of a policy they had come to find increasingly embarrassing. In view of the tenacity with which Mr. Roosevelt held to his major program, there can hardly be any doubt that had he wanted to pursue the major policy objective involved in the NRA codes, as he did, for example, with the labor provisions, he would not have been stopped by the Court's special theory of the Constitution. As to the seven other cases,[10] it is entirely correct to say, I think, that whatever some of the eminent justices might have thought during their fleeting moments of glory, they did not succeed in interposing a barrier to the achievement of the objectives of the legislation; and in a few years most of the constitutional interpretation on which the decisions rested had been unceremoniously swept under the rug.

The remainder of the thirty-eight cases where the Court has declared legislation unconstitutional within four years of enactment tend to fall into two rather distinct groups: those involving legislation that could reasonably be regarded as important *from the point of view of the lawmaking majority* and those involving minor legislation. Although the one category merges into the other, so that some legislation must be classified rather arbitrarily, probably there will be little disagreement with classifying the specific legislative provisions involved in eleven cases as essentially minor from the point of view of the lawmaking majority (however important they may have been

[8] Booth v. United States, 291 U.S. 339 (1934), involved a reduction in the pay of retired judges. Lynch v. United States, 292 U.S. 571 (1934), repealed laws granting to veterans rights to yearly renewable term insurance; there were only twenty-nine policies outstanding in 1932. Hopkins Federal Savings & Loan Ass'n v. Cleary, 296 U.S. 315 (1935), granted permission to state building and loan associations to convert to federal ones on a vote of fifty-one per cent or more of votes cast at a legal meeting. Ashton v. Cameron County Water Improvement District, 298 U. S. 513 (1936), permitting municipalities to petition federal courts for bankruptcy proceedings.

[9] Schechter Poultry Corp. v. United States, 295 U. S. 495 (1935).

[10] United States v. Butler, 297 U.S. 1 (1936); Perry v. United States, 294 U.S. 330 (1935); Panama Refining Co. v. Ryan, 293 U.S. 388 (1935); Railroad Retirement Board v. Alton R. Co., 295 U.S. 330 (1935); Louisville Joint Stock Land Bank v. Radford, 295 U.S. 555 (1935); Rickert Rice Mills v. Fontenot, 297 U.S. 110 (1936); Carter v. Carter Coal Co., 298 U.S. 238 (1936).

TABLE 4. Number of Cases Involving Legislative Policy Other than Those Arising Under New Deal Legislation Holding Legislation Unconstitutional Within Four Years After Enactment.

Interval in Years	Major Policy	Minor Policy	Total
2 or Less	11	2	13
3 to 4	4	9	13
Total	15	11	26

as constitutional interpretations).[11] The specific legislative provisions involved in the remaining fifteen cases are by no means of uniform importance, but with one or two possible exceptions it seems reasonable to classify them as major policy issues from the point of view of the lawmaking majority.[12] We would expect that cases involving major legislative pol-

[11] United States v. Dewitt, 9 Wall. (U.S.) 41 (1870); Gordon v. United States, 2 Wall. (U.S.) 561 (1865); Monongahela Navigation Co. v. United States, 148 U.S. 312 (1893); Wong Wing v. United States, 163 U.S. 228 (1896); Fairbank v. United States, 181 U.S. 283 (1901); Rassmussen v. United States, 197 U.S. 516 (1905); Muskrat v. United States, 219 U.S. 346 (1911); Choate v. Trapp, 224 U.S. 665 (1912); Evans v. Gore, 253 U.S. 245 (1920); Untermyer v. Anderson, 276 U.S. 440 (1928); United States v. Lovett, 328 U.S. 303 (1946). Note that although the specific legislative provisions held unconstitutional may have been minor, the basic legislation may have been of major policy importance.

[12] Ex parte Garland, 4 Wall. (U.S.) 333 (1867); United States v. Klein, 13 Wall. (U.S.) 128 (1872); Pollock v. Farmers' Loan & Trust Co., 157 U.S. 429 (1895), rehearing granted 158 U.S. 601 (1895); Employers' Liability Cases, 207 U.S. 463 (1908); Keller v. United States, 213 U.S. 138 (1909); Hammer v. Dagenhart, 247 U.S. 251 (1918); Eisner v. Macomber, 252 U.S. 189 (1920); Knickerbocker Ice Co. v. Stewart. 253 U.S. 149 (1920); United States v. Cohen Grocery Co., 255 U.S. 81 (1921); Weeds, Inc. v. United States, 255 U.S. 109 (1921); Bailey v. Drexel Furniture Co., 259 U.S. 20 (1922); Hill v. Wallace, 259 U.S. 44 (1922); Washington v. Dawson & Co., 264 U.S. 219 (1924); Trusler v. Crooks, 269 U.S. 475 (1926).

TABLE 5. Type of Congressional Action Following Supreme Court Decisions Holding Legislation Unconstitutional Within Four Years After Enactment (Other than New Deal Legislation).

Congressional Action	Major Policy	Minor Policy	Total
Reverses Court's Policy	10a	2d	12
Changes Own Policy	2b	0	2
None	0	8e	8
Unclear	3c	1f	4
Total	15	11	26

Note: For the cases in each category, see footnote 13.

[13]a Pollock v. Farmers' Loan & Trust Co., 157 U.S. 429 (1895); Employers' Liability Cases, 207 U.S. 463 (1908); Keller v. United States, 213 U.S. 138 (1909); Hammer v. Dagenhart, 247 U.S. 251 (1918); Bailey v. Drexel Furniture Co., 259 U.S. 20 (1922); Trusler v. Crooks, 269 U.S. 475 (1926); Hill v. Wallace, 259 U.S. 44 (1922); Knickerbocker Ice Co. v. Stewart, 253 U.S. 149 (1920); Washington v. Dawson & Co., 264 U.S. 219 (1924).

b Ex parte Garland, 4 Wall. (U.S.) 333 (1867); United States v. Klein, 13 Wall. (U.S.) 128 (1872).

c United States v. Cohen Grocery Co., 255 U.S. 81 (1921); Weeds, Inc. v. United States, 255 U.S. 109 (1921); Eisner v.

Macomber, 252 U.S. 189 (1920).

d Gordon v. United States, 2 Wall. (U.S.) 561 (1865); Evans v. Gore, 253 U.S. 245 (1920).

e United States v. Dewitt, 9 Wall. (U.S.) 41 (1870); Monongahela Navigation Co. v. United States, 148 U.S. 312 (1893); Wong Wing v. United States, 163 U.S. 228 (1896); Fairbank v. United States, 181 U.S. 283 (1901); Rassmussen v. United States, 197 U.S. 516 (1905); Muskrat v. United States, 219 U.S. 346 (1911); Choate v. Trapp, 224 U.S. 665 (1912); United States v. Lovett, 328 U.S. 303 (1946).

f Untermyer v. Anderson, 276 U.S. 440 (1928).

icy would be propelled to the Court much more rapidly than cases involving minor policy, and, as [Table 5] shows, this is in fact what happens.

Thus a lawmaking majority with major policy objectives in mind usually has an opportunity to seek for ways of overcoming the Court's veto. It is an interesting and highly significant fact that Congress and the president do generally succeed in overcoming a hostile Court on major policy issues.

It is particularly instructive to examine the cases involving major policy. In two cases involving punitive legislation enacted by Radical Republican Congresses against supporters of the Confederacy during the Civil War, the Court faced a rapidly crumbling majority whose death knell as an effective national force was sounded with the election of 1876.[14] Three cases are difficult to classify and I have labelled them "unclear." Of these, two were decisions made in 1921 involving a 1919 amendment to the Lever Act to control prices.[15] The legislation was important, and the provision in question was clearly struck down, but the Lever Act terminated three days after the decision and Congress did not return to the subject of price control until World War II, when it experienced no constitutional difficulties arising from these cases (which were primarily concerned with the lack of an ascertainable standard of guilt). The third case in this category successfully eliminated stock dividends from the scope of the Sixteenth Amendment, although a year later Congress enacted legislation taxing the actual income from such stock.[16]

The remaining ten cases were ultimately followed by a reversal of the actual policy results of the Court's action, although not necessarily of the specific constitutional interpretation. In four cases,[17] the policy consequences of

the Court's decision were overcome in less than a year. The other six required a long struggle. Workmen's compensation for longshoremen and harbor workers was invalidated by the Court in 1920;[18] in 1922 Congress passed a new law which was, in its turn, knocked down by the Court in 1924;[19] in 1927 Congress passed a third law, which was finally upheld in 1932.[20] The notorious income tax cases[21] of 1895 were first somewhat narrowed by the Court itself;[22] the Sixteenth Amendment was recommended by President Taft in 1909 and was ratified in 1913, some eighteen years after the Court's decisions. The two child labor cases represent the most effective battle ever waged by the Court against legislative policy-makers. The original legislation outlawing child labor, based on the commerce clause, was passed in 1916 as a part of Wilson's New Freedom. Like Roosevelt later, Wilson was somewhat unlucky in his Supreme Court appointments; he made only three appointments during his eight years, and one of these was wasted, from a policy point of view, on McReynolds. Had McReynolds voted "right," the subsequent struggle over the problem of child labor need not have occurred, for the decision in 1918 was by a Court divided five to four, McReynolds voting with the majority.[23] Congress moved at once to circumvent the decision by means of the tax power, but in 1922 the Court blocked that approach.[24] In 1924 Congress returned to the engagement with a constitutional amendment that was rapidly endorsed by a number of state legislatures before it began to meet so much resistance in the states remaining that the enterprise mis-

[14] Ex parte Garland, 4 Wall. (U.S.) 333 (1867); United States v. Klein, 13 Wall. (U.S.) 128 (1872).
[15] United States v. Cohen Grocery Co., 255 U.S. 81 (1921); Weeds, Inc. v. United States, 255 U.S. 109 (1921).
[16] Eisner v. Macomber, 252 U.S. 189 (1920).
[17] Employers' Liability Cases, 207 U.S. 463 (1908); Keller v. United States, 213 U.S. 138 (1909); Trusler v. Crooks, 269 U.S. 475 (1926); Hill v. Wallace, 259 U.S. 44 (1922).
[18] Knickerbocker Ice Co. v. Stewart, 253 U.S. 149 (1920).
[19] Washington v. Dawson & Co., 264 U.S. 219 (1924).
[20] Crowell v. Benson, 285 U.S. 22 (1932).
[21] Pollock v. Farmers' Loan & Trust Co., 157 U.S. 429 (1895).
[22] Nicol v. Ames, 173 U.S. 509 (1899); Knowlton v. Moore, 178 U.S. 41 (1900); Patton v. Brady, 184 U.S. 608 (1902); Flint v. Stone Tracy Co., 220 U.S. 107 (1911).
[23] Hammer v. Dagenhart, 247 U.S. 251 (1918).
[24] Bailey v. Drexel Furniture Co., 259 U.S. 20 (1922).

carried. In 1938, under a second reform-
ist president, new legislation was passed,
twenty-two years after the first; this a
chastened Court accepted in 1941,[25] and

[25] United States v. Darby, 312 U.S. 100
(1941).

thereby brought to an end a battle that
had lasted a full quarter-century.

The entire record of the duel between
the Court and the lawmaking majority,
in cases where the Court has held legislation unconstitutional within four years
after enactment, is summarized in Table 6.

TABLE 6. Type of Congressional Action After Supreme Court Decisions Holding
Legislation Unconstitutional Within Four Years After Enactment (Including New
Deal Legislation).

Congressional Action	Major Policy	Minor Policy	Total
Reverses Court's Policy	17	2	19
None	0	12	12
Other	6*	1	7
Total	23	15	38

* In addition to the actions in Table 5 under "Changes Own Policy" and "Unclear," this figure includes the NRA legislation affected by the *Schechter
Poultry* case.

Thus the application of the majority
criterion seems to show the following:
First, if the Court did in fact uphold
minorities against national majorities, as
both its supporters and critics often seem
to believe, it would be an extremely
anomalous institution from a democratic point of view. Second, the elaborate "democratic" rationalizations of the
Court's defenders and the hostility of its
"democratic" critics are largely irrelevant,
for lawmaking majorities generally have
had their way. Third, although the Court
seems never to have succeeded in holding
out indefinitely, in a very small number
of important cases it has delayed the application of policy up to as much as
twenty-five years.

V

How can we appraise decisions of the
third kind just mentioned? Earlier I referred to the criterion of Right or Justice
as a norm sometimes invoked to describe
the role of the Court. In accordance with
this norm, it might be argued that the
most important policy function of the
Court is to protect rights that are in some
sense basic or fundamental. Thus (the
argument might run) in a country where
basic rights are, on the whole, respected,
one should not expect more than a small
number of cases where the Court has had
to plant itself firmly against a lawmaking

majority. But majorities may, on rare occasions, become "tyrannical"; and when
they do, the Court intervenes; and although the constitutional issue may,
strictly speaking, be technically open, the
Constitution assumes an underlying fundamental body of rights and liberties which
the Court guarantees by its decisions.

Here again, however, even without examining the actual cases, it would appear,
on political grounds, somewhat unrealistic
to suppose that a Court whose members
are recruited in the fashion of Supreme
Court justices would long hold to norms
of Right or Justice substantially at odds
with the rest of the political elite. Moreover, in an earlier day it was perhaps
easier to believe that certain rights are so
natural and self-evident that their fundamental validity is as much a matter of
definite knowledge, at least to all reasonable creatures, as the color of a ripe
apple. To say that this view is unlikely to
find many articulate defenders today is,
of course, not to disprove it; it is rather
to suggest that we do not need to elaborate the case against it in this essay.

In any event the best rebuttal to the
view of the Court suggested above will be
found in the record of the Court's decisions. Surely the six cases referred to a
moment ago, where the policy consequences of the Court's decisions were
overcome only after long battles, will not

appeal to many contemporary minds as evidence for the proposition under examination. A natural right to employ child labor in mills and mines? To be free of income taxes by the federal government? To employ longshoremen and harbor workers without the protection of workmen's compensation? The Court itself did not rely upon such arguments in these cases, and it would be no credit to their opinions to reconstruct them along such lines.

So far, however, our evidence has been drawn from cases in which the Court has held legislation unconstitutional within four years after enactment. What of the other forty cases? Do we have evidence in these that the Court has protected fundamental or natural rights and liberties against the dead hand of some past tyranny by the lawmakers? The evidence is not impressive. In the entire history of the Court there is not one case arising under the First Amendment in which the Court has held federal legislation unconstitutional. If we turn from these fundamental liberties of religion, speech, press and assembly, we do find a handful of cases—something less than ten—arising under Amendments Four to Seven in which the Court has declared acts unconstitutional that might properly be regarded as involving rather basic liberties.[26] An inspection of these cases leaves the impression that, in all of them, the lawmakers and the Court were not very far apart; moreover, it is doubtful that the fundamental conditions of liberty in this country have been altered by more than a hair's breadth as a result of these decisions. However, let us give the Court its due; it is little enough.

Over against these decisions we must put the fifteen or so cases in which the Court used the protections of the Fifth, Thirteenth, Fourteenth and Fifteenth Amendments to preserve the rights and liberties of a relatively privileged group at the expense of the rights and liberties of a submerged group: chiefly slave-holders at the expense of slaves,[27] white people at the expense of colored people,[28] and property holders at the expense of wage earners and other groups.[29] These cases, unlike the relatively innocuous ones of the preceding set, all involved liberties of genuinely fundamental importance, where an opposite policy would have meant thoroughly basic shifts in the distribution of rights, liberties, and opportunities in the United States—where, moreover, the policies sustained by the Court's action have since been repudiated in every civilized nation of the Western world, including our own. Yet, if our earlier argument is correct, it is futile —precisely because the basic distribution of privilege *was* at issue—to suppose that the Court could have possibly acted much differently in these areas of policy from the way in which it did in fact act.

VI

Thus the role of the Court as a policy-making institution is not simple; and it is an error to suppose that its functions can be either described or appraised by means of simple concepts drawn from democratic or moral theory. It is possible, nonetheless, to derive a few general conclusions about the Court's role as a policy-making institution.

National politics in the United States, as in other stable democracies, is domi-

[26] The candidates for this category would appear to be Boyd v. United States, 116 U.S. 616 (1886); Rassmussen v. United States, 197 U.S. 516 (1905); Wong Wing v. United States, 163 U.S. 228 (1896); United States v. Moreland, 258 U.S. 433 (1922); Kirby v. United States, 174 U.S. 47 (1899); United States v. Cohen Grocery Co., 255 U.S. 81 (1921); Weeds, Inc. v. United States, 255 U.S. 109 (1921); Justices of the Supreme Court v. United States ex rel. Murray, 9 Wall. (U.S.) 274 (1870); United States ex rel. Toth v. Quarles, 350 U.S. 11 (1955).

[27] Dred Scott v. Sandford, 19 How. (U.S.) 393 (1857).

[28] United States v. Reese, 92 U.S. 214 (1876); United States v. Harris, 106 U.S. 629 (1883); United States v. Stanley (Civil Rights Cases), 109 U.S. 3 (1883); Baldwin v. Franks, 120 U.S. 678 (1887); James v. Bowman, 190 U.S. 127 (1903); Hodges v. United States, 203 U.S. 1 (1906); Butts v. Merchants & Miners Transportation Co., 230 U.S. 126 (1913).

[29] Monongahela Navigation Co. v. United States, 148 U.S. 312 (1893); Adair v. United States, 208 U.S. 161 (1908); Adkins v. Children's Hospital, 261 U.S. 525 (1923); Nichols v. Coolidge, 274 U.S. 531 (1927); Untermyer v. Anderson, 276 U.S. 440 (1928); Heiner v. Donnan, 285 U.S. 312 (1932); Louisville Joint Stock Land Bank v. Radford, 295 U.S. 555 (1935).

nated by relatively cohesive alliances that endure for long periods of time. One recalls the Jeffersonian alliance, the Jacksonian, the extraordinarily long-lived Republican dominance of the post-Civil War years, and the New Deal alliance shaped by Franklin Roosevelt. Each is marked by a break with past policies, a period of intense struggle, followed by consolidation, and finally decay and disintegration of the alliance.

Except for short-lived transitional periods when the old alliance is disintegrating and the new one is struggling to take control of political institutions, the Supreme Court is inevitably a part of the dominant national alliance. As an element in the political leadership of the dominant alliance, the Court of course supports the major policies of the alliance. By itself, the Court is almost powerless to affect the course of national policy. In the absence of substantial agreement within the alliance, an attempt by the Court to make national policy is likely to lead to disaster, as the *Dred Scott* decision and the early New Deal cases demonstrate. Conceivably, the cases of the last three decades involving the freedom of Negroes, culminating in the now famous decision on school integration, are exceptions to this generalization; I shall have more to say about them in a moment.

The Supreme Court is not, however, simply an *agent* of the alliance. It is an essential part of the political leadership and possesses some bases of power of its own, the most important of which is the unique legitimacy attributed to its interpretations of the Constitution. This legitimacy the Court jeopardizes if it flagrantly opposes the major policies of the dominant alliance; such a course of action, as we have seen, is one in which the Court will not normally be tempted to engage.

It follows that within the somewhat narrow limits set by the basic policy goals of the dominant alliance, the Court *can* make national policy. Its discretion, then, is not unlike that of a powerful committee chairman in Congress who cannot, generally speaking, nullify the basic policies substantially agreed on by the rest of the dominant leadership, but who can, within these limits, often determine important questions of timing, effectiveness, and

subordinate policy. Thus the Court is least effective against a current lawmaking majority—and evidently least inclined to act. It is most effective when it sets the bounds of policy for officials, agencies, state governments or even regions, a task that has come to occupy a very large part of the Court's business.[30]

Few of the Court's policy decisions can be interpreted sensibly in terms of a "majority" versus a "minority." In this respect the Court is no different from the rest of the political leadership. Generally speaking, policy at the national level is the outcome of conflict, bargaining, and agreement among minorities; the process is neither minority rule nor majority rule but what might better be called *minorities* rule, where one aggregation of minorities achieves policies opposed by another aggregation.

The main objective of presidential leadership is to build a stable and dominant aggregation of minorities with a high probability of winning the presidency and one or both houses of Congress. The main task of the Court is to confer legitimacy on the fundamental policies of the successful coalition. There are times when the coalition is unstable with respect to certain key policies; at very great risk to its legitimacy powers, the Court can intervene in such cases and may even succeed in establishing policy. Probably in such cases it can succeed only if its action conforms to and reinforces a widespread set of explicit or implicit norms held by the political leadership; norms which are not strong enough or are not distributed in such a way as to insure the existence of an effective lawmaking majority but are, nonetheless, sufficiently powerful to prevent any successful attack on the legitimacy powers of the Court. This is probably the explanation for the relatively successful work of the Court in enlarging

[30] "Constitutional law and cases with constitutional undertones are of course still very important, with almost one-fourth of the cases in which written opinions were filed [in the two most recent terms] involving such questions. Review of administrative action . . . constitutes the largest category of the Court's work, comprising one-third of the total cases decided on the merits. The remaining . . . categories of litigation . . . all involve largely public law questions." Frankfurter, *op. cit. supra* note 1, at 793.

the freedom of Negroes to vote during the past three decades and in its famous school integration decisions.[31]

Yet the Court is more than this. Considered as a political system, democracy is a set of basic procedures for arriving at decisions. The operation of these procedures presupposes the existence of certain

[31] Rice v. Elmore, 165 F.2d 387 (C.A. 4th, 1947), cert. denied 333 U.S. 875 (1948); United States v. Classic, 313 U.S. 299 (1941); Smith v. Allwright, 321 U.S. 649 (1944); Grovey v. Townsend, 295 U.S. 45 (1935); Brown v. Board of Education, 347 U.S. 483 (1954); Bolling v. Sharpe, 347 U.S. 497 (1954).

rights, obligations, liberties and restraints; in short, certain patterns of behavior. The existence of these patterns of behavior in turn presupposes widespread agreement (particularly among the politically active and influential segments of the population) on the validity and propriety of the behavior. Although its record is by no means lacking in serious blemishes, at its best the Court operates to confer legitimacy, not simply on the particular and parochial policies of the dominant political alliance, but upon the basic patterns of behavior required for the operation of a democracy.

SUGGESTED ADDITIONAL READINGS

1. Abraham, Henry J., *The Judicial Process,* Chap. IX, "Coda: A Realistic Bulwark," pp. 309–328, New York: Oxford University Press, 1962. Identification and explanation of sixteen maxims of judicial self-restraint followed by the Supreme Court.

2. Barnard, Chester I., *The Functions of the Executive,* Chap. 17, "The Nature of Executive Responsibility," pp. 258–284, Cambridge: Harvard University Press, 1954. Consideration of responsibility as conformity with moral codes in the individual, rather than with public codes; a valuable contribution to the broader aspects of the problem.

3. Burnham, James A., *Congress and the American Tradition,* pp. 262–278, Chicago: Henry Regnery, 1959. Strong defense of the Congress and its allegedly slow, inefficient, and undemocratic procedures, in terms of its basic functions.

4. Congressional Quarterly Service, "Congressional Reform: An Examination of the Structure, Operation, Rules, and Customs of Congress, and Proposals for Revision," *Congressional Quarterly Special Report,* revised April 1, 1964, 61 pp. A comprehensive and informative survey of congressional procedures; covers all important aspects, including apportionment.

5. ———, "Suburban Areas Most Under-represented in the House," *Congressional Quarterly Weekly Report,* XX, No. 5 (February 2, 1962), 153–169.

6. Eulau, Heinz, *et al.,* "The Role of the Representative: Some Empirical Observations on the Theory of Edmund Burke," *American Political Science Review,* LIII, No. 3 (September 1959), 742–756. Critical examination of the theoretical problem of representation, using Burkian theory as a convenient example, in an effort to clarify some of the ideological assumptions and postulates for use in empirical research.

7. Fairlie, John A., "The Nature of Political Representation," *American Political Science Review,* XXXIV (April–June, 1940), 236–248, 456–466. Comprehensive survey of the variety of approaches to definition of representation.

8. *Federalist Papers,* Nos. 47–51. Description of the separation of powers and checks and balances by Alexander Hamilton, John Jay, and James Madison, members of the Constitutional Convention of 1787.

9. Finer, Herman, "Administrative Responsibility in Democratic Government," *Public Administration Review,* Vol. 1 (Summer 1941), 335–350. Thorough review

of many of the problems relating to administrative responsibility and maintaining an effective and controlled bureaucracy.

10. Freeman, J. Leiper, "The Bureaucracy in Pressure Politics," *The Annals of the American Academy of Political and Social Science,* Vol. 319 (September 1958), 10–19. Discusses the ways in which some administrative agencies resemble and behave like political interest groups.

11. Froman, Lewis A., Jr., *Congressmen and Their Constituencies,* Chicago: Rand McNally, 1963, 127 pp. Demonstrates how constituency pressures affect the way congressmen act so as to maximize their chances of being re-elected.

12. Goodwin, George, Jr., "The Seniority System in Congress," *American Political Science Review,* LIII, No. 3 (June 1959), 412–436. Describes and analyzes the seniority system—the mechanics, history, pros and cons, effects and alternatives. Sees the seniority system as one of the more defensible of the conservative checks in our government.

13. Harris, Joseph P., *The Advice and Consent of the Senate,* Berkeley: University of California Press, 1953, 457 pp. The leading work on the Senate's role in confirmation of presidential appointments.

14. Jacob, Herbert, *Justice in America: Courts, Lawyers, and the Judicial Process,* Chap. 1, "Courts in the Political Arena," pp. 3–14, and Chap. 3, "Policy-Making by the Courts," pp. 25–33, Boston: Little, Brown, 1965. Brief but precise discussion of the political nature of the courts, their policy-making role, and the differences between policy-making by courts and other agencies of government.

15. Kelley, Stanley, Jr., "The Presidential Campaign," in *The Presidential Election and Transition 1960–1961,* ed. Paul T. David, pp. 57–87, Washington, D. C.: The Brookings Institute, 1961. The 1960 presidential election analyzed to demonstrate the context, organizations, strategies, and issues of political campaigns.

16. Key, V. O., Jr., *Politics, Parties, and Pressure Groups,* 5th ed., Chapter 6, "Role and Techniques of Pressure Groups," pp. 128–161, New York: Thomas Y. Crowell, 1964. Discusses the place of political interest groups in the political system; their techniques in manipulating public opinion, persuading legislators, influencing administrators and the courts.

17. ———, *Public Opinion and American Democracy,* Chap. 1, "Introduction," pp. 3–18, New York: Alfred A. Knopf, 1961. A definitive survey of the nature of publics and public opinion. Public opinion defined as "those opinions held by private persons which governments find it prudent to heed." Reviews major approaches by other authors.

18. Knebel, Fletcher, *Night of Camp David,* New York: Harper and Row, 1965. A fictional account of the problem facing the nation when a president becomes mentally unbalanced. Highlights the question of presidential disability.

19. Manwaring, David R., *Render Unto Caesar: The Flag-Salute Controversy,* Chicago: University of Chicago Press, 1962, 321 pp. Scholarly and readable study of the Jehovah's Witnesses' struggle in the courts against the compulsory flag-salute.

20. Massel, Mark S., "The Regulatory Process," *Law and Contemporary Problems,* Spring 1961, pp. 181–202. Examines the political nature of the administrative regulatory process, with special emphasis on the independent regulatory commissions and their effect on policy.

21. Moos, Malcolm, *Politics, Presidents, and Coattails,* Baltimore: Johns Hopkins Press, 1952, 237 pp. Definitive study of the effect of a presidential candidate's electoral fortune on the campaigns of lesser candidates.

22. Neustadt, Richard E., *Presidential Power: The Politics of Leadership,* New

York: John Wiley, 1960, 224 pp. Scholarly and readable study of the ways in which the president leads and controls. Three case studies: President Truman's removal of General MacArthur (1951); President Truman's seizures of the steel mills (1952); and President Eisenhower's use of troops in Little Rock (1957).

23. Robinson, James A., *The House Rules Committee,* New York: Bobbs-Merrill, 1963, 142 pp. A brief but thorough consideration of the committee—powers, organization, history, and proposed reforms.

24. Rogers, Lindsay and Jacob K. Javits, "The Filibuster Debate," *The Reporter,* January 8, 1959, pp. 21–25. A defense and a critique of unlimited debate in the Senate by two knowledgeable observers. States the opposing positions succinctly.

25. Rossiter, Clinton, *The American Presidency,* 2d ed., Chap. 6, pp. 182–206, "The Hiring of Presidents," New York: Harcourt Brace, 1960. Explains the procedures for nominating and electing a president; evaluates the criticisms of the electoral college; discusses characteristics considered desirable in a presidential candidate.

26. Schubert, Glendon, *Reapportionment,* Part III, "Congress," New York: Scribner's, 1965. A thorough research anthology, including articles covering every aspect of reapportionment. Part III reprints sixteen of the best sources on reapportionment as it affects Congress.

27. Shils, Edward A., "Congressional Investigations: The Legislator and His Environment," *The University of Chicago Law Review,* 18 (Spring 1951), 571–584.

28. Truman, David D. *The Governmental Process: Political Interests and Public Opinion,* Chaps. 11, 12, 14, and 15, pp. 321–394, 437–498, New York: Alfred A. Knopf, 1955. Chapters 11 and 12 examine the role and technique of political interest group access to Congress; the factors influencing the degree of access; they establish the theme that "even a temporarily viable legislative decision usually must involve the adjustment and compromise of interests." Chapter 14 examines interest group access in the administrative process; Chapter 15, in the judiciary.

29. Vose, Clement E., "Litigation as a Form of Pressure Group Activity," *The Annals of the American Academy of Political and Social Science,* Vol. 319 (September 1958), 20–31. The standard reference on the role of political interest groups in the courts; discusses *amicus curiae,* test cases, and the activities of the NAACP, the American Liberty League, and the National Consumers' League.

30. ———, "NAACP Strategy in the Covenant Cases," *Western Reserve Law Review,* 6 (Winter 1955), 101–145. Analysis of the Negroes' use of the courts to change public policy on residential segregation through the restrictive covenant.

31. Williams, Irving G., *The American Vice-Presidency: New Look,* New York: Random House, 1954, 82 pp. An excellent short discussion of the vice-presidency—history of the office, relationship to the president, as a Senate officer, in relation to presidential succession, and prospects for the future.

FOR FURTHER CONSIDERATION

1. ". . . [P]olitical interest groups are an indispensable adjunct to the formal process of representation." Identify the kinds of political interest groups which might help represent *you* in the policy-making process. Consider to what extent your interests are better represented by the activities of these groups than by voting in periodic elections.

2. Take a major public policy question, such as Medicare, foreign aid, income tax cut, and (without doing any research) attempt to trace the process through which it might have been developed. What institutions of government do you think were involved, and how? Did the president play a role? Is it probable that administrators were involved? How and when? How about the courts? When and how might they become involved? And what political interest groups might you expect to have been participants in this process? How? Now, how do you respond to the familiar election-year editorial that in a democracy the purpose of elections is to allow the voters to make basic policy decisions? How would you restate this?

3. Speculate as to how our society would be different if we allowed the legislative majority to have its way at all times. Would this be desirable? Would it be possible?

4. "Governmental institutions in a democracy are in the business of translating public demands into public policy . . . Public policy in a democratic society is the nearest possible approximation of what the people want as expressed through imperfect mechanisms for representing these demands." What "mechanisms for representing these demands" can you now identify? How effective are they? What improvements might we consider?

5. "Government provides institutionalized means to arrive at politically acceptable solutions to politically important problems" but "this does not necessarily result in *correct* solutions to such problems" or any solutions to politically unimportant problems. In a democracy, can we devise institutional means to insure we arrive at *correct* solutions? How would "correctness" be determined? And how can "politically unimportant problems" be solved if they are too big or complex for solution without organized governmental action? Can they become "politically important"? How? What if they do not? Is democracy then unable to cope with these problems? Can you identify any problems of this nature? Does our slowness in solving the problems of racial discrimination, for instance, really testify to the ineffectiveness of American democracy? If not, how do you explain it to our critics in other countries?

Economic Realities and American Democracy 6

Thus far in this volume the major theoretical, institutional, and political characteristics of American democracy have been examined. It has been concluded that democracy is characterized by a competitive struggle for political power in which the privilege of making public policy is at stake; that government provides institutionalized means to arrive at politically acceptable solutions to politically important problems; and that the struggle for power is central to the development of answers to such problems.

In Chapter 5 the policy-making process was examined in both its theoretical and institutional aspects. The three remaining chapters will analyze the subject-matter of that process—the substantive problems of public policy, for example: what is our public policy in major areas of concern; what problems do we face now and in the future in insuring that public policy is both politically acceptable and as nearly "correct" as the democratic process will allow? Chapter 6 considers economic policy; Chapter 7, foreign policy; and Chapter 8, civil liberties and civil rights—the areas of public policy of major concern in the 1960's.

This country, as we have seen, has made great strides in the development of political institutions and broadening the democratic base. There was a time when it seemed that expanding economic opportunity would keep abreast of political development. Then came the Great Depression of the 1930's, suggesting serious limitations to the dream of an economy of abundance. [2] During the past thirty years or so faith in a self-regulating economy has been shaken; our nation has had to meet the economic challenges imposed by both domestic and international crises—depression, war, post-war reconstruction of a large part of Europe, permanent international commitments attendant upon our newly acquired role of world leadership, the strains of a continuous cold war. We had already come a long way from the classical laissez-faire socio-economic-political philosophy of nineteenth-century liberalism; we had already seen widespread use of governmental power to regulate various aspects of the economy. But today, more than a quarter of a century after the "new economics" was first aggressively applied to the economic challenge of the Great Depression, problems remain.

There is a substantial problem of want in the wealthiest nation in the world. [9] There is a serious problem of maldistribution of wealth. There is danger that we may cancel out the advantages of economic growth through overpopulation. Can we avoid another depression? The choice of the means by which full employment and prosperity are to be maintained presents perplexing problems, involving political as well as economic considerations. At one level it is a question of protecting freedom while providing security. At another level it is a question of which groups in our society shall be the main beneficiaries of public policy. At the most imaginative level it is a question of where we want to go, what kind of country we really want. We may have the technical ability to make the good life possible for all our citizens, but can we agree on what is the good life?

The idea of equality of opportunity is one of the basic themes underlying democratic social philosophy—not absolute equality but equal opportunity to move up the social, political, or economic ladder on the basis of ability and desire.

The present chapter will discuss the major problems of American economic democracy: (1) the emergence of the United States as a welfare state; (2) labor-management relationships and public policy; (3) government-business relationships and public policy; and (4) the special problem of American agriculture.

EMERGENCE OF THE WELFARE STATE

The United States today is a welfare state. But in order to understand the meaning and significance of that fact—and fact it is—one must first be aware of the historical background of our economic society.

THE HISTORICAL PERSPECTIVE

Thomas Jefferson dreamed of a great rural republic of independent people, a nation free from the degradation of life in the great industrial cities and the slavery of factories or coal pits that he had seen in England, and from the serfdom that had horrified him in France and Italy. "While we have land to labor," he wrote, "let us never wish to see our citizens occupied at the work bench or twirling a distaff."[1] He had helped found, so he thought, an agrarian democracy and had provided for its expansion through the Louisiana Purchase.

As Jefferson's successors moved into the White House and his followers

[1] Philip S. Foner (ed.), *Basic Writings of Thomas Jefferson* (Garden City, N.Y.: Halycon House, 1950), pp. 161–162.

took over the Congress, his dream seemed well on the road to fulfillment. As the nation's boundaries moved westward agriculture expanded far more rapidly than industry. Even in 1860 the nation was still predominantly rural, and many observers viewed the Civil War not as a contest between a rising industrialism and an expanding agriculture but as a struggle between King Cotton and King Wheat.

Around the middle of the nineteenth century, however, American life was dramatically transformed by the Industrial Revolution. Greatly increased industrial productivity caused the national wealth to soar and raised the standard of living significantly. The merchant capitalism of the earlier days gave way to industrial capitalism and finance capitalism. [6]

As the nation became increasingly industrialized, certain long-established values served as rallying points for large segments of the population. Some groups, such as the Progressives and the Populists, sought to remake society to reflect what they believed to have existed previously. [1]

The general tone of the Progressive movement "was the effort to restore a type of economic individualism and political democracy that was widely believed to have existed earlier in America and to have been destroyed by the great corporation and the corrupt political machine; and with that restoration to bring back a kind of morality and civic purity that was also believed to have been lost."[2] Traditional American democracy had its roots on the farm and in the small village, and it was here that the Populist movement gathered strength. The rapidly expanding industrialism of the nineteenth century challenged the sanctity of an agrarian society.

The growth of powerful corporate structures and the rise of trusts such as Carnegie Steel and Standard Oil created a system of absentee ownership more far-reaching than anything known in history. Vast properties of coal, copper, iron, timber, and railroads were owned and directed by New York corporations. Centered in the hands of a few men was power over the fortunes of millions of people, greater than that wielded by many monarchs. Economic control of the nation was concentrated in a small section of the Northeast. Ownership was separated from management; the tens of thousands of owners—stockholders— had little responsibility for the financial or labor policies of their companies. New aggregations of capital were created, powerful enough to dictate policies to state and national government bodies and to influence both domestic and foreign policies. Some benefits were undoubtedly realized—a good deal of cutthroat competition was eliminated, greater efficiency was achieved, money was made available for research, and mass production brought lower prices—but all at a heavy cost to society. [12]

When Herbert Spencer came from England and delivered a number of lectures on his theory of social Darwinism,[3] a philosophy was provided to justify the social evils of industrialism. It was in accord with the laws of nature that

[2] Richard Hofstadter, *The Age of Reform* (New York: Alfred A. Knopf, 1955), p. 5.
[3] Charles Darwin (*Origin of Species,* 1859) takes credit for developing the biological theory of survival of the fittest, but Spencer made the application of the biological theory to social development. This application, passionately advanced by William Graham Sumner, a professor of sociology at Yale and the leading American spokesman for social Darwinism, required considerable interpretation if not misreading of Darwin's original argument.

big business arose and survived, and man cannot or should not oppose these laws or interfere with the process. [11]

If government did not interfere with business, business soon began to interfere with government. The wealth of the corporations enabled them to maintain paid lobbyists in Washington to prevent any action by Congress detrimental to their interests. They sometimes "bought" state judges. [25] They appealed, successfully in large measure, to the Supreme Court to declare unconstitutional, under the Fourteenth Amendment, state laws which they claimed deprived them of their property without due process of law.

The latter half of the nineteenth century, then, was characterized by social Darwinism and economic conservatism. But the transition period between the two centuries brought the beginnings of revolt against the old order, demands for reform, and the rising force of organized labor. [20]

Labor in colonial America had been essentially feudal in its outlook. Workmen had no necessity to organize. The laborer thought of himself as a thrifty, industrious Puritan and deplored being on public and private charity designed for orphans and widows. The general growth of industrialism and the resulting urbanization made labor organization inevitable. Urbanization brought with its pauperism, starvation, delinquency, and disillusionment with the lot of the laborer in his relationship to the corporate giants. Jefferson's dreams of an agrarian democracy and his warnings of the evils of urban life came into sharp relief as industry changed both the face of the nation and the lives of its people.

Workingmen's parties arose, including mechanics, craftsmen, and farmers. Their platforms reflected a desire to resist industrialization, banking, and capitalism. They advocated a shorter workday, abolition of imprisonment for debt, abolition of compulsory military service, simplified court procedures, regulation of credit houses, tax reform, tax-supported public education, and land reforms enabling all men to own personal property. Their demands represented embryonically all that the growing force of organized labor was to demand for the American people during its long struggle for recognition in the ensuing century.

The industrialization process has changed America from an individual-oriented society based on the Protestant ethic to a society of mass economic values rooted in the corporate structure. It is remarkable, however, that the traditional agrarian values and the classic ideas of self-centered capitalism have continued to exist, although ideologically rather than practically. [5, 15]

WHAT IS THE WELFARE STATE?

Speaking at Boise, Idaho, on August 20, 1952, presidential candidate Dwight D. Eisenhower concluded his talk saying,

. . . Now, ladies and gentlemen, this middle way today starts off with certain very definite assumptions. It assumes that all Americans of all parties have now accepted and will forever support what we call social gains, the security that people are entitled to in their old age and to make certain they are adequately cared for, insurance against unemployment, equal opportunity for everybody, regardless of race, religion, where he was born or what is his national origin.

We have accepted a moral obligation—the education of our young, decent housing, the rights of working men and working women to be productive, the rights of each of us to earn what we can and to save it as far as taxes will let him. We accept as part of these social gains the fact that Americans must have adequate insurance against disaster.

No one counts that thing a political issue any more. That is part of America.

We are never going to surrender these human, these moral obligations that we hold for everyone, the least one of our people. That is America.

No one is going to struggle about that. Every party is going to agree on that.[4]

For all practical purposes this speech marked the end of a great debate which had occupied Americans since the advent of the New Deal. There are, of course, lingering echoes of that debate still to be heard in an occasional academic hall and, with strange persistence, in some political campaigns. Let it be clearly understood, however, that in the real world no one seriously doubts the fact that America is a welfare state. But in one sense it has always been so. The term welfare state, as used here, does not apply only to the agencies and programs designed to aid needy individuals or groups—such as the aged, infirm, uneducated, unemployed—but includes also all activities of government designed to advance the welfare of its people—such as regulation of trusts and monopolies, establishment of fair rates and charges in interstate commerce, and setting purity standards for foods and drugs. Thus, to call the United States a welfare state is to acknowledge that public policy has expressed an intention to use government to promote aggressively the maximum economic and social benefits for the people. Differences arise, of course, as to the nature of "maximum benefits," the techniques best calculated to accomplish them, priorities of the tasks to be accomplished and how far we should go.

Our welfare state arose not as the result of a particular philosophy but in response to the needs created by an industrialized society in which people were exposed to the chaos of technological change, economic fluctuations, war, and social revolution. The term welfare state and socialism are not interchangeable. While a socialistic state may certainly be a welfare state, all welfare states are not necessarily socialistic. [24] Public ownership and control of the means of production and distribution are not a prerequisite to welfare. This is demonstrated by our own economy. The American economy is a "mixed economy," that is, it has elements which occur at various points along a continuum from pure socialism to pure capitalism. Many enterprises popularly described as private or free actually have a greater degree of government control than some of those thought of as public or socialized, and vice versa. There is, for instance, a greater degree of government control of public utilities, which are commonly considered free enterprise, than there is in government contracts with private producers for public housing projects, regarded as very much in the public sphere. Thus it is increasingly unproductive to argue in terms of public ownership and operation or control. In essence, what constitutes our welfare state is planning to accomplish defined social ends, and such planning does not necessarily imply public ownership. [17]

The basic goal of the welfare state is not to redistribute income but to guarantee equality of opportunity and a minimum standard of living. This in-

[4] *Vital Speeches,* Vol. XVIII, September 1, 1952, p. 677.

cludes not only the traditional material minimum; it implies, in addition, a psychological component—self-respect.[5]

The welfare state represents society's efforts to balance the needs of individuals, business enterprise, and the total economy. It is based on the assumption that the success of business need not be at the expense of, nor deny the legitimacy of, the needs and happiness of individuals; that governmental efforts are as legitimately applied to serving the needs of individuals in developing the "good life" [21] as to promoting and protecting the interests of economic enterprise. Furthermore, it is inevitable that some people are not going to have the foresight, desire, or ability to provide for themselves and will eventually become burdens on their family or society. Society, for the common good, is compelled to provide for them.

The government plays a vital role in providing economic stabilizers. Partial redistribution of income through taxing and spending, government regulation, and welfare programs are designed to ameliorate and prevent many of the extremes of the business cycle. [10]

Active governmental involvement in the economic life of the country has strengthened local governments through the expenditure of federal grants. Grants-in-aid have tended to even out some of the inequalities in ability to cope with problems between the various state and local governments, a significant factor in a political structure where the system of representation leaves major areas of public policy to these levels.

While the welfare state in the United States involves a certain amount of public ownership, a good deal of economic regulation, and some redistribution of income, the essentials of a free market system have been maintained. Indeed, the evidence suggests that rather than damaging private enterprise, our particular style of modified free enterprise system—our welfare state, as we have termed it—has brought us the highest standard of living of any people in history, an ever-increasing gross national product, higher corporate profits, and decreasing extremes in the distribution of both the necessities and luxuries of life. Predictions by some of economic chaos, loss of individual rights—such as the right to hold private property—serious diminution of individual initiative, and bureaucratic domination of the economic life of the country simply have not been verified by experience in the United States. [14, 24] Yet, when we seem to have been successful in maximizing the benefits of both a free enterprise system and governmental activity in the economic arena, it is still possible to hear predictions of impending disaster associated with the continuance of the articulated public policy of the welfare state. [18] But one thing is clear: the choice has been made; we will see more rather than less government involvement in the economy.

Prior to 1933, most presidents of the United States adhered strongly to

[5] Some argue that "self-respect" is a basic democratic ideal. Riker contends that ". . . Democracy is self-respect for everybody. Within this simple phrase is all that is and ought to be the democratic ideal. . . . If self-respect is the democratic good, then all things that prevent its attainment are democratic evils. . . . Democracy is a form of government in which the rulers are fully responsible to the ruled to realize self-respect for everybody. . . ." William H. Riker, Democracy in the United States, 2d ed. (New York: The Macmillan Company, 1965), pp. 1–34.

conservative economic values. Former President Herbert Hoover postulated one of the cardinal precepts of conservatism. Upon hearing President Roosevelt's famous "Four Freedoms" speech—freedom of speech and expression, freedom of religion, freedom from fear, freedom from want—Mr. Hoover commented that there is a fifth freedom—economic freedom—without which none of the other four freedoms will be realized. This statement does not mean that Mr. Hoover advocated going back to a laissez-faire economy; rather, he meant that citizens "must be free to engage in enterprise so long as each does not injure his fellow man."[6] Among other important conservative economic values [18] are: (1) liberty is superior to security; (2) political freedom cannot exist without economic freedom; (3) government should function with maximum thrift and efficiency, and within its means; and (4) primary responsibility for welfare lies with the individual, the community, and the states, not the federal government. Most advocates of the welfare state, whatever their ideological convictions, would have little serious argument with these beliefs. They do not necessarily lead to a rejection of the idea that government should function to promote the welfare of its people to the maximum.

The Great Depression of the early thirties, however, prompted the American people to elect a president and Congress who promised emergency measures to help the economically prostrate country. [2] Because of the inability of local agencies to meet the economic crisis and the human problems attendant to it, the federal government intensified its activity in the economic affairs of the nation.

New Deal policy consisted of emergency measures designed to get the economy moving as soon as possible. While the plans were not enthusiastically endorsed by conservatives, the situation was critical enough to warrant immediate action by the federal government. After the crisis had passed many of the temporary relief measures became permanent programs, thus arousing the concern of many. [23]

For over thirty years liberals have built their programs on the idea that the federal government should be involved in welfare. Their conservative critics have charged that the end result of so much welfare legislation will be a collectivist society. Conservatism has emerged recently after a lengthy dormant period with such articulate spokesmen as William Buckley, Russell Kirk, John Dos Passos, and Barry Goldwater. [18] Most conservatives view the proliferation of welfare services as undermining individual initiative and the moral strength of the nation. Their basic position toward welfare programs is that it is better to provide for the needy through private means, individual or cooperative, or by local government programs.

It is important to note that the criticism is directed with far more enthusiasm against the pejoratively termed welfare agencies and programs (social security, old-age benefits, unemployment programs) than against the regulatory and promotional agencies. This discussion has correctly included under the term welfare state all aspects of aggressive government intervention in the economic sphere—the regulatory commissions, agencies designed to promote various segments of the economy, the use of the courts (to redefine due process and the

---

[6] Herbert Hoover, "The Fifth Freedom," in *Free Government in the Making*, ed. Alpheus T. Mason (New York: Oxford University Press, 1965), p. 819.

contract clause, for instance), as well as those programs and agencies designed to aid the needy and the aged. The failure to recognize that the welfare state embraces governmental intervention in almost all aspects of economic life often leads to selective criticism of certain programs while ignoring their counterpart programs aiding or regulating other segments of the economy. For instance, many oppose federal aid to education as "welfare statism" while failing to consider the economic involvement of government through federal subsidies to rail or water transport; or, editorialize about the income-leveling effects of the progressive income tax while ignoring the extensive subsidies built into the internal revenue statutes for businesses, private enterpreneurs, and professionals.

The debate will continue, but the evidence is quite clear: the competitive struggle for political power has resulted in development of a public policy that has shaped the government's active participation in the economic life of the nation.

LABOR-MANAGEMENT RELATIONS AND PUBLIC POLICY

Our society is characterized by economic interdependence, and this interdependence is nowhere more evident than in the relations of labor and management. A major unsettled labor-management dispute in a basic industry may seriously affect not only the nation's economy but the lives and well-being of thousands of workers directly and many more thousands indirectly. Both groups, labor and management, have become such an important part of our society that conflict between them is of national concern. Management and unions have come to recognize their interdependence and their responsibility to the community.

A basic premise to labor-management relations is that the cost of agreement must always be lower to the parties involved than the cost of disagreement. Selection of techniques in bargaining is always relative to the demands made. Also important is the "guess" that each side must make on the costliness of the proposals to each. The costs to management and labor ultimately can be traced back to their objectives; the cost of foregoing or altering them is a major consideration in negotiations and selection of techniques. In sum, the main determinants in any labor-management dispute are the strengths, attitudes, and goals of the parties.

Collective bargaining is a business compact, a treaty, and a code of honor. There are relatively few legal controls on collective bargaining. Its success depends on mutual trust, good will, and intelligence. [7]

A relatively new phenomenon has emerged both to plague and puzzle the proponents of social democracy in America. The problem derives from the emergence of a new labor-management alliance based on the nature of the union growth and the realities of current economic life.

Organized labor today is a large, private institution, consciously approved of by society, whose power is maintained in a loose framework of prescribed rules, agencies, and government regulations. [16, 20] As the American labor unions have matured, they have become solid institutions within the central economic power structure.

The post-New Deal era saw the increasing institutionalization of the labor unions. Official recognition of labor's support of the government, the right to bargain, governmental efforts at arbitration in labor-management disputes, manpower shortages of the war, and postwar prosperity gave labor slow, steady gains that made militant unionism seem unnecessary. The postwar era saw labor fully matured in its institutional role. Restricted by the Taft-Hartley Act, labor retreated to a middle-of-the road economic position rather than engaging in radical reaction, in large part to avoid the possibility of even more restrictive legislation.

Today's labor unions accept the basic American democratic system and operate within it. Economically, they are as dedicated to the free enterprise ideology as is business, and politically they are within the mainstream of American society.

Labor no longer acts as a countervailing power to the large corporations. Labor is now involved and intertwined with management. Common lines of thought have led to cooperative action and economic unity between the two ostensibly opposing forces. Labor has ceased to be a competitor for power with management. [13] The new role of labor is one indication of the change in the American economic structure. It is no longer capitalistic, nor is it socialistic. Rather, as noted above, a mixed economy has developed, extending into the political sphere as well. The outstanding feature of the mixed economy is the interlocking of the major power centers within society—the military, industry, government, and labor. These power centers are merging at the upper levels, creating "the power elite" which C. Wright Mills has described.[7] As a result, conflict over basic ideology is dying out; the significant disputes are about means and administration. Labor is as interested in a higher Gross National Product as management, though they may want to attain it for different reasons and by somewhat different methods.

The historical trend of labor from social militancy toward a conservative position within the corporate structure has been accelerated in recent years. There is a close connection between this development and the instability of the labor force due to increasing automation. Labor's attempt to combat unemployment caused by automation has not been radical, first, because of the traditions of the labor movement, and second, because labor's relative success has kept it from becoming militant. [4] Nor is the majority of the labor force out of work or ill-paid or living under sweatshop conditions. However, there is a dormant threat—sometimes of a shift in public acceptance of labor's gains, always of potential unemployment—hanging over the unions. Consequently, the unions seek to increase economic, as well as political, stability in the hope of preventing the loss of jobs or public disfavor. To do this they seek to bolster the industries within which they operate. A basic premise of labor is that the welfare of the worker depends upon the welfare of the industry in which he works.[8] Its

[7] C. Wright Mills, *The Power Elite* (New York: Oxford University Press, 1959), especially pp. 269–297.
[8] Sidney Lens, *The Crisis of American Labor* (New York: Sagamore Press, 1959), p. 81.

corollary is that labor's welfare requires that it contribute to the success of American capitalism.

A result of this trend toward labor-management cooperation has been the growth of the corporate power elite and a decline in the vitality of the democratic process—a decline of conflict in the development of economic policy. As the labor unions and management diminish the areas of conflict between them, together they increase their control over the economic and political life of the society.[9] [13]

GOVERNMENT, BUSINESS, AND PUBLIC POLICY

The relationship between government and business is one of the most important determinants of public policy on economic matters. Two interacting variables of this relationship will concern us here: (1) the political role of business, and (2) governmental regulation of business.

THE POLITICAL ROLE OF BUSINESS

"The proper role for business in American political life is debated with great heat. At one extreme are those who would erect an impregnable barrier between business and politics. Others would rigidly restrict the political activities of business. Still others urge the necessity and merit of business intervention to give direction to our national life."[10] But regardless of one's feeling about business, it does have a direct impact on politics and policy determination.

Overt partisan political action traditionally has been avoided by businessmen. The attitude of the businessman has been, until recently, that business and politics are separate worlds. [8] Legislative lobbying, party contributions, (often to both parties), community relations, and utilization of the mass media have been the chief methods through which businessmen have influenced public policy.

In recent years, however, there has been a new trend toward direct political involvement by business. Managerial employees have begun working for the party of their choice and are more frequently running for office. Efforts have been made to gain representation in the Congress and state legislatures, to insure that the views of business may have equal representation with those of labor.

The recent involvement of business in politics takes many forms, among which the following is not atypical: the company takes a public stand on con-

[9] The danger to society as a whole which this new collaboration may present is stated by Clark Kerr: "The balance of power center in our industrial system is being endangered by the growing areas of collusion in labor-management relations. Prices, entrance to the trade, business practices are jointly controlled in a surprising number of industries already. The old conflict of industry against labor is giving way to a new conflict of industry plus labor against the consuming public." Clark Kerr, *Managing the Manager—The Distribution of Power in American Industrial Society* (Berkeley: Institute of Industrial Relations, 1960), p. 96.
[10] Harry R. Hall, in *Vital Speeches,* Vol. XXVIII, No. 2 (Nov. 1, 1961).

troversial issues and identifies this position in its advertising and public relations programs; people "down the line" are informed that direct political activity is not only permitted but officially approved; "business climate" programs, in which local groups are encouraged to present to employees an analysis of political, economic, and social conditions are developed; programs consisting of workshops and seminars running from a few days to several weeks are conducted to teach the relatively uninformed businessman the political facts of life. A not untypical feature: a practical, step-by-step guide on how to take control of a party precinct organization.

The most visible political trend during the past twenty years has been the extensive involvement of the wealthy in the political process. Today, for both major parties, nominees for the presidency are generally men of wealth; not only can they contribute toward the tremendous expenses involved in a campaign but they have business, professional, and personal associates who are wealthy. It is almost axiomatic in politics that second only to the need for exposure is the need for money. Indeed, without the latter, achievement of the former is highly doubtful. Campaigns at all levels are prohibitively expensive, and this has placed a premium on the financial friendship of corporate giants, both the successful businessman and the business itself. The financial factor is tremendously important in assessing the role of business in direct political action.

Mass propaganda indulged in by business has been both widespread and effective. Business has been one of the oldest practitioners of "institutional advertising." Businesses that attempt to mold public opinion often use three basic devices: (1) the corporation is humanized—for instance, by referring to the "members of the Inland Steel Family"—dispelling any idea that the sixth largest steel producer in the United States might have bureaucratic characteristics; (2) the corporation is localized by describing neighbors as stockholders and hometown businesses as suppliers—A.T. & T. is a "hometown business"; (3) the corporation implies that there is a complete community of interests between large and small business. It is a fundamental dogma of the national Chamber of Commerce that it effectively represents all business regardless of size. Principal contributors to the Small Business Economic Foundation include some of the largest national corporations. These efforts make big business appear as the ally of the small businessman, and, by extension, the promoter of individual initiative, and all that's good in American life. The fact that business and its aims are almost above reproach in the mind of the average American is due, in no small measure, to the image big business has projected of itself.

Direct involvement in political campaigns by business is considerably circumscribed by law. Still the areas in which a corporation may legally act are many. Corporate activities may involve: (1) sponsoring educational courses in politics and economics; (2) taking part in registration and get-out-the-vote drives; (3) discussion meetings, publication of house organs of political opinion; (4) publication of a congressman's voting record; (5) letters to employees urging them to vote for a particular candidate and encouraging employees to run for office. Most small businesses do not engage in any of these activities; big businesses participate in almost all. The small companies' reluctance to engage in legitimate political activity puts them at an even greater disadvantage than their relative size would indicate. Businesses of all sizes and types have an important role to play in the political struggle and in the influencing of public policy that is important to their future.

GOVERNMENT REGULATION OF BUSINESS

There are seven recognized purposes behind government regulation of economic enterprise: (1) maintenance of competition; (2) prevention of the "curse of bigness"; (3) protection of labor; (4) protection of the consumer; (5) protection of the investor; (6) promotion of economic enterprise; and (7) promotion of social justice and the "good life." Around these purposes has been developed a complex and efficient network of regulations in five key areas: (1) transportation, communication, and other public utilities; (2) mining, crude petroleum, and gas; (3) agriculture, forestry, and fishing; (4) banking and insurance; (5) food, drugs, and cosmetics. [3]

Government regulatory practices have been based upon the premise that through regulation, economic enterprise, honestly performed, would be promoted and assisted in its development.

Almost all of the states now prohibit combinations in restraint of trade, whether such a combination takes the form of pool, trust, association, partnership, holding company, or otherwise. Usually the state prohibition is statutory, though some states have included the provisions in their constitutions. The state antitrust laws have been partially successful in preventing purely local combinations. They have had little effect on large corporations which operate across state boundaries or on pooling agreements of nation-wide scope.

Price legislation is more effective on the state level than are antitrust laws. Price legislation is designed principally to control the growth of chain stores and to protect independent retailers. State unfair practices acts prohibit sales by retailers below cost. State fair practices acts permit manufacturers to prescribe minimum prices at which their products may be sold to consumers. In other words, they make legal the practice of resale-price maintenance.

The most important economic regulations, however, have originated at the national level, mostly in the form of antitrust laws. Because of the rapid growth of big business and the inability of the common law and state legislation to curb concentrations of economic power and its abuses, the federal government enacted certain laws to preserve free competition. The most important of these is the Sherman Antitrust Act of 1890, which has come to be regarded as the country's economic constitution, an expression of national faith in competitive free enterprise. With respect to activities affecting interstate and foreign commerce, the Sherman Act prohibits two broadly phrased practices: (1) contracts, combinations, and conspiracies in restraint of trade, and (2) monopolization and attempts and conspiracies to monopolize.

The proscription of various agreements in restraint of trade was judicially restricted in 1911 to *unreasonable* restraint of trade. Under this "rule of reason," the burden was placed on the party attacking a restrictive practice to prove that its detrimental effects upon competition outweighed the business justification supporting the practices.

This dilution of the first of the Sherman Act's prohibitions was countered by three developments. Congress responded in 1914 with the Clayton Act which applied more stringent standards to certain kinds of practices—exclusive dealing arrangements, contracts tying the sale of one product to another, and discriminatory price-fixing. In the same year Congress created the Federal Trade Commission and authorized it to forbid "unfair" competitive practices. The courts, operating within the rule of reason, defined several categories of particularly obnoxious restraints as unreasonable per se—unlawful without regard to their merits or demerits in the particular case. Practices thus condemned include agreements among different firms fixing prices or dividing markets, group boycotts, and the use of patent rights to gain advantages with respect to unpatented articles. The trend is toward expansion of the categories illegal per se and contraction of areas in which practices must be shown to be unreasonable in their particular economic setting.

The second of the Sherman Act's prohibitions—directed at monopolization—was used principally to challenge concentrations of power in a *single* business organization. Where a single firm achieved such dominance that it had control of more than 65 percent of a recognized industry or market, a charge of monopolization might be prosecuted, although not always successfully. But where dominance rested in several firms—the situation described as oligopoly—the charge of monopolization could not be sustained. And under the rule of reason, the courts generally refused to find that merger agreements and other transactions leading to oligopolistic concentration constituted unreasonable restraint of trade.

In the Clayton Act Congress took further action in the area of monplies. The Sherman Act had provided for punishment of monopolistic practices; the Clayton Act attempted to prevent them. It sought to curtail holding companies, interlocking directorates, and other business concentrations, which were new threats to free competition since the enactment of the Sherman Act. The Act specifically prohibited price discrimination, the acquisition of stock by one company in another, interlocking directorates where the aggregate capitalization was a million dollars or more, and contracts which prevented purchasers from dealing with the seller's competitors.

Important modifications of the Sherman Act in respect to labor and agricultural organizations were also provided. The antitrust legislation was not to be construed as forbidding the existence or operation of labor unions and agricultural associations, nor were such organizations to be construed as illegal combinations in restraint of trade. It also limited the use of the injunction in labor disputes and legalized strikes, picketing, and boycotts under federal jurisdiction.

Other acts were passed which are not antitrust legislation but nonetheless affect business directly. The Securities Acts of 1933 and 1934 require the registration of all securities sold or exchanged through interstate commerce with the Securities Exchange Commission. The Public Utility Holding Company Act of 1935 was designed to correct numerous abuses which had been practiced by utilities[11] during the period preceding the depression, and which had been ex-

[11] A public utility is a business "affected with a public interest," usually because it provides an indispensable service to the public in the absence of economically justifiable competition. Since normal competition cannot be used to regulate rates and services, the business is subject to governmental regulation to insure continuance of adequate service, fair and reasonable rates, and a fair return to investors. Utilities, then, are publicly regulated monopolies.

posed by investigations and reports of the Federal Trade Commission between 1929 and 1935. This law prohibits holding companies from purchasing and/or issuing securities without the consent of the Securities Exchange Commission. Also, the entire holding company system was to be simplified. The Chandler Act of 1938 increased the authority of the Securities Exchange Commission by requiring that corporate reorganization plans be submitted to the courts and the Commission for approval. The Investment Company Act of 1940 put the investment companies under the control of the Securities Exchange Commission.

Other legislation, such as the Pure Food and Drug Act and the Meat Inspection Act, became necessary when producers flooded the markets with food products, drinks, and drugs which were adulterated. These practices were induced by the desire of manufacturers to increase their profits and resulted in wholesale frauds upon the public which had unwittingly bought inferior articles labeled as goods of standard quality. They also involved a serious menace to public health, inasmuch as food products and drugs, particularly meat, were sold which were impure, diseased, or otherwise unfit for consumption. State regulation, though fairly extensive, was not wholly effective, primarily because of the interstate nature of commerce in such products. In 1906 the Pure Food and Drug Act and Meat Inspection Act were enacted. The former provided for a Pure Food and Drug Administration to insure the public healthful foods and to prevent false advertising. The Meat Inspection Act insured the public of safe and disease-free meat by requiring that all meat products be inspected before being sold on the market.

Regulatory acts of both the state and federal levels, therefore, are numerous. [14] They have evolved from the desire to insure the economic stability and growth of the nation and to protect both business and individuals. Along with the regulatory acts have come the independent regulatory agencies for their administration and enforcement. The "Big Six" regulatory commissions are the Federal Communications Commission (FCC), the Civil Aeronautics Board (CAB), the Federal Power Commission (FPC), the Federal Trade Commission (FTC), the Interstate Commerce Commission, (ICC), and the Securities and Exchange Commission (SEC). [22]

The activities of the Federal Trade Commission have become particularly noteworthy since, in team with the Justice Department, it has undertaken action seemingly inconsistent with the Johnson Administration's attempt to woo and win the support of the business community. Many businessmen are protesting a rash of charges and complaints issued from the Justice Department and the FTC which appear to them to be a stepped-up attack by the government "trust-busters." Some of the biggest names in industry have been involved: most of the leading steel producers, the aluminum companies, chemical and petroleum firms, and the auto industry. According to federal officials, the increase in antitrust activity is justified by evidence of a trend toward monopoly in many types of business.

Looking ahead, businessmen have every reason to expect more trouble from the antitrust agencies. Investigations are continuing in many areas, especially foods, chemicals, paper, petroleum, iron and steel, electrical and non-electrical machinery, and the auto industry. Business leaders have thus far refrained from blaming the president for the trustbusting assault, and have, instead, directed their protests against the officials of the antitrust agencies.

It would seem, therefore, that the future relationship between government and business depends upon which of the following factors predominates: (1) the anti-big business activities of the Justice Department and the Federal Trade Commission, or (2) the pro-big business policies, proposals, and programs of the president and Congress.

In opposition to the anti-monopolists, economist John Kenneth Galbraith supports oligopolies, contending that the nature of the competition they stimulate is more realistic than the old-style competition derived from laissez-faire free enterprise which is no longer characteristic of the American economy. The doctrine of countervailing power asserts

. . . that competition, of sellers against sellers and of buyers against buyers, had indeed ceased to be the main regulatory process by which prices were set and resources allocated in the economy. Instead, huge producer aggregates of economic power, such as the United States Steel Corporation, were confronted by other consumer aggregates of economic power, such as the General Motors Corporation, in the pricing process for steel.[12]

This conception of competition between oligopolies assumes that "the driving force of our economic life is now large business; no amount of nostalgia for the good old days can change that fact.'[13] In the traditional sense countervailing power does not reflect competition, but neither is it characteristic of monopoly. However, if we accept Lilienthal's contention that big business is the heart of our economy, and Galbraith's contention that oligopoly automatically begets countervailing power,[14] then the net results serve to regulate business without the necessity of government intervention.

In order to exercise countervailing power successfully, sellers and buyers must be prevented from combining to such an extent that monopoly results:

The power exerted by large buyers will vary directly with the numbers of the sellers with whom they deal. The more numerous the sellers, the better is the chance that one can be played off against another and a better price obtained.[15]

As long as equality is maintained between the strengths of the buyer and the seller, the theory of countervailing power can exist without control as a benefit to the consumer.

This discussion of attempts to regulate big business enterprise in the interest of maximum welfare to both business itself and the public-at-large, and the concern for countervailing power raises the idea that the development of public policy is the end product of a conflict for power between those interested in the outcome of policy decisions. Application of the analysis presented in Chapter 3, "The Political Process," to the problems of regulation of business

[12] Calvin B. Hoover, *The Economic Liberty and the State* (New York: Doubleday, 1961), p. 242.

[13] David E. Lilienthal, *Big Business: A New Era* (New York: Harper, 1953), p. 6.

[14] John Kenneth Galbraith, *American Capitalism* (Boston: Houghton-Mifflin, 1952), pp. 134–135.

[15] Claire Wilcox, *Public Policies Toward Business* (Homewood, Ill.: Richard P. Irwin, 1960), p. 316.

should contribute materially to better understanding of the relationships between free enterprise, government control, and democratic processes which make up our mixed economy.

THE SPECIAL PROBLEM OF AGRICULTURE

The farm and the city have never been closer. In this age of specialization, each depends on the other. [19, 26] The city worker expects the farmer to provide basic raw materials and food for his consumption, and the farmer, in turn, expects the continuance of the urban dweller's historical role as a consumer of farm products. If continued indefinitely, this supplier-consumer relationship would exhibit parallel growth without either becoming more or less dependent on the other. Such has not been the case, however. The relationship between rural and urban life has been convergent, and the farmer has become increasingly dependent on the city for his livelihood.

The subsidization of the farmer by the urban population has been a source of much controversy in the twentieth century. It arose both from the urbanite's need for farm products and the long-standing tradition of the farmer's integral place in American life. This management of farm economy has been attacked by many critics as "socialistic" and "un-American." In fact, however, concern for the farmer far antedates socialism in the American tradition and, in fact, has been evident since the meeting of the First Congress in 1789, if not since the passage of the Northwest Ordinance in 1787.

Much of the present farm program came into existence at a time when agriculture was near bankruptcy during the depression of the 1930's. "It embodies efforts to maintain prices at which farm commodities should sell sufficient to maintain agriculture in a reasonable income relationship with other segments of the economy."[16] In 1929, under the Hoover Administration the Federal Farm Board was set up. Subsequently, under various other agencies the government has increased its intervention in the "natural laws of supply and demand" as they pertain to farming. In order to increase and stabilize farm income, rigid controls were instituted to prevent overproduction of farm products.

It seems evident, therefore, that the concept of government involvement in agriculture is in no way foreign to traditional American principles. But the fact that present policy conforms to the general standards within which our body politic can legitimately operate is not enough to justify its retention. Has it been effective? How does it relate to the problems as they exist? What are the alternatives available? These are the questions we must ask in any discussion of the relative merits of contemporary farm policy.

The importance of agriculture's continued viability is great. Despite a rapidly diminishing farm population, the secondary effects of farm problems are inevitably reflected throughout the nation—through increased migration to the cities, higher prices for food, higher taxes for rural relief, loss of farm purchasing power and diminishing consumer demands for other goods, and unemployment. "In the long view, the interests of our country, as well as our primary goal

---

[16] Committee on Agriculture, U. S. House of Representatives, "Government Subsidy—Historical Review," 86th Cong. 2nd Sess., May 10, 1960, p. 5.

of individual betterment, demand that these maladjustments be adjusted and that this lagging sector of our economy be restored to a dynamic place in our national life."[17]

ROOTS OF AGRICULTURAL DISCONTENT

"Agriculture is in trouble, faced by the same nagging surpluses and low net income that have plagued farmers for the last four decades."[18] In the years since World War I, the technological revolution that rearranged the means of industrial production has radically affected agriculture. We are not faced so much with scarcity as with surplus; and this in spite of significant successes in reducing surpluses in recent years by increased shipment of agricultural products overseas in the form of aid, massive sales by Canada and Australia to the USSR and Red China allowing U. S. products larger overseas markets, and domestic policies providing subsidies for conservation and non-production. This is the basis of the farm problem: farmers can produce more than can be sold at a price sufficient to provide a farm income comparable to that of other economic groups in our society. Low prices, caused by an excess supply, invite additional production in order to supplement income, which in turn aggravates the oversupply.

The problem of surplus production has existed in one form or another since the 1930's. Up to that time, however, the growth of agricultural production had followed a normal arithmetical rate of progression. Surplus existed, but it was primarily due to an inability to get the food to the consumer rather than a lack of demand. The high price supports of World War II provided a catalyst for increased production that exceeded the normal demand schedule. At the end of the war, production remained constant while demand decreased. Perhaps the term constant is inaccurate, for if production had remained stable the current agricultural crisis would have been easily resolved. A fixed production lends itself to planned disposal. The greatly magnified problem facing agriculture is that a lessened demand has been accentuated by ever-increasing production.

The basis of farm surplus has been uncontrolled output. Individual farms are so numerous (approximately four million) that they cannot act together to control production. With fixed resources of labor and land, each farmer seeks to increase income by operating at full capacity. In other industries differing circumstances induce firms to operate at varying levels of production, thereby promoting a market stability that agriculture lacks. Steel or automobile manufacturers would never operate at full capacity at all times, regardless of market conditions, yet this is exactly what farmers normally do.

The second basic problem facing the farmer is that of declining income. Even as production has increased at an exponential rate, per capita income has declined. On the surface it would seem that a shrinking rural population (over one million in the last decade) would encourage larger individual shares from the "revenue pool" for those remaining on the farm. This has *not* been the case. The

[17] Rockefeller Panel, *Prospects for America* (New York: Doubleday, 1961), p. 297.
[18] The American Assembly, *Goals for Americans* (Englewood Cliffs, N.J.: Prentice-Hall 1960), p. 207.

decline in farm population has not been sufficient to cope with the decline in prices. There are two basic reasons for the income decline: less demand and higher costs of production.

A third problem, although perhaps more properly a corollary of declining income, has been rural poverty.[19] Many poor farms have not shared in technological growth, nor have they been aided by price supports. Many small, mainly southern, farm units are so tiny that income is always low regardless of the market fluctuations. Since for these farmers rural life offers neither a decent standard of living nor a viable occupation, it is often proposed that such farmers be retrained for urban employment. The problem of surplus production receives much attention, but the problem of surplus population is sometimes overlooked. Regardless of the alternative chosen to alleviate the lot of almost two million poor farmers, the solution to rural poverty is not a farm problem. It is a problem for the nation as a whole.

In November 1959, President Eisenhower and Secretary of Agriculture Ezra Taft Benson agreed that five steps were needed to improve the farm situation: (1) a bigger conservation program, (2) more research to find new markets and new uses for farm products, (3) increased use of surpluses in the Food for Peace Program, (4) a larger program of assistance to rural areas, and (5) a better price support program. Price support levels were to be realistically related to production controls and to be set at levels that would not "stimulate still more population," nor reduce domestic markets or increase subsidies required to hold world outlets. Since 1960, three of the above steps have been taken: Food for Peace, rural development, and a research program.

The five steps proposed by Eisenhower and Benson in 1959 were to become the five major areas that both Presidents Kennedy and Johnson were to stress in their agricultural programs, with emphasis on conservation and rural development. Both men hoped to be able to employ a more stringent supply management program in order to increase sharply government controls over production, keeping farm prices high by preventing oversupply.

Present policy assumes that farm income can be maintained at a high level if a carefully scheduled program of surplus liquidation can be carried out. This can take place only if farm production is limited for several years to less than market demand, thereby enabling the government to sell its stored surpluses[20] and return to a better balance between farm production and market demand. In contrast to President Eisenhower, who had stressed a free market, Presidents Kennedy and Johnson wanted more government control on production and conversion of surplus land to conservation projects and recreational facilities for a growing urban community.

THE FUTURE OF AGRICULTURE?

As we look forward to the years ahead, what are the choices in agricultural policy? What short-term and long-range goals should we seek?

---

[19] "U.S. Farm Policy," *Editorial Research Reports,* November 1955, p. 782.
[20] Under programs existing for many years government agencies under specified circumstances obtain title to certain surplus crops to keep them off the market.

The long-range goals must fulfill two basic tasks. First, we must maintain a strong and progressive agricultural segment of the economy. Secondly, there must be equalization of rural income with that earned for equivalent labor in urban areas.

The National Agricultural Advisory Commission has recommended to the president, and he has in turn recommended to Congress, that the following objectives guide future farm policy: (1) an abundant supply of quality food and other farm products at reasonable prices; (2) a level of farm income enabling efficient producers to earn returns on their labor and investment comparable with returns realized outside agriculture; (3) democratic procedures in making and executing farm policy, together with maximum freedom for individual farm operators within the limits of farm programs; (4) consistency with other national policies of the United States; (5) maintenance of the family farm structure of agriculture; and (6) maintenance of adequate reserves of farm products.[21]

The problem of agriculture, of course, is only one part of the much larger issue—the extent and nature of governmental intervention in the economy. This intervention has been justified in a broad sense by the interdependent nature of our economy. A failure in one segment of the economy, such as agriculture, sooner or later affects the rest. Whether the government restrains or permits the concentration of economic power of any one group directly affects the prosperity of every other group in the economy.

Specific justification for governmental intervention has been found in the commerce clause of the Constitution delegating such authority to Congress. The Supreme Court has consistently sustained the government's power under the commerce clause to institute a program for the control and regulation of agriculture. Once one has justified the role of the government in agriculture, both theoretically and pragmatically, the question then arises: has this intervention been successful? Have surpluses been visibly reduced by such programs? Have government-stored commodities been a boon or a detriment to the free market? Critics of governmental intervention can point to the ever-increasing surpluses as evidence of failure, but, on the other hand, how much worse might the situation today have been had there been no controls?

American agriculture is a diverse industry, and it has become evident that no one method of stabilization will work for all parts of it. A dogmatic approach is thus doomed to failure—be it a strict free market approach or a strict supply-management approach. To develop useful public policy on the special problems of agriculture remains one of the major challenges to American democratic processes today.

The three selections reprinted below elaborate, in depth and detail, some of the issues discussed in this chapter. The selection by Heilbroner ("The Worldly Philosophers") is a summary of Keynesian economics and its relationship to post-depression America. Ferry ("The Economy Under Law") poses as the central issue of the immediate future the question of the role and responsibility of government within the context of today's technological world. Berle

[21] The American Assembly, *Goals for Americans, op. cit.*, pp. 214–216.

("Property, Production and Revolution"), a leading scholar in the field of democracy in its relation to the corporation and business world, discusses much the same subject, with particular emphasis on the interrelationship of property, production, and revolution.

The Worldly Philosophers

ROBERT L. HEILBRONER

An economist and journalist of note, Robert Heilbroner has written many articles on economics and social affairs which have appeared in leading American journals. Many students know him through his very popular work, The Worldly Philosophers.

Dramatic as it was, it was not the wild decline of the stock market which most damaged the faith of a generation firmly wedded to the conviction of never-ending prosperity. It was what happened at home. A few items from those dreary years may serve to illustrate. In Muncie, Indiana—the city made famous by its selection as "Middletown"—*every fourth factory worker lost his job by the end of 1930.* In Chicago the majority of working girls were earning less than twenty-five cents an hour and a quarter of them made less than ten cents. In New York's Bowery alone, two thousand jobless crowded into breadlines every day. In the nation as a whole, residential construction fell. Eighty-five thousand businesses failed. The national volume of salaries dwindled forty per cent; dividends fifty-six per cent; wages sixty per cent.

And the worst of it, the most depressing aspect of the Great Depression, was that there seemed to be no end to it, no turning point, no relief. In 1930 the nation manfully whistled "Happy Days Are Here Again," but the national income precipitously fell from $87 billions to $75 billions. In 1931 the country sang "I've Got Five Dollars"; meanwhile its income plummeted to $59 billions. In 1932 the song was grimmer: "Brother Can You Spare a Dime?"—national income had reached an incredible $42 billions.

By 1933 the nation was virtually prostrate. The income of the country was down to $39 billions. Over half the prosperity of only four years back had vanished without a trace; the average standard of living was back where it had been twenty years before. On street corners, in homes, in Hoovervilles, 14 million unemployed sat, haunting the land. It seemed as if the proud spirit of hope had been permanently crushed out of America.

It was the unemployment that was hardest to bear. The jobless millions were like an embolism in the nation's vital circulation; and while their indisputable existence argued more forcibly than any text that something was wrong with the system, the economists wrung their hands and racked their brains and called upon the spirit of Adam Smith, but could offer neither diagnosis nor remedy. Unemployment—this kind of unemployment—was simply not listed among the possible ills of the system: It was absurd, impossible, unreasonable, and paradoxical. But it was there. . . .

The trouble is so important—so central to the problem of depression—that we must take a moment to make it clear.

We must start out by understanding how we measure the prosperity of a nation. It is not by its gold—poverty-stricken India is rich in gold. Nor is it by its physical assets—buildings, mines, factories, and forests did not evaporate in 1932. Prosperity and depression are not so much matters of past glories but of present accomplishments; therefore they are measured by the *incomes* that we earn. When most of us individually (and therefore most of us collectively) enjoy high incomes, the nation is well off; when our total individual (or national) income drops, we are in depression.

But income—national income—is not a static concept. Indeed, the central characteristc of an economy is the *flow* of incomes from hand to hand. With every purchase that we make, we transfer a part of our incomes into someone else's pocket. Similarly every penny of our own incomes, be it wages, salaries, rents, profits, or interest, ultimately derives from money which someone else has spent. Consider any portion of the income which you enjoy and it will be clear that it has originated from someone else's pocket: when he engaged your services, or patronized your store, or helped maintain the corporation in which you own bonds or stock.

It is by this process of handing money around—taking in each other's wash, it has been described—that the economy is constantly revitalized.

Now to a large extent this process of handing income around takes place quite naturally and without hindrance. All of us spend the bulk of our incomes on goods for our own use and enjoyment— on consumption goods, so-called—and since we go on buying consumption goods with fairly consistent regularity, the handing around of a large portion of our national income is assured. The fact that we must eat and clothe ourselves, and that we crave enjoyment, ensures a regular and steady spending on the part of all of us, and thus further ensures a regular and steady receiving on the part of others.

So far everything is quite simple and direct. But there is one portion of our incomes which does *not* go directly out onto the market place to become another's income: that is the money we save.

If we tucked our savings into mattresses or hoarded them in cash, we should obviously disturb the evenness of the circular flow of income. For then we should be simply freezing some part of the income stream that was handed to us, and returning to society less than it gave to us. If such a freezing process were wide-spread and continued, there would soon be a cumulative fall in everybody's money income, as less and less was handed around at each turn. We should be suffering from a depression.

But this dangerous break in the income flow does not in fact take place. For in a civilized community we do not freeze our savings. We put them into stocks or bonds or banks and in this way make it possible for them to be used again. Thus, if we buy new stock we give our savings directly to business; if we put our savings in a bank, they can be used on loan by businessmen who seek capital. Whether we bank our savings or use them to buy insurance or securities, the channels exist for those savings to go back into circulation via the activities of business. For when our savings are taken up and spent by business, they again turn up as someone's wages, someone's salary, or someone's profit.

But—and notice this vital fact—there is nothing *automatic* about this savings-investment channel. Business does not ordinarily need savings to carry on its operations; it works within its regular budget and pays its expenses from the proceeds of its sales. Business only needs savings if it is *expanding* its operation— for its regular receipts will not usually provide it with enough capital to build a new factory or to add substantially to its equipment.

And here is where the trouble enters. A thrifty community will always attempt to save some part of its income. But business is not always in a position to expand its operations. To take an obvious case, it is apparent that the days of great expansion for the radio industry— as contrasted with the television industry —are pretty much a thing of the past. Now *if*—for reasons we must look into later—all industry is in the position of the radio industry, then obviously investment will be very small.

And therein lies the possibility of depression. *For if our savings do not become invested by expanding business firms, our incomes must decline.* We should be in the same spiral of contraction as if we had frozen our savings by hoarding them.

Can such an eventuality come to pass?

We shall see. But note meanwhile that this is a strange and passionless tug of war. Here are no greedy landlords, no avaricious capitalists. There are only perfectly virtuous citizens prudently attempting to save some of their incomes, and perfectly virtuous businessmen who are just as prudently making up their minds whether the business situation warrants taking the risk of buying a new machine or building a new plant. And yet, on the outcome of those two sensible decisions the fate of the economy hangs. For if the decisions are out of joint— if businessmen invest less than the community tries to save, for example—then the whole economy will have to readjust to the crimp of depression. The enormous question of boom or slump depends —more than on anything else—on this. . . .

For the seesaw theory of savings and investment failed at one central point: it did not explain how an economy could *remain* in a state of prolonged depression. Indeed, as the very analogy of the seesaw indicates, it seemed as if an economy which was weighted down by surplus savings must, in fairly short order, right itself and swing the other way.

For savings and investment—Thrift and Enterprise—were not utterly unconnected economic activities. On the contrary, they were tied together in the market where businessmen "bought" savings—or at least borrowed them: the money market. Savings, like any other commodity, had its price: the rate of interest. Therefore (so it seemed), at the bottom of a slump when there was a flood of savings, its price should decline —exactly as when there was a glut of shoes, the price of shoes declined. And as the price of savings cheapened—as the rate of interest went down—the *incentive* to invest appeared very likely to increase: if a new factory was too expensive to build when the money for it would cost six per cent, might it not look much more profitable when money could be had for a payment of only three per cent?

Hence the seesaw theory seemed to promise that there would be an automatic safety switch built right into the business cycle itself; that when savings became too abundant, they would become cheaper to borrow, and that there-

by business would be encouraged to invest. The economy might contract, said the theory, but it seemed certain to rebound.

But that was exactly what failed to happen in the Great Depression. The rate of interest declined, but nothing happened. The old nostrums were trotted out—a pinch of local relief and a large dose of hopeful waiting—and still the patient failed to improve. For all its intellectual elegance, something was patently missing from the neat formulation of the swing of savings and investment with the rate of interest always hovering over the seesaw to see that it was kept in motion. Something else must be holding the economy back. . . .

[Keynes] had a startling and dismaying conclusion. There was no automatic safety mechanism after all! Rather than a seesaw which would always right itself, the economy resembled an elevator: it could be going up or down, but it could also be standing perfectly still. And it was just as capable of standing still on the ground floor as at the top of the shaft. A depression, in other words, might not cure itself at all; the economy could lie prostrate indefinitely, like a ship becalmed.

But how could this be? Would not the flood of savings at the bottom of the slump push down the rate of interest, and would this not in turn interest business in the possibility of using cheap money to expand its plant?

Keynes found the solution to the problem in the simplest and most obvious (once it had been pointed out) fact of economic life: *there would be no flood of savings at the bottom of the trough.* For what happened when an economy went into an economic tailspin was that its income contracted, and what happened as its income contracted was that its savings were squeezed out. How could a community be expected to save as much when everyone was hard up as when everyone was prosperous, asked Keynes. Quite obviously, it could not. The result of a depression would not be a glut of savings, but a drying-up of savings; not a flood of saving, but a trickle.

And so it was, in fact. In 1929 the American private citizenry put aside $3.7

billions out of its income; by 1932 and 1933 it was saving *nothing*—in fact it was even drawing down its old savings made in the years before. Corporations, which had tucked away $2.6 billions at the top of the boom *after* paying out taxes and dividends, found themselves losing nearly $6 billions three years later. Quite obviously Keynes was right: saving was a kind of luxury which could not withstand hard times.

But the practical consequence of that decline in saving was more portentous than the individual tragedies which accompanied it. It resulted in a paralyzing situation where the economy was in perfect *economic* balance, even though it was in the throes of social agony. For if there was *no* surplus of savings, there would be *no* pressure on interest rates to encourage businessmen to borrow. And if there was *no* surplus of investment (and the very essense of depression, as we have seen, is that investment is not large enough), then there would be *no* impetus for expansion. The economy would not budge an inch.

Thus the paradox of poverty amidst plenty and the anomaly of idle men and idle machines. To be sure, at the bottom of a slump there is a heartless contradiction between a crying need for goods and an insufficiency of production. But the contradiction is purely a moral one. For the economy does not operate to satisfy human *wants*—wants are always as large as dreams. It turns out goods to satisfy *demand*—and demand is as small as a person's pocketbook. Hence the unemployed are little more than economic zeros; they might as well be on the moon for all the economic influence they exert on the market place.

Once investment has declined and the economy has shrunk in size, social misery appears. But not—as Keynes points out—*effective* social misery: the nation's conscience will not do as an effective subsitute for enough investment. And since savings decline along with investment, the economic machine turns over evenly, quite unperturbed by the fact that it is a smaller machine than it used to be.

A peculiar state of affairs, indeed; a tragedy without a villain. No one can blame society for saving, when saving is so apparently a private virtue; it is equally impossible to chastise businessmen for not investing when no one would be so happy to comply as they—if they saw a reasonable chance for success. No, the difficulty is no longer a moral one; this is no question of justice, exploitation, or even human foolishness. It is a technical difficulty, almost a mechanical fault. But its price is no less high for all of that. For the price of inactivity is unemployment.

But worse follows. Keynes had explained how an economy in the trough of depression could fail to generate its own automatic recovery. That was gloomy enough. But when you turned the Keynesian proposition around, it spelled trouble at the top of the business cycle as well.

For just as savings contracted when the economy contracted, so they would expand when the economy expanded. And that simple fact had a frightening consequence: it meant that *every boom was constantly threatened with collapse.* For if at any time investment slowed down, the nation's swollen savings would again exert the upper hand; the chain of handing around incomes would be broken, and the process of contraction would begin.

Hence in the final analysis, the economy hung on the amount of investment which business carried out. When investment was low, the economy shrank in size; when investment was high, it pulled the nation up with it; if investment failed to *remain* high, it permitted the cycle of contraction to begin. Riches and poverty, boom and slump, all depended on the willingness of business to invest.

And here was the most indigestible fact of all. That willingness to invest could not go on indefinitely. Sooner or later, investment was *bound* to contract.

For at any time, an industry is limited by the size of the market to which it caters. Let us take the example of the railroads in the 1860's—a time of vast investment in new railroad lines. The early railway magnates were not building for the markets of 1950; had they proceeded to lay the trackage the economy would need ninety years hence, they would have been building lines to nonexistent cities in uninhabited territory. So they built what could be used—and then they stopped. Similarly with the auto industry. Even if Henry Ford had been able to find the capital to build the present-day River Rouge plant in 1910, he would have gone bankrupt in a hurry: the roads, the gas stations, the *demand* for that many cars was simply lacking. Or to bring the matter to the present, the country's utility plants are now spending $4 billions a year to add to their capacity; but they cannot spend $40 or even $14 billions—although someday they may have to. Today no one could use *that* much power.

Not only is investment limited in size, but it proceeds in spurts. You cannot build a railway line mile by mile to keep pace with demand: you build one entire line at a time. You cannot enlarge an auto plant piecemeal beyond a certain size: then you must build an entirely new plant. And having built that line, having constructed that plant, you have satisfied the market for a time. You cease investing.

Ancient Egypt [wrote Keynes] was doubly fortunate and doubtless owed to this its fabled wealth, in that it possessed *two* activities, namely pyramid-building and the search for the precious metals, the fruits of which, since they could not serve the needs of man by being consumed, did not stale with abundance. The Middle Ages built cathedrals and sang dirges. Two pyramids, two masses for the dead are twice as good as one; but not so two railways from London to York.

And so investment typically has its pattern: at first eagerness to take advantage of a new opportunity; then caution lest enthusiasm lead to overbuilding; then inactivity when the market has been satisfied for the time being.

If, as each separate investment project came to a halt, another immediately appeared, there need never be a slump. But such is not likely to be the case. The mere fact that human wants are vast does not mean that *any* investment will pay for itself: the economy is littered with businesses which have died of rash and foolhardy overexpansion. No, most investment needs more than the stimulus of sanguine expectations; it needs something

more concrete: some new invention, some better way of doing things, some intriguing product to catch the public eye. And such opportunities, as any businessman will tell you, are not always there.

Hence when one investment project dies, there may not be another ready to step into the breach. If there is—if investment maintains its size, although it changes its complexion—the economy will sail smoothly along. But if there is no ready substitute for each investment casualty, the pressure of savings will make itself felt and contraction will begin. And needless to say, investment does not thrive in such a dwindling market.

All this was the gloomy diagnosis of *The General Theory.*

First, that an economy in depression might well stay there; there was nothing inherent in the situation to pull it out.

Second, that prosperity depended on investment; for if savings were not put to use, the dread spiral of contraction began.

And third, that investment was an undependable drive wheel for the economy; through no fault of the businessman it was constantly threatened with satiety, and satiety spelled economic shrinkage.

In a word, the economy lived in the shadow of collapse.

Certainly it was a morbid outlook. But it would have been utterly unlike Keynes the man to content himself with making a diagnosis of gloom and letting it go at that. With all its prophecy of danger, *The General Theory* was never meant to be a book of doom. On the contrary, it held out a promise and it proposed a cure.

As a matter of fact, the cure had begun before its actual prescription was written; the medicine was being applied before the doctors were precisely sure what it was supposed to do. The Hundred Days of the New Deal had enacted a flood of social legislation that had been backing up for twenty years behind a dam of governmental apathy. These laws were meant to improve the social tone, the morale, of a discontented nation. But it was not social legislation which was designed to revitalize the patient. That tonic was something else: the deliberate undertaking of *government* investment.

It began not so much as investment as makeshift work-relief. Unemployment had reached the point at which some sort of action was dictated by pure political necessity—after all, this was a time when there had recently been riots in Dearborn and a ragged march on Washington, when families huddled for warmth in municipal incinerator buildings and even scrabbled for food in garbage trucks. Relief was essential and began under Hoover; then under Roosevelt relief turned into leaf-raking, and leaf-raking turned into constructive enterprise. The government was suddenly a major economic investor itself: roads, dams, auditoriums, airfields, harbors, and housing projects blossomed forth.

Keynes came to Washington in 1934 —this was when he made his notes on the impression of President Roosevelt's hands—and urged that the program be extended further. The satistics showed that the bottom had fallen out of private investment activity: business expansion, which had pumped out $15 billions in wages and salaries and profits in 1929, had fallen to the appalling figure of $886 *millions* in 1932—a drop of ninety-four per cent. Something had to boost the investment end of the seesaw up again, and he hoped that government spending would act as such a stimulus by bolstering the nation's general buying power—"priming the pump" it was called in those days.

Hence when *The General Theory* came out in 1936, what it offered was not so much a new and radical program as a defense of a course of action which was already being applied. A defense and an explanation. For *The General Theory* clearly pointed out that the catastrophe facing America and, indeed, the whole Western World, was only the consequence of a lack of sufficient investment on the part of business. And so the remedy was perfectly logical: if business was not able to expand, the government must take up the slack.

With his tongue only partly in his cheek Keynes had written:

If the Treasury were to fill old bottles with bank notes, bury them at suitable depths in disused coal mines which are then filled up to the surface with town rubbish, and leave it to private enterprise on well tried principles of *laissez-faire* to dig the notes up again . . . there need

be no more unemployment and with the help of the repercussions, the real income of the community would probably become a good deal larger than it is. It would, indeed, be more sensible to build houses and the like; but if there are practical difficulties in the way of doing this, the above would be better than nothing.

To some it no doubt appeared that many of the more unorthodox W.P.A. projects were no more sane than Keynes' whimsical proposal. But now, at least, they had a rationale behind them: if private enterprise found itself unable to carry forward with a big enough program of investment, then the government must fill in as best it could—the need for investment of some sort was so imperative that almost anything was better than nothing.

And if investment could not be directly stimulated, why then, at least consumption could. For while investment was the capricious element in the system, consumption provided the great floor of economic activity; hence the W.P.A. projects were thought to attack the problem with a two-edged sword: by directly helping to sustain the buying power of the otherwise unemployed, and by leading the way for a resumption of private business spending.

Keynes himself in a letter to *The New York Times* in 1934 wrote, "I see the problem of recovery in the following light: How soon will normal business enterprise come to the rescue? On what scale, by which expedients, and for how long is abnormal government expenditure advisable in the meantime?"

Note "abnormal." Keynes did not see the government program as a permanent intereference with the course of business or as anything but a helping hand to a system that had slipped and was struggling to regain its balance.

It seemed the essence of common sense; in fact it was the essence of common sense. And yet the pump-priming program never brought the results that the planners had hoped for. Total government spending, which had hovered at the $10-billion level from 1929 until 1933, rose to $12 billions, to $13 billions, then to $15 billions in 1936. Private investment picked itself up from the floor and recovered two-thirds of its loss: private firms invested $10 billions by 1936. The national income and national consumption rose by fifty per cent after three years of government injections. And yet unemployment lingered on; it was manageable now, but there were still at least 9 million out of work—hardly a mark of a new economic era.

There were two reasons why the cure did not work better. First, the government program of investment was never carried out to the full extent that would have been necessary to bring the economy up to full employment. Later, in the Second World War, government spending rose to the monumental figure of $103 billions: that brought not only full employment, but inflation. But within the framework of a peacetime economy in the thirties, such all-out spending was quite impossible; indeed, even a modest program of government investment soon brought murmurs that Federal power was overstepping its traditional bounds.

The second reason is closely allied with the first. Neither Keynes nor the government spenders had taken into account that the beneficiaries of the new medicine might consider it worse than the disease. Government investment was *meant* as a helping hand for business. It was *interpreted* by business as a threatening gesture.

Nor is this surprising. The New Deal had swept in on a wave of antibusiness sentiment; values and standards that had become virtually sacrosanct were suddenly held up to skeptical scrutiny and criticism. The whole conception of "business rights," "property rights," and the "role of government" was rudely shaken; within a few years business was asked to forget its traditions of unquestioned preeminence and to adopt a new and strange philosophy: cooperation with labor unions, acceptance of new rules and regulations, reform of many of its practices. Little wonder that it regarded the government in Washington as inimical, biased, and downright radical. And no wonder, in such an atmosphere, that its eager-

ness to undertake large-scale investment was dampened by the uneasiness it felt in this new and unfamiliar climate.

Hence every effort of the government to undertake a program of sufficient magnitude to mop up all the unemployed—perhaps a program twice as large as it did in fact undertake—was assailed as further evidence of socialist design. And at the same time, the halfway measures which the government did employ, were just enough to frighten business away from the undertaking of a full-scale effort by itself. It was a situation not unlike that found in medicine; the medicine cured the patient of one illness, only to weaken him with another. Government spending never truly cured the economy—not because it was economically unsound, but because it was ideologically upsetting.

It was not meant to be upsetting; it was a policy born of desperation rather than design. Had the government not begun to open the valve of public investment, eventually private business would surely once again have led the way: it always had in the past, and despite the severity of the Great Depression, it would in time unquestionably have found new avenues of adventure. But it was impossible to wait. The American people had waited for four long years, and they were in no mood to wait much longer. Not only were there disturbances in the land, but there were troubling voices in the air. The voice of Marx rang louder than it ever had in the past; many pointed to the unemployed as prima-facie evidence that Marx was right. The mumble of Veblen was discernible in the faddish vogue of the technocrats who wanted to call out not the proletariat but the engineers. And there was the still more chilling voice that never wearied of pointing out that Hitler and Mussolini knew what to do with *their* unemployed. In this welter of remedies and advocy of desperate action, the voice of *The General Theory*, the gentlemanly tones of Keynes, were certainly moderate and reassuring.

The Economy Under Law

W. H. FERRY

W. H. Ferry is now vice-president at the Center for the Study of Demo-cratic Institutions. He is principally an economist whose writings have appeared in many professional journals.

We are at the beginning of a thorough-going debate on principles of political economy. The central question, now as always, will be the role and responsibility of government. . . .

There is the Hands Off or absolute minimalist point of view, which is not only against further "encroachment" by government but also requires withdrawal of services, such as the Post Office, that it believes can and should be under private operation. Freedom and justice in this scheme are served by the absense of official restraint. They make their way by competition and the process of natural selection. This point of view derives from classical economics, is promoted by a respectable but not very numerous academic group, and profoundly affects all other viewpoints while itself remaining deaf to the arguments of others.

There is what might be called the National Weatherman position that government is to provide the surroundings and climate in which private enterprise can flourish. It takes the well-being of enterprise as a preliminary to any other kind of well-being. This does not prevent approval of government devices or plans designed to "help the business climate"; e.g., tariffs, quotas, subsidies, certain restrictions on production. Otherwise, proponents of this position display what Senator Joseph S. Clark calls an "anti-government fixation."

A third viewpoint is the one roughly denoted by "bumps and grinds" or "countervailing power." It makes government referee as well as participant in the economic game. The government represents some sort of balance among the

Reprinted by permission of the author.

powers and principalities in American life. This, in general, is the historic American way of producing the general welfare and enhancing freedom and justice.

A. A. Berle, Jr., has refined, expanded, and questioned the outlook of the "bumps and grinds" school, especially in his concept of the consensus. The consensus, says Berle, is the conscience of society speaking through an informed elite to those in and out of government who are responsible for the economy. The consensus also is connected by Berle in some as yet undefined way with the "transcendental margin," the extra portion of energy or taste which transforms ordinary accomplishment into extraordinary achievement. The voice of the consensus reminds leaders of their duties. It warns against excesses and calls for official action—law—when excesses are persisted in. It rewards as well as punishes; for example, it approves of the tendency of large corporations (and unions) to "social responsibility." The efficacy of the consensus as an instrument of control, it is argued, is to be seen in the recent development of social responsibility on the part of corporations—the "corporate conscience." With regard to intervention by government, this fourth attitude would say "as little as possible, as much as necessary," and it would place many now-neglected problems under the heading of necessity.

These four viewpoints are well mixed up in today's "conventional wisdom" about the economy, in J. K. Galbraith's useful phrase. Each is a partial description, each claims history and experience in some degree as its authority.

The views put forth in this paper are most closely related to the Berle analysis. They incorporate, for example, the notion of the need that large corporations feel for legitimacy. But the paper moves beyond these issues toward the idea of a political economy based on the purposive use of law, politics, and government on behalf of the common good.

The argument thus departs from Berle on the point of the consensus as general controller of economic affairs. Doubtless the consensus has operated in the past generation much as Berle says it has, as a report card for the behavior of powerful industrial and financial interests, presumably to keep the class in order. But a mere report card for the turbulent years ahead is inadequate in major ways. For one thing, the national economy is more than the sum of private interests. For another, the consensus depends on the awareness of economic developments and corporate behavior by a small but influential group. This awareness today is more and more frustrated by the techniques of public relations. Used by government or corporations or unions, these techniques filter information, and what gets through the filter is not all the news but merely the best of it as those who hold the filter see the best. The consensus is further stultified by the inability or unwillingness of the mass media to make pertinent information available. The reasons the mass media give for this neglect of important economic controversies range from mere lack of space to an indisposition to print dull materials.

Quite apart from these hindrances to the workings of the consensus, there is another powerful argument for departing from Berle. This is the argument that this paper adopts: We have come to the point where the economy can be purposefully ordered to serve the common good. According to this argument, the deep expectations of the consensus can be summoned forth and, by means of law and political invention, can be made explicit and commanding.

To state it another way, we would no longer congratulate ourselves on how well we have done compared with the rest of the world. We would ask how well we could do in articulating the highest aims of a civilized political community and in providing the political and social means for achieving these aims.

Finally, the argument of this paper is based on grounds of urgency, the complete novelty of today's technologized world, and the inevitability of drastic change in all political and economic arrangements as America speeds into a new world order.

The assumptions in the following discussion are these:

The United States is at the beginning of the democratic constitutional experiment, not at its high point or end.

The acceleration in productivity provided by technology will continue through the cold war and beyond it.

Americans expect increasing services and goods, public and private.

Americans see the economy as the main means to social justice and equality, stability and security, and opportunity for the pursuit of happiness.

Basic changes in the economic order can be effected without frustrating or abandoning democratic ideals.

Technology and bureaucracy within a generation will transform present economic practice, theory, dogma, and institutions, whether or not the cold war has been terminated.

THE NEED FOR FRESH STYLES

Since the end of World War II it has been the general but by no means universal opinion that the American economic system works well and, in the main, meets popular expectations. The customary view is that by any measure we are the best-provided of countries. Almost any conceivable good or service may be had, for a price. There is no simmering unrest; the lack of it is the usual complaint of intellectuals. We are told that the nation is prosperous and more settled and content than the cold war warrants. Monopoly is said to be no longer a problem; neither are the money and security markets. A balance of sorts is believed to exist among the largest power centers.

There is persuasive evidence, moreover, that most of the underpinnings of the *status quo* have been made secure. Federal concern for the aged, for maintenance of reasonable levels of employment, for control of depression, and many like activities are irrevocable policies. Unions and corporations are becoming more "soulful" and socially responsible; solicitude has replaced indifference to the problems of employees and others in the corporate family.

Altogether it is a picture of ease and good living, of steady development, and apparent satisfaction with things as they are. At least for the moment we seem to have no need for change in the fundamental arrangements of the economy.

But there are too many new elements in the picture to believe that a self-satisfied "business as usual" attitude can persist:

A swelling population, conscious that it holds citizenship not only in a country but in a world.

Oligarchic control of power, in unions, the media of communication, trade associations, corporations, and scientific development.

Urbanization (more than four-fifths of the country already off the farm and the proportion increasing yearly), with none of the old city-farm problems solved, and new ones besides.

A growing feeling of responsibility for helping out less fortunate nations, propelled by international political competition, if not by conscience.

Technology, already dictating our international relations and dominating our domestic life in ways yet uncomprehended.

The changing character of work, and the rise of leisure.

Bureaucracy, especially in a welfare government occupied more and more with planning and with administration of new services.

The absence of any widely held and systematic theory capable of explaining our economic and technical society, and bewilderment about national aims in general.

An increasingly opulent society, with no criterion for deciding between public needs and private wants.

The progress of the Soviet economy, the spread of non-capitalistic methods for industrializing under-developed economies, and the resulting demolition of Western ideas of inherent superiority.

The need for resolving matters of political economy on a multi-national level.

Finally, the prospect of an economy from which the military machine has been permanently removed: the problem of economic order in a warless world.

Singly and collectively, these factors suggest that so complicated a society demands fresh political styles. Freedom, justice, and the general welfare can no longer be regarded as the accidental benefits or by-products of a political economy. The political economy should be designed to produce them.

THE NOVELTY OF CAPITALISM

One striking feature of American capitalism has been its novelty. Whether looked at against the backdrop of eighteenth century expectations, or turn-of-the-century practices, or developments elsewhere in the world, it presented an utterly new picture. This has been true however one cared to examine it: the proportion of employable people at work, the level and kinds of goods and services, income and consumption, the proliferation of voluntary agencies, the marginal role of poverty, the speed with which basic research has been translated into commercial development, hours of work and

leisure, the relation of power groups to one another.

It has also been remarkable in America that economic activity should now have come to occupy the whole national stage, so to speak, and not merely the most conspicuous place on it: a domination confirmed by "the business of America is business," and by the clamor against governmental intervention. Economic activity has been looked on not as a problem in housekeeping but almost as a theological proposition.

An outstanding and novel characteristic of American life today is generalized irresponsibility. We turn the important decisions over to the experts and retire to our home workshops or television sets. Many people use the Soviet menace as an excuse for political listlessness. Russia is surrogate for national purpose. The deafening debate as to whether we should be able to annihilate the Reds two dozen times over or only a dozen permits us to postpone urgent domestic decisions indefinitely. Labor unions, like corporations, are rich, established, and tormented about where they go from here. Most men, however successful, are not satisfied with their lives. An epidemic of alienation spreads as people feel their own destinies slipping out of their control.

The sense of unease is pervasive, because there seems to be only trifling choices to be made about central issues. Our well-being in a world of want makes us feel guilty, but not guilty enough to make a profound political issue out of it. We ignore poverty and hardship and inequality in our own midst. (As of mid-1959 the poorest one-third of Americans owned 1 per cent of the wealth of the United States. The next 23 per cent up the scale owned 5 per cent. Thus, well over half the population owns 6 per cent of the wealth of the United States. The richest 1.6 per cent own nearly one-third of the country's material assets.) Administrative agencies show signs of wear and misuse, so we lay on a coat of whitewash. Corporations are private governments without any effective politics.

We have not appreciated the significance of our attitude and situation because we are too much part of it. Yet questions are beginning to be asked: Is this all there is to the United States? Is it proper that our best educated and most talented people should devote their lives to supplying goods and services? What shall we think about the vast amount of meaningless effort called for by the present economic scheme? When every trace of poverty has been eliminated and a domestic ranch-wagon and foreign sports car sit in every garage, will national purpose have been accomplished? Since we can only eat and consume so much, what shall we do with what is left over? Why should we not decide on a proper rate of national growth, make plans for achieving it, and see to a reasonable distribution of the result between public and private needs?

It is beginning to be realized, in short, that the present economic arrangements are not part of a divinely ordained scheme which mechanically supplies both the means and the ends of the economic order. A "self-regulating economy" guided by an invisible hand—observably faulty in premise and operation—is economic fatalism, the creed of the affluent, the satisfied. This group is growing smaller as a consensus begins to form that economy-by-accident is not good enough for our complicated domestic and international society.

PUBLIC CONTROL AND PRIVATE DECEPTION

The United States began to ignore the chief injunction of economy-by-accident, "thou shalt not intervene," many years ago. The Welfare State is a late product of the industrial brigandage that followed the Civil War. Populism and the bringing of railroads and the trusts under public control marked its infancy. Today the economy is controlled and directed in ways unrecognized even by those who are most affected. Yet the idea that there are "economic laws" connected remotely but unbreakably with an eternal order still occupies a prominent place in American thought.

This persistent self-deception has often been referred to by A. A. Berle, Jr., J. K. Galbraith, and others. In his most recent book, *Beyond the Welfare State*, Gunnar Myrdal is explicit:

. . . our national economies have become increasingly regulated, organized, and coordinated, i.e., "planned," to an extent nobody would have dreamed of a century, or even half a century, ago . . . this all happened in a piecemeal and almost offhand way . . . governments, parliaments, and the citizenry at large have never made up their minds that this type of society was what they wanted. On the contrary, its gradual emergence through induced changes, all working in the direction of more and more social controls, all requiring an everincreasing degree of planned coordination, has mostly proceeded to the accompaniment of loud proclamations from almost all sides that it was not to happen and that ours was a "free" economy.

. . . these formulae have been the gospel for businessmen and politicians whose daily labor it was to regulate markets and frame new public interventions and also, in more recent times, to participate in the efforts to improve the coordination of all those acts of intervention with one another . . .

. . . in the Western countries people generally tend to keep themselves unaware of how far they have proceeded from a "free" economy: how very much regulatory intervention by organized society there actually is in their countries, and how important national economic planning of a pragmatic, non-comprehensive type has in fact become.

We have come to a juncture where, if we are to keep control of our own destiny, we shall have to direct our political processes deliberately and openly to the rational control of our economic affairs. Preservation of traditional values in our domestic life calls for inventiveness, fresh approaches, and new methods—most of which will have to bring in government in unprecedented ways. The steel strike in 1959 mightily involved the public welfare, and most proposals to keep it from happening again focused on government action. The "personal summitry" of the industry and union leaders and the Vice-President can scarcely be considered a pattern for the future settlement of such issues. Yet the public interest was so involved that both sides recognized the need for some "public" resolution. Automation and such technological advances as chemical or mechanical control of behavior are affected with a public interest, and this means ultimate intervention in one form or other.

The Employment Act of 1946 marks the acceptance of "purposive government" as a respectable doctrine. It is a proclamation that the people collectively hold themselves responsible for the maintenance of high employment. Government cannot any longer play a minimal or negative role even if it wanted to; the immense power of the federal purse would not permit it. The power is there, and it will be used. The move from negative and minimal notions about government to affirmative concepts is in more or less direct relation to the growth of the national budget, and it may be expected to become more pronounced as budgets get larger. Before World War I the budget was a housekeeping account and played no part in the forming and quality of economic life. Government was looked on as a policeman of economic affairs, walking a longer and longer beat as the country expanded, but still a policeman.

As the budget and the nation grew, government began to be perceived in a larger way; and the New Deal and World War II removed forever the image of federal authority as policeman only. The budget today moves into the economy as contracts for billions of dollars' worth of goods and services. These contracts bristle with stipulations about minimum wages, non-discrimination and safety in employment, record-keeping, excessive profits, security, and a host of other matters. Such conditions are usually the result of Congressional mandate, and while they are muttered about in corporate corridors, they are rarely resisted as undue intervention. There is little debate about the right of government to impose standards for the performance of public business.

THE PRIMACY OF POLITICS

The kind of government argued for here asserts the primacy of politics; that is to say, it calls for the use of political rather than private decisions in economic issues that affect the whole country. It denies the sufficiency of classical economic theory. The private corporation is a flexible and efficient means of producing goods and services, but not the only one. Government seen in this light disclaims the absolute autonomy of the market, the necessity for allocation of resources mainly by private decisions, competition and incentive as the only adequate organizers of economic activity, and profit as the only criterion. It recognizes the importance of such ideas in history and their continuing value in wide areas, but it believes that the possibilities in cooperative economic effort and in national planning deserve far more examination than they have received. The Constitution embodies the principle that the people are the repository of power over policies and institutions that touch the entire community. This power can be used whenever needed, democratic direction of economic power can be achieved, and economic activity can thus be rationalized.

The Labor-Management Reporting and Disclosure Act of 1959, requiring public reports and minimal democratic procedures in unions and giving members certain explicit rights, is an example of this tendency in action. This is a move to "constitutionalize" the union, as some people speak of "constitutionalizing" the corporation. The aim is to enhance freedom and justice in a complex society; to use political freedom and democratic techniques and constitutional procedures to decide and carry out economic plans; to create a political community, not to further the ends of an acquisitive society.

The movement is already under way sufficiently so that new law is not so much needed, at least in the initial stages, as coordination of what already exists. The work of such present devices as the Federal Reserve Board, credit authorities, farm and industry subsidies, regulatory and conservation bodies, anti-trust and price statutes, needs to be made more coherent. Myrdal believes with Berle that the effort toward coordination would itself give national planning a great boost toward respectability.

The largest American corporations are the most influential of non-governmental agencies and the largest allocators of resources. Thus, a principal question would center around what devices would be needed to obtain political accountability from the corporation for such matters as:

Decisions about the investment, use, and distribution of goods and services; the allocation of resources, human and material;

The introduction of significant new technology;

Stabilization of production and employment;

The creation of standards of due process for employees and others directly affected by corporate action, and a judicial system to enforce them.

Federal responsibility for the health of the banking system is already established, and few additional steps would be needed to bring the money and credit apparatus into the scheme of government here proposed. In this case, the grounds would be extension of the rationale of "public interest, convenience, and necessity" which is at the heart of utility regulation. There is no law that says transportation, telephone, water, gas, electric, and one or two other services exhaust the idea of public utility.

Government could describe and mark off industries or corporations whose indispensability to the general welfare is beyond dispute. The aim would be accountability, but the pattern would not necessarily be that of utility regulation or regulation by government agency. This is a field virtually untilled by political invention, although Carl Kaysen in an unpublished paper and Bayless Manning in different ways have made a case for turning the most powerful corporations into quasi-utilities.

Decisions affecting the country could be transferred from the corporate conscience via Congress to the public conscience. The argument that this would be unwarranted intervention in technical and "private" matters does not stand up, quite apart from the importance to the public of some of the largest corporations. The principal decisions taken by the enormous corporations are political, or what Richard Eells in *The Meaning of Modern Business* calls "strategic," decisions: e.g., the steel industry's recent decision to "fight inflation," that of the automobile companies to produce heavier, wider, and more powerful cars with resounding effects on highway, parking, and safety programs, decisions to look for oil in the Sudan or to build a new plant in Mississippi. All of these decisions are political in meaning and in results. A company that has 150,000 employees, 300,000 stockholders, and 15,000 suppliers and dealers (and their employees), and that sells to millions of customers, can only by tradition be considered a "private" company. The large company is something new as to size, numbers, and influence. There is little question any more that it is a private government, or semi-sovereign state.

Whatever the shortcomings of the present system may be, it is still an efficient way of raising capital and producing and distributing goods. It will be argued therefore that more accountability by law will mean less efficiency because of bureaucracy and lack of incentive. Yet there is surprisingly little evidence to support either the general bias against government as inefficient or the general presumption in favor of industry as efficient. Several apposite situations may be noted:

The prosperous situation of utilities (railroads perhaps excepted) and the blue-chip standing of their stocks and bonds;

The success of the industries that work in the closest way with government and under the closest supervision, such as the airplane and missile companies;

The record of efficiency of most (not all) new-style public authorities—highway, seaport, valley, airport—in financing, building and operating facilities, and in meeting obligations;

"White collar featherbedding" and other bureaucratic practices in large corporations;

The apparent efficiency of the governmentally controlled Soviet industrial machine.

CONSTITUTIONALIZING THE ECONOMY

Many methods are available for bringing the economic order under political guidance. Once the decision to do so is taken, legislative inventiveness will produce others. For the source of action must be Congress, as the direct instrument of the people. For example, a fourth branch of government might at the instigation of Congress be created by constitutional amendment, charged with initiating measures essentially economic in effect, as the House of Representatives now initiates appropriation measures. This is a drastic idea, and one not likely to appeal to Congress. But it is intended as a reminder of the revolutionary differences between the problems of the First and Eighty-sixth Congresses. Domination of the American scene by a highly industrialized order was scarcely anticipated in the late eighteenth century. Anyone rewriting the Constitution today might well conclude that such imposing power deserves formal representation in government.

A less dramatic form of constitutionalization might be the formation by statute of a commonwealth of corporations, an "association of free, self-governing nations." This would call for federal charters, or "constitutions," which would recognize the autonomy of the member-corporations but charge them collectively with specific powers and responsibilities. An effective judicial process might be erected in such a framework to safeguard the rights of the various constituencies of the member-corporations.

Along some such route might also come the legitimacy that Berle believes the modern corporation is seeking. Establishing a commonwealth or federation of corporations would necessitate, for example, a review of corporate charters. These instruments are now the slenderest of connections between the people as the sovereign authorizers of power and the great corporations as the privileged deployers thereof. If they were transformed into federal charters, or constitutions, they might thereby be re-charged with meaning. Constitutions conferred by the federal government would confer and legitimize powers that corporations are now exercising with doubt and discomfort. The limitations and duties of corporations would be defined. Constitutions would enable the members of a commonwealth of corporations to carry more economic responsibility than they are now carrying, while relieving them of their ungainly social burdens. The biggest and most powerful of corporate organizations might thus, for example, be reminded (and might remind one another) that the resources of the nation are not inexhaustible, and that the general welfare includes that of future generations.

A more modest vision would extend the duties of the government's Council of Economic Advisers into planning and coordination of existing agencies and means. Changing the Council from its present appointive, expert, and partisan character into a representative political body (perhaps to be elected on a regional basis) might in time be done.

Some of the institutional innovations of the cold war might be taken as models for the coordination and enforcement of national economic policies. Counterparts of such agencies as the National Security Council and the Operations Coordinating Board would be erected. The need for a Central Statistical Bureau has been apparent to economists for years, and it seems likely that the requirements of the cold war will bring it into being before long. A cluster of these agencies, including a much-strengthened Council of Economic Advisers, could serve as the center of a great range of planning efforts

stretched across the nation at every level and operating both publicly and privately. The need exists, the organizations and machines are ready; all that is required is the will. But the case for national planning has been put before, and need not be repeated. Wassily Leontief, specialist in input-output economic analysis at Harvard, has summarized the current situation:

Under such names as "operations research," "logistics analysis," or "management science," the new techniques are now being used by most large American corporations in the solution of production scheduling, inventory control, investment planning and many other of their internal problems which hitherto were met by routine application of conventional and mostly rather wasteful rules of thumb. But certain business circles in the U. S. have viewed with unconcealed alarm the application of these methods to the traditional problems of the economic system as a whole—the very purpose for which some of the most powerful of the new analytic devices were designed in the first place. No doubt this attitude reflects the fear that too close and too detailed an understanding of the structure of the economic machine and of its operation might encourage undesirable attempts to regulate its course.

PATHOLOGY OF THE CORPORATION

There is, it is true, formidable opposition to any extension of government into the economic sphere. Some of the more familiar arguments follow.

Statutes and administrative law, it is said, cannot bear the weight. The political processes daily show their frailty. Private interest transforms public interest into its own forms and uses before our eyes. The government set forth in the Constitution was designed to be minimal. A new kind of government might require extensive redrafting of the Constitution. Americans have become cynical about law and politics. Moreover, Americans take these terms to signify restraint, and restraint is popularly supposed to be the opposite of freedom. The main set of American mythology and experience is against political regulation of economic affairs.

There is also the opposition of the business community, which deeply believes that contemporary capitalism, with all its paradoxes and contradictions, represents the finest and final flowering of economic organization. "Letting corporations alone" is regarded as the best contribution that the government can make to the economic order. Managers believe that they are making rapid progress toward "the well-tempered corporation" and that benign oligarchy is the only way of bringing efficient production and the claims of diverse constituencies into step. The business community holds that the sovereignty of the consumer and similar tenets of the "conventional wisdom" have been proved by experience. It regards management as a mystical art whose subtleties cannot be shared, least of all by those in government. There is, they say, the greatest opportunity for initiative and for the uncommon man in the corporation. Sweetening the atmosphere by tariffs, tax concessions, and the like is the limit of constructive activity by government. Every encroachment by government means diminishing efficiency. Through the prerogatives of "unfettered management" the greatest good of the greatest number is accomplished. Above all, business says, the rights of property and the principle of economic freedom are paramount and are to be equated with the theory of least government.

But the corporation, especially the modern mastodon, also has deep perplexities and troubles. . . . The large corporation is a pre-eminent fact of American life, but it is not sure of what it is about. Lawyers are beginning to point out that the large corporation, in essence, is unowned. When we speak of the large corporation we mean the managers, and there is no widely accepted "apologetic of manageralism." Is its reason for existence to employ as many people as possible as long as possible? To maximize profits? To serve freedom and justice by removing inequalities? To support education and other good works? To countervail labor and governmental power? To produce and distribute goods? To survive and expand? All of these things? Management is notably unsure, as its intensive investigation of corporate pathology demonstrates.

The large corporation's effort to cope simultaneously with these often conflicting mysteries of life is constantly complicated by new factors, of which automation and the prospect of disarmament are examples. Both involve the possibilities of massive alterations, and both are substantially beyond the control and influence of the corporation itself. Some experts think automation can in twenty-five years go far toward eliminating "middle management," to say nothing of its impact in the factory. Students of collective bargaining agree that automation cannot be dealt with at the negotiating table except in a temporary and limited way. There is evidence that managers themselves do not feel up to the new tasks they are asked to perform. The most refined corporate conscience or sense of social responsibility may not be able to handle many of the demands produced by the mere size and influence of the large organization. More and more loath to throw its economic weight around, it cannot help but do so; automobile dealers, to give an example, felt it so necessary to protect themselves from the arbitrariness of manufacturers that they lobbied a federal statute onto the books.

A riskless and seemingly eternal organization, dominating the public and personal lives of thousands of people and institutions, possessing the power to tax and make other political decisions, and devoted to the welfare of its constituents and that of the society it serves: this is not only a description of a large industrial corporation but also of a government. Amidst the growing perception of the corporation as a government, the murmurings about the need for "corporate" due process grow louder. The organized employee has grievance procedures to appeal to, but there is no course against arbitrary or capricious action for the swelling army of unorganized "management people" nor for small suppliers nor for the prospective employee denied a job for irrelevant reasons.

As part of this interest in due process within the corporation there is the shift in theories about property. Only recently has the idea been seriously entertained that employees have some kind of property right in their jobs. Traditional concepts about private property in all its forms are being questioned, a movement that started slowly with Berle and Means' *The Modern Corporation* in 1932 and has been gathering force. An assertion of property rights in jobs was inevitable as soon as three things happened: first, when it became clear that the "ownership" of the corporation was not the same thing as management; second, when banks, finance companies, and other credit sources began to treat jobs as security (the installment buying apparatus is built, perhaps unconsciously, on the notion that men have some right in their employment); and third, when evidences began to abound of what David T. Bazelon calls "the paper economy" that jiggling world of legal transformations of property, persons-as-corporations, power without property, and artful accounting practices. Against such now-you-see-it-now-you-don't aspects of property the idea of a property right in the job takes on a certain concreteness.

A promising vein of inquiry opens up with the proposition that the large corporation is a private government. Berle and others have pointed to the "taxing power" of the big firm, for example, and the question arises, by what right? Expansion and new development are being more and more financed out of earnings, and there is less recourse to the stock market and other sources of capital by the large firms. Thus, present customers are buying new plant and equipment for Corporation A without receiving anything in return; while a stockholder in Corporation A who has done nothing except give his broker an order is said to be an "owner" whose equity is hereby increased.

CAPITALISM AS AMERICAN POLICY ABROAD

There is the further fact that virtually every large American corporation does a great deal of business in other countries. In an earlier day such activity did not have the importance it has now, nor were managers as self-conscious about their non-economic roles as they now are when they operate in overseas markets. James M. Fulton, counsel to Merck, Sharp and Dohme International, answering the question, "What is the responsibility of Big Business to the world at large?", related his firm's attitude in starting up in India:

The company realized that drugs and pharmaceuticals were and would be of social and political significance to India. We were also well aware of the significance of India to the Free World, and of the struggle between Russia and the Free World for the allegiance of India. These circumstances injected a higher degree of urgency into the picture, to be sure, but the point is that our primary business is drugs, not international politics, and we mean to keep it that way.

Mr. Fulton seems to be saying that his company is providing for the common defense and conducting foreign policy as well as getting into the drug business in India.

Living in the world community means living with state-controlled economies and with under- and semi-developed nations, in all of which the state carries the main weight of industrial and social development. ("The Soviets have set up a shop that looks very much like it is going to be in business for a long time to come. What is more, their shop is working better all the time. . . . I very much fear that whatever theory of consumer economies we now have in this country is the most underdeveloped part of our economic system. I also fear that without some modification of our marketplace-directed allocation of resources, we shall be severely handicapped in the competitive struggle. Our most pressing problem is to develop agencies of rational allocation, at multiple private and government levels, to keep the whole task from eventually going to the federal government by default. Such a default would leave little to choose between our way and theirs." Haig Babian, *Economic Affairs,* Institute of Economic Affairs, NYU, June 30, 1960.) Capitalism, regularly associated with colonialism, would not seem to be the ideal instrument for dealing with the expectations of these rising blocs. ("The economic power of Western Europe and North America owes its superiority to the intense exploitation of the natural resources of Africa and Asia at prices and salaries far below standard . . . the brunt [of war preparations] is borne by these very peoples, supplying cheap raw materials or cheap labor. The wealth accumulated by the rulers through centuries imposed duties to provide technical and economic assistance . . . free from any political strings." Lebanese delegate at the United Nations, quoted in *Wall Street Journal,* September 26, 1960.) It is a bizarre proposition in any case that this nation's policies in such circumstances should be largely developed and explicated by private managers. Here as elsewhere the large corporation is to be seen as usurping the powers and duties of government. Perhaps it would be as accurate to call it a failure of governmental responsibility. Yet until we develop some more effective way of carrying our economic burdens overseas, the problem remains whether the ambassadorial function of the large corporation should not be recognized, with suitable accountability then demanded of it.

The similarities of the large national and international corporation to government are, in short, becoming more pronounced while the question of the final legitimacy of power in these private governments grows more and more troubling. The formulation can be power without property or responsibility.

THE NEED FOR A NEW THEORY

The important point is not the machinery of economic regulation but rather the widespread recognition that the basic characteristics of the economy are matters of public interest and responsibility. The sovereign importance of the market is a thing of the past. Even if it were to furnish a perfectly equilibrated price structure, the market would resolve few if any of our fateful dilemmas. No one has claimed that it would provide full employment, housing, schools, an equitable distribution of wealth, or a proper division between public needs and private wants. No one has claimed that an "unintervened" market would result in a rate of national growth commensurate with obligations to our own citizens and to those abroad whose situation is both desperate and of selfish importance to us. Such basic economic decisions will have to be brought into the realm of public responsibility. This means bringing economic activity under the legal order and making it a first responsibility of government and law. Otherwise our future as a nation will be determined by economic choices made privately, choices having to do with domestic matters such as the rate of growth and type of capital investment and internationally with the amount of foreign investment and the type of regime with which business is to be done.

How to achieve general acceptance of the necessity for purposive governmental policies in the economic order is a hard question. Americans want to feel free of constraints and obligations, especially those of government, but their world is increasingly and inescapably crisscrossed with the strands of mutuality. The biggest facts of their lives—air, water, power, security, noise, traffic, communication, income, homebuilding, crops, education, milk, drugs—are so complicated that government has already had to become heavily involved in them. Americans do not want to be caught up in multinational responsibilities; they prefer not to think about the intricacies of multinational trade and finance. Yet these too are the necessary conditions of their existence and far more so those of their children. Since such momentous matters cannot be left in private hands, they end in government's hands. And since the decisions about such urgent and difficult matters are more and more to govern our common life, a new philosophy of government is necessary to meet the need.

Political inventiveness seems to be on a long vacation. In the Thirties it was needed to head off disaster and in the early Forties it was needed to mobilize swiftly for a world struggle. The argument cannot be advanced that innovation is to be called on only when domestic or international Armageddon occurs. A radically new situation needs radical theory for its life and growth. Instead of radical theory we now have political *stare decisis*. There is a general flight from politics. Political freedom is the least used of many unused freedoms. This was not the result foreseen when, in 1789, the people covenanted a community dedicated to peace, order, freedom, and justice. The formula for today's problems can be expressed positively: purpose produces political invention.

The unavoidable problem is that of finding ways to give law greater standing and of disposing of the anachronism of least government, best government. Perhaps it cannot be done. Yet it is a minimum condition for keeping popular government afloat. While the physical and international world has been evolving with dizzy speed, we have been content with a political outlook and an attitude toward law dating from before the first world war. Government, as the institution organized by the people from their town councils to the national capital, needs to be rescued from desuetude and made not only a respectable mechanism but the purposeful means of securing the general welfare. A good deal of the necessary political apparatus is already present, although it is fragmented, hidden behind anomalous titles, and often aimed not at public and general ends but private and local ones. Planning boards, chambers of commerce, state development and conservation authorities, trade associations, labor councils, associations of parent-teachers and taxpayers, all these and dozens more private and public devices are at hand, ready to become parts of the inner structure of government attuned to the demands of the second half of the twentieth century.

To these organizations can be added the New Leisure. Like the old leisure of the Greeks and the Founding Fathers the New Leisure can provide an essential condition for successful self-government. In the early days of the republic, politics and government largely occupied the wealthy and leisured. It is an absorbing speculation whether the New Leisure can in some way be diverted into similiar channels. It may be remarked that in all the din about the results of the New Leisure there has been little or no suggestion that it be regarded as the first great opportunity for self-government and public service by the multitudes who until now have been fully occupied making a living. Turning the New Leisure into political activity would be one way to dispel the anxiety that man's lot henceforth will be pleasure-seeking, dull, and long rather than nasty, brutish, and short.

The kind of government envisioned in this paper asserts that men can modernize their political apparatus and can consciously control their political and economic destinies. It argues that the machinery for effective political participation on a wider basis than ever before can be invented. It asserts, that is to say, that democracy is not senescent but in an early stage.

Perhaps the dialogue can be reconstructed around this proposal:

Freedom, justice, and the general welfare cannot be regarded as the accidental benefits or by-products of a political economy: the political economy should therefore be directed to their attainment: to bring the economic order under the political order, a new theory of government is necessary.

Property, Production, and Revolution

ADOLPH A. BERLE

A professor at Columbia University, Adolph A. Berle has achieved fame as a writer and analyst of modern American capitalism. His special area of expertise is the role of the corporation in our current economy.

More than thirty years ago, in the preface of *The Modern Corporation and Private Property,* I wrote:

The translation of perhaps two-thirds of the industrial wealth of the country from individual ownership to ownership by the large, publicly financed corporations vitally changes the lives of property owners, the lives of workers, and the methods of property tenure. The divorce of ownership from control consequent on that process almost necessarily involves a new form of economic organization of society.[1]

Reprinted from *Columbia Law Review* (January 1965), 1–20, by permission of the author and publisher.

[1] *Preface* to BERLE & MEANS, THE MODERN CORPORATION AND PRIVATE PROPERTY at vii–viii (1932).

Dr. Means and I had pointed out that the two attributes of ownership—risking collective wealth in profit-seeking enterprise and ultimate management of responsibility for that enterprise—had become divorced. Accordingly we raised the questions:

Must we not, therefore, recognize that we are no longer dealing with property in the old sense? Does the traditional logic of property still apply? Because an owner who also exercises control over his wealth is protected in the full receipt of the advantages derived from it, must it *necessarily* follow that an owner who has surrendered control of his wealth should likewise be protected to the full? May not this surrender have so essentially changed his relation to his wealth as to have changed the logic applicable to his interest in that wealth? An answer to this question cannot be found in the law itself. It must be sought in the economic and social background of law.[2]

We based these questions on the growing dominance of the corporate form, the increasing decision-making power of corporate management, the increasingly passive position of shareholders, and the increasing inapplicability of the ethical and economic justifications given (rightly enough at the time) by classic economics.

The object of this essay is to review some aspects of this conception in the light of a generation of experience and consequent developments.

[2] BERLE & MEANS, *op. cit. supra* note 1, at 338–39.

THE CONTINUING CURRENT OF CHANGE TO "COLLECTIVE CAPITALISM"

Factually, the trend towards dominance of that collective capitalism we call the "corporate system" has continued unabated. Evolution of the corporation has made stock-and-security ownership the dominant form by which individuals own wealth representing property devoted to production (as contrasted with property devoted to consumption).[3] The last great bastion of individually-owned productive property—agriculture—has been dramatically declining in proportion to the total production of the United States,[4] and even in agriculture, corporations have been steadily making inroads. Outside of agriculture, well over ninety percent of all the production in the country is carried on by more than a million corporations. In all of them, management is theoretically distinct from ownership. The directors of the corporation are not the "owners"; they are not agents of the stockholders and are not obliged to follow their instructions.[5] This in itself is not determinative. Numerically most of the million corporations are "close"—the stockholders are also the directors or are so related to them that the decision-making power rests with the stockholders. Quantitatively, however, a thousand or so very large corporations whose stockholders' lists from 10,000 up to 2,500,000, as in the case of American Telephone and Telegraph, account for an overwhelmingly large percentage both of asset-holders and of operations. *Fortune* Magazine tabulated the 500 largest United States industrial corporations and found their combined sales were 245 billion dollars in 1963 or about sixty-two percent of all industrial sales.[6] The factor of concentration is, of course, higher in the public service industries: communications, transportation and public utilities. It is not unfair to suggest that if these industries were included (they are not in

[3] See note 11 *infra* and accompanying text.
[4] Agricultural employment declined dramatically from 11.4 million in 1920 to 5.7 million in 1960. Value of owned farms and equipment rose—but far more slowly than the value of assets, chiefly corporate, employed in industry. See BERLE, THE AMERICAN ECONOMIC REPUBLIC 233 n.24 (1963).

[5] Manson v. Curtis, 223 N. Y. 313, 322, 119 N. E. 559, 562 (1918); Peabody v. Interborough Rapid Transit Co., 121 Misc. 647, 651, 202 N. Y. Supp. 287, 291 (1923) (Lehman, J.), *modified on other grounds,* 212 App. Div. 502, 209 N. Y. Supp. 380 (1st Dep't 1925).
[6] *The Fortune Directory,* Fortune, July 1964, P. 179.

the *Fortune* tabulation), 600 or 700 large corporations, whose control nominally is in the hands of their "public" stockholders (actually, of their managers), account for seventy percent of commercial operation of the country—agriculture aside. There has been a slow but continuing trend toward corporate concentration reckoned by the percentage of industry thus controlled. Actually the total trend is more marked because, in contrast to total economic growth, the proportion of American economic activity represented by individually controlled agriculture has been relatively declining.[7] American economics at present is dominantly, perhaps overwhelmingly, industrial.

The effect of this change upon the property system of the United States has been dramatic. Individually-owned wealth has enormously increased. It is today reckoned at somewhat more than 1,800 billion dollars.[8] Of more importance is the distribution of that figure. Relatively little of it is "productive" property—land or things employed by its owners in production or commerce—though figures are hazy at the edges. The largest item of individually-owned wealth, exclusive of productive assets, is described as "owner-occupied homes" (approximately 520 billion dollars).[9] These, of course, are primarily for consumption though a fraction of them are probably farmsteads. The next largest item—consumer durables—accounts for 210 billion dollars more;[10] these are chiefly automobiles and home equipment, again chiefly used for personal convenience and not for capital or productive purposes.

The property system as applied to productive assets breaks down (as of the end of 1963) as follows: 525 billion dollars of shares of corporate stock; 210 billion dollars in fixed income financial assets (federal, state and local government securities, corporate and foreign bonds, life insurance values, etc.); and 360 billion dollars in liquid assets, chiefly cash in banks.[11] These figures mean that, far and away, the largest item of personally owned "property" representing productive assets and enterprise is in the form of stock of corporations. In addition, a substantial amount of other assets held by individuals consists of claims against intermediate financial institutions —banks, insurance companies and the like, whose holdings include large amounts of corporation stocks, bonds and securities. "Individually-owned" enterprise is thus steadily disappearing. Increasingly, the American owns his home, his car, and his household appliances; these are for his consumption. Simultaneously, he increasingly owns stocks, life insurance, and rights in pension funds, social security funds and similar arrangements. And he has a job, paying him a wage, salary or commission.

Comparable figures do not run back to 1932; no one prior to Franklin D. Roosevelt had been vividly interested in developing a first-rate system of social statistics. My own crude figures, worked out in 1934 at the Columbia Law School in a little-noted volume, *Liquid Claims and National Wealth,*[12] showed that the total of all domestic stocks and bonds reached a peak of 100.7 billion dollars in 1929—to which must be added 54 billion dollars of net liquid claims (chiefly bank balances), and 12.6 billion dollars of life insurance values;[13] but there was no division between individually-owned and corporate-owned wealth at that time. My co-author, V. E. Pederson and I estimated that in a single decade (1922–1932) more than one-sixth of the entire national wealth had shifted from individual hands into managerial—that is, corporate—hands,[14] and we suggested that at that rate forty years would see the wealth of the entire country split, most of it being operated by corporate management, though its "ownership" would be represented by individual "hold-

---

[7] See note 4 *supra* and accompanying text.
[8] First Nat'l City Bank, Monthly Economic Letter, July 1964, p. 78.
[9] *Ibid.*
[10] *Ibid.*
[11] *Ibid.*
[12] BERLE & PEDERSON, LIQUID CLAIMS AND NATIONAL WEALTH (1934).
[13] *Id.* at 73.
[14] *Id.* at 82.

ings" of stocks, bonds, and other liquid claims.[15]

Based on the figures to date, that development has gone far toward accom-

plishment. In crude summation, most "owners" own stock, insurance savings and pension claims and the like, and do not manage; most managers (corporate administrators) do not own. The corporate collective holds legal title to the tangible productive wealth of the country—for the benefit of others.

The word "revolutionary" has been justifiably applied to less fundamental change. The United States is no longer anticipating a development. It is digesting a fact.

[15] In addition, we noted that owners of stock would be so far separated from the producing property that they would be "substantially at the mercy of the mechanism of liquidity, such as the stock exchange," adding that, "in terms of organization of society, [it poses] . . . a problem far beyond the ability of any purely private mechanism to handle in case of heavy weather." *Id.* at 83.

THE EMERGING CONCEPTION OF PROPERTY

Lawyers are accustomed to conceive of poperty in terms of ancient classification. If tangible, it was "real"—that is, land or rights derived from land; or it was "personal"—mobile, capable of being used, taken away, moved, transferred and so forth by its owners. If intangible, it was a "chose in action"—a claim on or against other individuals or entities capable of being enforced or protected in the courts. Some of this was "negotiable," passing under the law-merchant or adaptations thereof. The *proprietas* (the relation of the individual or owner to this property—real, personal or chose in action) was assumed to be fixed.

There is no occasion to change these classic definitions. They do quite well for the purposes of defining rights, methods of transfer, handling intervening claims, and the myriad minor problems of transmission and adjustment. What has changed is the conception of *proprietas*. I here suggest that a new classification has been superimposed on the old theory.

My thesis is that "property" is now divided into two categories: (a) consumption property on the one hand and (b) productive property on the other—property devoted to production, manufacture, service or commerce, and designed to offer, for a price, goods or services to the public from which a holder expects to derive a return.

In respect of productive property, the *proprietas* has now been made subject to an overall, political determination as to the kind of civilization the American

state in its democratic processes has decided it wants. This is an on-going process, not yet complete.

As a corollary, productive property has been divided into two layers: (1) that fraction which, though not managed by active owners, is administered to yield a return by way of interest, dividends or distribution of profit, and (2) that layer dominated and controlled by the representatives or delegates of the passive owners whose decisions are now subject to the political process just noted. In this category, social development is at present intense and likely to continue.

This essay does not deal with forces present and emerging that now bear on or will later affect consumptive property. Unquestionably these exist. As population, urbanization and congestion steadily increase, one man's consumptive use may become another man's privation, and the enjoyment of consumptive property may depend upon facilities as well as regulations provided by the state. Thus automobiles require both roads and traffic rules; suburban homes can become untenantable unless land use control is provided by the community; and the right to sell or transfer may be restricted by the antidiscrimination laws.

In general . . . the impact of modern and economic evolution seems to be an expansion of a very old common-law maxim: *Sic utere tuo ut alienum non laedas.* The essential aim is to preserve the greatest available degree of consumption and choice as empty land fills up, roads become congested, and the capacity to invade others' lives by esthetic horrors is enlarged by technique. American law and law schools have, happily, developed a growing number of scholars and experts in this field. Let us confine (the word is scarcely apt) ourselves to the impact of economic and social evolution on *productive* property in its two aspects: (1) managerial-productive (management) and (2) passive-receptive (stock and security ownership).

THE CHANGING CONTENT OF PROPERTY[16]

We must note an enormous expansion of the scope of the term "property" in this connection. Not only is it divorced from the decision-making power of its supposedly beneficial holders (stockholders and their various removes), but it has come to encompass a set of conceptions superimposed upon the central reality of domination over tangible things. Businessmen describe an enterprise, great or small, as "the property." They do not mean merely the physical plant. They include access to all the facilities necessary to produce, transport, distribute and sell. They mean an entire organization of personnel without which the physical plant would be junk; they mean a hierarchy of executives, technical experts, sales managers and men; as well as the dealer organization and the labor relations habits. These relationships are increasingly protected, not merely by the law of contract, but by an increasing body of law imposing upon individuals a measure of loyalty to the central enterprise. For example, they may not acquire and sell to others as part of their personal capacity or equipment, confidential technical information, data on sales, or customer goodwill. Underlying this extension of the property concept to management relationships is recognition of the fact that the "capital" has been projected far into the realm of intangibles. The central enterprise is spending good money—often in immense amounts—building this organization, this technical information, these relationships; it is entitled to be protected against their appropriation by individuals.

A counterforce registers the impact of this extension. Literally enormous quantities of technical information have been accumulated by government and thrust into fields of non-statist enterprise. Resources of nuclear energy and nuclear physics are the most dramatic—but by no means the only or even perhaps the most significant—of these intrusions. Nearly two-thirds of all technical research is now financed by the federal government. Through a great number of modern industries—one thinks at once of electronics, of aviation, and of space satellite communication—this government-financed technique enters the process of corporate explosion. By no stretch of imagination can it be described as property primarily created by private enterprise. Like it or not, these assets are social and statist in origin. Complete turnover of these assets to "private" (that is, non-statist) ownership seems wholly unlikely. Illustration of the impact—and of a compromise—is found in the Communications Satellite Act[17] authorizing creation of ComSat, a corporation owned one-half by the federal government and one-half by private investors. The proportion of investment by current communications enterprises such as A.T.&T. was severely limited,[18] despite the fact that the primary function of the new facilities to be provided in outer space was to offer A.T.&T. and like corporations new avenues of communication.

Earlier discovery that electromagnetic

[16] The rapid increase in technical development necessarily downgrades the position of physical or tangible things and upgrades the factors of organization and technical knowledge. Organization is not reducible to a formula. Technical knowledge is rarely if ever assignable to any single individual, group of individuals or corporation. It is part of the heritage of the country and of the race. In neither case do the traditional formulae applicable to common-law property fit the current fact.

[17] 76 Stat. 419 (1962), 47 U. S. C. §§ 701–44 (Supp. V, 1964).

[18] §§ 303–04, 76 Stat. 423, 47 U. S. C. §§ 733–34 (Supp. V, 1964).

energy could be used for radio and later television resulted in an odd and undetermined new form of property. It took the form of short-term exclusive licenses, granted by the Federal Communications Commission, to use specific wave lengths. These were granted to private companies but rapidly ripened into an uncodified but thoroughly recognized expectancy (if not right) that the licensee companies, through renewal of their licenses, would continue to enjoy the wave length frequencies assigned them. Temporary licenses, plus expectancy of their renewal became the basis for dollar-value markets for radio and TV stations, big and little. The statist right thus became engulfed in a "private property" institution. The ComSat debate and the resulting statute sufficiently indicate resistance to this process, and the compromises reached between the state and the non-statist users of the assets developed by the state.

"Property" when used in connection with and as adjunct to legal (that is, corporate) ownership is thus changing its import not because the old rules relating to ownership of a plant have changed, but because of the addition of an enormous proportion of new content differing both in kind and in origin from the old. The Research Institute of America in a private report observed:

A third industrial revolution is in the making, as dramatic as those which followed the harnessing of steam power and the proliferation of electricity. This one will be sired by the release of nuclear and thermonuclear energy, the electronic conversion of energy to work, and the use of cybernetics and computers to free human energy from routine decision-making. By 1980, the industrial world will be as different from today's as today is different from the 19th century.[19]

To project this discussion would take us into the realm of science fiction far beyond the competence of this writer. One observation nevertheless appears warranted. Whatever the fantasy of the science fiction writers, it will probably be outstripped both in scope and speed by the fact. In the light of what has already been achieved, the Jules Vernes and the H. G. Wellses of yesterday seem like children.[20] Can the science fiction writers of today expect a better fate?

As technology and its organization for production and use evolve, so will property. The "private," and still more individualized, aspects will become increasingly attenuated. Elisha Gray having developed the embryonic idea of telecommunication, organized a private company to put it to productive use and asked private investors to join him and risk their capital in the venture. Today's Elisha Gray or Alexander Graham Bell would be a team, working in a great research center, more often than not financed by the federal government. Such techniques as they emerge are "property" of a government that does not need the private investor to supply risk capital—although as a gesture towards old times, it may offer participation as was done in the ComSat legislation. Plainly we are moving towards a new phase fundamentally more alien to the tradition of profit even than that forecast in *The Modern Corporation and Private Property*.

A shift in attitude toward corporate property arises in part from the changed origin of finance-capital. The property of corporations is dedicated to production, not to personal consumption; but, even more significant, that property is no longer the result of individual effort or choice. This change has come silently. Its implications even yet are not understood.

Corporations were originally groups of investors pooling their individual contributions of risk capital to organize and carry on an enterprise. Since they had saved their earnings or gains and had risked them in the undertaking, they were assimilated to the owner of land, who cleared and cultivated it, and sold

[19] Research Institute of America, *Your Business in the Next 15 Years,* June 30, 1964.

[20] Jules Verne's submarine was a marvel for the nineteenth century but his Nautilus would not be impressive today. 20,000 LEAGUES UNDER THE SEA (1871). H. G. Wells, in 1899, forecast a battle over London between a dirigible and an airplane, expecting it might take over a century or so before such a confrontation occurred. WHEN THE SLEEPER WAKES (1899). Such a battle actually happened over London in World War I. Both types of imagined aircraft, of course, are obsolete now.

its products. As the economics of the time went, this was justifiable. They had sacrificed, risked and, to some extent, worked at the development of the product. Presumably they had done something useful for the community, since it was prepared to pay for the product.

A mature corporation typically does not call for investor-supplied capital. It charges a price for its products from which it can pay taxation, costs, depreciation allowances, and can realize a profit over and above all these expenses. Of this profit item, approximately half goes as income taxes to the federal government, and sixty percent of the remaining half is distributed to its shareholders. It accumulates for capital purposes the undistributed forty percent and its depreciation charges. This is a phenomenon not of "investment," but of market power. Since corporations legally have perpetual life, this process can continue indefinitely. The result has been that more than sixty percent of capital entering a particular industry is "internally generated" or, more accurately, "price-generated" because it is collected from the customers. Another twenty percent of the capital the corporation uses is borrowed from banks chiefly in anticipation of this accumulative process. The corporations in aggregate do indeed tap individual "savings," but for only a little less than twenty percent of their capital, and mainly through the issuance of bonds to intermediate savings-collecting institutions (life insurance companies, trust funds, pension trusts and savings banks).[21]

The corporation becomes the legal "owner" of the capital thus collected and has complete decision-making power over it; the corporation runs on its own economic steam. On the other hand, its stockholders, by now grandsons or great-grandsons of the original "investors" or (far more often) transferees of their transferees at thousands of removes, have and expect to have through their stock the "beneficial ownership" of the assets and profits thus accumulated and realized, after taxes, by the corporate enterprise. Management thus becomes, in an odd sort of way, the uncontrolled administrator of a kind of trust having the privilege of perpetual accumulation. The stockholder is the passive beneficiary, not only of the original "trust," but of the compounded annual accretions to it.

Not surprisingly, therefore, we discover a body of law building up to protect and deal with this remarkable phenomenon. To that fact itself perhaps is due a continuing tendency: subjection of property devoted to *production*—that is, chiefly in managerial hands—to legal rules requiring a use of it, more or less corresponding to the evolving expectations of American civilization.

[21] Gorman & Shea, *Capital Formation, Savings & Credit,* Survey of Current Bus., May 1964, p. 11.

DEVELOPMENT OF PROPERTY LAW

Inevitably, the common-law legal system moves to normalize the new areas thus comprehended within the general head of "productive property." Two major lines are observed. The first (primarily outside the scope of this essay) proceeds through taxation. The principle has been established that the federal government—and in lesser measure, state governments—both may and should take a portion of the profits of corporations through the device of direct corporate income tax. Under the recent tax reduction, the federal government presently taxes corporate profits above 25,000 dollars at the rate of fifty percent; that percentage will be reduced to forty-eight percent in 1965.[22] This virtually makes the state an equal partner as far as profits are concerned. Factually, though silently, the process recognizes a fundamental and entirely demonstrable economic premise. Corporations derive their profits partly indeed from their own operations, but partly also from their market position and increasingly from techniques resulting from state expenditures of taxpayers' money. In this sense, the American state is an investor in practically every substantial enterprise; without its activity, the enterprise, if it could exist at all, would be or would have been compelled

[22] INT. REV. CODE of 1954, §§ 11(b), (c).

to spend money and effort to create position, maintain access to market, and build technical development it currently takes for granted. Under these circumstances, there is little reason or justification for assuming that *all* profits should automatically accrue to stockholders. Put differently, stockholders—not having created the entire enterprise—are no longer the sole residuary legatees (after production costs and depreciation) of all the profits of an industrial progress, much of which is derived from state outlay.

A second line of development impinges directly on management operation. It arises from an evolving social concept of what American civilization should look like. It began with the minimum wage legislation[23] and the Wagner Act,[24] later revised by the Taft-Hartley Act[25] and modified by the Landrum-Griffin Act.[26] These statutes, and the growing body of case and administrative law under them, limit the decision-making power of corporate managements with respect to wages and labor relations. Of interest is the fact that these laws in the main (though not univerally) are applied to general enterprise for profit-making operations in production or commerce. Slowly a distinction began to develop between both expenditures and activities for personal consumption, and enterprises directed towards the offer of goods or services to the public from whose purchase or payment a profit is expected.

The later, it increasingly appears, are subject to the imposition of rules derived

essentially from the Bill of Rights. These rules are designed to assure that the market power of enterprise shall not be used so as to create or perpetuate conditions which the state itself is forbidden to create or maintain. Thirteen years ago, the writer drew attention to this tendency, noting:

[T]here is being generated a quiet translation of constitutional law from the field of political to the field of economic rights. The main outlines of this new body of law are only scarcely discernible now; yet its future history is certain to be important. . . . The emerging principle appears to be that the corporation, itself a creation of the state, is as subject to constitutional limitations which limit action as is the state itself. If this doctrine, now coming into view, is carried to full effect, a corporation having economic and supposedly juridical power to take property, to refuse to give equal service, to discriminate between man and man, group and group, race and race, to an extent denying "the equal protection of the laws," or otherwise to violate constitutional limitations, is subject to direct legal action.[27]

The doctrine had been applied to municipal corporations by the Supreme Court in *Jones v. Opelika*[28] and extended to a private corporation performing the equivalent of public functions through the operation of a company town.[29] It has been gradually expanded in a number of directions.[30]

Dramatically, the recently enacted Civil Rights Act[31] has forthrightly moved into this field. It provides among other things that certain enterprises offering goods and services or accommodations to the public may not discriminate against any member of the public because of racial origin. Gone is the old rule that merchandiser, purveyor of accommoda-

[23] See, *e.g.*, Fair Labor Standards Act of 1938 § 6, 52 Stat. 1062, as amended, 29 U. S. C. § 206 (Supp. V, 1964); District of Columbia Minimum-Wage Law, ch. 174, 40 Stat. 960 (1918), held unconstitutional in Adkins v. Children's Hosp., 261 U.S. 525 (1923), in turn overruled by West Coast Hotel Co. v. Parrish, 300 U.S. 379 (1937); Mass. Acts 1912, ch. 706.

[24] National Labor Relations Act, 49 Stat. 453 (1935), as amended, 29 U. S. C. §§ 151–68 (1959), as amended, 29 U. S. C. §§ 153–64 (Supp. V, 1964).

[25] Labor Management Relations Act, 61 Stat. 136 (1947), as amended, 29 U. S. C. §§ 141–87 (1959), as amended, 29 U. S. C. §§ 153–87 (Supp. V, 1964).

[26] Labor-Management Reporting and Disclosure Act of 1959, 73 Stat. 519, 29 U. S. C. §§ 153–87 (Supp. V, 1964).

[27] Berle, *Constitutional Limitations on Corporate Activity—Protection of Personal Rights from Invasion Through Economic Power,* 100 U. Pa. L. Rev. 933, 942 (1952).

[28] 319 U. S. 103 (1942), *adopting on rehearing* 316 U. S. 584, 600–10 (1942) (Stone, J., dissenting).

[29] Marsh v. Alabama, 326 U. S. 501 (1946).

[30] See, *e.g.,* Burton v. Wilmington Parking Authority, 365 U. S. 715 (1961); Steele v. Louisville & N. R. R., 323 U. S. 192 (1944).

[31] 78 Stat. 241 (1964).

tions or provider of services (above an insignificant size) may do what he likes with his own, may sell or decline to sell, serve or decline to serve, choose between customer and customer at least on the basis of race.[32] State statutes like those prevailing in New York[33] has already set up this rule. Now the federal government enters alongside the state.

Property devoted to other than commercial or productive use is not dealt with in a similar manner. A man may refuse to entertain anyone within his home or admit anyone to ride in his car. Consumption for personal use is an expression of personality, guarded from in-

vasion. Property (in the extruded sense we have been using the term) devoted to production and commerce is not; neither in employment of labor nor in the sale of goods and services can the ancient absolute property right of domination—decision-making in the current phase—be unqualified. What happened is sufficiently clear. The political ideal invested in the Constitution and reflected in the Bill of Rights, and the fourteenth and fifteenth amendments, contemplated individuals whose personality was not to be invaded, save for police purposes designed to protect other personalities from invasion. In the simpler days of the eighteenth century, the state was the principal threat: the Bill of Rights restrained the federal government and by the fourteenth amendment extended the restraints to the state governments. As the twentieth century entered its later half, it was clear that personal freedom could be abridged or invaded by denial of economic facilities offered or provided by privately-owned enterprises. Such facilities indeed were chiefly in private hands—overwhelmingly, in fact, offered or conducted by corporations. Yet they were essential to life and personality. The result was gradual, judicial extension of constitutional law, complemented now by such statutes as the Civil Rights Act of 1964 which covers the fields of lodging, restaurant facilities, places of entertainment, establishments serving or offering to serve food, gasoline or other products. The Civil Rights Act does not extend, even remotely, to the whole field of commerce; it does not affect all productive property. Yet the point is clear: such property may by statute, if not by constitutional extension, be made subject to those limitations which inhibit state action to protect individual freedom.

A third state constraint upon management results from the current interpretation of the antitrust legislation and more specifically the Clayton Act.[34] Under *Brown Shoe Co. v. United States,*[35] the Supreme Court established that any merger which appreciably limits compe-

---

[32] It is interesting to note the basis from which title II of the Civil Rights Act of 1964 proceeded. Most of the accommodations involved—hotels, restaurants, gasoline stations, possibly even places of amusement—could have been assimilated to the old concept of "public utilities." At least from the time of the Stuart monarchy, the duty to serve all comers had been imposed on inns and ferries and had been extended to the whole public utility field. See, *e.g.,* King v. Mayor of London, 1 Show. K. B. 251, 89 Eng. Rep. 558 (1692); White's Case, 2 Dyer 158, 73 Eng. Rep. 343 (K. B. 1682); Rex v. Collins, Palm. 373, 81 Eng. Rep. 1130 (K. B. 1623). Extension to gasoline stations would have been entirely possible. Congress might well have taken this approach under the interstate commerce clause. Congress, however, used the rationale of the Bill of Rights and of the fourteenth amendment to support § 201 (a) of the act. That section provides:

All persons shall be entitled to the full and equal enjoyment of the goods, services, facilities, privileges, advantages, and accommodations of any place of public accommodation, as defined in this section, without discrimination or segregation on the ground of race, color, religion, or national origin.

78 Stat. 243 (1964). The House debate dealt with the public utility origin of the nondiscrimination rule, but made clear that the Bill of Rights basis provided one of the primary thrusts. Senator Goldwater based his argument against the bill on the theory that the federal government should not extend public-utilities regulatory authority into this field—that should be left to the states. 110 CONG. REC. 13825 (daily ed. June 18, 1964). Senator Javits, replying, believed the bill could be supported as regulation of interstate commerce, but he came down squarely for the proposition that the public accommodations title, and any possible intrusion into the field of state action, was justified by the fourteenth amendment, *Id.* at 13943-44 (daily ed. June 19, 1964).

[33] N. Y. CIV. RIGHTS LAW § 40.

[34] 38 Stat. 730 (1914), as amended, 15 U. S. C. §§ 12, 13, 14-21, 22-27 (1959), as amended, 15 U. S. C. §§ 13, 21 (Supp. V, 1964).

[35] 370 U. S. 294 (1962).

tition is prohibited. The writer considers the policy retrogressive; competition enforced to that extent is more likely to cripple production and distribution than increase it. That, however, is a matter for legislative determination, whether judicial or congressional. The significant fact is that the law (as construed in *Brown Shoe*) endeavors to assure that productive property will not be used to prevent carrying on production along the lines and subject to the conditions of the competitive process as conceived by classical economics. It thus seeks to maintain a picture of civilization to which a powerful current of American thought appears to be committed. Rightly, this is not construed as an invasion of liberty or personal right. It is construed as—and, of course, is—a direct attempt to mold, control or inhibit certain dispositions of productive property, maintaining the historical conception that highly competitive markets are generally beneficial to human liberty. In modern context, the premise may, of course, be disputed. Yet the enforcement of such a conception unquestionably imposes limitations on the disposition and operation of productive property. Cognate limitations have not yet been applied to property used only for individual consumption. Although the state considers that it can control the framework and bases of production and commerce, it has not attempted (aside from police limitations) to tell a man what or how he should consume—that would constitute an intolerable invasion of his private life.

THE INSTITUTION OF PASSIVE PROPERTY

Increased size and domination of the American corporation has automatically split the package of rights and privileges comprising the old conception of property. Specifically, it splits the personality of the individual beneficial owner away from the enterprise manager. The "things" themselves—including the intangible elements noted earlier in this essay—"belong" to the corporation which holds legal title to them. The ultimate beneficial interest embodied in a share of stock represents an expectation that a portion of the profits remaining after taxes will be declared as dividends, and that in the relatively unlikely event of liquidation each share will get its allocable part of the assets. The former expectation is vivid; the latter so remote that it plays little part in giving market value to shares. Stockholders do have a right to vote which is of diminishing importance as the number of shareholders in each corporation increases—diminishing in fact to negligible importance as the corporations become giants. As the number of stockholders increases, the capacity of each to express opinions is extremely limited. No one is bound to take notice of them, though they may have quasi-political importance, similar to that of constituents who write letters to their congressman. Finally, they have a right, difficult to put into operation, to bring a stockholders' action against the corporation and its management, demanding that the corporation be made whole from any damage it may have suffered in case of theft, fraud, or wrongdoing by directors or administrators. Such actions are common, though few stockholders are involved in them. They are a useful deterrent to dishonesty and disloyalty on the part of management.

These shares nevertheless have become so desirable that they are now the dominant form of personal wealth-holding because, through the device of stock exchanges, they are acquired "liquidity"—that is, the capability of being sold for ready cash within days or hours. The stockholder, though no longer the sole residuary legatee of all profits, is the residuary legatee of about half of them, and that is a vast stake. (Sophisticated estimates indicate that dividends combined with increase in market value of shares have yielded better than eight percent per annum during the generation past.) The package of passive property rights and expectations has proved sufficiently satisfactory to have induced an increasing number of Americans to place their savings in this form or property. In 1929 perhaps one million Americans owned common stock. At the close of 1963, a conservative estimate would place that figure at between seventeen and twenty million stockholders.[36] These holdings represent 525 billion dollars of current market value, comprising slightly less than one-third of individually-owned wealth in the United States.[37] Projecting the trend, one would expect twenty years from now to find between forty and fifty million Americans directly owning shares. The aggregate market value of personally owned shares now approximates ten to fifteen percent more than the annual personally-received income in the United States (the latter will be nearly 500 billion dollars for the year 1964). We can expect that the total market value of personally-owned shares twenty years hence will far surpass the trillion dollar mark.

Yet this is only the "top level" of passive property-holding. A very large number of shares are not held by individuals, but by intermediate fiduciary institutions which in turn distribute the benefits of shareholding to participating individuals. One of the two largest groups of such intermediary institutions is that of the pension trust funds maintained by corporations or groups of corporations for the benefit of employees; these collect savings in regular installments from employers to be held in trust for their employees and subsequently paid to them as old age or other similar benefits. The second is the relatively smaller group of institutions known as mutual funds; these buy a portfolio of assorted stocks and sell participations in the portfolio to individuals desiring to hold an interest in diversified groups of stock instead of directly holding shares in one or more companies. Through the pension trust funds not less than twenty million (probably a great many more) employees already have an indirect beneficial claim both to the dividends proceeding from shares and to the rise in market value in the pension portfolio—even though their interest is nonliquid, and is received only on retirement, death or (occasionally) other con-

tingency. Perhaps two million holders of shares in mutual funds are likewise indirect beneficiaries, although they receive current return, and can promptly convert their shares into cash.[38]

In addition to these two categories there are other intermediate institutions which are also holders (though less significant) of stocks—namely, life insurance companies which invest about three percent of their assets in stocks, and fire and casualty companies which invest a considerably larger percentage. Comparatively speaking, all these institutions combined probably own a relatively small fraction of all stocks outstanding—perhaps between seven and ten percent.[39] Yet the rapidity of their growth—especially striking in the case of pension trusts —indicates that this form of stockholding is likely to become dominant in future years.

The significance of the intermediate institutions is twofold. First, they vastly increase the number of citizens who, to some degree, rely on the stockholding form of wealth. Second, they remove the individual still further from connection with or impact on the management and administration of the productive corporations themselves.

As might be expected, the law has moved to protect the holders of this form of wealth. It has not unnaturally moved along the lines of the interest that most preoccupies shareholders—that is, "liquidity" (capacity to turn the holding into cash), and market price. Since liquidity turns not on underlying property, but on resale of shares, legal protection is chiefly involved with the processes of the market place. Hence its preoccupation with information enabling buyers and sellers to

---

[36] The 1962 figure is 17,010,000 stockholders. U. S. DEP'T OF COMMERCE, STATISTICAL ABSTRACT OF THE UNITED STATES 474 (1964).

[37] See note 11 *supra* and accompanying text.

[38] See generally HARBRECHT, PENSION FUNDS AND ECONOMIC POWER (1959).

[39] No one really knows the exact percentage of institutional holdings of stocks. Mutual investment funds are wholly invested in stock: they are reported to aggregate about $29 billion. No figures are available on pension trust holdings and insurance company holdings (such holdings are small due to statutory limitation on this kind of investment). A sophisticated guess on the generous side would be total holdings of around $50 billion or less than 10% of the value of outstanding stocks—hence the rough estimate. The percentage is probably slowly rising.

determine the price at which they are willing to buy or sell. The entire battery of legislation set up by the Securities and Exchange Acts[40] has essentially little to do with the conduct of the corporation's affairs beyond requiring regular publication of information considered accurate by accounting standards, and prohibiting speculative activities by corporate administrators. Even more directly, this legislation deals with conduct of the stock exchanges themselves and with practices of their members who buy or sell as brokers for the public.

Both in direction and effect, this preoccupation of the Securities and Exchange Acts recognizes a new economic fact: that stock markets are no longer places of "investment" as the word was used by classical economists. Save to a marginal degree, they no longer allocate capital. They are mechanisms for liquidy. The purchaser of stock, save in rare instances, does not buy a new issue. The price he pays does not add to capital or assets of the corporation whose shares he buys. Stock markets do not exist for, and in general are not used for (in fact are not allowed to be used for), distribution of newly-issued shares. Their rules commonly prevent shares from being listed and traded until *after* they have been sold by some other means. Occasionally, it is true, large new issues are distributed which shortly after make their way into markets (one thinks at once of the American Telephone and Telegraph Company issue of new stock in 1964). But such operations perform an insignificant percentage of the work of stock exchanges. The exchanges are institutions in which shares, arising from investment made long ago, are shifted from sellers who wish cash to buyers who wish stock. Purchases and sales on the New York and other stock exchanges do not seriously affect the business operations of the companies whose shares are the subject of trading.

We have yet to digest the social-economic situation resulting from this fact. Immense dollar values of stocks are brought and sold every day, month and year. These dollars—indeed hundreds of billions of dollars—do not, apparently, enter the stream of direct commercial or productive use. That is, they do not become "capital" devoted to productive use. A seller of stocks more likely desires to buy other stocks than to use the capital for a business he himself owns.[41]

Dr. Paul Harbrecht, at Columbia and now at Georgetown University, has been elaborating a theory that we have evolved a new wealth-holding and wealth-circulating system whose liquidity is maintained through the exchanges but is only psychologically connected with the capital gathering and capital application system on which productive industry and enterprise actually depend.[42] If this is the fact, one effect of the corporate system has been to set up a parallel, circulating "property-wealth" system, in which the wealth flows from passive wealth-holder to passive wealth-holder, without significantly furthering the functions of capital formation, capital application, capital use or risk bearing. Yet these functions were the heart of the nineteenth century "capitalist" system. Both the wealth and the wealth-holders are divorced from the productive—that is, the commercial—process though, at long last, the estimate of this wealth turns on an estimate of the productiveness, the

[40] Securities Act of 1933, 48 Stat. 74, as amended, 15 U. S. C. §§ 77a–77aa (1959), as amended, 15 U. S. C. §§ 77b, 77c, 77h (Supp. V, 1964), as amended, Securities Acts Amendments of 1964, § 12, 78 Stat. 580; Securities Exchange Act of 1934, 48 Stat. 881, as amended, 15 U. S. C. §§ 77b–77e, 77j, 77k, 77m, 77o, 77s, 78a–78o, 78o–3, 78p–78hh (1959), as amended, 15 U. S. C. §§ 78c, 78d, 78s (Supp. V, 1964), as amended, Securities Acts Amendments of 1964, §§ 2–11, 78 Stat. 565.

[41] Though accurate figures are not available, it is estimated that between 20% and 25% of all trading on the New York Stock Exchange is for "institutional" accounts. It represents investment funds or other institutions selling blocks of securities and buying others. In addition, there is a substantial volume of such trading which goes on off the exchange—the so-called "third market." But this trading comprises only an insignificant amount of "new" stock issues. It is a shift in ownership—from the previous holder to a new holder—gradually indeed from individual investors to institutional investors.

[42] See HARBRECHT, PENSION FUNDS AND ECONOMIC POWER 273–89 (1959); Harbrecht, *The Modern Corporation Revisited*, 64 COLUM. L. REV. 1410 (1964).

character and effectiveness of the corporation whose shares are its vehicles.

Now, clearly, this wealth cannot be justified by the old economic maxims, despite passionate and sentimental arguments of neoclassic economists who would have us believe the old system has not changed. The purchaser of stock does not contribute savings to an enterprise, thus enabling it to increase its plant or operations. He does not take the "risk" of a new or increased economic operation; he merely estimates the chance of the corporation's shares increasing in value. The contribution his purchase makes to anyone other than himself is the maintenance of liquidity for other shareholders who may wish to convert their holdings into cash. Clearly he can not and does not intend to contribute managerial or entrepreneurial effort or service.

This raises a problem of social ethics that is bound to push its way into the legal scene in the next generation. Why have stockholders? What contribution do they make, entitling them to heirship of half the profits of the industrial system, receivable partly in the form of dividends, and partly in the form of increased market values resulting from undistributed corporate gains? Stockholders toil not, neither do they spin, to earn that reward. They are beneficiaries by position only. Justification for their inheritance must be sought outside classic economic reasoning.

It can be founded only upon social grounds. There is—and in American social economy, there always has been—a value attached to individual life, individual development, individual solution of personal problems, individual choice of consumption and activity. Wealth unquestionably does add to an individual's capacity and range in pursuit of happiness and self-development. There is certainly advantage to the community when men take care of themselves. But that justification turns on the distribution as well as the existence of wealth. Its force exists only in direct ratio to the number of individuals who hold such wealth. Justification for the stockholder's existence thus depends on increasing distribution within the American population. Ideally, the stockholder's position will be impregnable only when every American family has its fragment of that position and of the wealth by which the opportunity to develop individuality becomes fully actualized.

Such distribution is indeed proceeding —rather dramatically in terms of statistics, all too slowly in terms of social ethics. The generation since 1932 has multiplied the number of direct stockholders tenfold. If indirect stockholdings through intermediate institutions are included, a vast indirect sector has grown up as well. Yet distribution of wealth generally is still in its infancy. One percent of the American population owns perhaps twenty-five percent of all personally-owned wealth[43] and undoubtedly more than that percentage of common stocks. Plainly we have a long way to go. The intermediate institutions, notably pension trusts, justify themselves not merely because they increase the benefits of the stockholder-position, but because they rationalize it as well. Through direct ownership, Nym who bought railroad stocks twenty years ago lost money, Bardolph who bought A.T.&T. trebled his stake, while Pistol who bought I.B.M. stock has multiplied it fiftyfold. This is an irrational result. The pension trust, possibly holding all of these stocks, distributes the losses and the benefits (the latter being considerably greater) among a broad category of employees.

One would expect therefore that the law would increasingly encourage an ever wider distribution of stocks—whether through tax policy or some other device. It would encourage pension trust or social security trust entry into stockholder position. The time may well come when the government social security funds are invested, not wholly in government bonds as at present but in a broadening list of American stocks. As social security and pension trusts increasingly cover the entire working population of the United States, the stockholder position, though having lost its ancient justification, could become a vehicle for rationalized wealth distribution corresponding to and serving the American ideal of a just civilization.

[43] LAMPMAN, THE SHARE OF TOP WEALTHHOLDERS IN NATIONAL WEALTH 1922–1926, at 208 (1962).

The institution of passive property has an advantage which, so far as we know, is new to history in that distribution and redistribution of wealth-holding can take place without interruption of the productive process. Ancient Hebrew law required redistribution of land every half-century through the institution of the "Jubilee Year," [44] but ran into operational difficulties, as might have been expected. The great revolutionary movements of 1848 and, in our time, in Russia, China and Cuba, involved extreme productive losses, none of which has yet been recouped (though after nearly half a century the Soviet Union may finally be at the point of doing so). The corporate system, accompanied by reasonably enlightened tax policies and aided by continuously growing productivity, can achieve whatever redistribution the American people want.

Few observers would seriously deny that greater production is inevitable as well as needed. President Lyndon B.

Johnson boldly embraced the proposition that "poverty" (referring to families with income of less than three thousand dollars a year[45]) can and should be abolished, making a first tentative approach toward meeting the problem in 1964. It is scarcely open to question that present and potential productive capacity offers adequate tools to the American economy when and if the American public really desires to "abolish poverty." That is, the tools are at hand insofar as the problems are economic. Actually it is clear that problems deeper than economic—for example, problems of education and automation—will have to be met. What can be said is that the deeper problems cannot readily be met unless productive capacity can be maintained and increased to finance their solution, and unless the present technical organization of wealth can permit the shifting process to go on without interrupting or handicapping production. Both these conditions do exist.

[44] *Leviticus* 25:8–34.

[45] See N. Y. Times, March 18, 1964, p. 31, col. 1.

THE INSTITUTIONAL ECONOMIC REVOLUTION

Though its outline is still obscure, the central mass of the twentieth century American economic revolution has become discernible. Its driving forces are five: (1) immense increase in productivity; (2) massive collectivization of property devoted to production, with accompanying decline of individual decision-making and control; (3) massive dissociation of wealth from active management; (4) growing pressure for greater distribution of such passive wealth; (5) assertion of the individual's right to live and consume as the individual chooses.

Of this revolution, the corporation has proved a vital (albeit neutral) instrument and vehicle. It has become, and now is, the dominant form of organization and production. It has progressively created, and continues to create, a passive form of wealth. It is, in great measure, emancipated from dependence on individual savings and "capital" markets. Nevertheless, like the slave of Aladdin's lamp, it

must increasingly follow the mandate of the American state, embodied in social attitudes and in case, statute and constitutional law. This mandate changes and evolves as a consensus is developed on values and their priorities in American life.

This revolution is no longer just a possibility, as was the case when *The Modern Corporation and Private Property* was published in 1932. It is at least half-way along. In historical terms, it is moving rapidly. Some may dread, others may welcome it. But its existence and its advance can not be seriously denied. The property system has decisively changed and there is no ground for believing the change is reversible. Tentative beginnings are apparent in the companion area of distribution, chiefly through taxation.

A closely related trend (not here discussed) is, of course, emergence of the American state partly as an administrator of wealth distribution, partly as a direct distributor of certain products. In notable areas production for use rather than production for profit is emerging as the norm. Education, scientific research and development, the arts, and a variety of services ranging from roads and low-income housing to nonprofit recreation and television constitute a few illustrative fields. Health will probably be—in part now is—such a field. Increasingly it is clear that these noncommercial functions are, among other things, essential to the continued life, stability and growth of the non-statist corporate enterprise.

In typical American fashion, the revolution has come not through a single ideological or utopian burst, conceived and imposed by a few, but through an evolving consensus that insists equally on enjoying the results of mass production and on the primacy of individual life. It will go forward—as it inevitably must—as fast and as far as that consensus demands.

CONCLUSION

In summary, we are well underway toward recognition that property used in production will be made to conform to the conception of civilization worked out through American constitutional democratic processes. The Civil Rights Act of 1964[46] was a notable step in this process, though it originated at least a generation or more ago.[47] This could, as I think it does, include recognition that collective operations—predominantly conducted by corporations—as they attain size and power, are assimilable to statist operations, and are governed by the same constitutional limitations. Having attained size and economic power surpassing individual operations, corporations are essentially political constructs, having perpetual life and a continued legitimacy that depends on their performance as productive and distributive mechanisms. But in intra-corporate operations (the corporation and its officers, agents, labor and employees) and in productive and distributive functions (relations with suppliers and customers), they will not be allowed to invade personality and freedom, or to discriminate for or against categories of men.

Passive property, on the other hand, loses its "capital" function and becomes increasingly an exclusive means for distributing liquid wealth, and a channel for distributing income whose accumulation for capital purposes is not required. Norms for that distribution are beginning to change. The antipoverty campaign suggests a beginning, setting minimum standards of distributed income. Beyond that (police regulation aside) the right to choose consumption—to spend if and as you please—will be guarded as a defense of the individual's right to order his own life.

So far, so much. Yet, far beyond this summary, the real revolution of our time is yet faintly perceived. If the current estimate that by 1980 (only fifteen years off) our total productivity will double (approximately 1.2 trillion of 1960 dollars) and personally-received income will reach approximately one trillion dollars, proves true, the entire emphasis of American civilization will appreciably change. Philosophical preoccupation will become more important than economic. What is this personal life, this individuality, this search for personal development and fulfillment intended to achieve? Mere wallowing in consumption would leave great numbers of people unsatisfied; their demand will be for participation. This means, in substance, a growing demand that significant jobs be available for everyone, at a time when automation may diminish the number of all commercially created jobs as we presently know them. It may well mean that the state will be expected to create jobs wherever

---

[46] 78 Stat. 241.

[47] The passage of the Civil Rights Act does not, of course, prevent the application of constitutional limitations along the lines suggested in my article, *Constitutional Limitations on Corporate Activity—Protection of Personal Rights from Invasion Through Economic Power,* 100 U. Pa. L. Rev. 933 (1952).

a social need is recognized, and irrespective of the classic requirement for a commercial base. Is it possible, as Walt Rostow maintains,[48] that the population will merely become bored? Perhaps; but if so, it will be because esthetics, the arts, the endeavor to understand and enjoy the thrilling prospects opened by science, and the endless research for meaning, will have tragically lagged far behind economic advance. Not impossibly, the teacher, the artist, the poet and the philosopher will then set the pace.

Meantime, quite obviously—as a glance at Harlem (ten blocks from Columbia University) or the Appalachian coal fields or the other spotted areas of rural and urban decay will forcefully demonstrate —there is plenty to be done.

[48] ROSTOW, THE STAGES OF ECONOMIC GROWTH 91–92 (1960).

SUGGESTED ADDITIONAL READINGS

1. Aaron, Daniel, *Men of Good Hope,* New York: Oxford University Press, 1961, 329 pp. (paper). An excellent series of short biographies of leading American progressives from Emerson and Parker through Theodore Roosevelt.

2. Allen, Frederick Lewis, *Only Yesterday,* New York: Bantam Books, 1946 (paper), pp. 322–398. A very vivid and colorful description of the 1930's Depression, its prelude and aftermath.

3. Anderson, James E., *The Emergence of the Modern Regulatory State,* Washington, D. C.: Public Affairs Press, 1962 (paper), pp. 72–143. An excellent source on government regulation lucidly written.

4. Buckingham, Walter, *Automation,* New York: New American Library, 1961 (paper), pp. 88–119. A discussion of automation's effect upon the American worker; and the issue of employment and automation.

5. Carr, E. H., *The New Society,* New York: St. Martin's Press, 1957, pp. 61–76. A serious study calling for a re-evaluation of our political mythology insofar as it is based on Lockean theses and principles that no longer exist. We have moved from an individualistic to a collectivistic economic base and need to accommodate to it politically.

6. Cochran, Thomas C., *The Age of Enterprise,* New York: Harper, 1961, Rev. ed. (paper), pp. 129–154, 181–211. A short historical summary of the use of railroad power, trusts, and corporations, and the whole phenomenon of "finance capitalism."

7. Daugherty, C. R., *The Labor Problems of American Society,* Boston: Houghton Mifflin, 1952, pp. 435–481. A standard text which presents in simple language a comprehensive account of the intricacies of collective bargaining. (For a more current analysis of collective bargaining see Jacobs, Paul, *Old Before its Time: Collective Bargaining at 28,* Santa Barbara: The Center for the Study of Democratic Institutions, 1963, 46 pp. (paper).

8. Grunewald, Donald, and Henry L. Bass (eds.), *Public Policy and the Modern Corporation,* New York: Appleton-Century-Crofts, 1966 (paper), pp. 347–361. Two articles on opposite sides of the question: Should businessmen stay out of politics or become active in politics?

9. Harrington, Michael, *The Other America,* New York: Macmillan, 1962, 186 pp. (paper). A trail-blazer in its field; brought the problem of poverty in the United States in open view. A categorization, description, and definition of the

segments of our population who are the poor and, in the author's conclusion, a separate nation within a nation.

10. Harris, Seymour, "U. S. Welfare Programs and Policies," in *The Nation's Economic Objectives,* Chicago: University of Chicago Press, 1964, pp. 123–150. A detailed, statistical analysis by a leading economist of the nature and scope of our welfare programs. Includes a description of insurance financing, welfare tax systems, payroll taxes, educational programs, and medical services.

11. Hofstadter, Richard, *Social Darwinism in American Thought,* Boston: Beacon Press, Rev. ed. 1965, (paper), pp. 67–85. A definitive work; recommended several times in this volume's annotations. Here the reference is to a chapter on the life and thought of Lester Ward.

12. Josephson, Matthew, *The Robber Barons,* New York: Harcourt, Brace, 1934, 474 pp. A vividly written account of the era 1861–1901. Subtitled "The Great American Capitalists"; describes the social milieu within which the captains of industry came into being and flourished. A valuable contribution to the literature of this colorful era.

13. Kariel, Henry S., *The Decline of American Pluralism,* Stanford: Stanford University Press, 1961, pp. 49–67. These pages describe the incorporation of labor and its new role in our society; particularly valuable for its detailing of the union's inner organization and factional strife.

14. Krislov, Samuel, and Lloyd Musolf (eds.), *The Politics of Regulation,* Boston: Houghton Mifflin, 1964, 261 pp. (paper). A collection of readings dealing with every major phase of regulation: patterns of regulation, its relation to capitalism, populism and democracy, responsibility and responsiveness. Among its readings are selections from Hayek, Lasswell, Redford, Landis, Clark, Hamilton and many others.

15. Lerner, Max, *America As a Civilization,* New York: Simon and Schuster, 1957, pp. 465–540, 621–700. Two chapters in a major work by a leading social critic and essayist. Subjects dealt with include the open-class society, profiles of the new middle class and the workers, the democratic class struggle, belonging and joining.

16. McConnell, Grant, *Private Power and American Democracy,* New York: Alfred A. Knopf, 1966, pp. 246–297. A discussion of "Self-Regulation: The Politics of Business"; describes the process of decentralization and decreasing size of the constituencies in the politics of business.

17. Merriman, Charles, "The Possibilities of Planning," *American Journal of Sociology,* Vol. 49, March 1944, pp. 397–407. One of the deans of American political science presents a defense of the compatability of planning and democracy.

18. Meyer, Frank S. (ed.), *What is Conservatism?,* New York: Holt, Rinehart and Winston, 1964, 242 pp. (paper). A superb collection of essays representing all phases of current conservative thought; includes selections from Kirk, Kendall, Röpke, Possony, Chamberlain, and Hayek.

19. Monsen, Joseph, Jr., and Mark W. Cannon, *The Makers of Public Policy,* New York: McGraw-Hill, 1965, pp. 96–132. In a book concerned with American power groups and their ideologies, this chapter deals with the various elements making up the agricultural power groups—the Farmers' Union, the National Grange, and the Farm Bureau. Also contains a prognosis for future farm policies.

20. Pelling, Henry, *American Labor,* Chicago: University of Chicago Press, 1964,

147 pp. (paper). A succinct history of American labor, from labor movements in colonial times through the post-Taft-Hartley days. There is a particularly interesting closing chapter on labor as a permanent minority, and a helpful "important dates" section.

21. Roosevelt, Franklin D., "Commonwealth Club Address," September 23, 1932, in Samuel I. Rosenman, ed., *The Public Papers and Addresses of Franklin D. Roosevelt,* New York: Random House, 1938, Vol. I, pp. 742–756. Delivered during the presidential campaign of 1932, this speech contained the first use and delineation of the term New Deal.

22. Salomon, Leon I. *The Independent Federal Regulatory Agencies,* New York: H. W. Wilson, 1959, 195 pp. An excellent source book for a detailed description of the operation of the "big six" agencies.

23. Schlesinger, Arthur M., Jr., *The Coming of the New Deal,* Boston: Houghton Mifflin, 1959, 669 pp. The second volume of the prize-winning work, *The Age of Roosevelt.* Describes in detail the "hundred days" and the entire first phase of the New Deal.

24. Viner, Jacob, "The United States as a 'Welfare State,' " in *The Nation's Economic Objectives,* note 10, pp. 151–167. A portrayal of the American version of the welfare state as compared to other such societies elsewhere in the world; very good contrast of the American welfare state to Marxist ideology.

25. Weinberg, Arthur and Lila (eds.), *The Muckrakers,* New York: Simon and Schuster, 1961, pp. 1–39, 67–174. The editors have assembled (and commented on) some of the leading "muckraking" articles from such journals as *McCall's* and *Collier's,* by Baker, Tarbell, Steffens, Irwin, Sullivan, and others.

26. Ziegler, Herman, *Interest Groups in American Society,* Englewood Cliffs, N. J.: Prentice-Hall, 1964, pp. 163–199. A brief chapter dealing with agrarian politics and emphasizing what the author refers to as "the triumph of formal organizations." Can be read in conjunction with *The Makers of Public Policy.* See also *Poverty on the Land,* National Advisory Committee on Farm Labor, 1965, 64 pp., which is particularly useful for its discussion of farm problems as they relate to the general problems of poverty and race.

FOR FURTHER CONSIDERATION

1. Does bigness in business and labor organization pose a threat to American freedoms? Are they simply inevitabilities which we have to learn to live with? To what degree is organized political action by labor unions and business associations "legitimate"?

2. Is the average American consumer disadvantaged as a result of new developments in labor-management relations? What, if anything, can he do about it? What, if anything, should the government do about it?

3. If President Eisenhower was correct in his assessment of the degree to which we have accepted the necessity of active promotion of social gains, how do you account for the continued persistence. as a political issue, of the "welfare state"?

4. What would you add to or delete from the following statement?

"For there is nothing mysterious about the foundations of a healthy and strong democracy. The basic things expected by our people of their political and economic systems are simple. They are: Equality of opportunity for youth and

for others. Jobs for those who can work. . . . Persons deserving or needing
gainful employment may obtain it . . . security for those who need it . . . the
ending of special privilege for the few . . . the preservation of civil liberties for
all . . . the enjoyment of the fruits of scientific progress in a wider and constantly rising standard of living . . ." (F. D. Roosevelt, 1941)

How would you suggest we go about accomplishing these objectives?

5. Our experience of the past thirty-five years in agriculture suggests to some that
the familiar economic principles of a capitalistic system (supply and demand,
for instance) might not be applicable. Increasingly, and in spite of the tendency
toward development of large cooperative and corporative farming enterprises,
aggressive governmental programs have been necessary to meet the basic problems of agriculture. What avenues of approach can you suggest toward solution
to these problems? Is the interdependence of the various segments of the economy a crucial factor to be considered? Does this problem-solving effort offer
any insights on the complexity of policy-making? What political forces do you
suspect would be operative in the development of policy in this regard?

Foreign Policy — Real and Ideal   7

In recent history the world has been divided along ideological lines. Yet all nations purport to be seeking peace. The schism has been intensified and exacerbated by increased industrial, social, and political changes. Depressed peoples are waking up to the possibilities that a society may offer its members— educational, agricultural, and political, as well as industrial. This coming-to-life of peoples heretofore buried in ignorance, superstition, and economic and political deprivation is causing perhaps the greatest social upheaval the world has ever known. [2, 5]

Contemporary world society contrasts sharply with that of the past. Never before have so many peoples begun to attain national consciousness. Never before have populations grown so explosively. Never before have so many people crowded into huge cities where they live divorced from direct knowledge of their means of sustenance. Never have people been so vulnerable to wars, natural disasters, civil commotions, and unpredictable disruptions of their complex economies. But perhaps most important, never before in modern times has so much of the world been gripped for so long in the continuing conflict between two dominating power blocs. At the same time that levels of human aspiration are rising so rapidly throughout the world, the world scene is characterized by ideological and political dichotomization exceeding anything seen or perhaps even dreamed of in all history. [8, 12]

The present chapter will analyze major aspects of American foreign policy, particularly the underlying considerations that may help us to understand better the day-to-day problems in relation to long-range policies and their consequences. The chapter will consider (1) cultural differences as they affect foreign policy, (2) the "realist" and "idealist" approaches to foreign policy, (3) the role of the

Some material in this chapter introduction appeared previously, in somewhat different form, in Carol Fisher and Fred Krinsky, *Middle East in Crisis* (Syracuse, N.Y.: Syracuse University Press, 1959), pp. 62–69.

public in foreign policy, (4) the institutional framework of foreign policy, and (5) some special considerations of foreign policy in the mid-twentieth century.

CULTURAL DIFFERENCES AND FOREIGN AFFAIRS

In an environment so entirely new, history has little to teach us. As a result of many anthropological studies, we know only that diverse customs and moral standards abound throughout the world, and that such emotions as fear, suspicion, and antagonism are the common responses to outsiders.[1] Since the differences which lead men to fear and hate others are clearly learned rather than innate, it becomes clear that the key to understanding other men and other societies lies in the study and comprehension of their systems of value and behavior. If nothing else, such study can provide us with insights as to how and why *they* see *us* as they do.

While foreign policy must be understood as primarily designed to maximize the national self-interest, the world is too complex today to permit correct assessment of national self-interest in the absence of clear understanding of the national self-interest of all other nations, as *they* see it, and the values which that self-interest articulates or assumes. The policymaker must never cease to study foreign customs, mentality, values, and goals, and must constantly ask the question, How do other people feel about us? [11, 13]

Creating a foreign policy for the United States is one of the most difficult tasks which faces any administration. Beginning with President Washington, each chief executive has had to meet the dual responsibility of developing a foreign policy consistent with the national self-interest as interpreted in his time, while simultaneously placating political opposition within and without his own party. This dual undertaking calls for a combination of the proverbial wisdom of Solomon and the patience of Job.

Our foreign policy traditionally has been rooted in domestic affairs: its constant aim has been to preserve and protect our institutions and values and an environment congenial to their vitality. [1] Since World War II the questions of foreign and military policy, and their costs in taxes, military service, and inflation, have moved into the very center of domestic affairs. Many people want to know: What is involved in making foreign policy? What is the machinery for making foreign policy? How well does the machinery operate and what are its weaknesses?

In foreign affairs a nation confronts conditions shaped largely by factors lying beyond its direct control. In making policy, therefore, the task is to decide how the nation can and should use its resources to modify external conditions in ways favorable to its interests.

The policymaker works in the uneasy world of prediction and probability. On the basis of the available intelligence, his job is (1) to determine what alternative courses of action are feasible and (2) to choose which to pursue. [10] Identifying and formulating alternatives requires both analysis and imagination. And in choosing among them, one must guard against disaster should the unex-

---

[1] For many of the ideas expressed in this section we are indebted to Professor Douglas Haring, formerly of Syracuse University.

pected occur, while avoiding the cautious hedging which forfeits the advantages of any single course by straddling several.

What are the main objectives to be pursued? What measures are most likely to be effective for those purposes? What means—military, economic, political, diplomatic, psychological—can be made available? What other nations can be induced to work together for the same ends? Will other nations consider the proposed measures as imperiling their interests, and how will they react? Will the proposed action help or harm other foreign or domestic policies or programs and how much?

REALISM AND IDEALISM IN FOREIGN POLICY

The development of American foreign policy has generally taken place within the context of an ideological struggle between what may be termed realism and idealism.

Representative of the viewpoint of political realism are the following quotations from Alexander Hamilton and the contemporary political analyst, Hans J. Morgenthau, respectively:

Self-preservation is the first duty of a nation . . . Indeed, the rule of morality in this respect is not precisely the same between nations as between individuals. The duty of making its own welfare the guide of its actions, is much stronger upon the former than upon the latter; in proportion to the greater magnitude and importance of national compared with individual happiness, and to the greater permanency of the effects of national than of individual conduct.[2]

The fundamental error which has thwarted American foreign policy in thought and action is the antithesis of national interest and moral principles. The equation of political moralism with morality and of political realism with immorality is itself untenable. The choice is not between moral principles and the national interest devoid of moral dignity, but between one set of moral principles, divorced from political reality, and another set of moral principles derived from political reality. The basic fact of international politics is the absence of a society able to protect the existence, and to promote the interests of the individual nations. For the individual nations to take care of their own national interests is, then, a political necessity. There can be no moral duty to neglect them; for as the international society is at present constituted, the consistent neglect of the national interest can only lead to national suicide. Yet it can be shown that there exists even a positive moral duty for the individual nation to take care of its national interests.
Self-preservation for the individual as well as for societies is not only a biological and psychological necessity, but in the absence of an overriding moral obligation a moral duty as well. . . .[3]

Typical of the idealistic approach are the following quotations from President Woodrow Wilson and President Franklin D. Roosevelt, respectively.

We dare not turn from the principle that morality and not expediency is the thing that must guide us, and that we will never condone iniquity because it is most convenient to do so.[4]

[2] *The Collected Works of Alexander Hamilton,* Henry Lodge, ed. (New York: G. P. Putnam's, 1904), Vol. IV, p. 457.
[3] Hans J. Morganthau, "The Mainsprings of American Foreign Policy: The National Interest vs. Moral Abstractions," *The American Political Science Review,* XLIV, No. 4 (December 1950), 261–262.
[4] *The Political Thought of Woodrow Wilson,* E. David Cronon, ed., p. 282. Copyright © 1965 by The Bobbs-Merrill Co., Inc., and reprinted by permission of the College Division.

We are committed to the proposition that principles of morality—and considerations for our own security—will never permit us to acquiesce in a peace dictated by aggressors and sponsored by appeasers. We know that enduring peace cannot be bought at the cost of other people's freedom . . .

In the future days, which we seek to make secure, we look forward to a world founded upon essential human freedoms. The first is freedom of speech and expression . . . everywhere in the world.

The second is freedom of every person to worship God in his own way . . . everywhere in the world.

The third is freedom from want . . . everywhere in the world.

The fourth is freedom from fear . . . anywhere in the world. . . . Our support goes to those who struggle to gain those rights or keep them.[5]

It becomes obvious that each of these approaches to making foreign policy is based upon a series of tacit assumptions and value judgments. It is necessary, therefore, to examine both the realistic and idealistic viewpoints in order to determine their basic soundness.

At the outset it would seem that the realistic viewpoint advocates dealing with each issue on its own merits and reaching conclusions on the basis of an assessment of gains and costs involved. The realist bases his approach upon acceptance of a prevailing Hobbesian conflict among nations. Strife rather than harmony is seen as the general rule in international relations. In the absence of an "overawing power" the goal of valid diplomacy is a comparatively limited one. It consists of the limitations of struggles and the restriction of their scope. Hence, the emergence of the containment policy under the authorship of Mr. Kennan.[6] Here, as always, the realist seeks not the utopian society which he believes can exist only on a blueprint, but rather the means of attaining a balance of power and an adjustment to existing conditions. He therefore emphasizes balance, compromise, and maintenance of a flexible bargaining position. He acknowledges that in international diplomacy there often exists a discrepancy between means and ends. Above all, he believes that the struggle for power is a permanent condition and that the best we can do is try to limit the over-concentration of power and relieve the tensions which make for war. Britain, for example, for over one hundred years maintained peace in Europe through a carefully controlled balance of power.

The political idealist believes that some formal moral criterion must be established as an a priori basis for policy determination. He ascribes all great controversies in history to the clash between incompatible ideals and principles rather than to a drive for power or purposeful assessment of gains and costs. [18] The idealist looks for alternatives to a policy of international competition to maximize the national self-interest. These often include world government, forswearing relations with "bad" countries, or some form of neutralism or isolationism.

Political commentators are pretty much in agreement that regardless of whether one is essentially an idealist or a realist there exists an underlying consensus as to the ends and means of American foreign policy today. Both schools adhere to a broad policy which includes the containment of the Soviet Union and Red China, establishment of a peaceful world order in which American

---

[5] *The Public Papers and Addresses of Franklin D. Roosevelt,* (New York: Macmillan, 1941), pp. 663 ff.

[6] George F. Kennan, "The Sources of Soviet Conduct," *Foreign Affairs,* XXV, No. 4 (July 1947), pp. 566–582.

ideological and material interests are secure, and the recognition that a reasonable reconciliation of individual freedom and mass welfare is desirable.

American foreign relations in the twentieth century have most often been affected by the idealistic approach. Thus, for example, we find the refusal to recognize first the Soviet Union and then Red China on the grounds that they are "evil and corrupt powers." Our wars have been fought to eliminate and extirpate the evildoers. When we go into battle, our goal is "unconditional surrender" and our motto "make the world safe for democracy." The implication is that once evil men are destroyed, evil too will disappear.

Realism and idealism are not unrelated. Indeed, a realistic foreign policy must take account of the value of idealistic commitment. Yet today foreign policy determinations will appear quite different to observers of the two schools. Basically the question may be: are we attempting to achieve a peaceful world in which all men may determine their own destiny, or are we attempting to create a world in which our national self-interest may be maximized? Perhaps the latter (realistic goal) is the reason for the former (idealistic goal).

There is an emerging eclecticism within contemporary United States foreign policy—an attempt to combine both the realistic and idealistic approach—which is reflected in the following statements. The first is from an address to the nation by President Dwight D. Eisenhower, delivered on April 16, 1953:

The way chosen by the United States was plainly marked by a few clear precepts, which govern its conduct in world affairs—First: no people on earth can be held, as a people, to be an enemy, for all humanity shares the common hunger for peace and fellowship and justice.
Second: no nation's security and well-being can be lastingly achieved in isolation but only in effective cooperation with fellow nations.
Third: any nation's right to a form of government and an economic system of its own choosing is *inalienable*.
Fourth: any nation's attempt to dictate to other nations their form of government is *indefensible*.
And fifth: a nation's hope of lasting peace cannot be firmly based upon a race in armaments but rather upon just relations and honest understanding with all other nations.[7]

For the second quotation we turn to the words of Mr. George Kennan:

It is clear that the United States cannot expect in the foreseeable future to enjoy political intimacy with the Soviet regime. It must continue to regard the Soviet Union as a rival, not a partner, in the political arena. It must continue to expect that Soviet policies will reflect no abstract love of peace and stability, no real faith in the possibility of a permanent happy coexistence of the Socialist-Capitalist worlds, but rather a cautious, persistent pressure toward the disruption and weakening of all rival influence and rival power. Balanced against this are the facts that Russia, as opposed to the Western world in general, is still by far the weaker party, that Soviet policy is highly flexible, and that Soviet policy may well contain deficiencies which will eventually weaken its own total potential. This would of itself warrant the United States entering with reasonable confidence upon a policy of firm containment designed to confront the Russians with unalterable counterforce at every point where they show signs of encroaching upon the interests of a peaceful and stable world.[8]

[7] *Theory and Practice of American Foreign Policy,* Martin Gordon and Kenneth N. Vines, eds. (New York: Thomas Y. Crowell, 1955), p. 463.
[8] George F. Kennan, *American Diplomacy 1900–1950,* (Chicago: University of Chicago Press, 1951), p. 126.

How as a nation are we prepared to meet the demands of such a foreign policy? It is common to note that we have taken on reluctantly the role of world leadership [3] and that the American rise to its present position has been accompanied by the concomitant rise of a ruthless, amoral, power-hungry Soviet Union. The question naturally arises as to how capable we are of making the necessary decisions which will achieve for us the maximum national security. These decisions are vital to us, but it does not necessarily follow that there is a direct relationship between a successful American foreign policy—successful in terms of maximization of our national self-interest—and the political and economic well-being of the rest of the world.

Where would the idealists now direct us? What role would the realists demand of us? Does either approach in itself really provide reliable guidelines? What will the political effect be of the propaganda and votes of the interested pressure groups in this country? Is our foreign policy a valid representation of articulated public demands? Is United States foreign policy flexible enough to cope with emergencies as they arise?

THE PUBLIC AND FOREIGN POLICY

In the development of foreign policy, a democratic nation faces one of its most difficult dilemmas. In traditional democratic thought the executive position must somehow reflect the consensus of the electorate. But the electorate is often contradictory and the existence of a consensus is problematical. With so many involved in the creation of foreign policy, and so many more affected by its direction, it is to be wondered if *any* policy can clearly reflect the will of the people.[16]

The root of the problem lies in the relationship between the need for incisive and intelligent decision-making by an informed leadership and a democratic myth that insists that the people, in their inherent wisdom, can make the decisions vital to their survival. Can the American people make wise judgments about the complex and often remote problems of contemporary foreign policy? The question is complicated by the traditional pattern of American abstention from foreign problems except in periods of great stress. [1] The average American citizen is deeply involved in private pursuits. In fact, it is in this involvement that men like T. V. Smith insist one finds the secret of American freedom.[9] The average American develops political views on matters that affect him directly, such as tax laws, social security, and wage and price legislation, and only incidentally and nonspecifically is he involved in matters of foreign policy. As a result, there is often marked instability in his foreign policy views.

We come face to face, then, with the dual problem of what is the role of the public in policymaking, and how to make official leadership responsible to the public. No less a problem is posed by the institutionalized executive-congressional struggle over program direction and leadership, a normal result of the structure of our government, [4] further complicated by the recurring demands of conflicting pressure groups. [16] The average citizen who wants to form an intelligent opinion about foreign policy needs to know not only what the chief executive and the Con-

[9] T. V. Smith, *Constructive Ethics,* (New York: Appleton-Century-Crofts, 1948), Books I-III.

gress are striving to achieve but also what pressure groups are behind what policy and for what reasons.

In American democracy, foreign policy must, in the long run, reflect the viewpoints of the articulate publics. In the words of Paul H. Appleby, "Every expression of opinion on public affairs—in the barber shop or beauty parlor, in a taxicab, at a party, union meeting, farm organization meeting, or wherever—is a contribution to the climate of opinion within which the government acts in its constant effort to achieve or maintain consent."[10]

THE INSTITUTIONAL FRAMEWORK OF FOREIGN POLICY

Under our system, the mechanics of policy-making require close collaboration between the executive and Congress. The president, as head of the executive branch, has a central role. [4] Speaking for the nation, he is charged with the direction of our foreign relations. Leadership must come primarily from him. Congress, however, must provide the means of foreign policy. Only it can appropriate money, draft men, approve treaties and other commitments, confirm ambassadors and enact required legislation. But at all times the president has a tremendous advantage over the Congress in developing foreign policy because of his superior sources of information and his position as the only official with a national constituency.

The Constitution has only a 320-word section outlining the functions and duties of the office of the president, and the strength of our nation lies in part in the imprecise wording of the original document, allowing for elasticity in interpretation. The major roles of the president as outlined in the Constitution are as commander-in-chief and chief executive. These vague terms have allowed for fantastic growth and power of the office. Through a train of complicated events in our history including a technological revolution, strong presidents acting in times of crisis, Supreme Court interpretations, congressional action, and the support of the people, the modern president finds himself in what is undoubtedly one of the most powerful positions in the world today.

The major powers of the president in foreign affairs are these: recognizes foreign nations; appoints ambassadors and lesser foreign officials with advice and consent of the Senate; negotiates treaties with foreign nations with advice and consent of the Senate; has the sole authority to speak in foreign affairs for the United States; is commander-in-chief of the armed forces; and can negotiate executive agreements with foreign nations without the consent of the Senate.

To obtain essential support in the form of funds, commitments, or legislation, the executive must convince Congress of the necessity and wisdom of proposed policies. The president and appropriate Cabinet members meet informally with leaders of Congress and the relevant committees from time to time for briefings and consultation. Sometimes the president may address the Congress. Usually members of the Cabinet and other officials will appear before congressional committees to testify regarding requested actions.

[10] Paul H. Appleby, *Policy and Administration*, (University: University of Alabama Press, 1949), p. 145.

Infrequently, Congress may take the initiative in foreign affairs, as it did with the Vandenburg resolution which laid the foundation for the North Atlantic Treaty Organization (NATO) structure. More often, its role is to approve, reject, or modify proposals of the executive, or to influence its proposals by investigations or reports.

During times of crisis the presidential influence in foreign affairs grows. Lincoln used vaguely articulated emergency powers during the Civil War, and Franklin D. Roosevelt greatly augmented executive power during World War II. The United States does not have clearly defined emergency powers as many other nations do, but controversy over what authority the president has in foreign affairs has been somewhat clarified by major Supreme Court decisions. The executive agreement used so effectively by F. D. R. was declared constitutional in 1937 in *U. S.* v. *Belmont*.[11] In the previous year in *U. S.* v. *Curtiss, Wright Export Co.*,[12] the Court pointed out that the president has sole power to regulate foreign affairs. The president is the leader of the nation in the area of foreign affairs. What then are the drawbacks to effective presidential leadership in world affairs?

Robert Dahl, a contemporary political scientist, contends that the overworked congressman scuffling to satisfy the multitude of services his constituents demand—spending his time being re-elected, confused by lack of correct information on complex foreign issues, and receiving distorted foreign policy views from constituents—is not in a position to make careful foreign policy judgments.[13] The individual congressman does, nevertheless, retain his role in debating issues, serving as a critic and, ultimately, giving or withholding his support. But Congress is more important as a forum, a publicity tool, a sounding board than as a policy-making agency.

Allies are consulted in various ways and at various stages in the making of policy. In part, such consultation is done through normal diplomatic channels, using foreign ambassadors in Washington or our ambassadors in foreign capitals. Nowadays, however, agencies such as the NATO Council are often used as a convenient forum to discuss a proposed action which is of interest to its members. The United Nations provides a general arena for consulting other nations, friendly or otherwise. Much of this activity goes on behind the scenes, in sounding out other nations to develop common positions and to work out proposals and compromises. [15]

In appraising our foreign policy machinery, one should remember what little time our nation has had to master its current role. We emerged from World War II with ill-defined notions about our position and our interests and the direction of foreign policy. Most great powers have had an extended period to develop the techniques of foreign policy-making. Our nation has had less than a quarter-century, in times of unprecedented change and turmoil. In evolving its policies the United States had to learn from experience, and rapidly.

However, history awards no prizes for effort, no matter how creditable, if the results are not adequate to the need. We must therefore recognize that our process for foreign policy development suffers from several weaknesses.

[11] 301 U. S. 324 (1937).
[12] 299 U. S. 304 (1936).
[13] Robert A. Dahl, *Congress and Foreign Policy*, (New York: W. W. Norton, 1950). See Chaps. II, III, VI, XI, XII, *passim*.

(1) It is obviously ponderous. In running the gamut of the presidency, the federal bureaucracy, Congress and its committees, and the counterpart agencies of our allies, an analysis or proposal is likely to be diluted or blurred by compromise. Moreover, the time and energy required to initiate a policy doubtless create strong inertia against changing existing positions.

(2) The machinery has not always assured a realistic appraisal of conditions. The tendency of some to discount persuasive evidence of Soviet economic progress and Soviet ability to produce complex weapons probably resulted in part from reluctance to believe that a system repugnant in its methods could succeed as well as it has. Again, the full sweep of the Soviet threat has been hard for some to grasp because its purposes and methods are so foreign to our own. The increasing concern for Red China involves similar problems.

(3) The machinery has not produced a balanced allocation of resources among essential activities. The Sino–Soviet challenge is many-sided. It is not merely a military threat but also a political, diplomatic, and propaganda offensive throughout the world. The most obvious of these threats, however, is the military. Since it is easy to dramatize, there has been a dangerous tendency to emphasize military programs at the expense of other programs in allocating resources. It has been much more difficult to secure support for economic and technical assistance programs and for reciprocal trade agreements. Their results are more gradual and less dramatic. Yet failure to carry on a balanced program with necessary stress on non-military measures will expose us to grave dangers even though we maintain an adequate military posture. [8, 17]

(4) The Communist offensive is essentially long term. The Communist leaders view competitive co-existence as a struggle for an indefinite time. Even if peace is preserved they clearly intend to probe for weak spots and to exploit them fully. Our programs must be planned and carried out on a long-term basis. [14]

The policy-making machinery is not well-suited to planning in these terms. In the executive branch day-to-day crises constantly demand immediate action and divert attention from analysis of more basic problems. The budget procedure also tends to shorten the focus within which programs are presented and judged. With elections to Congress every two years, members on the lookout for election "issues" are likely to stress short-run policy effects. Then too the president's actions in foreign affairs must be related to his and his party's political welfare. Finally, the press has a similar bias for the immediate effect: the dramatic crisis is newsworthy, and gradual success seldom makes the headlines. All these factors tend to foreshorten the perspective in which programs are judged.

There is no simple cure for the weaknesses outlined. They flow in part from the very methods of consent and dispersion of power which underlie our political system. Their correction depends largely on better understanding of the defects and of the necessity for steady, persistent efforts to counter them.

FOREIGN POLICY—TODAY AND TOMORROW

The particular foreign policy questions will vary as world conditions change, but there are some special considerations bearing on any policy decisions which will continue over time. Five have been selected for discussion as of major significance to understanding the complexities of twentieth-century international relations: (1) the interrelationship of foreign policies; (2) the assumption of sincerity; (3) rejection of one-factor analysis; (4) the disutility of modern warfare; (5) the complexity of United States' policy in the 1960's. [6]

INTERRELATIONSHIP OF FOREIGN POLICIES

No nation stands alone in the twentieth century. Hence, the actions of one inevitably affect others. The foreign policy determinations of one nation will unavoidably involve the interests of some other nations, and, in the case of major nations, will indirectly affect the interests of all. Thus, to say that the primary purpose of foreign policy is the maximization of national self-interest requires that we recognize also that this attempt may, and often does, affect the efforts of other nations to maximize their national self-interest.

Our foreign policy goals are both determined by and determine the foreign policy goals of other nations. Conflicts of interest are inevitable, and the problems of interrelationship of interests will not disappear through an insistence on our own virtues or condemnation of the interests of other nations. For any nation to insist on full realization of its own interests without recognition of their effect upon the vital interests of other nations has proved in history to be an almost sure guarantee of its ultimate demise.

THE ASSUMPTION OF SINCERITY

Analysis of international relations can proceed profitably only upon an assumption that each nation is operating within a general commitment to the maximization of its national self-interest. Each nation defines for itself what its goals are and what means will best accomplish them. No nation is, of course, free to operate without recognition of the interrelationship of its goals and means with those of other nations. But it must be assumed that each nation is attempting to do in the international community that which it defines for itself to be best in its own interest. That all nations may at some time have to modify their goals and redefine their means in recognition of the goals and means of others is, of course, axiomatic.

From this viewpoint there are no "good guys" and "bad guys" in the international community. Obviously, from the point of view of the interests of any one nation and the ease or difficulty of their accomplishment, the actions of other nations may be unacceptable. From the standpoint of one nation's view of morality or humanitarianism, the actions of another may be immoral and inhumane. But explanations of the actions of nations simply in terms of morality or humanity, without recognition of their interests, will not produce very reliable assessments of the probable courses of action of the nations involved.

Specifically, it is highly doubtful that such terms as "peace-loving," "democratic," "self-determination," "freedom for the oppressed," and the like really explain a nation's actions without being related to the basic interests being advanced. For example, all nations profess to be for world peace, but these same nations repeatedly find it necessary to make war in order to accomplish their goal of peace. More accurately we might restate the position: any nation will favor peace as a goal *so long as it is not at the expense of uncompromisable national interests.*

To say we must assume the sincerity of all nations does not mean we must accept their goals or their means but only that we must analyze both on the assumption that they are trying sincerely to maximize their interests as they see them. Thus, for other nations to doubt the United States' sincerity in guaranteeing the national self-determination of various peoples is not surprising, but for them to fail to recognize the relationship of such a policy to the accomplishment of our own national interests would be quite another matter. Equally important, we must recognize that our goals of peace, self-determination, etc., are related directly to the accomplishment of our national interests in the international community—and the same is presumably true of all other nations—and consequently we do not have a monopoly of virtue, we are not always right and other nations always wrong.

REJECTION OF ONE-FACTOR ANALYSIS

It is popular today to view all international relations as reflecting the basic conflict between communism and democracy. Such a view, however, does not accurately represent the complexity of the problems of foreign policy. There is no doubt that the world has been dominated by two major power blocs since the end of World War II. But to view all relationships, all international programs, all national interests as determined by this conflict between the United States and the Soviet Union is both a colossal oversimplification and a serious handicap to efforts to devise realistic foreign policies.

The present conflict between communism and democracy, while it has its own peculiar characteristics, is not unique as a type of relationship. Basically the historical pattern is as follows: Major nations differ in their assessment of their interests and the means of maximizing them, and their conflicting assessments bring them into sharp conflict in their efforts to effect their foreign policies. Other nations are drawn in as their assessment of the best means of maximizing their interests dictates. Economic, political, ideological, and military conflict follows.

The goal of the foreign policy of the United States is not destruction of communism. Even if that were possible, challenges to American foreign policy would continue as this nation, in concert or conflict with others, redefined its interests and attempted to maximize them.

It is likewise unproductive to assume the homogeneous nature of communism. All nations which call themselves communist are not the same; particularly are they not the same in their impact on United States' foreign policy objectives. To split the world into communist and non-communist is an over-simplification which makes it impossible to appraise validly alternative policies. Not all nations calling themselves communist are our mortal enemies; indeed, the problem is to get behind such question-begging labels to assess precisely how the interests of each nation relate to our interests and their maximization. The USSR, China, Yugoslavia, and Cuba all call themselves communist, but failure to recognize their differences, and failure to relate our policies to theirs as separate entities can lead to paralysis in foreign policy development. As George F. Kennan, former U. S. ambassador to the Soviet Union, says,

. . . [T]he term 'Communist' does not serve adequately either to bring out the differences that prevail as between the various 'Communist' countries or to make clear the growing degree in which the problems they present for American diplomacy are similar to, or identical with, those presented for us by other countries which do not go by the name of 'Communist.' To the extent the term may still be useful, the usefulness is a rapidly declining one; and when we insist on deciding things simply according to whether we conceive ourselves to be dealing with something 'Communistic' or something 'non-Communistic' it is often only ourselves we are deceiving and our own responses we are distorting.[14]

THE DISUTILITY OF MODERN WARFARE

War in the mid-twentieth century is capable of destroying whole nations and perhaps civilization itself. Mankind has finally reached the point at which his capability to destroy is far beyond his capacity to survive. The nuclear age has brought the possibility of death to whole peoples, without corresponding hope for survival of the killers. It is the magnitude of this destructive potential that has made nuclear war a doubtful part of any realistic foreign policy today. [7, 9]

Conventional warfare is possible, for its costs are calculable and it can be survived. But conventional war can be engaged in only under these conditions: (1) one or both of the opposing sides is incapable of the use of large-scale nuclear warfare techniques; and (2) those capable of nuclear warfare find their basic interests either served by conventional war or not endangered by it. If the nuclear potential is present, any serious threat to the vital self-interest (say, survival or victory) of a nuclear-potential nation may be expected to escalate the scale of the war to the use of the maximum force necessary to win, i.e., to maximize the national interest. The history of war and of international relations suggests the validity of this expectation.

The tragic consequences of nuclear warfare suggests our best hope for its non-use: it is disutilitarian in its results. Death to, say, 125 million people of one nation would bring perhaps equal devastation to the killing nation through air pollution, even with a "clean" bomb, water pollution, disease, and food contamination resulting from the death of so many humans and animals. The inability to survive may be our best hope of avoiding the use of nuclear weapons.

But what of limited use? Small "pops" can be controlled, the results calculated, and survived. Limited use is possible if two conditions apply: (1) if one of the combatants has no nuclear potential; *and* (2) if all nuclear nations find the use of nuclear weapons by the using nation to be in their self-interest. Under any other circumstances, escalation to the point of disutility may be predicted.

What of a deterrent nuclear force? Deterrence may be meaningful if in fact the existence of massive retaliatory force does deter one nation from initiating a first-strike. But once that first-strike is on its way, regardless of the reason, the deterrence is no longer a deterrent; its use becomes simple retaliation. Retaliation, a counter-blow of equal or greater strength, is useful only if it can be calculated to maximize the gain to the interests of the using nation. The question now becomes: Is the retaliatory death of, say, 125 million of the other nation's people going to contribute in any constructive fashion to enabling the attacked nation to

[14] George F. Kennan, *On Dealing with the Communist World*, (New York: Harper & Row, 1964, for the Council on Foreign Relations, pp. viii–ix.

survive the effects of the first-strike? It may likewise be suggested, given these considerations, that even the threat of the use of nuclear power is becoming of less value as a device of foreign policy.

These are not simply questions of right or wrong but questions of survival, not only of one nation but of all. Impassioned demands that we use our nuclear capability to rid the world of potential threats—Red Chinese domination, for example—are based on failure to recognize the limitations imposed by condition (2) above when applied to nuclear warfare. In other words, use of nuclear weapons by any single nation is possible only if its use agrees with the interests of other nuclear powers. Even then, however, the using nation would share the tragedy of the costs of nuclear warfare.

What does this mean for foreign policy? Essentially our analysis of foreign policy does not change. The purpose of foreign policy is to maximize the national self-interest of the nation in relation to the same effort by all other nations. The awful specter of nuclear destruction makes the consequences of foreign policy more frightening but does not change its nature.

THE COMPLEXITY OF UNITED STATES' POLICY

Recognition of the complexity of United States' foreign policy involves consideration of a diverse range of factors. Here we call attention to only a few. First, in analyzing foreign policy we would have to take into account such factors as United States' investments, mostly of private corporations, in foreign countries. The welfare of these investments is of major concern in our relations to other nations, often more important than the country's ideological commitments. United States military intervention in the Dominican Republic, for instance, cannot be understood simply in terms of preservation of democracy or protection against communist takeover.

The existence of non-committed nations—those neither in the Soviet bloc nor the United States' bloc (and now, probably, one has to include a third, the China bloc)—and our relationships with them constitute another area of great complexity. How do the interests of the United States relate to the interests of each of these nations? To treat them as a homogeneous group will lead to miscalculation of both their actions and ours. In one sense it is as crucial to evaluate correctly the interests of the individual non-committed nations as it is the interests of the "committed" nations. In the non-committed nations may lie the balance of power in the continuing struggle between the power blocs.

The relationship between domestic and international affairs is also significant. A healthy, growing economy, a happy and basically satisfied people, an optimistic and constructive outlook are all vitally related to the foreign relations of a nation. And a viable democracy, capable of solving, or at least moving toward the solution of, its major problems, is directly connected to our foreign policy objectives. Serious inability to make democracy work, or failure to maximize freedom and equality for our own people, cannot fail to reflect in our efforts in the international community.

Finally, a word about the United Nations. The UN, like its forerunner the League of Nations, is an instrument of the foreign policy of the member nations.

It is not a world government; it has no governing powers. It is an arena for reconciliation of conflict, for exposition of interests, for accomplishment of national purposes. It is not designed to solve all problems, or to replace the individual national definition of vital interests. It is a potential instrument for their accomplishment.

The UN is a part of the foreign policy machinery of the United States. It has served our interests well, on the whole; but if and when it ceases to be useful, the United States will find alternative mechanisms. To expect, however, that an international tribunal made up of many nations with many approaches to governing should operate on democratic principles and with the machinery of democracy reflects an inability to see the world as it is.

There are undoubtedly other areas of major concern contributing to the complexity of United States' foreign policy today. The aim has not been to exhaust the possibilities but to suggest the necessity of searching out such questions so as to avoid oversimplification of a complex problem area.

The first two selections reprinted below, by Hans Morgenthau ("Another 'Great Debate': The National Interest of the United States"), and William V. O'Brien ("Basic Issues of International Ethics"), respectively, are representative, in much greater detail, of the two broad positions described above as realist and idealist. They present two alternative positions from which a choice, or synthesis, can be made. The third selection, by Arthur Herzog, ("The War-Peace Establishment"), moves into the field of debate over arms and arms control. Herzog summarizes and analyzes the approaches to disarmament—a problem that many believe to be the major one facing the nation today.

Another "Great Debate": The National Interest of the United States

HANS J. MORGENTHAU

The Albert A. Michelson Distinguished Service Professor of political science and modern history at the University of Chicago, Hans J. Morgenthau is also director of the Center for the Study of American Foreign and Military Policy. He has written many books and articles, and is generally accepted as one of the nation's leading authorities in the field of international relations.

The controversy which has arisen on the occasion of Ambassador Kennan's and my recent publications differs from the great historical debates on American foreign policy in two significant respects. It raises an issue more fundamental to

Reprinted from *The American Political Science Review* Vol. XLVI, No. 4 (December 1952), 961–988, by permission of the author and publisher.

the understanding of American foreign policy and of all politics than those with which the previous "great debates" were concerned, and it deals with the issue largely in terms which are not conducive to understanding.

The great debates of the past, such as the one over intervention vs. neutrality in 1793, expansion vs. the status quo before the Mexican and after the Spanish-

American War, international cooperation vs. isolation in the 'twenties, intervention vs. abstention in the late 'thirties—all evolved around clear-cut issues of foreign policy. In 1793 you were in favor of going to war on the side of France or of remaining neutral. In the 1840's you approved of the annexation of Texas or you did not. At the turn of the century you supported overseas expansion or you were against it. In the 'twenties you advocated joining the League of Nations or staying out of it. In the late 'thirties you wanted to oppose the Axis Powers by all means short of war or you wanted to abstain from intervening. What separates the "utopian" from the "realist" position cannot be so sharply expressed in terms of alternative foreign policies. The very same policies can be and are being supported by both schools of thought. What sets them apart is not necessarily a matter of practical judgment, but of philosophies and standards of thought.

The issue which the present debate raises concerns the nature of all politics and, more particularly, of the American tradition in foreign policy. The history of modern political thought is the story of a contest between two schools which differ fundamentally in their conception of the nature of man, society, and politics. One believes that a rational and moral political order, derived from universally valid abstract principles, can be achieved here and now. It assumes the essential goodness and infinite malleability of human nature and attributes the failure of the social order to measure up to the rational standards to lack of knowledge and understanding, obsolescent social institutions, or the depravity of certain isolated individuals or groups. It trusts in education, reform, and the sporadic use of force to remedy these deficiencies.[1]

The other school believes that the world, imperfect as it is from the rational point of view, is the result of forces which are inherent in human nature. To improve the world one must work with those

forces, not against them. This being inherently a world of opposing interests and of conflict among them, moral principles can never be fully realized, but at best approximated through the ever temporary balancing of interests and the ever precarious settlement of conflicts. This school, then, sees in a system of checks and balances a universal principle for all pluralist societies.[2] It appeals to historic precedent rather than to abstract principles, and aims at achievement of the lesser evil rather than of the absolute good.

This conflict between two basic conceptions of man and politics is at the bottom of the present controversy. It is the same conflict which found its classic expression in the polemic of Burke against the philosophy of the French Revolution. Given the sad state of political thought in our time, it would be vain to expect the spokesmen of political realism to speak with the voice of Burke and the defenders of political utopianism to measure up to the standards of Condorcet and Rousseau. Yet one has a right to expect that scholars discuss the issue without resort to invective and with proper regard for established facts.[3]

[1] This is the ideal type of the utopian position rather than the empirical description of any particular historic type. In actuality, and this is true particularly of the present, the utopian position in international affairs is not always consistent with its philosophic premises.

[2] It ought not to need special emphasis that a principle of social conduct, in contrast to a law of nature, allows of, and even presupposes, conduct in violation of the principle. Robert W. Tucker, in "Professor Morgenthau's Theory of Political 'Realism'" in this REVIEW, Vol. 46, pp. 214–224 (March, 1952), has missed this and many other points in his zeal to find contradictions where there are none.

[3] "This [the realist] doctrine," writes one historian—Frank Tannenbaum, "The Balance of Power versus the Coördinate State," Political Science Quarterly, Vol. 67, p. 173 (June, 1952)—"is confessedly, nay gleefully, amoral. It prides itself upon being realistic and takes Machiavelli as its great teacher. It is contemptuous of the simple beliefs of honest men, jeers at the sentimentalism of those who believe that men may strive for peace among nations, and looks upon democracy as a hindrance to skilled diplomacy. It looks with a certain derisive superiority upon the great leaders of this nation from Jefferson and John Quincy Adams to Woodrow Wilson and Franklin Delano Roosevelt and describes them as moralistic and sentimental, and suggests that our models ought to be Richelieu, Clemenceau and Bismarck. Its adherents believe that international wars instead of being made by men and supported by institutions humanly contrived have their

I

In order to refute a theory which pretends to be scientific, it is first necessary to understand what a scientific theory is. A scientific theory is an attempt to bring order and meaning to a mass of phenomena which without it would remain disconnected and unintelligible. Any one who disputes the scientific character of such a theory either must produce a theory superior in these scientific functions to the one attacked or must, at the very least, demonstrate that the facts as they actually are do not lend themselves to the interpretation which the theory has put upon them. When a historian tells us that the balance of power is not a universal principle of politics, domestic and international, that it was practiced in Europe only for a limited period and never by the United States, that it ruined the states that practiced it,[4] it is incumbent upon him to tell us how we can dispose by means of theory of the historic data by which, for instance, David Hume demonstrated the universality of the balance of power and Paul Scott Mowrer[5] and Alfred Vagts[6] its practice by the United States; what Kautilya was writing about in the fourth century B. C. when he summarized the theoretical and practical tradition of Indian statecraft in terms of the balance of power; what the Greek city states, the Roman republic, and the medieval emperors and popes were doing if they did not apply the principles of the balance of power; and how the nations which either neglected these principles or applied them wrongly suffered political and military defeat and even extinction, while the nation which applied these principles most consistently and consciously, that is, Great Britain, enjoyed unrivalled power for an unparalleled length of time.

The historian who wishes to replace the balance of power as the guiding principle of American foreign policy with the "humanitarian and pacific traditions" of the "coördinate state"[7] must first of all explain how it has come about that the thirteen original states expanded into the full breadth and a good deal of the length of a continent, until today the strategic frontiers of the United States run parallel to the coastline of Asia and along the River Elbe. If such are the results of policies based upon "humanitarian and pacific traditions," never in the history of the world has virtue been more bountifully rewarded! Yet our historian must explain not only the great sweep of American expansion, but also the specific foreign policies which in their historic succession make up that sweep. Is it easier to explain the successive shifts of American support from Great Britain to France and back again from the beginning of King George's War in 1744 to the War of 1812 in terms of the "coördinate

origin in the nature of man himself and are inevitable."

Another historian, Arthur Schlesinger, Jr., in "Policy and National Interest," *Partisan Review,* Vol. 18, p. 709 (Nov.–Dec., 1951), however, gives Ambassador Kennan a clean bill of moral health. "But what differentiates," he writes, "the Kennan approach from that of, for example, the followers of Professor Hans J. Morgenthau is that he takes the revelations of international amorality in his stride; more than that, he comprehends them in his understanding of the tragedy of history. Mr. Kennan, in other words, is deeply moral, rather than moralistic, like Judge Hull, or immoral, like the boys who have just discovered that politics involve power."

"This dreadful doctrine," we are told (by Tannenbaum, pp. 173–174), "has now won wide acceptance by teachers and scholars in the field of international relations and has, in fact, become the leading theme in such circles in many of our largest universities. It has become the *science* of international relations—and who would quarrel with science, especially when it comes packaged in good clear English and from high sources? But it is not science. It is, in fact, only poor logic based upon false premises, and its claim to be a science is only a bit of unholy conceit."

It may be remarked in passing that to dispose of a scientific theory as "fashionable" or a "fad," as some do with regard to political realism, may reveal something about the state of mind of the writer, but reveals nothing at all about the scientific value of the theory.

[4] Tannenbaum, in the article cited above, and in "The American Tradition in Foreign Relations," *Foreign Affairs,* Vol. 30, pp. 31–50 (Oct., 1951).

[5] *Our Foreign Affairs* (New York, 1924), pp. 246 ff.

[6] "The United States and the Balance of Power," *The Journal of Politics,* Vol. 3, pp. 401–449 (Nov., 1941).

[7] Tannenbaum, "The Balance of Power versus the Coördinate State," (cited above, note 3), p. 173.

state" than in terms of the balance of power? The same question might be asked about the postponement of the recognition of the independence of the Spanish colonies until 1822, when the Floridas had been acquired from Spain and Spain had thereby been deprived of the ability to challenge the United States from within the hemisphere. The same question might be asked about the Monroe Doctrine itself, about Lincoln's policies toward Great Britain and France, and about our successive policies with regard to Mexico and the Caribbean. One could go on and pick out at random any foreign policy pursued by the United States from the beginning to 1919 and one would hardly find a policy, with the exception perhaps of the War of 1812, which could not be made intelligible by reference to the national interest defined in terms of power—political, military, and economic —rather than by reference to the principle of the "coördinate state." This inevitable outcome of such an inquiry is well summarized in these words:

Ease and prosperity have made us wish the whole world to be as happy and well to do as ourselves; and we have supposed that institutions and principles like our own were the simple prescription for making them so. And yet, when issues of our own interest arose, we have not been unselfish. We have shown ourselves kin to all the world, when it came to pushing an advantage. Our action against Spain in the Floridas, and against Mexico on the coasts of the Pacific; our attitude toward first the Spaniards, and then the French, with regard to the control of the Mississippi; the unpitying force with which we thrust the Indians to the wall wherever they stood in our way, have suited our professions of peacefulness and justice and liberality no better than the aggressions of other nations that were strong and not to be gainsaid. Even Mr. Jefferson, philanthropist and champion of peaceable and modest government though he was, exemplified this double temper of the people he ruled. "Peace is our passion," he had declared; but the passion abated when he saw the mouth of the Mississippi about to pass into the hands of France. Though he had loved France and hated England, he did not hesitate then what language to hold. "There is on the globe," he wrote to Mr. Livingston at Paris, "one

single spot the possessor of which is our natural and habitual enemy. The day that France takes possession of New Orleans seals the union of two nations, who, in conjunction, can maintain exclusive possession of the sea. From that moment we must marry ourselves to the British fleet and nation." Our interests must march forward, altruists though we are; other nations must see to it that they stand off, and do not seek to stay us.

This realist appraisal of the American tradition in foreign policy was published in 1901 in the *Atlantic Monthly*. Its author was a professor of jurisprudence and political economy at Princeton by the name of Woodrow Wilson.[8]

Nothing more needs to be said to demonstrate that facts do not support a revision of American diplomatic history which tries to substitute "humanitarian and pacifist traditions" and the "coördinate state" for power politics and the balance of power as the guiding principle of American foreign policy. What, then, does support it? Three things: the way American statesmen have spoken about American foreign policy; the legal fiction of the "coördinate state"; finally, and foremost, an emotional urge to justify American foreign policy in humanitarian, pacifist terms.

It is elementary that the character of a foreign policy can be ascertained only through the examination of the political acts performed and of the foreseeable consequences of these acts. Thus we can find out what statesmen have actually done, and from the foreseeable consequences of their acts we can surmise what their objectives might have been. Yet examination of the facts is not enough. To give meaning to the factual raw material of history, we must approach historical reality with a kind of rational outline, a map which suggests to us the possible meanings of history. In other words, we put ourselves in the position of a statesman who must meet a certain problem of foreign policy under certain circumstances and ask ourselves, what are the rational alternatives from which a statesman may choose who must

[8] "Democracy and Efficiency," *Atlantic Monthly*, Vol. 87, pp. 293–294 (March, 1901).

meet this problem under these circumstances, presuming always that he acts in a rational manner, and which of these rational alternatives was this particular statesman, acting under these circumstances, likely to choose? It is the testing of this rational hypothesis against the actual facts and their consequences which gives meaning to the facts of history and makes the scientific writing of political history possible.

In the process of writing the history of foreign policy the interpretations by statesmen of their own acts, especially if they are made for public consumption, must needs have a strictly subsidiary place. The public self-interpretation by actors on the political scene is itself, of course, a political act which seeks to present a certain policy to its presumed supporters in terms of their moral and political folklore and to those against which it is directed in terms which intend to embarrass and deceive. Such declarations may indeed shed light upon the character and objectives of the policy pursued if they are considered in conjunction with, and in subordination to, rational hypotheses, actions, and likely consequences. Yet it is quite a different matter to interpret the American tradition of foreign policy in the light of a collection of official statements which, like most such statements, present humanitarian and pacifist justifications for the policies pursued. If anybody should be bold enough to write a history of world politics with so uncritical a method he would easily and well-nigh inevitably be driven to the conclusion that from Timur to Hitler and Stalin the foreign policies of all nations were inspired by the ideals of humanitarianism and pacifism. The absurdity of the result is commensurate with the defects of the method.

It is only from a method which accepts the declarations of statesmen as evidence of the character of the policies pursued, that the principle of the "coördinate state" receives a semblance of plausibility. Statesmen and international lawyers have been wont to speak of the "equal dignity" of all states, regardless of "wealth, power, size, population or culture," [9]

which I take the principle of the "coördinate state" to mean. It is also referred to as the principle of "federalism in international relations." [10] As its prime examples are cited the relations amongst the states of the Union, the states of the American system, the members of the Commonwealth of Nations, and the members of the Swiss Confederation. If the whole world were organized in accordance with this principle, as are already these four political entities, it is assumed that the freedom, dignity, and peace of all nations would then be assured.

There is no need to examine the theoretical and practical merits of the principle of the "coördinate state," because for none of the four political entities mentioned does the idea of the "coördinate state" provide the principle of political organization. The equality of the states as the political foundation of the United States became obsolescent when Chief Justice Marshall's Supreme Court resolved the ambiguity of the Constitution in favor of the federal government, and it became obsolete when the Civil War proved Chief Justice Marshall's point. The equality of the states survives today only in the shadow and by virtue of the federal government's political supremacy, and without the cohesive force of that supremacy there would be no union of equal states to begin with. That these powers of the federal government are limited and qualified by the principle of federalism, that is, by the constitutionally granted powers of the states, is quite a different matter; it concerns the distribution of powers between federal government and states within a general system of checks and balances, but has nothing to do with the equality of the states as the alleged political foundation of the American system of government. With the exception of the equality of senatorial representation, the principle of the equality of the states is today, as it has been for almost a century, devoid of political content. It serves only as a principle of regional organization, of administrative decentralization, and, above all, of constitutional rhetoric. What it really signifies was pointed out more than fifty years ago by

[9] Tannenbaum, p. 177.

[10] *Ibid.*

W. A. Dunning when he summarized his answer to the question "Are the states equal under the Constitution?" by saying that "the theory of equal states falls to the ground." [11]

Similarly, the federalism of Switzerland is the result of a long series of civil wars, the last one fought a little more than a century ago, which established the predominance of the German-speaking cantons within the confederation. Here too, it is the existence of predominant power, located in one segment of the federal system, which makes federalism possible in the first place.

By the same token, the unchallengeable supremacy of the United States within the Western Hemisphere has throughout been the backbone of the system of American states. As long as this supremacy is secure, there is, on the one hand, no need for the United States to assert it in the political and military sphere, and, taking it for granted, the United States can well afford to pursue a policy of the Good Neighbor; and there is, on the other hand, no opportunity for the other members of the system to challenge that supremacy effectively. This is what the principle of the "coördinate state" amounts to in the Western Hemisphere. Consequently, whenever there was even a remote possibility that the supremacy of the United States might be challenged, generally through instigation from outside the hemisphere, the United States asserted its superior power within the hemisphere and acted as all states must act under similar conditions.

Whatever possibility for common political action there remains among the members of the Commonwealth of Nations is the result of the interests which these members may have in common. In other words, the member states may work together or each of them may work with other nations, as their interests dictate. Their membership in the Commonwealth, as the examples of India, South Africa, Australia, and New Zealand clearly show, has no influence upon this decision; that membership is but a faint remembrance of the times when Great

Britain could secure cooperation among the member states on its terms by virtue of its superior power.

What, then, have these four examples of the "coördinate state" in common which would establish them as a distinct type of interstate relationship, and what conclusions can be drawn from them for the organization of the world? The only thing that these four examples seem to have really in common is the legal stipulation of the equality of the members of the respective systems and this characteristic is not peculiar to them, but a general principle of international law applicable to all sovereign states. In the political sphere they seem to have nothing in common at all. What they tend to show, however, is the decisive importance of the distribution of political power for the operation of federal and egalitarian relations among states. The political cohesion of a federal system is the result of superior power located in some part of it. It is by virtue of its superior power that the predominant part can afford to grant the other members of the federal system a measure of equality in the non-political sphere. These observations bring us back to power politics and the balance of power to which the principle of the "coördinate state" was supposed to be the alternative.

In truth, it is not the disinterested consideration of facts which has given birth to the theory of the "coördinate state." That theory is rather the response to an emotional urge, and since this emotion is not peculiar to a particular author but typical of a popular reaction to the new role which the United States must play in world affairs, it deserves a brief analysis.

One of the great experiences of our time which have impressed themselves upon the American mind is the emergence of the United States as a nation among other nations, exposed to the same opportunities, temptations, risks, and liabilities to which other nations have been traditionally exposed. This experience becomes the more shocking if it is compared with the expectation with which we fought the Second World War. We expected from that war a reaffirmation of the secure, detached, and independent

[11] William Archibald Dunning, *Essays on the Civil War and Reconstruction and Related Topics* (New York, 1931), p. 351.

position in world affairs which we had inherited from the Founding Fathers and which we had been successful in preserving at least to the First World War. By avoiding what we thought had been Wilson's mistakes, we expected to emerge from that war if not more independent, certainly more secure than we were when we entered it. In fact, probably not even in the early days of the Republic were we more exposed to danger from abroad than we are today, and never had we less freedom of action in taking care of our interests than we have today.

It is naturally shocking to recognize that a happy chapter in the history of the nation and in one's own way of life has come to an end. There are those who reconcile themselves to the inevitable, albeit with sorrow rather than with glee, and try to apply the lessons of the past to the tasks at hand. There are others who try to escape from a disappointing and threatening reality into the realm of fantasy. Three such escapist fantasies have arisen in our midst in response to the challenge of American world leadership and power: the fantasy of needless American participation in war, the fantasy of American treason, and the fantasy of American innocence.

The first of these fantasies presumes that the present predicament is a result not of necessity but of folly, the folly of American statesmen who needlessly intervened in two world wars. The second of these fantasies attributes the present predicament to treason in high places whereby the fruits of victory were handed to the enemy. The third of these fantasies denies that the predicament is real and prefers to think of it as an intellectual fraud perpetrated upon the American people. To support this fictional denial of the actualities of the present, it draws upon a fictional account of the past. The United States does not need to bear at present the intellectual, moral, and political burdens which go with involvement in power politics and the maintenance of the balance of power; for it has never borne them in the past, never having been thus involved. The golden age of past political innocence sheds its glow upon a but seemingly less innocent pres-

ent and promises a future in which all the world will follow the example of America, forswear power politics and the balance of power, and accept the principle of the "coördinate state." Our rearmament program, as exemplified in the Atlantic Security Pact, we are told, has nothing to do with the balance of power but aims at the "organization of as much of the world as we can upon the basis of the coördinate state. . . . It may prove impossible under present conditions to build such a system without having to fight a war with Russia, but then at least we will be fighting, as we did before, for the thing we consider worth defending with our lives and treasure."[12] Thus a fictional account of the American past, begun as an act of uncalled-for patriotic piety, issues in an ideology for a third world war. Escape we must from the unfamiliar, unpleasant, and dangerous present, first into the political innocence of the past and from there into the immediate future of a third world war, beyond which the revived and universalized innocence of the more distant future will surely lie.

We have said that to present the American tradition in foreign policy as having been free from concern with power politics and the balance of power is not warranted by the facts of American history. Yet it might still be argued, and it is actually being argued, that, regardless of the evidence of history, the American people will not be reconciled to power politics and the balance of power and will support only policies based upon abstract moral principles. While in the past the United States might have pursued balance of power policies and while it might be a good thing if it did do so again, the American people will not stand for it. Here the emotional appeal to patriotic piety is joined by calculations of political expediency. Yet the case for misrepresenting American history has nothing to gain from either.

There is a strong tendency in all historiography to glorify the national past, and in popular presentations that tendency takes on the aspects of the jingoist whitewash. Even so penetrating a mind

[12] Tannenbaum, pp. 195–196.

as John Stuart Mill's could deliver himself of an essay in which he proved, no doubt to the satisfaction of many of his English readers but certainly of few others, that Great Britain had never interfered in the affairs of European nations and had interfered in those of the Indian states only for their own good.[13] Yet it is the measure of a nation's maturity to be able to recognize its past for what it actually is. Why should we not admit that American foreign policy has been generally hardheaded and practical and at times ruthless? Why should we deny Jefferson's cunning, say, in the Puget Sound affair, the cruelty with which the Indians were treated, and the faithlessness with which the treaties with the Indians were cast aside? We know that this is the way all nations are when their interests are at stake—so cruel, so faithless, so cunning. We know that the United States has refrained from seeking dominions beyond the seas not because it is more virtuous than other nations, but because it had the better part of a continent to colonize.

As has been pointed out elsewhere at greater length, the man in the street, unsophisticated as he is and uninformed as he may be, has a surer grasp of the essentials of foreign policy and a more mature judgment of its basic issues than many of the intellectuals and politicians who pretend to speak for him and cater to what they imagine his prejudices to be. During the recent war the ideologues of the Atlantic Charter, the Four Freedoms, and the United Nations were constantly complaining that the American soldier did not know what he was fighting for. Indeed, if he was fighting for some utopian ideal, divorced from the concrete experiences and interests of the country, then the complaint was well grounded. However, if he was fighting for the territorial integrity of the nation and for its survival as a free country where he could live, think, and act as he pleased, then he had never any doubt about what he was fighting for. Ideological rationalizations

and justifications are indeed the indispensable concomitants of all political action. Yet there is something unhealthy in a craving for ideological intoxication and in the inability to act and to see merit in action except under the stimulant of grandiose ideas and far-fetched schemes. Have our intellectuals become, like Hamlet, too much beset by doubt to act and, unlike Hamlet, compelled to still their doubts by renouncing their sense of what is real? The man in the street has no such doubts. It is true that ideologues and demagogues can sway him by appealing to his emotions. But it is also true, as American history shows in abundance and as the popular success of Ambassador Kennan's book demonstrates, that responsible statesmen can guide him by awakening his latent understanding of the national interest.

II

Yet what is the national interest? How can we define it and give it the content which will make it a guide for action? This is one of the relevant questions to which the current debate has given rise.

It has been frequently argued against the realist conception of foreign policy that its key concept, the national interest, does not provide an acceptable standard for political action. This argument is in the main based upon two grounds: the elusiveness of the concept and its susceptibility to interpretations, such as limitless imperialism and narrow nationalism, which are not in keeping with the American tradition in foreign policy. The argument has substance as far as it goes, but it does not invalidate the usefulness of the concept.

The concept of the national interest is similar in two respects to the "great generalities" of the Constitution, such as the general welfare and due process. It contains a residual meaning which is inherent in the concept itself, but beyond these minimum requirements its content can run the whole gamut of meanings which are logically compatible with it. That content is determined by the political traditions and the total cultural context within which a nation formulates its foreign policy. The concept of the national

---

[13] "A Few Words on Non-Intervention," *Dissertations and Discussions: Political, Philosophical, and Historical* (London, 1875), pp. 153–178.

interest, then, contains two elements, one that is logically required and in that sense necessary, and one that is variable and determined by circumstances.

Any foreign policy which operates under the standard of the national interest must obviously have some reference to the physical, political, and cultural entity which we call a nation. In a world where a number of sovereign nations compete with and oppose each other for power, the foreign policies of all nations must necessarily refer to their survival as their minimum requirements. Thus all nations do what they cannot help but do: protect their physical, political, and cultural identity against encroachments by other nations.

It has been suggested that this reasoning erects the national state into the last word in politics and the national interest into an absolute standard for political action. This, however, is not quite the case. The idea of interest is indeed of the essence of politics and, as such, unaffected by the circumstances of time and place. Thucydides' statement, born of the experiences of ancient Greece, that "identity of interest is the surest of bonds whether between states or individuals" was taken up in the nineteenth century by Lord Salisbury's remark that "the only bond of union that endures" among nations is "the absence of all clashing interests." The perennial issue between the realist and utopian schools of thought over the nature of politics, to which we have referred before, might well be formulated in terms of concrete interests vs. abstract principles. Yet while the concern of politics with interest is perennial, the connection between interest and the national state is a product of history.

The national state itself is obviously a product of history and as such destined to yield in time to different modes of political organization. As long as the world is politically organized into nations, the national interest is indeed the last word in world politics. When the national state will have been replaced by another mode of organization, foreign policy must then protect the interest in survival of that new organization. For the benefit of those who insist upon discarding the na-

tional state and constructing supranational organizations by constitutional fiat, it must be pointed out that these new organizational forms will either come into being through conquest or else through consent based upon the mutual recognition of the national interests of the nations concerned; for no nation will forego its freedom of action if it has no reason to expect proportionate benefits in compensation for that loss. This is true of treaties concerning commerce or fisheries as it is true of the great compacts, such as the European Coal and Steel Community, through which nations try to create supranational forms of organization. Thus, by an apparent paradox, what is historically relative in the idea of the national interest can be overcome only through the promotion in concert of the national interest of a number of nations.

The survival of a political unit, such as a nation, in its identity is the irreducible minimum, the necessary element of its interests vis-à-vis other units. Taken in isolation, the determination of its content in a concrete situation is relatively simple; for it encompasses the integrity of the nation's territory, of its political institutions, and of its culture. Thus bipartisanship in foreign policy, especially in times of war, has been most easily achieved in the promotion of these minimum requirements of the national interest. The situation is different with respect to the variable elements of the national interest. All the cross currents of personalities, public opinion, sectional interests, partisan politics, and political and moral folkways are brought to bear upon their determination. In consequence, the contribution which science can make to this field, as to all fields of policy formation, is limited. It can identify the different agencies of the government which contribute to the determination of the variable elements of the national interest and assess their relative weight. It can separate the long-range objectives of foreign policy from the short-term ones which are the means for the achievement of the former and can tentatively establish their rational relations. Finally, it can analyze the variable elements of the national interest in terms of their legitimacy and their compatibility with other national values and with the national interest of other nations. We shall address ourselves briefly to the typical problems with which this analysis must deal.

The legitimacy of the national interest must be determined in the face of possible usurpation by subnational, other-national, and supranational interests. On the subnational level we find group interests, represented particularly by ethnic and economic groups, who tend to identify themselves with the national interest. Charles A. Beard was emphasized, however one-sidedly, the extent to which the economic interests of certain groups have been presented as those of the United States.[14] Group interests exert, of course, constant pressure upon the conduct of our foreign policy, claiming their identity with the national interest. It is, however, doubtful that, with the exception of a few spectacular cases, they have been successful in determining the course of American foreign policy. It is much more likely, given the nature of American domestic politics, that American foreign policy, insofar as it is the object of pressures by sectional interests, will normally be a compromise between divergent sectional interests. The concept of the national interest, as it emerges from this contest as the actual guide for foreign policy, may well fall short of what would be rationally required by the overall interests of the United States. Yet the concept of the national interest which emerges from this contest of conflicting sectional interests is also more than any particular sectional interest or their sum total. It is, as it were, the lowest common denominator where sectional interests and the national interest meet in an uneasy compromise which may leave much to be desired in view of all the interests concerned.

The national interest can be usurped by other-national interests in two typical ways. The case of treason by individuals, either out of conviction or for pay, needs only to be mentioned here; for insofar as treason is committed on behalf of a

[14] *The Idea of National Interest: An Analytical Study in American Foreign Policy* (New York, 1934).

foreign government rather than a supranational principle, it is significant for psychology, sociology, and criminology, but not for the theory of politics. The other case, however, is important not only for the theory of politics but also for its practice, especially in the United States.

National minorities in European countries, ethnic groups in the United States, ideological minorities anywhere may identify themselves, either spontaneously or under the direction of the agents of a foreign government, with the interests of that foreign government and may promote these interests under the guise of the national interest of the country whose citizens they happen to be. The activities of the German-American Bund in the United States in the 'thirties and of Communists everywhere are cases in point. Yet the issue of the national interest vs. other-national interests masquerading as the national interest has arisen constantly in the United States in a less clear-cut fashion.

A country which had been settled by consecutive waves of "foreigners" was bound to find it particularly difficult to identify its own national interest against alleged, seeming, or actual other-national interests represented by certain groups among its own citizens. Since virtually all citizens of the United States are, as it were, "more or less" foreign-born, those who were "less" so have frequently not resisted the temptation to use this distinction as a polemic weapon against latecomers who happened to differ from them in their conception of the national interest of the United States. Frequently, this rationalization has been dispensed with and a conception of foreign policy with which a writer happened to disagree has been attributed outright to foreign sympathy or influence or worse. British influence and interests have served as standard arguments in debates on American foreign policy. Madison, in his polemic against Hamilton on the occasion of Washington's Neutrality Proclamation of 1793, identified the Federalist position with that of "the foreigners and degenerate citizens among us, who hate our republican government, and the French revolution," [15] and the accusation met with a favorable response in a majority of Congress and of public opinion. However, these traditional attempts to discredit dissenting opinion as being influenced by foreign interests should not obscure the real issue, which is the peculiar vulnerability of the national interest of the United States to usurpation by the interests of other nations.

The usurpation of the national interest by supranational interests can derive in our time from two sources: religious bodies and international organizations. The competition between church and state for determination of certain interests and policies, domestic and international, has been an intermittent issue throughout the history of the national state. Here, too, the legitimate defense of the national interest against usurpation has frequently, especially in the United States, degenerated into the demagogic stigmatization of dissenting views as being inspired by Rome and, hence, being incompatible with the national interest. Yet here, too, the misuse of the issue for demagogic purposes must be considered apart from the legitimacy of the issue itself.

The more acute problem arises at the present time from the importance which the public and government officials, at least in their public utterances, attribute to the values represented and the policies pursued by international organizations either as alternatives or supplements to the values and policies for which the national government stands. It is frequently asserted that the foreign policy of the United States pursues no objectives apart from those of the United Nations, that, in other words, the foreign policy of the United States is actually identical with the policy of the United Nations. This assertion cannot refer to anything real in actual politics to support it. For the constitutional structure of international organizations, such as the United Nations, and their procedural practices make it impossible for them to pursue interests apart from those of the member-states which dominate their policy-forming bodies. The identity between the interests of the United Nations and the United States can only refer to the successful policies of the United States within the United Nations through which the support of the United Nations is being secured for the policies of the United States.[16] The assertion, then, is mere polemic, different from the one discussed previously in that the identification of a certain policy with a supranational interest does not seek to reflect discredit upon the former, but to bestow upon it a dignity which the national interest pure and simple is supposed to lack.

The real issue in view of the problem that concerns us here is not whether the so-called interests of the United Nations, which do not exist apart from the interests of its most influential members, have superseded the national interest of the United States, but for what kind of interests the United States has secured United Nations support. While these interests cannot be United Nations interests, they do not need to be national interests either. Here we are in the presence of that modern phenomenon which has been variously described as "utopianism," "sentimentalism," "moralism," the "legalistic-moralistic approach." The common denominator of all these tendencies in modern political thought is the substitution for the national interest of a supranational standard of action which is generally identified with an international organization, such as the United Nations. The national interest is here not being usurped by sub- or supranational interests which, however inferior in worth to the national interest, are nevertheless real and worthy of consideration within their proper sphere. What challenges the national interest here is a mere figment of the imagination, a product of wishful thinking, which is postulated as a valid

[15] "Helvidius, in Answer to Pacificus, on President Washington's Proclamation of Neutrality," in *Letters and other Writings of James Madison* (Philadelphia, 1867), Vol. 1, p. 611.

[16] See, on this point, Hans J. Morgenthau, "International Organizations and Foreign Policy," in *Foundations of World Organization: A Political and Cultural Appraisal,* Eleventh Symposium of the Conference on Science, Philosophy and Religion, edited by Lyman Bryson, Louis Finkelstein, Harold D. Lasswell, R. M. MacIver (New York, 1952), pp. 377–383.

norm for international conduct, without being valid either there or anywhere else. At this point we touch the core of the present controversy between utopianism and realism in international affairs; we shall return to it later in this paper.

The national interest as such must be defended against usurpation by non-national interests. Yet once that task is accomplished, a rational order must be established among the values which make up the national interest and among the resources to be committed to them. While the interests which a nation may pursue in its relation with other nations are of infinite variety and magnitude, the resources which are available for the pursuit of such interests are necessarily limited in quantity and kind. No nation has the resources to promote all desirable objectives with equal vigor; all nations must therefore allocate their scarce resources as rationally as possible. The indispensable precondition of such rational allocation is a clear understanding of the distinction between the necessary and variable elements of the national interest. Given the contentious manner in which in democracies the variable elements of the national interest are generally determined, the advocates of an extensive conception of the national interest will inevitably present certain variable elements of the national interest as though their attainment were necessary for the nation's survival. In other words, the necessary elements of the national interest have a tendency to swallow up the variable elements so that in the end all kinds of objectives, actual or potential, are justified in terms of national survival. Such arguments have been advanced, for instance, in support of the rearmament of Western Germany and of the defense of Formosa. They must be subjected to rational scrutiny which will determine, however tentatively, their approximate place in the scale of national values.

The same problem presents itself in its extreme form when a nation pursues, or is asked to pursue, objectives which are not only unnecessary for its survival but tend to jeopardize it. Second-rate nations which dream of playing the role of great powers, such as Italy and Poland in the interwar period, illustrate this point. So do great powers which dream of remaking the world in their own image and embark upon world-wide crusades, thus straining their resources to exhaustion. Here scientific analysis has the urgent task of pruning down national objectives to the measure of available resources in order to make their pursuit compatible with national survival.

Finally, the national interest of a nation which is conscious not only of its own interests but also of that of other nations must be defined in terms compatible with the latter. In a multinational world this is a requirement of political morality; in an age of total war it is also one of the conditions for survival.

In connection with this problem two mutually exclusive arguments have been advanced. On the one hand, it has been argued against the theory of international politics here presented that the concept of the national interest revives the eighteenth-century concept of enlightened self-interest, presuming that the uniformly enlightened pursuit of their self-interest by all individuals, as by all nations, will of itself be conducive to a peaceful and harmonious society. On the other hand, the point has been made that the pursuit of their national interest by all nations makes war the permanent arbiter of conflicts among them. Neither argument is well taken.

The concept of the national interest presupposes neither a naturally harmonious, peaceful world nor the inevitability of war as a consequence of the pursuit by all nations of their national interest. Quite to the contrary, it assumes continuous conflict and threat of war, to be minimized through the continuous adjustment of conflicting interests by diplomatic action. No such assumption would be warranted if all nations at all times conceived of their national interest only in terms of their survival and, in turn, defined their interest in survival in restrictive and rational terms. As it is, their conception of the national interest is subject to all the hazards of misinterpretation, usurpation, and misjudgment to which reference has been made above. To minimize these hazards is the first task of a foreign policy which seeks the defense of the national interest by peaceful means. Its second task is the defense of the national interest, restrictively and rationally defined, against the national interests of other nations which may or may not be thus defined. If they are not, it becomes the task of armed diplomacy to convince the nations concerned that their legitimate interests have nothing to fear from a restrictive and rational foreign policy and that their illegitimate interests have nothing to gain in the face of armed might rationally employed.

III

We have said before that the utopian and realist positions in international affairs do not necessarily differ in the policies they advocate, but that they part company over their general philosophies of politics and their way of thinking about matters political. It does not follow that the present debate is only of academic interest and without practical significance. Both camps, it is true, may support the same policy for different reasons. Yet if the reasons are unsound, the soundness of the policies supported by them is a mere coincidence, and these very same reasons may be, and inevitably are, invoked on other occasions in support of unsound policies. The nefarious consequences of false philosophies and wrong ways of thinking may for the time being be concealed by the apparent success of policies derived from them. You may go to war, justified by your nation's interests, for a moral purpose and in disregard of considerations of power; and military victory seems to satisfy both your moral aspirations and your nation's interests. Yet the manner in which you waged the war, achieved victory, and settled the peace cannot help reflecting your philosophy of politics and your way of thinking about political problems. If these are in error, you may win victory on the field of battle and still assist in the defeat of both your moral principles and the national interest of your country.

Any number of examples could illustrate the real yet subtle practical consequences which follow from the different positions taken. We have chosen two: collective security in Korea and the liberation of the nations that are captives of Communism. A case for both policies can be made from both the utopian and realist positions, but with significant differences in the emphasis and substance of the policies pursued.

Collective security as an abstract principle of utopian politics requires that all nations come to the aid of a victim of aggression by resisting the aggressor with all means necessary to frustrate his aims. Once the case of aggression is established, the duty to act is unequivocal. Its extent may be affected by concern for the nation's survival; obviously no nation will commit outright suicide in the service of collective security. But beyond that elemental limitation no consideration of interest or power, either with regard to the aggressor or his victim or the nation acting in the latter's defense, can qualify the obligation to act under the principle of collective security. Thus high officials of our government have declared that we intervened in Korea not for any narrow interest of ours but in support of the moral principle of collective security.

Collective security as a concrete principle of realist policy is the age-old maxim, "Hang together or hang separately," in modern dress. It recognizes the need for nation A under certain circumstances to defend nation B against attack by nation C. That need is determined, first, by the interest which A has in the territorial integrity of B and by the relation of that interest to all the other interests of A as well as to the resources available for the support of all those interests. Furthermore, A must take into account the power which is at the disposal of aggressor C for fighting A and B as over against the power available to A and B for fighting C. The same calculation must be carried on concerning the power of the likely allies of C as over against those of A and B. Before going to war for the defense of South Korea in the name of collective security, an American adherent of political realism would have demanded an answer to the following four questions: First, what is our interest in the preservation of the independence of South Korea; second, what is our power to defend that independence against North Korea; third, what is our power to defend that independence against China and the Soviet Union; and fourth, what are the chances for preventing China and the Soviet Union from entering the Korean War?

In view of the principle of collective security, interpreted in utopian terms, our intervention in Korea was a foregone conclusion. The interpretation of this principle in realist terms might or might not, depending upon the concrete circumstances of interest and power, have led us to the same conclusion. In the execution of the policy of collective security the utopian had to be indifferent to the possibility of Chinese and Russian intervention, except for his resolution to apply the principle of collective security to anybody who would intervene on the side of the aggressor. The realist could not help weighing the possibility of the intervention of a great power on the side of the aggressor in terms of the interests engaged and the power available on the other side.[17]

The Truman administration could not bring itself to taking resolutely the utopian or the realist position. It resolved to intervene in good measure on utopian grounds and in spite of military advice to the contrary; it allowed the military commander to advance to the Yalu River in disregard of the risk of the intervention of a great power against which collective security could be carried out only by means of a general war, and then refused to pursue the war with full effectiveness on the realist grounds of the risk of a third world war. Thus Mr. Truman in 1952 is caught in the same dilemma from which Mr. Baldwin could extricate himself in 1936 on the occasion of the League of Nations sanctions against Italy's attack upon Ethiopia only at an enormous loss to British prestige. Collective security as a defense of the status quo short of a general war can be effective only against second-rate

[17] The difference in these two attitudes is well illustrated by the following passage from a recent Moon Mullins cartoon. An elderly representative of the utopian school asks little Kayo: "Remember the golden rule. Now, supposing that boy slapped you on the right cheek, what would you do?" Whereupon Kayo replies realistically: "Jest how big a boy are you supposin'?"

powers. Applied against a major power, it is a contradiction in terms, for it means necessarily a major war. Of this self-defeating contradiction Mr. Baldwin was as unaware in the 'thirties as Mr. Truman seems to be in 1952. Mr. Churchill put Mr. Baldwin's dilemma in these cogent terms: "First, the Prime Minister had declared that sanctions meant war; secondly, he was resolved that there must be no war; and thirdly, he decided upon sanctions. It was evidently impossible to comply with these three conditions." Similarly Mr. Truman had declared that the effective prosecution of the Korean War meant the possibility of a third world war; he resolved that there must be no third world war; and he decided upon intervention in the Korean War. Here, too, it is impossible to comply with these three conditions.

Similar contradictions are inherent in the proposals which would substitute for the current policy of containment one of the liberation of the nations presently the captives of Russian Communism. This objective can be compatible with the utopian or realist position, but the policies designed to secure it will be fundamentally different according to whether they are based upon one or the other position. The clearest case to date for the utopian justification of such policies has been made by Representative Charles J. Kersten of Wisconsin who pointed to these four "basic defects" of the "negative policy of containment and negotiated coexistence":

It would be immoral and unchristian to negotiate a permanent agreement with forces which by every religious creed and moral precept are evil. It abandons nearly one-half of humanity and the once free nations of Poland, Czechoslovakia, Hungary, Rumania, Bulgaria, Albania, Lithuania, Latvia, Esthonia and China to enslavement of the Communist police state.

It is un-American because it violates the principle of the American Declaration of Independence, which proclaims the rights of all people to freedom and their right and duty to throw off tyranny.

It will lead to all-out World War III because it aligns all the forces of the non-Communist world in military opposition to and against all the forces of the Communist world, including the 800,000,000 peoples behind the Iron Curtain.

The policy of mere containment is uneconomic and will lead to national bankruptcy.[18]

This statement is interesting for its straightforwardness and because it combines in a rather typical fashion considerations of abstract morality and of expediency. The captive nations must be liberated not only because their captivity is immoral, unchristian, and un-American, but also because its continuation will lead to a third world war and to national bankruptcy. To what extent, however, these considerations of expediency are invalidated by their utopian setting will become obvious from a comparison between the utopian and the realist positions.

From the utopian point of view there can be no difference between the liberation of Esthonia or Czechoslovakia, of Poland or China; the captivity of any nation, large or small, close or far away, is a moral outrage which cannot be tolerated. The realist, too, seeks the liberation of all captive nations because he realizes that the presence of the Russian armies in the heart of Europe and their cooperation with the Chinese armies constitute the two main sources of the imbalance of power which threatens our security. Yet before he formulates a program of liberation, he will seek answers to a number of questions such as these: While the United States has a general interest in the liberation of all captive nations, what is the hierarchy of interests it has in the liberation, say, of China, Esthonia, and Hungary? And while the Soviet Union has a general interest in keeping all captive nations in that state, what is the hierarchy of its interests in keeping, say, Poland, Eastern Germany, and Bulgaria captive? If we assume, as we must on the historic evidence of two centuries, that Russia would never give up control over Poland without being compelled by force of arms, would the objective of the liberation of Poland justify the ruin of western civilization, that of Poland included, which would be the certain result of a third world war? What

[18] *New York Times,* August 14, 1952, p. 1.

resources does the United States have at its disposal for the liberation of all captive nations or some of them? What resources does the Soviet Union have at its disposal to keep in captivity all captive nations or some of them? Are we more likely to avoid national bankruptcy by embarking upon a policy of indiscriminate liberation with the concomitant certainty of war or by continuing the present policy of containment?

It might be that in a particular instance the policies suggested by the answers to these questions will coincide with Representative Kersten's proposals, but there can be no doubt that in its overall character, substance, emphasis, and likely consequences a utopian policy of liberation differs fundamentally from a realist one.

The issue between liberation as a utopian principle of abstract morality vs. the realist evaluation of the consequences which a policy of liberation would have for the survival of the nation has arisen before in American history. Abraham Lincoln was faced with a dilemma similar to that which confronts us today. Should he make the liberation of the slaves the ultimate standard of his policy even at the risk of destroying the Union, as many urged him to do, or should he subordinate the moral principle of universal freedom to considerations of the national interest? The answer Lincoln gave to Horace Greeley, a spokesman for the utopian moralists, is timeless in its eloquent wisdon. "If there be those," he wrote on August 22, 1862,

who would not save the Union unless they could at the same time save slavery, I do not agree with them. If there be those who would not save the Union unless they could at the same time destroy slavery, I do not agree with them. My paramount object in this struggle *is* to save the Union, and is *not* either to save or to destroy slavery. If I could save the Union without freeing *any* slave I would do it, and if I could save it by freeing *all* the slaves, I would do it; and if I could save it by freeing some and leaving others alone I would also do that. What I do about slavery, and the colored race, I do because I believe it helps to save the Union; and what I forbear, I forbear because I do *not* believe it would help to save the

Union. I shall do *less* whenever I shall believe what I am doing hurts the cause, and I shall do *more* whenever I shall believe doing more will help the cause. I shall try to correct errors when shown to be errors; and I shall adopt new views so fast as they shall appear to be true views.

I have here stated my purpose according to my view of *official* duty; and I intend no modification of my oft-expressed *personal* wish that all men everywhere could be free.

IV

The foregoing discussion ought to shed additional light, if this is still needed, upon the moral merits of the utopian and realist positions. This question, more than any other, seems to have agitated the critics of realism in international affairs. Disregarding the voluminous evidence, some of them have picked a few words out of their context to prove that realism in international affairs is unprincipled and contemptuous of morality. To mention but one example, one eminent critic summarizes my position, which he supposes to deny the possibility of judging the conduct of states by moral criteria, in these words: "And one spokesman finds 'a profound and neglected truth,' to use his words, in the dictum of Hobbes that 'there is neither morality nor law outside the state.' "[19] These are indeed my words, but not all of them. What I actually said was this:

There is a profound and neglected truth hidden in Hobbes's extreme dictum that the state creates morality as well as law and that there is neither morality nor law outside the state. Universal moral principles, such as justice or equality, are capable of guiding political action only to the extent that they have been given concrete content and have been related to political situations by society.[20]

It must be obvious from this passage and from all my other writings on the subject[21] that my position is the exact

opposite from what this critic makes it out to be. I have always maintained that the actions of states are subject to universal moral principles and I have been careful to differentiate my position in this respect from that of Hobbes. Five points basic to my position may need to be emphasized again.

The first point is what one might call the requirement of cosmic humility with regard to the moral evaluation of the actions of states. To know that states are subject to the moral law is one thing; to pretend to know what is morally required of states in a particular situation is quite another. The human mind tends naturally to identify the particular interests of states, as of individuals, with the moral purposes of the universe. The statesman in the defense of the nation's interests may, and at times even must, yield to that tendency; the scholar must resist it at every turn. For the light-hearted assumption that what one's own nation aims at and does is morally good and that those who oppose that nation's policies are evil is morally indefensible and intellectually untenable and leads in practice to that distortion of judgment, born of the blindness

[19] A. H. Feller, "In Defense of International Law and Morality," *The Annals of the American Academy of Political and Social Science*, Vol. 282, p. 80 (July, 1952).

[20] *In Defense of the National Interest: A Critical Examination of American Foreign Policy* (New York, 1951), p. 34.

[21] See, for instance, "The Machiavellian Utopia," *Ethics*, Vol. 55, pp. 145–147 (Jan., 1945); "Ethics and Politics," in *Approaches to Group Understanding*, Sixth Symposium of the Conference on Science, Philosophy and Religion, edited by Bryson, Finkelstein, and MacIver (New York, 1947), pp. 319–341; "The Escape from Power in the Western World," in *Conflicts of Power in Modern Culture*, Seventh Symposium of the Conference on Science, Philosophy and Religion, edited by Bryson, Finkelstein, and MacIver, pp. 1–12; *Scientific Man vs. Power Politics* (Chicago, 1946), Chaps. 7, 8; "Views of Nuremberg: Further Analysis of the Trial and Its Importance," *America*, Vol. 76, pp. 266–267 (Dec. 7, 1946); "The Twilight of International Morality," *Ethics*, Vol. 58, pp. 79–99 (Jan., 1948); "The Political Science of E. H. Carr," *World Politics*, Vol. 1, pp. 127–134 (Oct., 1948); *Politics Among Nations* (New York, 1948), Ch. 14; "National Interest and Moral Principles in Foreign Policy: The Primacy of the National Interest," *The American Scholar*, Vol. 18, pp. 207–212 (Spring, 1949); "The Pathology of Power," *American Perspective*, Vol. 4, pp. 6–10 (Winter, 1950); "The Moral Dilemma in Foreign Policy," in *The Year Book of World Affairs, 1951* (London, 1951), pp. 12–36.

of crusading frenzy, which has been the curse of nations from the beginning of time.

The second point which obviously needs to be made again concerns the effectiveness of the restraints which morality imposes upon the actions of states.

A discussion of international morality must guard against the two extremes either of overrating the influence of ethics upon international politics or else of denying that statesmen and diplomats are moved by anything else but considerations of material power.

On the one hand, there is the dual error of confounding the moral rules which people actually observe with those they pretend to observe as well as with those which writers declare they ought to observe. . . .

On the other hand, there is the misconception, usually associated with the general depreciation and moral condemnation of power politics, discussed above, that international politics is so thoroughly evil that it is no use looking for ethical limitations of the aspirations for power on the international scene. Yet, if we ask ourselves what statesmen and diplomats are capable of doing to further the power objectives of their respective nations and what they actually do, we realize that they do less than they probably could and less than they actually did in other periods of history. They refuse to consider certain ends and to use certain means, either altogether or under certain conditions, not because in the light of expediency they appear impractical or unwise, but because certain moral rules interpose an absolute barrier. Moral rules do not permit certain policies to be considered at all from the point of view of expediency. Such ethical inhibitions operate in our time on different levels with different effectiveness. Their restraining function is most obvious and most effective in affirming the sacredness of human life in times of peace.[22]

In connection with this passage we have given a number of historic examples showing the influence of moral principles upon the conduct of foreign policy. An example taken from contemporary history will illustrate the same point. There can be little doubt that the Soviet

Union could have achieved the objectives of its foreign policy at the end of the Second World War without antagonizing the nations of the West into that encircling coalition which has been the nightmare of Bolshevist foreign policy since 1917. It could have mitigated cunning for its own sake and the use of force with persuasion, conciliation, and a trust derived from the awareness of a partial community of interests and would thereby have minimized the dangers to itself and the rest of the world which are inherent in the objectives of its policies. Yet the Soviet Union was precluded from relying upon these traditional methods of diplomacy by its general conception of human nature, politics, and morality. In the general philosophy of Bolshevism there is no room for honest dissent, the recognition of the intrinsic worth of divergent interests, and genuine conciliation between such interests. On all levels of social interaction opposition must be destroyed by cunning and violence, since it has no right to exist, rather than be met half way in view of its intrinsic legitimacy. This being the general conception of the political morality of Bolshevism, the foreign policy of the Soviet Union is limited to a much more narrow choice of means than the foreign policies of other nations.

The United States, for instance, has been able, in its relations with the nations of Latin America, to replace military intervention and dollar diplomacy with the policy of the Good Neighbor. That drastic change was made possible by the general conception of political morality which has been prevalent in the United States from its very inception. The United States is a pluralist society which presupposes the continuing existence and legitimacy of divergent interests. These interests are locked in a continuing struggle for supremacy to be decided by force only as a last resort, but normally through a multitude of institutional agencies which are so devised as to allow one or the other interest a temporary advantage but none a permanent supremacy at the price of the destruction of the others. This morality of pluralism allows the United States, once it is secure in that minimum of vital interests to which we

[22] Morgenthau, *Politics Among Nations*, pp. 174–175.

have referred above, to transfer those principles of political morality to the international scene and to deal with divergent interests there with the same methods of genuine compromise and conciliation which are a permanent element of its domestic political life.

The third point concerns the relations between universal moral principles and political action. I have always maintained that these universal moral principles cannot be applied to the actions of states in their abstract universal formulation, but that they must be, as it were, filtered through the concrete circumstances of time and place. The individual may say for himself: *"Fiat justitia, pereat mundus"*; the state has no right to say so in the name of those who are in its care. Both individual and state must judge political action by universal moral principles, such as that of liberty. Yet while the individual has a moral right to sacrifice himself in defense of such a moral principle, the state has no moral right to let its moral disapprobation of the infringement of liberty get in the way of successful political action, itself inspired by the moral principle of national survival. There can be no political morality without prudence, that is, without consideration of the political consequences of seemingly moral action. Classical and medieval philosophy knew this and so did Lincoln when he said: "I do the very best I know how, the very best I can, and I mean to keep doing so until the end. If the end brings me out all right, what is said against me won't amount to anything. If the end brings me out wrong, ten angels swearing I was right would make no difference." The issue between utopianism and realism, as it bears on this point, has been put most succinctly by Edmund Burke, and what he has to say in the following passage about revolution, that is, civil war, may well be applied *mutatis mutandis* to all war.

Nothing universal can be rationally affirmed on any moral or any political subject. Pure metaphysical abstraction does not belong to these matters. The lines of morality are not like the ideal lines of mathematics. They are broad and deep as well as long. They admit of exceptions; they demand modifications. These exceptions and modifications are not made by the process of logic, but by the rules of prudence. Prudence is not only the first in rank of the virtues political and moral, but she is the director, the regulator, the standard of them all. Metaphysics cannot live without definition; but Prudence is cautious how she defines. Our courts cannot be more fearful in suffering fictitious cases to be brought before them for eliciting their determination on a point of law than prudent moralists are in putting extreme and hazardous cases of conscience upon emergencies not existing. Without attempting, therefore, to define, what never can be defined, the case of a revolution in government, this, I think, may be safely affirmed—that a sore and pressing evil is to be removed, and that a good, great in its amount and unequivocal in its nature, must be probable almost to a certainty, before the inestimable price of our own morals and the wellbeing of a number of our fellow-citizens is paid for a revolution. If ever we ought to be economists even to parsimony, it is in the voluntary production of evil. Every revolution contains in it something of evil.[23]

Fourth, the realist recognizes that a moral decision, especially in the political sphere, does not imply a simple choice between a moral principle and a standard of action which is morally irrelevant or even outright immoral. A moral decision implies always a choice among different moral principles, one of which is given precedence over others. To say that a political action has no moral purpose is absurd; for political action can be defined as an attempt to realize moral values through the medium of politics, that is, power. The relevant moral question con-

[23] *The Works of The Right Honorable Edmund Burke,* 4th ed. (Boston, 1871), Vol. 4, pp. 80–81. Cf. also Burke, "Speech on A Bill for Shortening the Duration of Parliaments," May 8, 1780, in *Works,* Vol. 7, p. 73: "I must see, to satisfy me, the remedies; I must see, from their operation in the cure of the old evil, and in the cure of those new evils which are inseparable from all remedies, how they balance each other, and what is the total result. The excellence of mathematics and metaphysics is, to have but one thing before you; but he forms the best judgement in all moral disquisitions who has the greatest number and variety of considerations in one view before him, and can take them in with the best possible consideration of the middle results of all."

cerns the choice among different moral values, and it is at this point that the realist and the utopian part company again. If an American statesman must choose between the promotion of universal liberty, which is a moral good, at the risk of American security and, hence, of liberty in the United States, and the promotion of American security and of liberty in the United States, which is another moral good, to the detriment of the promotion of universal liberty, which choice ought he to make? The utopian will not face the issue squarely and will deceive himself into believing that he can achieve both goods at the same time. The realist will choose the national interest on both moral and pragmatic grounds; for if he does not take care of the national interest nobody else will, and if he puts American security and liberty in jeopardy the cause of liberty everywhere will be impaired.

Finally, the political realist distinguishes between his moral sympathies and the political interests which he must defend. He will distinguish with Lincoln between his "*official* duty" which is to protect the national interest and his "*personal* wish" which is to see universal moral values realized throughout the world.

The issue has been admirably put by Father Wilfred Parsons of Catholic University in defending Ambassador Kennan's position:

Mr. Kennan did not say state behavior is not a fit subject for moral judgment, but only that it should not sway our realization of the realities with which we have to deal. Msgr. Koenig continues: "Should we accept power realities and aspirations without feeling the obligation of moral judgment?" And he appeals to the present writer and other political scientists to say whether this doctrine agrees with Pope Pius XII's messages on peace.

I am sure that most political scientists, and also Mr. Kennan, would agree with the monsignor that we should not accept those realities "without feeling the obligation of moral judgment." But there is a difference between *feeling* this obligation (and even expressing it) and allowing this feeling to sway our actions in concrete negotiations that deal with the national or world common good. We can still feel and yet deal.

To make my meaning clearer, I understood Mr. Kennan to hold that we went off the beam with Woodrow Wilson, when we began to make our moral disapprobation an *essential part* of our foreign relations, even sometimes at the expense of our own and the world's common good. Logically, such an attitude would inhibit our dealing with Britain, France and a host of countries. Pius XI, speaking of Mussolini after the Lateran Treaty, said he would deal with the devil himself if he must. Here was moral disapprobation, but it was not "carried over into the affairs of states."

This relative position, and not the absolute one of Msgr. Koenig (with which in itself I agree), is, I think, the issue raised by Mr. Kennan, and it is worth debating on that basis.[24]

The contest between utopianism and realism is not tantamount to a contest between principle and expediency, morality and immorality, although some spokesmen for the former would like to have it that way. The contest is rather between one type of political morality and another type of political morality, one taking as its standard universal moral principles abstractly formulated, the other weighing these principles against the moral requirements of concrete political action, their relative merits to be decided by a prudent evaluation of the political consequences to which they are likely to lead.[25]

[24] *America*, Vol. 86, p. 700 (March 29, 1952). See also Algernon Cecil, "The Foreign Office," in *The Cambridge History of British Foreign Policy, 1783–1919* (New York, 1923), Vol. 3, p. 605, concerning Lord Salisbury: "Always, however, the motive of his policy was to be found in the political interests as opposed to the political sympathies of Great Britain; and in this way his treatment of Foreign Affairs is at the opposite policy from that of Palmerston or Gladstone." Cf. also the general remarks in Alexander H. Leighton, *Human Relations in a Changing World* (New York, 1949), pp. 155 ff.

[25] See, on this point, Shirley R. Letwin, "Rationalism, Principles, and Politics," *The Review of Politics*, Vol. 14, pp. 367–393 (July, 1952); L. Susan Stebbing, *Ideals and Illusions* (London, 1941); Vernon H. Holloway, *Religious Ethics and the Politics of Power* (New York, 1951); and Dorothy Fosdick, "Ethical Standards and Political Strategies," *Political Science Quarterly*, Vol. 57, pp. 214 ff. (1942).

These points are re-emphasized by the foregoing discussion. Which attitude with regard to collective security and to the liberation of the captive nations, the utopian or the realist, is more likely to safeguard the survival of the United States in its territorial, political, and cultural identity and at the same time to contribute the most to the security and liberty of other nations? This is the ultimate test—political and moral—by which utopianism and realism must be judged.

Basic Issues of International Ethics

WILLIAM V. O'BRIEN

Chairman of the Institute of World Polity, Georgetown University, William V. O'Brien has written extensively in the field of international law.

INTRODUCTION

Foreign and domestic critics have traditionally criticized the American propensity for "moralizing" about international relations. Too often this criticism, much of which is probably justified, is productive of the attitude that there is no such thing as international ethics. This conclusion is not justified, but, unhappily, so little effort has been made to produce a sound and meaningful international ethic that so-called idealists and realists continue to exchange barren criticisms and to go their separate ways, seldom finding any central points for discourse and mutual enlightenment.

Too often debates over the ethical implications of international affairs are carried on in a fortuitous fashion with respect to some specific policy problem, e.g., "Should aid be discontinued," "Should the United States support the UN bond issue," "Should nuclear testing be discontinued," "Are we intervening too much or too little in Vietnam," etc. But to the extent that one's ethical views are the product of informed reason and not mere emotion or prejudice, they presumably have some bases, or ought to,

Paper originally prepared for use in Seminars on Ethics and Foreign Policy conducted by the Council on Religion and International Affairs. Reprinted by permission of the author and the Council on Religion and International Affairs.

in fundamental attitudes about man and the world in which he lives.

My purpose is not to convince you of the rectitude of some bundle of principles, institutions and programs for the ethical conduct of foreign affairs. Rather it is to present for consideration and discussion some of the basic issues which ought to be faced by anyone seriously concerned with ethics and foreign policy.

International relations are carried out by men who represent large numbers of their fellow men in societies which we call states. Increasingly, international relations also involves relations between social entities within states and international and supra-national organizations. But it should be quite clear that international relations are simply one part, an extremely important part, of the totality of human activity. As such they are subject, generally speaking, to very much the same ethical principles which govern human activity within individual states, groups, organizations and families. This is an essential point which is widely misunderstood and controverted.

On the one hand, there are those who deny the existence or the possibility of any ethics in international affairs. It seems curious that whatever faith we hold would bind us strictly from the levels of individual, family, group to national ethics but would suddenly permit unlimited pursuit of power in the international arena. However, many hold essentially this view. Even more take the attitude that they would *prefer* that international relations be subjected to ethical limitations but this is simply impossible. The best of statesmen has no choice but to play the power game as best he can so that the evil done in the process will at least be balanced by the good achieved for his nation.

On the other hand there are those who attempt to apply their principles taken from personal ethics or even the ethics of domestic society to international elations. Pacifism, for example, often results from this kind of thinking. To do this is to reason rather in the fashion of the individual whose concepts of public finance are drawn from his own simple experiences and who, ignoring the complexities of political economy, argues that the government should never go into debt because he himself never does.

The problems of establishing and applying a realistic international ethic are neither so hopeless as the first opinion portrays them nor so simple as the second opinion believes. One can come down at various points between these ex-tremes but the most elementary point to be made at the outset is that it does not really matter whether it is extremely difficult or quite easy, or moderately difficult or easy, to formulate ethical principles to guide the conduct of international relations. The real point is that since international relations are a part of human activity they *must* be subject to some ethical principles and our task is to find such principles and apply them as best we can.

If this ethical imperative be accepted, what are some of the basic issues which must be discussed in international ethics, whatever the viewpoint taken? They are old, very familiar issues: (1) What is the nature of man? (2) What is the nature of the state? (3) What is the nature of the international society? (4) What is the nature of politics? (5) What is the nature of law? (6) What is the role of force in domestic and in international society?

I would like to indicate what difference it makes for international ethics how each of these questions is answered. Then I will try to illustrate the practical relevance of these issues to some contemporary problem areas.

THE NATURE OF MAN

All political, legal and ethical theory must deal with the question, "What is the nature of man?" I shall not presume to do more than recall some of the prevailing theories of human nature and to suggest their relevance to international ethics. Some theories emphasize man's sinfulness, his weakness, the need to control him by balancing selfish interests and by naked coercion. Some theories view man optimistically. They see him as capable of a high degree of perfection which can be reached through the development of his reason. This means that a high level of social organization is possible wherein the sheer reasonableness of blueprints for peace, law and order will ensure their acceptance without the necessity of dirty politics and coercion. Then naturally there are theories of human nature which strike a balance between the two foregoing extremes. Usually such middle of the road theories combine an awareness for the need for coercion with a solid but cautious respect for the practical potentialities of human reason. I have but to mention a subject of importance in international relations to make clear the relevance of such theories to international ethics, disarmament. Is it not clear *prima facie* how an exponent of each type of theory of human nature would view the feasibility of an agreement between the United States and the Soviet Union to achieve general and complete disarmament?

Thus far I have mentioned theories of human nature that are essentially religious or metaphysical in their origin. For better or worse they have exercised an historic influence on the attitudes of the American and other peoples towards ethics and foreign policy. They have exercised this influence in part precisely because they hold the nature of man to be perennial, immutable. Accordingly, the nature of the state, of international society, of politics, law, force, are all perennial and immutable. A Hans Morgenthau, Reinhold Niebuhr, John Courtney Murray, or Louis Sohn has a foreseeable view on most basic issues of international ethics because he holds a definite view of human nature which he applies consistently throughout his political thought.

Today, however, there appears to be a trend towards a scientific relativism that rejects or at least strongly questions the notion of an immutable human nature. Human nature is thought to be largely a product of environment, circumstances, and scientific manipulation. Thus none of the basic issues raised here could be resolved definitively because the central issue, the nature of man, is never resolved definitively. What is the nature of man? It all depends. Should we be optimistic or pessimistic about the prospects for an ethical ordering of the world society? It all depends. In any event, what *is* "ethical"? That all depends too.

Naturally, those who believe that their theological and metaphysical beliefs do accord with reality would hope that the gap between rational and experimental psychology can be closed. There is no question but that traditional philosophies are being challenged to confirm and elaborate their basic concepts in the light of findings of the behavioral sciences. But the task is a difficult one, not only because of potential conflicts but because there is some uncertainty as to just how scientific the behavioral sciences really are.

Interestingly enough, scientific relativism is perhaps strongest in the United States, a country wherein the whole basis for government and law is found in natural law-natural rights theories which are often explicitly traced to religion, e.g., the Declaration of Independence. The American system assumes immutable rights based upon an immutable human nature. It will be embarrassing if American social scientists prove, at least to their own satisfaction, that empirical reality does not coincide with the concepts on which this country was founded.

THE NATURE OF THE STATE

I shall not discuss the nature of the state in terms of its origins or of the mutual rights and duties of citizen and government. Rather I will raise the question of the interrelationships between a state and other states and, in the next section, between a state and the total world society.

Traditional political theory has dealt with the state as the *civitas maxima,* the highest, the most perfect form of human organization. Particularly since the emergence of sovereign nation-states in modern times, the state has been recognized as possessing virtually unlimited power within its own jurisdiction. The state was also accorded a right to preserve its existence and to enhance its power. Until the establishment of the League of Nations there really was no effort to limit these prerogatives. One of the reasons for this indulgence with respect to states was the conviction that broad powers were justified by the fact that the state assured adequately the security and welfare of its subjects.

Anoter reason for the tolerance of rather unrestrained pursuit of national interests was the belief in the essential worth of so-called "nations." Both of these reasons are increasingly open to question today. No state except the United States and the Soviet Union can assure its own security unilaterally. Very few states can provide the good life for their subjects without the cooperation of many other states and supranational organizations. The traditional nation-states, Great Britain, France, Germany, Italy, etc., are inclining more and more towards organizations such as NATO, EEC. Meanwhile the great majority of the new nations are capable neither of self-defense, of maintaining minimal standards with respect to the necessities of life, or, in some instances, of assuring domestic order. The term, "the state" is used to describe entities as diverse as Chad and the Soviet Union.

At the same time the concept of "nationalism" has been so stretched and abused that one wishes that Woodrow Wilson had not elevated self-determination

FOREIGN POLICY—REAL AND IDEAL

from the level of political aspirations to that of a fundamental norm of international ethics. Presumably one of the ethically significant features of older nationalisms was that, despite all the trouble they caused, nationalism contributed the cohesive human basis for political society. Many of the new nations are accidents of the arbitrary geography of colonialism. They do not unite a "nation" in the sense of the French, Italian, or German nations at all.

This is not to say that the sovereign nation-state is dead. Obviously it lives even where its existence is against common sense. But this fact cannot conceal the clear evidence that the state in the sense of the typical 19th century nation-state is definitely not the highest, most perfect level of political-economic organization to which men can aspire. The trend, however blurred by emotional outbreaks of "nationalism," is towards supranational regional organizations, security organizations, functional international organizations all in the context of an acute realization of the essential interdependence of the peoples of the world with respect to every problem from avoiding mass nuclear destruction to avoiding mass starvation. This fact is obviously of fundamental importance to the consideration of international ethics.

THE NATURE OF THE INTERNATIONAL SOCIETY

To those who consider the state the true *civitas maxima,* the highest "good" in politics is the national interest. Yet the older traditions in political thought, even when they accepted the state as the *civitas maxima,* always recognized the higher good of the totality of states, the international common good. It is hard enough to define the common good of the United States; to speculate on the international common good would seem to be a difficult if not hopeless task. But as we have said earlier, it is a task which cannot be avoided. Moreover, what used to be considered to be at best a highly speculative invention of obtuse medieval minds is increasingly conspicuous in the reasoning of practical statesmen. Nuclear testing, exploration of space, exploitation of the continental shelf and of the world's fisheries, the conservation of world resources, these are all problems of the international common good. A state acts for its selfish short-range national interest and against the international common good at its peril, even in the worst moments of the Cold War.

And, indeed, the United States has been careful to defer to the international common good in its declarations and practices. When, as in the case of nuclear testing, it has acted in such a way as to threaten the international common good, it has sought to justify its act as being required for the defense of that same common good. Thus we argued that nuclear weapons were needed to protect the Free World and to maintain equilibrium. Testing was necessary in order that this could be accomplished. Thus we sought to identify our national interests with the international common good.

Like any concept of "good" or "justice" or "reasonableness" there can be no formula for defining the international common good. In practice it is defined over time by the states of the world as they react to problems of common concern. The underlying point, however, is that the very concept of an international common good has a reality and an effectiveness in and of itself. Once it is admitted that there is an end *somewhere* to the pursuit of national interests, that at some point the requirements of the whole world society must prevail over those of any one member of it, then the beginnings of an international ethic are in sight.

THE NATURE OF POLITICS

Thus far we have been talking mainly about the institutional structure of domestic and international politics. But what makes the wheels turn over? What are the dynamic forces which make up politics? Here we must return to our root concepts of human nature. The realist, as we have seen, thinks of politics in terms of setting up one selfish "faction" (as Madison put it in Federalist #10) against the other in a balance-of-power system which turns the very divisive elements of society into instruments for maintaining minimum justice and order. The idealist, confident in man's rationality and goodness, scorns the very subject of politics to which he tends to attach a degree of odium. He would prefer scientific decision-making by enlightened managers supported by enlightened public-spirited citizens. Model constitutions, statutes, organization charts, tribunals, administrative machinery of all kinds are held out as the means to achieve the proper objectives of political society.

These extremes are particularly evident in the field of foreign relations. One part of our people revels in the grimy details of power political *coups de main* executed by wily, hard-headed American diplomats. Another segment of our people is convinced that all international disputes can be solved provided that (1) we really try, and (2) adequate machinery is available. The latter are the more able to indulge their dreams since they are seldom treated seriously by practical statesmen and it is therefore always possible to point out that "we have not really tried" to have—world government now, unilateral disarmament or some other panacea.

It would certainly seem that blue-prints and machinery without practical political expertise are ineffectual means for the application of ethical values. On the other hand, the power political approach is always in danger of (1) getting out of hand and leading to self-defeating power rampages, or, (2) drifting into a succession of purely pragmatic technical exercises in the manipulation of power without any sense of deeper purpose other than the preservation of the particular political unit at hand. Clearly a marriage of elements of the two approaches is needed. Political activity is not an end in itself, it needs institutions, constitutions, laws, governmental machinery to channel it as coherently as possible so that long term values are pursued in an intelligent way. But the grease of politics is needed to make the wheels of the political system work. Thus the informal compromises and alignments of politics must precede the erection of formal legal institutions and laws. Politics in itself is a neuter phenomenon. It is neither an end in itself nor a grubby reminder of sinfulness soon to be removed by social engineering. What we need is not the elimination of power politics but the channeling of power politics so as to support useful international institutions and laws.

THE NATURE OF LAW

Controversy and misunderstanding over the nature of law rivals that found with respect to the nature of politics. The realist approaches limit the concept of law to that which is enforced by coercive authority. The idealists, as we have said, think of law in terms of enlightened legislation. The printed word is highly respected; all problems are soluble if the right terms of agreement can only be found.

The realist argues briefly and devastatingly: law requires enforcement by a supreme authority; there is no such authority in the international society; there is, then, no international law in the strict sense at all. However, admittedly states do agree to the restrictions of posi-tive international law. But these restrictions are always subject to removal without notice when the higher interests of a state so require. In any event, the restrictions themselves are of a modest, peripheral kind. The idealist wants the same kind of sophisticated legislation that a very advanced domestic law produces when it is at its best. He fails to recognize that the problems of developing international law in a primitive, de-centralized international juridical order are very different from those of law in an advanced legal order. He is also inclined to forget that even the most advanced legal orders experience grave difficulties when formal laws outrange the willingness of society to accept them. Surely this has been the

American experience in dealing with problems of economic, social and racial justice.

In truth law combines elements of coercion, rationality, social engineering, social mores, and the propensity of the subjects of the law to obey or not to obey the law as a matter of general practice. As in politics, higher goals and selfish interest interact. Law grows out of politics and survives to the extent that it has political, economic, social and ethical foundations within the society which it purports to govern. If it has such foundations, it can exist with comparatively little in the way of coercive sanctions. But any law which is to deal comprehensively with the great problems of inernational relations needs enforcement and there is visible the beginning, however crude and inadequate, of a trend towards the enforcement of international law by force employed on behalf of the international juridical order, e.g., Korean War, UN interventions in the Middle East and the Congo.

The point is that law is not a magic force which either does or does not exist. It is a human creation that requires the meshing of the highest of ideals with the most practical questions of politics, as well as the development of the will and the means to enforce it when more peaceful methods have failed. Failure to understand this is as much responsible for ridicule of international law as for the propagation of well-intentioned but utterly unrealistic slogans enjoining us to establish world peace through world law.

THE ROLE OF FORCE

From what I have said about the nature of politics and law you will not be surprised to hear that I believe the concept of the elimination of war is an illusory one. Every society with which we are familiar requires force to maintain law and order. It is inconceivable to me that even the most idyllic projection of general and complete disarmament could be envisaged without the continued existence of armed forces of some kind. The means of war cannot be uninvented, there will always have to exist community forces to put down revolts against world order. Perhaps there should also exist forces in individual parts of the world order to ensure that the guardians of the world peace do not decide to exploit their advantage.

In any event, one of the most fundamental issues of international ethics is this question of the role of force. Obviously one's position on this question depends, just as in the case of the debates over the nature of politics and law, on one's fundamental assumptions about human nature and the nature of political society. But one fact of life affects all approaches to the question. Widespread recourse to force, even in the era of impressive efforts to outlaw war, is the rule rather than the exception in international relations. This is the "given" of our problems and we must work from it. We cannot ignore this given if we are to develop an international ethic that is relevant to the real problems of international relations.

APPLICATION: ECONOMIC, SOCIAL AND RACIAL JUSTICE

We should now turn to some indications as to how these fundamental concepts of international ethics are applied. Let us begin with the problem area of economic, social and racial justice. There is presently much disillusionment in this country over the results of our foreign aid programs. These programs were sold to the Congress primarily on the strength of the following arguments: (1) they would produce stronger and happier societies and thereby prevent the internal spread of Communism; (2) they would bolster up the military capacity of the recipients, thus preventing Communist military aggression; (3) they would enhance America's prestige and produce friends and allies all over the world. It was also occasionally added that aid would produce future customers for American Trade.

Now we find that many of the recipients of our aid are not safe from internal or external Communist pressures. We find that almost all of them are by our standards, spectacularly ungrateful, even spiteful and treasonable in their behavior towards us on matters of grave importance. Americans traditionally like to be liked and we find that hardly anybody likes us. We even find statesmen such as Prince Norducing Sihanouk of Cambodia who not only does not thank us for building him a "Friendship Highway" but who bluntly says he does not want our aid at all. Our feelings are so hurt that we hardly notice that on the other side of the world the Soviet Union is smarting under similar rebuffs.

An approach to the aid problem based on the fundamentals of international ethics would have avoided some of these peaks and valleys of euphoria and despair. First of all, to the extent that aid has been designed for military purposes it can hardly be considered either as a "give-away" or as a charitable benefaction. It is simply an instrument in America's global security. Like all such investments, it involves risks. The establishment of alliances and the hiring and supplying of mercenaries (for that is what the armed forces of some of our allies are in a very real sense) have always been rather speculative undertakings.

Shakespeare has already warned us about the potentialities of man's ingratitude to man; we shall simply have to become more mature on that score. The real point is that the Congress has seldom been willing to admit that underneath all of the arguments for aid there was a vague, inarticulate but very potent ethical impulse to help our neighbors. Aside from the limited objective of deterring Communist expansion, our arguments for aid should be twofold, one primarily self-ish, the other ethical. First we should help the less fortunate because we cannot prosper in the long run if we are an island of affluence in a sea of human misery. Second, we have an ethical obligation to feed the hungry, to clothe the naked, to nurse the weak and diseased. This obligation is more complicated, to be sure, than the obligation which the individual has to do these things for his neighbors. There are serious questions, for example, about our techniques in giving aid, questions that become quasi-ethical themselves. If there is an ethical obligation to give aid there would seem to be an obligation to give it as wisely and as efficiently as possible.

If we view aid in this light we will not be side-tracked by emotional reactions. It would be nice if our efforts brought friendly responses but the important point is whether they meet the requirements of an ethical imperative to help our fellow men.

There is not time to trace the implications for the problem of foreign aid of all of the various theories with respect to the basic issues of international ethics. But it should be evident that one's basic assumptions about these issues will strongly influence one's approach to aid. For example, the optimistic idealist will be much more confident about the possibilities for raising the political, economic and social levels of underdeveloped countries than the pessimist who takes a dim view of human nature. One's view of the nature of politics, law and force will color one's reaction to behavior by aid-receiving governments which is far removed from American standards. In short, the contribution of international ethics to the debate over foreign aid would be the introduction of some comparatively objective standards of judgment in an area where selfish short-term motives and confused emotional reactions are all too prevalent.

APPLICATION: ARMS CONTROL AND DISARMAMENT

The greatest single problem before the world is that of arms control and disarmament. Adequate analysis of this problem requires a searching confrontation with all of the great issues of international ethics. Man cannot but question the meaning of his existence and the requirements of his nature when he confronts the H-bomb. In order to find the limits of the right of the state to defend itself, he is forced to re-examine the nature of the thing to be defended at such great risk. The implications of political blunders and failures necessitate a harder, less condescending look at the nature of politics. The crying need for world law and the contrasting record of failures in modern international law and organization demand that the nature of law and the dynamics of the law-making process be understood much more clearly and by many more people. Finally, the paradox that overall effective power seems to decrease rather than increase with the development of nuclear capabilities raises in the most acute form all of the traditional questions about the nature of force.

Underlying prevailing differences of opinion about American defense preparations, the test-ban, further negotiations at Geneva, the problem of nuclear proliferation and the like are disagreements over and misconceptions about these basic issues. More important, unwillingness to face these issues is the root cause of the scandalous state of American thought on the morality of modern war and deterrence. Surely historians of other ages and civilizations will be puzzled and indignant when they attempt to understand how the Christian world has been able to co-exist with the A and H bomb for nearly twenty years without coming to any real moral consensus except that something ought to be done about them!

What are the limits to rights of states to endanger their own subjects and the subjects of other nations, friendly, hostile and neutral, to the dangers of nuclear war? How important is it for any particular state to continue to exist, if necessary by recourse to nuclear war? How ought politics to be viewed in an era when political intercourse is a matter of life and death? If we must build a world law for the nuclear age, how do we go about it? All theorizing aside, how do you build a legal system when there is no monolithic political unit to enforce it? Is it really feasible to eliminate armed force from international relations? If so, how can this be accomplished? If not, what methods of limiting force are most promising?

APPLICATION: THE PROCESS OF INFUSING ETHICS INTO FOREIGN POLICY

This survey of the basic issues of international ethics and of some of the problems of application may seem to be primarily a call to scholars and moralists to study and develop the subject of international ethics with much greater diligence and zeal. That is one of the purposes of the paper. But the main purpose is to call to your attention the significance of fundamental political, legal and ethical concepts in the formulation of practical foreign policies. Most of us stand in the ranks of what might be called the middle *elite*. We are not of the highest intellectual, cultural, political, business, social *elite* that gives a society its distinctive characteristics nor are we identified entirely with the great masses who accept our civilization without much question and who are "led" by the upper *elites*. We both follow the upper *elites* and, in one way or another, lead some portion of the masses, whether as clergymen, educators, civic leaders or whatever.

I think that it is probably too much to expect the generality of citizens to ponder over the great issues we have been discussing. I do think that we have a right to ask the members of the middle *elites* to do so. The average citizen should be given programs to approve or disapprove, e.g., aid, an arms control agreement, continued participation in the UN. The middle *elite* should be required to think through these issues of international ethics and apply the products of his meditations to current problems. He should not, for example, be for or against the slogan "World Peace Through World Law." Rather he should be prepared to inquire just what is meant by "peace" and "law" and how all of this is to come about. He should not be for or against an aid program without looking at its underlying rationale, the methods it is employing and the results it seems to be getting. The member of the middle *elite* should not be "absolutely opposed to" or "in favor of" any arms control and disarmament agreement with the Soviet Union. He should analyze any proposed agreement in the light of a reasoned and informed view of the political limits of the situation, the limits of international law in our time, the potentialities for law-making precedents and the extent to which the United States would be able to live with such precedents, and the necessities of force for security and force for the enforcement of the agreement itself.

Above all the community leader of the middle *elite* should be able to understand the normative guidance of the moralist, the lawyer, and the scholar as well as the practical difficulties of the statesman. In a sense he should act as a bridge between the two and at times he should act as judge of the quality of their interaction. If, as I believe to be the case with respect to nuclear war the moralist and the academician fail to give the statesman the kind of relevant guidance which he needs, the middle *elite* should be asking insistently why this is so. If the statesmen appear to have created an air-tight world of their own, complete with its own morality or amorality (as may have been the case in the Second World War), the middle *elite* should be making their dissatisfaction evident through the many potent means at their disposal. If enough community leaders are in disagreement with national policies, politicians at all levels take notice and change is possible.

Whether in fact this kind of role is within the capacity of our clergymen, educators and civic leaders is another question. The study and application of international relations and international ethics is an endless process requiring great patience. It is an undertaking usually bereft of clear-cut successes and rewards. It is much easier to be an isolationist or a nationalist or a ritualistic one-worlder than it is to study international problems deeply and to try to make your mind conform to the dimensions of the problems rather than the problems to the dimensions of your mind.

Can the American democratic society cope with these problems? Walter Lippmann and others have said that on the great issues of war and peace in this century the people were almost always wrong. All critics of modern American foreign policy have scored our propensity for over-simplifying foreign policy issues and for zigzagging from positions of naive idealism to brute power politics. There is evidence, however, that this is changing somewhat. Indeed I feel that the era of criticizing American policy on these terms has probably ended. There is reason to believe that as a people we are capable of sustaining our leaders through crises such as the Bay of Pigs, the show-downs over Berlin, the Cuban missile crisis and the messy turning points in the counter-insurgency efforts in Laos and Vietnam.

Whether this insight is entirely accurate or not, I think that it is clearly time to put aside criticism of the past and to concentrate on positive measures that can be taken to develop a meaningful international ethic which recommends itself in different forms to statesmen, to the middle *elite,* and to the generality of the citizenry. In a pluralistic society this must be an interfaith undertaking. In a democracy, it must involve the education of opinion-making *elites* and the mobilization of political and other forces on behalf of sound ethical principles in our foreign policy. In a country which, despite all talk of the post-Christian era, still looks to its churches and universities for ethical guidance, the development of a relevant international ethic requires the allocation of brains and money in some degree proportionate to the magnitude of the problems we face. The Council on Religion and International Affairs is doing a service to all of us in its role as catalyst and clearing house for all of these activities.

Still there is much to do. If we were to compare the amount of research, publication, and discussion of ethics and foreign policy with the corresponding amounts of activity in other problem areas such as racial problems to the population explosion, juvenile delinquency and conservation, we could hardly fail to be struck by the pitifully small dimensions of efforts in international ethics. Unless we bring more enlightenment to our efforts to solve these international problems it may not matter very much whether we solve these other problems or not.

Since the outbreak of the Cold War we have heard much of acting and negotiating from "positions of strength." *The* position of strength of America is her ethical tradition. Without it we cannot win any victory that is meaningful. By applying it and improving it we can win the only victories that are meaningful.

The War-Peace Establishment

ARTHUR HERZOG

Arthur Herzog was a former magazine editor who is now a full-time journalist. His articles have appeared in leading newspapers and magazines in the United States and England.

I suffer, I hasten to say, from nucleomitophobia, the fear of atomic attack, and my quest for a cure has led me to grapple with the great debate on war and peace as it is being carried on in the United States. James R. Newman, the noted science writer, has said, "The duty to press forward in the search for peace binds everyone. This is the dictate of common sense and morality."

I agreed with that directive, but at the same time I shared the confusion of Reinhold Niebuhr, the eminent theologian, who asked, "We have come into the tragic position of developing a form of destruction which, if used by our enemies against us, would mean our physical annihilation, and if used by us against our enemies would mean our moral annihilation. What shall we do?"

I was perfectly agreeable to writing my Congressman or carrying a placard, but whose, and what would my letter recommend? It is clear that there are important divisions of viewpoint in the United States, especially among those who have concerned themselves most with it, on the question of what to do about the threat of thermonuclear war. To some, risks must not be run; to oth-

ers, great risks must be taken; and to still others, we have reached the point of absurdity either way. "We are of course all guessing here," says Hans J. Morgenthau, the political scientist, "but I would have to make the guess that Western civilization would not survive such a catastrophe. If this estimate is correct, then obviously an all-out nuclear war in defense of Western civilization is a contradiction in terms, an absurdity. I must say that this absurdity may occur, but if it should occur I would still say that it was an absurdity."

But I wasn't content to have my placard, if I was to carry one, merely say "DOWN WITH THE ABSURD." Edmund Wilson, who is not only a leading literary critic but an informed student of political affairs, offers more specific advice. "To one who was born in the nineteenth century, and so still retains some remnants of the belief in human progress of a moral as well as a mechanical kind," Wilson writes, "It is especially repugnant to be forced to accept preparations for the demise of our society or of a damage to it so appalling that it is not possible to see beyond it." Wilson's search for peace concludes that one should consider paying no more taxes to support the defense effort, an action which our ungrateful government would reward by putting the tax resister in jail. Well, sacrifices for peace may be necessary.

Then I turned to the philosopher Sidney Hook, who asks, "Is it true that our system of nuclear defense is a greater threat to the survival of free institutions in the world today than the Communist movement in all its manifestations—a movement whose aggressive acts brought the present system of defense of the free world into being?"

Who is right in such debates? It's evidently important to make up one's mind. According to Jeremy J. Stone, a military policy analyst, "In areas where we lack understanding or confidence, we prefer inertia or arms race, or both, to arms control and disarmament. It is important for the Soviet Union to understand this fact about us, as it is for us to do so." According to P. M. S. Blackett, the English scientist, "In order to study possible ways in which each country might alter its military posture so as to facilitate a multilateral agreement, it is necessary for individuals to subject their government's defense and disarmament policies to a critical examination." That is a worthy goal, but how is the ordinary citizen to go about it?

The American citizen in the mid-twentieth century has an enormous difficulty on his hands if he wants to understand contemporary foreign and military policy. The military strategies are often complicated and couched in a new and forbidding vocabulary: "first strike," "second strike," "damage-limiting capability," and even "spasm war." Foreign policy, it seems, is no longer straight and simple foreign policy—if it ever was—but must be considered in relation to technology and military strategy. And then even informed opinion seems all split up, into armers and disarmers, cold warriors and arms controllers, realists and idealists, and making a choice between them is hard indeed.

I did not find, unfortunately, that the newspapers throw any considerable light on the complexities of the nuclear age, an observation I was to hear confirmed again and again by those who have specialized in the problems of the cold war. Some publishers, no doubt, emphasize some aspects of the situation instead of presenting the whole, but, even more important, the reporters appear little better informed than the rest of us.

The papers, moreover, make little effort to integrate the news. On the same front page, for instance, you read that the U. S. and Britain are willing to discuss a 10 percent reduction in military budgets with the Soviet Union, the Department of Defense announces that European armies must raise their combat strength, and President Johnson says that the cold war must end "once and for all." On the one hand, the United States wants disarmament, but, on the other, it espouses a multilateral nuclear naval force and is prepared to expand its military commitments to underdeveloped countries. There is, I felt sure, a key to such seeming inconsistencies, but the newspapers fail to offer it. Most disturbing to one who is prepared to exercise his civic obligations and decide among available policies, the newspapers give little indication of the alternatives. Perhaps there aren't any good ones, but at least one likes to decide for oneself.

To be sure, there is no shortage of literature on the subject of the atomic age—if anything, there is too much. More, it seems, has been written on war and peace in our times than in all previous decades combined. A peace research institute reports that no less than 100,000 pieces of literature—articles, reports, books and so on—have been written on the topic since World War II, most of it in the United States and most of it, significantly, in the last few years. This figure, moreover, is exclusive of what must be an Everest-size collection of classified material in government files. One independent study group, the RAND Corporation, for instance, turned out reports for the government at the rate of one a day for ten years. Nothing but a computer could assort all this material, and nobody, I'm afraid, but a mechanical man (with a security clearance) could read it, written as most of it is in the most unapproachable style. Considering the many difficulties, I could see why so many people have turned their backs on the subject of peace.

My feeling was one of bewilderment, and I despaired at ever being able to subject my government's policies to a "critical examination," as Professor Blackett recommends. At this point, I decided to tackle the problem head on: to ferret out and talk to the nation's leading theoreticians on war and peace of varying opinions, to see who they are, what they want and why, and to ask them what hopes for permanent peace they foresee. I determined to conduct this intellectual mission with an open mind, to listen to the arguments of all sides with as much objectivity as I could, though bearing in mind the arguments others had made against this or that position. In this way I hoped to be able to lay out the whole range of choices presently available to the U.S., and, in the end, to reach some logical decisions myself, as befits my obligations as a citizen.

One conclusion can be stated in advance. Debates similar to the one under way in the United States are without doubt occurring in the Soviet Union, China, France, the United Kingdom, Germany and elsewhere, though with different perspectives and vocabularies, and, in some places, with less freedom. (And with less sophistication, too, for nowhere is war-peace theory as advanced as it is here.) It may be useful to foreigners to know what American specialists are thinking, and, in no small sense, on the outcome of these world-wide debates depends the future. "Man has taken his life in his hands," says Gerard Piel, editor of *Scientific American,* and life will never get back to normal. "However long this age may last, even if it should last forever," says Günther Anders, the Austrian philosopher, "it is the Last Age, for there is no possibility that its *differentia specifica,* the possibility of our self-extermination, can ever end—but by the end itself." What gives urgency to the debates, then, is not only the seriousness of the present situation, but also the question of how to avoid the cold war's recurrence. It may be that a cold warless world will require that we reshape a host of notions. Such, at any rate, were some of my thoughts as I set out on the journey I've come to think of as a search for peace.

* * * *

For the people of the United States the twenty years since World War II have been years of international crisis virtually uninterrupted. Many of us (the author included) have never lived out from under the shadow of nuclear war, and in this period we have all come to know the Bomb in our bones. Despite protestations of peace emanating from leaders the world over, no one can say we are markedly nearer disarmament than we were a decade or two ago. What, if anything, shall we do?

The choices are not simple, and they are even less so when one has finally come to understand the arguments. When we speak of war and peace, the avoidance of one and the achievement of the other, we are dealing with a complicated set of appraisals about the world, our adversaries and ourselves, and all philosophy bears on our decisions. Everybody says he wants peace and hates war, and the differences on this question cannot be accounted for by easy assertions that this position is bellicose or that simple-minded.

As evidence of the complexities of the war-peace debate, I offer the following chart—itself tentative and oversimplified—on how the dominant groups in the U. S. separate in their appraisals of the three central issues of power, probability and time.

One sympathizes with the lady who announced at a peace meeting, "I'm tired of all these arguments about peace. Let's throw them into a computer and get the answer." Unfortunately we are left with the difficult task of sifting our answers for ourselves. The choices are partly imposed on us by others, but it is also ours to choose, even if it is the assent indicated by our silence. That choice is particularly significant today, because the world appears to have reached a kind of historical plateau from which the path may be up or down. Should we further arm, in the name of peace? Should we be content, even gratified, with a nuclear standoff, under the name of stabilized deterrence? Or should we seek disarmament, either gradual or precipitate? Which?

What follows is the writer's own attempt to answer these questions.

It must be said at the outset that the arguments of the American theoreticians on war and peace have been made to seem more isolated and abstract than they are in the real world. "Certainly," as Robert Levine says, "the values and analyses on which real policy is dependent can never be sorted out completely neatly or satisfactorily." There is no reason why

	POWER	PROBABILITIES	TIME
Deterrers	Power urge inevitable in states and people. Expresses itself as military power. Military power must be deterred by counterpower. Fear controls power. Nations operate in terms of self-interest as defined by power. They cannot take the "long view" or be "reasoned with" except in these terms. Hostility is a normal part of the international order. War arises out of clashes of self-interest. It can't be abolished, therefore must be deterred.	Thermonuclear war: moderate so long as we deter. Aggression by Communist or other states without nuclear deterrence: high. Sweeping changes in state system, states or people: generally, low. Serious disarmament: very low, in foreseeable future.	Enough, under present policies, to find alternatives to thermonuclear war. Buy more through deterrence. Hope for, in the long run, changes in the Communist world. Work, generally, for short-run stability.
Experimentalists	States can be made to see that their self-interest lies in the absence of military power. Thermonuclear weapons are responsible for this. Power urge not inevitable. People and states are modifiable. War arises out of misunderstanding and habitual reliance on military systems. Fear increases tension. Try generosity instead. Nonetheless, habits are deeply ingrained so move with deliberate speed. Can war be abolished? Cautiously, yes.	Thermonuclear war under present policies: high. Aggression by Communists: low, but hedge with minimum deterrence. Sweeping changes in state system: good. Serious disarmament: good.	Not enough under present policies. Buy more through change. Work for drastic change in war system now.
Peace Movement	Return to humanistic values of man. Concept of "natural" power urge is false. Military power not symptom of hostility but cause of it. Do away with military power. War is a habit. Either centralize existing military power in international institution or disperse. War can be abolished.	Thermonuclear war; very high as long as weapons are in national hands. Aggression by Communists: low, but be prepared to deal with through nonviolent means. Sweeping changes in states and people: good.	Very little. Nuclear disarmament the only hope. But in long run go beyond disarmament to the real problem of war, which lies in social organization and/or people.

one cannot be unneatly eclectic in one's approach, as are many of the war-peace intellectuals themselves. It may even be possible, by borrowing from various positions, to reach a satisfactory synthesis.

I, for one, will have to put the forward strategy behind me. Its reliance on force or the threat of force appears excessive—its "model" awards too high a role to the power of unfriendly persuasion. The forward strategist position seems to be based on the superiority of Western values, leading to a parochial self-righteousness that puts those very values in doubt. It appears to me that the forward strategists have exaggerated the malignity of the Communist world and underestimated the probability of nuclear war if the arms race should continue, as they insist it must. I *am* attracted by the forward strategist notion of a stronger tie between the U. S. and Europe, even if it means forgoing elements of national sovereignty, but I am dismayed that so transcendentally important an event should be seen by the forward strategists in military, anti-Communist terms. This view accepts as semipermanent the division of the world into two or more armed camps.

Of course, there is the logical possibility that the forward strategists are right in this and still another idea—that modern technology, at least in the confines of the present international situation, is more or less uncontrollable. But rather than accepting this as given, I would bend every effort to find out if the opposite might not be correct. If we are to be manipulated by a weapons science in a world of implacable hostility, then I would be strongly tempted to vote for the unilateral disarmament of the United States as the slim but sole hope of avoiding catastrophe. But I do not accept the forward strategist evaluation of the world.

Therefore I am compelled to part company with the radicals of the peace movement who advocate unilateral American disarmament. In seeking a correlation between personal and national pacifism, the radicals are guilty of too much consistency. There is nothing to suggest that any nation is going to disarm unilaterally, unless so compelled, and the radicals demand too much of the mass of wills known as a nation. The blunt morality of the radicals leads them to overlook some of the important intangibles as well. What would happen to the self-confidence, and with it the economy, of a unilaterally disarmed United States? Nor is it certain that nonviolence is always an effective way of defending oneself or asserting those interests one holds to be vital. And so I am forced to strike unilateral disarmament from my platform, and I think the radicals would be wise to do the same.

This being said, I would not want to overlook what the radicals have to offer. Because I conclude, painfully, that force is a necessary feature of justice does not mean that nonviolence must be rejected, and I would be pleased if my country resorted to armed violence only when it could bear the strain and risk no longer. It seems to me that the radicals are right in saying that the answer to war, in the long run, can come only in deep changes in our style of governing, even in ourselves, and to me the utopian vision, what Martin Buber calls the "wish picture," is a real power in human affairs, giving us energy and pointing out the goals. I share the radical hope that someday a new world will come to pass.

To turn to my synthesis proper, I begin with the analysts. The peace movement is seriously misguided in talking about the analysts, with their strategies and game theories, as though they favored, or even caused, wars. On the contrary, the analysts deserve high marks for years of careful study and planning. On the whole, they have tried to deal with the facts of the matter and tried not to indulge in long-range speculations or moralistic cries. They raise a difficult question. Suppose, they say, the cause of the present crisis *is* "politics" or "misunderstanding"; the weapons still exist and are not likely to be gotten rid of soon. That being the case, the analysts insist on a careful management of force. Even in deterrence, the analysts declare, nations can cooperate to avoid war.

Where I am forced to doubt analytic thinking is over the question of strategic deterrence itself. As worked out with statistical precision, nuclear deterrence tends to assume that military strategy is itself fearful enough to dominate the logic of the other side. This in turn assumes that fear will keep both sides at nuclear peace at least. There is no doubt that we want to be logical and rational in this situation, but there is a great deal of doubt as to whether we can depend on the mathematics of destruction to keep the peace. Too much of our experience points to illogic and self-destructiveness. The analytic "model" has led it to acquiesce to high levels of nuclear arms as a method of controlling the opponent and managing war. I think these ideas are too narrow, and I wonder if the analysts have fought hard enough for change away from the use of military threats.

When we reach the realists, we are deep in the speculations of philosophy, and here, truly, it is one person's logic against that of another. But one piece of realist thought I must add to my synthesis—that the collective will, though stemming from the sum of individual wills, may have characteristics quite different from those of individual wills. To me, the realists are right in saying that nations cannot help acting in terms of power and self-interest. It follows that nations must seek to protect themselves, that they will change only slowly, and that they will disarm only when they feel utterly safe. One must not expect too much from them. My reservation about realism is one of degree—I think realism is too pessimistic about the possibilities of change. And I'm afraid that the realist view of man, as afflicted by original sin, the power-urge, and ignorance, leads too easily to the conclusion that man must be deterred against himself. Before long, realism hardens into the view that man is controlled only by the fear of force.

Government idealism, as we have identified it, may be described as the realism of a nation-state overlaid with the country's ideological aspirations. (This observer thought it rather a tribute to the ability of our public officials that they are able to function, and apparently effectively, amid the rush and harassment of modern Washington.) I am suspicious of the present practice of justifying our international commitments in terms of safeguarding freedom and democracy around the world, and uncertain as to the necessity or wisdom of trying to secure a democratic world environment. I, for one, would remove the ideological labels from our policies, on the grounds that liberty, democracy, free enterprise, and so on, have specialized meanings in the U. S. not necessarily applicable or even helpful elsewhere. To be sure, I am concerned, and I hope the country is, with the welfare of the peoples of the world, but rather than justifying our actions with ideology I would have us try to meet human needs as such, whatever they are.

And I think the peaceful aspirations of our country would be more convincing were its disarmament objectives better codified. Crucial to my synthesis is a change away from high-level deterrence, and here I am buttressed by the minimum deterrers' declaration that national security would not be jeopardized, and world security increased, by reducing the nation's nuclear armory. It is not that I believe the U. S. will start a nuclear war, or that counterforce strategy is wicked; it's just that I see no long-term stability in large numbers of these devices, and I believe the U. S. must abandon its notion of nuclear superiority if it is to get arms agreements. Finally, I am in essential agreement with those we have called experimentalists that in the long stretch deterrence through fear is no very adequate way of dealing with an opponent.

Some experimentalists believe that international conflict is rooted in misunderstandings and that only strong unilateral initiatives will clear them away. I approach this point of view with caution. For one thing, it may be that instead of misunderstanding each other in this world we understand each other only too well. For another, I sympathize in my imagination with a President who had to explain to the American right wing why a bold and generous series of unilateral initiatives failed. Nonetheless, though I wouldn't put all my faith or face in them, I would support unilateral American initiatives for peace, and to my synthesis I will add the experimentalists' conviction that imagination, along with a spirit of trial and error, is needed. I would have the United States (and the Communist nations, too) be more boldly experimental in searching for peace.

Embedded in war-peacy theory in the nuclear age are two questions of enormous difficulty and import, and if one is to take a position at all (as opposed merely to resting one's case on hope or despair), one must try to confront them in full self-honesty. The first, simply stated, is whether one is prepared to employ nuclear weapons even in self-defense. As we have seen, a deterrent doesn't qualify as such if we are not prepared to authorize its actual use. The other is whether, to achieve peace, we must demand the abolition of war. Let us see what answers to these questions are offered by the survivalists of the peace movement.

I must begin my characterization of the peace movement by admitting to a certain bewilderment. Though the survivalists want to be practical, their policies often sound like wish-fulfillment. I am depressed by the peace movement's overuse of fear in some of its propaganda, and its way of considering people who don't agree with it as warmongers. (On the other hand, the peace movement has been quick sometimes to press into service certain arguments of people it might not otherwise accept—its habit, for instance, of quoting President Eisenhower on the dangers of the "military-industrial complex.") Those who struggle for peace in the name of humanism do not always seem to understand the problems imposed by modern science, technology and military strategy. And I find myself unimpressed with moral cries, ethical fulminations, neat nostrums, and so on, against "war" and for "peace"—we've had all this before without a visible shift away from the "war system."

Having entered these caveats, I cannot turn my sympathies away from the peace movement altogether. I find myself agreeing with its argument that the United States, since World War II (perhaps in the course of overcoming its isolationism), has relied too heavily on the seemingly simple and expeditious instrument of military force to solve its international problems. And I am grateful to the peace movement for what I believe to be its fundamental stand, on values, on generosity, charity, purity of purpose. I am thankful that it has raised, again and again, the question of the whole future of the human race. I am glad it has been willing to act.

The peace movement has been no more successful than any other group in solving what I take to be the essential contradiction of the nuclear age—our agreement to hold on to these weapons and what I assume is a near-universal rejection of their use. But its philosophers have at least made the contradiction clear, and helped us to understand that we are balanced uneasily between today and tomorrow, between reality and hope. Our situation contains much of the absurd, and only as we begin to recognize the full measure of the contradiction, as we come to grips with the nuclear absurdity, will we begin to find that many things are possible which seem impossible now.

So I return to the question with which I began my search for peace—what should my banner say? I know now that its legend will offer nothing simple or final, nothing pleasant or easy. It will eschew slogans like "Abolish war" because of my apprehensions about the likelihood of armed conflict, the constant clash of interests between men and nations, the necessity to use force at times, indeed, the immaturity of the human race; it will reject "peace through military strength" for exactly the same reasons. In composing it, I will bear in mind both the deterrers' desire for the management of force and the peace movement's call for morality. But my banner will say experimentalism. It will accept, for a time at least, the contradictions of the nuclear age as being insoluble. As a first step, it will ask for a minimum deterrent leading from there by stages to genuine universal nuclear disarmament. It will insist that the United States has not been aggressive enough in searching for peace. It will have us conduct that search in a manner both open and optimistic, with strong imagination and bold inquiry, in a spirit of humility about the rightness of our own positions, and it will have us understand more clearly that others, as well as ourselves, suffer from nucleomitophobia, the fear of atomic attack.

SUGGESTED ADDITIONAL READINGS

1. Almond, Gabriel A., *The American People and Foreign Policy,* New York: Harcourt, Brace, 1950, pp. 29–115. An older but still very useful examination of the relationship of the American character and mood to foreign policy. Deals with general American attitudes towards foreign policy and the specific factors which make for changes in those attitudes.

2. Arendt, Hannah, *On Revolution,* New York: The Viking Press, 1963, 334 pp. (paper). A theoretical and philosophical study of the nature and meaning of revolution. Not easy reading but the student should attempt the Introduction ("War and Revolution"), Chapter One, ("The Meaning of Revolution"), and Chapter Six ("The Revolutionary Tradition").

3. Brandon, Donald, *American Foreign Policy,* New York: Appleton-Century-Crofts, 1966 (paper), pp. 3–13, 269–88. A description and analysis of the historical circumstances within which America has come to the fore in international affairs. A particularly good closing section on what America must do to "come of age."

4. Crabb, Cecil V. Jr. (ed.), *American Foreign Policy in the Nuclear Age,* New York: Harper and Row, 2nd ed., 1965, pp. 42–65, 91–128. Book deals with various aspects of American foreign policy, especially since World War II. Describes the executive-legislative relationship in foreign policy-making, with particular stress upon bipartisan techniques and procedures, barriers to unity, and the various executive agencies.

5. Dean, Vera Micheles, *The Nature of the Non-Western World,* New York: New American Library, 1957, 284 pp. (paper). Excellent survey of the revolutionary factors at play in various parts of the world; discusses Russia, Middle East, India and Pakistan, Southeast Asia, China, and other troublespots. Of particular value are Chapters 1, 10–12.

6. Fulbright, J. W., *Old Myths and New Realities,* New York: Random House, 1964, 147 pp. (paper). The dynamic and often controversial senator takes a deeply critical look at the myths pervading American public life, particularly as they relate to foreign policy and the cold war, and suggests a series of new approaches.

7. Grodzins, Morton, and Eugene Rabinowitch (eds.), *The Atomic Age,* New York: Basic Books, 1963, 616 pp. A series of articles taken from the *Bulletin of the Atomic Scientists* during the years 1945–1962. The authors constitute a "who's who" of American science, and their subject matter covers such diverse topics as "Before Hiroshima," "Disarmament, Deterrence, Arms Control," "Loyalty and Security," and "Bases for Hope."

8. Heilbroner, Robert L., *The Future as History,* New York: Grove Press, 1961 (paper), pp. 1–114. An attempt to "establish a sense of order and continuity in the face of the historic realities which confront us." Deals with the forces changing our lives, the waning of confidence and optimism in the Western world, the impact of the atomic bomb, the awakening of the colonial world, and the role of communism and socialism.

9. Kissinger, Henry A., *Nuclear Weapons and Foreign Policy,* New York: Harper, 1957, 463 pp. Published for the Council on Foreign Relations by a recognized authority. Deals with several major problem areas: the challenge of the nuclear age; the dilemma of American security; limited war; NATO; the prospects for the future; the need for doctrine.

10. ———— (ed.), *Problems of National Strategy,* New York: Frederick A. Praeger, 1965, 477 pp. (paper). A book of readings by noted authors from the worlds of science and politics in which five major areas of strategy are discussed in full detail: strategic doctrine, alliances, neutrality and insurgency, weapons control, and national security.

11. Lens, Sidney, "Leadership for a World in Revolution," *The Progressive,* January 1965, pp. 29–32. An attack upon what has served as the accepted rationale of the cold war. Contends we are losing ground in the developing areas because we are afraid of radical nationalism; that Europe is withdrawing from the cold war; that the communist world is experiencing profound social, political, and economic change.

12. Manis, Jerome G. and Samuel I. Clark (eds.), *Man and Society,* New York: Macmillan, 1960, pp. 81–173. A major collection of readings in the social sciences. The two sections referred to ("How Men Differ" and "Why Men Hate"), bring together a series of short, effective essays by biologists, anthropologists, psychologists, and sociologists on the problems of cultural heterogeneity and human interrelationships.

13. Northrop, F. S. C., *The Meeting of East and West,* New York: Macmillan, 1946, 531 pp. Written by one of America's leading professors of philosophy; difficult but very worthwhile reading. Examines in depth some of the underlying philosophical foundations for Eastern and Western socio-political systems, and concludes with suggestions on how to bridge some of the gaps.

14. Osgood, Charles E., "Suggestions for Winning the Real War Against Communism," *Conflict Resolution,* Vol. III, No. 4 (November 1959), pp. 295–325. Written by a psychologist; lengthy, difficult, and excellent analysis. Brings a relatively new approach to the field of political writing. Main theme is that we are engaged in a war to preserve our way of life and that many of our strategies in combating communism do not support our way of life. Moves from an examination of these policies to a consideration of alternatives.

15. Ransom, Harry H. (ed.), *An American Foreign Policy Reader,* New York: Thomas Y. Crowell, 1965 (paper), pp. 527–613. A series of articles by scholars and diplomats describing the nature, problems, and future of American diplomacy.

16. Rosenau, James N., *Public Opinion and Foreign Policy,* New York: Random House, 1961, 118 pp. (paper). A brief, authoritative, incisive discussion of the various "publics" and opinion-makers and their relationships to foreign policy.

17. Rostow, W. W., *The Stages of Economic Growth,* London: Cambridge University Press, 1960, 179 pp. (paper). A "non-Communist Manifesto" describing five basic stages of economic growth. In addition to rejecting Marxist determinism, the author offers a comprehensive alternative to the Marxist theory of how societies evolve.

18. Tannenbaum, Frank, "The Balance of Power versus the Coordinate State," *Political Science Quarterly,* LXVII, (June 1952), pp. 173–197. Part of the literature of the great debate between "idealism" and "realism" as approaches to American foreign policy; a classic representation of the idealist position.

FOR FURTHER CONSIDERATION

1. To what degree does idealism in foreign policy represent naïvete? Is it akin to facile utopianism? Can it be defended on other than moral grounds?

2. If you were called upon to rewrite the sections of the American Constitution dealing with foreign policy formation and control, what changes, if any, would you make?

3. How much importance would you ascribe to cultural differences as an obstacle to the development of a successful American foreign policy in the underdeveloped world? Is it important for nations to be liked? What criteria would you develop for the measurement of a successful foreign policy?

4. Given the overwhelming importance of the military factor in the contemporary world, would you be willing to give our top military people a greater voice in the formulation of foreign policy? How much policy discretion would you allow field commanders? Can you construct a hypothetical situation in which your answers to this question would have specific relevance?

5. What do you consider the most pressing problem in American foreign policy today? Present a position paper to the State Department outlining your suggestions on how to meet the problem.

With Liberty
and Justice for All 8

Democracy requires that people be able to participate in the governing process. Throughout this volume we have been examining democracy in both its theoretical and institutional aspects. We have recognized both the intangibles of values, beliefs, myths, power, and the tangibles of votes, structures, rules, laws. We conclude this discussion of the theory and practice of American democracy with what may well be its starting point—freedom and civil liberties.

Central to democracy is the freedom of the individual. The present chapter will consider the following aspects of individual freedom: (1) government as an instrument of freedom; (2) the necessity of freedom; (3) civil liberties in historical perspective; (4) the absolute or relative nature of rights; (5) the challenge of anti-democrats; and (6) the problem of civil disobedience.

GOVERNMENT AS AN INSTRUMENT OF FREEDOM

One of the oldest debates in American politics—the question of the proper role of the national government—is being carried on today with as much fervor as it was nearly two centuries ago when men were faced with the question of what form of government to establish for the new nation. Today, however, the debate seems almost futile, for time and circumstances have determined government's role in twentieth-century America.

Many of those who condemn the national government picture it in fantasy as a huge machine-like monster with tentacles reaching into every state, city, and home, whose aim is to crush or at least curtail individual freedom. In reality, government's function is a positive one designed to help and enrich the individual, not hinder or destroy him. Despite its expansion, the national government is still basically the instrument of the people it serves. It is made up of citizens who serve only as long as their fellow citizens wish them to. Critics of the federal government also are prone to overlook the fact that it has most often been state and local governments which have imposed the most stringent restraints on freedom—for instance, on religion, speech, assembly, and the press. Government per se neither promotes nor hinders freedom; but American government at all levels, and particularly the national, has more often been an instrument of expansion of freedom than curtailment.

John Locke, the seventeenth-century English political philosopher, believed that man's social instincts impelled him toward political society but that no man entered this society except by consent. Locke held that the purpose of this man-created and man-maintained government was to preserve the rights which man already possessed. In Locke's mind, government should rule only by the consent of the governed. Locke's ideas greatly influenced the founding fathers who embodied the concept of government by consent in the Constitution. [11] Government in the United States today remains a government made up of the people, operated and staffed by the people, governing for the people. Government is an instrument of society, existing to protect the freedom and advance the opportunities of its citizens. Its purpose, as stated in the preamble to the Constitution, is to promote the general welfare and secure the blessings of liberty.

Although the founding fathers could not possibly have foreseen the tremendous changes the future would bring, they managed to give us a constitutional system which has survived a turbulent 180 years. Under the constitution, we have expanded the role of government beyond anything they may have imagined. In spite of the pessimism of those who foresee the death of liberty at the hands of the government they have lost faith in and through the democratic process they do not understand, it is well to remember that at no time in recorded history has one country been the home of so many people who have enjoyed such a great degree of individual freedom as the United States today. Historically governments have often been instruments of oppression; all governments have that potentiality. But the history of this nation clearly demonstrates that we have little reason to fear government and much reason to commend it for its contribution to freedom.

THE NECESSITY OF FREEDOM

Democracy is a way of governing which combines majority rule and minority rights, allows universal suffrage and a secret ballot, preaches equalitarianism (interpreted as equal opportunity), establishes free speech and other freedoms, and provides for constitutional checks on governmental power while at the same time allowing government to function. It provides unity without destroying diversity. It makes room for freedom *and* government. In short, it provides order without destroying freedom.

Our government is also limited in what we expect it to do for men:

government is not intended to do all things but primarily one thing—provide a framework which combines order and freedom so that change can take place without violence. We have been able to get along for almost 200 years without full agreement on fundamentals because our institutions have been designed to allow for possible disagreement without the destruction of government.

If democracy is thought of as a system of institutionalized competition for power, then the *ability* to compete is indispensable to that process. It was suggested earlier that democracy assumes unrestricted participation and freedom to compete, including freedom to organize, criticize, and differ. The classical democratic theorists' interest in freedom and liberty is germane when individual freedoms are seen not simply as desirable, ethical, or normative goals but as essential to the nature of the democratic political process. Competition cannot be meaningful unless it is based on a genuine freedom to compete. Freedom and democracy are inherently linked.

THE HISTORICAL PERSPECTIVE

Throughout our history we have been philosophically dedicated to the maximization of freedom, yet in times of crisis it becomes apparent that we have recurring doubts about the nature of freedom and its limits.

Every society that claims to be a free society embodies a system of ordered liberty in which there are certain guarantees of rights and immunities against arbitrary state power. As noted earlier, the political philosophy of the seventeenth and eighteenth centuries strongly emphasized the doctrine of natural rights, which declared "self-evident" the existence of natural law that endowed each person in society with a body of unalienable rights. In following John Locke, Jefferson and his colleagues who wrote the bills of rights for the national and various state governments were in effect initiating what has come to be called the "open society." [17] All the evidence indicates clearly their fervent belief in a society of individuals free to pursue their own welfare as they saw fit with as few controls as possible by government. Their concepts included freedom of conscience and religious belief, freedom of movement, freedom of speech and press, freedom of economic choice. Theirs was *not* a rejection of government but rather an insistence that the state ought to exist ultimately to serve the individuals who collectively made up the social order. [1]

To achieve these ends legal guarantees had to be established within a framework of administrative justice. Thus, the American people by the end of the eighteenth century had evolved a system of justice which gave body to the abstractions of individual freedoms. [6] The guarantees against arbitrary destruction of life, liberty, or property included such things as guarantee of a fair trial, prohibition against bills of attainder, the right to the writ of habeas corpus, and protection against arbitrary state power in taxation, unreasonable search and seizure, and the use of military power.

All in all the American people showed their practical wisdom in realizing, as Zechariah Chafee, Jr., was to state a century and a half later, that it is necessary

. . . in discussing any situation where freedom of speech or some other form of liberty is involved, to examine the existing legal machinery and if this is unsatisfactory to canvass the merits of possible alternatives. Three aspects of such machinery at least are important: (1) its nature; (2) the persons who constitute it, for we have no mechanical devices or litmus paper for detecting unpermissable speech and writings but must always rely on human beings; (3) the speed and expense with which the line is drawn.[1]

Throughout the early development of the ideas and laws on rights one common goal can be seen—and that is, whether the point at issue was censorship or libel, religious freedom or the meaning of commerce, the purpose was to remove whole areas of human activity from control by the state. Thomas Jefferson summed it up for his generation when he defined good government in his First Inaugural Address:

A wise and frugal government which shall restrain men from injuring one another shall leave them otherwise free to regulate their own pursuits of industry and improvement, and shall not take from the mouth of labor the bread it has earned.[2]

What was the basis of this Jeffersonian faith? Henry Steele Commager, the eminent contemporary historian, tells us clearly that both the "Jeffersonian faith in the ability of the individual to fend for himself and the Jeffersonian fear of government" were based on realities of historical experience. Men of the day could take care of themselves, and there was little need for government. The country was rich, land was available, there was little poverty, no unemployment, no standing army to support, no established church, no idle aristocracy to subsidize. At the same time they had the experience of tyranny under the rule of George III, and the Revolution had been fought to free them from tyrannical government. History taught them, as they read it, "that any government tends to tyranny, that no government is to be trusted, and that government is best which governs least." They translated both this faith and this fear into constitutional doctrines, creating "governments checked and balanced and limited in every conceivable way."[3]

But Commager points out that much of this was misleading or irrelevant:

Fear of government, for example, was misleading, for in a democracy men did not need to fear government. After all they were the government. A complex system of checks and balances was in a sense misleading. It assumed that the business of government was purely negative whereas in fact the business of government was positive. It assumed that government was a compartmentalized thing, whereas in fact government was a unit. Even the abounding richness of Nature was in a sense misleading—certainly the sense of infinity was. Jefferson said there would be land enough forever, but the best land was gone in a hundred years, and more and more the natural resources of the nation fell into the hands of small privileged groups or corporations[4]

It is important to remember that while Jefferson and his like-minded contemporaries had great confidence in the individual's ability to tend to his

[1] Zechariah Chafee, Jr., "Liberty and Law," in *Freedom and the Modern World,* Horace M. Kallen, ed. (New York: Coward-McCann, 1928), p. 85.
[2] Philip S. Foner, ed., *Basic Writings of Thomas Jefferson,* (Garden City, N. Y.: Halyson House, 1950), p. 334.
[3] Henry Steele Commager, *Living Ideas in America* (New York: Harper, 1951), p. 315.
[4] *Ibid.,* p. 316.

own needs, they recognized that this ability was nourished by individual freedom —intellectual, political, and economic. Theirs was not a doctrinaire fear of government but a passion for democracy and freedom. The present-day Jeffersonian school encourages *positive* governmental action in behalf of freedom. It believes that the Bill of Rights should promote and ensure human welfare, and that while "negative government" may have been justified by the circumstances of an earlier age, it is not appropriate today.

What is important is to maintain the open society by whatever techniques best serve the goal of human freedom. Ultimately, this type of society is dependent upon faith in man, the calculated risk that in the open market of ideas he will choose wisely. [8] The history of democratic societies, however, gives many examples of "rational man" concurring in the suspension of democratic processes for the supposed service of a social or economic ideal. Our own generations have seen the successful manipulation of the masses and the abortive death of democratic processes by the demagoguery of a Hitler and Mussolini and the cynicism of a Stalin. It is the fear of such political catastrophe occurring here that has caused so much recent concern about the philosophy of the open society and the application, in practice, of the Bill of Rights, particularly the First Amendment.[5]

It is not our intention here to examine in detail either the historical development or the present meaning of the various guarantees of the Bill of Rights. Excellent sources are available for such purposes, the demands of which are beyond the limitations imposed by the size of this volume. [2, 6, 7, 16, 21] Rather, the remainder of this chapter will consider three questions that are basic to the problem of the place of civil liberties in our democratic society: Are rights absolute or relative? What is democracy's answer to freedom for non-democratic elements? What is the role of civil disobedience?

BILL OF RIGHTS: RELATIVE OR ABSOLUTE?

If we reflect carefully upon the contemporary significance of the Bill of Rights, we are reminded that the concept of liberty implied is more important than any specific guarantee. Yet there is considerable debate as to the substance of liberty. [4, 9] There is, for example, a close relationship between civil liberty and public opinion. Each has been proved indispensable to the existence of the other. We have by now learned the lesson that civil liberties are safe only when placed beyond the reach of temporary majorities. But we may tend to forget, as Robert Cushman reminds us, that

public opinion can exist only where and when civil liberty is kept alive . . . [and] civil liberty will exist only so long as it is supported and defended by public opinion . . . [P]ublic opinion with respect to civil liberty today shows dangerous signs of being confused, timid, and complacent . . . [C]ourageous leadership and sound education are vitally necessary if we are to keep alive a public opinion which values civil liberty and will demand its effective protection.[6]

[5] See the writings of Russell Kirk, William F. Buckley, Jr., Henry J. Taylor, and James S. Kilpatrick, especially their nationally-syndicated newspaper columns.
[6] Robert F. Cushman, "Civil Liberty and Public Opinion," in *Safeguarding Civil Liberty Today,* (Ithaca, N. Y.; Cornell University Press, 1945), p. 85.

What Cushman is saying is that it is all too common for many people to believe that civil liberties ought to belong not by right to everybody but only to those who deserve them. In the last two decades large numbers of Americans have demonstrated that they believe in freedom of speech only for those "on our side." For example, the prevailing judicial test holds that to be obscene, a book must be, among other things, "utterly without redeeming social importance." While many regard this rule as unduly permissive, it is, in fact, presumptive of the necessity of social importance or value in order to justify freedom to write or distribute such a book. Only "good" or "clean" or "valuable" ideas are to be granted constitutional protection. Obscenity is beyond constitutional protection. The question-begging nature of such an assertion is obvious, and the implications for democratic processes serious.

Are the guaranteed rights absolute? [6, 7, 16, 21] Before American independence, the freedoms later to be embodied in the First Amendment were simply political principles. Once incorporated within the national and state constitutions they became principles of law. What, then, do we mean when we say, "Congress shall make no law . . .?" One of our country's most esteemed spokesmen for civil liberty, Alexander Meiklejohn, implies that *any* act which restricts thinking, talking, and printing would, or should, be unconstitutional:

When men govern themselves, it is they and no one else who must pass judgment upon unwisdom and unfairness and danger . . . Just so far as, at any point, the citizens who are to decide an issue are denied acquaintance with information or opinion or doubt or disbelief or criticism which is relevant to that issue, just so far the result must be ill-considered, ill-balanced planning for the general good. *It is that mutilation of the thinking process of the community against which the First Amendment to the Constitution is directed.*[7]

This is, however, a minority opinion. The prevailing view is that constitutional freedoms cannot be regarded as absolute. They must instead be allotted a weight according to their respective social values and then, balanced one against the other, receive the appropriate legal expression. We are faced continually with situations of conflict between community interest and individual interest. How, for example, do we resolve the demand of the individual to practice his religion freely with the demand of society that he refrain from doing certain acts such as committing adultery or engaging in snake rituals? How can the individual's freedom not to engage in war be reconciled with the nation's security demands?

The Supreme Court has repeatedly rejected the absolutist interpretation of the First Amendment. In the words of the late Chief Justice Vinson,

Both the majority of the Court and the dissenters in particular cases have recognized that this is not an unlimited, unqualified right, but that the societal value of speech must, on occasion, be subordinated to other values and considerations.[8]

The majority view tends to look upon the prohibitions of the Bill of Rights more as admonitions to Congress than unequivocal commands. Thus Congress may, in the presence of a "clear and present danger," abridge a constitutional right. Or, a right may be abridged if the feeling prevails that its exercise would

[7] Alexander Meiklejohn, *Free Speech and Its Relation to Self-Government* (New York: Harper, 1948), p. 26.
[8] *Dennis v. U. S.,* 341 U. S. 494 (1951).

cause so much injury to the public as to outweigh the injury caused to the individual in denying him his right. Under this interpretation, all constitutional problems become questions of reasonableness, proximity, and degree.

Despite the preponderance of opinion favoring the anti-absolutist interpretation, Supreme Court Justice Hugo Black has consistently supported the idea of absolute liberties. Writing in 1960 he said,

It is my belief that there *are* "absolutes" in our Bill of Rights, and that they were put there on purpose by men who knew what words meant, and meant their prohibitions to be "absolutes." The whole history and background of the Constitution and Bill of Rights . . . point to the creation of a government which was denied all power to do some things under any and all circumstances, and all power to do other things except precisely in the manner prescribed. . . . Neither as offered nor as adopted is the language of this [First] Amendment anything less than absolute. . . . [T]he history and language of the Constitution and the Bill of Rights . . . make it plain that one of the primary purposes of the Constitution with its amendments was to withdraw from the Government all power to act in certain areas—whatever the scope of those areas may be. If I am right in this then there is, at least in those areas, no justification whatever for "balancing" a particular right against some expressly granted power of Congress. If the Constitution withdraws from Government all power over subject matter in an area, such as religion, speech, press, assembly, and petition, there is nothing over which authority may be exerted. . . .[9]

Perhaps there is a middle ground. Perhaps we may recognize the necessity of the maximization of freedom and, consequently, the necessity of abridgement or restraint on the exercise of freedom *in the interest of its maximization*. Thus, restraints on freedom could be justified *only* for the purpose of making possible the maximum exercise of freedom—not to promote morality, or godliness, or to purify language or eliminate evil. The test would be: can society tolerate this specific conduct from the standpoint of its effect on the freedom of others? Does it (1) curtail another's freedom or (2) endanger the system which makes such freedom possible? The exercise of freedom would be relative, not to vaguely defined social values or norms of good conduct, but to the exercise of freedom by others. One may not drive down the wrong side of the highway because it necessarily curtails others' freedom to move safely along the highway; one can read pornographic literature without infringing on another's freedom; a communist can speak without endangering the system which allows him to speak. Can one commit suicide without abridging another's freedom, or engage in illicit sexual relations with other willing adults without curtailing someone else's freedom? Can economic restraints—production quotas, pure food laws, etc.—be justified under such a rule?

The problems posed by the question of the nature of rights are not simple ones. Recognition of their nature may be the first step toward enlightened participation in the continuous development of workable answers.

THE CHALLENGE OF ANTI-DEMOCRATS

Closely allied to the matter of interpreting the quality of rights is the problem of non- or anti-democratic individuals and groups and their freedom. Here we are placing in a contemporary setting a familiar and recurrent issue. Should

[9] Hugo L. Black, "The Bill of Rights," *New York University Law Review,* Vol. 35 (April 1960), pp. 867, 874–875. Delivered as the 1960 James Madison Lecture at New York University School of Law, and reprinted with permission of the copyright owner—New York University.

the freedoms guaranteed in the Bill of Rights, and especially the freedom of speech, be granted to those who are avowedly intent upon substituting an entirely different set of political principles for the prevailing democratic ones? [4, 9] There were, after all, neither communists nor fascists in 1800 who openly threatened to destroy democratic institutions. Since our problem today is security and survival as well as liberty, can we afford the luxury of maintaining in our midst men and movements who will use the guarantees of freedom to undermine the society granting them?

Three varying and at least partially contradictory policies have been espoused at different times to deal with the issue of civil liberties and anti-democrats of both the left and the right: (1) complete and unrestricted freedom of expression; (2) total denial of free expression to all who oppose the processes of democratic government; or (3) a pragmatic approach which grants full freedom and rights except under conditions recognized as being dangerous or detrimental to the national welfare.

There are many sources which may be cited as setting the philosophical basis for the first policy position—complete freedom of expression. The two most frequently mentioned are the essay *On Liberty* by John Stuart Mill and *Areopagitica* by John Milton. Zechariah Chafee, Jr., has brought together some of the arguments from this latter classic, published in 1644:

1. The chief value of freedom of speech is to the community.
'And though all the winds of doctrine were let loose to play upon the earth, so Truth be in the field, we do injuriously by licensing and prohibiting to misdoubt her strength. Let her and Falsehood grapple; who ever knew Truth put to the worse, in a free and open encounter. Her confuting is the best and surest suppressing.'
2. We all run the risk of condemning good ideas as bad, simply because they are new and strange to us.
'. . . if it come to prohibiting, there is not aught more likely to be prohibited than truth itself; whose first appearance to our eyes bleared and dimmed with prejudice and custom, is more unsightly and unplausible than many errors . . .'
3. The sources of evil are numerous, and many of them cannot be prevented by law from reaching men even if books are censored.
'. . . evil manners are as perfectly learned without books a thousand other ways which cannot be stopped . . . And he who were pleasantly disposed, could not well avoid to liken it to the exploit of that gallant man, who thought to pound up the crows by shutting his part gate.'[10]

The proponents of this policy argue further that speech is either free or it is not and that to deny freedom to speak to those whose ideas are repugnant to us is a denial of freedom itself. If one can say only those things, advocate only those ideas, use only those words that most people find acceptable, he has no real freedom of speech. In addition, the argument continues, once a democracy begins to curb the freedoms of those who oppose it, and is no longer willing to risk democracy's future in the marketplace of ideas, it degenerates into a kind of totalitarianism.

Those who would choose to deny freedoms to the opponents of constitutional liberty take their lead from Sidney Hook's now-famous work *Heresy, Yes; Conspiracy, No.* Hook wrote that the failure to distinguish between heresy and conspiracy is dangerous, for

[10] Zechariah Chafee, Jr., *Freedom of Speech and Press* (New York: Carrie Chapman Catt Memorial Fund, 1955), pp. 32–34. Reprinted by permission of Harper & Row.

. . . the inescapable consequence of their identification is either self-destruction, when heresies are punished as conspiracies, or destruction at the hands of their enemies, when conspiracies are tolerated as heresies.

A heresy is a set of unpopular ideas or opinions on matters of grave concern to the community. The right to profess publicly a heresy of any character, on any theme, is an essential element of a liberal society. . . .

A conspiracy . . . is a secret or underground movement which seeks to attain its ends not by normal political or educational processes but by playing outside the rules of the game. Because it undermines the conditions which are required in order that doctrines may freely compete for acceptance, because where successful it ruthlessly destroys all heretics and dissenters, a conspiracy cannot be tolerated without self-stultification in a liberal society.[11]

In addition, the argument runs, the communists (and with them, for a time, the Nazis and fascists), forfeited their rights by operating outside the democratic framework and, in effect, at war against it. Once we have ample and clear-cut evidence of conspiracy against democracy we need not wait for an attempted overthrow of its institutions before taking restrictive action against the conspirators. However, it has been precisely this effort "to defend the state against communists" that has been the rationalization advanced by right-wing, fascist elements in modern times to justify their utilization of non-democratic methods and, ultimately, their assumption of governmental power.

The arguments of those who favor the pragmatic approach are presented in this excerpt from the writings of an eminent American political scientist, Jack W. Peltason:

In the United States the ballot is the alternative to force. Everyone is free to try to achieve his goals by voting; and this requires that all, including the Communists, be given freedom of speech and of the press. To outlaw any group engaged in political activities, however objectionable its goals, is to deny this basic democratic premise and to open the way for such a group to insist that only subversive tactics are possible.

Rather than outlaw the Party and deny Communists the right to express their ideas, we should try to drive them out into the open, encourage them to express their ideas, protect their meetings. Not only can we thus better expose the fallacies of Communism, but our own belief in democracy will be strengthened as it will have to be defended rather than accepted merely as an article of faith. . . . Merely because Communists are a highly disciplined group and advocate programs which we find objectionable does not give us grounds, consistent with our democratic principles, to prevent them from engaging in normal political action. . . .

Of course, there is a risk in letting Communists talk. But there are even greater risks in suppressing them.[12]

Loyalties in a democratic society are varied and multiple. One has allegiances on many levels—friendship, kinship, church, lodge, union, etc. These pluralistic loyalties are not only welcome but are essential to the health of a dynamic society. But one qualification must be added. Each citizen must respect the right of all other citizens to maintain loyalties of *their* choosing. Hence the highest loyalty in the free society is to the democratic process which enables us to choose freely, in the surety that none will disturb us in our right to be ourselves.

One may draw on analogy between this argument and the choice of rooters on the baseball scene. One group of fans may choose to support the

[11] Sidney Hook, *Heresy, Yes; Conspiracy, No,* (New York: John Day, 1953), pp. 21–22.
[12] Jack W. Peltason, *Constitutional Liberty and Seditious Activity* (New York: Carrie Chapman Catt Memorial Fund, 1954), p. 56. Reprinted by permission of Harper & Row.

Dodgers and another set of fans may opt for the Giants, but the highest loyalty of each is neither to the Giants nor to the Dodgers but to the game, which allows for the continual competition of the Dodgers and Giants. To complete the analogy, the anti-democrats refuse to abide by the higher loyalty to the democratic process. They are, instead, committed to "ending the game" by becoming the only players. [18]

J. Edgar Hoover, the Chief of the FBI, writing in 1962, declared,

An analysis of Communist tactics in undermining of laws of our land should give us an insight into how to cope with this danger. The answer must be an increased reliance on law, a renewed faith in the democratic processes of government. Just because the Communists have no respect for law and order does not mean that we should retaliate in kind. Cries for legal shortcuts, vigilante methods and less reliance on legal processes, though based on the most patriotic of motives, are most short-sighted. These would undermine our cause. . . .

Our fight against communism must be a sane, rational understanding of the facts. Emotional outbursts, extravagant name-calling, gross exaggerations hinder our efforts. We must remember that many non-Communists may legitimately on their own oppose the same laws or take positions on issues of the day which are also held by the Communists. Their opinions—though temporarily coinciding with the Party line—do not make them Communists. Not at all. We must be very careful with our facts and not brand as a Communist any individual whose opinion may be different from our own. Freedom of dissent is a great heritage of America which we must treasure.

Today far too many self-styled experts on communism are plying the highways of America giving erroneous and distorted information. This causes hysteria, false alarms, misplaced apprehension by many of our citizens. We need enlightenment about communism—but this information must be factual, accurate and not tailored to echo personal idiosyncrasies. To quote an old aphorism, we need more light and less heat.[13]

Mr. Hoover's warning should be heeded; we must recognize that enthusiasm for defense of democracy, regardless of how well-meaning and sincere, against actual or potential enemies does not justify the use of non-democratic techniques. Democracy may be lost as well through the misguided efforts of its friends as through the deliberate efforts of its enemies. The solution to the misuse of freedom by non-democrats is more democracy, not less. The answer to the challenges of the non-democrats of either the right or the left is not suppression, curtailment of participation, restriction of freedom, but a more vital competition by democrats.

CIVIL RIGHTS AND CIVIL DISOBEDIENCE

The civil rights movement in the United States has many facets. It is being advanced in the courts and legislatures as well as in the streets of our cities. [2] A vast literature has developed in an attempt to describe this movement in its many moods and manifestations. [12, 13, 14] Our concern here will be limited to the relationship between the civil rights movement and the philosophy and practice of civil disobedience.

The militant civil rights movement has made extensive use of civil disobedience as a technique. The history of civil disobedience must be as old as society itself. [20] It was the theme of Sophocles' tragedy, *Antigone;* Aristotle speaks of it; Plato discusses it at length in at least three of the dialogues. The

---

[13] J. Edgar Hoover, "Shall It Be Law or Tyranny?" *American Bar Association Journal,* February 1962, pp. 120 ff.

subject is dealt with by Pascal, Hobbes, Locke, and Hegel. In our own history, the "transcendentalist revolt," which took place roughly from 1835 to 1855 [5], was probably the most extraordinary movement of civil disobedience prior to its current recurrence. Henry David Thoreau stands as the foremost exponent of transcendentalist civil disobedience. Thoreau was the forerunner of both Ghandi and Martin Luther King.

Thoreau accepted the motto, "That government is best which governs least." His essay *On the Duty of Civil Disobedience* has served as an inspiration to later generations.

Must the citizen ever for a minute, or in the least degree resign his conscience to the legislator? Why has every man a conscience? I think that we should be men first, and subjects afterward. It is not so desirable to cultivate a respect for the law, so much as for the right. The only obligation which I have a right to assume, is to do at any time what I think right. . . .

How does it become a man to behave toward this American government today? I answer that He cannot without disgrace be associated with it. I cannot for an instant recognize that political organization as my government which is the slaves' government also.

All men recognize the right of revolution; that is, the right to refuse allegiance to and to resist the government, when its tyranny or its inefficiency are great and unendurable.[14]

Democracy affords citizens a fair opportunity within the law to make their grievances known; why, then, are the techniques of civil disobedience thought necessary? Often individuals and groups in a democratic state will plead a cause they feel is just, and yet be rebuffed by the majority. Usually the decision of the majority is acceptable, or at least tolerable. However, if the complainants feel that their basic rights and freedoms are endangered or denied, if the decision compels individuals to violate their moral consciences, or if the impact of the decision is to deny the basic procedures of the democratic process, (such as the opportunity to participate in the competition for power to change the policy), compliance may not be justified.

Nearly all Americans accept the right of free expression. Exception, when it is taken, is to the form of its exercise. The general rule is that protest is permissible unless it upsets the orderly routines of society. Yet, obviously, protest will have no results unless it does precisely that. Protest which does not disturb is futile; protest which does may be unacceptable to the majority. Thus the lot of the protester is an uneasy one. [15] Yet the vitality of the democratic process requires that those with grievances be willing to demand redress and that those against whom their protests are directed permit them to do so. This is not difficult when the matters involved are unimportant and of no great moment to the majority. But when the protests involve basic questions of interest to significant segments of the society, or when serious challenges to vested interests or power positions are involved, the democratic process faces its most serious test. To demand that the protesters accept "the law," to castigate them as disturbing elements, or to otherwise avoid entertaining their protests on the merits, is to short-circuit the democratic process.

[14] Quoted in Alpheus T. Mason (ed.), *Free Government in the Making,* 3rd ed. (New York: Oxford University Press, 1965), p. 487.

Non-violent disobedience presumes a measure of democratic humanitarianism on the part of the authorities. Those who employ non-violent methods do so with the conviction that they are pleading a just cause, one which will gain the support of others if only they can be made aware of the true situation. But the success of such methods depends to a great extent on the condition that the demonstrators will not be repressed. The overriding values of our democratic system dictate that those who are driven outside the law in following their own notion of right be allowed considerable latitude, short of the point of endangering the system itself. If the practice of this idea seems doubtful in the light of the way in which many present-day demonstrators have been treated, we need only remind ourselves that their treatment falls well short of the all-out use of physical violence characteristic of non-democratic societies under similar circumstances. We can scarcely conceive, for instance, that the police might have employed machine guns instead of fire hoses against civil rights demonstrators; and it is the fact that we can scarcely conceive it that gives non-violent demonstrations some chance of success in affecting public policy. [15]

Another major assumption of those in the civil rights movement who have consciously practiced civil disobedience is that a society which professes commitment to the rule of law, as ours most certainly does, need not be inflexible in its demand for the observance of the law. The source of this assumption is the long-standing acceptance, both in American theory and law, of the existence of a "higher law," [10] higher even than constitutional law. The right of appeal to that higher law is vital to the understanding of the civil rights movement, for the leaders of the movement contend that violation of specific laws is justified precisely because of their moral invalidity. The only way, it has been argued, that such invalid laws can be tested is by clearly and purposefully violating them. From this perspective civil disobedience, far from being a disruptive force, is, within proper limits, essential to the democratic process.

What, though, constitutes "proper limits"? Under what circumstances should civil disobedience be accepted or even encouraged? These once-academic questions have been terribly real in light of recent events and, more particularly, since segments of the civil rights movement have begun to advocate violent protest. The movement towards greater activism is a result of the conclusion that discrimination ceases or diminishes more readily in response to more dramatic forms of protest. [19]

Yet there is little doubt that, given the American milieu, civil disobedience cannot go on indefinitely. Sooner or later it reaches a point of diminishing returns. Having contributed appreciably to such successes as the Civil Rights Act of 1964 [3] and its subsequent additions; having helped galvanize public opinion in support of its general position through such dramatic incidents as the march on Washington and the march from Selma to Montgomery; having proved the courage of its adherents in Birmingham, Mobile, and many other areas throughout the country; how much longer can the civil rights movement continue *outside* the framework of law without alienating much of its hard-won sympathy?

Certainly the history of similar movements, in America and elsewhere, points to the fact that perpetual disorder is an intolerable condition. The civil rights movement has unquestionably aroused the interest of many segments of the American community formerly content to ignore the problems. It has greatly broadened the base of active workers in the civil rights struggle and has given new hope to long-time participants. And, most important, it has been able to influence the body politic to write many of its demands into the law. It now is at a crossroads where its choice of tactics for the future can lead to further solidification of gains or to a new form of isolation from the mainstream of American life. Again we must remind ourselves that there is no guarantee that the democratic process will produce correct answers to important questions. But the history of civil rights in the United States gives us reason to believe that the democratic process is our best hope to arrive at such answers.

In the three selections reprinted below, Mill ("On Liberty") presents what has come to be accepted as the definitive statement in favor of absolute freedom of speech; Kristol ("'Civil Liberties,' 1952—A Study in Confusion") discusses some of the confusions which arise, particularly among liberals, when the Mill doctrine becomes applicable policy; Rustin, a leading Negro intellectual and organizer of the march on Washington ("From Protest to Politics: The Future of the Civil Rights Movement"), discusses the future of the civil rights movement.

On Liberty

JOHN STUART MILL

A nineteenth-century British philosopher (1806–1873) best known for his writings on liberalism and utilitarianism, John Stuart Mill's most important works include: Principles of Political Economy, On Liberty *and* Utilitarianism.

OF THE LIBERTY OF THOUGHT AND DISCUSSION

The time, it is to be hoped, is gone by, when any defence would be necessary of the "liberty of the press" as one of the securities against corrupt or tyrannical government. No argument, we may suppose, can now be needed, against permitting a legislature or an executive, not identified in interest with the people, to prescribe opinions to them, and determine what doctrines or what arguments they shall be allowed to hear. This aspect of the question, besides, has been so often and so triumphantly enforced by preceding writers, that it needs not be specially insisted on in this place. Though the law of England, on the subject of the press, is as servile to this day as it was in the time of the Tudors, there is little danger of its being actually put in force against

political discussion, except during some temporary panic, when fear of insurrection drives ministers and judges from their propriety and, speaking generally, it is not, in constitutional countries, to be apprehended, that the government, whether completely responsible to the people or not, will often attempt to control the expression of opinion, except when in doing so it makes itself the organ of the general intolerance of the public. Let us suppose, therefore, that the government is entirely at one with the people, and never thinks of exerting any power of coercion unless in agreement with what it conceives to be their voice. But I deny the right of the people to exercise such coercion, either by themselves or by their government. The power itself is illegitimate. The best government has no more title to it than the worst. It is as noxious or more noxious, when exerted in accordance with public opinion, then when in opposition to it. If all mankind minus one, were of one opinion, and only one person were of the contrary opinion, mankind would be no more justified in silencing that one person, than he, if he had the power, would be justified in silencing mankind. Were an opinion a personal possession of no value except to the owner; if to be obstructed in the enjoyment of it were simply a private injury, it would make some difference whether the injury was inflicted only on a few persons or on many. But the peculiar evil of silencing the expression of an opinion is, that it is robbing the human race; posterity as well as the existing generation; those who dissent from the opinion, still more than those who hold it. If the opinion is right, they are deprived of the opportunity of exchanging error for truth: if wrong, they lose, what is almost as great a benefit, the clearer perception and livelier impression of truth, produced by its collision with error.

It is necessary to consider separately these two hypotheses, each of which has a distinct branch of the argument corresponding to it. We can never be sure that the opinion we are endeavoring to stifle is a false opinion; and if we were sure, stifling it would be an evil still.

First: the opinion which it is attempted to suppress by authority may possibly be true. Those who desire to suppress it, of course deny its truth; but they are not infallible. They have no authority to decide the question for all mankind, and exclude every other person from the means of judging. To refuse a hearing to an opinion, because they are sure that it is false, is to assume that *their* certainty is the same thing as *absolute* certainty. All silencing of discussion is an assumption of infallibility. Its condemnation may be allowed to rest on this common argument, not the worse for being common.

Unfortunately for the good sense of mankind, the fact of their fallibility is far from carrying the weight in their practical judgment which is always allowed to it in theory; for while every one well knows himself to be fallible, few think it necessary to take any precautions against their own fallibility, or admit the supposition that any opinion, of which they feel very certain, may be one of the examples of the error to which they acknowledge themselves to be liable. Absolute princes, or others who are accustomed to unlimited deference, usually feel this complete confidence in their own opinions on nearly all subjects. People more happily situated, who sometimes hear their opinions disputed, and are not wholly unused to be set right when they are wrong, place the same unbounded reliance only on such of their opinions as are shared by all who surround them, or to whom they habitually defer; for in proportion to man's want of confidence in his own solitary judgment, does he usually repose, with implicit trust, on the infallibility of "the world" in general. And the world, to each individual, means the part of it with which he comes in contact; his party, his sect, his church, his class of society; the man may be called, by comparison, almost liberal and large-minded to whom it means anything so comprehensive as his own country or his own age. Nor is his faith in this collective authority at all shaken by his being aware that other ages, countries, sects, churches, classes, and parties have thought, and even now think, the exact reverse. He devolves upon his own world the responsibility of being in the right against the dissentient worlds of other people; and it never troubles him that mere accident has decided which of these numerous worlds is the object of his reliance, and that the same causes which make him a Churchman in London, would have made him a Buddhist or a Confucian in Pekin. Yet it is as evident in itself, as any amount of argument can make it, that ages are no more infallible than individuals; every age having held many opinions which subsequent ages have deemed not only false but absurd; and it is as certain that many opinions now general will be rejected by future ages, as it is that many, once general, are rejected by the present.

The objection likely to be made to this argument would probably take some such form as the following. There is no greater assumption of infallibility in forbidding the propagation of error, than in any other thing which is done by public authority on its own judgment and responsibility. Judgment is given to men that they may use it. Because it may be used erroneously, are men to be told that they ought not to use it at all? To prohibit what they think pernicious, is not claiming exemption from error, but fulfilling the duty incumbent on them, although fallible, of acting on their conscientious conviction. If we were never to act on our opinions, because those opinions may be wrong, we should leave all our interests uncared for, and all our duties unperformed. An objection which applies to all conduct, can be no valid objection to any conduct in particular. It is the duty of governments, and of individuals, to form the truest opinions they can; to form them carefully, and never impose them upon others unless they are quite sure of being right. But when they are sure (such reasoners may say), it is not conscientiousness but cowardice to shrink from acting on their opinions, and allow doctrines which they honestly think dangerous to the welfare of mankind, either in this life or in another, to be scattered abroad without restraint, because other people, in less enlightened times, have persecuted opinions now believed to be true. Let us take care, it may be said, not to make the same mistake: but governments and nations have made mistakes in other things, which are not denied to be fit subjects for the exercise of authority: they have laid on bad taxes, made unjust wars. Ought we therefore to lay on no taxes, and, under whatever provocation, made no wars? Men, and governments, must act to the best of their ability. There is no such thing as absolute certainty, but there is assurance sufficient for the purposes of human life. We may, and must, assume our opinion to be true for the guidance of our own conduct: and it is assuming no more when we forbid bad men to pervert society by the propagation of opinions which we regard as false and pernicious.

I answer, that it is assuming very much more. There is the greatest difference between presuming an opinion to be true, because, with every opportunity for contesting it, it has not been refuted, and assuming its truth for the purpose of not permitting its refutation. Complete liberty of contradicting and disproving our opinion is the very condition which justifies us in assuming its truth for purposes of action; and on no other terms can a being with human faculties have any rational assurance of being right.

When we consider either the history of opinion, or the ordinary conduct of human life, to what is it to be ascribed that the one and the other are no worse than they are? Not certainly to the inherent force of the human understanding; for, on any matter not self-evident, there are ninety-nine persons totally incapable of judging of it, for one who is capable; and the capacity of the hundredth person is only comparative; for the majority of the eminent men of every past generation held many opinions now known to be erroneous, and did or approved numerous things which no one will now justify. Why is it, then, that there is on the whole a preponderance among mankind of rational opinions and rational conduct? If there really is this preponderance—which there must be unless human affairs are, and have always been, in an almost desperate state—it is owing to a quality of the human mind, the source of everything respectable in man, either as an intellectual or as a moral being, namely that his errors are corrigible. He is capable of rectifying his mistake, by discussion and experience. Not by experience alone. There must be discussion, to show how experience is to be interpreted. Wrong opinions and practices gradually yield to fact and argument: but facts and arguments, to produce any effect on the mind, must be brought before it. Very few facts are able to tell their own story, without comments to bring out their meaning. The whole strength and value, then, of human judgment, depending on the one property, that it can be set right when it is wrong, reliance can be placed on it only when the means of setting it right are kept constantly at hand. In the case of any person whose judgment is really deserving of confidence, how has it become so? Because he has kept his mind open to criticism of his opinions and conduct. Because it has been his practice to listen to all that could be said against him; to profit by as much of it as was just, and expound to himself, and upon occasion to others, the fallacy of what was fallacious! Because he has felt, that the only way in which a human being can make some approach to knowing the whole of a subject, is by hearing what can be said about it by persons of every variety of opinion, and studying all modes in which it can be looked at by every character of mind. No wise man ever acquired his wisdom in any mode but this; nor is it in the nature of human intellect to become wise in any other manner. The steady habit of correcting and completing his own opinion by collating it with those of others, so far from causing doubt and hesitation in carrying it into practice, is the only stable foundation for a just reliance on it: for, being cognisant of all that can, at least obviously, be said against him, and having taken up his position against all gainsayers—knowing that he has sought for objections and difficulties, instead of avoiding them, and has shut out no light which can be thrown upon the subject from any quarter—he has a right to think his judgment better than that of any person, or any multitude, who have not gone through a similar process. . . .

But, indeed, the dictum that truth always triumphs over persecution is one of those pleasant falsehoods which men repeat after one another till they pass into commonplaces, but which all experience refutes. History teems with instances of truth put down by persecution. If not suppressed for ever, it may be thrown back for centuries. To speak only of religious opinions: the Reformation broke out at least twenty times before Luther, and was put down. Arnold of Brescia was put down. Fra Dolcino was put down. Savonarola was put down. The Albigeois were put down. The Vaudois were put down. The Lollards were put down. The Hussites were put down. Even after the era of Luther, wherever persecution was persisted in, it was successful. In Spain, Italy, Flanders, the Austrian empire, Protestantism was rooted out; and, most likely, would have been so in England, had Queen Mary lived, or Queen Elizabeth died. Persecution has always succeeded, save where the heretics were too strong a party to be effectually persecuted. No reasonable person can doubt

that Christianity might have been extirpated in the Roman Empire. It spread, and became predominant, because the persecutions were only occasional, lasting but a short time, and separated by long intervals of almost undisturbed propagandism. It is a piece of idle sentimentality that truth, merely as truth, has any inherent power denied to error of prevailing against the dungeon and the stake. Men are not more zealous for truth than they often are for error, and a sufficient application of legal or even of social penalties will generally succeed in stopping the propagation of either. The real advantage which truth has consists in this, that when an opinion is true, it may be extinguished once, twice, or many times, but in the course of ages there will generally be found persons to rediscover it, until some one of its reappearances falls on a time when from favourable circumstances it escapes persecution until it has made such head as to withstand all subsequent attempts to suppress it. . . .

It is the opinions men entertain, and the feelings they cherish, respecting those who disown the beliefs they deem important, which makes this country not a place of mental freedom. For a long time past, the chief mischief of the legal penalties is that they strengthen the social stigma. It is that stigma which is really effective, and so effective is it, that the profession of opinions which are under the ban of society is much less common in England, than is, in many other countries, the avowal of those which incur risk of judicial punishment. In respect to all persons but those whose pecuniary circumstances make them independent of the goodwill of other people, opinion, on this subject, is as efficacious as law; men might as well be imprisoned, as excluded from the means of earning their bread. Those whose bread is already secured, and who desire no favours from men in power, or from bodies of men, or from the public, have nothing to fear from the open avowal of any opinions, but to be ill-thought of and ill-spoken of, and this ought not to require a very heroic mould to enable them to bear. There is no room for any appeal *ad misericordiam* in behalf of such persons. But though we do not now inflict so much evil on those who think differently from us, as it was formerly our custom to do, it may be that we do ourselves as much evil as ever by our treatment of them. Socrates was put to death, but the Socratic philosophy rose like the sun in heaven, and spread its illumination over the whole intellectual firmament. Christians were cast to the lions, but the Christian church grew up a stately and spreading tree, overtopping the older and less vigorous growths, and stifling them by its shade. Our merely social intolerance kills no one, roots out no opinions, but induces men to disguise them, or to abstain from any active effort for their diffusion. With us, heretical opinions do not perceptibly gain, or even lose, ground in each decade or generation; they never blaze out far and wide, but continue to smolder in the narrow circles of thinking and studious persons among whom they originate, without ever lighting up the general affairs of mankind with either a true or a deceptive light. And thus is kept up a state of things very satisfactory to some minds, because, without the unpleasant process of fining or imprisoning anybody, it maintains all prevailing opinions outwardly undisturbed, while it does not absolutely interdict the exercise of reason by dissentients afflicted with the malady of thought. A convenient plan for having peace in the intellectual world, and keeping all things going on therein very much as they do already. But the price paid for this sort of intellectual pacification is the sacrifice of the entire moral courage of the human mind. A state of things in which a large portion of the most active and inquiring intellects find it advisable to keep the general principles and grounds of their convictions within their own breasts, and attempt, in what they address to the public, to fit as much as they can of their own conclusions to premises which they have internally renounced, cannot send forth the open, fearless characters, and logical, consistent intellects, who once adorned the thinking world. The sort of men who can be looked for under it, are either mere conformers to commonplace or time servers for truth, whose arguments on all great subjects are meant for their hearers, and are not those which have convinced themselves. Those who

avoid this alternative, do so by narrowing their thoughts and interest to things which can be spoken of without venturing within the region of principles, that is, to small practical matters, which would come right of themselves, if but the minds of mankind were strengthened and enlarged, and which will never be made effectually right until then: while that which would strengthen and enlarge men's minds, free and daring speculation on the highest subjects, is abandoned.

Those in whose eyes this reticence on the part of heretics is no evil, should consider in the first place, that in consequence of it there is never any fair and thorough discussion of heretical opinions; and that such of them as could not stand a discussion, though they may be prevented from spreading, do not disappear. But it is not the minds of heretics that are deteriorated most by the ban placed on all inquiry which does not end in the orthodox conclusions. The greatest harm done is to those who are not heretics, and whose whole mental development is cramped, and their reason cowed, by the fear of heresy. Who can compute what the world loses in the multitude of promising intellects combined with timid characters, who dare not follow out any bold, vigorous, independent train of thought, lest it should land them in something which would admit of being considered irreligious or immoral? Among them we may occasionally see some man of deep conscientiousness, and subtle and refined understanding, who spends a life in sophisticating with an intellect which he cannot silence, and exhausts the resources of ingenuity in attempting to reconcile the promptings of his conscience and reason with orthodoxy, which yet he does not, perhaps, to the end succeed in doing. No one can be a great thinker who does not recognize, that as a thinker it is his first duty to follow his intellect to whatever conclusions it may lead. Truth gains more even by the errors of one who, with due study and preparation, thinks for himself, than by the true opinions of those who only hold them because they do not suffer themselves to think. Not that it is solely, or chiefly, to form great thinkers, that freedom of thinking is required. On the contrary, it is as much and even more indispensable, to enable average human beings to attain the mental stature which they are capable of. There have been, and may again be great individual thinkers, in a general atmosphere of mental slavery. But there never has been, nor ever will be, in that atmosphere, an intellectually active people. Where any people has made a temporary approach to such a character, it has been because the dread of heterodox speculation was for a time suspended. Where there is a tacit convention that principles are not to be disputed; where the discussion of the greatest questions which can occupy humanity is considered to be closed, we cannot hope to find that generally high scale of mental activity which has made some periods of history so remarkable. Never when controversy avoided the subjects which are large and important enough to kindle enthusiasm, was the mind of a people stirred up from its foundations, and the impulse given which raised even persons of the most ordinary intellect to something of the dignity of thinking beings. Of such we have had an example in the condition of Europe during the times immediately following the Reformation; another, though limited to the Continent and to a more cultivated class, in the speculative movement of the latter half of the eighteenth century; and a third, of still briefer duration, in the intellectual fermentation of Germany during the Goethean and Fichtean period. These periods differed widely in the particular opinions which they developed; but were alike in this, that during all three the yoke of authority was broken. In each, an old mental despotism had been thrown off, and no new one had yet taken its place. The impulse given at these three periods has made Europe what it now is. Every single improvement which has taken place either in the human mind or in institutions, may be traced distinctly to one or other of them. Appearances have for some time indicated that all three impulses are well-nigh spent; and we can expect no fresh start, until we again assert our mental freedom.

Let us now pass to the second division of the argument, and dismissing the supposition that any of the received opinions may be false, let us assume them to be true, and examine into the worth of the manner in which they are likely to be held, when their truth is not freely and openly canvassed. However unwillingly a person who has a strong opinion may admit the possibility that his opinion may be false, he ought to be moved by the consideration that however true it may be, if it is not fully, frequently, and fearlessly discussed, it will be held as a dead dogma, not a living truth.

There is a class of persons (happily not quite so numerous as formerly) who think of it enough if a person assents undoubtingly to what they think true, though he has no knowledge whatever of the grounds of the opinion, and could not make a tenable defence of it against the most superficial objections. Such persons, if they can once get their creed taught from authority, naturally think that no good, and some harm, comes of its being allowed to be questioned. Where their influence prevails, they make it nearly impossible for the received opinion to be rejected wisely and considerately, though it may still be rejected rashly and ignorantly; for to shut out discussion entirely is seldom possible, and when it once gets in, beliefs not grounded on conviction are apt to give way before the slightest semblance of an argument. Waiving, however, this possibility—assuming that the true opinion abides in the mind, but abides as a prejudice, a belief independent of, and proof against, argument—this is not the way in which truth ought to be held by a rational being. This is not knowing the truth. Truth, thus held, is but one superstition the more accidentally clinging to the words which enunciate a truth. . . .

If, however, the mischievous operation of the absence of free discussion, when the received opinions are true, were confined to leaving men ignorant of the grounds of those opinions, it might be thought that this, if an intellectual, is no more evil, and does not affect the worth of the opinions, regarded in their influence on the character. The fact, however, is, that not only the grounds of the opinion are forgotten in the absence of discussion, but too often the meaning of the opinion itself. The words which convey it cease to suggest ideas, or suggest only a small portion of those they were originally employed to communicate. Instead of a vivid conception and a living belief, there remain only a few phrases retained by rote; or, if any part, the shell and husk only of the meaning is retained, the finer essence being lost. The great chapter in human history which this fact occupies and fills, cannot be too earnestly studied and meditated on. . . .

The same thing holds true, generally speaking, of all traditional doctrines—those of prudence and knowledge of life, as well as of morals or religion. All languages and literatures are full of general observations on life, both as to what it is, and how to conduct oneself in it; observations which everybody knows, which everybody repeats, or hears with acquiescence, which are received as truisms, yet of which most people first truly learn the meaning when experience, generally of a painful kind, has made it a reality to them. How often, when smarting under some unforeseen misfortune or disappointment does a person call to mind some proverb or common saying, familiar to him all his life, the meaning of which, if he had ever before felt it as he does now, would have saved him from the calamity. There are indeed reasons for this, other than the absence of discussion: there are many truths of which the full meaning cannot be realized, until personal experience has brought it home. But much more of the meaning even of these would have been understood, and what was understood would have been far more deeply impressed on the mind, if the man had been accustomed to hear it argued *pro* and *con* by people who did understand it. The fatal tendency of mankind to leave off thinking about a thing when it is no longer doubtful, is the cause of half their errors. A contemporary author has well spoken of 'the deep slumber of a decided opinion.' . . .

It still remains to speak of one of the principal causes which make diversity of opinion advantageous, and will continue to do so until mankind shall have entered a stage of intellectual advancement which at present seems at an incalculable distance. We have hitherto considered only two possibilities: that the received opinion may be false, and some other opinion, consequently, true; or that, the received opinion being true, a conflict with the opposite error is essential to a clear apprehension and deep feeling of its truth. But there is a commoner case than either of these when the conflicting doctrines, instead of being one true and the other false, share the truth between them; and the nonconforming opinion is needed to supply the remainder of the truth, of which the received doctrine embodies only a part. Popular opinions, on subjects not palpable to sense, are often true, but seldom or never the whole truth. They are a part of the truth; sometimes a greater, sometimes a smaller part, but exaggerated, distorted, and disjointed from the truths by which they ought to be accompanied and limited. Heretical opinions, on the other hand, are generally some of these suppressed and neglected truths, bursting the bonds which kept them down, and either seeking reconciliation with the truth contained in the common opinion, or fronting it as enemies, and setting themselves up, with similar exclusiveness, as the whole truth. The latter case is hitherto the most frequent, as, in the human mind, one-sidedness has always been the rule, and many-sidedness the exception. Hence, even in revolutions of opinion, one part of the truth usually sets while another rises. Even progress, which ought to superadd, for the most part only substitutes, one partial and incomplete truth for another; improvement consisting chiefly in this, that the new fragment of truth is more wanted, more adapted to the needs of the time, than that which it displaces. Such being the partial character of prevailing opinions, even when resting on a true foundation, every opinion which embodies somewhat of the portion of truth which the common opinion omits, ought to be considered precious, with whatever amount of error and confusion that truth may be blended. No sober judge of human affairs will feel bound to be indignant because those who force on our notice truths which we should otherwise have overlooked, overlook some of those which we see. Rather, he will think that so long as popular truth is one-sided, it is more desirable than otherwise that unpopular truth should have one-sided asserters too; such being usually the most energetic, and the most likely to compel reluctant attention to the fragment of wisdom which they proclaim as if it were the whole. . . .

In politics, again, it is almost a commonplace, that a party of order or stability, and a party of progress or reform, are both necessary elements of a healthy state of political life; until the one or the other shall have so enlarged its mental grasp as to be a party equally of order and of progress, knowing and distinguishing what is fit to be preserved from what ought to be swept away. Each of these modes of thinking derives its utility from the deficiencies of the other but it is in a great measure the opposition of the other that keeps each within the limits of reason and sanity. Unless opinions favourable to democracy and to aristocracy, to property and to equality, to co-operation and to competition, to luxury and to abstinence, to sociality and individuality, to liberty and discipline, and all the other standing antagonisms of practical life, are expressed with equal freedom, and enforced and defended with equal talent and energy, there is no chance of both elements obtaining their due; one scale is sure to go up, and the other down. Truth, in the great practical concerns of life, is so much a question of the reconciling and combining of opposites, that very few have minds sufficiently capacious and impartial to make the adjustment with an approach to correctness, and it has to be made by the rough process of a struggle between combatants fighting under hostile banners. On any of the great open questions just enumerated, if either of the two opinions has a better claim than the other, not merely to be tolerated, but to be encouraged and countenanced, it is the one which happens at the particular time and place to be in a minority. That is the opinion which, for the time being, represents the neglected interests, the side of human well-being which is in danger of obtaining less than its share. I am aware that there is not, in this country, any intolerance of differences of opinion on most of these topics. They are adduced to show by admitted and multiplied examples, the universality of the fact, that only through diversity of opinion is there, in the existing state of human intellect, a chance of fair play to all sides of the truth. When there are persons to be found, who form an exception to the apparent unanimity of the world on any subject, even if the world is in the right, it is always probable that dissentients have something worth hearing to say for themselves, and that truth would lose something by their silence. . . .

I do not pretend that the most unlimited use of the freedom of enunciating all possible opinions would put an end to the evils of religious or philosophical sectarianism. Every truth which men of narrow capacity are in earnest about, is sure to be asserted, inculcated, and in many ways even acted on, as if no other truth existed in the world, or at all events none that could limit or qualify the first. I acknowledge that the tendency of all opinions to become sectarian is not cured by the freest discussion, but is often heightened and exacerbated thereby; the truth which ought to have been, but was not, seen, being rejected all the more violently because proclaimed by persons regarded as opponents. But it is not on the impassioned partisan, it is on the calmer and more disinterested bystander, that this collision of opinions works its salutary effect. Not the violent conflict between parts of the truth, but the quiet suppression of half of it, is the formidable evil; there is always hope when people are forced to listen to both sides; it is when they attend only to one that errors harden into prejudices, and truth itself ceases to have the effect of truth, by being exaggerated into falsehood. And since there are few mental attributes more rare than that judicial faculty which can sit in intelligent judgment between two sides of a question, of which only one is represented by an advocate before it, truth has no chance but in proportion as every side of it, every opinion which embodies any fraction of the truth, not only finds advocates, but is so advanced as to be listened to.

We have now recognized the necessity to the mental well-being of mankind (on which all their other well-being depends) of freedom of opinion, and freedom of the expression of opinion, on four distinct grounds; which we will now briefly recapitulate.

First, if any opinion is compelled to silence, that opinion may, for aught we can certainly know, be true. To deny this is to assume our own infallibility.

Secondly, though the silenced opinion be an error, it may, and very commonly does, contain a portion of truth; and since the general or prevailing opinion on any subject is rarely or never the whole truth, it is only by the collision of adverse opinions that the remainder of the truth has any chance of being supplied.

Thirdly, even if the received opinion be not only true, but the whole truth: unless it is suffered to be, and actually is, vigorously and earnestly contested, it will, by most of those who receive it, be held in the manner of a prejudice, with little comprehension or feeling of its rational grounds. And not only this, but fourthly, the meaning of the doctrine itself will be in danger of being lost, or enfeebled, and deprived of its vital effect on the character and conduct: the dogma becoming a mere formal profession, inefficacious for good, but cumbering the ground, and preventing the growth of any real and heartfelt conviction, from reason of personal experience.

Before quitting the subject of freedom of opinion, it is fit to take some notice of those who say that the free expression of all opinions should be permitted on condition that the manner be temperate, and do not pass the bounds of fair discussion. Much might be said on the impossibility of fixing where these supposed bounds are to be placed; for if the test be offence to those whose opinions are attacked, I think experience testifies that this offence is given whenever the attack is telling and powerful, and that every opponent who pushes them hard, and whom they find it difficult to answer, appears to them, if he shows any strong feeling on the subject, an intemperate opponent. But this, though an important consideration in a practical point of view, merges in a more fundamental objection. Undoubtedly the manner of asserting an opinion, even though it be a true one, may be very objectionable, and may justly incur severe censure. But the principal offences of the kind are such as it is mostly impossible, unless by accidental self-betrayal, to bring home to conviction.

The gravest of them is, to argue sophistically, to suppress facts or arguments, to misstate the elements of the case, or misrepresent the opposite opinion. But all this, even to the most aggravated degree, is so continually done in perfect good faith, by persons who are not considered, and in many other respects may not deserve to be considered, ignorant, or incompetent, that it is rarely possible on adequate grounds conscientiously to stamp the misrepresentation as morally culpable; and still less could law presume to interfere with this kind of controversial misconduct. With regard to what is commonly meant by intemperate discussion, namely invective, sarcasm, personality, and the like, the denunciation of these weapons would deserve more sympathy if it were ever proposed to interdict them equally to both sides; but it is only desired to restrain the employment of them against the prevailing opinion: against the unprevailing they may not only be used without general disapproval, but will be likely to obtain for him who uses them the praise of honest zeal and righteous indignation. Yet whatever mischief arises from their use is greatest when they are employed against the comparatively defenceless; and whatever unfair advantage can be derived by opinion from this mode of asserting it, accrues almost exclusively to received opinions. The worst offence of this kind which can be committed by a polemic, is to stigmatize those who hold the contrary opinion as bad and immoral men. To calumny of this sort, those who hold any unpopular opinion are peculiarly exposed, because they are in general few and uninfluential, and nobody but themselves feels much interested in seeing justice done them; but this weapon is, from the nature of the case, denied to those who attack a prevailing opinion: they can neither use it with safety to themselves, nor, if they could, would it do anything but recoil on their own cause. In general, opinions contrary to those commonly received can only obtain a hearing by studied moderation of language, and the most cautious avoidance of unnecessary offence, from which they hardly ever deviate even in a slight degree without losing ground: while unmeasured vituperation employed on the side of the prevailing opinion really does deter people from professing contrary opinions, and from listening to those who profess them. For the interest, therefore, of truth and justice, it is far more important to restrain this employment of vituperative language than the other; and, for example, if it were necessary to choose, there would be much more need to discourage offensive attacks on infidelity, than on religion. It is, however, obvious that law and authority have no business with restraining either, while opinion ought, in every instance, to determine its verdict by the circumstances of the individual case; condemning every one, on whichever side of the argument he places himself, in whose mode of advocacy either want of candour, or malignity, bigotry, or intolerance of feeling manifest themselves; but not inferring these vices from the side which a person takes, though it be the contrary side of the question to our own; and giving merited honour to every one, whatever opinion he may hold, who has calmness to see and honesty to state what his opponents and their opinions really are, exaggerating nothing to their discredit, keeping nothing back which tells, or can be supposed to tell, in their favour. This is the real morality of public discussion: and if often violated, I am happy to think that there are many controversialists who to a great extent observe it, and a still greater number who conscientiously strive towards it.

"Civil Liberties," 1952 — A Study in Confusion

IRVING KRISTOL

Formerly the managing editor of Commonwealth *magazine, Irving Kristol is now co-editor of* The Public Interest.

DO WE DEFEND OUR RIGHTS BY PROTECTING COMMUNISTS?

*Heard ye not lately of a man
That went beside his witt,
And naked through the citty rann
Wrapt in a frantique fitt?*

The above tantalizing bit of 17th-century verse was quoted recently in the London *Times Literary Supplement,* in the same issue in which there appeared, elsewhere in its pages, a review of the English edition of Alan Barth's *The Loyalty of Free Men.* This fortuitous juxtaposition was not without its ironic relevance, Mr. Barth's book having been provoked by the "frantique fitt" of McCarthyism, beneath which he saw a cool

and calculating assault on the American democracy, and his defense being couched in a cool and calculating eloquence that turns out, upon close examination, to be not nearly the exercise in pure reason it seems.

A close examination, however, Mr. Barth's book and others of its kind have not received. It was hardly to be expected from Senator McCarthy and his friends, who are less famous for their habits of meticulous reading than for their preference for arguing in the large, while the more scholarly sections of American opinion have been so delighted to see the Senator get his, and so soothed by the cadences of a familiar tone, that they have not so much read these books as permitted themselves to be enchanted by them. This enchantment has had its political sequel, for as a result of it there has been drawn a line of battle. On the one side are the men of intellect and sensibility, fairminded and generous-hearted and confessedly not infallible: the Alan Barths, the Henry Steele Commagers, the Zechariah Chafees, the Howard Mumford Joneses, the Ralph Barton Perrys, the William O. Douglases, and, rather more tentatively committed, the Francis Biddles. On the other side are the mindless men, the kind who get elected to office when the spirit of the age reverts to primitivism, and who wish, under cover of fighting Communism, to squeeze the nation into a Know-Nothing strait-jacket.

The line is drawn—and those liberals who have rallied to their positions on the left of it find themselves ever more pressed against the outer walls of the city. The ready quotations from Jefferson about the trees of liberty and the blood of tyrants, the sonorous repetition of Justice Holmes' dissenting opinions, the schoolmaster's measured accents alternating with prophetic indignation—the whole battery has failed significantly to make an impression on the dominant American mood. Senator McCarthy remains blithely on the offensive and his critics give ground before him. It is a most exasperating and melancholy situation for liberals to be in; yet in proportion as they fail in strength, they gain in their sense of petulant righteousness.

Is it conceivable that the line was incorrectly drawn in the first place? The liberals are loath to weigh the possibility lest it give comfort to the enemy; Senator McCarthy for his part has no cause for dissatisfaction with things as they are; but those of us who are the displaced persons of this war might reflect on this question to our advantage. Perhaps it is a calamitous error to believe that because a vulgar demagogue lashes out at both Communism and liberalism as identical, it is necessary to protect Communism in order to defend liberalism. This way of putting the matter will surely shock liberals, who are convinced that it is only they who truly understand Communism and who thoughtfully oppose it. They are nonetheless mistaken, and it is a mistake

on which McCarthyism waxes fat. For there is one thing that the American people know about Senator McCarthy: he, like them, is unequivocally anti-Communist. About the spokesmen for American liberalism, they feel they know no such thing. And with some justification.

With what justification, can be seen from an illustrative incident involving Professor Henry Steele Commager, a distinguished historian who never was a Communist and never will be. In the May 1947 issue of *Harper's,* Professor Commager wrote a spirited article that began as follows:

"On May 6 a Russian-born girl, Mrs. Shura Lewis, gave a talk to the students of the Western High School of Washington, D. C. She talked about Russia—its school system, its public health program, the position of women, of the aged, of the workers, the farmers, and the professional classes—and compared, superficially and uncritically, some American and Russian institutions. . . . Mrs. Lewis said nothing that had not been said a thousand times, in speeches, in newspapers, magazines and books. She said nothing that any normal person could find objectionable."

What greatly disturbed Professor Commager was that this inoffensive speech did give rise to a furor in Washington. Congressmen bellowed that our schools were being subverted, the principal of the school came forward with a humble apology, the superintendent of schools for the nation's capital swore it would never happen again, and the speech itself was reprinted (after some discussion of the wisdom of exposing the public to inflammation) in the Congressional Record as a horrible example. Professor Commager saw in this a reflection of an anti-Communist hysteria that threatened to engulf all civil liberties, and he pleaded earnestly that reason control the anti-Communist passion, lest we find ourselves saddled with an anti-Communist orthodoxy no less reprehensible than the Communist one. His article was hailed as a kind of liberal manifesto, and was reprinted—alongside John Stuart Mill and John Milton—in Howard Mumford Jones' *Primer of Intellectual Freedom* (1949). Evil won a transient victory in the seats of power and Good won a permanent niche in the anthologies—a familiar tale.

Familiar, that is, until one goes to the Congressional Record and reads through this speech that no "normal person could find objectionable." Mrs. Lewis' English was broken, but her sentiments were whole:

"They call it collective farm—the peasants farm and divide up products according to work put in by each individual during the years. As a result of planning, unemployment is completely wiped out. . . .

"In Russia right now people absolutely do not worry about today or tomorrow. They never think 'All of a sudden I lose a job.' That fear doesn't exist among Russian people. . . .

"No matter where you live you have to work. What the Russian people have, they are more secure about this. They work. They need not worry much about losing the job. They are free to travel from one place to another, and each person must work 25 years for after that he is able to get a pension. No matter where you work—in this plant or another, 25 years and then you get 50% of your salary and live the rest of your life. . . .

"I never appreciated the life in Russia until I live here. Here you have to work hard in order to live, use all your courage not to die. . . .

"I read all the papers here and occasionally I go to the Library of Congress and read all papers printed in Moscow. It is very interesting, and when I read these papers always you can see here evidence of press where people talk all the time about having a war, to throw the atomic bomb on Russia, to destroy because they have a system which is very prideful. At the present time Russians are busy to restore all those houses, all those cities, all those towns. Russian people make streets, plants, produce new style of shoes, new fashion of dress, new production, and never they talk about having a war."

The echoes this awakened in Congress may have been exaggerated, but they were not factitious or beside the point. Obviously, Professor Commager can argue that it will not harm American school children to encounter an occasional

Communist apologist in the flesh; one may even go further and say it would do them good. However, in the first place, Mrs. Lewis was not introduced as a Communist apologist but as an informed reporter, and, in the second place, everything she said should have been objectionable to every normal person, and especially to a historian like Professor Commager—for the good and sufficient reason that it was a tissue of lies. For Professor Commager to defend the rights of Communists to free speech is one thing, for him to assert that there is nothing objectionable in mendacious pleading in support of Communism is quite another. The conclusion "any normal person" will draw from such behavior is that, for whatever reason, his critical faculties are less alert when he looks out of the left corner of his eye.

Indeed, the heart of the matter is exactly that he looks at Communism out of the *left* corner of his eye. Professor Commager seems to be seduced by the insidious myth according to which Communism is a political trend continuous with liberalism and democratic socialism, only more impatient and inclined to the fanatical, only more "radical" than its companions who are not quite so "left." It is a myth that Senator McCarthy, for his own ends, is happy to accept, since it allows him to tag a New Dealer as being by nature an embryonic Communist. Neither the Professor nor the Senator is concerned to see that the antithesis of "left" and "right" no longer suits the political realities; that measured by the ideals of the French or even Russian Revolution, Communism today is as counter-revolutionary as Louis XVI or Kolchak ever was; that if one wishes to defend the civil liberties of Communists (as the Senator does not), one must do so on the same grounds that one defends the civil liberties of Nazis and fascists—no more, no less.

Professor Commager might retort that he knows all this full well, and that he is for civil liberties for everyone, fascist, Communist, or what-have-you. But if a Nazi had, in 1938, addressed a high-school audience in this country, extolling the accomplishments of Hitler's regime, presenting a thoroughly fictitious account of life in Nazi Germany, never once mentioning the existence of concentration camps—would Professor Commager find in such a speech "nothing that any normal person could find objectionable"? It is doubtless an injustice to him even to conceive of the possibility.

This notion of Communism as "left" and therefore at an opposite pole from fascism, which is "right," appears to have become intrinsic to the liberal outlook. It is imbedded in the meretricious historical analogies, in the rolling phrases about "the forces of freedom and those of fear," beneath which there lies the gross metaphysic of the liberal Manichee, apportioning the universe to "forward-looking" and "backward-looking" demiurges. It helps explain how Professor Commager can permit himself to write: "After all, it is no accident that the nations dedicated to freedom won the two great wars of the 20th century and those committed to totalitarianism went under" —when it is not only no accident, it is not even a fact. The same notion is evidenced in Zechariah Chafee's explanation (in his essay in the recent symposium *Civil Liberties Under Attack*) of the origin of Communist fronts: "It is inevitable that the membership of organizations formed to bring about change should include some persons who want a great deal of change"—as if Professor Chafee and the Communists were agreed on the direction of the change, quarreling only over the measure. It is the presupposition from which Ralph Barton Perry (in his new book *The Citizen Decides*) can deduce that Communism is "democratic" by virtue of being a revolt of the "masses" against the "classes," that the Soviet regime is a government "for the people with the consent of the people" though not by the people, and that the Chinese Communist leaders are "hostages" of a popular revolution.

Moreover, after staring out of the left corner of the eye for any length of time, there comes an irrepressible inclination to wink. How else explain, for instance, the attitude Alan Barth takes toward the Hiss-Chambers affair? He can begin a sentence: "Insofar as Chambers may be credited with having told the truth. . . ."; or: "whatever the guilt of Alger Hiss and

whatever the utility of exposing it and punishing it a decade later. . . ." About Whittaker Chambers and the Communist "informer" in general, he is no longer judiciously bland but is knowingly tart: "The ex-Communists, conscious of their betrayal of American values, wanted the comfort of company; they had to show that many others, even many who were highly respected, had been as recreant as they." In other words, Chambers in telling the truth is a man of malice, Hiss in denying it is his defenseless victim. Hiss's guilt is problematic and, in any case, not important; Chambers' wickedness is certain.

On Owen Lattimore, there is liberal unanimity: he got a raw deal. Professor Commager believes (in his contribution to *Civil Liberties Under Attack*) that the attack on Lattimore was an attack on "independence and non-conformity." Professor Chafee laments: "Owen Lattimore did his own thinking and look how his services were appreciated." Alan Barth is casually positive: "Dr. Lattimore's ordeal was, of course, only the most spectacular instance of legislative punishment of teachers for expressing their opinions." About the worst that can be said for such arrant nonsense is that it is uttered in all sincerity. For the incontrovertible facts of the case are, "of course," that Owen Lattimore did *not* do his own thinking; that his "ordeal" was the public demonstration of this fact; that he was a faithful and enormously influential fellow-traveler who for more than a decade followed the Communist line as if magnetized by it, including a docile zig-zag during the Stalin-Hitler pact. Is it really no legitimate concern of Congress that such a man was appointed advisor to Chiang Kai-shek, that he accompanied Vice-President Wallace during his tour of Asia, that he was admired and listened to by important people in the State Department?

In his denunciation of Lattimore's pro-Communist record and in hurling unsubstantiated charges against him (chief of Soviet espionage, etc.), Senator McCarthy may well have been aiming a blow against independence of mind and non-conformity of spirit. For Messrs. Commager, Barth, and Chafee to defend

Lattimore's pro-Communist record in order to defend such independence and nonconformity, is for them to play the Senator's game, on the losing side.

It is equally futile for liberals to try to match Senator McCarthy's irresponsible declamations with a crafty rhetoric of their own, especially when this rhetoric, while not designedly pro-Communist, is compelled by the logic of disingenuousness and special pleading to become so in effect. The need for disingenuousness arises out of a refusal to see Communism for what it is: a movement guided by conspiracy and aiming at totalitarianism, rather than merely another form of "dissent" or "nonconformity." Hence the liberal argument runs askew of reality and must clothe itself with neat obfuscation.

Once again, Professor Commager obliges with a superior specimen:

"The House Un-American Activities Committee has launched an attack on the Lawyers' Guild as a pro-Communist or 'subversive organization. The chief basis for this attack is, as far as we know, that the Guild has proffered its services to the defense of Communists under indictment for violation of the Smith Act. We need not inquire into the accuracy of this charge or into the degree of zeal displayed by the Lawyers' Guild. Let us ask rather what are the logical conclusions to be drawn by the position which the House Committee has adopted? They are two: that certain criminals are so despicable that they are not entitled to counsel, and that a lawyer who defends a criminal is himself sympathetic to crime."

That phrase in the second sentence, "as far as we know," is curious. It implies strongly that the only conceivable explanation of the Committee's attitude is the action of the Guild in providing lawyers to defend indicted Communists, and that there is no public information which gives plausibility to the Committee's belief that the Guild is a "front" organization, controlled and run by Communists. On the contrary, however, "as far as we know," and we know much further than Professor Commager suggests, the Lawyers' Guild is a Communist creation that, as A. A. Berle stated when he resigned from it in 1940, "is not prepared to take any stand which conflicts with the Communist party line." Moreover, the House Committee on Un-American Activities has collected and published sufficient evidence to demonstrate this beyond cavil—which leads one to think that if Professor Commager spent nearly as much time reading the records of Congressional hearings as he does denouncing them, we should all be better off.

The entire third sentence is even more curious: "We need not inquire into the accuracy of this charge or into the degree of zeal displayed by the Lawyers' Guild." If we take "zeal" to mean pro-Communism (in the context, that is all it can mean), then the degree of this zeal and the accuracy of the charge of pro-Communism are precisely what we *do* need to inquire into. How can we know whether to sanction or condemn the Committee's investigation of the Guild as a pro-Communist organization unless we make an effort to find out if the Guild is or is not, in fact, a pro-Communist organization? Even Professor Commager surreptitiously ignores his own disclaimer, as the last two sentences of his paragraph show. Obviously, the two "logical conclusions" flow, not from the Committee's premise, but his own: namely, that the Lawyers' Guild is neither pro-Communist nor subversive. From the Committee's own premise, quite other logical conclusions may be inferred—one of them being that the Committee is engaged in showing up Communist fronts for what they are. Professor Commager's "logic" is a sleight-of-hand whereby premises that are prejudiced in favor of the Communist interpretation of affairs are made to pass for natural conclusions.

In the same vein, there is a liberal rhetoric of insinuation that works under cover of a high moral posture. Its net effect is to give a backhanded credence to the Communist assertion that it is impossible to oppose Communism vigorously without walking into the arms of Black Reaction. It is the kind of thing represented in the following observation of Alan Barth's:

"In the New York trial of eleven Communist Party leaders in 1949, a number of FBI undercover operatives who had joined the party appeared as prosecution witnesses. How widely such agents have been dispersed in labor unions, in lawful voluntary associations, and in political groups is a matter of mere conjecture. But it is certainly a matter of legitimate concern to Americans who care about preservation of the traditional rights of privacy."

A noble sentiment, and the unwary reader assents—who is against the right to privacy, and who is not prepared to be concerned with its violation? Only the exceptionally attentive will note that the supposed threat to "the traditional rights of privacy" is "a matter of mere conjecture." Whose conjecture? We are not told. Is here any ground for such a conjecture? We are not told that either. Is Mr. Barth against the use of undercover agents in principle? He does not say so. Is he against the use of undercover agents in Communist organizations? He does not say this, either. He would seem to be against dispersing FBI agents in bona fide labor unions, lawful voluntary associations, and political groups, and reminds us of the consequences. But who is for it? The answer, which he does not bother to give, is: nobody—and that is why the FBI is doing no such thing and why the whole business is a "matter of mere conjecture." In the course of Mr. Barth's innuendoes, however, the onus has been neatly shifted from the Communist conspirators to the FBI agents who identified them.

The same technique of persuasion is at work in such a statement as this one by Professor Commager: "It will be useful to determine, a generation from now, whether those universities that have purged their faculties are actually stronger than they were before the purges occurred —stronger in those essentials that go to make a university." This has about it so trembling an air of bittersweet wisdom that it seems positively boorish to ask: just which universities would Professor Commager describe as "purged"? Surely Columbia is not one of them, for Professor Commager is not the kind of man who would retain his post on a "purged" faculty. Is it Yale? Princeton? Harvard? University of Chicago? The list could be extended indefinitely, and never provoke an affirmative response, for there is not a single university in the United States that can be said to have been, in any meaning-

ful sense of the word, "purged." There has been no more than a handful of cases where Communist college teachers have been dismissed, and less than a handful of cases where non-Communists have been unjustly fired as "Reds." To call this a "purge"—even regardless of whether or not one thinks Communists have a right to teach in colleges—is to echo Communist propaganda.

Perhaps Professor Commager had in mind the University of California, where several dozen (out of a total of more than a thousand) teachers found the idea of a special loyalty oath—the content of which was irrelevant to their action—so offensive and intolerable that they exercised their constitutional right to refuse to swear it, and consequently had to seek other employment. Granting that the notion of a special oath for teachers is obnoxious, and even conceding that this minority was correct and courageous in its particular reaction to it—is it the part of sobriety to insist, as Professor Commager goes on to do, that the philosophy behind the actions of California's Board of Trustees does not differ "in any essentials" from the philosophy behind the totalitarian control of university teaching? One swallow does not make a spring, or one injustice an apocalypse.

Despite their fondness for clichés of Communist manufacture, all these liberal spokesmen are sincerely anti-Communist —otherwise, what they have to say would be of little interest to anyone. But their rejection of Communism has all the semblance of a preliminary gesture, a repudiation aiming to linger in the memory as a floating credential. It has little relation to all the ensuing scenes of the political drama, where bad conscience and stubborn pride join to guide the liberal through his role.

Did not the major segment of American liberalism, as a result of joining hands with the Communists in a Popular Front, go on record as denying the existence of Soviet concentration camps? Did it not give its blessing to the "liquidation" of millions of Soviet "kulaks"? Did it not apologize for the mass purges of 1936–38, and did it not solemnly approve the grotesque trials of the Old Bolsheviks? Did it not applaud the massacre of the non-

Communist left by the GPU during the Spanish Civil War? All this carries no weight with Alan Barth who knows that, though a man repeat the Big Lie, so long as he is of a liberal intention he is saved. On the participation of non-Communists in Communist fronts during the 30's, he writes:"In the main, their participation, while it lasted, was not only innocent but *altogether* praiseworthy." (My italics.)

Even Francis Biddle, who is generally cautious, remarks in his book *The Fear of Freedom*: "What makes an organization subversive? If a vast majority of its members are Communists but its conduct has always been exemplary, advocating desirable social reforms which Communists usually back, it can hardly fit the description."

One surmises that Mr. Biddle is not really so politically naive as this statement, on the face of it, would lead one to believe. He must know what it means to be "subversive," since it was he who, as Attorney General, sent eighteen members of a minuscule Trotskyist sect to jail in 1942 for being just that; he must know how Communists work, how front organizations act as an ancillary to the Communist party apparatus, since this is a matter of common knowledge and Mr. Biddle is uncommonly literate and intelligent. No, it was no elevated unsophistication that urged him on, but rather a sense of shame and a cowardliness to confess that shame. Mr. Biddle, like Mr. Barth, refuses to admit what is now apparent: that a generation of earnest reformers who helped give this country a New Deal should find themselves in retrospect stained with the guilt of having lent aid and comfort to Stalinist tyranny. This is, to be sure, a truth of hindsight, an easy truth. But it is the truth nonetheless, and might as well be owned up to. If American liberalism is not willing to discriminate between its achievements and its sins, it only disarms itself before Senator McCarthy, who is eager to have it appear that its achievements *are* its sins.

There is a false pride, by which liberals persuade themselves that no matter what association a man has had with a Communist enterprise, he is absolutely guiltless of the crimes that Communism has committed so long as he was moved to this association by a generous idealism. There is a political mythology, by which liberals locate Communism over on the "left," in a zone exempt from the unsparing verdict directed against the totalitarian "right." There is also a fear, a fear that the American democracy in an excess of anti-Communism will gather its abundant energy into a wave of "conformism" that will drown all free thought. This pride, this mythology, this fear all unite for a liberal prejudgment of issues (e.g., the cases of Alger Hiss, Owen Lattimore, William Remington, Harry Dexter White) which is not easy to explain on a purely rational view. It is what stimulates a flood of irrelevant and gaudy prose about loyalty in the abstract ("like love it must be given freely," etc.) while it shuns a careful discussion of Communist disloyalty in the concrete.

Of the three factors, the fear of "conformism" or "orthodoxy" is probably the most influential in its appeal, for it is founded in some degree on objective fact. Alexis de Tocqueville and John Stuart Mill, both friendly critics of the egalitarian trend, pointed out long ago that in every democratic society there is an inherent tendency toward a "despotism of public opinion"; where the majority makes the laws, it may also wish—especially in feverish and unsettled times—to make opinion, lauding the popular and extirpating the unpopular. In America, where the people are more powerful than elsewhere, and where there is, too, a significant tradition of vigilante-ism, the danger of a despotism of public opinion is proportionately greater. When the State Department is forced to suspend an exhibition abroad of modern American art because some Congressmen denounce it as "Communistic," the danger of such a despotism seems more than academic, and many otherwise sensible people are led to reprehend any attempt to unveil Communist activities or Communist beliefs as a malignant form of "punishment by publicity," which will soon be extended to all opinions that illiterate and narrowminded Congressmen detest.

What these people do not see is that Communism, because it is a conspiratorial movement, has not the faintest interest in any genuine resistance to the despotism of public opinion. These martyrs whose testament is—"I refuse to answer on the grounds that it might incriminate me"! These "intellectuals" of Hollywood and radio who are outraged at a Congressman's insistence that they say what they actually believe, and who wail that they are in danger of—being excluded from well-paying jobs! Is this the vibrant voice of "nonconformity" and "dissent"? Are these the American rebels of today? Oddly enough, the majority of American liberals seem to think so: they have been moved to indignation by the questions, but never moved to disgust by the answers. Presumably, this is what they think a dissenter looks like, and no sadder commentary is possible on the corruption they have inflicted on themselves. And not only on themselves—for this image of a dissenter happens to coincide with the image held by Joseph McCarthy and Pat McCarran, for whom the dissenter is *per se* a scheming subversive. No greater spur to the despotism of public opinion can be imagined than this identification of free thought with underground conspiracy.

There is only one way the despotism of public opinion can be resisted. That is for a person with unpopular views to express himself, loudly, brazenly, stubbornly, in disregard of the consequences. Such a person may have to suffer for his convictions, as others have suffered before him, and as others will suffer after. But the responsibility for the mind's freedom in a democracy lies with the intransigent thinker, with his courage to shout the truth in the face of the mob, with his faith that truth will win out, and with his maddening commitment to the truth, win or lose. Yet, during all the occasions of the past several years, not a single liberal voice was to say to these strange "victims": "Speak up and damn the consequences! Let them take your job—as they certainly will anyway; tell the truth —you have nothing to lose and honor to gain!" Instead, there were erudite essays on the "right to a job" that would have corroborated William James in his mournful conviction that "the prevalent fear of poverty among our educated classes is the worst moral disease from which our civilization suffers."

Still, unworthy as these "victims" are, may they not, despite themselves, represent the right of the individual to hold whatever opinions he pleases without having to give a public accounting of them? Even if these Communists and Communist sympathizers are despicable, don't they have the right to believe privately anything they please? This is the way the question is frequently put, and it reveals a total misapprehension as to what Communism really is.

Communism is an idea, beyond question. Indeed, it is an Idea, and it is of the essence of this Idea that it is also a conspiracy to subvert every social and political order it does not dominate. It is, furthermore, an Idea that has ceased to have any intellectual status but has become incarnate in the Soviet Union and the official Communist parties, to whose infallible directives unflinching devotion is owed. A person who is captive to this Idea can, at any time, in any place, be called upon to do whatever the Idea, i.e., the Party, thinks necessary. Since this is so, it is of considerably more than private interest if a person is held by the Idea—he is, all appearances to the contrary, a person with different loyalties, and with different canons of scrupulousness, from ours. To grant him an "immunity by silence" is to concede the right to conspiracy, a concession no government ever has made or ever will make.

This sounds exaggerated, as it must, being so foreign to the nature of American political experience. Many of us have known Communists, and most of them conveyed no impression of being conspirators. But then, some of us have known Nazis too, and they conveyed no immediate association with gas chambers. It is quite impossible to judge a political movement by the personality of an individual member. Roosevelt certainly didn't see in Stalin any symptoms of blood lust. Hermann Goering in jail struck one as a clever clown. And there are still plenty of people who can't believe that Alger Hiss ever did any such thing.

No doubt there are some present members of the Communist party who would, in a showdown, break free of the Idea and rally to the democratic cause. Unfortunately, we have no way of knowing who they are. No doubt there are some present members and fellow-travelers of the Communist party who would sooner or later get disillusioned with Communism if they were permitted to hold down their present jobs as teachers, civil service workers, etc., whereas they are likely to harden in the face of persecution. Unfortunately, it is quite as impossible to tell the citizens of Oshkosh, some of whom have suffered personal loss as a result of the war in Korea, that there is no harm in having their children taught the three R's by a Communist, as it would have been to persuade the citizens of Flatbush in 1939 that there was no cause for excitement in their children being taught by a Nazi, or to convince a businessman that it is smart practice for him to pay a handsome salary to someone pledged to his "liquidation." No doubt some of these people became Communists after having suffered during the depression, or during a labor conflict, or as a result of race prejudice, and society must bear its share of the blame. Unfortunately, as Fitzjames Stephens remarked many decades ago: "It does not follow that because society caused a fault it is not to punish it. A man who breaks his arm when he is drunk may have to cut it off when he is sober."

The problem of fighting Communism while preserving civil liberties is no simple one, and there is no simple solution. A prerequisite for any solution, however, is, firstly, a proper understanding of Communism for what it is, and secondly, a sense of proportion. So long as liberals agree with Senator MCarthy that the fate of Communism involves the fate of liberalism, and that we must choose between complete civil liberties for everyone and a disregard for civil liberties entirely, we shall make no progress except to chaos. So long as one is either for or against "guilt by association," it is hopeless to try to distinguish between a sober and silly definition of that concept—sober when it is taken to mean, as for instance the Canwell Committee of the State of Washington

took it to mean, that anyone who is a member of three or more organizations officially declared subversive is to be considered a Communist; silly when it is taken to mean, as many government loyalty boards take it to mean, that if you have a friend or a relation who is sympathetic to Communism, you are a "bad security risk." So long as Senator McCarthy and the liberals agree that the right of a Communist to teach or be a government employee is a matter of principle, we shall remain distant from that intelligent discrimination between one case and another, and one situation and another, which alone can give us our true bearings. And so long as Senator McCarthy and the liberals are enmeshed in this confusion, the Senator will grow the stronger, for such confusion is the sap of his political life.

Inevitably, liberals will disagree among themselves about the appropriateness of specific actions with regard to Communism and Communists. Inevitably, too, there will always be a basic division and antagonism between liberalism (which is solicitous of freedom) and McCarthyism (which is not). But if a liberal wishes to defend the civil liberties of Communists or of Communist fellow-travelers, he must enter the court of American opinion with clean hands and a clear mind. He must show that he knows the existence of an organized subversive movement such as Communism is a threat to the consensus on which civil society and its liberties are based. He must bluntly acknowledge Communists and fellow-travelers to be what they are, and then, if he so desires, defend the expediency in particular circumstances of allowing them the right to be what they are. He must speak as one of *us*, defending *their* liberties. To the extent he insists that they are on our side, that we can defend our liberties only by uncritically defending theirs, he will be taken as speaking as one of them.

From Protest to Politics:
The Future of the
Civil Rights Movement

BAYARD RUSTIN

Bayard Rustin is a nationally respected leader of the civil rights movement. He has served at intervals as personal assistant to Martin Luther King, Jr.; he has been an editor of Liberation; *and he organized the 1963 march on Washington. During World War II he spent three years in federal prison as a conscientious objector.*

The decade spanned by the 1954 Supreme Court decision on school desegregation and the Civil Rights Act of 1964 will undoubtedly be recorded as the period in which the legal foundations of racism in America were destroyed. To be sure, pockets of resistance remain; but it would be hard to quarrel with the assertion that the elaborate legal structure of segregation and discrimination, particularly in relation to public accommodations, has virtually collapsed. On the other hand, without making light of the human sacrifices involved in the direct-action tactics (sit-ins, freedom rides, and the rest) that were so instrumental to this achievement, we must recognize that in desegregating public accommodations, we affected institutions which are relatively peripheral both to the American socio-economic order and to the fundamental conditions of life of the Negro people. In a highly industrialized, 20th-century civilization, we hit Jim Crow precisely where it was most anachronistic, dispensable, and vulnerable—in hotels, lunch counters, terminals, libraries, swimming pools, and the like. For in these forms, Jim Crow does impede the flow of commerce in the broadest sense: it is a nuisance in a society on the move (and on the make). Not surprisingly, therefore, it was the most mobility-conscious and relatively liberated groups

in the Negro community—lower-middle-class college students—who launched the attack that brought down this imposing but hollow structure.

The term "classical" appears especially apt for this phase of the civil rights movement. But in the few years that have passed since the first flush of sit-ins, several developments have taken place that have complicated matters enormously. One is the shifting focus of the movement in the South, symbolized by Birmingham; another is the spread of the revolution to the North; and the third, common to the other two, is the expansion of the movement's base in the Negro community. To attempt to disentangle these three strands is to do violence to reality. David Danzig's perceptive article, "The Meaning of Negro Strategy," correctly saw in the Birmingham events the victory of the concept of collective struggle over individual achievement as the road to Negro freedom. And Birmingham remains the unmatched symbol of grass-roots protest involving all strata of the black community. It was also in this most industrialized of Southern cities that the single-issue demands of the movement's classical stage gave way to the "package deal." No longer were Negroes satisfied with integrating lunch counters. They now sought advances in employment, housing, school integration, police protection, and so forth.

Thus, the movement in the South began to attack areas of discrimination which were not so remote from the Northern experience as were Jim Crow lunch counters. At the same time, the interrelationship of these apparently distinct areas became increasingly evident. What is the value of winning access to public accommodations for those who lack money to use them? The minute the movement faced this question, it was compelled to expand its vision beyond race relations to economic relations, including the role of education in modern society. And what also became clear is that all these interrelated problems, by their very nature, are not soluble by private, voluntary efforts but require government action—or politics. Already Southern demonstrators had recognized that the most effective way to strike at the police brutality they suffered from was by getting rid of the local sheriff—and that meant political action, which in turn meant, and still means, political action within the Democratic party where the only meaningful primary contests in the South are fought.

And so, in Mississippi, thanks largely to the leadership of Bob Moses, a turn toward political action has been taken. More than voter registration is involved here. A conscious bid for *political power* is being made, and in the course of that effort a tactical shift is being effected: direct-action techniques are being subordinated to a strategy calling for the building of community institutions or power bases. Clearly, the implications of this shift reach far beyond Mississippi. What began as a protest movement is being challenged to translate itself into a political movement. Is this the right course? And if it is, can the transformation be accomplished?

II

The very decade which has witnessed the decline of legal Jim Crow has also seen the rise of *de facto* segregation in our most fundamental socio-economic institutions. More Negroes are unemployed today than in 1954, and the unemployment gap between the races is wider. The median income of Negroes has dropped from 57 per cent to 54 per cent of that of whites. A higher percentage of Negro workers is now concentrated in jobs vulnerable to automation than was the case ten years ago. More Negroes attend *de facto* segregated schools today than when the Supreme Court handed down its famous decision; while school integration proceeds at a snail's pace in the South, the number of Northern schools with an excessive proportion of minority youth proliferates. And behind this is the continuing growth of racial slums, spreading over our central cities and trapping Negro youth in a milieu which, whatever its legal definition, sows an unimaginable demoralization. Again, legal niceties aside, a resident of a racial ghetto lives in segregated housing, and more Negroes fall into this category than ever before.

These are the facts of life which generate frustration in the Negro community and challenge the civil rights movement. At issue, after all, is not *civil rights*, strictly speaking, but social and economic conditions. Last summer's riots were not race riots; they were outbursts of class aggression in a society where class and color definitions are converging disastrously. How can the (perhaps misnamed) civil rights movement deal with this problem?

Before trying to answer, let me first insist that the task of the movement is vastly complicated by the failure of many whites of good will to understand the nature of our problem. There is a widespread assumption that the removal of artificial racial barriers should result in the automatic integration of the Negro into all aspects of American life. This myth is fostered by facile analogies with the experience of various ethnic immigrant groups, particularly the Jews. But the analogies with the Jews do not hold for three simple but profound reasons. First, Jews have a long history as a literate people, a resource which has afforded them opportunities to advance in the academic and professional worlds, to achieve intellectual status even in the midst of economic hardship, and to evolve sustaining value systems in the context of ghetto life. Negroes, for the greater part of their presence in this country, were forbidden by law to read or write. Second, Jews have a long history of family stability, the importance of which in terms of aspiration and self-image is obvious. The Negro family structure was totally destroyed by slavery and with it the possibility of cultural transmission (the right of Negroes to marry and rear children is barely a century old). Third, Jews are white and have the *option* of relinquishing their cultural-religious identity, intermarrying, passing, etc. Negroes, or at least the overwhelming majority of them, do not have this option. There is also a fourth, vulgar reason. If the Jewish and Negro communities are not comparable in terms of education, family structure, and color, it is also true that their respective economic roles bear little resemblance.

This matter of economic role brings us to the greater problem—the fact that we are moving into an era in which the natural functioning of the market does not by itself ensure every man with will and ambition a place in the productive process. The immigrant who came to this country during the late 19th and early 20th centuries entered a society which was expanding territorially and/ or economically. It was then possible to start at the bottom, as an unskilled or semi-skilled worker, and move up the ladder, acquiring new skills along the way. Especially was this true when industrial unionism was burgeoning, giving new dignity and higher wages to organized workers. Today the situation has changed. We are not expanding territorially, the western frontier is settled, labor organizing has leveled off, our rate of economic growth has been stagnant for a decade. And we are in the midst of a technological revolution which is altering the fundamental structure of the labor force, destroying unskilled and semi-skilled jobs —jobs in which Negroes are disproportionately concentrated.

Whatever the pace of this technological revolution may be, the *direction* is clear: the lower rungs of the economic ladder are being lopped off. This means that an individual will no longer be able to start at the bottom and work his way up; he will have to start in the middle or on top, and hold on tight. It will not even be enough to have certain specific skills, for many skilled jobs are also vulnerable to automation. A broad educational background, permitting vocational adaptability and flexibility, seems more imperative than ever. We live in a society where, as Secretary of Labor Willard Wirtz puts it, machines have the equivalent of a high school diploma. Yet the average educational attainment of American Negroes is 8.2 years.

Negroes, of course, are not the only people being affected by these developments. It is reported that there are now 50 per cent fewer unskilled and semi-skilled jobs than there are high school dropouts. Almost one-third of the 26 million young people entering the labor market in the 1960's will be dropouts. But the percentage of Negro dropouts nationally is 57 per cent, and in New York City, among Negroes 25 years of age or over, it is 68 per cent. They are without a future.

To what extent can the kind of self-help campaign recently prescribed by Eric Hoffer in the *New York Times Magazine* cope with such a situation? I would advise those who think that self-help is the answer to familiarize themselves with the long history of such efforts in the Negro community, and to consider why so many foundered on the shoals of ghetto life. It goes without saying that any effort to combat demoralization and apathy is desirable, but we must understand that demoralization in the Negro community is largely a common-sense response to an objective reality. Negro youths have no need of statistics to perceive, fairly accurately, what their odds are in American society. Indeed, from the point of view of motivation, some of the healthiest Negro youngsters I know are juvenile delinquents: vigorously pursuing the American Dream of material acquisition and status, yet finding the conventional means of attaining it blocked off, they do not yield to defeatism but resort to illegal (and often ingenious) methods. They are not alien to American culture. They are, in Gunnar Myrdal's phrase, "exaggerated Americans." To want a Cadillac is not un-American; to push a cart in the garment center is. If Negroes are to be persuaded that the conventional path (school, work, etc.) is superior, we had better provide evidence which is now sorely lacking. It is a double cruelty to harangue Negro youth about education and training when we do not know what jobs will be available for them. When a Negro youth can reasonably foresee a future free of slums, when the prospect of gainful employment is realistic, we will see motivation and self-help in abundant enough quantities.

Meanwhile, there is an ironic similarity between the self-help advocated by many liberals and the doctrines of the Black Muslims. Professional sociologists, psychiatrists, and social workers have expressed amazement at the Muslims' success in transforming prostitutes and dope addicts into respectable citizens. But every prostitute the Muslims convert to a model of Calvinist virtue is replaced by the ghetto with two more. Dedicated as they are to maintenance of the ghetto, the Muslims are powerless to affect substantial moral reform. So too with every other group or program which is not aimed at the destruction of slums, their causes and effects. Self-help efforts, directly or indirectly, must be geared to mobilizing people into power units capable of effecting social change. That is, their goal must be genuine self-help, not merely self-improvement. Obviously, where self-improvement activities succeed in imparting to their participants a feeling of some control over their environment, those involved may find their appetites for change whetted; they may move into the political arena.

III

Let me sum up what I have thus far been trying to say: the civil rights movement is evolving from a protest movement into a full-fledged *social movement*—an evolution calling its very name into question. It is now concerned not merely with removing the barriers to full *opportunity* but with achieving the fact of *equality*. From sit-ins and freedom rides we have gone into rent strikes, boycotts, community organization, and political action. As a consequence of this natural evolution, the Negro today finds himself stymied by obstacles of far greater magnitude than the legal barriers he was attacking before: automation, urban decay, *de facto* school segregation. These are problems which, while conditioned by Jim Crow, do not vanish upon its demise. They are more

deeply rooted in our socio-economic order; they are the result of the total society's failure to meet not only the Negro's needs, but human needs generally.

These propositions have won increasing recognition and acceptance, but with a curious twist. They have formed the common premise of two apparently contradictory lines of thought which simultaneously nourish and antagonize each other. On the one hand, there is the reasoning of the New York *Times* moderate who says that the problems are so enormous and complicated that Negro militancy is a futile irritation, and that the need is for "intelligent moderation." Thus, during the first New York school boycott, the *Times* editorialized that Negro demands, while abstractly just, would necessitate massive reforms, the funds for which could not realistically be anticipated; therefore the just demands were also foolish demands and would only antagonize white people. Moderates of this stripe are often correct in perceiving the difficulty or impossibility of racial progress in the context of present social and economic policies. But they accept the context as fixed. They ignore (or perhaps see all too well) the potentialities inherent in linking Negro demands to broader pressures for radical revision of existing policies. They apparently see nothing strange in the fact that in the last twenty-five years we have spent nearly a trillion dollars fighting or preparing for wars, yet throw up our hands before the need for overhauling our schools, cleaning the slums, and really abolishing poverty. My quarrel with these moderates is that they do not even envision radical changes; their admonitions of moderation are, for all practical purposes, admonitions to the Negro to adjust to the status quo, and are therefore immoral.

The more effectively the moderates argue their case, the more they convince Negroes that American society will not or cannot be reorganized for full racial equality. Michael Harrington has said that a successful war on poverty might well require the expenditure of a $100 billion. Where, the Negro wonders, are the forces now in motion to compel such a commitment? If the voices of the moderates were raised in an insistence upon a reallocation of national resources at levels that could not be confused with tokenism (that is, if the moderates stopped being moderates), Negroes would have greater grounds for hope. Meanwhile, the Negro movement cannot escape a sense of isolation.

It is precisely this sense of isolation that gives rise to the second line of thought I want to examine—the tendency within the civil rights movement which, despite its militancy, pursues what I call a "no-win" policy. Sharing with many moderates a recognition of the magnitude of the obstacles to freedom, spokesmen for this tendency survey the American scene and find no forces prepared to move toward radical solutions. From this they conclude that the only viable strategy is shock; above all, the hypocrisy of white liberals must be exposed. These spokesmen are often described as the radicals of the movement, but they are really its moralists. They seek to change white hearts—by traumatizing them. Frequently abetted by white self-flagellants, they may gleefully applaud (though not really agreeing with) Malcolm X because, while they admit he has no program, they think he can frighten white people into doing the right thing. To believe this, of course, you must be convinced, even if unconsciously, that at the core of the white man's heart lies a buried affection for Negroes—a proposition one may be permitted to doubt. But in any case, hearts are not relevant to the issue; neither racial affinities nor racial hostilities are rooted there. It is institutions—social, political, and economic institutions—which are the ultimate molders of collective sentiments. Let these institutions be reconstructed *today,* and let the ineluctable gradualism of history govern the formation of a new psychology.

My quarrel with the "no-win" tendency in the civil rights movement (and the reason I have so designated it) parallels my quarrel with the moderates outside the movement. As the latter lack the vision or will for fundamental change, the former lack a realistic strategy for achieving it. For such a strategy they substitute militancy. But militancy is a matter of posture and volume and not of effect.

I believe that the Negro's struggle for equality in America is essentially revolu-tionary. While most Negroes—in their hearts—unquestionably seek only to enjoy the fruits of American society as it now exists, their quest cannot *objectively* be satisfied within the framework of existing political and economic relations. The young Negro who would demonstrate his way into the labor market may be motivated by a thoroughly bourgeois ambition and thoroughly "capitalist" considerations, but he will end up having to favor a great expansion of the public sector of the economy. At any rate, that is the position the movement will be forced to take as it looks at the number of jobs being generated by the private economy, and if it is to remain true to the masses of Negroes.

The revolutionary character of the Negro's struggle is manifest in the fact that this struggle may have done more to democratize life for whites than for Negroes. Clearly, it was the sit-in movement of young Southern Negroes which, as it galvanized white students, banished the ugliest features of McCarthyism from the American campus and resurrected political debate. It was not until Negroes assaulted *de facto* school segregation in the urban centers that the issue of quality education for *all* children stirred into motion. Finally, it seems reasonably clear that the civil rights movement, directly and through the resurgence of social conscience it kindled, did more to initiate the war on poverty than any other single force.

It will be—it has been—argued that these by-products of the Negro struggle are not revolutionary. But the term revolutionary, as I am using it, does not connote violence; it refers to the qualitative transformation of fundamental institutions, more or less rapidly, to the point where the social and economic structure which they comprised can no longer be said to be the same. The Negro struggle has hardly run its course; and it will not stop moving until it has been utterly defeated or won substantial equality. But I fail to see how the movement can be victorious in the absence of radical programs for full employment, abolition of slums, the reconstruction of our educational system, new definitions of work and leisure. Adding up the cost of such programs, we can only conclude that we are talking about a refashioning of our political economy. It has been estimated, for example, that the price of replacing New York City's slums with public housing would be $17 billion. Again, a multi-billion dollar federal public-works program, dwarfing the currently proposed $2 billion program, is required to reabsorb unskilled and semi-skilled workers into the labor market—and this must be done if Negro workers in these categories are to be employed. "Preferential treatment" cannot help them.

I am not trying here to delineate a total program, only to suggest the scope of economic reforms which are most immediately related to the plight of the Negro community. One could speculate on their political implications—whether, for example, they do not indicate the obsolescence of state government and the superiority of regional structures as viable units of planning. Such speculations aside, it is clear that Negro needs cannot be satisfied unless we go beyond what has so far been placed on the agenda. How are these radical objectives to be achieved? The answer is simple, deceptively so: *through political power.*

There is a strong moralistic strain in the civil rights movement which would remind us that power corrupts, forgetting that the absence of power also corrupts. But this is not the view I want to debate here, for it is waning. Our problem is posed by those who accept the need for political power but do not understand the nature of the object and therefore lack sound strategies for achieving it; they tend to confuse political institutions with lunch counters.

A handful of Negroes, acting alone, could integrate a lunch counter by strategically locating their bodies so as *directly* to interrupt the operation of the proprietor's will; their numbers were relatively unimportant. In politics, however, such a confrontation is difficult because the interests involved are merely *represented*. In the execution of a political decision a direct confrontation may ensue (as when federal marshals escorted James Meredith into the University of Mississippi —to turn from an example of non-violent coercion to one of force backed up with the threat of violence). But in arriving at a political decision, numbers and organizations are crucial, especially for the economically disenfranchised. (Needless to say, I am assuming that the forms of political democracy exist in America, however imperfectly, that they are valued, and that elitist or putschist conceptions of exercising power are beyond the pale of discussion for the civil rights movement.

Neither that movement nor the country's twenty million black people can win political power alone. We need allies. The future of the Negro struggle depends on whether the contradictions of this society can be resolved by a coalition of progressive forces which becomes the *effective* political majority in the United States. I speak of the coalition which staged the March on Washington, passed the Civil Rights Act, and laid the basis for the Johnson landslide—Negroes, trade unionists, liberals, and religious groups.

There are those who argue that a coalition strategy would force the Negro to surrender his political independence to white liberals, that he would be neutralized, deprived of his cutting edge, absorbed into the Establishment. Some who take this position urged last year that votes be withheld from the Johnson-Humphrey ticket as a demonstration of the Negro's political power. Curiously enough, these people who sought to demonstrate power through the non-exercise of it, also point to the Negro "swing vote" in crucial urban areas as the source of the Negro's independent political power. But here they are closer to being right: the urban Negro vote will grow in importance in the coming years. If there is anything positive in the spread of the ghetto, it is the potential political power base thus created, and to realize this potential is one of the most challenging and urgent tasks before the civil rights movement. If the movement can wrest leadership of the ghetto vote from the machines, it will have acquired an organized constituency such as other major groups in our society now have.

But we must also remember that the effectiveness of a swing vote depends solely on "other" votes. It derives its power from them. In that sense, it can never be "independent," but must opt for one candidate or the other, even if by default. Thus coalitions are inescapable, however tentative they may be. And this is the case in all but those few situations in which Negroes running on an independent ticket might conceivably win. "Independence," in other words, is not a value in itself. The issue is which coalition to join and how to make it responsive to your program. Necessarily there will be compromise. But the difference between expediency and morality in politics is the difference between selling out a principle and making smaller concessions to win larger ones. The leader who shrinks from this task reveals not his purity but his lack of political sense.

The task of molding a political movement out of the March on Washington coalition is not simple, but no alternatives have been advanced. We need to choose our allies on the basis of common political objectives. It has become fashionable in some no-win Negro circles to decry the white liberal as the main enemy (his hypocrisy is what sustains racism); by virtue of this reverse recitation of the reactionary's litany (liberalism leads to socialism, which leads to Communism) the Negro is left in majestic isolation, except for a tiny band of fervent white initiates. But the objective fact is that *Eastland and Goldwater* are the main enemies—they and the opponents of civil rights, of the war on poverty, of medicare, of social security, of federal aid to education, of unions, and so forth. The labor movement, despite its obvious faults, has been the largest single organized force in this country pushing for progressive social legislation. And where the Negro-labor-liberal axis is weak, as in the farm belt, it was the religious groups that were most influential in rallying support for the Civil Rights Bill.

The durability of the coalition was interestingly tested during the election. I do not believe that the Johnson landslide proved the "white backlash" to be a myth. It proved, rather, that economic interests are more fundamental than prejudice: the backlashers decided that loss of social security was, after all, too high a price to pay for a slap at the Negro. This lesson was a valuable first step in re-educating such people, and it must be kept alive, for the civil rights movement will be advanced only to the

degree that social and economic welfare gets to be inextricably entangled with civil rights.

The 1964 elections marked a turning point in American politics. The Democratic landslide was not merely the result of a negative reaction to Goldwaterism; it was also the expression of a majority liberal consensus. The near unanimity with which Negro voters joined in that expression was, I am convinced, a vindication of the July 25th statement by Negro leaders calling for a strategic turn toward political action and a temporary curtailment of mass demonstrations. Despite the controversy surrounding the statement, the instinctive response it met with in the community is suggested by the fact that demonstrations were down 75 per cent as compared with the same period in 1963. But should so high a percentage of Negro voters have gone to Johnson, or should they have held back to narrow his margin of victory and thus give greater visibility to our swing vote? How has our loyalty changed things? Certainly the Negro vote had higher visibility in 1960, when a switch of only 7 per cent from the Republican column of 1956 elected President Kennedy. But the slimness of Kennedy's victory—of his "mandate"—dictated a go-slow approach on civil rights, at least until the Birmingham upheaval.

Although Johnson's popular majority was so large that he could have won without such overwhelming Negro support, that support was important from several angles. Beyond adding to Johnson's total national margin, it was specifically responsible for his victories in Virginia, Florida, Tennessee, and Arkansas. Goldwater took only those states where fewer than 45 per cent of eligible Negroes were registered. That Johnson would have won those states had Negro voting rights been enforced is a lesson not likely to be lost on a man who would have been happy with a unanimous electoral college. In any case, the 1.6 million Southern Negroes who voted have had a shattering impact on the Southern political party structure, as illustrated in the changed composition of the Southern congressional delegation. The "backlash" gave the Republicans five House seats in

Alabama, one in Georgia, and one in Mississippi. But on the Democratic side, seven segregationists were defeated while all nine Southerners who voted for the Civil Rights Act were re-elected. It may be premature to predict a Southern Democratic party of Negroes and white moderates and a Republican Party of refugee racists and economic conservatives, but there certainly is a strong tendency toward such a realignment; and an additional 3.6 million Negroes of voting age in the eleven Southern states are still to be heard from. Even the *tendency* toward disintegration of the Democratic party's racist wing defines a new context for Presidential and liberal strategy in the congressional battles ahead. Thus the Negro vote (North as well as South), while not *decisive* in the Presidential race, was enormously effective. It was a dramatic element of a historic mandate which contains vast possibilities and dangers that will fundamentally affect the future course of the civil rights movement.

The liberal congressional sweep raises hope for an assault on the seniority system, Rule Twenty-two, and other citadels of Dixiecrat-Republican power. The overwhelming of this conservative coalition should also mean progress on much bottlenecked legislation of profound interest to the movement (e.g., bills by Senators Clark and Nelson on planning, manpower, and employment). Moreover, the irrelevance of the South to Johnson's victory gives the President more freedom to act than his predecessor had and more leverage to the movement to pressure for executive action in Mississippi and other racist strongholds.

None of this *guarantees* vigorous executive or legislative action, for the other side of the Johnson landslide is that it has a Gaullist quality. Goldwater's capture of the Republican party forced into the Democratic camp many disparate elements which do not belong there, Big Business being the major example. Johnson, who wants to be President "of all people," may try to keep his new coalition together by sticking close to the political center. But if he decides to do this, it is unlikely that even his political genius will be able to hold together a coalition so inherently unstable and rife with contradictions. It must come apart. Should it do so while Johnson is pursuing a centrist course, then the mandate will have been wastefully dissipated. However, if the mandate is seized upon to set fundamental changes in motion, then the basis can be laid for a new mandate, a new coalition including hitherto inert and dispossessed strata of the population.

Here is where the cutting edge of the civil rights movement can be applied. We must see to it that the reorganization of the "consensus party" proceeds along lines which will make it an effective vehicle for social reconstruction, a role it cannot play so long as it furnishes Southern racism with its national political power. (One of Barry Goldwater's few attractive ideas was that the Dixiecrats belong with him in the same party.) And nowhere has the civil rights movement's political cutting edge been more magnificently demonstrated than at Atlantic City, where the Mississippi Freedom Democratic Party not only secured recognition as a bona fide component of the national party, but in the process routed the representatives of the most rabid racists—the white Mississippi and Alabama delegations. While I still believe that the FDP made a tactical error in spurning the compromise, there is no question that they launched a political revolution whose logic is the displacement of Dixiecrat power. They launched that revolution within a major political institution and as part of a coalitional effort.

The role of the civil rights movement in the reorganization of American political life is programmatic as well as strategic. We are challenged now to broaden our social vision, to develop functional programs with concrete objectives. We need to propose alternatives to technological unemployment, urban decay, and the rest. We need to be calling for public works and training, for national economic planning, for federal aid to education, for attractive public housing—all this on a sufficiently massive scale to make a difference. We need to protest the notion that our integration into American life, so long delayed, must now proceed in an atmosphere of competitive scarcity instead of in the security of abundance which technology makes possible. We cannot claim to have answers to all the complex problems of modern society. That is too much to ask of a movement still battling barbarism in Mississippi. But we can agitate the right questions by probing at the contradictions which still stand in the way of the "Great Society." The questions having been asked, motion must begin in the larger society, for there is a limit to what Negroes can do alone.

SUGGESTED ADDITIONAL READINGS

1. Bailyn, Bernard, "Political Experience and Enlightenment Ideas in Eighteenth-Century America," *American Historical Review*, Vol. LXVII, No. 2, January 1962, pp. 339–351. Summarizes pertinent data and discusses the relationship of ideas to experience—i.e., is there a cause-and-effect relationship and, if so, which if either comes first.

2. Barker, Lucius J. and Turley W. Barker, Jr., *Freedoms, Courts, Politics: Studies in Civil Liberties,* Englewood Cliffs, N. J.: Prentice-Hall, 1965, 324 pp. Six chapters, each dealing very effectively with a different aspect of civil liberties—religion and the schools, speech and assembly, obscenity and free expression, security and communism, racial problems and rights of the accused—in both their political and judicial contexts.

3. Bickel, Alexander M., "The Civil Rights Act of 1964," *Commentary,* Vol. 38, August 1964, pp. 33–39. Review of the historical background as well as a summary of major provisions of this landmark legislation. Also contains some interesting prognostications.

4. Biddle, Francis, *The Fear of Freedom,* Garden City, N. Y.: Doubleday, 1952, 263 pp. Written during the time of a great anti-communist crusade; a strong plea for maximum liberty for all in our society. Chapters 1, 4, 5, 13 are especially useful.

5. Blau, Joseph M., *Men and Movements in American Philosophy,* Englewood Cliffs, N. J.: Prentice-Hall, 1952, pp. 110–150. A definition and description of transcendentalism; also includes short, critical sketches of Emerson, Thoreau, and the elder Henry James.

6. Bragdon, Henry Wilkinson, Samuel P. McCutcher, Stuart Gerry Brown, *Frame of Government,* New York: Macmillan, 1962, 293 pp. A profusely annotated description of the chief documents upon which the American political system is based. Each document is accompanied by an introduction and general explanation.

7. Brant, Irving, *The Bill of Rights,* Indianapolis: Bobbs-Merrill, 1965, 567 pp. Probably the best single-volume study on the origins of the Bill of Rights; contains a very useful bibliographical section.

8. Brown, Stuart Gerry, "The Meaning of Democracy," in Brown, Stuart Gerry (ed.), *We Hold These Truths,* New York: Harper, 2nd ed., 1948, pp. 1–9. An introductory essay to a book of readings on American democracy; presents a lucid and provocative definition of "democracy as process."

9. Cook, Thomas I., *Democratic Rights versus Communist Activity,* New York: Random House, 1954, 56 pp. In opposition to Biddle and others, Cook presents a strong argument for suppression of types of Communist activities, particularly in the areas of speech and propaganda.

10. Corwin, Edward S., *The "Higher Law" Background of American Constitutional Law*, Ithaca, N. Y.: Cornell University Press, 1928, 89 pp. (paper). A classic; required reading for anyone interested in the effect of "higher law" doctrine on the development of the American Constitution.

11. Curte, Merle, "The Great Mr. Locke, America's Philosopher, 1783–1861," *The Huntington Library Bulletin*, No. 11, April 1937, pp. 107–151. One of America's leading historians details the influence of John Locke on our early history and the ensuing years up to the Civil War.

12. Goodman, Paul, (ed.), *Seeds of Liberation*, New York: George Braziller, 1964, pp. 175–370. A series of essays and articles, excerpted from the magazine, *Liberation*. Includes among its authors Martin Luther King, James Baldwin, James Farmer, and Bayard Rustin. Treasury of source material on civil rights, non-violence and the "new left."

13. Lewis, Anthony and The New York Times, *Portrait of a Decade,* New York: Random House, 1964, 322 pp. A famous journalist (he has won two Pulitzer prizes) and a famous newspaper combine their talents and resources to portray the "second American revolution," the decade 1954–1964.

14. Lomax, Louis E., *The Negro Revolt,* New York: New American Library, 1963, 288 pp. (paper). A history of the Negro revolution by one of its most outspoken proponents. The fiery and forthright Negro journalist attempts a clarification of the current forces in the Negro revolt as well as its antecedents and goals.

15. McKay, Robert B., "Racial Protests, Civil Disobedience, and the Role of Law," *Arts and Sciences*, Winter, 1964–1965. A leading professor of law (New York University) discusses the implications of civil disobedience for a society tied to the idea of "rule by law." The author shows a sensitive understanding of the human factor in many so-called legal issues.

16. Pfeffer, Leo, *The Liberties of An American,* Boston: Beacon Press, 1956, 309 pp. One of America's leading constitutional lawyers, who has presented some of the major briefs in civil liberties cases before the Supreme Court, reviews civil liberties historically and judicially.

17. Popper, Karl, *The Open Society and its Enemies,* Princeton, N. J.: Princeton University Press, 1950, pp. 165–198, 443–464. A masterpiece of political theory; the pages referred to contain the author's now-famous statement of the open society, as well as a general review of the meaning of history.

18. Royce, Josiah, *The Philosophy of Loyalty,* New York: Macmillan, 1908, 409 pp. The source of Royce's statement on "loyalty to loyalty." Having defended loyalty as a supreme goal, he speaks of the necessity of deciding upon what causes are worthy of loyalty and suggests that a worthwhile cause is one which has concern for the individual and is, at the same time, superpersonal.

19. Sackett, Russell, "Plotting A War on Whitey," *Life,* June 10, 1966, pp. 100 ff. An article representative of the growing mood of anti-white sentiment in the Negro community. Consult *Readers' Guide to Periodical Literature,* for more contemporary articles in this rapidly-developing problem area.

20. Sibley, Mulford Q., (ed.), *The Quiet Battle,* Garden City, N. Y., Doubleday, 1963, 390 pp. (paper). A noted political scientist and pacifist has brought together an excellent collection of readings on the theory and practice of non-violence. Draws from historical and non-American, as well as from contemporary and American, sources.

21. Weinberger, Andrew D., *Freedom and Protection, The Bill of Rights,* San Francisco: Chandler, 1962, 180 pp. (paper). A short statement on the history of the Bill of Rights and judicial review followed by a series of abridged opinions on the Bill of Rights today; contains a short but useful section of appendices.

FOR FURTHER CONSIDERATION

1. If anybody is denied freedom, is this not a violation of the spirit of a free society as well as the letter of the American Constitution? Is it true that the real subversive is the one who denies full freedom to a communist? On the other hand, do I have to wait until somebody hits me before I can have him arrested? Where is the line? When he thinks about hitting me? When he advocates it? Teaches it? Threatens me? Picks up a rock? Draws back his arm? In what respects are civil liberties and civil rights threatened today? Does the threat come mainly from communists, fascists, patriots, or other sources?

2. In the mid-twentieth century, when the demand for freedom and independence sweeps in floodtide fashion across the world, can a significant sector of the American population be asked to wait for the slow processes of democratic political change and social evolution to free them from a century-old position of second-class citizenship? In an age in which American democracy faces the most formidable enemy in its history and in which the price of losing any important technological or political contest to this enemy might mean annihilation, must security be placed above freedom in any issue in which there is a possible conflict of these two concepts? Can American democracy survive if this is done?

3. Suppose you were an officer in the United States Armed Forces at the beginning of World War II. You are ordered to take part in the removal of thousands of Japanese-Americans from their homes in California to barren relocation centers in the western desert. You have read Harold Laski's statement that "the only ground for obedience to the state is where its purpose is morally superior to that of its opponents. The only ground upon which the citizen can give his support for the state is upon the conviction that what he is aiming at is, in each particular action, good." Are you justified in refusing to take part in an enforced relocation operation, feeling that it is grossly inequitable and that thousands of loyal Americans will suffer from it?

4. Mosher T. Kingsley is the legal guardian of a third-generation mental defective, Oscar Jukes. Kingsley and Jukes belong to a religious faith which argues that for government to interfere with reproduction is to interfere with spiritual integrity. In the face of a constitutional law providing for the sterilization of third-generation defectives, is Kingsley justified morally and ethically in spiriting his client Jukes away from the state insane asylum to protect him from the sterilization operation? At what point should you refuse to accept a political decision on moral or religious grounds?

5. The following statement was made several years ago by Dr. Martin Luther King during the course of an NBC Television debate. Do you agree or disagree? Why?

I would say also that on this question of whether individuals have a moral right to obey what they consider just law, I think we all should do that, but I think the individual who discovers on the basis of conscience that a law is unjust and is willing in a very peaceful sense to disobey that unjust law and willingly and voluntarily suffers the consequences, I think at this moment he is expressing the highest respect for law.

Index for Commentaries